Recent Advances in
Speech Understanding and
Dialog Systems

NATO ASI Series

Advanced Science Institutes Series

A series presenting the results of activities sponsored by the NATO Science Committee, which aims at the dissemination of advanced scientific and technological knowledge, with a view to strengthening links between scientific communities.

The Series is published by an international board of publishers in conjunction with the NATO Scientific Affairs Division

A Life Sciences **B Physics**	Plenum Publishing Corporation London and New York
C Mathematical and Physical Sciences **D Behavioural and Social Sciences** **E Applied Sciences**	Kluwer Academic Publishers Dordrecht, Boston and London
F Computer and Systems Sciences **G Ecological Sciences** **H Cell Biology**	Springer-Verlag Berlin Heidelberg New York London Paris Tokyo

Series F: Computer and Systems Sciences Vol. 46

Recent Advances in Speech Understanding and Dialog Systems

Edited by

H. Niemann

Universität Erlangen-Nürnberg
Martensstr. 3
D-8520 Erlangen, FRG

M. Lang

Siemens AG, ZT ZTI SYS 5
Otto-Hahn-Ring 6
D-8000 München 83, FRG

G. Sagerer

Universität Erlangen-Nürnberg
Martensstr. 3
D-8520 Erlangen, FRG

Springer-Verlag
Berlin Heidelberg New York London Paris Tokyo
Published in cooperation with NATO Scientific Affairs Division

Proceedings of the NATO Advanced Study Institute on Recent Advances in Speech Understanding and Dialog Systems, held in Bad Windsheim, FRG, July 5–18, 1987.

ISBN-13: 978-3-642-83478-3 e-ISBN-13: 978-3-642-83476-9
DOI: 10.1007/978-3-642-83476-9

Softcover reprint of the hardcover 1st edition 1988

2145/3140-543210

PREFACE

This volume contains invited and contributed papers presented at the NATO Advanced Study Institute on "Recent Advances in Speech Understanding and Dialog Systems" held in Bad Windsheim, Federal Republic of Germany, July 5 to July 18, 1987. It is divided into the three parts Speech Coding and Segmentation, Word Recognition, and Linguistic Processing. Although this can only be a rough organization showing some overlap, the editors felt that it most naturally represents the bottom-up strategy of speech understanding and, therefore, should be useful for the reader.

Part 1, SPEECH CODING AND SEGMENTATION, contains 4 invited and 14 contributed papers. The first invited paper summarizes basic properties of speech signals, reviews coding schemes, and describes a particular solution which guarantees high speech quality at low data rates. The second and third invited papers are concerned with acoustic-phonetic decoding. Techniques to integrate knowledge-sources into speech recognition systems are presented and demonstrated by experimental systems. The fourth invited paper gives an overview of approaches for using prosodic knowledge in automatic speech recognition systems, and a method for assigning a stress score to every syllable in an utterance of German speech is reported in a contributed paper. A set of contributed papers treats the problem of automatic segmentation, and several authors successfully apply knowledge-based methods for interpreting speech signals and spectrograms. The last three papers investigate phonetic models, Markov models and fuzzy quantization techniques and provide a transition to Part 2.

Part 2, WORD RECOGNITION, contains 3 invited and 16 contributed papers. This part starts with an invited paper presenting a full introduction to and overview of all aspects of hidden Markov models and their application to isolated word recognition and continuous speech understanding. The second invited paper gives an approach to the unification of cognitive and information-theoretic approaches to speech recognition and its application to letter and digit recognition. The third invited paper is devoted to the problem of isolated word recognition in very large vocabularies. The first set of contributed papers concerns the problem of isolated word recognition, and the second set concerns word recognition in continuous speech. The last set of papers treats the problem of adaptation or learning in order to achieve speaker independence. One paper suggests an approach to the evaluation of speech recognizer performance.

Part 3, LINGUISTIC PROCESSING, contains 3 invited and 7 contributed papers. This section makes explicit that linguistic processing has become an integral part of speech understanding systems. It covers both the continuous speech recognition task with the help of linguistic models and the speech understanding task based on explicitly represented linguistic knowledge. Syntactic, semantic, and pragmatic aspects in the design of on-line language understanding systems are addressed by the first invited paper. The second one evaluates the state of the art in semantic representation and linguistic analysis techniques as far as they are used in speech understanding systems. System architectures for knowledge-based speech understanding and the problem of knowledge representation for such systems are discussed in the third paper. Both papers also concern the integration and cooperation of linguistic and acoustic analysis for speech understanding. The problems of continuous speech recognition are treated in the first set of contributed papers. A second part deals with the understanding task, and a third one suggests models for oral dialog systems.

The editors would like to thank the authors for their effort to provide papers of high scientific quality, the participants of the NATO ASI for their active support of a stimulating meeting, the publisher for preparing this volume, and last but not least the NATO Office of Scientific Affairs in Brussels, Siemens AG München, and the University of Erlangen-Nürnberg for support of the ASI.

H. Niemann, M. Lang, and G. Sagerer
Erlangen and München

Spring 1988

TABLE OF CONTENTS

PART 1: Speech Coding and Segmentation

INVITED PAPERS

CONTRIBUTED PAPERS

PART 2: Word Recognition

INVITED PAPERS

CONTRIBUTED PAPERS

PART 3: Linguistic Processing

INVITED PAPERS

CONTRIBUTED PAPERS

RECENT ADVANCES IN SPEECH CODING

D. Wolf and H. Reininger

Institut für Angewandte Physik der Universität Frankfurt a.M.
D-6000 Frankfurt a. M., Robert-Mayer-Straße 2-4, FRG

Abstract: After a short summary of some basic properties of speech signals and of speech signal models the effect of linear prediction and vector quantization for data compression in speech coding is outlined. Some well-known coding schemes are reviewed. The recently developed RELP-S schemes based on speech analysis by synthesis are discussed in more detail. In particular a scheme using stochastic excitation sequences is expected to guarantee high speech quality at data rates far below 8 kb/s.

1. INTRODUCTION

Today speech coding techniques are considered not only in connection with all kinds of communication services but also for automatic speech recognition, voice request, and voice storage systems. Thus, speech coding has become one of the most exciting topics of signal processing both from a theoretical and a practical point of view [2,16,24,29]. Improved mathematical models of the physical phenomena of speech production as well as advanced concepts of data compression have led to new speech coding schemes which allow digital speech processing at medium or low bit rates with high speech quality. On the other hand the rapid progress in microelectronics particularly in the development of highly integrated signal processors has provided the basis for efficient and economic realizations of more and more complex speech encoding algorithms.

In this review an attempt is made to illustrate the recent development in the field of speech coding without the claim for completeness. After a brief summary of the basic signal properties emphasizing the stochastic nature of speech signals, the speech synthesis models, and the fundamental principles of data compression in speech coding, linear prediction and vector quantization, are discussed. Finally a survey of the most important digital speech coding schemes will be presented. The currently studied schemes performing speech analysis by synthesis will be treated in detail. Trends of actual research which aims at low bit rate high quality speech coding down to 2.4 kb/s will be outlined.

2. SPEECH SIGNALS AND MODELS

Speech signals - an example is shown in Fig. 3 - are characterized by their amplitude distribution and the specific type of statistical dependency between signal amplitudes at different time points. Referring to speech signals in standard telephone channels with a frequency bandwidth of 300 Hz to 3400 Hz sampled at a rate of 8 kHz, one observes the typical shape of the univariate amplitude density $p_\xi(x)$ as given in Fig. 1 together with some analytical approximations. Another basic result is that the contour lines of the bivariate densities

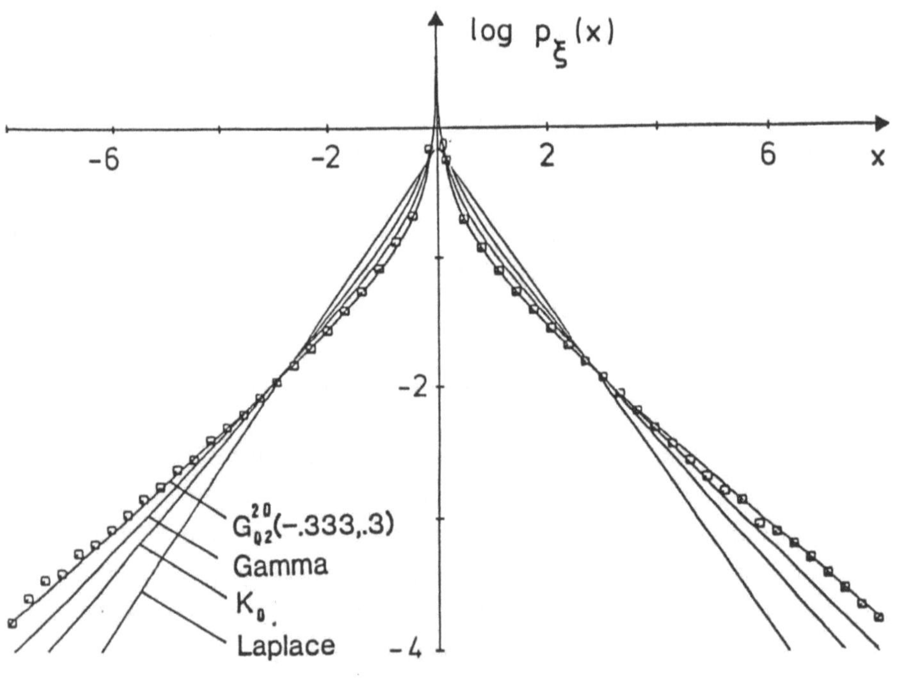

Fig. 1: Univariate density $p_\xi(x)$ of speech together with analytical approximations (after Brehm [4])

$p_{\xi_1,\xi_2}(x_1,x_2)$ for two speech samples x_1 and x_2 separated by a time distance $\tau \leq 5$ ms are found to be ellipses. These statements have led to a well-known stochastic speech signal model [4,30]. From the point of view of this model speech signals may be considered to be sample functions of a stochastic process $\xi(t)$ which is at least short-time stationary and spherically invariant. As has been shown $\xi(t)$ can be represented by a random mixture of Gaussian processes [4]. The amplitude densities of the process $\xi(t)$ are obtained by averaging the randomly varying variances s^2 of the Gaussian processes applying a suitable weighting function $p_\sigma(s)$. As shown in Fig. 1 the best representation of the observations is given bei Meijer's G-function $G_{02}^{20}(.)$ with $p_\sigma(s) \sim G_{12}^{20}(.)$ while for the simple assumption that $p_\sigma(s)$ is Gaussian $p_\xi(x)$ becomes K_0-distributed [30].

The stochastic signal model corresponds with the speech synthesis scheme of Fig. 2. White Gaussian noise n(t) of the generator N is "modulated" by a function $\sigma(t)$ in G^{-1}, thus being transformed into a spherically invariant signal x(t), which is finally filtered by a time-variant linear filter F. The filter F defined by a set of parameters S introduces the specific correlations of the synthesized speech signal s(t).

The RELP-S schemes with stochastic innovation sequences as described in 5.2 may be regarded as realizations of this model. The model of Fig. 2 is also a more generalized version of the popular vocoder model that generates speech by exciting the linear filter F with white noise or a series of pulses.

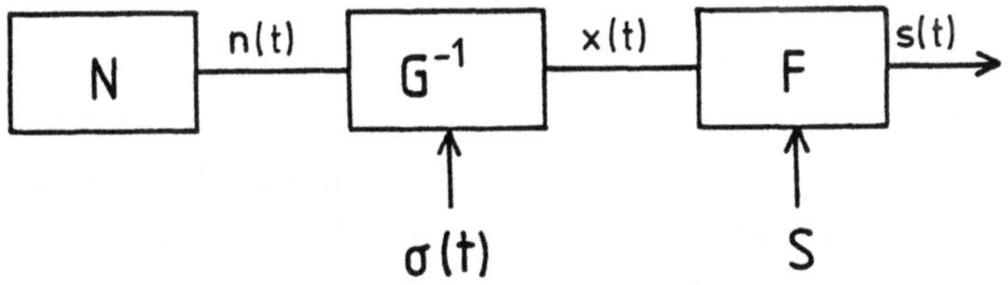

Fig. 2: Model of speech synthesis

3. LINEAR PREDICTION

Linear prediction [22,23] provides a simple and widely used method to remove linear statistical dependencies and thus to reduce the data rate.

A linear predictor of order p estimates an actual speech sample s(n) by an optimized linear combination

$$\hat{s}(n) = \sum_{k=1}^{p} a_k \, s(n-k)$$

of p preceding speech samples. In a predictive speech coding scheme the prediction error (or residual) signal

$$e(n) = s(n)-\hat{s}(n)$$

is encoded and transmitted to the receiver together with the predictor coefficients a_k or equivalent data such as the parcor coefficients or the log-area-ratios. The effect of linear prediction can be characterized as a linear filtering of the signal s(n) by the "prediction error filter" with the system function

$$A(z) = 1 - \sum_{k=1}^{p} a_k z^{-k} \quad .$$

At the receiver an inverse prediction error filter allows to reconstruct the speech signal from the residual signal.

According to the time-varying characteristics of a speech waveform, which is shown in Fig. 3, the parameters of the linear predictor are adapted periodically to speech segments of 10 to 25 ms duration. In Fig. 3 the error signal e(n) derived from the speech signal s(n) by a linear predictor of order p=8 is depicted. The waveform e(n) illustrates that with an 8th-order predictor, a so-called short-delay predictor, decorrelation can be achieved within a range of about 8 adjacent samples. However, e(n) also illustrates that rather large errors occur due to rapid changes of the waveform mainly in voiced segments of the signal s(n). These errors can be reduced by a

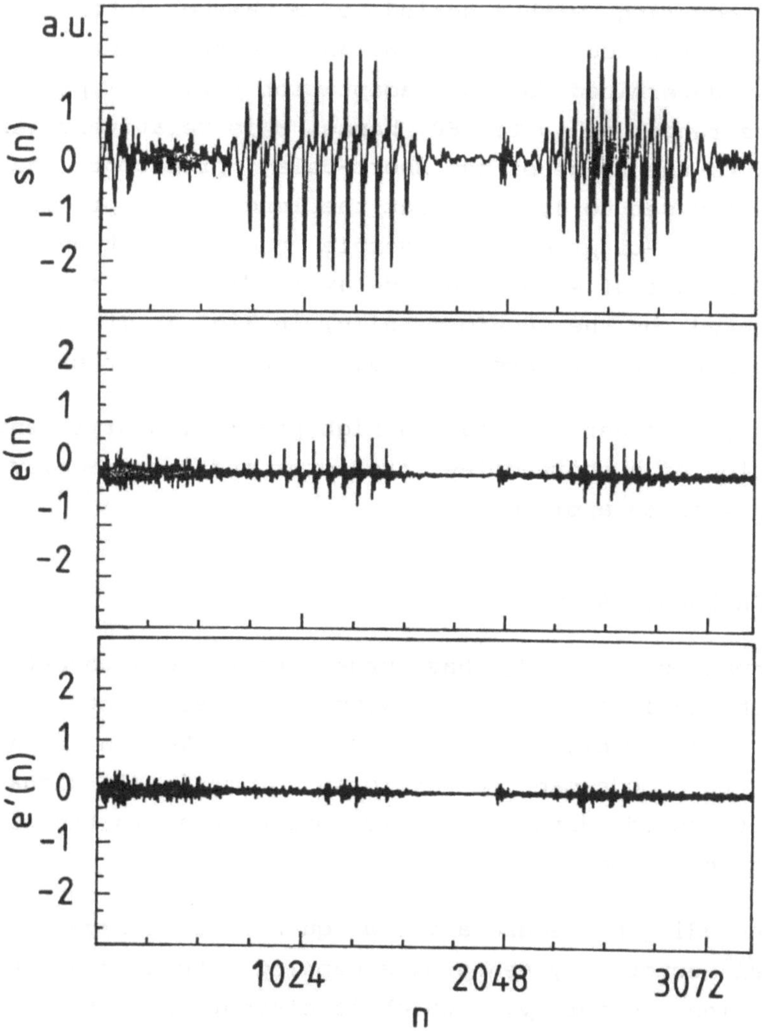

Fig. 3: Speech signal s(n), prediction error signal e(n) after short-delay prediction with p=8, and error signal e'(n) after long-delay prediction with q=3

long-delay predictor or pitch predictor [10,25] of order q=2k+1, k∈N, which is represented by the system function

$$P(z) = 1 - \sum_{i=-k}^{k} \beta_i z^{-M-i} \quad .$$

The pitch predictor exploits the quasi-periodicity of these

changes occuring with a period of M sample intervals. The pitch predictor coefficients β_i and the "pitch period" M are optimally determined for each adaptation period. Typically, M is in the range of 40 to 160, hence M is relatively large as compared to the range of the short-delay predictor. The order q is usually set to 3, i.e. that the long-delay prediction is based on the M-th preceeding sample and its next neighbours. The performance of such a long-delay predictor of order q=3 is demonstrated by the waveform e'(n) in Fig. 3. It can be seen that the large errors are eliminated almost completely.

Therefore, in order to obtain a high prediction efficiency the combination of a short-delay predictor and a long-delay predictor has to be applied.

4. VECTOR QUANTIZATION

Vector quantization (VQ) has turned out to be a powerful tool in speech and image coding allowing the development of coding schemes for low bit rates [11,13,21,26]. VQ can be applied directly to encode sampled waveforms or residual signals as well as to encode data and system parameters in the time and the frequency domain.

In the encoding procedure a vector quantizer assigns an n-dimensional vector $\underline{x}$ by means of a mapping Q to an n-dimensional reproduction vector $\underline{y}_i$, which is element of a reproduction alphabet $C=\{\underline{y}_1,\ldots,\underline{y}_K\}$ called "codebook". A vector quantizer is completely defined by the codebook C and the mapping Q. The mapping Q is chosen such that a given distortion measure $d(\underline{x},\underline{y})$ is minimized. The index i of the optimum codebook vector $\underline{y}_i$, for which $d(\underline{x},\underline{y}_j)$, $j=1,\ldots,K$, is minimum, is transmitted to the receiver and decoded into the vector $\underline{y}_i$ using a local copy of C. The code rate R resulting by a VQ scheme with a codebook C consisting of K n-dimensional vectors is $R=\frac{1}{n}\mathrm{ld}(K)$ bit per sample.

An appropriate codebook C is derived by minimizing the mean quantization error $E\{d(\underline{x},\underline{y})\}$ with respect to the joint probability density $p(\underline{x})$. In general, the joint probability density $p(\underline{x})$ is not known or the resulting minimization problem cannot be treated analytically. Therefore, an iterative procedure known as LBG-algorithm [20] is used to derive a codebook from a sequence $\{\underline{x}_j\}$ of training data, sufficient in length to represent the statistical properties of the underlying information source. In the first iteration step the training sequence $\{\underline{x}_j\}$ is encoded using an initial codebook containing arbitrarily chosen or previously optimized codebook vectors. This implies a partition of the training sequence into subsets $S_i=\{\underline{x}_j | Q(\underline{x}_j)=\underline{y}_i\}$, $i=1,...,K$. The "centroid" of each subset S_i is used to replace the codebook vector $\underline{y}_i$ for the next iteration step; thus the total distortion does not increase from one iteration step to the next. This procedure is repeated until the relative distortion of two successive iteration steps falls below a certain threshold. Codebooks designed by means of the LBG-Algorithm are in general at least locally optimum in a sense that a local minimum of the quantization error is achieved [12].

Typical results of the signal-to-quantization noise ratio (SNR) obtained by VQ of speech signals using a quadratic distortion measure are shown in Table 1. In parallel Fig. 4 shows the similarity of the original and of the vector quantized waveforms in dependence on the dimension n for a rate of R=1 bit per sample. For a constant code rate R the SNR values increase monotonously with increasing dimension n. Correspondingly, the quantized waveforms y(n) closely approach the original waveform s(n) even at that low rate of R=1 bit per sample.

For a given bit rate R per sample the quantization error of VQ decreases with increasing vector dimension n. Unfortunately, in full-search VQ schemes (FSVQ) the number of distortion calculations increases exponentially with the value of n. Therefore, recent investigations have been focused on VQ algorithms achieving the same performance as FSVQ but with a reduced number of distortion calculations [7,27]. Those fast search algo-

Table 1: SNR values for VQ of speech signals

Dimension	Iterations	SNR(dB)
R=1 bit per sample		
1	6	2.12
2	8	6.94
3	10	9.08
4	10	10.03
5	11	11.18
6	8	11.80
7	9	12.56
8	8	13.15
R=2 bit per sample		
1	6	7.42
2	15	13.12
3	16	15.63
4	14	17.24

rithms have been developed on the basis of structured codebooks. Two different types of fast search VQ schemes have been proposed: First, algorithms with parameter-structured codebooks which reduce the number of distortion calculations by analyzing only that part of a FSVQ codebook which contains with high probability the optimum codebook vector. This part of the codebook is characterized by a scalar parameter extracted from the codebook vectors. Second, algorithms where the codebook structure is imposed by choice of the codebook design procedure [27]. One method of the second kind is to design a tree-structured codebook (TSVQ). This type of codebook consists of a sequence of small codebooks organized like a tree. The more the depth of the tree is increased the preciser an incoming vector is approximated. Tree-structured codebooks are characterized by a linear increase of the number of distortion calculations with n. In principle, the performance of TSVQ is below that of FSVQ, since the partition of the n-dimensional vector space, defined by the tree-structured codebook and the distortion measure, cannot be optimum. Another method of reducing the computational costs by the choice of specific code-

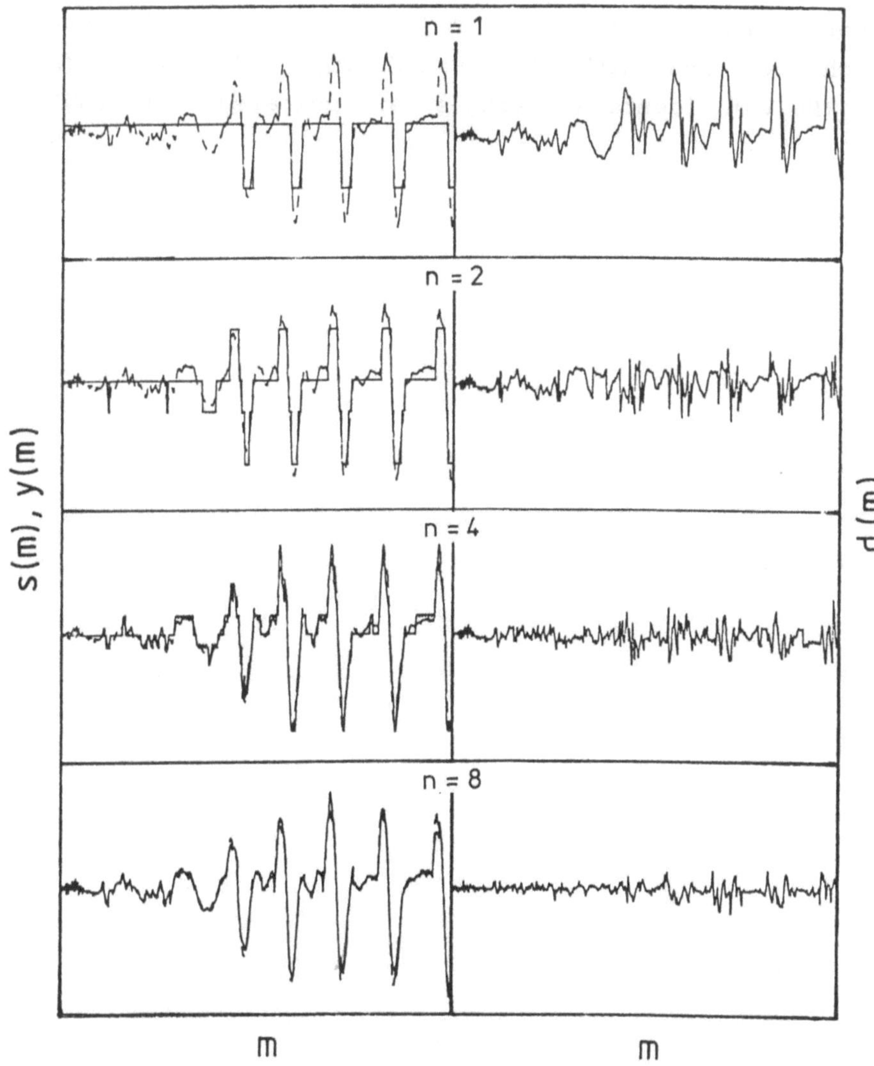

Fig. 4: Original signals s(m) (---), vector quantized signals y(m) (——), and error signals d(m) as functions of n

book structures is multistage VQ (MSVQ). A data vector $\underline{x}$ is quantized by a sequence of vector quantizers, where each vector quantizer encodes the quantization error of the preceding VQ-stage. The optimum codebook vector of a data vector $\underline{x}$ in a MSVQ scheme is given by the sum of the best vectors of all VQ stages.

The performances of TSVQ with 2 (TS_2VQ) and 4 (TS_4VQ) branches in each level and only 2 levels ($TS_{2L}VQ$), MSVQ with 2 (MS_2VQ) and 4 (MS_4VQ) identical stages are compared with FSVQ at a

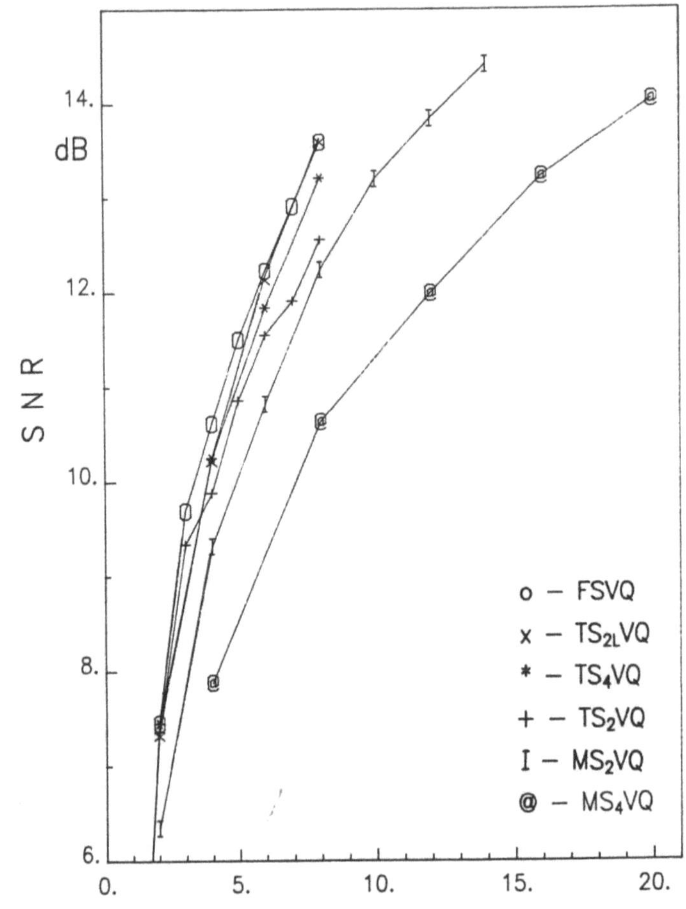

Fig. 5: SNR values for various VQ schemes obtained with speech signals at a rate of R=1 bit per sample

rate of R=1 bit per sample in Fig. 5. It can be seen that for all of the algorithms the SNR values increase with increasing dimension n. $TS_{2L}VQ$ approaches the values of FSVQ very closely while MSVQ schemes yield SNR values as high as FSVQ only at higher dimensions. However, MSVQ schemes may exceed the SNR values of FSVQ if the number of codebook vectors in each stage is sufficiently large to achieve a small quantization error. Table 2 demonstrates the amount of reduction in computational complexity achieved by the introduction of structured codebooks. The numbers of distortion calculations are presented for several values of n.

Table 2: Number of distortion calculations for VQ schemes

n	FSVQ	TS_2VQ	TS_4VQ	$TS_{2L}VQ$	MS_2VQ	MS_4VQ
8	256	16	16	32	32	16
10	1024	20	20	64	64	-
12	4096	24	24	128	128	32
16	65536	32	32	512	512	64

Another successful application of VQ is the encoding of predictor parameters. A set of p predictor parameters of an adaptive linear predictor, considered as a p-dimensional vector, is encoded via a codebook consisting of K predictor parameter sets by minimizing the distortion based on a modified Itakura measure [5,14,15]. The codebook is calculated by applying the LBG-algorithm to a training sequence of predictor parameter sets in a similar manner as in the case of sampled waveforms, only the centroid calculation is slightly different. Fig. 6 gives the prediction gain PG obtained with quantized parameters of an 8th-order linear predictor using FSVQ and TSVQ techniques in comparison with the optimum PG value. The results show that FSVQ with K=1024 codebook vectors yields about 95% of the maximum prediction gain obtained with unquantized parameters. The values achieved by TSVQ schemes are very close to those of FSVQ demonstrating that the number of distortion calculations can be drastically reduced with these schemes without any significant degradation of the quantization accuracy.

Therefore - using VQ in a predictive coding scheme - the predictor parameters can efficiently be encoded at a rate of about 0.5 kb/s to 0.8 kb/s.

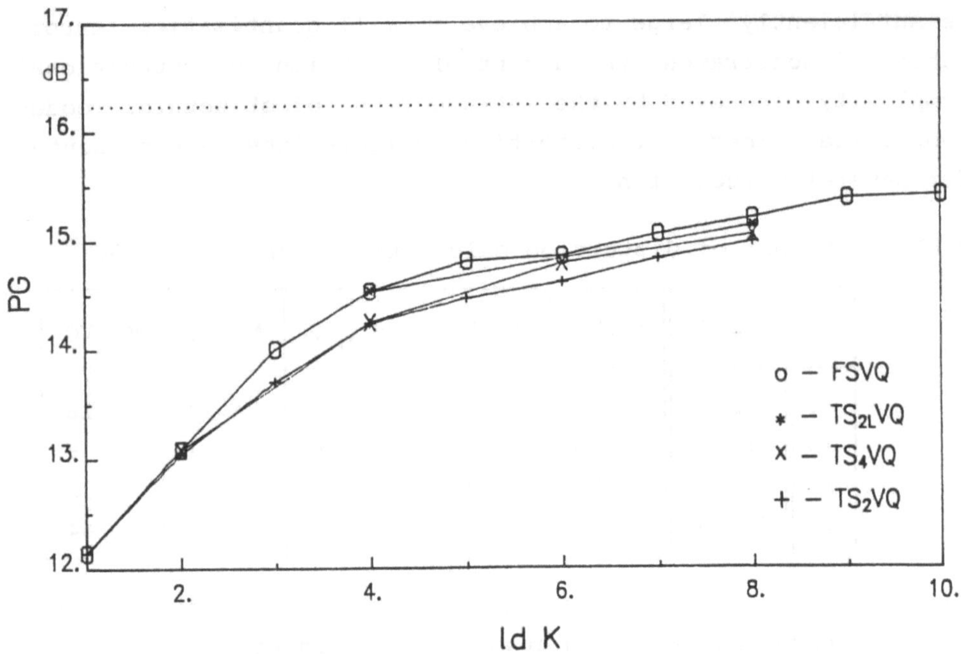

Fig. 6: PG as functions of K for various VQ schemes compared to the optimum value (···)

5. CODING SCHEMES

5.1 General Survey

As illustrated by Fig. 7 most speech coding methods proposed up to now can be regarded either as a waveform coding scheme or as a scheme based on source modeling, usually called vocoding.

Waveform coding schemes are optimized for facsimile reconstruction of the speech waveform at the decoder. Well-known time-domain waveform coding schemes such as PCM, DPCM, and ADPCM lead to high quality speech at rates between 64 kb/s and 32 kb/s by utilizing statistical properties and correlations of speech signals [10,17]. Two schemes operating in the frequency domain, namely SBC and ATC have successfully been

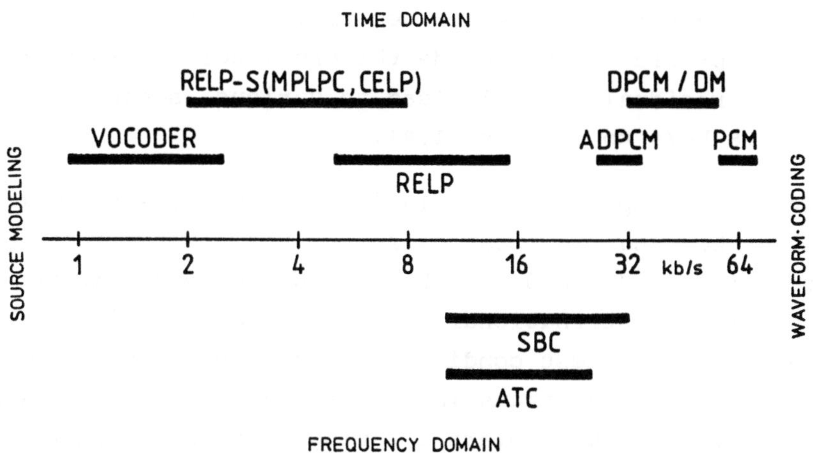

Fig. 7: Properties of speech coding methods

applied for waveform coding. They are able to produce high quality speech at rates of 16 kb/s down to 10 kb/s by exploiting specific properties of the speech spectrum [17].

The second type of speech encoding methods, the source modeling concepts are based on the modeling of the speech production process. Parameters of a digital filter modeling the vocal tract and parameters of an optimum excitation function are estimated from the speech signal to be encoded. In the classical vocoder the excitation consists of pulses or of white noise depending on the classification of a speech segment to be voiced or unvoiced, resp. These schemes yield an intelligible but synthetically sounding speech at 2.4 kb/s [9]. Recent progress in the development of speech coding schemes with high speech quality at rates of 2.4 kb/s to 10 kb/s has been achieved by the so-called RELP-S schemes. They use a more sophisticated way to determine an excitation function as described subsequently in 5.2.

Finally, it should be noted that a lot of hybrid coding schemes combining waveform coding and source modeling have been designed. Especially, various kinds of residual excited linear predictive (RELP) coders which decorrelate the speech signal by a linear predictor and encode the predictor parameters as well as the residual signal lead to various schemes in the range of 4.8 kb/s to 16 kb/s [1,8].

Recently, in a competition of 16 kb/s speech codecs presented for the forthcoming European cellular radio network the performances of four SBC and two RELP-S schemes were compared to each other in an international test. The mean opinion scores (MOS) under various test conditions ranged between 3 and 4 in the case of error free transmission and about 2 to 3 with 1% bit error rate. The best overall ratings have been achieved by the two RELP-S schemes. A certain combination of both codecs is now proposed as final scheme for standardization.

5.2 RELP-S Schemes

A novel approach for the encoding of speech with high speech quality at rates below 10 kb/s is based on the concept of analysis by synthesis. The principle of operation of the so-called RELP-S schemes is shown in Fig. 8.

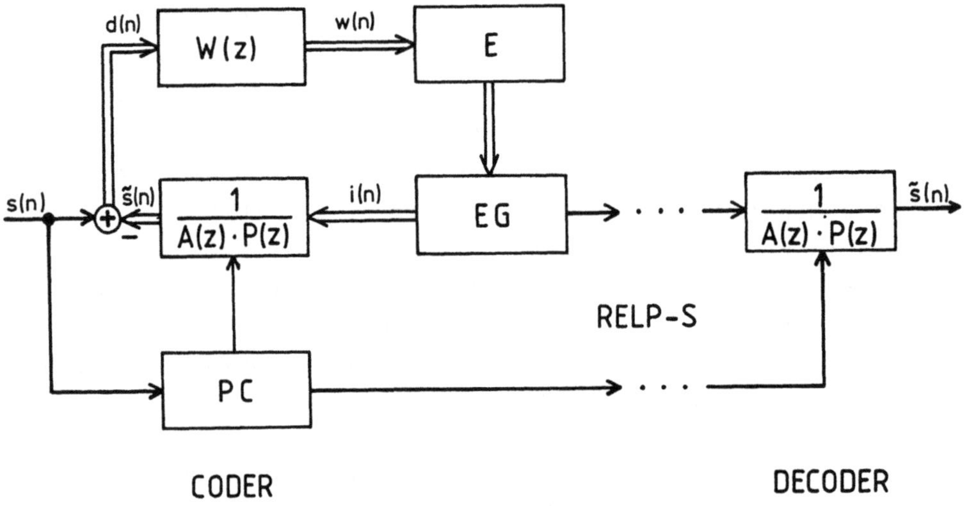

Fig. 8: RELP-S scheme

The innovation sequence i(n) produced by an excitation generator is filtered by a combination of inverse prediction error filters $(A(z)P(z))^{-1}$ to obtain a speech signal $\tilde{s}(n)$. The difference d(n) of the actual speech signal s(n) and the synthesized speech signal $\tilde{s}(n)$ is filtered by a weighting filter W(z) offering the possibility to introduce a perceptually meaningful distortion measure into the encoding procedure. Minimizing the power E of the weighted difference signal w(n) either by iteratively improving the innovation sequence or by searching over all possible innovation sequences leads to the optimum innovation sequence for the speech signal s(n). This innovation sequence is transmitted to the receiver together with the parameters specifying the adaptive inverse prediction error filters. Finally the speech signal is reconstructed by filtering of the optimum innovation sequence by $(A(z)P(z))^{-1}$.

At present two types of RELP-S schemes using different excitation generators are in the focus of research. In the so-called MPLPC [3,6,19] schemes a pulse generator is used which produces a sequence of pulses with variable pulse distances and pulse amplitudes. For a speech segment of N samples the innovation sequence with a given number of pulses is iteratively optimized by applying a procedure called sequential pulse placement. The pulses are placed one by one. For each single pulse the power E is calculated for all of the N possible positions and that position and amplitude is selected which yields the minimum of E. The SNR values obtained by a MPLPC scheme using this procedure is shown in Fig. 9 as a function of the number R_p of pulses per second. The parameters of the 12th- and 3rd-order inverse prediction error filters as well as the innovation sequences were adapted to speech segments of 15 ms durations. It can be seen that the SNR increases monotonously with increasing R_p and reaches about 22 dB in the case of 2000 pulses per second. About 750 to 1000 pulses per second are sufficient to obtain a high speech quality, resulting in a data rate of 6 to 8 kb/s, if 8 bits are used to encode the amplitude and position of each pulse. The parameters of the prediction error filters can be encoded with about 2 kb/s

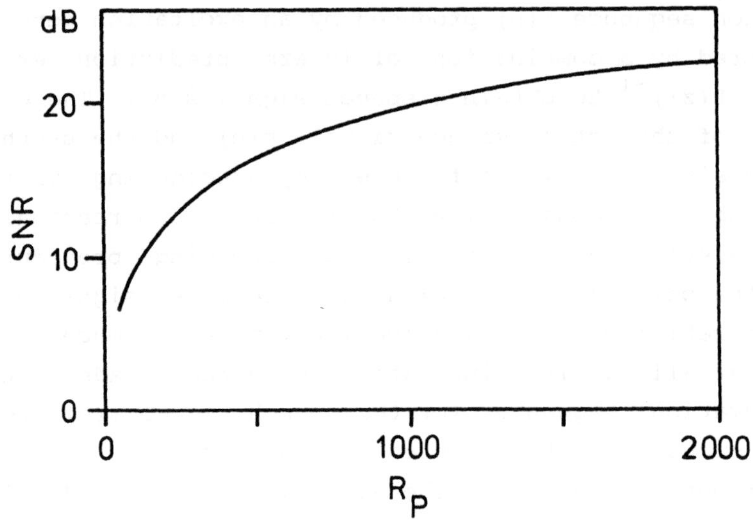

Fig. 9: SNR in dB for a MPLPC scheme

using VQ from which a total rate of 8 to 10 kb/s follows for these MPLPC schemes. Fig. 10 shows an example of an innovation sequence i(n) and the synthesized speech segment $\tilde{s}(n)$ for a MPLPC scheme at a data rate of 8 kb/s together with the original speech segment s(n). Obviously an innovation sequence consisting of 750 pulses per second allows to reproduce the waveform very well, especially in the voiced parts. At pulse rates lower than 500 pulses per second the SNR values as well as the speech quality of MPLPC decrease rapidly indicating that for excitation a pulse generator is no longer adequate.

A further reduction of the data rate without degrading the speech quality can be obtained by using RELP-S schemes with stochastic innovation sequences [18,28]. In the so-called CELP schemes a random number generator combined with a gain control is used as excitation generator. The generator produces a given number K of innovation sequences each consisting of n Gaussian distributed random numbers. The K innovation sequences can be considered to be vectors of an n-dimensional codebook. In order to encode a speech segment containing n samples

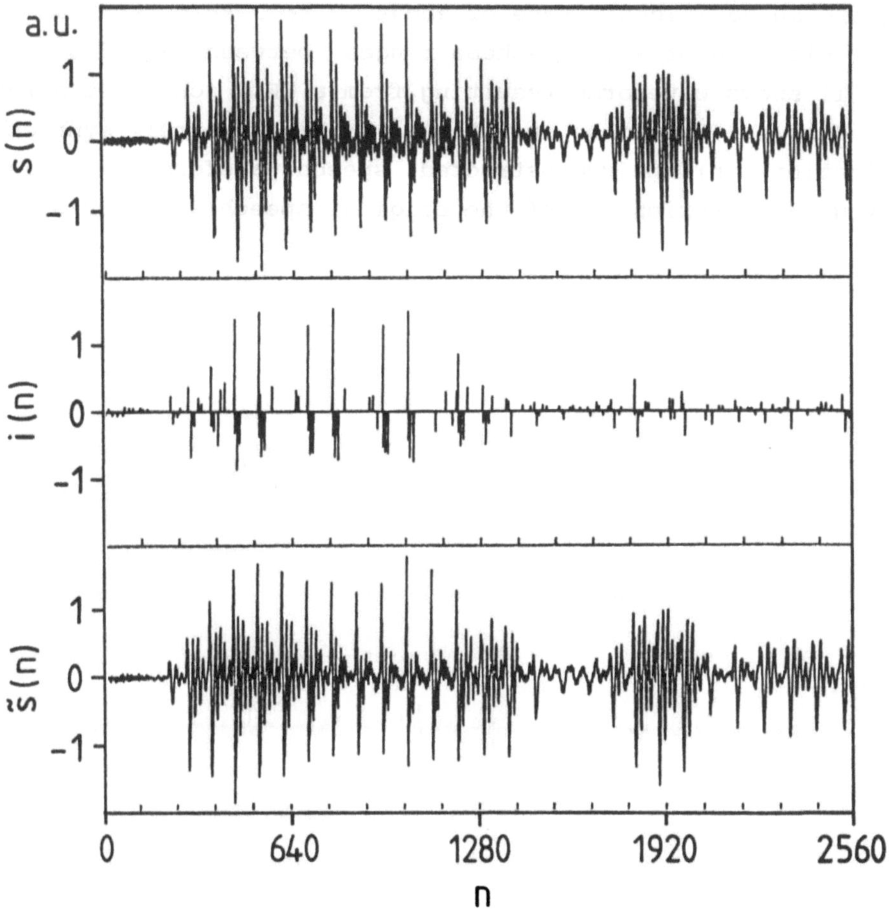

Fig. 10: Waveforms of a MPLPC scheme with 8 kb/s

each codebook vector combined with an optimum gain factor is used to excite the inverse prediction error filters and thus produces a speech segment $\tilde{s}(n)$. That codebook vector together with its gain factor yielding the minimum error power E is the optimum innovation sequence which is transmitted to the receiver. The rate needed to encode the optimum innovation sequences is ld(K)/n bit per sample. Typical values for a CELP scheme with high speech quality are K=1024 and n=40 resulting in a bit rate of 2 kb/s for the excitation. The gain factors and the parameters of the inverse prediction error filters require an additional rate of about 2 to 3 kb/s so that the total bit rate of a CELP scheme ranges between 4 and 5 kb/s. Fig. 11 shows waveforms resulting from a CELP scheme at a rate of 4.8 kb/s. It can be seen that even with a purely synthetic excitation i(n) the reconstructed speech waveform $\tilde{s}(n)$ is a very good approximation of the original speech waveform s(n).

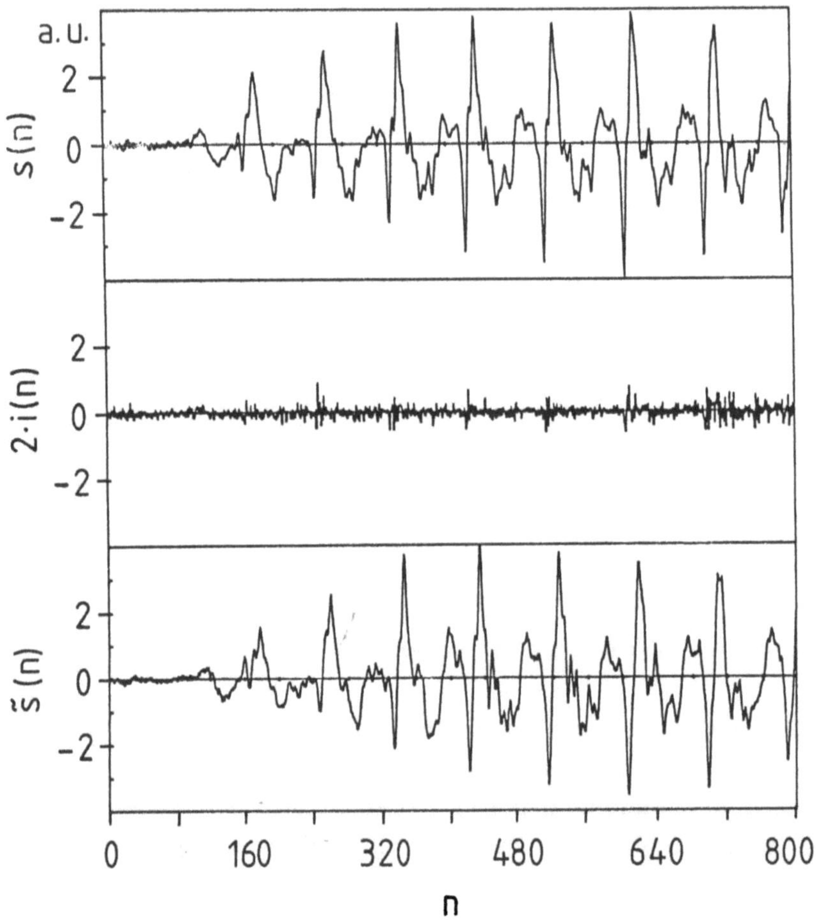

Fig. 11: Waveforms of a CELP scheme at 4.8 kb/s

6. CONCLUSION

Comparing the performances of the various speech coding schemes on the basis of MOS ratings one is led to the statements illustrated by Fig. 12. The traditional schemes PCM, DPCM, ADPCM, SBC, ATC provide an excellent speech quality at rates above 16 kb/s, while the quality rapidly decreases at rates below 10 kb/s. On the other hand the classical vocoder schemes operating in the low-bit-rate range at 4.8 kb/s and far below achieve a quality which is at best only fair. This is due to the limitations of the speech production model used so far.

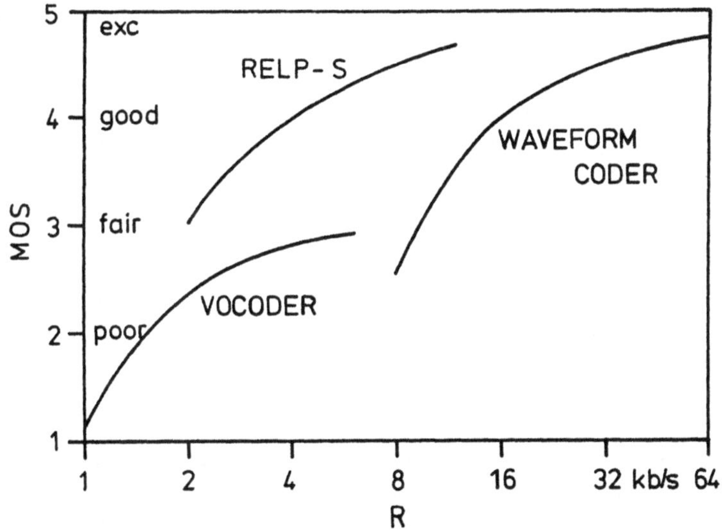

Fig. 12: MOS ratings for speech coding schemes

The recent concepts of RELP-S (MPLPC, CELP) coders which follow the principle of speech analysis by synthesis promise to fill this gap in performance at medium and low data rates. Today the practical realizations of these concepts suffer from their extreme complexity which is about ten times as high as that of the conventional coding schemes. However, the rapid progress in microelectronics will help to overcome this problem in the near future.

REFERENCES

[1] Atal, B.S., "Predictive Coding of Speech at Low Bit Rates", IEEE Trans. on Communications, COM-30, (1986) pp. 600-614.

[2] Atal, B.S., and Rabiner, L.R., "Speech Research Directions", AT&T Techn. Journal 65, (1986) pp. 75-88.

[3] Atal, R., and Remde, J.R., "A New Model of LPC Excitation for Producing Natural-Sounding Speech at Low Bit Rates", Proc. IEEE Int. Conf. Acoust., Speech, and Signal Processing, Paris 1982, pp. 614-617.

[4] Brehm, H., and Stammler, W., "Description and Generation of Spherically Invariant Speech-Model Signals", Signal Processing 12, (1987) pp. 119-141.

[5] Buzo, A., Gray, H., Gray, R.M., and Markel, J.D., "Speech Coding Based upon Vector Quantization", IEEE Trans. on Acoust., Speech, and Signal Processing ASSP-28, (1980) pp. 562-574.

[6] Caspers, B., and Atal, B.S., "Role of Multi-Pulse Excitation in Synthesis of Natural-Sounding Voiced Speech", Proc. IEEE Int. Conf. Acoust., Speech, and Signal Processing, Dallas 1987, pp. 2388-2394.

[7] Cheng, D.Y., Gersho, A., Ramamurthi, B., and Shoham, Y., "Fast Search Algorithms for Vector Quantization and Pattern Matching", Proc. Int. Conf. Acoust., Speech, and Signal Processing, San Diego (CA) 1984, pp. 9.11.1-9.11.4.

[8] Cuperman, V., and Gersho, A., "Adaptive Differential Vector Coding of Speech", Conference Record Globe-Com 82, (1982) pp. 1092-1096.

[9] Flanagan, J.L., "Speech Analysis, Synthesis, and Perception", Springer-Verlag Berlin, Heidelberg, New York 1972.

[10] Flanagan, J.L., et al., "Speech Coding", IEEE Trans. on Communications, COM-27, (1979) pp. 710-736.

[11] Gersho, A., "On the Structure of Vector Quantizers", IEEE Trans. Inform. Theory, IT-28, (1982) pp.157-166.

[12] Gray, R.M., and Karnin, E.D., "Multiple Local Optima in Vector Quantizers", IEEE Trans. Inform. Theory, IT-28, (1982) pp. 256-261.

[13] Gray, R.M., "Vector Quantization", IEEE ASSP Magazine 1, (1984) pp. 4-29.

[14] Guth, P., Reininger, H., und Wolf, D., "Zur Vektorquantisierung der Prädiktorparameter", Kleinheubacher Berichte 29, (1986) pp. 91-94.

[15] Itakura, F., and Saito, S., "Analysis Synthesis Telephony Based upon the Maximum Likelihood Method", Reports on the 6th Int. Cong. Acoust., ed. by Y. Kohasi, Tokyo, (1968) pp. C-5-5 - C17-20.

[16] Jayant, N.S., "Coding Speech at Low Bit Rates", IEEE Spectrum 23, (1986) pp. 58-63.

[17] Jayant, N.S., and Noll, P., "Digital Coding of Waveforms", Prentice Hall, Inc., Englewood Cliffs, New Jersey 1984.

[18] Kroon, P., and Atal, B.S., "Quantization Procedures for the Excitation in CELP Coders", Proc. IEEE Int. Conf. Acoust., Speech, and Signal Processing, Dallas 1987, pp. 1649-1652.

[19] Kroon, P., Deprettere, E.F., and Sluyter, R.J., "Regular-Pulse Excitation - A Novel Approach to Effective and Efficient Coding of Speech", IEEE Trans. on Acoust., Speech, and Signal Processing, ASSP 34, (1986) pp. 1054-1063.

[20] Linde, Y., Buzo, A., and Gray, R.M., "An Algorithm for Vector Quantizer Design", IEEE Trans. on Communications, COM-28, (1980) pp.84-95.

[21] Makhoul, J., Roucos, S., and Gish, H., "Vector Quantization in Speech Coding", Proc. IEEE, 73, (1985) pp. 1551-1588.

[22] Makhoul, J., "Linear Prediction: A Tutorial Review", Proc. IEEE, 63, (1975) pp. 561-580.

[23] Markel, J.D., and Gray Jr., A.H., "Linear Prediction of Speech", Springer-Verlag, Berlin, Heidelberg, New York 1976.

[24] Rabiner, L.R., and Schafer, R.W., "Digital Processing of Speech Signals", Prentice-Hall, Inc., Englewood Cliffs, New Jersey 1978.

[25] Ramachandran, R.P., and Kabal, P., "Stability and Performance Analysis of Pitch Filters in Speech Coders", IEEE Trans. Acoust., Speech, and Signal Processing, ASSP-35, (1987) pp. 937-946.

[26] Reininger, H., "Prinzipien der digitalen Sprachcodierung und ihre Anwendung zur Sprachübertragung über Fadingkanäle bei mittleren Datenraten", Dissertation, Institut für Angewandte Physik, Universität Frankfurt am Main, 1987.

[27] Reininger, H., and Wolf, D., "Fast Search Algorithms for Speech Coding Schemes Using Vector Quantization", Signal Processing III: Theories and Applications, North Holland, Amsterdam 1986, pp. 453-456

[28] Schroeder, M.R., and Atal, B.S., "Code-Excited Linear Prediction (CELP): High-Quality Speech at Very Low Bit Rates", Proc. IEEE Int. Conf. Acoust., Speech, and Signal Processing, Tampa 1985, pp. 937-940.

[29] Wolf, D., "Speech Coding", Proc. Zürich Seminar on Digital Communications, (1984) pp. 1-5.

[30] Wolf, D., "Statistical Models of Speech", NTG-Fachberichte 65, (1978) pp. 1-9.

Acoustic-Phonetic Decoding of Speech

(Statistical Modeling for Phonetic Recognition)

Richard M. Schwartz*
Y. Chow, M. Dunham, O. Kimball, M. Krasner,
F. Kubala, J. Makhoul, P. Price, S. Roucos

BBN Laboratories Inc.
10 Moulton Street
Cambridge, MA, 02238
USA

Abstract: Several methods for acoustic-phonetic decoding are reviewed. Emphasis is placed on the need for mathematical methods for speech recognition. Several examples of statistical methods are described. The author presents several techniques for incorporating "speech knowledge" into these statistical models, and provides a simple formalism for using multiple knowledge sources in a coherent speech recognition system.

1. Introduction

A wide variety of approaches for acoustic-phonetic decoding have been proposed in the literature of the past three or four decades. All of these techniques attempt to capture the similarities among different repetitions of the same words, while allowing for what can appear to be random variation between repetitions. This mapping of variable events onto a discrete set of classes is the basic pattern recognition problem in speech recognition. Success requires that we have both good models for the phenomena in speech and good recognition techniques for distinguishing among the different classes.

Many efforts in speech recognition try to simplify the problem by defining words in terms of phonemes. A phoneme is the basic acoustic unit of speech in any given language, such that a different phoneme implies a different word. The existence of the phoneme is based on the psycholinguistic evidence that, at some level, people produce most words in terms of a sequence of simpler (smaller) units. Linguists identify from 30 to 50 phonemes that comprise each language. However, the phonemes of one language do not necessarily map directly to

*While this paper was organized, written, and presented by the first author, several paragraphs of this paper are taken directly from several conference papers written by various combinations of all the authors.

NATO ASI Series, Vol. F46
Recent Advances in Speech Understanding
and Dialog Systems
Edited by H. Niemann et al.

the phonemes of another language. In addition, it is difficult to find invariant features that correspond to these phonemes; the acoustic realization of a phoneme varies considerably due to coarticulation with the phonetic environment, as well as with several other factors. Consequently, while phonemes are certainly statistically separable no one has yet devised an automatic method for unambiguously recognizing the phonetic sequence in a passage of speech.

Why then should we use phonemes as the basic recognition unit? First, much of the variation in speech can be expressed easily in terms of regular phonological variations modeled as string substitutions among phonemes. Second, and perhaps more important, since each phoneme occurs more frequently than most words we can estimate a good model for them from a relatively small amount of training speech. Furthermore, to the extent that the phonetic model of words is correct, we can predict how a person will say new words, based on an acoustic-phonetic analysis of other words with the same phonemes.

The phonemes that we use for speech recognition need not necessarily be those defined by linguists. There has been recent interest and exciting research into finding a more natural set of units automatically to improve the accuracy of the speech model /BAH 88/. However, while the methods presented in this paper could apply equally to automatically derived units, all the examples are based on more conventional phonetic units.

This chapter begins with a brief review of several (but not all) common approaches to acoustic-phonetic decoding followed by some observations and suggestions about the requirements for a successful approach to acoustic-phonetic decoding. Section 3 presents and compares two statistical models for phonetic recognition. In Section 4 we describe several particular ways in which structural speech knowledge can be incorporated into the statistical models thus reducing the effective dimensionality and thereby improving the accuracy of the recogniton. There are several different logical components in a speech recognition system. In Section 5 we discuss various search algorithms and describe the use of multiple knowledge sources in the BYBLOS speech recognition system /CHO 87/.

In addition to presenting several particular methods for phonetic decoding, the author offers several strong opinions on some of the features of a system that he feels will be essential to good performance. Most of these opinions are flagged clearly as such, but some others may have slipped through unlabeled. Hopefully the reader will agree that the arguments supplied support the opinions given.

2. Methods for Acoustic-Phonetic Decoding

The many methods for speech recognition can be broken down into two categories based on the techniques used. Generally, they fall into:

- Heuristic/Rule-Based Approaches
- Distance-Based Approaches
- Probabilistic Approaches

The heuristic approach attempts to use expert system techniques to immitate the ability of some people to recognize speech by examining spectrogram or parameter plots of speech. These methods usually fall into two categories: bottom-up, and top-down. Typically, in the bottom-up approach, a sequence of heuristic rules are applied to the parameters of a sentence to segment and label different regions of the speech. The rules are usually applied in a hierarchical manner, to successively divide the speech into finer and finer regions. Figure 1 illustrates the hierarchical segmentation of a sentence into broad phonetic classes based on the gross features in three bands of energy.

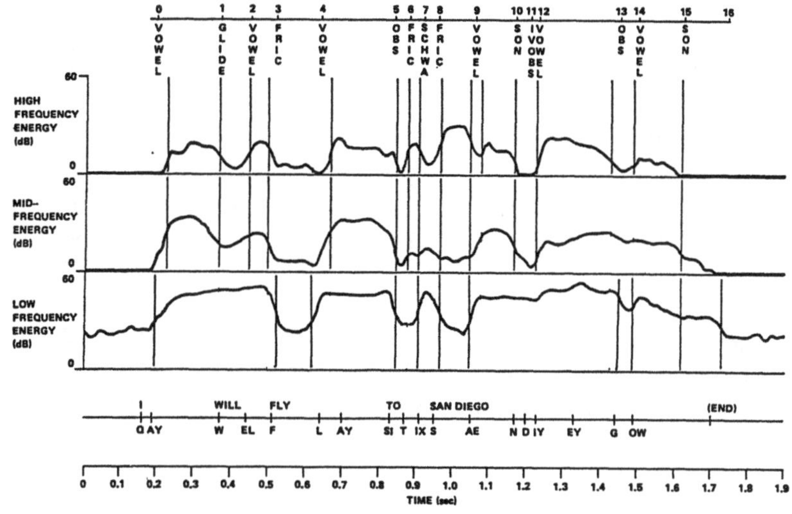

FIGURE 1: Plot of several band energy functions with dip detector output shown. The dip detector results can be used to segment the utterance into regions of acoustic similarity.

The hierarchical nature of the rules means that they can be tailored to specific kinds of speech phenomena. At the same time, since each rule depends on previous decisions, they are vulnerable to possible errors in those decisions. This will be discussed further below. It is also possible to apply a set of production rules to the speech input to parse the parameter tracks into the likely sequences of phonetic units. These production rules can be applied in either a top-down or bottom-up manner. To the extent that the rules correctly describe all the possible realizations of the parameters for a given phoneme, without accepting too many other other phonemes, these production rules can serve as a viable recognition approach. The attractiveness of this approach is that one can write production rules based on subjective observations and intuitions. In addition, it is possible to learn the parameters of the rules statistically from large amounts of speech.

The distance-based approach is commonly used for matching whole word templates, although it can be used for phonetic units as well. This method is based on the very reasonable assumption that if the parameters of two speech events are very similar, they are probably the same kind of (word or phoneme) event. As the distance increases, the likelihood that the two are the same decreases. Usually, some time-warping of the pattern to the input is necessary to allow for varying duration of the different phonemes.

Figure 2 illustrates a network of diphone templates that can be used both to recognize and synthesize speech. Between each phoneme center there is a directed arc which represents a typical parameter trajectory from the middle of the first phoneme to the middle of the second phoneme. The problem with the distance based approach is that it is not always true that the smaller of two large distances corresponds to the more likely class, since the distance metric may not accurately reflect either probability or perceptual distance. However, due to its inate simplicity the distance-based approach is quite popular.

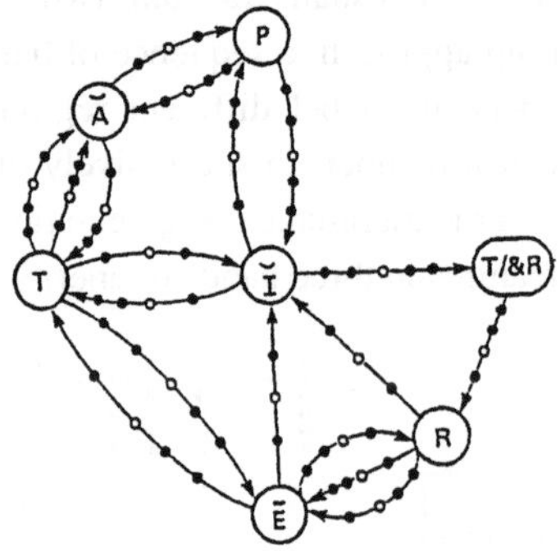

FIGURE 2: Network of Diphone Templates for Recognition or Synthesis. Each template represents the diphone from the center of one phoneme to the center of the next.

The probabilistic approach requires that we have a statistical model for the acoustic realization of each phonetic unit. This means that it should be possible to compute for any observed speech, the probability that the observed parameters were produced by any particular sequence of hypothesized speech models. Then, using the maximum likelihood assumption, we can choose the sequence of classes such that this probability is maximized. Two examples of probabilistic models for phonetic decoding are the hidden Markov model (HMM) and the stochastic segment model. Figure 3 illustrates a 3-state HMM model for a phoneme.

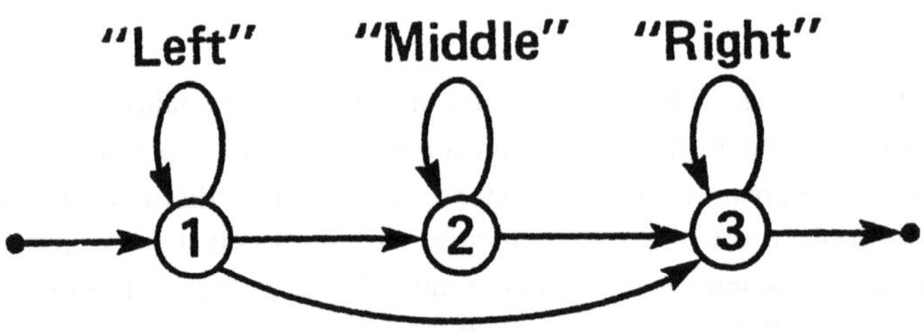

FIGURE 3: Hidden Markov Model of a Phoneme. States 1, 2, and 3 are assumed to correspond approximately to the left, middle, and right portion of a phoneme.

The circles represent states of the model. Associated with each state is a probability distribution for the possible speech spectra.

$$b_i(v) = p(v_t = k | s_t = i);\ i=1,2,3;\ \text{for all } k \tag{1}$$

For each allowed transition (indicated by the arrows in Figure 3) we have a transition probability

$$a_{ij} = P\ (s_t = j | s_{t-1} = i) \tag{2}$$

the probability of state i being followed by state j. While the relation is not direct, we find it useful to think of the states as corresponding to the beginning, middle, and end of a phoneme. The parameters for each of the phonetic models are estimated from a large training set of speech using the forward-backward algorithm. For recognition, we use the Viterbi algorithm or a similar algorithm to find the most likely sequence of phonetic models that are consistent with the phonetic lexicon and the grammar. This method is attractive because it is largely automatic, requiring no manual labeling of data, or painstaking discovery and formulation of hundreds or thousands of rules. The use of hidden Markov models for speech recognition is described quite well in /BAH 83/, /RAB 87/.

A second probabilistic method for phonetic modeling is the stochastic segment model. This model differs from the HMM model in that it does not make the Markov assumption of independent observations within a phoneme. Instead, it models the whole phonetic segment as a single stochastic unit. To do this, it first warps the hypothesized phonetic segment to a fixed length so that it can be compared more easily with each phonetic model. The time-warping depends only on the input segment, so that it is only done once. With 14 spectral features per time-warped frame and a 10-frame model, each segment is a 140-dimensional vector. This entire vector can then, in principle, be modeled as a whole to capture dependence between successive frames.

2.1 Discussion

The features of these and other methods can be discussed independently of the particular methods themselves. For example, we can compare bottom-up and top-down methods.

In bottom-up methods, local decisions are made which guide further processing. This can result in a substantial data reduction, and thus reduce computation. It can also simplify the later stages of processing in that the environment for each decision has been determined by previous decisions. However, errors made in earlier stages will propagate to later stages, causing irrecoverable errors.

Top-down methods consider all possible hypotheses, given the constraints of the problem (grammar, lexicon, continuity, etc.). Low level acoustic parameters are consulted in a verification (hypothesize and score) paradigm. This method will suffer much less from early decisions, since very few are made. Of course, the top-down approach may require more computation than the bottom-up approach.

Consider, for a moment, what requirements would be placed on a bottom-up approach for it to perform well. In current phonetic recognition systems, the first choice decisions are typically correct about 60%-80% of the time. Let's say that, to reduce this problem, our bottom-up phonetic recognition system allows several choices (but not all choices) for phoneme segmentation and labeling. If the average sentence is 40 phonemes long, and want 95% of the sentences to have any possibility of being correct (i.e. the correct sequence of phonemes are among the many choices) then 99.9% of the correct phonemes must be among the choices because

$$0.999^{40} = 0.96$$

This argument quickly leads to the clear conclusion that hard decisions must be avoided wherever possible.

From the discussions above we might list what seem to us to be desirable properties for a speech recognition system:

- The system should use a consistent scoring metric, such as probability, because many scores are combined to decide on the final answer.
- The system should take phonetic context into account as much as possible.
- The system should combine spectral parameters and acoustic-phonetic features within the same formalism.
- It must be possible to train the parameters of the system automatically to allow for retraining after some condition (e.g. microphone, speaker, environment) has changed.
- The search strategy should use global decisions rather than local decisions to optimize accuracy.

3. Statistical Methods for Acoustic Decoding

In this section we present a more detailed description of the two probabilistic methods defined above. But first we offer a short discussion with several of the author's opinions concerning the use of mathematical models in general and probabilistic models in particular.

3.1 Mathematical Models

There are several advantages for using a mathematical model (as opposed to a heuristic one) as the basis for phonetic and speech recognition. First, a mathematical model enables us to make mathematical (i.e. precise) statements about the behavior of the system and often provides a method for optimizing some performance criterion. Two such criteria - though not the only ones - would be to minimize the probability of errors, or maximize the possibility of a correct answer. Second, automatic training algorithms with well-behaved convergence criteria exist or can be devised for systems with a well-understood mathematical basis. As stated before, this feature is probably essential for any practical system. Third, a mathematical basis for understanding the system makes it easier to describe a system to others or to understand its behavior and how to improve it. When an entire system can be described in terms of a few diagrams and equations then people can easily share detailed experiences and ideas with others. Thus, the techniques can be easily taught and the field progresses from an art to a science. Fourth, the system is more likely to be generalizable to all conditions and languages if the assumptions are only in the mathematical structure of the system. For example, a completely different set of phonemes (as in the change from one language to another) would only require retraining the parameters of the mathematical models.

Now for some specific opinions about the use of probabilistic models for speech recognitions. We will try to answer most of the criticisms of the probabilistic approach:

- There are many ways to incorporate our "speech knowledge" in probabilistic systems. They need not be "dumb".
- The computations needed for such top-down search algorithms is indeed large, but within the capabilities of currently available chip technology.
- The methods apply equally well to speaker-independent as well as speaker-dependent recognition (as shown by Rabiner /RAB 87/, Lee /LEE 87/, and others at this conference).
- These models are capable of making fine phonetic distinctions.
- The probabilistic approach will *not* always choose the most likely (a priori) event, no matter what is said. It *will* correctly weigh the a priori probability and the a posteriori evidence to optimize performance.

Some additional advantages of the probabilistic models are that they

- represent a good model of variability in speech,
- Provide a unified framework for scoring,
- Facilitate the combination of knowledge sources,
- Separate the data from the algorithms,
- Allow for automatic training and adaptation.

3.2 HMM Phonetic Models

In this section we describe a procedure for using HMMs as the basic phonetic recognition model in a continuous speech recognition system. Hidden Markov Models (HMMs) have been shown to provide an effective statistical formalism for speech recognition. They have been used to model whole words in both isolated /LEV 83/, /RAB 87/ and continuous /BAK 75/ speech recognition. They have also been used to model phonemes for continuous speech recognition /BAK 75/, /BAH 75/, /BAH 83/. Rabiner /RAB 87/ gives a thorough treatment of the mathematics and use of HMM models. The Hidden Markov Model has two important advantages over many other models for speech. First, it provides a well-defined structural model for variability in both time and in frequency (spectral variation), both of which occur in speech. Second, once the structure of the models are specified, the parameters of the models can be estimated automatically with a large amount of speech data using the forward-backward or Baum-Welch algorithm /BAU 67/.

As mentioned several times, we would like to train the phonetic HMMs in as automatic a procedure as possible. First we record a training set of speech. The speech is divided into sentences for convenience. For each sentence spoken we have only the digitized speech and the text. The text contains only the list of words spoken without any time information. Next, we must initialize all the phonetic models. This initial estimate can be constructed manually or automatically. For discrete HMMs this initial estimate can simply be a flat distribution

$$b_i(v) = \frac{1}{N_k} \text{ for all } k.$$

Next, we consult a phonetic lexicon for the phonetic spellings of each of the words in the text. We then construct a model for each word in the sentence by concatenating the appropriate phonetic models. If a word has more than one pronunciation then a network of phonetic HMMs is constructed. Similarly, a single hidden Markov model for each sentence is created by concatenating the word models.

The forward-backward algorithm is applied to all the training data - sentence by sentence - collecting and distributing "counts" to the phonetic models. At the end of each pass through all the data, all the parameters of the phonetic models are reestimated and the next iteration begins. We find that five to six iterations are sufficient for convergence. The resulting parameters maximize the likelihood of the speech observed in the training data, given the models.

For recognition we can use the concatenated phonetic models for each word as whole-word models. If each phonetic model is used in many words, then the word models refer to the appropriate phonetic models rather than duplicating them. The effect is still equivalent to constructing word models.

The HMM is a basic mathematical tool that can be used in many ways. The "outputs" in the model can be spectral parameters or features. It provides a good model for variations in both time and spectral space. The training process is largely automatic. As we will see later on, it can be made to model a large number of coarticulation effects and the search strategy can be global in nature. However, there are (at least) two possible limitations of the simple HMM model described above. First, in the Markov model successive frames are assumed to be conditionally independent. This is known not to be true. Second, the model given with self-loops and skips has very weak durational constraints. Even when explicit duration PDFs are used, the relative state durations and total phoneme duration are ignored. Next, we discuss a more complex model that tries to deal with some of these deficiencies.

3.3 Stochastic Segment Model

Evidence of the importance of spectral correlation over the duration of a segment can be found in the success of segment-based vocoding systems /ROU 82/. Consequently, we investigated an alternate approach, called stochastic segment modeling to better capture the spectral/temporal relationship over the duration of a phoneme. Below, we define the Stochastic Segment Model followed by a description of the segment-based recognition and training algorithms. Then, we present experimental results for phoneme and word recognition, comparing the results to HMM recognition results for the same tasks. This work is described in more detail in /ROU 87/.

A speech "segment" is a variable-length sequence of feature vectors, $X = [x_1 \, x_2 \ldots \, x_L]$, where x_i is a k-dimensional feature vector (e.g. cepstral coefficients). We can think of this observation as a variable-length realization of an underlying fixed-length spectral trajectory $Y = [y_1 \, y_2 \ldots \, y_m]$ where the duration of X is variable due to variation in speaking rate. Given X, we define the fixed-length representation $Y = XT_L$ where the $L \times m$ matrix T_L, called the resampling transformation, represents a time-warping. The best recognition results have been obtained using linear time sampling without interpolation. The segment Y, called a *resampled* segment, is an m-long sequence of k-dimensional vectors (or a $k \times m$ matrix). The stochastic segment model for each phoneme α is based on the resampled segment Y and is a conditional probability density function $p(Y|\alpha)$. The density $p(Y|\alpha)$ is assumed to be a km-dimensional multivariate Gaussian model for the entire fixed-length segment Y.

3.3.1 Discussion

In this work, typically k=14 and m=10. Consequently, the segment model has 140 dimensions. Because of insufficient training, we cannot estimate the full phoneme-dependent covariance matrix, so we must make some simplifying assumptions about the structure of the problem. For the experiments reported here, we assume that the m samples of the resampled segment are independent of each other, which gives a block diagonal covariance structure for Y, where each block in the segment covariance matrix corresponds to the $k \times k$ covariance of a sample. The block-diagonal structure saves a factor of m in storage and training and a factor of m^2 in computation. The disadvantage of this simplification is that it reinstates the invalid assumption of independence that we were trying to avoid.

There are two aspects of the stochastic segment model which might be useful properties for a speech recognition system. First, the transformation T_L, (e.g. the linear time-warping function) which maps the variable-length observation to a fixed-length segment, can be designed to constrain the temporal structure of a phoneme model. To achieve this constraint with a HMM model would require a very large model. Second, the whole-segment model provides a good structure for incorporating additional segment-based acoustic-phonetic features in a statistical (rather than rule-based) recognition system.

3.3.2 Recognition Algorithm

The recognition algorithm can be formulated in a time-synchronous dynamic programming procedure that finds the best matching sequence of segment models for an input passage. The procedure is somewhat more complicated than for HMM recognition, since the alignment of the input depends on the entire phoneme. For each new frame we consider all preceding frames as a possible starting time for a segment. The algorithm simply keeps track of the best scoring sequence of segments to account for the interval from the beginning of the sentence to each time. If there is a grammar, the search algorithm must be modified accordingly. The extra loop (with respect to the typical HMM viterbi search) of beginning times for the segment increases the computation considerably.

3.3.3 Training Algorithm

The training algorithm for estimating the segment models from continuous speech iterates between two steps: first, the maximum probability phonetic segmentation of the training speech is obtained, then new maximum likelihood density estimates of the segment models are derived based on the aligned speech. We assume that the phonetic transcription of the training data is known and that we have an initial Gaussian model $p_0(Y|\alpha)$ for all phonemes. (Phonetic transcriptions can be generated automatically from the word sequence that corresponds to the speech by using a word pronunciation dictionary.) The iteration can continue until convergence. However, in most of our experiments we have used only one iteration for training due to the large computational requirement. In limited experiments, more iterations made little difference.

3.3.4 Experimental Results

In this section we present results for a phoneme recognition task, as well as word recognition results for a segment-based recognition system and an HMM-based system. All experiments use $m = 10$ samples per segment and $k = 14$ mel-frequency cepstral coefficients per sample. These values are based on work in segment quantization /ROU 83/, and limited experimentation confirmed that these values represent a reasonable compromise between complexity and performance. The spectral analysis used was the same for both the HMM and segment-based systems.

3.3.4.1 Phoneme Recognition

Phoneme recognition tests were run on one speaker using five minutes of training data. The phonetic recognition accuracy using 61 context-independent phonetic segment models was 74% correct with 8% insertions. For reference /SCH 85/, a discrete hidden Markov model with 3 states/phoneme and using a codebook with 256 entries has 62% phonetic recognition rate with 12% insertions on the same database. The HMM recognition performance on this database is higher when phoneme models are conditioned on left context, 75% correct with 12% insertions /SCH 85/. In the latter case, 600 left-context phonetic models are used in the HMM system while 61 phonetic models are used in the stochastic segment model.

3.3.4.2 Word Recognition

The segment-based word recognition system consists of a dictionary of phoneme pronunciation networks and a collection of segment phoneme models. The recognition algorithm searches for the most likely sequence of words. Each phonetic model need only be scored against each region of speech once, as the phonetic models are shared by several words.

We used a 334 word vocabulary, speaker-dependent database based on an electronic mail task. The database included three different male speakers. The initial segment models were obtained on training with segmentations given by the discrete hidden Markov model recognition system. Fifteen minutes of speech was used for training the 61 phoneme models for each speaker. An additional 30 sentences (187 words from each speaker) from each speaker were used for recognition. No grammar was used.

The average word recognition accuracy for the segment system was 83%, as compared with 76% for the simple HMM system. However, the HMM system improved to 88% using phoneme models conditioned on left and right context. The segment-based recognition has not improved with the use of context-dependent models - possibly because the increased number of parameters in the segment model cannot be well estimated from the limited training data available.

4. Building Speech Knowledge into Statistical Models

While the statistical models presented above are appealing, it is desirable to be able to account for the wealth of knowledge that we have gathered about the nature of the speech process. The need for additional knowledge comes from the inability to estimate accurate statistical models from the limited amounts of training data that are feasible. Knowledge about the speech process can be used to determine the structure of our statistical models so that they have fewer free parameters that need to be estimated. Then, the power of the statistical framework is used to model that variation for which we have no deterministic model. That is, it is used to model our ignorance. The proper combination of structural models based on our knowledge and statistical models of our ignorance has lead to fairly high recognition accuracy in recent years.

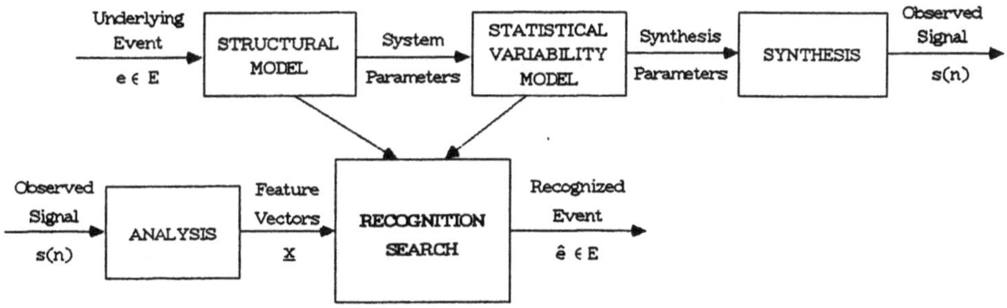

FIGURE 4: General Synthesis/Recognition Model. Recognition attempts to determine the most likely event e given the observed parameters, using the structural model and the statistical variability model.

Figure 4 illustrates a general synthesis/recognition process. We assume that there is a structural model (based on our knowledge) that transforms a sequence of events into some system parameters. These then undergo random (or unexplained) variation, which we model as statistical variability. The output parameters are used to synthesize speech. The recognition model begins with parameter analysis which attempts to recover the synthesis parameters. Then, the recognition search must use both the structural model and the statistical model to attempt to find the most likely event, given the observed signal.

The choice of the HMM as the basic phonetic model is consistent with our speech knowledge. It models variability in both time and spectral space, both of which are known to occur readily in speech. In this section we present several other specific examples of algorithms that incorporate our knowledge of speech into the model without increasing the number of free parameters too much.

4.1 Robust Model of Phonetic Coarticulation

As stated at the beginning of this chapter, the coarticulation effects on the acoustic realization of a phoneme are very large. To obtain high recognition accuracy it is important to model phonetic coarticulation as well as possible. The topic of modeling coarticulation is covered in the sequence of ICASSP papers: /SCH 84/, /SCH 85/, /CHO 86/.

As stated earlier we often decompose words into sequences of basic speech sounds or phonemes, to try to reduce the problem of modelling many words to the problem of modelling a smaller number of units. We observe that these basic units exhibit systematic acoustic variation as a function of their phonetic environment. These the coarticulation effects bridge all the phoneme boundaries. If we chose to use a larger basic unit, such as the syllable, we could model coarticulation within the syllable, but we would be making the false assumption that there are no coarticulatory effects between syllables. If, instead, we allow the coarticulatory dependency of each speech unit to extend beyond its duration, then we can model any amount of dependency that we wish. To capture this systematic variation we must first define *context-dependent* allophones or variants of each phoneme. An allophone is defined as any variant of a phoneme, which may be statistically different from other allophones of that phoneme. We commonly use allophones defined by the preceding and following contexts. (We will often use the terms "left" and "right" instead of "preceding" and "following".) This idea of context-dependent units - as opposed to larger units - is key to the modeling of coarticulation.

4.1.1 Training Problem

For any units with context-dependency larger than the phoneme, we will have a training problem. While some of the contexts may occur frequently, many will not occur with sufficient frequency to estimate a robust acoustic model. In fact, large numbers of the possible contexts will not occur at all in any particular set of training speech. A simple solution would be to use the most detailed context-dependent model with a sufficient number of training samples. This algorithm for choosing the model, however, does not make optimal use of the training data, and does not properly account for coarticulatory phenomena. To solve this problem, we must examine more closely how coarticulation interacts with our 3-state model for a phoneme.

4.1.2 Weighted Context-Dependent Models

Both experience and reason tell us that the coarticulatory effect of an adjacent phoneme is greatest in the part of the phoneme closest to that adjacent phoneme. For example, a phoneme to the left will have the most effect on the left part (state 1) of a phoneme, and the least effect on the right part (state 3). Therefore we use a combined context model as shown for the example model of the /e^y/ in "whales":

$$
\begin{aligned}
\hat{p}(\underline{x}|e^y \text{ in whales}) = \; & \\
& +\lambda_1 \; p(\underline{x}|\, e^y) \\
& +\lambda_2 \; p(\underline{x}|w\, e^y) \\
& +\lambda_3 \; p(\underline{x}|\, e^y\, l) \\
& +\lambda_4 \; p(\underline{x}|w\, e^y\, l) \\
& +\lambda_5 \; p(\underline{x}|\, e^y \text{ in whales})
\end{aligned}
$$

where $\underline{\lambda} = f(\#\ \text{Occurrences, State})$

$$\text{and} \sum_{k=1}^{5} \lambda_k = 1$$

That is, the combined model, $\hat{p}$, is a linear combination of the various context-dependent models. The weight vector, $\underline{\lambda}$, depends on the state of the phoneme model (left, middle, right), and the amount of training for each type of model.

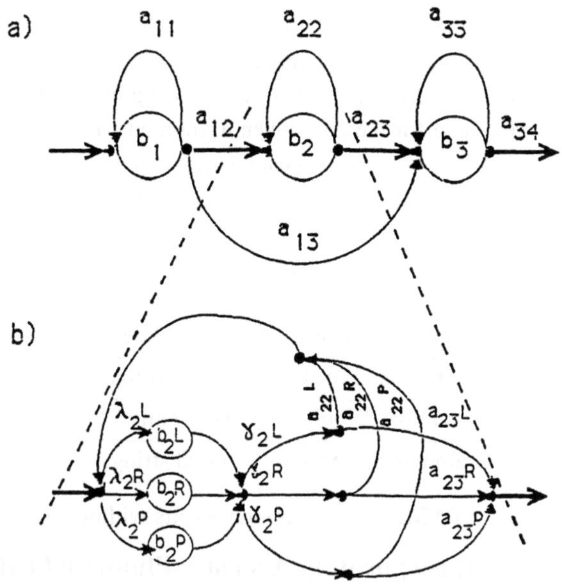

FIGURE 5: Expanded Hidden Markov Model. a) Model of a phoneme b) Expanded model for state 2.

That is, to avoid the lack of robustness due to insufficient amounts of training, we can smooth these detailed context-dependent models with well trained context-independent models. Thus, the phonetic modeling is not tied to any particular level of context, such as the diphone or syllable. It attempts to use the information in the training data to the extent possible. Figure 5a above shows the basic HMM model for a phoneme. In Figure 5b, the second state and all its transitions are replaced by a subnetwork of three different context models in parallel, with weights to combine them. For the case of /e^y/ in *whales*, we define some terms below:

$$b_2L = p(v_t|s_t = 2, we^y) \tag{1}$$

$$\lambda_2L = \textit{weight of left–context model for state 2 which is a function of } N_{we^y}$$

where N_c is the number of occurrences of context c in the training data. During forward-backward training the models are kept separate. Prior to recognition, the models for a state can be combined into a single pdf to save computation.

4.1.3 Experiments With Context

Below we summarize the results of experiments designed to demonstrate the effectiveness of the coarticulation model proposed above. The isolated E-set experiment, which is described in /SCH 84/, illustrates the use of phonetic context directly for the case of minimal pair distinctions. The continuous phonetic recognition experiment, described in /SCH 85/, shows the generalization to arbitrary phoneme sequence recognition. The word recognition experiments, described in /CHO 86/, extend the model to word-dependent context. In each experiment, the recognition accuracy is measured using context-independent phonetic models and various combinations of context-dependent models.

In the interest of brevity, Table 1 compares the recognition accuracy for the context-independent phonetic model with that for the appropriate context-dependent model for each of these experiments. The word recognition and sentence recognition accuracies are also presented for the case when a grammar (test set perlexity of 31) was used. In all cases, the benefit of using the robust coarticulation model over the simple context-independent phonetic model was a reduction of the error rate by at least a factor of two and often more.

Experiment	*Complexity*	*No Context*	*With Context*
Isolated E-Set	9 letters	93%	97%
Continuous Phonetic	50 phones	62%	81%
Continuous Word	334 words	76%	90%
Grammar-Word	Perplexity 31	95%	99%
Grammar-Sentence	word strings	66%	90%

TABLE 1: Recognition results without and with context-dependent models.

4.2 Incorporating Acoustic-Phonetic Features

Several acoustic-phonetic recognition systems are based on the use of complex acoustic-phonetic features that are found to perform quite well at particular phonetic distinctions. These are typically higher level features that can be computed or abstracted from the frame parameters. Some examples of such features are: total phoneme duration, voice-onset-time between the burst of a plosive and the following vowel, formant trajectories, characteristic burst frequency, etc. Typically, different features are used for different phonetic distinctions. There are several motivations for using segmental features rather than the frame-by-frame parameters typically used in statistical recognition systems. They allow the use of expert knowledge which reduces the effective dimensionality, and thus reduces the training data needed to estimate reliable models. These features, which are computed over larger regions than a single frame, account directly for dependence of parameters within a phoneme or between phonemes. In addition, some of these parameters may be more robust to changes in the speaker or the environment, since they can focus on those projections of the original parameters that are relatively invariant to these changes.

The question then is how to use these acoustic-phonetic features in a well-motivated statistical framework combined with the frame-by-frame parameters. The reasons for using a statistical framework have already been discussed. The reason for combining these features with the frame parameters is that the features chosen are rarely a complete set. That is, there may be some features for particular distinctions, but they are not a sufficient set to enable reconstruction of the speech, and hence are often lacking in many areas. The frame-by-frame parameters provide a covering set to which we can add segmental acoustic-phonetic features to enhance particular distinctions. As discussed earlier the Stochastic Segment Model offers one mechanism, since each segment is considered as a single unit. Unfortuantely, the segment model as presented has problems of parameter estimation, large computation, and does not perform as well as the HMM system. In /SCH 85/ we present a method for using these features within an HMM as illustrated in Figure 6.

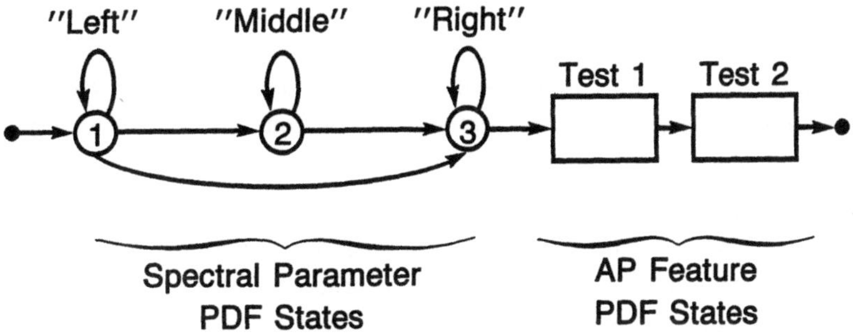

FIGURE 6: Addition of Acoustic-Phonetic Features to HMM.

The figure shows the typical phonetic 3-state HMM followed by a sequence of special feature-states represented by the rectangles. The feature-states contain arbitrary procedures for computing acoustic-phonetic features. During the recognition search, when a theory gets to the end of the 3-state model, it executes the procedures specified on the feature-states linked to that phoneme. These procedures have available the beginning and ending time of the hypothesized phoneme for each different alignment. The features computed are compared with conditional probability densities of those same features that were computed from the training set. Since each phoneme, in general, has different features, and therefore, the scores of different paths through the HMM network are no longer directly comparable, we normalize all the probabilities by the average over the phonemes that use that particular feature.

In a few cases, we were able to find segmental acoustic-phonetic features that radically improved the distinction among certain phonemes. For example the distinction among /p,t,k/ was improved from 83% to 91% using the burst frequency, burst energy, VOT, and formant transitions. Unfortunately, we found that it was quite hard to identify specific groups of phonemes with enough errors to fix. That is, the frame-based HMM performance was typically quite good, and we often could not find features that were as good. In addition, the HMM recognition keeps on improving as we make changes to the overall structure of the recognition. Because of this, we typically do not use these acoustic-phonetic features in our system.

4.3 Rapid Speaker Adaptation

To achieve the high recognition accuracy presented in previous sections, each speaker read 300 training sentences or about 15 minutes of training speech. Some speech recognition applications have a need for a new speaker to begin using the system with reasonable accuracy without investing a long time to train the system on their voice. However, as we will see below, the speaker-dependent performance degrades dramatically when the amount of training speech is reduced using the standard training procedure. A different training procedure is needed if we are to have robust and rapid speaker adaptation with only a few training sentences.

The approach that we take here is to normalize well-trained models from a "prototype" speaker to model the speech of the new speaker. The normalization requires only a few sentences (referred to as "normalization speech") from the new speaker. Below, we present a procedure for estimating a probabilistic spectral mapping from one speaker to another. This algorithm is described in more detail in /SCH 87/, /FEN 88/.

4.3.1 Probabilistic Mapping

Here we present the basis for the probabilistic transformation and show it to be equivalent to an expanded HMM model for each state of the original HMM. The transformation is generalized to be partially dependent on the particular phoneme.

4.3.1.1 Mapping From Prototype to New Speaker

We can view the discrete pdf for each state s of a discrete HMM as a probability row vector

$$\underline{p}(s) = [p(k_1|s),\ p(k_2|s),\ ...,\ p(k_N|s)], \tag{2}$$

where $p(k_i|s)$ is the probability of spectral template k_i at state s.

If we define a quantized spectrum for the prototype speaker as k_i, $1 \le i \le N$, where i is the index of the spectral template and a quantized spectrum for the new speaker as k'_j, $1 \le j \le N$, then we denote the probability that the new speaker will produce quantized spectrum k'_j, given that the prototype speaker produced spectrum k_i, as $p(k'_j|k_i)$ for all i,j. The set of probabilities $p(k'_j|k_i)$ for all i and j form an $N \times N$ matrix $\mathbf{T}$ that can be thought of as a probabilistic transformation from one speaker's spectral space to another's. If we assume that the matrix $\mathbf{T}$ is independent of the state s we can compute each discrete pdf $\underline{p}'(s)$ for the new speaker as the product of the row vector $\underline{p}(s)$ and the matrix $\mathbf{T}$

$$\underline{p}'(s) = \underline{p}(s)\ \mathbf{T}; \qquad \mathbf{T}_{ij} = p(k'_j|k_i) \tag{3}$$

We can relax the independence assumption mentioned above by using a different matrix $\mathbf{T}(ph)$ for all the HMM models involving phoneme ph. As always to avoid estimation problems we interpolate the *phoneme-dependent* transformation matrix with the *phoneme-independent* transformation matrix. The weight for the phoneme-dependent matrix depends on the number of observed frames of the particular phoneme.

$$\mathbf{T}(s) = \lambda(N_{ph})\,\mathbf{T}(ph) + [1-\lambda(N_{ph})]\mathbf{T} \quad \text{for } s \text{ in } ph$$

$$\lambda(N_{ph}) = \mathrm{MIN}(1, \mathrm{SQRT}(N_{ph}/500))$$

4.3.1.2 Expanded HMM Formulation

The probabilistic transformation can also be described in terms of an expanded HMM model for the state. Figure 7b shows a single state of the HMM for a new speaker. It contains a single discrete probability vector, $\underline{p}'(s)$. Figure 7a shows an expanded model in which the single state is replace by N parallel paths.

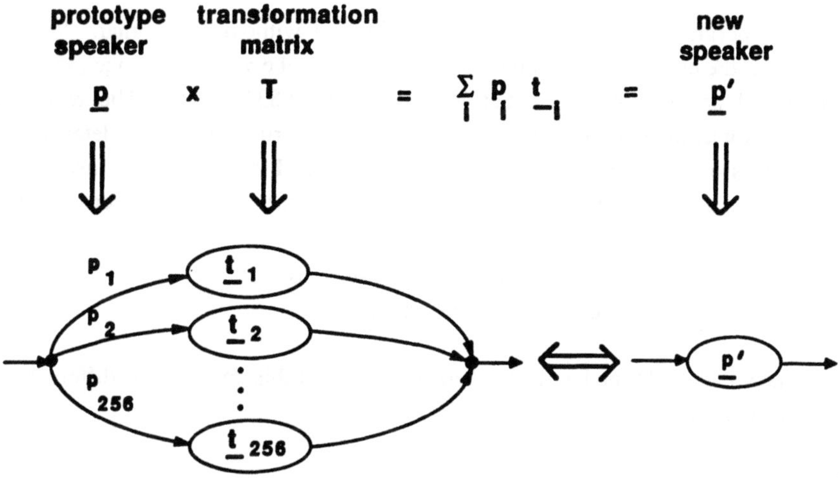

FIGURE 7: Expanded HMM. a) expanded model separating prototype pdf and transformation matrix; b) single state of the HMM.

The transition probability for path i is $p(k_i|s)$. The discrete pdf on that path is $\underline{p}(k'|k_i)$, which corresponds to row i of the transformation matrix.

We leave it as an exercise for the reader to show that the probability of any new-speaker spectrum k'_j for the expanded HMM shown is a summation of the jth probability over all N paths. Therefore, Figure 7b represents $\underline{p}'(s)$ (the left side of equation (3)), while figure 7a represents $\underline{p}(s)$ **T** (the right side). Now that we have decomposed each pdf for the new speaker into its components, we can use the forward-backward algorithm to estimate the transformation matrix while keeping the prototype pdf (the transition probabilities in figure 7a) fixed. Then, once the matrix has been determined, we can replace the expanded HMM by the single pdf resulting from the vector-matrix multiplication in (3).

Some modifications and optimizations to reduce memory and computation for the forward-backward estimation of the transformation matrix are given in /SCH 87/. In addition, an improved algorithm, using a text-dependent mapping is given by Feng /FEN 88/.

4.3.2 Adaptation Experiments

We have performed experiments on a 350-word subset of a Resource Management task. One male prototype speaker recorded 300 sentences (about 15 minutes of speech), which was used, together with the phonetic dictionary, to estimate *context-dependent* and *context-independent* phonetic models. Each of 6 new speakers also recorded the training sentences and, in a separate session, 30 test sentences. The 6 speakers included one female, one non-native speaker, one experienced speaker, and three inexperienced speakers.

The speech models for the new test speakers were computed in two ways: Speaker-Dependent training and Speaker Normalization. In addition we also performed control experiments using the prototype speaker's models without any change. These unaltered models are designated as "Cross-Speaker" models.

Recognition experiments were performed both with and without a grammar. When no grammar was used, the effective branching factor was equal to the vocabulary size (350). The grammar used had an estimated Test Set Perplexity /BAH 83/ of 20. The recognized sequence of words was then compared automatically to the correct answer to determine the percentage of errors of each type: substitutions, deletions, and insertions. We use an error measure that reflects all three types of errors in a single number. The percent error is given by

$$\%error = 100 \frac{\text{substitutions} + \text{deletions} + \text{insertions}}{\text{total words} + \text{insertions}} \tag{4}$$

The word accuracy is then defined as 100 - *%error*. Note that this definition is different from the percent correct words.

4.3.2.1 Results

Figure 8 shows the recognition error as a function of the amount of training speech (on a log scale) for both training conditions. For reference, the results using the Cross-Speaker models are also shown. The recognition error varied less with the duration of speech for speaker normalization than for speaker-dependent training - particularly when a grammar was used. The error rate with 15 seconds of normalization speech was about the same as achieved by the speaker-dependent training method with 6 to 10 minutes of training speech. In particular, when a grammar was used, the word recognition error with only 5 sentences (15 seconds) of normalization speech from each speaker was 4% (97% correct words with 1% insertions.)

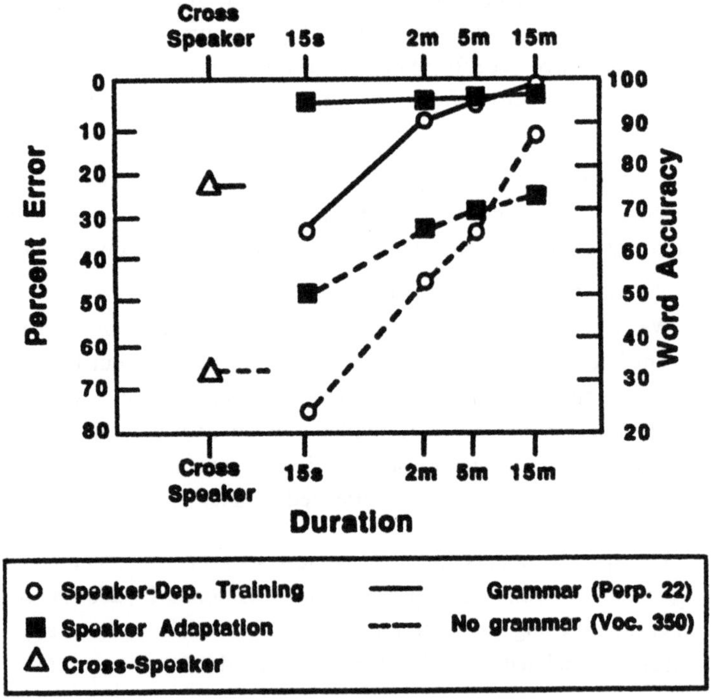

FIGURE 8:

Speaker-Dependent Training vs Normalization.

4.4 Summary

In summary, we have shown several methods for exploiting our knowledge of the nature of speech to improve the recognition accuracy under different conditions. The examples given include the choice of the HMM model to represent variability in spectrum and timing, the use of context-dependent phonetic models to capture coarticulatory effects, the inclusion of segmental acoustic-phonetic features to represent detailed knowledge about particular phonetic distinctions, and a rapid speaker adaptation algorithm based on a transformation from one speaker to another. In each case it was essential that the algorithm take into account the basic relation between dimensionality and training set size.

5. Use of Statistical Phonetic Models in Speech Recognition Systems

In this section we discuss some of the practical issues of using statistical phonetic models in speech recognition systems. Foremost among these issues is the search strategy used to find the most likely answer. Below, we discuss a few alternate search algorithms, with particular emphasis on one that has several advantages. Next, we describe how one can integrate the several different knowledge sources into a single speech recognition system.

5.1 Search Algorithms

The simple purpose of a search strategy is to find the best scoring sequence of models for the input. The reason an explicit search strategy is needed, is that for any but the simplest of recognition tasks, the number of possible answers is far to large to search exhaustively. And yet, we would like to believe that we could get the same answer as if we did perform that exhaustive search. The primary goals of a good search algorithm are thus to minimize overall computation while causing almost no "search errors". In addition we would prefer algorithms that could be computed in parallel, since parallelism is one easy way to get improved computer speed. Finally, the algorithm should result in only a small delay from the end of speaking to displaying or acting on the answer. This means that most of the computation should be able to take place while the speaker is still speaking.

Figure 9 compares three different search algorithms. In each case, the system must compute the scores for several states at different times through an utterance. The Level-Building algorithm described by Rabiner in this book computes the scores for the set of possible first words spanning all plausible times first. Then, it goes on to compute the scores for possible next words for all times, given the different ending scores and times for first words, and so on. This algorithm must wait until the entire utterance has been spoken before it can begin the computations. The second general algorithm suggested by Vintsyuk /VIN 76/

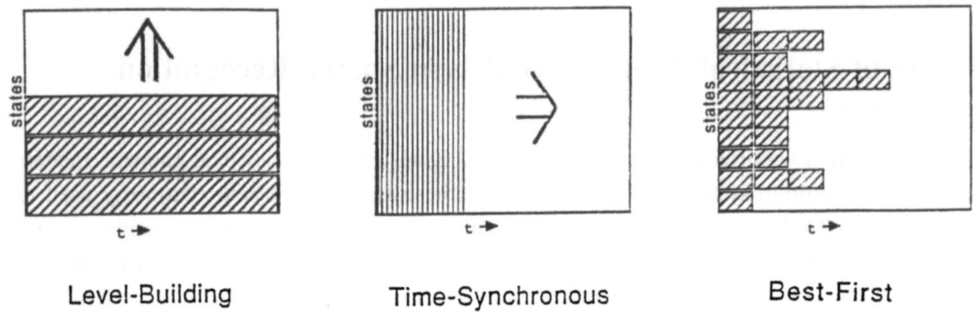

FIGURE 9: Three Different Search Algorithms: a. Level-Building, b. Time-Synchronous, c. Best-First

and Bridle /BRI 79/ is most closely related to the Viterbi algorithm. It updates the scores for all plausible states within all words given each frame. Computation proceeds to the right with all computations being performed on only one frame at a time. Therefore, computation can begin as soon as speech starts. Also, since all theories span the same input, the scores can be compared directly for an effective pruning algorithm, such as a beam search. The third algorithm is often called the "Best-First Search". This algorithm, used in the Tangora system of IBM /BAH 83/, keeps a stack of partial word-sequence theories for the sentence. It advances by one word the theory that currently seems most likely to be the correct one. A fairly complex evaluation function is necessary to be able to compare theories of different length. If there is not too much backtracking, this method can result in less computations than the other methods. However, it can also end up thrashing, or spending all its time shifting from one theory to another.

The time-synchronous Viterbi search algorithm is attractive in terms of its simplicity and the fact that it involves no delay. Unfortunately, the straightforward Viterbi search does not compute the most likely sequence of models. Instead, it only computes the most likely sequence of states through any sequence of models. In practice, we have found that the performance of the Viterbi search is slightly worse than a search that finds the most likely sequence of models. Therefore, we devised a new hybrid search algorithm that more nearly finds the most likely sequence of models. This algorithm is described more fully in /SCH 85/. Figure 10 illustrates the new algorithm for the case of phonetic models, but it can be extended trivially to word models.

In the Viterbi algorithm, when two scores come from two different states into one state, one remembers only the maximum of the scores and which path resulted in that maximum. In this new algorithm, we remember which path resulted in the maximum, but the score remembered is the sum of the several path scores that come into the state. Thus, within each model of interest (in this case within each phoneme model), we sum scores, while in

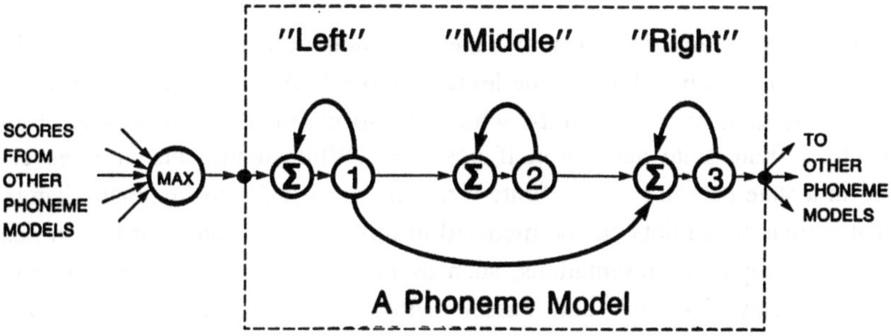

FIGURE 10: Hybrid Time-Synchronous Search Algorithm. Within the model probabilities are added. Between models, only maximum probability is preserved.

transitions between models that we are trying to distinguish, we only keep the maximum score. This algorithm has all the implementation advantages of the Viterbi algorithm and also most of the advantage of computing the most likely sequence of models.

5.2 Integrating Multiple Knowledge Sources

Now that we have described several specific algorithms and enhancements for phonetic decoding, we will propose a method for integrating all the various knowledge sources into a single speech recognition system. The various knowledge sources that must be included are: the acoustic-phonetic models, the phonetic pronunciations given by the lexicon, and the linguistic constraints given by syntactic, semantic, and pragmatic considerations. In addition, we must use an efficient search strategy that takes all these knowledge sources into account before making any irreversible decisions.

The approach that we have taken in the BYBLOS system /CHO 87/ is to precompile as much knowledge as possible into data structures. Then, at the time of recognition, we use a brute force search (with conservative pruning strategies to reduce computation) to find the most likely sequence of words, given all the constraints. Figure 11 shows the various components of the BYBLOS system. The system can be divided into three basic functions. The first (shown on top) is the training function. In this section, data (in the form of speech and corresponding text) is used together with a phonetic lexicon to estimate the parameters of the phonetic HMM models. The training method can either be based on a large amount of speech from the speaker, using speaker-dependent techniques, or a small amount of speech, in which case rapid speaker adaptation techniques are used, or on a large amount of speech from many speakers to estimate speaker-independent models.

The next major function of the system is the precompilation phase. The context-dependent phonetic models are combined, using the lexicon into HMM models for all the words in the vocabulary. The linguistic constraints, which are specified in terms of sets of rules, are compiled into a finite state automaton if possible. While many sets of rules cannot be represented in a state network of any finite size, one can usually make small changes to the rules so that similar constraints can be modeled in this way. Of course, it is also possible to use other more compact representations, such as the context-free notation directly for the recognition (see Ney /NEY 87/ and Paeseler /PAE 87/), but these are somewhat more complicated. The tradeoffs between computation and storage must be considered for each case.

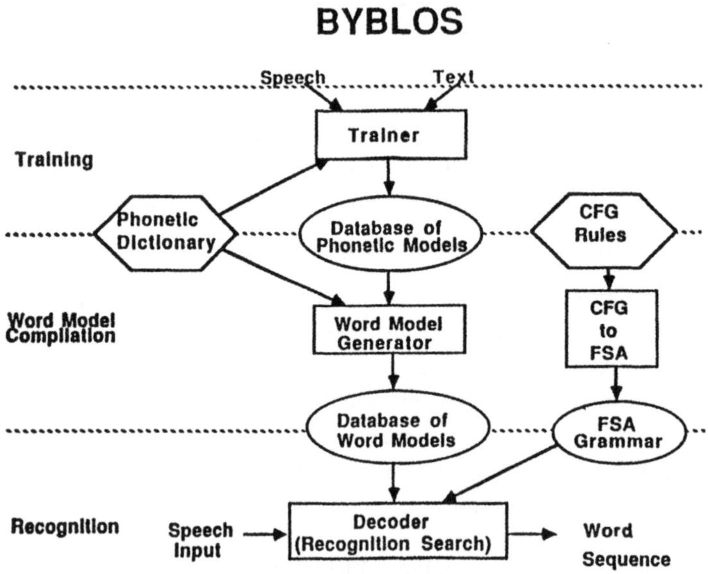

FIGURE 11: Components of the BYBLOS System: Training, Compilation of Knowledge Sources, Recognition.

Finally, the compiled word models and language model are used with the time-synchronous search algorithm to find the most likely sequence of words for any input utterance.

While the computation and storage needed for this approach to speech recognition can be quite large, it is not too large for the hardware that is either currently available, or will be available within a very short time. The advantages of simplicity and global use of constraints result in very high recognition performance.

The recognition accuracy of the BYBLOS system has been tested in speaker-dependent /KUB 88/, and speaker-adapted /FEN 88/ mode with different grammars using the DARPA Resource Management Database collected at TI /PRI 88/. On average, in speaker-dependent mode the percent word errors is given by the square root of the perplexity (e.g. 32% error with perplexity 1000; 7% error with perplexity 60). For speaker-adapted mode, the error rate is about 1.5 times as much.

5.2.1 Current Work

There is still very much work to be done. If we are to achieve our long-term goal of very large vocabularies and grammars, the acoustic decoding must be improved further for acceptable performance. This will happen as we find improved structural models for phonetic recognition. In addition, we continue to search for speaker adaptation methods that can work using very little speech from the new speaker. The integration between the speech recognition components and very large natural language inferencing models must be improved. Finally, more efficient search strategies on fast parallel processors will need to be developed to handle the large problems of the future.

6. Summary/Conclusions

In conclusion, we have given several arguments and examples that support a particular methodology for acoustic-phonetic decoding. We list them here.

- Speech recognition is a pattern recognition problem.
- Statistical phonetic models yield high accuracy.
- It is possible to build our speech knowledge into the structure of statistical models. (This is the primary research area.)
- Issues of dimensionality and training set size are very important.
- Systems must be trainable.
- Search strategies must be global.
- All knowledge sources can be integrated in a top-down predictive system.

As stated at the beginning of the chapter, several of these conclusions are, in fact, the opinions of the author. However, it is hoped that the foregoing arguments and discussions will convince the reader that these conclusions are warranted.

References

/BAH 75/ L.R. Bahl and F. Jelinek. Decoding for Channels with Insertions, Deletions, and Substitutions with Applications to Speech Recognition. IEEE Trans. Inform. Theory IT-21(4):404-411, July, 1975.

/BAH 83/ L.R. Bahl, F. Jelinek, and R.L. Mercer. A Maximum Likelihood Approach to Continuous Speech Recognition. IEEE Trans. Pattern Analysis and Machine Intelligence PAMI-5(2):179-190, March, 1983.

/BAH 88/ L.R. Bahl, P.F. Brown, P.V. deSouza, R. L. Mercer, and M.A. Picheny. A Method for the Construction of Acoustic Markov Models for Words. In IEEE Int. Conf. Acoust., Speech, Signal Processing. New York, NY, April, 1988.

/BAK 75/ J.K. Baker. Stochastic Modeling for Automatic Speech Understanding. In Raj Reddy (editor), Speech Recognition, chapter Part Five:systems Organization and Analysis Systems, pages 521-542. Academic Press, New York, 1975.

/BAU 67/ L.E. Baum and J.A. Eagon. An Inequality with Applications to Statistical Estimation for Probabilistic Functions of Markov Processes and to a Model of Ecology. Amer. Math Soc. Bulletin 73, :360-362, 1967.

/BRI 79/ J.S. Bridle and M.D. Brown. Connected Word Recognition Using Whole Word Templates. In Proc. of the Inst. of Acoustics. Autumn, 1979.

/CHO 86/ Y.L. Chow, R.M. Schwartz, S. Roucos, O.A. Kimball, P.J. Price, G.F. Kubala, M.O. Dunham, M.A. Krasner, and J. Makhoul. The Role of Word-Dependent Coarticulatory Effects in a Phoneme-Based Speech Recognition System. In IEEE Int. Conf. Acoust., Speech, Signal Processing, pages 1593-1596. Tokyo, Japan, April, 1986. Paper No. 30.9.

/CHO 87/ Y.L. Chow, M.O. Dunham, O.A. Kimball, M.A. Krasner, G.F. Kubala, J. Makhoul, P.J. Price, S. Roucos, and R.M. Schwartz. BYBLOS: The BBN Continuous Speech Recognition System. In IEEE Int. Conf. Acoust., Speech, Signal Processing, pages 89-92. Dallas, TX, April, 1987. Paper No. 3.7.

/FEN 88/ M.W. Feng, F. Kubala, R.M. Schwartz, and J. Makhoul. Improved Speaker Adaptation using Text-Dependent Spectral Mappings. In IEEE Int. Conf. Acoust., Speech, Signal Processing. New York, NY, April, 1988.

/KUB 88/ F. Kubala, Y. Chow, A. Derr, M.Feng, O.Kimball, J. Makhoul, P. Price, J. Rohlicek, S. Roucos, R. Schwartz, and J. Vandegrift. Continuous Speech Recognition Results of the BYBLOS System on the DARPA 1000-Word Resource Management Database. In IEEE Int. Conf. Acoust., Speech, Signal Processing. New York, NY, April, 1988.

/LEE 87/ K.F. Lee. Speaker-Independent Continuous Speech Recognition Using Hidden Markov Models. In NATOAdvancedStudyInstitute. Bad Windheim, FR Germany, July, 1987. elsewhere in this volume.

/LEV 83/S.E. Levinson, L.R. Rabiner, and M.M. Sondhi. Speaker Independent Isolated Digit Recognition Using Hidden Markov Models. In IEEE Int. Conf. Acoust., Speech, Signal Processing, pages 1049-1052. Boston, MA, April, 1983.

/NEY 87/ H. Ney. Dynamic Programming Speech Recognition Using a Context Free Grammar. In IEEE Int. Conf. Acoust., Speech, Signal Processing, pages 69-72. Dallas, TX, April, 1987. Paper No. 3.2.

/PAE 87/ A. Paeseler. Modification of Earley's Algorithm for Speech Understanding. In NATOAdvancedStudyInstitute. Bad Windheim, FR Germany, July, 1987. elsewhere in this volume.

/PRI 88/ P.Price, W. Fisher, J. Bernstein, and D. Pallett. The DARPA 1000-Word Resource Management Database for Continuous Speech Recognition. In IEEE Int. Conf. Acoust., Speech, Signal Processing. New York, NY, April, 1988.

/RAB 87/ L.R. Rabiner. Mathematical Foundations and Applications of HMM. In NATOAdvancedStudyInstitute. Bad Windheim, FR Germany, July, 1987. Invited paper. Elsewhere in this volume.

/ROU 82/ S. Roucos, R. Schwartz, and J. Makhoul. Segment Quantization for Very-Low-Rate Speech Coding. In IEEE Int. Conf. Acoust., Speech, Signal Processing, pages 1565-1569. Paris, France, May, 1982.

/ROU 83/ S. Roucos, R. Schwartz, and J. Makhoul. A Segment Vocoder at 150 B/S. In IEEE Int. Conf. Acoust., Speech, Signal Processing, pages 61-64. Boston, MA, April, 1983.

/ROU 87/ S. Roucos and M.O. Dunham. A Stochastic Segment Model for Phoneme-Based Continuous Speech Recognition. In IEEE Int. Conf. Acoust., Speech, Signal Processing, pages 73-89. Dallas, TX, April, 1987. Paper No. 3.3.

/SCH 84/ R.M. Schwartz, Y. Chow, S. Roucos, M. Krasner, and J. Makhoul. Improved Hidden Markov Modeling of Phonemes for Continuous Speech Recognition. In IEEE Int. Conf. Acoust., Speech, Signal Processing, pages 35.6.1-35.6.4. San Diego, CA, March, 1984.

/SCH 85/ R.M. Schwartz, Y.L. Chow, O.A. Kimball, S. Roucos, M. Krasner, and J. Makhoul. Context-Dependent Modeling for Acoustic-Phonetic Recognition of Continuous Speech. In IEEE Int. Conf. Acoust., Speech, Signal Processing, pages 1205-1208. Tampa, FL, March, 1985. Paper No. 31.3.

/SCH 87/ R.M. Schwartz, Y.L. Chow, G.F. Kubala. Rapid Speaker Adaptation using a Probabilistic Spectral Mapping. In IEEE Int. Conf. Acoust., Speech, Signal Processing, pages 633-636. Dallas, TX, April, 1987. Paper No. 15.3.

/VIN 76/ T.K. Vintsiuk. Generative Grammars and Dynamic Programming in Speech Recognition with Learning. In IEEE Int. Conf. Acoust., Speech, Signal Processing, pages 446-449. Philadelphia, PA, April, 1976.

KNOWLEDGE-BASED APPROACHES IN ACOUSTIC-PHONETIC DECODING OF SPEECH

Jean-Paul HATON
INRIA / CRIN
B.P. 239
54506 Vandoeuvre les Nancy cedex, France

Summary :

The level of acoustic-phonetic decoding (i.e. the transformation of the acoustic continuum of speech into a description under the form of discrete, linguistic units) represents an important step and a major bottleneck in the overall process of automatic speech recognition.

A number of different approaches have been proposed so far for solving problem. After a brief recall of these approaches based on pattern matching and/or stochastic modelling, we introduce a new class of methods based on Artificial Intelligence knowledge-based techniques that make an explicit use of all available kinds of knowledge in order to carry out the phonetic decoding of a sentence. The various issues involved in this approach are discussed and illustrated by the presentation of APHODEX, an expert system for acoustic-phonetic decoding.

1. INTRODUCTION

The recognition and understanding of continuous speech is not presently satisfactorily achieved by automatic systems. In fact this knowledge based activity represents one of the major challenge of Artificial Intelligence (AI). In order to deal more efficiently with the problem, the process of understanding a spoken sentence is usually considered as a sequence of steps from the acoustic level up to the semantic level. In this overall organization the level of phonetic decoding (PD) represents an important step and a major bottleneck in the design of speech recognizers even for single speaker applications. We refer to phonetic decoding as to the different processes involved in the transformation of the continuous, acoustic data coming from a microphone into a description under the form of discrete, linguistic units such as phonemes, syllables, diphones, etc.

NATO ASI Series, Vol. F46
Recent Advances in Speech Understanding and Dialog Systems
Edited by H. Niemann et al.

A large number of PD systems have been designed for different languages, based on several approaches. In this chapter we consider the AI approach based on the use of several kinds of knowledge. After having presented in section 2 the position of the PD problem, we will briefly recall in section 3 the main different approaches that attempt at solving the PD problem. Then section 4 will introduce the various aspects of the knowledge-based approach. This approach will finally be illustrated in section 5 by the presentation of the APHODEX expert system presently under development in Nancy.

2. POSITION OF THE PROBLEM

2.1. The Speech Recognition Paradigm

The speech signal can be regarded as the result of a hierarchical encoding process at successive levels among which important ones are the pragmatic, semantic, syntactic, phonological, articulatory levels. This signal presents specific characteristics that make its interpretation difficult, especially : continuity (which necessitates to take segmentation decisions at one time or another), variability (which complexifies the multi-speaker phonetic decoding of speech) and redundancy.

One possible approach to the automatic recognition of speech consists in referring to the above mentioned encoding process and in taking into account the various corresponding knowledge pieces. This knowledge-based approach, though not the only one possible, has been widely used /LEA 80/ /HAT 85a/. In this framework the importance of the acoustic-phonetic level is presently widely admitted /KLA 77/.

2.2. Variability of Speech

A language such as French or English has a relatively low number of phonemes (about some tens) but the variety of corresponding acoustic speech patterns is very high and difficult to characterize for several reasons :

- factors like speaking rate, loudness, prosody, etc. have an influence on speech sounds,
- the acoustic patterns depend on the speech production manner,
- coarticulation effects, context and speaker dependencies make the diversity of acoustic realizations very large.

The contextual variability in the acoustic structure of phonetic segments is particularly important, due to several major processes /LON 87/ :

- unvoicing of voiced glides in contact with a voiceless fricative or stop,
- labial coarticulation : figure 1 shows that the low frequency cut-off of /s/in labial context of /y/ is brought down to the level of /ʃ/,
- tongue coarticulation,
- nasal coarticulation,
- differences in vocal tract length,
- variations in the vocal source spectrum.

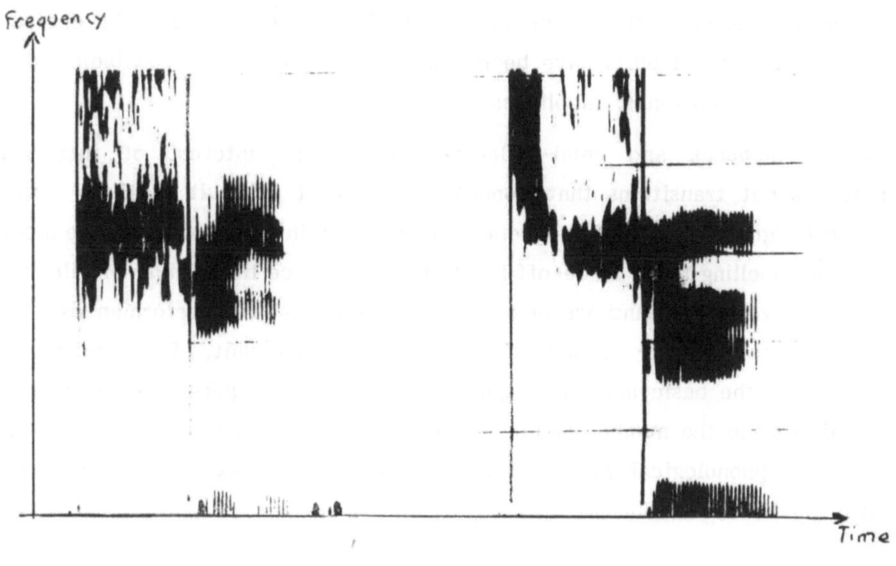

Example of phonological alteration (/ʃi/ vs /sy/)
Figure 1

2.3. Acoustic-Phonetic Decoding of Speech

The causes and examples of variability just described illustrate the difficulty of the acoustic-phonetic decoding of speech. However it is of primary importance to design robust and efficient PD techniques since the overall performances of any sentence recognizer rely heavily on the quality of this decoding.

The activity of PD comprises two complementary subtasks that can be carried out sequentially or concurrently, according to the approach :

- a task of segmentation of the speech wave into acoustic segments,
- a task of phonetic identification or labeling of these segments.

An important point in the design of a phonetic decoder concerns the choice of a phonetic unit. Several units have been concurrently used so far : syllables, demi-syllables, diphones, phonemes, allophones.

Syllables, diphones and demi-syllables present the interest of integrating information about transitions that constitute the most difficult parts to identify in the speech signal. The use of allophones can to a certain extent simplify the process of automatic labelling but a trade-off has to be found since the number of allophones is unlimited (several thousand are necessary for obtaining good performances). Many systems use at one stage or another phonemes as a decoding unit, for several reasons. The phoneme is the basic unit of language production. It requires less training and storage space since the number of phonemes in a given language is rather low (less than 100). The phonological variations of phonemes can be predicted by contextual rules within and between sounds.

3. TECHNIQUES OF ACOUSTIC-PHONETIC DECODING

3.1. Feature Selection and Extraction

Signal processing techniques (FFT, LPC, cepstrum, filter bank, auditory models, etc.) applied to a portion of speech signal yield a set of parameters which are specific to each technique. These sets or vectors of acoustic parameters can usually not be directly related to some phonetic knowledge : an interpretation of these vectors is requested. Phonetician experts have a long experience for relating acoustics to articulatory phenomena based on the study of speech spectrograms ; position and trajectory of formants, bursts, VOT, etc. Such correlations must be computed in in order to interpret the speech signal in terms of acoustic-phonetic elements.

Phonetics has proposed models for phoneme classification from acoustic and articulatory models. The classification system based on distinctive features is well known /JAK 51/. The distinctive features of this model constitute a minimal system for all languages but, unfortunately, they are not directly related to the acoustic reality and, therefore, cannot be practically implemented for automatic PD.

However a feature-based approach to automatic PD has been very often used in all languages. We will briefly review in this section the different techniques that make it possible to efficiently combine features for labelling speech. Some of these acoustic-phonetic are redundant. Since speakers do not always articulate carefully all features are not always present in the speech signal. It is therefore important to use a reasonable number of parameters (as far as it is computationnally tractable) event though these parameters are not statistically independent.

3.2. Segmentation

Segmentation is a fundamental process of PD. A major issue concerns the choice of the segmental unit. The different units already mentioned have been used for this purpose :

- phones /CAE 83/ : phones are subphonemic units which are then merged together in order to produce larger units ;
- phonemes /HAT 74/ /MEL 82/ : a human listener is able to identify phoneme-like segments in continuous speech. However segmentation at phoneme level is very difficult and introduces errors of under - and over - segmentation ;
- diphones /LIE 72/ /SCA 83/; demi-syllables /RUS 82/ and syllables /FUJ 76/ /PER 92/ /DEM 83/ /MER 83/ /FOH 85/ : such supra-phonemic units make it possible to incorporate coarticulatory phenomena but their identification is complex and recognition errors can have dramatic consequences in the understanding process.

Segments can be obtained synchronously by analyzing fixed-length samples of speech ("centisecond" samples) /BAK 77/ or asynchronously /GOL 75/.

The segmentation process is usually based on the study of the variations of a function measuring the discontinuities of the speech wave or of its spectra. Articulatory criteria have also been used /VON 71/. Segmentation refers to acoustic-phonetic knowledge that can alternatively been explicited in a declarative way. This representation leads to segmentation systems based on parsers using rewriting rules /BAU 78/ /DEM 80/, and also to knowledge-based segmentation /MIZ 84/. This latter approach makes it easier to embed heuristic knowledge that a phonetician has and to enforce the segmentation algorithms through symbolic manipulation.

Most speech segmenters use a bottom-up strategy going from acoustic data to abstract linguistic representations but some attempts have also been done toward a top-down segmentation based on a prediction of the phonetic string /LEN 83/.

3.3. Segment Identification techniques

We have seen in paragraph 3.1. that the identification or labelling of phonetic segments is often based on a set of acoustic-phonetic features extracted from a parametric representation of the speech wave. We will now review the different techniques, more or less related to classification and/or pattern recognition algorithms, that are usually used in PD systems :

- **vector quantization** : this technique consists of taking into account the statistical properties of sounds in a representation space. It is widely used for speech coding and synthesis but it does also present some interest in PD for carrying out a first, rough classification of segments into broad classes /ROU 82/,

- **statistical pattern recognition** : a large number of PD systems are classical pattern recognition systems. The identification of a segment is made by comparing this segment to a set of reference segments described by their acoustic and phonetic features with some statistical information. These techniques necessitate to define an efficient distance measure between patterns. Dynamic programming algorithms can be used in order to compensate for non-linear time distorsions, especially for long units (diphones or syllables). The major importance of contextual phenomena in the speech production process (cf. section 2) makes it necessary to use an extremely large number of reference patterns (at least 10 000). That constitutes a basic limitation of the approach, especially for multi-speaker applications since the reference patterns are essentially speaker-dependent.

- **structural pattern recognition** : structural pattern recognition is concerned with the description of complex patterns in terms of simple, primitive patterns. This technique has been used in PD /BAU 78/ /DEM 80/ but the limitations encountered in statistical pattern recognition still exist. Once again the problem of multi-speaker recognition is solved by clustering prototypes among a large number of different speakers. This solution is not satisfactory and drastically limits the use of pure pattern matching techniques in PD.

- **stochastic modelling** : the acoustic-phonetic decoding of speech formally consists of finding the best string or lattice of speech units by optimally matching an input utterance against every possible concatenation of reference patterns or speech unit production models. This can be expressed in terms of stochastic processing, especially in the framework of Markov sources, more precisely with Hidden Markov Models (HMM) /BAK 75/ /JEL 76/. Initially proposed for larger units (i.e. words) the method can be generalized to phonetic decoding /CRA 86/ /LEV 83/. An important advantage of this approach is the possibility to capture in a statistical way broad speech and speaker variances. This is carried out automatically by processing of huge amount the speech data coming from a large variety of speakers. HMMs provide one of the most efficient framework for multi-speaker PD. However these models are purely mathematical, without any explicit use of phonetic knowledge.

- **knowledge-based reasoning** : the explicit use of linguistic knowledge constitutes an alternative solution to the PD problem that will now be presented.

4. KNOWLEDGE-BASED METHODOLOGY

4.1. Position of the problem

We have just seen that the acoustic-phonetic decoding of a sentence can be carried out by purely mathematical models such as Markov models. However the interpretation of the speech signal necessitates to take into account knowledge and information that are not present in the signal itself. therefore it is interesting to design PD methods which allow for the integration of some knowledge in the recognition process, possibly in conjunction with other models. This knowledge will usually be coded simultaneously under a procedural form (e.g. procedures for detecting a feature in the speech signal) and a declarative form (e.g. the knowledge used by some control structures for reasoning). A knowledge-based approach to PD makes it possible not only to take into account relevant knowledge (phonotactic constraints, allophonic variations, phonological constraints, etc.) but also to implement more realistic decoding strategies. Such strategies can be inspired from the observation of expert phoneticians reading spectrograms (cf. paragraph 4.2.) : opportunistic reasoning with forward and backward processing according to the context, focus of attention on pertinent events (e.g. burst of plosives, formant transitions, etc.).

The implementation of a knowledge-based system for PD raises two problems that will now be considered, i.e.

- the acquistion and formalization of the knowledge involved in PD,
- the representation of this knowledge.

4.2. Knowledge Acquisition

The knowledge used by a human listener for decoding speech is mostly unconscious and implicit, and therefore quite impossible to formalize. It is then necessary to consider activities in which there exists conscious knowledge related to acoustics and phonetics. Speech spectrogram reading by skilled phoneticians represents a typical example of such activities. Early attempts at spectrogram reading were rather pessimistic and usually concluded on the enormous difficulty of the task due to the contextual variations of the acoustic signal /COL 80/. In fact recent studies have proven that the phonetic decoding was feasible without any high level linguistic knowledge with an average accuracy of 80-85%, i.e. far better than the one of present automatic systems /ZUE 79/ /LON 87/. Of course spectrogram readers do not proceed in a way similar to the auditory system but the interest for an AI approach to PD is that the visual features used by these experts are clearly specifiable and that the knowledge involved in their reasoning is explicit. We have carried out an experiment, with F. Lonchamp as expert phonetician, which is described below.

4.2.1. Description of the experiment

The knowledge and decoding strategies used by experienced spectrogram readers are not easy to elucidate, in-as-much as spectrogram decoding involves visual cues and, therefore, requires perceptive knowledge and competence, which are by nature difficult to explain and/or to convey. This led us to develop specific observation and analysis methods that are fully reported in /CAR 84/ and will just be summarized here.

We requested our experienced spectrogram reader to decode one hundred spectrograms representing different sentences from Combescure's corpus of phonetically balanced French sentences /COM 81/. Ten male untrained speakers were chosen among computer scientists in our laboratory ; we only rejected voluntary subjects with strong provincial accent or too high pitch (> 200 Hz). The recording took place in a sound attenuated room.

In order to obtain a rather brisk and natural rythm of elocution from the speakers (12 to 20 phonetic units per second), each sentence was read aloud by a trained speaker to the subject who had to repeat it from short-term memory. Each subject recorded ten sentences from the corpus. Spectrograms were produced on a Voiceprint 700, with a frequency range from 0 to 5 Hz.

The expert, who only knew that the spectrograms represented meaningful sentences was asked :

- not to use linguistic knowledge, such as lexical, syntactic or semantic information,
- to proceed from left to right, since on his own account this constraint does not hamper him,
- not to make precise measurements with instruments such as a ruler, but the frequency scaling lines were obviously used.

No time constraints were put on the expert : on average it took him between 5 and 10 minutes to identify 20 to 30 sounds.

He freely chose the way to give out his results : a segment is often given more than one phonetic label but the alternative solutions are rank-ordered according to the expert's degree of confidence.

4.2.2. The expert's approach and strategies

We discovered that the expert's strategy consists of two consecutive steps :
- first, a brief global survey of the whole spectrogram,
- then, a close scanning from left to right.

A. Global survey

During this stage, the expert determines rough thresholds in the time and frequency domains, which enable him to tune various acoustic parameters to inter- and intra-speaker variations. When processing spectrograms from different untrained speakers, this stage is most important.

For instance, he attempts to assess global energy thresholds. More precisely, he first estimates the effective range of temporal variations of energy by comparing the darkest and lightest areas on the spectrographic representation ; he then determines the scale of grey levels corresponding to the significant energy variations in the speaker's utterance ; this scale, for instance, will enable him later to distinguish nasal vowels from oral ones, the former being usually uttered less energetically and therefore showing up lighter on the spectrogram than the latter.

During this overall glance he also tries to detect vocalic nuclei and to appraise their average duration ; this information plays a crucial part in the segmentation of non-vocalic parts of the signals : since the boundaries of vocalic sounds are usually easy to detect while those of other sounds are often more difficult to determine, the estimation of the mean vocalic duration for a given spectrogram helps him to segment non-vocalic portions of the spectrogram.

B. Local strategies and identification rules

The second stage which consists of a left to right analysis is usually devoted simultaneously to :

- the refinement of the segmentation provided by the global survey,
- the identification (phonetic labeling) of the different segments.

If the expert has succeeded in unambiguously parsing a sound stretch, using the mean vocalic duration as well as his knowledge of transitional patterns, then the phonetic identification of the segment(s) is attempted. In such cases, which occur most frequently, his strategy appears relatively simple.

But, sometimes, the segmentation is ambiguous, which leads him to use a more complex strategy : for each possible representation he tries to identify the segment(s) ; if he fails, the hypothetized segmentation is rejected. For example, if a vocalic segment whose duration is twice the mean vocalic duration is under analysis, he tests the two following hypotheses : the segment is composed of two identical contiguous vowels or it is constituted by a single vowel occuring in a lengthening phonetic context.

In these complex cases identification closely interacts with segmentation.

During the identification process, the expert first looks for one or more non-ambiguous acoustic cue(s). Then, from this reliable information, he deduces a list of potential hypotheses as to the phonetic nature of the segment. Finally, he validates or rejects these hypotheses according to the following criterium : for each hypothesis, he compares all the visible cues in the current segment with the stored list of acoustic features that characterize the hypothetized phonetic class or phoneme ; if most of these features do not show on the spectrogram or if one of them is in contradiction with the cues provided by the spectral representation of the segment, the hypothesis in either rejected or pushed down the list of rank-ordered hypotheses.

Thus, the expert never relies on one single acoustic cue. Since linguistic knowledge (lexical, syntactic and semantic) makes it possible to eliminate most wrong hypotheses but proves of little help in cases when the right interpretation has been overlooked, our expert tries to include all possible hypotheses into the list of phonetic interpretations he proposes for each segment ; he only rejects the ones that contradict one or more cues on the spectrogram. By ordering the ones he has validated, he takes into account their relative degrees of plausibility and expresses the degree of confidence he has in each one.

Nb. occ. in transcript.		correct 1st rank	correct 2nd rank	correct 3rd rank	correct	%*	omission no answer	Nb. errors
p	44	17	18	3	38	86	2	4
b	13	5	1	-	6	(46)	-	7
t	62	54	5	-	59	95	-	3
d	37	17	1	-	18	49	1	18
k	41	34	2	2	38	93	-	3
g	6	6	-	-	6	(100)	-	-
F	13	5	2	-	7	(54)	-	6
v	29	20	2	-	22	76	3	4
s	68	59	2	-	61	90	-	7
z	11	7	-	-	7	(64)	-	4
ʃ	13	11	1	-	12	(92)	-	1
ʒ	22	16	4	-	20	91	-	2
L	76	53	5	1	59	78	4	13
R	86	55	8	2	65	76	13	8
J	22	14	2	-	16	73	-	6
w	19	12	-	-	12	(63)	5	2
ɥ	5	2	-	-	2	(40)	1	2
m	41	30	6	2	38	93	1	2
n	38	22	10	1	33	87	1	4
μ	4	1	0	1	2	(50)	1	1
	650	440	69	12	521	80.2	32	97

Table I : Spectrogram reader's performance on consonants.
* % based on less than 20 tokens are within brackets.

Nb. occ. in transcript.		correct	%*	missed	Main feature errors			
					High/low	Round	Nasal	Front/back
i	55	47	85	5	2	-	-	1
e	70	66	94	-	-	4	-	-
ɛ	42	32	76	-	6	4	-	(2)
a	99	75	76	4	20	(12)	(1)	-
ɔ	20	10	50	1	6	-	3	(2)
o	21	16	76	-	4	-	-	1
u	32	21	66	1	(4)	(5)	(3)	10
y	22	14	64	-	(1)	8	-	-
ø	4	3	(75)	-	1	(1)	-	(1)
œ	7	1	(14)	-	5	1	-	-
ə	67	43	64	-	10	8	2	4
ã	35	23	66	1	3	-	8	-
ɔ̃	29	23	79	-	-	-	1	5
ɛ̃	15	5	(33)	-	-	-	6	-
œ̃	4	0	(0)	-	(4)	-	2	-
	522	379	73 %					

Table II : Spectrogram reader's performance on vowels.
* % based on less than 20 tokens are within brackets.

4.2.3. The expert's recognition performances

The rates given here bear on fifty sentences uttered by five different speakers.

Consonant recognition results

The overall recognition rate for consonants is 80%. Detailed results are given in table I. As voicing is often not clearly visible on spectrograms, the expert often reported both voiced and voiceless consonants (i.e. |p-b|). The following pairs are also hard to distinguish : |b-v, m-n|. In these cases, the answer is tallied as correct when either consonant appears in the aural transcript. The mean number of symbols or pair of symbols for consonants is 1.51. 75 extra consonantal segments were wrongly hypothetized, but 39 were explicitly marked as dubious. 32 consonants were missed : 12 |R| out of 86, all, either in sentence final position, or next to a consonant ; 5 |w| out of 19, in all cases next to a voiceless consonant. 84% of all correct consonants were given as most preferred answers (1st rank). Mean recognition rates for individual subjects are 85.3, 83, 79.8 and 76.7%. The poorest results seem to be due to wide variations of energy within a sentence, with a loss of spectral details for the softly articulated consonants.

Vowel recognition results

As our expert was prevented from measuring the formant frequencies, we have used a rather lax criterion for assessing recognition rates for vowels. An answer is deemed correct when the high/low feature is wrong by at most one step (i.e. |e| reported instead of |i|) except for nasal vowels. A failure to detect either labiality |for y, ø or œ, ə |, nasality |ã, õ, ɛ̃, œ̃| or the front/back feature results in an error being tallied. Detailed results are given in table II. We have attempted to list main feature errors in this table, with less severe errors within brackets. Extra segments were posited in 19 cases, 7 of which being dubious. 12 vowels were missed, 5 |i| and 5 other vowels in vocalic sequences.

4.3. Issues in Knowledge Representation

The formalism of production rules is widely used for the development of knowledge-based expert systems in a large variety of domains. Production rules are declarative pieces of knowledge under the form :

IF Conditions THEN Conclusion/Action

which make it easy to represent the surface knowledge and rules of thumb used by human experts for various tasks. These rules have been introduced in PD (see for instance the APHODEX system in section 5, and also /DEM 84/ /MEM 83//JOH 83/)

in order to code the contextual variations of speech sounds as expressed by spectrogram readers. Similarly the use of PROLOG clauses has also been extensively studied /MEL 82/. Automatic learning of these rules has been tested, especially for extracting implicit knowledge from large sets of examples /GUI 87/.

However production rules do not enable to represent the deep linguistic knowledge underlying the PD process nor to structure the concepts involved in this process. Several solutions have been proposed for partly solving these problems : frame representations /HAT 85b/, object-oriented formalisms, speech sketch (an intermediate structure between the acoustic signal and the phonetic representations) /GRE 87/.

5. THE APHODEX SYSTEM

5.1. Overview of the Project

In order to illustrate some of the issues related to knowledge-based phonetic decoding we will now give functional and experimental data about the APHODEX system that we have been developping in Nancy for the past 4 years /CAR 87/.

APHODEX, Acoustic PHonetic Decoding EXpert, is an experimental tool designed for improving our knowledge about PD by the in-depth study of spectrogram reading activity. The knowledge gained from this study is coded in the system under three forms :

- procedures for segmentation and labeling of segments into gross phonetic classes,
- contextual production rules. Presently the knowledge base is made up of about 400 rules and it is regularly augmented.

  A typical rule is as follows :

  IF LEFT CONTEXT /y u ɛ œ o a œ o u w ʃ z/
  RIGHT CONTEXT /ã ɛ̃ d e a p t k b d g s v z m n r l/
  AND NOISE-LIMIT IS INCREASING
  AND FRICTION THRESHOLD |2800-3300|
  THEN s 1 / z 1.

The value 1 associated with the two conclusions of the rule represents the certainty factor (ranging from -1 (false) to 1 (true)) of these conclusions.

- decoding strategies that operate at two levels :
  . a global strategy which is roughly bottom-up from the speech signal to the gross phonetic labelinf of a sentence and then mixed top-down and bottom-up

for the refinement of the precise labeling,

. a strategy used for propagating constraints during the reasoning process.

The overall architecture of APHODEX is given in figure 2. The inference engine of the system uses both forward and backward chaining and carries out approximate reasoning by combination of certainty factors. It is completed by a constraint propagation algorithm which controls that the constraints that appeared in most production rules under the form of left and right contexts are satisfied.

The practical example shown below summarizes the different operations involved in the decoding of a sentence.

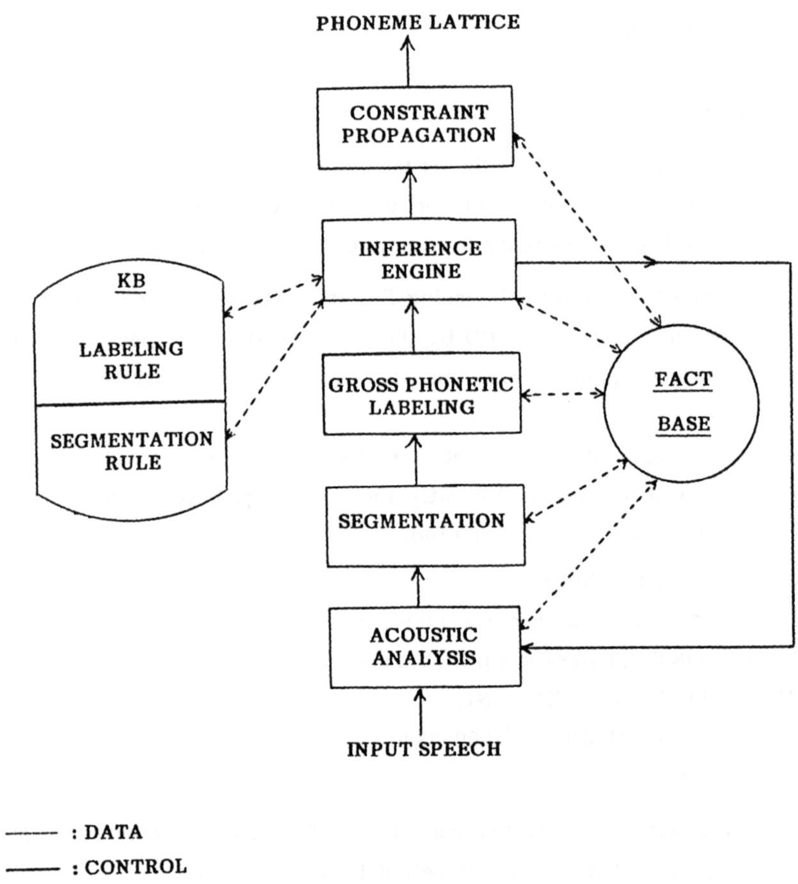

The architecture of APHODEX
Figure 2

5.2. Example of processing

APHODEX is implemented in C on a Masscomp computer. Figure 3 illustrates the different steps in the decoding of the French phrase "Beau chapeau" (Nice hat) pronounced by a male speaker.

In this figure are successively plotted

- the different facts (acoustic-phonetic features) extracted from the speech signal that are used by the expert system for reasoning (certainty factors associated with these facts also range from -1 to + 1),
- the phonetic label hypotheses emitted by the reasoning process and kept by the constraint propagation algorithm,
- the final phoneme lattice obtained by combining the different valid hypotheses.

Although precise performance figures cannot yet be given the different experiments carried out show that the system is robust and yield good results for multi-speaker phonetic decoding

6. CONCLUSION

The various approaches proposed to solve the difficult problem of acoustic-phoentic decoding have been briefly recalled, including the Hidden Markov Model which appears to be particularly efficient. We have then proposed to consider PD as a knowledge intensive process and we have envisaged the different issues involved in the knowledge-based approach to this problem. The APHODEX phonetic decoding expert system has been used in order to illustrate this approach. Results obtained show that the knowledge acquired from expert phoneticians can substantially improve the performances of PD systems. The incorporation of this knowledge into efficient operational models such as HMM represents a good compromise for further developments in the field /HAT 87/, that will also largely gain from the use of new, parallel models such as neural nets /LIP 87/.

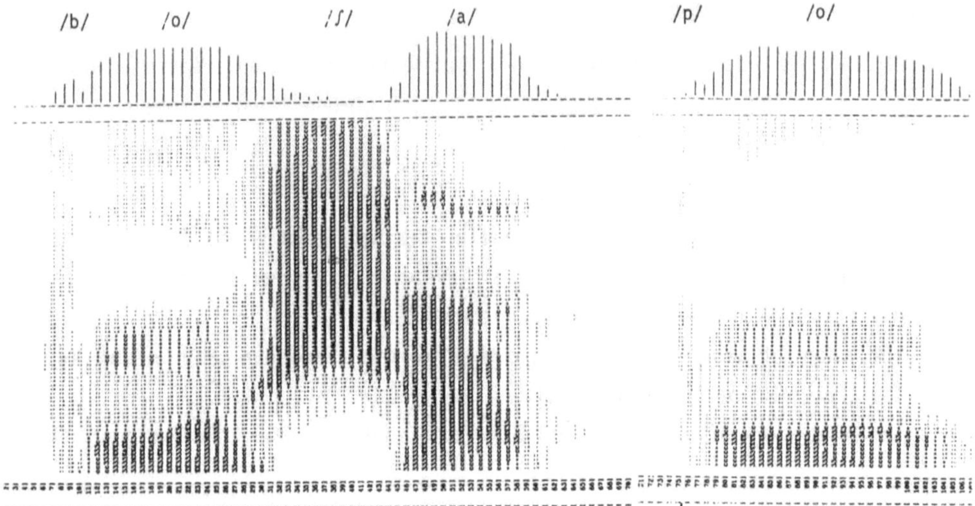

FACT BASE

PLOSIVE
PITCH 1
BURST 1
LOW-FRIC 1
BURST-2500.8
BURST-F1-F2.8
DOUBLE BURST-1
BURST-F1-1
BURST-F2-.5

VOWEL
PITCH 1
NOISE-LIM ↘ 0
F1 383
F2 872
F3 2285

FRICATIVE
PITCH-1
NOISE-LIM <–> 0
NOISE-LIM ↗ .4
FRIC-THRES.2200

VOWEL
PITCH 1
NOISE-LIM ↗ 0
F1 620
F2 1350
F3 2300

PLOSIVE
PITCH-1
BURST 1
LOW-FRIC.8
BURST-F1-1
BURST-F2.3
BURST F1-F2.5
BURST F3.5

VOWEL
PITCH 1
NOISE-LIM ↘ 0
F1 368
F2 812
F3 2300

RESULTS OF CONSTRAINTS PROPAGATION

b.5	0.24	ʃ.8	a.38	p.5	o.51
b.5				p.1	u.24
d.3					
d.5				p.8	o.21
b.8					

FINAL PHONEME LATTICE

b.94	0.24	ʃ.8	a.28	p.1	o.61
d.65					u.24

Figure 3 : Example of sentence decoding by APHODEX

REFERENCES

/BAK 75/ J. K. Baker : Stochastic Modelling for Automatic Speech Understanding. In "Speech Recognition", R. Reddy, editor, New York, Academic Press (1975).

/BAK 77/ R. BAKIS : Continuous Speech Recognition via centisecond Acoustic States. 91st Meeting ASA (1977).

/BAU 78/ M. Baudry : Etude du signal vocal dans sa représentation amplitude-temps. Algorithme de segmentation et de reconnaissance de parole. Doctorat d'Etat Thesis, University of Paris (1978).

/CAE 83/ J. Caelen, N. Vigouroux, G. Pérennou : Structuration des informations acoustiques dans le projet ARIAL. Speech Com., Vol. 2, N° 2-3 (1983), 219-222.

/CAR 84/ N. Carbonell, M.O. Cordier, D. Fohr, J.P. Haton, F. Lonchamp, J.M. Pierrel : Acquisition et formalisation du raisonnement dans un système expert de lecture de spectrogrammes vocaux. Colloque ARC, Orsay (1984).

/CAR 87/ N. Carbonell, D. Fohr, J.P. Haton : APHODEX, an Acoustic-Phonetic Decoding Expert System. Int. Journal of Pattern Recognition and Artificial Intelligence, Vol. 1, N° 2 (1987) 31-46.

/COL 80/ R.A. Cole et al. : Speech as Patterns on Paper. In "Perception and Production of Fluent Speech", R.A. Cole, editor, LEA (1980).

/COM 81/ P. Combescure : Vingt listes de dix phrases phonétiquement équilibrées. Revue d'Acoustique, 14, N° 56 (1981).

/CRA 86/ M. Cravero, R. Pieraccini, F. Raineri : Definition and Evaluation of Phonetic Units for Speech Recognition by Hidden Markov Models, Proc. ICASSP-86, Tokyo (1986), 2239-2242.

/DEM 80/ R. de Mori and G. Giordano : A Parser for Segmenting Continuous Speech into Pseudo-Syllabic Nuclei. Proc. ICASSP, Denver (1980).

/DEM 83/ R. De Mori : Extraction of Acoustic Cues using a Grammar of Frames. Speech Com., Vol. 2, N° 2-3 (1983), 223-225.

/DEM 84/ R. De Mori et al. : Integration of Acoustic, Phonetic, Prosodic and Lexical Knowledge in an Expert System for Speech Understanding. Proc. ICASSP (1984).

/FOH 85/ D. Fohr, J.P. Haton, F. Lonchamp, L. Sauter : Méthodes de segmentation syllabique en reconnaissance de la parole. XIV JEP, GALF, Paris (1985).

/FUJ 76/ O. Fujimura : Syllabes as Concatened Demi-syllabes and Affixes. 9th Meeting of ASA (1976).

/GOL 75/ H.G. Goldberg : Segmentation and Labelling of Speech : A Comparative Performance Evaluation. Ph. D. Thesis, Carnegie-Mellon University (1975).

/GRE 87/ P.D. Green et al. : A Speech Recognition Strategy Based on Making Acoustic Evidence and Phonetic Knowledge Explicit. Proc. European Conf. Speech Technology, Edinburgh (1987).

/GUI 87/ J. Guizol : Apport de l'apprentissage au décoage acoustico-phonétique en reconnaissance automatique de la parole. 7èmes Journées sur les Systèmes experts, Avignon (1987).

/HAT 74/ J.P. Haton : Contribution à l'analyse, la paramétrisation et la reconnaissance automatique de la parole. Doctorat d'Etat Thesis, University of Nancy (1974).

/HAT 85a/ J.P. Haton : Intelligence artificielle en compréhension automatique de la parole : état des recherches et comparaison avec la vision par ordinateur. TSI, Vol. 4, N° 3 (1985), 265-287.

/HAT 85b/ J.P. Haton and J.P. Damestoy : A Frame Language for the Control of Phonetic Decoding in Continuous Speech Recognition. Proc. ICASSP, Tampa (1985).

/HAT 87/ J.P. Haton, N. Carbonell, D. Fohr, J.F. Mari, A. Kriouile : Interaction between Stochastic Modeling and Knowledge-based Techniques in Acoustic-phonetic Decoding of Speech. Proc. ICASSP, Dallas (1987).

/JAK 51/ R. Jakobson, G. Fant and M. Halle : Preliminaries to Speech Analysis. MIT Press, Cambridge MA (1951).

/JEL 76/ F. Jelinek : Continuous Speech Recognition by Statistical Methods. Proc. IEEE, Vol. 64, N° 4 (1976).

/JOH 83/ J. Johanssen et al. : A Speech Spectrogram Reader. Proc. ICASSP (1983).

/KLA 77/ D. Klatt : Review of the ARPA Speech Understanding Project. JASA, 62 (1977), 1345-1366.

/LEA 80/ W.A. Lea : Trends in Speech Recognition. Prentice-Hall (1980).

/LEV 83/ S.E. Levinson, L.R. Rabiner, M.M. Sondhi : An Introduction to the Application of the Theory of Probabilistic Functions of a Markov Process to Automatic Speech Recognition. The Bell System Technical Journal, Vol. 62, N° 4 (1983), 1035-1074.

/LEV 96/ S.E. Levinson : Continuously Variable Duration Hidden Markov Models for Speech Analysis. Proc. ICASSP, Tokyo (1986), 1241-1244.

/LIE 72/ J.S. Liénard : Analyse, synthèse et reconnaissance automatique de la parole. Doctorat d'Etat Thesis, University of Paris (1972).

/LIP 87/ R.P. Lippmann : An Introduction to Computing with Neural Nets. IEEE ASSP Magazine (1987).

/LON 87/ F. Lonchamp : Reading Spectrograms : The View of the Expert. In "Fundamentals in Computer Understanding : Speech and Vision", J.P. Haton, editor, Cambridge University Press (1987).

/MEL 82/ H. Meloni : Etude et réalisation d'un système de reconnaissance automatique de la parole. Doctorat d'Etat Thesis, University of Marseille (1982).

/MEM 83/ D. Memmi, M. Eskénazi, J. Mariani and A. Nguyen-Xuan : Un système expert pour la lecture de sonagrammes. Speech Com., Vol. 2, N° 2-3 (1983), 234-236.

/MER 83/ G. Mercier : The KEAL Speech Understanding System. In "Spoken language Generation and Understanding", J.C. Simon, editor, D. Reidel (1983).

/MIZ 84/ R. Mizoguchi and O. Kakusho : Continuous Speech Recognition based on Knowledge Engineering Techniques. Proc. ICASSP-84 (1984), 638-640.

/PER 82/ G. Pérennou : The ARIAL II Speech Recognition System. In "Automatic Speech Analysis and Recognition", J.P. Haton, editor, D. Reidel Publishing Company (1982).

/ROU 82/ S. Roucos et al. : Vector Quantization for Very-Low-Rate. Proc. Global Telecom. Conf., Miami (1982).

/RUS 82/ G. Ruske : Automatic Recognition of Syllabic Speech Segments Using Spectral and Temporal Features. IEEE ICASSP, Paris (1982).

/SCA 83/ C. Scagliola : Continuous Speech Recognition without Segmentation : two Ways of using Diphones as basic Speech Units. Speech Com., Vol. 2, N° 2-3 (1983), 199-201.

/VON 71/ T.G. Von Keller : An On-line Recognition System for Spoken Digits. JASA, 49 (1971), 1288-1296.

/ZUE 79/ V. W. Zue and R.A. Cole : Experiments on Spectrogram Reading. IEEE-ICASSP (1979), 116-119.

THE USE OF PROSODIC PARAMETERS IN AUTOMATIC SPEECH RECOGNITION

J. Vaissière
Centre National d'Etudes des Télécommunications
22301 Lannion, France

KEYWORDS.

prosody/ suprasegmental/ automatic speech recognition/ stress/ boundaries/ junctures/ segmentation/ phrase/ sentence type

ABSTRACT.

The present communication concerns the use of prosodic parameters in automatic speech recognition (ASR), i.e. the feasibility of automatically extracting prosodic information from a set of acoustic measurements done on the signal, and the incidence of integrating such information on the performance of ASR. Prosodic parameters include pauses and contrasts in pitch, duration and intensity between successive segments (mainly the vocalic parts). This notion is also extended to number of syllables and to ratios of voiced to unvoiced portions of the words. Part one introduces the various aspects of prosody (linguistic and non linguistic) and the main problems to be solved in automatically extracting linguistic messages conveyed by prosodic features. Part two deals with word level and lexical search: it presents work done (1) on the feasibility of word stress detection (primary stress, estimation of its magnitude, and evaluation of the complete word stress pattern) and (2) on the estimation of the amount of lexical constraints imposed by stress information in lexical search, completed by other suprasegmental information (number of syllables, word boundaries, ratios between voiced and unvoiced portion in the word, etc.). Part three deals with phrase and sentence levels and syntactic constraints provided by the automatic detection of word, phrase and sentence boundaries. Part four relates a number of miscellaneous uses at the phonemic level: phonetic segmentation, identification of the voicing feature of consonants, and estimation of the "segmental quality" of the underlying segments.

It is observed that prosodic parameters have been exploited rather poorly compared to segmental aspects of speech. Integration of prosodic knowledge with segmental knowledge in an ASR system is a difficult problem: to know when and where to integrate the prosodic knowledge into the system and how to combine the evidence and scores obtained from different sources. The exact contribution of the use of prosody in ASR is still to be estimated in an ASR system flexible enough to efficiently test such an integration.

NATO ASI Series, Vol. F46
Recent Advances in Speech Understanding
and Dialog Systems
Edited by H. Niemann et al.

0. INTRODUCTION

In the early seventies there were a number of papers directed to specialists of automatic speech recognition (ASR), written by Wayne Lea [LEA 73a, 73b], pointing out the many possible uses of the prosodic parameters. As early as 1960 Lieberman showed that it is possible to automatically determine the stress pattern of bisyllabic words uttered in isolation with only 1 percent error [LIE 60]. As Lea suggested, prosodic parameters can be used at **all** levels in the decoding process of an ASR system: for example, at the **acoustic-phonetic** level to separate voiced from unvoiced stops, at the **lexical level** to detect word stress position, at the **syntactic level** to locate the principal phonological boundaries in sentences, and at the **pragmatic level** by locating the emphasized portion(s) of the discourse. Lea even suggested a prosodically guided speech understanding system and discussed some of the alternative strategies for using prosodics to aid speech recognition [LEA 75b].

Presently, despite the growing number of articles devoted to that subject in recent years, the effective use of prosody in ASR is rather limited. In particular, a number of papers have calculated the theoretical advantages of adding prosodic information to ASR systems, to restrict the lexical search and speed up the process of word retrieval in very-large-lexicon ASR. Studies have shown that automatic detection of word stress and main junctures in sentences is feasible with a very low error rate. The results obtained in terms of improvement of performance in ASR remain in most cases inconclusive for the following reasons: in some studies the process of extracting the basic prosodic parameters is not completely automatic, and automation is a necessary prerequisite for integration into an ASR system, at least in bottom-up systems; in others, the decision algorithms are manually run. More importantly, the value of integrating prosodically delivered information into strictly spectral information in isolated words and in continuous speech has not yet been tested in an ASR system flexible enough to combine different types of information and to run systematic tests.

However, it seems obvious that the use of all the information that can be automatically extracted from speech signals (including prosodic information) is necessary to achieve progress, particularly to ease the heavy constraints imposed by the existing recognizers: limited vocabulary size, restricted syntax, necessity to adapt the system to every new speaker, or obligation of the speaker to insert a pause between every word in the sentence.

As solicited by the organizer of this course, the purpose of this contribution is to provide a general survey of the use of prosodic knowledge in ASR. The first part includes introductory remarks on prosody which are relevant to the use of prosody in ASR. It aims at meeting the needs of readers wishing to quickly up to date about the state-of-the-art in this domain. The following parts provide a survey of the work already done in the field in English, French, Swedish, Italian and Japanese. Part two mainly concerns **word level** , specifically the detection of stress and the use of prosodic filtering in lexical search. Word level is the level at which most work has been done, particularly in the field of isolated-word systems. Part three deals with the detection of **phonological boundaries** in the continuum and part four summarizes some other uses at the phonemic level.

1. PART ONE: INTRODUCTORY REMARKS ON PROSODY

1.1 The four basic aspects of prosody

In a spoken sentence, the successive sounds (vowels and consonants) vary in pitch, duration and intensity. Such variations are conditioned by a number of factors which are reviewed succintly in the following paragraph.

a) Phonetically conditioned aspects: intrinsic values and coarticulation

Part of the observed variations in pitch, duration and intensity depend on sounds in sequence and are often called " phonetically-conditioned aspects of prosodic parameters". These variations are conditioned by differences in the physiological mechanism involved in the production of **each** individual sound, on one hand, and by temporal, **coarticulatory** constraints due to the overlapping of articulatory gestures corresponding to phonemes in sequence, on the other hand. Let us examplified briefly the two types of phonetically-conditioned variations: intrinsic characteristics of the phonemes and contextual modifications.

1) Intrinsic characteristics of the phonemes have been rather well investigated. In particular, duration, fundamental frequency (Fo) and intensity of the vowels are known to be correlated with tongue height. High vowels (such as /i/), for example, have an intrinsically higher pitch, a shorter duration and an inherently lower intensity than low vowels (such as /a/). Nasal vowels in French are intrinsically longer than oral vowels. Tense vowels in English are intrinsically long and lax vowels short. Duration of a vowel is therefore correlated with the degree of vowel openness in French and English, the feature oral/nasal in French and the feature tense/lax in English.

2) The immediate context also has an influence. Vowels in unvoiced consonantal context (such as /p-p/) have a relatively higher pitch and are shorter in duration than the same vowels in voiced context (such as /b-b/). The influence of voicing on the duration of the preceding vowel is increased when both the vowel and the following consonant belong to the same syllable. Duration of a vowel therefore depends on syllable boundary location and the voice-voiceless feature of the following consonant [See Lehiste 's book on suprasegmentals for an excellent review of phonetically-

conditioned aspects of prosodic parameters, LEH 70). Such aspects are mainly speaker-independent and, to a great extent, independent of the language spoken. They may indirectly contribute to the identification of the underlying sounds, but do not have a linguistic function per se. In automatic decoding of prosodic information, it would be advantageous to normalize the prosodic parameters for such variations (see details later), but this can only followed identification of the underlying segments.

b) Linguistic aspects of prosody: syntax and rhythm

The part of variations in pitch, duration and intensity which is not conditioned by purely articulatory constraints is the carrier of linguistic messages. Those linguistically-motivated aspects of prosody are of utmost interest for automatic decoding of sentences. They carry information concerning **individual** linguistic units at various levels (on phonemes, but also on syllables, on word stress, accent and word boundaries, on phrase and sentence types and boundaries), on one hand, and concerning the acoustic **structuring** of each unit into larger units (phonemes into a syllable, syllables into a prosodic word, prosodic words into a sentence), on the other hand. These linguistically conditioned aspects of prosodic parameters and the prosodic structuring of each spoken sentence which are, for a given language, speaker-independent also seem language-independent to a certain extent (see VAI 83 for further references).

The basic problem is the following: prosodic parameters are at the same time governed by the **syntactic-semantic** organisation of the sentence (KLA 76), and also by **rhythmic** principles (LEH 80). There may be a substantial difference between the units as defined by syntactic-semantic constraints and the rhythmic units (FOW 77). As a consequence, both influences may become conflicting. Syntactic influence results in **varying** duration and Fo to contrast the units in sequence to mark boundaries. Rhythmic influences results in a tendency for the syllables and the stresses to **succeed at regular temporal intervals.** The segments duration are compressed or expanded to preserve the global duration of the successive syllables as invariant (isosyllabicity) and to equalize the time-interval between two stressed syllables (isochrony). At the same time, they are shortened or lengthened to mark the syntactic-semantic organisation. The coexistence of the three types of influence, (phonetically-conditioned aspects, rhythmic tendencies and syntactic-semantic organisation) is the main source of difficulties for interpreting the cause of a striking lengthening or shortening phonemenon (at the level of a syllable, a vowel or a consonant).

Rhythmic tendencies could be exploited in a predicting way, for gaining information, for example, on syllable boundaries (Gerard Bailly, personal communication). The present use of prosody in ASR mainly concerns its syntactic aspects, and exploits the constrasts in Fo and duration in a down-up fashion. One of the most interesting functions of prosody from an ASR point of view, is the grouping of semantically related words such as a noun and an adjective preceding or following it into a single so-called prosodic word and to express different degrees of junctures between successive prosodic words. Segmentation and structuring by prosody do not allow recovery of the complete syntactic structure of sentences in every day conversation. It may happen (i.e., when isolated sentences are pronounced in a neutral but careful way) that the prosodic structuring exactly maps out the syntactic structure, but in most cases There is not a one-to-one correspondance. In a sentence like "The dog likes the small cat", or "le chien aime le petit chat" (this tendency is language- independent), the main (and only) boundary may be placed either after the subject noun phrase, or the verb. Or there may be an equivalent boundary after the subject noun phrase and the verb. The adjective and the following noun are lileky to be grouped into a single prosodic group and no boundary is expected between these two lexical words.

As a result, prosodic information decoded from the signal should be compatible with lexical hypotheses made by the lexical search and with hypotheses made on the sequence of words by the syntactic module. Because it is necessary to provide for possible inter- and intra-speaker variability, algorithms for compatibility checking at the lexical and syntactic levels (in a verification process) are easier to conceive than algorithms for prediction (in a hypothetisation process).

c) Non-linguistic aspects: speaker's feeling about what he says

A sentence may also be uttered in a non-neutral, but more or less **marked** manner. The prosodic variations are then knowingly controlled by the speaker to eventually communicate knowledge about his attitude towards what he is saying: doubt, irony, involvement, conviction, etc... or to direct his listener's attention toward the **more important** words of his discourse. There is a continuum between completely neutral and marked manners of uttering a sentence. The acoustic correlates of "doubt" or "irony" marking are not yet well investigated, and, no need to say, the sentences to be prosodically decoded should be uttered in a rather neutral way (see the work done on automatic classification of Halliday's tones superimposed to the words "yes", "no", "mmm" and "well" , AIN 87). The system has to be however flexible enough to handle a certain amount of **emphasis** (such as the assignment of emphatic stress or **focal accent** to particular word(s) in the sentence). This aspect of prosody is particularly important in a **dialogue** where the speaker tends to emphasize key words to clarify a question or an answer.

d) Paralinguistic aspects: physiological differences and dialects

Furthermore, deviations from commonly observed patterns may contribute to inform the listener(s) **about the speaker** himself: pathological accent, foreign accent, emotional state, physical condition, etc... (Note that these are generally not under the control of the speaker).

The last two aspects (non-linguistic and paralinguistic) of prosody, which are speaker-dependent, may obscure the linguistically conditioned aspects. None of the actual achievements have tackled the problem of automatic adaptation to the "abnormal" particularities of a speaker. The existing systems expect speakers to differ very little from each other.

1.2 Interactions on prosodic parameters and normalisations

a) A specific function is carried on by a combination of all cues

As stated before, the **relative** contribution of phonetically-conditioned variations and of each of the many functions of prosody to the determination of the observed quantitative values of the three physical variables (Fo, duration and energy) is not easily determined. One specific function (such as stress marking or juncture marking) is generally not defined by a single prosodic parameter but by a combination of all prosodic cues: duration, intensity and Fo (and eventually by the insertion of a pause). Furthermore, the exact contribution of each parameter varies as a **function of the context.** Let us illustrate the complexity of the phenomena.

In a stressed language (such as English or Italian), the **phonologically stressed syllable** of a word tends to have a relatively longer duration, a higher (often rising) pitch and a greater intensity than the surrounding unstressed syllables. These are only tendencies. The criterion of a **longer duration** may fail, and the cases of failure are predictable.

First, the criterion of a longer duration may fail. In cases where the stressed vowel is an intrinsically short vowel (such as /I/ in English) surrounded by intrinsically long vowels, and/or it belongs to a syllable with a larger number of phonemes than the surrounding syllables (the larger the number of units at one linguistic level, the shorter the length of each unit), and/or it is located next to a syllable which has been lengthened because it is a word-final or a phrase-final syllable, etc..., the stressed vowel may be shorter than the surrounding vowels.

Second, the criterion of a **higher intensity** may also fail when intrinsically low intensity vowels (such as /i/ and /I/) are surrounded by inherently high intensity vowels (such as /a/). The criterion of a **integrated intensity** over the vowel fails when the vowel is too short.

Third, the criterion of a **higher Fo** may fail. A pitch movement is often present on each stressed syllable. Depending on the position of the word in the phrase, Fo may be mainly rising or falling during the stressed syllable (When two words are regrouped into a single prosodic word, there is a (language-independent) tendency for Fo to rise during the first word and to fall during the second; see illustration later). An Fo rise, which is often concommitent to a stressed syllable, may also be found on an unstressed syllable (such as the realisation of a continuation rise on the final vowel before a non-final pause). There is also a natural tendency for Fo values to rise at the beginning of sentence, then to decline (the so-called "declination line") and for the pitch range to diminish throughout the sentence: the relative height of the stressed syllables and the amplitude of the pitch movement are to be interpreted according to the position of the syllables in the sentence. The largest Fo movements are expected near the beginning; if not, a word located elsewhere than at the sentence beginning is emphasized. The lowest Fo values are expected at the end of the utterance; if not, the sentence is marked (it might be an interrogative sentence).

There are three consequences: first, a combination of at least three parameters (pitch, duration and intensity) is desirable to achieve more reliable decisions, even for isolated words; second, contextual rules are necessary to achieve reliable decisions in continuous speech; third, a prosodic event (such as a vowel lengthening or an Fo rise) will often receive more than one interpretation.

b) Normalisation by articulatory and perceptual considerations

As expected, some algorithms attempt to substract the effect of **phonetically-conditioned** variations. Such normalisation requires identification of the sounds and possibly the position of syllable boundaries.

Ideally, compensation includes:

1. the intrinsic characteristics of the phonemes and the influence of the surrounding phonemes.
2. the number of phonemes in the syllable, of syllables in the word, and of words in the sentence.
3. the speech rate;
4. the correction for prepausal lengthening.

Present systems only include partial compensation of the phonetically-conditioned variations, i.e. of the ones which are the easiest to integrate. It is not clear whether or not such partial normalisation is better than no compensation at all (there is no known comparative studies). Indeed, complete compensations can be carried out only in a verification process. Details on compensation in present systems are described in Part II.

It has often been said (LEA 80c) that the raw data for prosodic decoding should not only be corrected for the phonetically-conditioned aspects but should also take into account knowledge about **speech perception.** It is evident that such a "normalisation" by perceptual considerations should lead to a more integrated view of the relative contribution of the three basic prosodic parameters, duration, Fo and intensity. However, knowledge on how duration, intensity and Fo are perceived and processed in continuous speech is not advanced enough to be applicable in an ASR system.

1.3 The role of prosody in speech decoding

a) Is prosody used by human listeners?

It is often argued that ASR systems should parallel, to a certain extent, the way humans perceive speech to be successful. One may question the real use of prosodic parameters by human listeners.
Do listeners use prosodic cues at all? How do they use them and when? And how far do the prosodic cues contribute to the understanding of the whole message?

Despite the apparent complex manifestation of the organisation of prosodic parameters, listeners seem to have no difficulties in decoding prosodically-carried information, at least in controlled experiments. The effective use of prosodic parameters in every day conversation and its exact contribution to the complete decoding of sentences are rather difficult to test. Despite the fact that it is easy to invent pairs of sentences which can only be made unambiguous by a single prosodic event (the position of a juncture or of a word stress), the cases where prosody cues are vital for comprehension of the message are rather rare in every day conversation. Because of that, prosodic aspects are often said to be **redundant** with spectral aspects, making the assumption that spectral aspects are sufficient for uniquely decoding the sentence. The assumption of redundancy may be questionned. It has been shown that listeners pay attention to prosodic continuity at the expense of semantic continuity (DAR 75). Nevertheless overall intelligibility systematically declines with an increased degree of time-compression; sentences heard in normal intonation are significantly more capable of withstanding the debilitating effects of compression than those heard in anamalous intonation (WIN 75). Understanding speech synthesis when there is no control of the prosodic parameters requires a particular effort from the listener. Deciphering a spectrogram without using temporal cues and Fo contour is much harder than using all cues available (personal experiment). It is equally reasonable to assume that not only the spectral aspects but also the temporal aspects and Fo are parallel inputs to the ears of the listener who simultaneously decodes them, and that a simultaneous treatment of both inputs might be absolutely necessary for automatic recognition of continuous speech. Such view is generally accepted in the psycho-linguistic literature.

b) The particular role of word stress

The exact part played by word stress in continuous speech processed by listeners is not clearly established. Nevertheless, a number of studies have investigated the potential use of stressed-syllable detection in an ASR system. The arguments are the following:

- 1) the position of word stress is **strictly necessary** to the differentiation of words uttered in isolation. Some words such as noun/verb pair (PERmit-perMIT) are distinguished from each other almost entirely on the basic of stress position (in English or Italian, for example). [In languages with fixed word stress position like French, syllables found as "stressed" by prosodic considerations, i.e. a longer duration and an higher Fo, may not only correspond to a phonological stress on the last word syllable, but also to emphasis at word onset].

- 2) in English stressed syllables seem to represent **islands of reliability** where the acoustic cues are relatively more robust. Experiments in spectrogram reading by experts and analysis of the phonetic confusions made by automatic acoustic-phonetic decoders confirm the fact that stressed vowels are more easily recognized than unstressed vowels (LEA 75a). Easier recognition is often explained by the fact that in word stress the syllables are lengthened. [Such an observation is compared to the notion of acoustic dominancy in French. In French, the "dominant" consonants, i.e. consonants which are located in portions of the sentence where Fo is rising, have characteristics closer to the norm than the same consonants in other contexts (VAI 86). Note that phoneme dominancy is an acoustic notion and it is determined by the actual position of phonemes in the prosodic structuring of the sentence, while stress is a phonological notion].

- 3) a number of theorical studies have demonstrated the usefulness of stress detection for a **multi-level access** to the lexicon. It has been shown that stress pattern information can reduce the lexical search in English and Italian. For **English**, dividing phonemes in stressed syllables into broad phonetic categories (manner of articulation) while "wild-carding' the unstressed syllables is almost as restrictive as representing the vocabulary by six broad phonetic classes (HUT 84; see also CAR 87). Stress information make thus restrictions that are potentially very useful for large-vocabulary, isolated-word speech recognition. Using a 15,000 word lexicon, and assuming a three level convention for the description of each syllable (stressed, unstressed and reduced) and a single stressed syllable per word, Aull showed that knowledge of only the number of syllables of the word yields an expected class size equal to approximately 41 percent of the size of the lexicon. When the stress pattern is known (i.e. the correct number of syllables and the correct assignment of stress for each syllable), the expected class size is reduced to 19 percent. If the number of syllables is known as well as the location of the stressed syllable in the word, then the expected class size is 22 percent [AUL 84]. The charateristics of lexical stress and their possible use in automatic speech recognition of the **Italian** language have been investigated at GSELT. A theoretical analysis of the constraints imposed by stress in the strategy of a large lexicon was conducted on the basis of a 12,000 word vocabulary: knowledge of the number of syllables and the stress location potentially allows reduction of the cohort size to 4.3 percent of the entire lexicon [PIE 87].

c) The basic function of alterning Fo rises and falls

Perhaps because a Fo rise is mainly realized by tensing the vocal folds and Fo fall by relaxing them, an upward change of Fo between two successive vowels seems to be associated with the notion of beginning and a downward movement with the notion of end in a number of languages (see VAI 83 for references; see also AIN 86, LIN 83). As a first result, a decrease in Fo usually occurs at the end of each major syntactic constituent and an increase in Fo occurs near the beginning of the following constituent (the so-called **fall-rise** pattern used as a boundary marker [disjuncture phenomena] (COO 77, LEA 72, LEA 80). As a second result, rise and fall often appear as a pair, and thus the schematized Fo pattern exhibits a so-called **hat-pattern** (MAE 76 for English) used for word grouping (juncture phenomena). In English, Fo movements are limited to the stressed syllables; in French, to word boundaries.

As noted before, there is more than one way to utter a given sentence. There are four basic ways to structure prosodically the following declarative:

THE CAT LIKES THE SMALL DOG. [1]

THE CAT LIKES THE SMALL DOG. [2]

THE CAT LIKES THE SMALL DOG. [3]

THE CAT LIKES THE SMALL DOG. [4]

(the pattern are schematized according to Maeda's method; see MAE 76 for further examples). The number of rises and falls depends on speech rate. As noted before, the number of large Fo movements decreases as rate of speech increases. [1] is more likely to correspond to slow speech, and [4] to rapid speech. Due to rhythmic constraints, there is also a tendency for the long words to correspond to a complete pattern, and for short words to be regrouped into a single pattern: a boundary (marked by a fall-rise pattern) between the subject noun phrase and the verb is more likely to happen when the subject noun phrase is long (in terms of number of syllables). As a consequence, for a given sentence and a given rate of speech, a certain type of prosodic patterning is more likely to occur than the others. It is however necessary to integrate the possibility of differences between speakers into the system.

d) Speaker-dependent variations

The same basic principles govern the determination of the prosodic parameters for all speakers, but the relative contribution of phonetically-conditioned variations, stress, rhythm, syntax, semantic, style and rate is speaker-dependent. Each speaker tends to be consistent, but there are regular differences between speakers. The study of speaker-dependent regularities is very important for ASR: the tuning of the system to the particular habits of the speaker is a prerequisite for a full extraction of the information.

Let us give some typical examples. I have compared the prosodic "habits" of two native speakers of English, JA and KNS, while reading long texts. The following represents the schematized Fo contours (schematisation is done using Maeda's method, MAE 76) for the first sentence of the first text (unpublished data). Only the Fo movements from the "plateau" to the "base-line" and vice-versa are schematized.

Schematized patterns for speaker JA:

THE MASSACHUSETTS INSTITUTE OF TECHNOLOGY [5]

IS A COEDUCATIONAL INDEPENDENT INSTITUTION, [6]

WHOSE PRINCIPAL INTERESTS ARE ENGINEERING SCIENCES, [7]

PURE SCIENCES AND ARCHITECTURE [8]

Schematized pattern for speaker KNS:

THE MASSACHUSETTS INSTITUTE OF TECHNOLOGY [9]

IS A COEDUCATIONAL INDEPENDENT INSTITUTION, [10]

WHOSE PRINCIPAL INTERESTS ARE ENGINEERING SCIENCES, [11]

PURE SCIENCES AND ARCHITECTURE [12]

There are at least four points for which the two speakers differ.

- 1) The **Fo falls** for JA are always rapid (that is superimposed to a single syllable) and concommitent to a stressed syllable (primary or secondary) (excepted at sentence end, where the fall is superimposed to the last syllables)(see Fo falls in [5] to [8]). In contrast, for KNS, the falls are rapid or gradual (see "coeducational" in [10], "principal" in [11]). Rapid falls are superimposed either to a stressed syllable or to a function word (a regularity observed in the remaining parts of the texts).

- 2) For JA, there may be a fall in a stressed vowel, directly followed by a Fo rise marking continuation in the next (unstressed) syllable (see "sciences", [3] and [4]). For KNS, when a continuation word is used on the word's last syllable, the fall on the preceding stressed vowel is always suppressed (see "sciences" in [10] and [11]).

- 3) For JA, there was no lexical word without at least an Fo movement superimposed on it, unless than it is uttered entirely in the upper Fo register (see "institute" [5]). For KNS, the lack of Fo movement on a lexical word mark its dependency with the surrounding lexical word (see the following paragraph).

- 4) For JA, adjective and following nouns are always regrouped into a single prosody word (by a rise during the first word and a fall during the last): "independant institution" in [6] , "principal interest" in [7], "engineering sciences" in [7], "pure sciences" in [8], etc... For KNS, adjective and following noun may be regrouped in the same way as used by the first speaker ("independent institution"), but in most cases, there is a rise in the first word, followed by a gradual fall, and there may be no Fo movement on the last word.

Such speaker differences are very important to grasp by rules. Such rules are a prerequisite for a full use of prosodic information in ASR. There is a need of more work in that direction (there is no known systematic work on modelling intra- and extra-speaker differences).

e) The use of pauses as boundary marker

The acoustic analysis of speech shows that speakers insert a large number of pauses while talking. **Respiratory pauses** represent only a part of all pauses; there are also **hesitation pauses** , but the majority of pauses (including the respiratory pauses) are located at **grammatical junctures.** The use of pauses as major boundary markers between and within sentences seem to be similar across those languages for which there is available data.

f) The use of lengthening as boundary marker

In a number of languages (English, German, French, Spanish, Italian, Russian and Swedish) there is a tendancy to lengthen the final elements in the linguistic structure, particularly the last vowel before a pause, as well as the final elements in words and phrases (see VAI 83 for references). It seems that lengthening, like Fo fall, is associated mainly with the notion of termination.

1.4 Conclusion

The preceding remarks on prosody are far from of being sufficient to introduce the complexity and richness of information carried by prosodic parameters. Articles concerning descriptive analysis of prosodic parameters corresponding to different speech styles, to different speakers and to different dialects, automatic generation of prosodic parameters for automatic synthesis-by-rules program, the rapidly developping area of non-linear phonology, psycho-acoustic and psycho-linguistic studies on the perception of pitch, duration and intensity in continuous speech; the articles on automatic segmentation of speech and on fundamental frequency detection, etc..., may be of utmost importance to those interested in adding prosodic parameters to their system. The proceedings of a seminar devoted to the role of prosody in ASR may also be of some interest [DIC 82, in French).

In modelling prosody for integration into an ASR system, it is essential to keep in mind the following points:

- (1) the speaker is expected to speak in a more or less **neutral way**
- (2) there is **more than one** neutral way to utter a single sentence although the number of ways is still limited;
- (3) the acoustic evidence of secondary marked junctures decreases as the **speech rate** increases: roughly speaking, the amount of prosodic information is inversely proportional to the number of syllables per second;
- (4) **vocalic** portions of the signal play a prominent part and are the main carriers of temporal and Fo contrasts; however, contrasting **syllable** duration and relative lengthening of **consonants** within a syllable are carriers of relevant information (word-initial marking for example),
- (5) **the binary division** between long and short vowels, or long and short syllables or stressed and unstressed syllables, often used to describe the perception of prosodic parameters is not entirely adequate in an ASR system; in continuous speech there is **continuous** variation in values,
- (6) **Adaptation to the speaker's** particular patterns is very useful to fully extract the information contained in continuous speech; Without adaptation, less information can be extracted and finally

- (7) there are some speaker differences in the amount of prosodic information that can be decoded from the signal (at least manually using present knowledge): sentences spoken by some speakers are more easily deciphered prosodically than sentences spoken by others, independently of the speech rate;

The following sections describe specific work done in the field. There are a large number of papers more or less related to the use of prosody in ASR in French and in English. Only those works where prosodic features are automatically extracted from speech signals are cited. As for the other languages (Swedish, Japanese, Italian), all papers known to the autor are cited (See also Noeth'es paper in the present volume, NOE 88).

2. PART TWO: STRESS DETECTION, STRESS MAGNITUDE AND PROSODIC FILTERING

A number of studies have been devoted to the role of stress in ASR systems. Despite differences, the systems follow approximately the same procedure. Thus the problem of detecting stressed syllables in isolated words or continuous speech can be divided into five steps:

- 1) segmentation of the speech wave into syllable-like units,
- 2) extraction of the prosodic features,
- 3) normalisation of the features,
- 4) detection of stressed syllables and
- 5) testing the effectiveness of the delivered information in a complete ASR system.

2.1 Syllabic nuclei detection

As noted before, most programs start by detecting the syllabic nucleus to locate the vocalic portions of the signal. A typical program of that kind, written by Mermelstein, can detect over 92 percent of the syllabic nuclei. The program uses a spectrally-weighted "loudness" function (the intensity of the speech wave is in the frequency range 500 to 4000 Hz) to compensate for different intrinsic energies in various vowels, and an interactive application of a "hull function" to first detect large energy dips then subdivide long segments between those big dips, by locating smaller dips within the chunks (MER 75). Segmentation can also be carried out by using the phonetic lattice produced by the acoustic-phonetic analyzer as in the French system, KEAL, used in my own studies (see the article by Mercier & al in the present book, MER 88) or the output of a broad classifier (such as in Aull's work). Interestingly enough, the segmentation errors are very similar, independently of the system used and of the language concerned. Segmentation is mainly based on abrupt discontinuity. Algorithms fail when segmental parameters are changing slowly over time. They fails often when two vowels or more are in sequence (vocalic linking) and when there is a problem with the separation of vowels with adjacent sonorants (/l/ and /r/). The problem is particularly acute when the vowels have a low first formant.

2.2 Features detection

Once the frontiers of the syllabic nuclei have been detected, the next step consists of calculating a certain number of parameters for each region (up to five, depending on the system). The calculated parameters are the following:

- 1) the **duration** of the sonorant portion of the segment or the duration between syllable boundaries defined by the onset of the sonorants of consecutive syllables [WAI 86];
- 2) the **energy integral** (average of energy level over the vowel);
- 3) the **fundamental frequency**, generally the pitch maximum [AUL 84; WAI 86]
- 4) a measure of **spectral change** for English (AUL, 84; WAI 86);

2.3 Normalisation of the features

A number of normalisations of the raw parameters can be made. Some of the systems include:

- 1) compensation for the **intrinsic** characteristic of the vowels: The average energy level is multiplied by a correction factor depending on the intrinsic intensity of the vowel when the vowel is identified (carried out by the acoustic-phonetic decoder or found in a dictionary when the word is known); in case the detailed identity of the vowel is not known, duration and pitch of the vowels are modified depending on an estimation of the first formant of the vowel (NIS 82; MEL 82) and the evidence of nasality (MEL 82). The values for the correction factors are often taken from LEH 60 for English and from ROS 67 for French (the tendencies are language-independent).

- 2) compensation for the **lengthening-before-voicing** phenomenon: Automatic detection of the voicing feature of the consonant following the vowel is relatively feasible, but a unique correction factor is hardly adequate in continuous speech. The magnitude of the effect varies as a function of the tense-lax feature of the vowel, the nature of the following consonant (stop or fricative), the position of the word and syllable boundaries and the position of pauses (CRY 85).

- 3) correction for **prepausal lengthening**.

  Such a correction is currently used in isolated words where the position of the pause is known (note that in this case, the correction includes not only prepausal lengthening but also the combined effect of word final lengthening); Dumuchel for example used a fixed factor (DUM 86), while in Aull's algorithm, the correction factor is adjusted depending on the gross category of the final context (AUL 84).

2.4 Algorithms for stress detection

2.4.1 Stress detection in isolated words:

a) The largest number of studies concerns stress detection for **English.** Medress & al (cited in LEA 80) showed that while 72 percent of stressed syllables in isolated words could be detected from higher peak energy levels, 70 percent and 68 percent could be detected from syllabic nucleus durations and Fo peaks, respectively. Cheung et al (CHE 77) presents an automatic method which estimates the magnitude of syllabic stress on a continuous scale in continuous speech using a composite of three acoustic parameters: F0, intensity and duration. Results showed that perceptual stress correlates highest with F0(r=0.683), then intensity (r=0.495) and lastly duration (r=0.306) and that a combination of the three cues provides a close approximation of the perceptual data (r= 0.876). In Aull's training data (350 words, 7 speakers), the most stressed syllable has the longest duration 65 percent of the time, the maximum amount of energy 84 percent of the time, and the maximum in Fo 76 percent of the time. Aull made two interesting observations: first, by reducing the duration of the final syllable to account for prepausal lengthening the maximally stressed syllable has the longest duration 90 percent of the time; second, the measurements were nearly as effective in separating stressed syllables from unstressed syllables if sonorants adjacent to the vowels were also included. The latter observation is important in automatic stress determination since it is often difficult to separate sonorants from adjacent vowels automatically (AUL 84). In Aull's final system for recognizing lexical stress patterns from speech signals, duration (compensated for prepausal lengthening), logarithms of the average energy measure in two frequency bands (400-5000Hz; 1200-3300Hz), maximum Fo on the syllable, and a measure of spectral change are computed for each sonorant syllable. The assignment of stress is made on a relative comparison of the syllables. In her study of 1,600 isolated words, Aull has shown that 98 percent of the primary stresses can be detected. For the remaining 2 percent that are mislabelled, nearly 40 percent of the labelling errors is due to the front-end processor. In 30 percent of the labeling errors, the stressed syllable is marked as an alternative choice for stress. The correct number of syllables and the correct position of the stressed syllable were found in 90 percent of the cases. The entire stress pattern (number of syllables, position of the stressed syllable and correct labeling of the remaining syllables as unstressed or reduced) was estimated in 87 percent of the cases (AUL 84). Dumuchel (DUM 86) examined the contribution of stress information in a HMM-based large vocabulary recognition system. The duration of the vowel part (normalized for lengthening-before-voicing phenomena and for prepausal lengthening) and the average energy level of the vowel (normalized for intrinsic energy) were used for estimating the probability of the correctness of the estimated stress pattern. After an initial training phase, tests on a new word list yielded 95 percent correct detection of the syllable carrying the primary stress. During word recognition, the likelihood of each word derived from acoustic data is modified by the probability that the required lexical stress pattern is supported by observed data. The rank of the correct word in the word hypothesis list improves by an average of 0.3 word positions when using the stress information. Excluding the two thirds of the list where the correct word was already ranked first, the improvement amounts to an average of 0.9 word positions. Dumuchel's experiments showed a (minor) improvement in the average word position in an HMM system by using stress information (DUM 86).

b) Some work has also be conducted for **Italian** An investigation into several thousands of words spoken by different speakers was made in order to extract the statistical properties of the main stress correlates in Italian. The results suggest that in Italian duration has the most importance for stress determination (after correction of prepausal lengthening, duration has a stress relevance of about 91 percent. PIE 87; see also KOR 87). By using durations of vowels, average log-energy of vowels, maximum Fo within vowels, and average spectral change (Euclidian distance between consecutive cepstral patterns), over 96 percent of stressed syllables are well detected in isolated words (PIE 87).

2.4.2 Stress detection in continuous speech

The particular problems in stress detection for continuous sentences are the following: first, the word boundaries are not known, and it is not possible to compensate for word-final lengthening; second, the grammatical, rhythmic and pragmatic aspects of prosody interact with word prosody; third, the words are not equally emphasized and the lexically stressed syllable may be not heard as "stressed" by listeners.

a) Lea and Waibel have proposed algorithms for stress detection in continuous speech for **English.**

Lea (LEA 73a) has shown that 89 percent of the syllables heard by listeners as stressed in continuous speech can be automatically detected. The procedure locates stressed syllables from an "archetype algorithm" that uses increases in Fo and energy integrals (with 21 percent false stress assignments). If durations of nuclei alone are used, 84 percent are located with 32 percent false alarms; by using Fo rise only, 77 percent are detected with 24 percent false alarms.

Waibel adopted a pattern-recognition approach to optimally combine intensity, duration, pitch and spectral changes into one minimum-error stressed syllable classifier. When a forced decision is imposed by setting a threshold at stress probability 0.5, error rates of 7.79% to 14.85% percent missed stresses were obtained. Waibel concludes that amplitude integrals are the strongest predictors of English stress in continuous speech (WAI 86).

b) The automatic detectability of syllables heard by listeners as stressed seems to be similar for English and for French. In a limited study, Martin (MAR 77) has shown that in **French** , ranking in continuous speech of the syllabic nuclei into decreasing integrated intensity is effective in 81 percent of cases in detecting syllables heard as stressed by a panel of listeners.

c) In applying the previously described GSELT's system to 51 **Italian** sentences, over 95 percent of the stressed syllables are detected but also about 16 percent of false stress (PIE 86).

d) A joint research project shared by the Phonetic Institutes at the Universities of Lund and Stockholm, "Prosodic Parsing for **Swedish** Recognition" has just started. The algorithms that are beginning to emerge are intrinsically more complex that the algorithms developed for stressed languages like English and Italian, simply because Swedish prosody seems to be of a more complex nature. In addition to the basic distinction between stressed and unstressed syllables, the primary stressed syllable is characterized by having one of two tonal accents: acute and grave. The Fo representation of initial juncture bears a strong resemblance to that of an acute focal accent, while the representation of a final juncture resembles that of a grave word accent. House et al (HOU 87), however show a promising 81 percent correct detection rate for grave accents.

2.5 Lexical filtering by suprasegmental patterns and prosodic cues

There are very few known studies on lexical filtering estimating the real contribution of the introduction of prosodic information at the word level in an existing ASR.

a) In a study by Waibel (WAI 87) on **English** , the suprasegmental features exploited were temporal cues (syllable ratios, ratios of unvoiced segment durations to syllable durations, voiced segment durations), intensity profiles and stress likelihoods. Using a multispeaker continuous-speech data base for evaluation, each suprasegmental feature is shown to hypothesize the correct word substantially better than chance. All suprasegmental features were then combined and compared with a speaker-independent acoustic-phonetic word hypothesizer. After applying the suprasegmental information, the correct word ranked on average 25th out of 252 words. The acoustic-phonetic knowledge alone yielded an average rank of 40 (out of 252) without the addition of suprasegmental information. After suprasegmental and phonetic KSs were combined the average rank was reduced to 15 out of 252. The results indicate that suprasegmental information indeed adds complementary information that substantially improves word hypothesization in speaker-independent continuous speech recognition.

b) One of my own studies (VAI 76, 82) has shown that about 60 percent of the lexical words in **French** are marked by an Fo rise at their beginning and 70 percent by an Fo fall at the end. Ninety-six cent of Fo falls occur on word-final syllables and never on word-initial syllables. Ninety-six percent of Fo rises occur at word-boundary syllables, either the first syllable in the word (word-initial rise) or the last syllable (a manifestation of continuation rise on the word-final syllable). Taking into account the fact that an Fo rise can only happen on the last or the first syllable in a word, the system was able to eliminate 33 percent of the word possiblities (consisting of more than two syllables) proposed by the lexical module from spectral knowledge only, leading to an appreciable reduction of the syntactic load (VIV 77). Only rather long words were suppressed, but no correct word was eliminated.

3. PART THREE: DETECTION OF SYNTACTIC BOUNDARIES

As seen before, prosodic knowledge provides a form of constraint on each word. Juncture phonemena (also called boundary phenomena) carry additional constraints on **word sequences**. While stress detection concerns both isolated-words and continuous speech systems, word- and phrase- boundary detection relates to continuous speech only. The basic prosodic features used for boundary detection are pauses, Fo typical movements and lengthening.

3.1 Pauses

O'Malley and his colleagues (OMA 73) have lead a study of the relationship between syntax and the position of pauses in spoken **algebraic** expressions. It was found that subjects were very consistent in their placement of pauses when reading algebraic expressions slowly. Furthermore, there was an almost perfect correlation between measured silence and perceived juncture. Rules were developed for inserting parentheses based on the location and measured duration of silence intervals in an utterance. Listeners were asked to insert parentheses given the spoken form, and the consistency of their answers was measured by a chi-square test. For those cases where there was listener agreement in a single answer, the rules were tested and found to agree with the listeners form 91 to 95 percent of the time.

In a study, Lea showed that 95 percent of the clauses and sentence boundaries are marked by a pause of 350 milliseconds or more (LEA 72).

3.2 Fo rises and falls

In one of his studies on cues to constituent structure and sentence boundaries in English, Lea (LEA 72) showed that 94 percent of the syntactic boundaries of 500 sentences were marked by a **fall-rise** pattern in the pitch contour. He also noticed that sentence boundaries were always accompanied by fall-rise Fo contours. The program searches for substantial decreases (7 percent) in Fo followed by substantial increases , and marks a boundary at the last of the lowest Fo values in the valley. A computer program (LEA 73b) correctly detected over 80 percent of all syntactically predicted boundaries.

3.3 Pauses and Fo movements

It is interesting to **combine** the information given by the position of **pauses** and the **Fo contour.**

Komatsu and his colleagues (KOM 86) recently presented an algorithm for detecting boundaries between grammatical units and for formulating structural hypotheses in **conversational** speech (the task of a PBX telephone operator) using Fo contour and the location of pauses. Pauses and Fo histogram are first used to detect sentence boundaries. Then, within a sentence, Fo contour is analyzed in detail by means of a piecewise linear approximation with a sequence of linear lines. A number of solutions is proposed for each sentence. The preliminary results are encouraging. Their analysis relies on Fujisaki's and co-workers' findings on Fo contours in Japanese. According to Fujisaki (FUJ 87), the Fo contour is composed of accent components and phrase accents. There already exists a fairly detailed account of the interaction between both components, but there is no known attempt as yet to automatically detect word accents in Japanese.

3.4 Lengthening

Lea (LEA 75a) estimated how far phrase boundaries can be detected from a measure of " **phrase-final** lengthening phenomena". It was found that 91 percent of all phrase boundaries heard by listeners in spoken sentences can be detected by finding vowels and sonorant consonants that are at least 20 percent above the median lengths of the same vowel or sonorant in all its speech occurences. The duration of interstress intervals tends to be short only when a word boundary intervenes but increasingly longer for syntactically predicted boundaries between phrases, clauses and sentences. He also noted that the phonetic error rate is more readily predictable from the interstress interval than from other measures.

Phrase-final lengthening affects both the duration of the successive vowels and syllables. In a previous study, I compared the use of syllable duration (automatically detected) with the use of the vocalic part alone. There was no clear advantage of one method over the other. In 97 percent of the cases, syllables (or vowels) detected as long by the program corresponded to first or last syllable of a lexical word and to monosyllabic grammatical words (VAI 77).

3.5 Fo movements and lengthening

Combining **Fo** and **duration** information is necessary to improve recovering of prosodic information. By using both duration and Fo in each vowel and a set of heuristic rules for detecting the **main boundaries** in sentences uttered without internal pauses in continuous French, a program was able to detect a main boundary in 86 percent of sentences (5 percent false alarms, most of them due to segmentation errors) (VAI 80).

Main boundary detection is probably the easiest to obtain automatically. To extract further information from duration and Fo contour and to determine **clause, phrase and word boundaries** , more complicated rules are necessary. PROSEIDON is an expert system developped for chunking the continuum into prosodic words [A prosodic word can contain one or several lexical words, preceded or not by grammatical words], for giving information about **sentence type** , position of the main boundary, left and right word boundaries and **dominant and dominated syllables** for a given sentence whenever possible. Connected to the acoustic-phonetic decoder (providing segmentation of the continuum into phoneme-size and syllable-size segments), the prosodic module uses both down-up and bottom-up informations. In particular, the number of syllables and a measurement of speech rate determines the number of boundaries the module is expected to find (about one boundary for four syllables). The main boundary is first detected, and the continuum is chunked into two parts. Extra boundaries in the each part are detected then, taking into account the number and the position of the segment relatively to the main boundary and the surrounding pauses. Figure 1 illustrates the input data to the phonetic module. Visualisation of the parameters computed directly from the signal is important for the expert who elaborates the rules. A "prosodic transcription" of the sentence to be interpreted is done automatically from (1) its temporal aspects (derived from calculation on relative length of the successive vocalic nuclei and syllables) and (2) its melodic aspects (derived from calculation on Fo relative height between vocalic nuclei and on Fo contour in lengthened vocalic parts). The principle on which the program is based is to interpret concommitently the rhythmic (temporal) aspects and its melodic (Fo) aspects. In a preliminary experiment, the program was able to give an average of 2.8 pieces of prosodically extracted information per sentence and to segment the continuum into chunks containing an average of 1.3 lexical words with an error rate of 3 percent (VAI 84). For example, for the sentence displayed in Fig.1, the running of the prosodic program PROSEIDON delivered the following information: (1) declarative sentence, (2) main boundary (//) on the fifth syllable (in fact, the offset of the subject noun phrase) and secondary boundary on the eigth syllable (the offset of the verb). The sentence was divided into three prosodic words (no error). The main weakness of the prosodic module is that it works in a top-down fashion starting calculation when the end of the

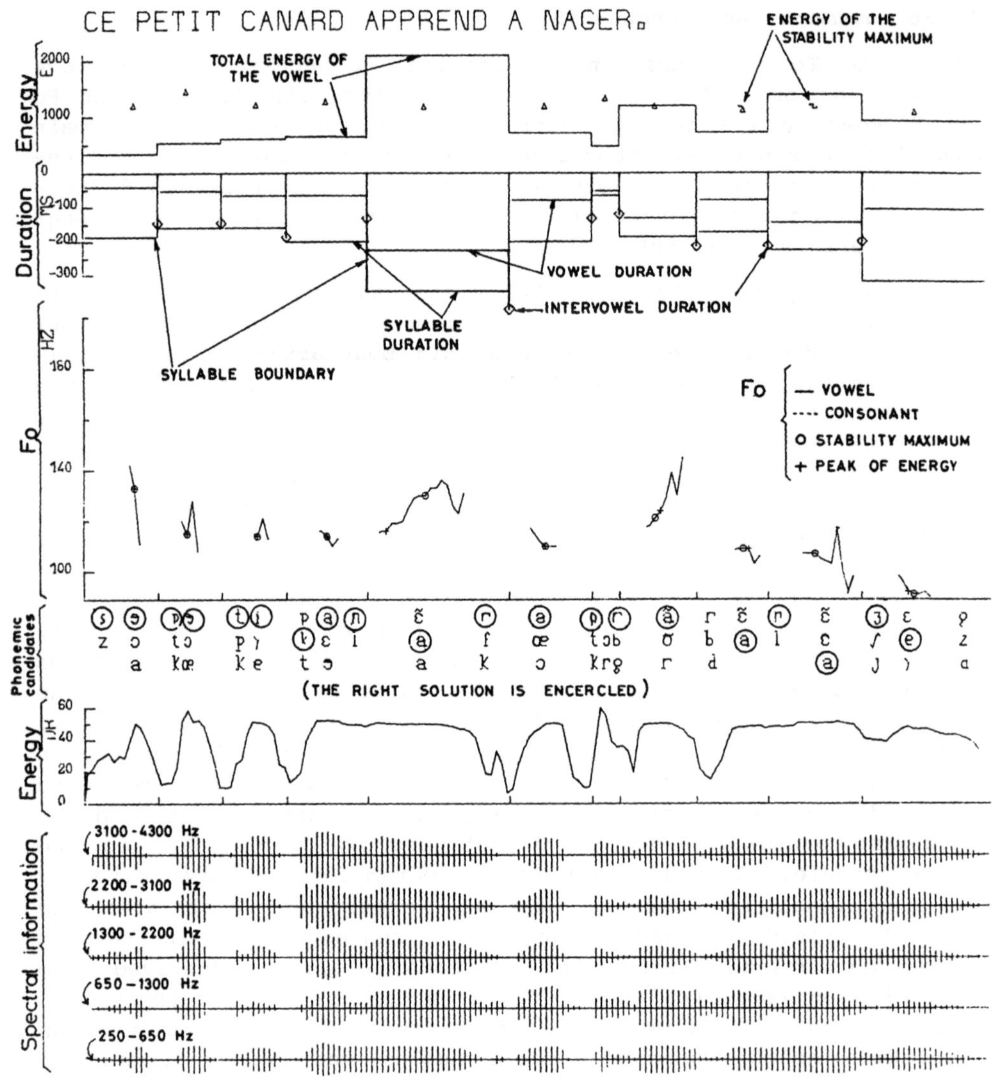

Figure 1: Visualisation of the prosodic parameters

This figure shows one possible output for the sentence :" Ce petit canard apprend à nager." (The little duck learns how to swim). It displays, from down to top,
1) SPECTRAL INFORMATION: energies in five frequency bands (bottom),
2) ENERGY,
3) PHONEMIC CANDIDATES: the three first candidates proposed by the phonemic analyzer,
4) MELODIC INFORMATION: Fo contour (+ indicates the selected value at the most stable part and the empty circle the selected value at the maximum of energy of each vowel),
5) RHYTMIC INFORMATION: the computed duration of the successive vowels and syllables, (vertical lines indicate syllable boundaries),
6) INTENSITY INFORMATION: the integrated energy over the vowel, and the intensity at the most stable part of the vowel.

sentence is reached. I am presently working on a new version of this program going strictly from left to right in order to be useful in a real time application by chunking incoming speech into logical sense-groups.

3.6 Integration of the information about boundaries in an ASR

Allmost no work is done yet in that direction. An attempt has been made to use Fo-detected phrase boundaries to aid the syntactic parser in the BBN HWIM system (LEA 80). This procedure involved marking first all the words in the grammar that were expected to be immediately preceded by Fo valleys (i.e., main verbs, first stressed syllables in noun phrases, adverbs,etc.). Only about one sixth of the words generated by the grammar was expected to be preceded by Fo-detected boundaries. If a word was expected to be preceded by a boundary and a boundary was acoustically detected, then the priority or "score" for that word was increased substantially; if the expected boundary was not detected, the word's score is decreased. Unfortunately, while BBN implemented Lea's ideas in a version of their HWIM system, their project terminated before any results were available. There is no attempt as yet to communicate the syntactic information delivered by PROSEIDON to KEAL's syntactic module.

As a consequence, it is not possible to conclude on the efficiency of integrating information on prosodic boundaries in automatic recognition of continuous speech.

4. PART FOUR: AID TO SEGMENTATING AND ACOUSTIC-PHONETIC DECODING

4.1 Segmentation

a) It is obvious that the error rate obtained by prosodic modules using duration as a parameter is very sensitive to segmentation errors. On the other hand, Vaissière has proposed how the **Fo contour** over the successive acoustic segments detected by the acoustic-phonetic analyzer of a ASR system can be used to estimate some cases of phoneme spreading and merging. For example, when a vowel is matched to a large Fo rise (generally a manifestation of the so-called continuation rise), it tends to be spread into two (or more) vocalic segments by the segmenter. In the verification process, if two contiguous but automatically segmented sonorant segments are superimposed on a continuously rising Fo contour, the two segments should correspond to a single phoneme (VAI 82b).

b) Bush (BUS 86) has examined the influence of **durational** constraints on recognition accuracy in an acoustic phonetically-based speaker-independent connected digit recognizer. The constraints are expressed using a set of finite-state pronunciation networks, together with specifications of minimum and maximum allowable durations for network primitives. In particular, a set of networks incorporates additional paths representing prepausal lengthening for the digits "oh" and "eight". The recognizers were tested on a corpus of 1232 5-digit and 7-digit strings with and without a priori knowledge of the string length. Recognition accuracies ranged from 33.9 percent to 94.6 percent and from 91.6 percent to 96.8 percent, for unknown and known string lengths, respectively, depending on the particular durational constraints incorporated in the network models.

4.2 Voiced-voiceless distinction

Fo and timing of the events may be used to distinguish between voiced and unvoiced consonants.

a) In a language like French, vibration of vocal cords during the entire or major portion of the consonant is the major cue distinguishing pairs of consonants like /p,b/, /t,d/, /k,g/. The **presence of Fo** and the concommitent presence of low frequency energy are generally used in knowledge-based ASR systems for French (such as in the Keal system).

b) In a language like English, the presence of Fo is a weak cue for voicing (Fujimura, 1961). The **shape of Fo at the vowel onset,** just after the release, is a cue that has been proposed by Lea (Lea, 1973) to distinguish between unvoiced and voiced consonants in ASR systems. The **timing** of the segmental events plays a preponderant part in distinction: **voice onset time, closure duration and vowel duration.** How far such cues are used in the existing knowledge-based ASR system for English is unknown.

4.3 Obstruent-non obstruent distinction

The **Fo shape during the voiced consonant** is very useful in the visual decoding of utterances for which the spectrographic representation is supplemented by Fo contour, at least for French (personal experience). During the occlusion period of the vocal tract for the realisation of obstruent consonants such as for stops and fricatives, there is a concommitent drop in transglottal pressure which lowers Fo (FAN 59). In other words, Fo is not expected to rise, nor to stay level during the realisation of the obstruent consonants. Moreover, the stop and fricative consonants, at least in French and particularly when the consonants are in a dominant position, are typically accompanied by a typical Fo fall-rise pattern which does not exist (or is much less marked) for non-obstruent consonants. Such a characteristic is not yet used in present ASRs, but is potentially useful for distinguishing between /m/ and /b/ or /v/, or /n/ and /d/.

4.4 Dominant-dominated phonemes

A given phoneme is ideally realized with a number of acoustic cues. In actual speech, a number of cues may not be clearly present. Even a phonologically-stressed syllable may be acoustically destressed.

Ongoing research at CNET by Roland Vives and myself has shown the absolute necessity of prosodic consideration before performing detailed verification on phonetic hypotheses to dramatically reduce the number of fatal errors (i.e. wrong suppression of the right solution). After word matching by the lexical analyzer, verification of the presence or absence of such acoustic cues corresponding to each matched phoneme is carried out depending not only on the position of the phoneme in the hypothesized word, but also on the position of the detected phoneme in the actual prosodic structuring of the sentence. For example, an unvoiced stop in a dominant position (the decision of dominancy is based on **Fo and duration** considerations) has to be realized with the absence of low-frequency energy for a period of time. In a dominated position, continued presence of low frequency energy is tolerated. The quantitative contribution of such prosodic considerations has not been systematically estimated since the work is far from being completed. The application of a first series of verification rules using a combination of segmental, suprasegmental and lexical knowledges leads to a suppressing of 45 percent of the lexical hypotheses. Three percent of right candidates are suppressed due to errors in segmentation and in Fo detection. Detailed verification of the acoustic attributes of phonemes without prosodic consideration leads to numerous fatal errors, i.e. the suppression of right candidates.

5. CONCLUDING REMARKS

It is not an easy task to come to a conclusion on the use of prosodic parameters in ASR. It is easy however to agree that very little has actually been done, that most studies are in fact preliminary, and that most of the work is still ahead. While prosody is potentially more useful in continuous speech recognition than isolated word recognition, less work has been done in the former direction. The feasibility (a small percentage of errors) and usefulness of stress detection of isolated words in ASR has already been rather well investigated. In constrast, there is a need for more research and experimentation in the domain of continuous speech and in dialogues. It has been shown that about eight out of ten syllables heard as stressed by listeners and most phonological boundaries are automatically detectable. Such information has not been however fully used. The state-of-the-art of the current ASR systems does not allow easy integration of prosodic information. Prosody needs a flexible host: it should be used both in a top-down and in a down-up fashion (for hypothetisation and verification), at all levels (acoustic-phonetic decoding, lexicon, syntax and pragmatics) and it requires feasibility of exchanging information between the different components of the recognizers.

The small amount of work done on prosody in ASR is by no means an indication that prosody is not important. Prosody is undoubtedly a necessary component for successful recognition of continuous speech. Prosodic knowldege can assist us in solving uncertainties arising from acoustic-phonetic errors and ambiguities. If properly exploited, such constraints could suggest promising hypotheses to pursue as well as eliminate unlikely interpretations from consideration. In more concrete terms, first, prosodic knowldege enables us to determine whether each word candidate has a prosodic profile compatible with the input signals. In particular, a prosodically stressed syllable should correspond to a "stressable" syllable as indicated by the lexicon. Second, it allows testing to find whether a particular sequence of hypothesized words can occur within a prosodically correct sentence. Word- and phrase- boundaries corresponding to hypothesized word sequence have to be compatible with the juncture and disjuncture phenomena detected from prosodic analysis. Two prosodically-regrouped words should correspond to two syntactically closed words. Conversely, detected major and minor boundaries should correspond to syntactic breaks. Third, prosodic knowldege provides a basis for predicting additional but unhypothesized fragment of sentences: a short, very low Fo frequency syllable often corresponds to a function word. Prediction of the presence of a word category is very useful in certain cases because it is often very difficult to hypothesize function words in a down-up fashion, from segmental information only. Fourth, the relationship between "segmental" quality of phonemes and their position in the acoustic structuring of sentences seem to be very crucial in attributing the acoustic evidence to other sources of knowledge. Automatic identification of phonemes in short, low Fo syllables should be given less weight. As described in this communication, there have been already some work in the former directions. Two other directions should be seriously investigated, concerning dialogue and quality control of incoming speech. First, sentence type (interrogative, declarative, ...) and emphasis phenomena detected within the sentence should be plausible and appropriate in the context of an ongoing dialogue. Second, prosody is the only way to control overall "quality" of incoming speech. Given the state-of-the-art of the current recognizers a sentence has to be uttered in a particular way to be recognized automatically. The proposals to use prosody in "guiding" the manner of speaking based on estimated speech rate, range and distribution of Fo movements, and the use of natural tendencies to emphasize important portions of the message (see VAI 86, pp 218) have not yet been tested.

It is often said that prosody is complex, too complex for straightforward integration into an ASR system. Complex systems are indeed required for full use of prosodic information. Lea's and my own experiments have clearly shown that it is not easy to integrate prosodic information into an already existing system such as HWIM or KEAL. It is necessary therefore to build an architecture flexible enough to test "on-line" integration of information arriving in parallel from different knowledge sources, particularly from prosodic aspects of the sentence.

Acknowledgements

I wish to thank Shinji Maeda, and Luc Mathan for kindly accepting to review a version of this paper, and particularly Gerard Bailly for his valuable suggestions.

REFERENCES:

(AIN 86) Ainsworth, W.A., (1986), "Pitch cahnge as cue to syllabification" J. of Phonetics, 14, 257-264.

(AIN 87) Ainsworth, W.A., & Lindsay, D., (1987), "Identification and discrimination of Halliday's primary tones", Proc. of Institute of Acoustic of Keele.

(AUL 84) Aull, A.M. (1984), "Lexical stress and its application to Large Vocabulary Speech Recognition", Master's Thesis, MIT. (See also Proc. ICASSP-85, 1449-1552).

(BUS 86) Bush, M.A., (1986), "Durational Contraints for Network-based Connected Digital Recognition", Proceedings of Montreal Symposium on Speech Recognition, McGill University, July 21-22, 89-90.

(CAR 82) Carbonell, N., Haton J.P., Lonchamp, F, & Pierrel, J.M., (1982), "Elaboration Experimentale d'Indices Prosodiques pour la Reconnaissance; Application à l'Analyse Syntaxico-sémantique dans le Système Myrtille II", in (DIC 82).

(CAR 87) Carter, D. Boguraev & Briscoe, T., (1987), "Lexical Stress and Phonetic Information: Which Segments are most Informative", Proc. European Conference on Speech Technology, Edinburgh, Vol. 2 234-238.

(CHE 87) Cheung, Y. J. & al, (1977), "Computer Recognition of Linguistic Stress Patterns in Connected Speech", Correspondence, IEEE Trans. on ASSP, 252-258.

(COO 77) Cooper, W.E. & Sorensen, J.M., (1977), "Fundamental frequency contours at syntactic boundaries", JASA, Vol. 62, No. 3, 683-692.

(CRY 86) Crystal, T.H. & House, A.S., (1986), "On the Availibity of Durational Cues", Proceedings of Montreal Symposium on Speech Recognition, McGill University, July 21-22, 71-72.

(DIC 82) Di Cristo, A., Haton, J.P., Rossi, M. & Vaissière, J., editors, PROSODIE ET RECONNAISSANCE AUTOMATIQUE DE LA PAROLE, GALF Groupe de la Communication Parlée, 289 pp.

(DAR 75) Darwin, C.J., (1975), "On the dynamic use of prosody in speech perception", In Cohen & Nooteboom, S. (eds), STRUCTURE AND PROCESS IN SPEECH PERCEPTION. Heidelberg: Springer.

(DUM 86) Dumouchel, P. & Lenning, M., (1986), "Using stress Information in Large Vocabulary Speech Recognition System", Proceedings of Montreal Symposium on Speech Recognition, McGill University, July 21-22, 75-76.

(FAN 59) Fant, G., (1959), "Acoustic Description and Classification of Phonetics Units", Ericsson Technics, No. 1.

(FAR 86) Fartenati, E. & Kori, S., (1986), "Effects of syllable and word structure on segmental durations in sopken Italian", Speech Communication 5, 17-34.

(FOW 77) Fowler, C.A., (1977), TIMING CONTROL IN SPEECH PRODUCTION, Ph.D. Thesis, University of Connecticut.

(FUJ 87) Fujisaki, H. & Kawai, H., (1987) "Realization of Word Accent in Connected Speech in Japanese", Eleventh International Congress of Phonetic Sciences, August 1-7, Tallinn, Estonia, U.S.S.R. Se 29.2.

(HOU 87) House, D., Bruce, G., Lacerda, F. and Lindblom, B., (1987), "Automatic Prosodic Analysis for Swedish Speech Recognition", Proc. European Conference on Speech Technology, Edinburgh, Vol. 2, 215-218.

(HUT 84) Huttenlocher, D., (1984), ACOUSTIC-PHONETIC AND LEXICAL CONSTRAINTS IN WORD RECOGNITION USING PARTIAL PHONETIC INFORMATION, S.M. Thesis, M.I.T., Cambridge, Mass.

(KLA 76) Klatt, D.H., (1976), "Linguistic uses of segmental duration in English: acoustic and perceptual evidence", JASA 59, 1208-1221.

(KOM 86) Komatsu A. &al, (1986), "Prosodic Aids to Structural Analysis of Conversational Speech" ICASSP 86, 2283-2285.

(KOR 87) Kori, S., Farnetani, E. & Cosi P., (1987), "A Perspective on Relevance and Application of Prosodic Information to Automatic Speech Recognition in Italian", Proc. European Conference on Speech Technology, Edinburgh, September 1987, Vol. 2, 211-214.

(LEA 72) Lea, W., (1972), "Use of Syntactic Segmentation and Stressed Syll-

able Location in Phonemic Recognition", 84th Meeting of the Acoustical Society of America, Miami, Florida.
(LEA 73a) Lea, W, (1973), "Segmental and Suprasegmental Influences on Fundamental Frequency Contours", in CONSONANT TYPES AND TONE, Southern California Occasional Papers in Linguistics No. 1, L. Hyman editor.
(LEA 73b) Lea W.A., (1973), "An Approach to Syntactic Recognition Without Phonemics", IEEE Trans. on Audio and Electroacoustics, Vol. AU-21, No. 3, 249-258.
(LEA 75a) Lea, W., (1975), "Isochrony and Disjuncture as Aids to Syntactic and Phonological Analysis", JASA, Vol. 57, 533.
(LEA 75b) Lea, W., Medress, M.F., and Skinner, T.E., (1975), "A prosodically Guided Speech Understanding Strategy", IEEE Trans. Vol. ASSP-23, 30-38.
(LEA 80a) Lea, W., (1980), "Prosodic Aids to Speech Recognition", in (LEA 80a), 166-205.
(LEA 80b) Lea, W., (1980), "Speech Recognition: What is needed now?", in (LEA 80a), 562-569.
(LEA 80c) W. Lea (editor), TRENDS IN SPEECH RECOGNITION, Prentice Hall Inc Englewoods Cliffs, New Jersey,
(LEH 70) Lehiste, I., (1970), SUPRASEGMENTALS, The MIT Press, Cambrdige, Mass. and London England.
(LEH 80) Lehiste, I., (1980), "Phonetic manifestation of syntactic structure in English", Ann. Bull. RILP, 14, 1-27.
(LIE 60) Lieberman, Ph., (1960), "Some Acoustic Correlates of Word Stress in American English", JASA, Vol. 32, No. 4.
(LIN 83) Lindsay, D., (1983), "A method of describing pitch phenomena" in INVESTIGATIONS OF THE SPEECH PROCESS (ed. Winkler), Bochum: Studienverlag Brockmayer, 189-210.
(MAE 76) Maeda, S., (1976), A CHARACTERIZATION OF AMERICAN ENGLISH INTONATION, PhD., M.I.T., Dpt of Electro-Engineering.
(MAR 79) Martin. Ph., (1979), "Automatic Location of Stressed Syllable in French", in Current Issues in Linguistic Theory, Vol. 9, p 1091-1094.
(MED 71) Medress, M.F., Skinner, T.E. and Anderson, D.E., (1971), "Acoustic correlates of word stress", presented to the 82nd Meeting of the Acoustical Society of America, Denver, Paper K3.
(MEL 82) Meloni, H. & Guizol, J., (1982), "Utilisation des Paramètres Prosodiques dans un Sysème de Reconnaissance Automatique de la Parole Continue", in (DIC 82), 93-120.
(MER 88) Mercier, G., Cozannet, A. & Vaissière, J., (1988), "Recognition of speaker-dependent continuous speech with Keal-Nevezh", in RECENT ADVANCES IN SPEECH UNDERSTANDING SYSTEMS, NATO ASIS, Springer Verlag.
(MER 75) Mermelstein, P., (1975), "Automatic Segmentation of Speech into Syllabic Units", JASA, Vol. 58, 880-883.
(NIS 81) Nishinuma, Y., Barber, S. & Hirst D.J., (1981), "Estimation de la Durée intrinsèque des Voyelles", XIIth Journées d'études sur la Parole, Montréal, 419-428.
(NOE 88) Noeth, E., (1988), "Prosodic features in German Speech" in RECENT ADVANCES IN SPEECH UNDERSTANDING SYSTEMS, NATO ASIS, Springer Verlag.
(OMA 73) O'Malley, M.H., Kloker, D.R., & Dara-Abrams B., (1973), "Recovering Parentheses from Spoken Algebraii Expressions", IEEE Trans. on Audio and Electroacoustics, Vol. AU-21, 217-220.
(PER 82) Perennou, G. & Caelen, G., (1982), "Utilisation de la Prosodie pour la Reconnaissance de la Parole Dictée", in /DIC 82/, 25-57.
(PIE 86) Pieraccini, R., (1986), "Lexical Stress and Speech Recognition", 112th Meeting of the Acoustical Society of America, Anaheim, 8-12 December.
(VAI 76) Vaissière, J., (1976), "Automatic Procedure for Segmenting Continuous Speech into Prosodic Words, in French", Recherches Acoustiques, Centre National d'Etudes des Télécommunications, Vol. 2, 193-208 [in French].
(VAI 77) Vaissière, J., (1977), "Premiers Essais d'Utilisation de la Durée pour la Segmentation en Mots dans un Système de Reconnaissance", VIIIth Journées d'Etudes sur la Parole, Aix-en-Provence, 345-352.
(VAI 82a) Vaissière, J., (1982), "A suprasegmental Component in a French Speech Recognition System: Reducing the Number of Lexical Hypotheses and Detecting the Main Boundary", Recherches Acoustiques, Centre National d'Etudes des Télécommunications, Vol. VII, 109-125.
(VAI 82b) Vaissière, J., (1982), "Utilisation des Paramètres Suprasegmentaux en Reconnaissance Automatique de la Parole comme Aide à la Segmentation en Phonèmes", in (DIC 82), 123-140.

(VAI 83) Vaissière, J., (1983), Language-Independent Prosodic Features", in PROSODY: MODELS AND MEASUREMENTS, (A.Cutler & R. Ladd, editors), Tokyo: Springer-Verlag, pp. 53-66

(VAI 84) Vaissiere, J., (1984), "PROSEIDON: Automatic Detection of Prosody Cues in Continuous Speech", Proceedings of the XIIIth Journées d"Etudes sur la Parole", Bruxelles, 28-30 May, 189-190.

(VAI 86) Vaissière, J., (1986), "Speech Recognition: a Tutorial", in COMPUTER SPEECH PROCESSING, F. Fallside and W.A. Woods, editors, Prentice Hall international, 191-236.

(VIV 77) Vives, R., Le Corre, C., Mercier, G. & Vaissière, J., (1977), "Use of Prosodic Markers in the Automatic Recognition of Continuous Speech", Proceedings of the VIIIth Journées d'Etudes sur la parole, GALF, Aix-en-Provence, 353-363.

(WAI 86) Waibel, A., (1986), "Recognition of Lexical Stress in a Continuous Speech Understanding System. A Pattern Recognition Approach", ICASSP 86, 2287-2290.

(WAI 87) Waibel, A., (1987), "Prosodic Knowledge Sources for Word Hypothesization in a Continuous Speech Recognition System", ICASSP-87, 856-859.

(WIN 75) Wingfield, A., (1975), "Acoustic Redundancy and the Perception of Time-compressed Speech", J. Speech Hearing Res., 18, 96-104.

Prosodic Features in German Speech: Stress Assignment by Man and Machine

E. Nöth, H. Niemann, S. Schmölz
Lehrstuhl für Informatik 5 (Mustererkennung)
Friedrich-Alexander-Universität Erlangen-Nürnberg
Martensstraße 3
8520 Erlangen, F.R. Germany

Abstract: We present a method for automatically assigning a stress score to every syllable in an utterance. The syllables are detected by looking at the energy in three energy bands. Based on features representing the prosodic parameters duration, intensity, and pitch, a stress assignment number for each syllable is calculated. The algorithm is tested on material collected from real dialogs. The automatic stress assignment is compared with the result of a stress perception experiment by human listeners.

1. STRESS AND PRAGMATIC IMPORTANCE

Even though there is little disagreement about the importance of the prosodic information in the human communication process, few automatic speech understanding projects use this knowledge source. Results on using prosodic information are presented in [LEA 80a] and [WAI 86a] for English and in [VAI 82a] for French. One of the most important contributions of a prosodic module to the analysis process could be to localize the stressed parts of an utterance. Practically all automatic speech understanding systems are information retrieval systems where a cooperative speaker can be expected. Therefore, the speaker will use sentence stress to guide the extraction of information by the listener. For this the speaker realizes the stress carrying syllable of the word representing the crucial information as perceptually striking. To achieve this, one or more of the three prosodic parameters duration, intensity, and pitch are used.

Our goal is to automatically detect the syllables in an utterance and to assign a stress score to each syllable. As a test set we collected eight real information retrieval dialogs (307 words with 458 syllables were spoken by the caller) from the application field of our speech understanding system (Intercity train information) [NIE 84a]. To obtain a reference contour we asked 15 people (phonetically untrained students and co-workers) to mark

NATO ASI Series, Vol. F46
Recent Advances in Speech Understanding and Dialog Systems
Edited by H. Niemann et al.

every syllable that they perceived as stressed. No definition of stress was provided. The average number of syllables that were marked by each person was about 23 percent. By summing up the results each syllable was assigned a number between 0 and 15. The numbers were compared with the result from a phonetician and good agreement was observed. Of course these numbers cannot be considered as a 16 level stress score but they can serve as a basis for a classification into 3 or 4 stress classes (i.e. unstressed, neutral, stressed).

We asked the co-worker who works on the pragmatic module in our project [EHR 88a], to mark the words that are pragmatically important. Under pragmatic importance, we understand words which represent domain dependent information that is crucial for the semantic analysis (i.e. place of destination). In the sense of [DIK 81a] these words carry a **topic** or **focus** function.

The average stress score for the word stress carrying syllable of the marked words was 12 vs. 2 for all syllables (21 percent of the words were marked by the pragmatics expert). We also asked her to pragmatically classify the words having a stress score of at least 8 (31 percent of the words). All of these words represented one of the concepts in the pragmatic network of our project (i.e. Intercity train station). The additional 10 percent of words realized structures for dialog control like in "**Hi**, my name is **Smith**" which fit into a pragmatic concept but were not considered to be pragmatically important.

2. AUTOMATIC DETECTION OF SYLLABLE NUCLEI

The first step in an automatic stress assignment algorithm is the detection of the syllable nuclei. This can either be done by another module (for instance optimal alignment paths from the word hypothesization module [KUN 88a]) or by the prosodic module itself. To do this we use the logarithmic energy in three energy bands. First the algorithm looks for local maxima in the median filtered output of the 300-2300 Hz energy band (the range of the first two formants). If certain criteria like minimum distance to the adjacent local maxima are satisfied, the peak is marked as a syllable nucleus. The beginning and the end of the syllable are set at half way between the maximum and the adjacent minima. Frequently, a strong fricative has enough energy in this band to show a maximum. Therefore the energy in the 300-2300 Hz band is compared with the energy in the 2300-5000 Hz band. If in a syllable the energy in the higher band exceeds the energy in the lower band, the syllable is deleted. The last step in the syllable detection algorithm is to look at the energy in the 100-300 Hz range. In the case of a syllabic nasal, the narrow and low first formant can often cause a maximum in this energy band while no local maximum can be found in the 300-2300 Hz band. Again, if certain criteria are satisfied, an additional syllable nucleus is inserted. Since reduction to a syllabic nasal is a safe indicator of the absence of stress, these nuclei are later automatically classified as unstressed.

3. AUTOMATIC STRESS ASSIGNMENT

Once the syllable nuclei are identified a stress assignment number between 0 (unstressed) and 1 (stressed) is calculated. This number is based on several features which are calculated for each nucleus and then compared with the features of the adjacent syllables. Each feature represents one of the prosodic parameters **duration, intensity**, and **pitch**.

The stress number is calculated in two stages. First the contribution of each of the three parameters to the overall stress is graded. As an example we will explain how the prosodic parameter **pitch** is calculated:

One can stress a syllable by **changing** the pitch. This can either be done very abrupt so that the pitch at the beginning of one voiced segment is very different from the pitch at the end of the previous one (i.e. tone-switch) or more slowly within a syllable (i.e. rise-fall). For each syllable nucleus the fundamental frequency is calculated at a frame rate of 12.5 msec. We use an algorithm based on [SEN 78a]. The maximum of the differences between the average f_0 within the nucleus and the average f_0 of the adjacent syllables is converted into semi-tones. With a fuzzy membership function this difference is assigned a number between 0 (no contribution to stress based on pitch) and 1 (very strong contribution).

The f_0 contour within each nucleus is approximated by one or two straight lines. The maximal slope of these lines is used to construct a stress number for this feature with the same range and interpretation. The maximum of these two numbers represents the contribution of the pitch to the overall stress.

The contribution of the other two prosodic parameters **intensity** and **duration** is graded in a similar way and the three partial stress numbers are combined to one stress assignment number. Both the fuzzy membership functions and the combination function were created heuristicly. A flow chart of the described stress assignment algorithm is shown in figure 3.1.

speech signal

↓

calculate logarithmic spectral energy for three energy bands:
300-2300 Hz 2300-5000 Hz 100-300 Hz

↓

apply 5 point median filter

↓

find local maxima in the 300-2300 Hz band and mark them as syllable nuclei

↓

eliminate nuclei with higher energy in the 2300-5000 Hz band

↓

find maxima in the 100-300 Hz band and mark them as reduced syllable nuclei
(if they don't touch a vocalic syllable nucleus)

↓

for each syllable:
calculate a stress assignment number between
0 ≙ unstressed and
1 ≙ very stressed
based on the following features of the nucleus:

- the length in comparison with the adjacent syllables

--> prosodic parameter **duration**

- the integral of the energy in the 300-2300 Hz band in comparison with the adjacent syllables
- the maximum of the energy in the 300-2300 Hz band in comparison with the adjacent syllables

--> prosodic parameter **intensity**

- the average fundamental frequency in comparison with the adjacent syllables
- the rate of change of the fundamental frequency within the syllable nucleus

--> prosodic parameter **pitch**

(reduced syllables automatically get the stress assignment number 0)

Fig. 3.1: Location of and stress assignment to syllable nuclei

4. RESULTS

The algorithm was trained with a set of read sentences and tested with another set of read sentences and with the above mentioned dialog parts. Table 4.1 shows the results for the detection of syllable nuclei for the two sets of test data. The different characteristics of the two sets of test materials led to significantly different results. While 94 percent of the syllables were found in the read sentences, only 87 percent were found in the dialog parts. This was largely due to the much higher speaking rate in unstressed parts of the utterance and to a higher degree of assimilation and reduction. Especially in a vowel-sonorant-vowel situation there was no significant minimum between the syllable nuclei and two unstressed syllables were merged to one syllable. 95 percent of the syllables that were not found were marked by a maximum of two people in the perception experiment described above.

test material	detected syllables	inserted syllables
read sentences	94 %	5 %
dialog parts	87 %	3 %

Table 4.1: Recognition rate of the syllable detection algorithm

In order to compare the automatic stress assignment number with the result of the perception experiment, we divided the range for the automatic stress number into 4 approximately equal intervals. Table 4.2 shows for each interval the average score in the perception experiment (Only the 87 percent of the syllable that were found by the algorithm were considered).

automatic score	0.0-0.2	0.2-0.4	0.4-0.8	0.8-1.0
average perception score	1.88	2.86	4.15	5.18
percentage of the syllables	22	24	25	30

Table 4.2: Average score of the listeners vs. automatic score

While the average scores show good agreement, there still is too high a number of syllables with contradicting scores (i.e. low perception score vs. high automatic score: 14 percent of the detected syllables had a perception score ≤ 2 and an automatic score $\geq .8$). About 30 percent of these cases were caused by merged syllables. The higher values for the temporal and dynamic features resulted both in higher scores for the unstressed syllables and in lower scores for adjacent stressed syllables. Another 30 percent were caused by the different intrinsic energy for central and front vowels. We currently work on improving the detection algorithm and on normalizing the dynamic features.

5. CONCLUSION

We presented an algorithm to automatically assign a stress number to every part of a given utterance. The algorithm identifies the syllable nuclei and assigns a number between 0 (unstressed) and 1 (very stressed) to each syllable. The number is based on several features representing the three prosodic parameters **pitch**, **intensity**, and **duration**. The algorithm was tested on parts from real dialogs and the result was compared to a human perception experiment.

BIBLIOGRAPHY

[DIK 81a] Dik, S. C.: "Functional Grammar", Foris Publications, Dordrecht, 1981.

[EHR 88a] Ehrlich, U., Niemann, H.: "Using Semantic and Pragmatic Knowledge for the Interpretation of Syntactic Constituents", in this volume.

[KUN 88a] Kunzmann, S., Kuhn, T., Niemann, H.: "An Experimental Environment for Generating Word Hypotheses in Continuous Speech", in this volume.

[LEA 80a] Lea, W.: "Prosodic Aids to Speech Recognition", in Lea, W.: "Trends in Speech Recognition", Prentice Hall, N. J., 1980.

[NIE 84a] Niemann, H., Brietzmann, A., Mühlfeld, R., Regel, P., Schukat, G.: "The Speech Understanding and Dialog System EVAR", in De Mori, R., Suen, C.: "New Systems and Architectures for Automatic Speech Recognition and Synthesis", Springer Verlag, Berlin, 1985.

[SCH 87a] Schmölz, S.: "Zur automatischen Bestimmung der Satzbetonung", Diplomarbeit, Lehrstuhl für Informatik 5 (Mustererkennung), Universität Erlangen, 1987.

[SEN 78a] Sennef, S.: "Real-time harmonic pitch detector", IEEE Trans. Acoust., Speech, Signal Processing, vol. ASSP-26, S. 358-364, 1978.

[VAI 82a] Vaissiere, J.: "A Suprasegmental Component in a French Speech Recognition System: Reducing the Number of Lexical Hypotheses and Detecting the Main Boundary", Recherches/Acoustique, CNET, Vol. 7, 1982/83.

[WAI 86a] Waibel, A.: "Prosody and Speech Recognition", Ph.D. thesis, Carnegie-Mellon University, Pittsburgh, USA, 1986.

RECOGNITION OF SPEECH USING TEMPORAL DECOMPOSITION

Gérard CHOLLET, Gunnar AHLBOM, Frédéric BIMBOT

ENST, Dept. Signal, CNRS UA-820
46 rue Barrault, 75634 PARIS cédex 13, FRANCE.

Abstract: *A natural approach to speech analysis is to attempt a segmentation of the speech signal into phoneme units. However, decomposition into phonemes is difficult, as they are context-dependent. Instead we propose a larger segmental unit, the "polysons" /BIM 86/.*

A technique is proposed for automatic labelling of speech, using a robust temporal decomposition, a technique originally proposed for speech coding. The spectral targets are evaluated by successive iterations on the computation of a set of compact interpolation functions, Ø(t), and corresponding spectra. These spectra are characterized by vectors of Log Area Ratios, LAR. A discussion on the choice of the representation may be found in /BIM 87/. Applications to speech recognition strategies are discussed.

1. INTRODUCTION

A natural approach to speech analysis is to attempt a segmentation into phone units. Coarticulation effects between such units is a source of failure for this approach. "Temporal decomposition" is a technique allowing for an overlap of the segments. This paper demonstrates its analytic power for speech recognition purposes.

1.1 Background

Following Atal's formulation /ATA 83/, some spectral representation, in our case the Log Area Ratios, $y_i(t)$, are given as a linear combination of a limited number of discrete spectra. These are tapered by compact interpolation functions $Ø_k(t)$

$$y_i(t) = \sum_{k=1}^{n} g_{ik}\ Ø_k(t) \qquad (1 \le i \le m\,,\, 1 \le k \le n)$$

with m being the number of LAR-parameters and n the number of interpolation functions. The Ø -functions are of limited duration (usually shorter than a syllable). They overlap in time to model the coarticulation of speech. A first estimation of the Ø - functions on the interval $[t_1, t_2]$ is achieved by using the Singular Value Decomposition, SVD, of the LAR - coefficients, contained in the matrix Y ($Y = U D V^t$).

NATO ASI Series, Vol. F46
Recent Advances in Speech Understanding and Dialog Systems
Edited by H. Niemann et al.

Only the first p collumns of the matrix U are retained to approximate the parameters $y_i(t)$ on the interval. Often (p = 4) is sufficient. Maximizing the energy of the Ø - functions on a compact, rectangular window then leads to the eigen value problem:

$$R\,b = \mu\,b$$

with
$$R_{ij} = \sum_{t=t_1}^{t_2} w(t)\, u_i(t)\, u_j(t) \qquad 1 \le i \le p,\ 1 \le j \le p$$

The Ø - function is then given by the eigenvector $\{b_i\}$ corresponding to largest eigenvalue:

$$\text{Ø}(t) = \sum_{i=1}^{p} b_i\ u_i(t) \qquad t_1 \le t \le t_2$$

Once a function is found an iterative procedure adapts the window w(t). Then we make a shift in time and calculate the next fonction Ø until the whole interval [1, T] has been analyzed. The spectral targets associated with a temporal decomposition are then obtained by minimizing the reconstruction error. Once the targets are found we can recalculate the Ø-functions. This procedure is then repeated until no significant improvement is gained.

1.2 Piece-wise linear approximation

The Ø-functions are approximated by three straight segments using a least square criterion. The spectra are calculated another time and the Ø-functions are normalized. Figure 1 shows the Ø-functions before and after such an approximation. It should be noted that this operation has a minor impact on the corresponding spectra, which are also given in the figure.

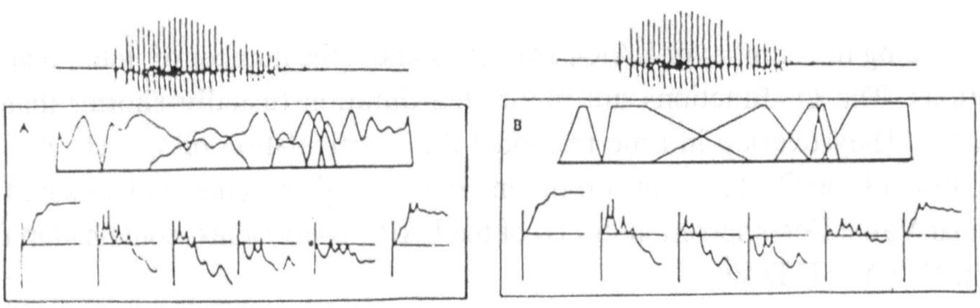

Figure 1. The temporal decomposition and corresponding spectral targets. A without, and B with the linear approximation.

2. RECOGNITION

The parameters used for recognition are not those resulting directly from the LPC analysis, but a result of the temporal decomposition. This reduces the dimension of the parameter space and decorrelates the extracted units.

2.1 Recognition using acoustic targets

Figure 2 shows the distance matrix for two utterances of the word "six" for a speaker, originating from the TI data base /DOD 81/. The euclidean distances are calculated for all combinations of targets. It should be observed that the number of targets is not the same in the two utterances. This matrix illustrates the consistency of the targets. Similar phonetic events correspond to similar targets, as given by the temporal decomposition technique. This allows the creation of a dictionary using known reference targets.

	1	2	3	4	5	6	7
1	4.8	13.1	19.1	18.5	14.6	17.1	3.9
2	20.7	14.0	8.0	8.7	15.1	12.4	18.3
3	21.3	17.0	9.3	10.8	17.0	10.4	17.3
4	15.4	6.7	16.7	13.9	3.4	16.4	13.5
5	22.7	12.2	15.8	12.4	13.9	10.6	20.5
6	9.0	12.7	19.8	19.9	14.6	17.7	5.2

Reference utterance

Test utterance

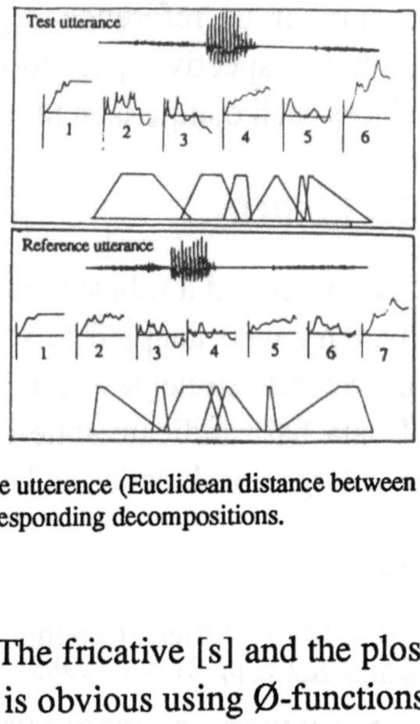

Figure 2. To the left a distance matrix for a test and a reference utterence (Euclidean distance between spectral targets) of the word 'six'. To the right the signals and the corresponding decompositions.

2.2 Recognition by labelling

The temporal information is essential. The fricative [s] and the plosive [t] have similar spectra, but the discrimination is obvious using Ø-functions. The learning phase of a system taking this into acount consists of calculating, for each phonetic reference unit i, the pair $(g, Ø)_i$. A reference word is represented by a sequence of such pairs.

A test word is then decomposed in such pairs. For each one, the distances to all possible reference pairs are calculated. The label associated to the test pair is the one, that corresponds to the minimum distance. Recognition of a word consists of comparing a sequence of labels and finally of deciding which reference word is the closest.

2.3 Recognition by inverse filtering

The 'polyson', defined as the segment bordered by two spectrally stable zones, is used as the unit for recognition. Each member k of a set of reference polysons is characterized by a sequence $(g_i^{ref}, \emptyset_i^{ref})_k$. During recognition, candidates for frontiers of polysons are hypothesized on spectrally stable zones. A test segment Y^{test} between these zones is inverse filtered by the sequence of targets $G_k^{ref} = (g_i^{ref})_k$, corresponding to a reference polyson k. The resulting $\emptyset_k^{test}$

$$\emptyset_k^{test} = (G_k^{ref\,t} . G_k^{ref})^{-1} G_k^{ref\,t} Y^{test}$$

is used to compute the reconstruction error : $Y^{test} - G_k^{ref} \emptyset_k^{test}$

for all polysons k, that match the hypothesized frontiers. A lattice of the recognized polysons is obtained by ordering the errors.

The number of reference segments $\{G_i^{ref}\}$ is in the order of 7000. However, their respective pseudo-inverses can be pre-calculated and stored, which reduces each comparison to a matrix multiplication.

3. CONCLUSION

We have described a robust version of a temporal decomposition technique. It is particulary well adapted to structure the output of an LPC analysis for recognition. Several strategies have been proposed. Preliminary results obtained on the TI data base indicate state of the art performances. Further testing is necessary on large vocabularies and connected speech.

References

/ATA 83/ B. ATAL: **Efficient coding of LPC parameters by temporal decomposition.** Proc. ICASSP-83, 2.6, pp 81-84. (1983)

/BIM 86/ F. BIMBOT, G. CHOLLET, S. MARCUS: **Localisation et représentation temporelle d'événements phonétiques: applications en étiquetage, segmentation et synthèse.** JEP-86, Aix en Provence, pp 27 - 29, (may 1986)

/BIM 87/ F. BIMBOT, G. AHLBOM, G. CHOLLET: **From segmental synthesis to acoustic rules using temporal decomposition.** XIth Int. Cong. Phon. Sciences, Tallinn. (1987)

/DOD 81/ G.R. DODDINGTON, T.B. SCHALK: **Speech recognition: turning theory to practice.** IEEE Spectrum, (sep 81), pp 26-32.

LONG TERM ANALYSIS-SYNTHESIS OF SPEECH BY NON-STATIONARY AR METHODS

Susanna Ragazzini
Fondazione Ugo Bordoni
Via Baldassarre Castiglione 59
00142 Rome
Italy

KEYWORDS / ABSTRACT : analysis-synthesis / non-stationary / AR algorithm / lattice predictor / frequency domain / source model

The use of non-stationary AR techniques for characterizing segments of speech of relatively long duration (e.g. 0.5 sec., a time duration that may include many bisillabic words) has been recently considered . A method has been proposed for this purpose, based on a non-stationary lattice, representing the dependence on time by a linear combination of functions of a suitable orthogonal basis. An iterative procedure for removing the bias of the formant frequencies due to the fundamental frequency is proposed in connection with the parametric non-stationary estimation of long-term segments of speech. The non-stationary tecnique can be extended to the identification of the excitation source; a method is described for recovering this signal from the residual of the lattice predictor. The efficiency of the resulting analysis-synthesis method is illustrated by real speech examples.

1. IDENTIFICATION OF THE VOCAL TRACT

In the present work we will use the same approach for determining the parameters regarding the vocal tract and the glottal waveform, based on representing the dependence on time by a linear combination of a suitable set of functions. In the case of the vocal tract, the parameters are the coefficients of the said decompositions of the reflection coefficients of the lattice model. The non-stationarity of the reflection coefficient k_i is modeled by expanding it into a linear combination of functions $g_j(n)$, $j=1,2,\cdots,L$ of a suitable base, i.e.

$$(1) \qquad K_i(n) = \sum_{j=1}^{L} K_{ij}\, g_j(n) \qquad i = 1,\cdots,P$$

where P is the lattice sections number . The choice of the basis can be guided by any a priori information on the properties of the AR process under consideration, such as, for instance, the presence of a jump in the coefficients at a given instant; in any case this method provides a model for smoothed but potentilly rapid evolution of the parameters.

The determination of the parameters k_{ij} of the predictor is usually carried out by solving the system of equations obtained by minimizing with respect to k_{ij} the sum ε of the variances

NATO ASI Series, Vol. F46
Recent Advances in Speech Understanding and Dialog Systems
Edited by H. Niemann et al.

of the forward and backward residuals at the output of the i-th section. The resulting system is

$$(2) \qquad \sum_{j=1}^{L} k_{ij} <A^i(n)\, g_j(n) g_r(n)> = -2 <B^i(n)\, g_r(n)> \qquad r = 1, ..., L$$

with $A^i(n) = [\, f_{i-1}(n)\,]^2 + [\, b_{i-1}(n-1)\,]^2$ and $B^i(n) = f_{i-1}(n)\, b_{i-1}(n)$

where $<\cdots>$ stands for mean value, $f_i(n)$ and $b_i(n)$ are the forward and backward residuals at the output of the i-th section.

The previous system (2) yields the value k_{ij} which minimizes ε without any control on the resulting magnitude of $k_i(n)$. It is possible to take into account the stability constraint by a method based on a mixed use of linear programming and least square procedures and taking advantage of the property of a function to be flat around its minimum. This property suggests to shift the solution from the minimum of ε under the physical constraint $|k_i(n)| \leq \rho$ for n=1,...N . The resulting algorithm [2] can be directly set under a form suitable to the application of linear programming techniques.

In the actual application of the previous algorithm it is convenient to reduce its computational cost at the expense of a less tight control on the magnitude of $k_i(n)$, since N is usually very large in the non-stationary case. A very simple way for accomplishing this goal is suggested by the remark that the maxima and minima of $k_i(n)$ are in correspondence with those of the basis functions $g_j(n)$. Consequently, we can limit the constraints to only the values n in the range $1 \div N$ which correspond to these maxima and minima. The number of parameters required by the present method for characterizing the vocal is much less than that required by the usual stationary predictors for short-term analysis of a comparable quality [1].

1.1. ELIMINATION OF THE PITCH BIAS

A fundamental assumption of the previous method is that the input to the model is white. Since this assumption is violated in the voiced segments of the speech, in some cases a significant pitch-related bias error will affect the estimated parameters of the lattice.This bias is quite equal both in the stationary and non-stationary analysis.

The procedure proposed in [3] is based on the remark that the contribution of the glottal signal to the signal to be processed is mainly concentrated in the lower part of its spectrum ($\approx 5 \div 10$ % of the spectrum). Consequently, the bias is automatically removed if the identification algorithm of the vocal tract requires only the remaining part of the spectrum.

The method proposed in [2] is transformed reformulating the LP algorithm in the frequency domain and using an iterative procedure in order to introduce the new frequency constraints.

When the power spectrum of the signal is completely available, applying the previous procedure that consists in solving section by section the LP problem in the frequency domain, we obtained the same values of the parameters as for the non-stationary lattice in the time domain. In the actual identification of a non-stationary AR process the power spectrum of the signal to be processed is only partially known, in this case we can apply an iterative procedure, trying to estimate the true spectrum in the range of frequencies where it is unknown (pitch range). At the k-th iteration the power spectrum in the unknown range is chosen to be proportional to the power spectrum of the signal at the output of the non-stationary lattice estimated at the (k-1)-th iteration .

The method followed for computing the spectrum of the input signal consists in :

1) driving the predictor calculated in the (k-1)-th step by a noise sequence;

2) determining the Fourier transform of the output sequence;

3) considering the magnitude of this transform as the power spectrum of the input signal in the unknown frequency range in correspondence to the k-th step.

As an example we can see in fig.1b the application of the non-stationary method in the time domain to a speech segment, all the figures 1 refer to the same sample time. Fig.1a represents the corresponding result of the stationary analysis.

The FFT spectra of the same time window is visible in fig.1c. It can be clearly seen from the figures that, if we compare the result of the FFT analysis in the pitch and first formant range, the estimates given by the previous methods are biased to an intermediate value between the frequency of the FFT peaks due to the pitch and the formant. To remove this bias we have applied the above mentioned recursive procedure in order to obtain a suitable AR model of the lower part of the spectrum. One iteration of the recursive procedure was sufficient to obtain the result fig.1d, where this bias is clearly removed.

2. IDENTIFICATION OF THE EXCITATION SOURCE

The complete characterization of the speech requires the simultaneous identification of the excitation source. This can be done starting from the predictor residual, in fact the source signal is given with acceptable approximation by the double integral of the predictor residual. It is important to note that the functions of the basis can be chosen arbitrarily. While this choice only sligthly affects the estimation of the vocal tract , in the case of the glottal signal, the situation is completely different, since the use of a trigonometric basis reduces both the computational cost and the number of parameter necessary to the representation.Using a technique similar to that used for identifying the vocal tract [4], the glottal signal is represented by the expression

$$s(n) = \sum_{k=1}^{H} [\, C_k \cos 2\pi F_k n + D_k \sin 2\pi F_k n \,] \qquad (6)$$

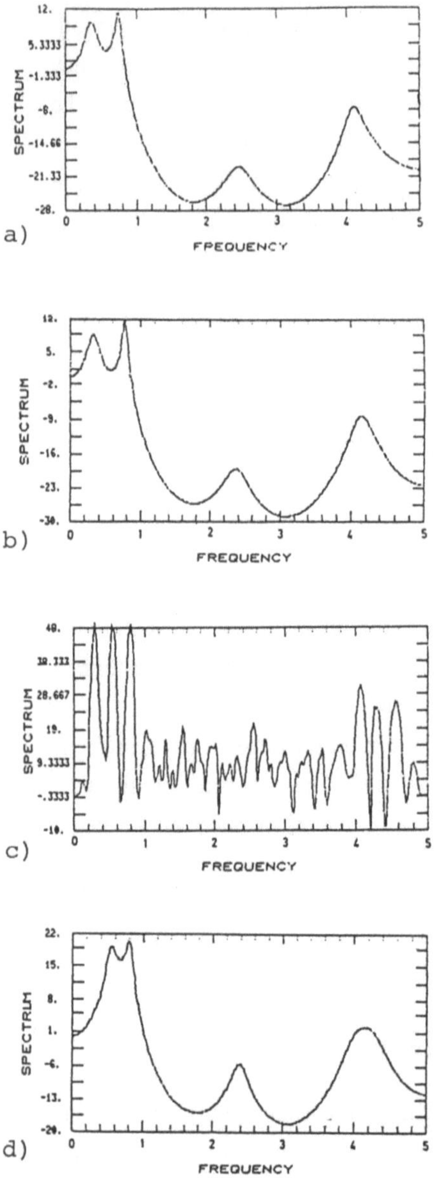

Fig. 1 Istantaneous spectrum
a) Stationary analysis
b) Non-stationary analysis in the time domain
c) FFT analysis
d) Non-stationary analysis in the frequency domain.

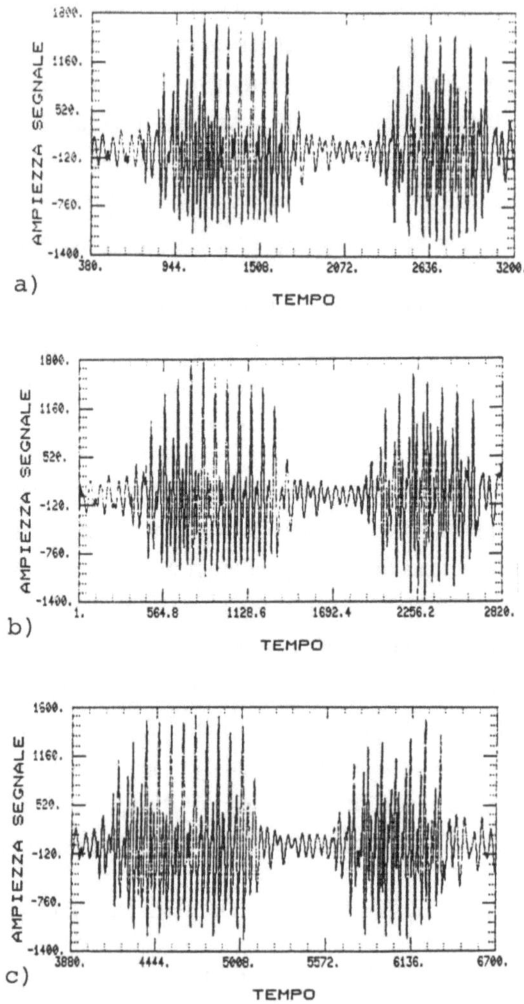

Fig. 2 Segment of 2048 samples of the italian word "vedo"
a) Original speech signal
Synthetic signal obtained with:
b) Proposed method
c) multipulse technique.

Since the determination of the parameters C_k and D_k can be afforted by an FFT, it requires a computational cost very reduced with respect to that necessary with a different basis. We have experimented a reduction of two orders of magnitude of the computational cost passing from a Chebyshev basis to (6).

In order to give an idea of the performances of the method from the point of view of resitution, we show in fig.2 the result obtained by applying our method of long term characterization of speech to a segment of 2820 samples of the italian word " vedo ", "I see" in english. Fig. 2a represents the original speech signal, fig. 2b the synthetic signal at the output of the proposed model and fig. 2c the synthetic signal obtained applying the multipulse technique.

3. CONCLUSION

The use of non-stationary techniques for characterizing long segment of speech has been considered in the present paper. In particular, the estimate of the parameters of the vocal tract in the frequency domain has proven to be effective to remove the formant bias due to the pitch frequency of speech. Moreover, its use impicitely reduces the interaction between the vocal tract and the glottal signal as the two sets of parameters are calculated in the only range of frequencies where they act.

REFERENCES

[1] G.Martinelli, G.Orlandi, L.Prina Ricotti, " Long term speech spectra of non-stationary AR models", IASTED Symposium on Applied Signal Processing and Digital Filtering, June 1985, Paris, paper 9.A.3.

[2] G.Martinelli, G.Orlandi, L.Prina Ricotti, S.Ragazzini, " Identification of stable non-stationary lattice predictors by linear programming ", Proc.IEEE, Vol.74, n.5, may 1986, pp. 759-760.

[3] S.Ragazzini, L.Prina Ricotti, G.Orlandi, G.Martinelli,"Elimination of the pitch bias in the non-stationary characterization of speech ", Proc.ICASSP'87 pp.940-944.

[4] G.Martinelli, G.Orlandi, L.Prina Ricotti, S.Ragazzini, " Excitation source identification in long term speech ", Signal Proc.III: Theories and Applications, I.T.Young et al.(ed.), Elsevier Science Pub.B.V.(North-Holland), EURASIP,1986, paper H3.1.

USING CONTEXTUAL INFORMATION IN VIEW OF FORMANT SPEECH ANALYSIS IMPROVEMENT

O. Al-Dakkak, G. Murillo, G. Bailly & B. Guérin.
Institut de la Communication Parlée. U. A. C.N.R.S. no. 368.
INPG 46, Av. Félix Viallet 38100 GRENOBLE FRANCE.

I. ABSTRACT :

Parallel formant synthesis of speech is a well known technique used in building performant synthesis systems. The fact that the synthesizer parameters can be closely controlled permits to obtain very high quality synthetic speech. However, the extraction of the parameters is not an easy task, usually semi-automatic methods are used for this purpose.

Our aim is to extract these parameters as automatically as possible. Hence, we use suitable signal processing procedures, together with a-priori and context knowledge on speech in order to guide the analysis and correct eventual errors where the automatic procedures are unable to give the correct results. The fact that we already have a whole French diphone dictionary ,analysed by an operator-controlled semi-automatic method will help us to gather the necessary a-priori knowledge of speech analysis. This analysis parameters are smoothed for all the diphones and then they are stored in a data-base form, we can then study the parameters' behavior and integrate them in the analysis system, the long term object being synthesis by rule.

II. FORMANT SYNTHESIS :

Parallel formant analysis by synthesis is one of the best methods to produce high quality synthetic speech because of the direct interpretation of the formant parameters in the acoustic representation of the speech signal [Badin & Murillo, 1983]. This good quality is obtained at the expense of a high cost both in time and human expertise.

Automatic analyses nowadys such as LPC produce better and better synthethic speech quality but have the shortcoming that the parameters

NATO ASI Series, Vol. F46
Recent Advances in Speech Understanding and Dialog Systems
Edited by H. Niemann et al.

are not directly interpretable on the signal and the naturalness of synthetic speech is not always as high as desired.

In the work described here formant analysis has been adopted; the use of a priori knowledge together with procedural signal processing will reduce the analyses costs.

Our formant synthesizer is controlled by twenty four parameters:

- four for a parametric elaborate voicing source,
- two for the noise source,
- fourteen for the formant parameters (amplitude, bandwidth and frequency for the first five formants in a parallel configuration),
- four for a pole-zero pair (frequency and bandwidth), in series with the first formant (see fig.1).

This synthesizer is implemented via a TI- TMS320 speech signal processor for real-time computation and piloted by a DEC computer. Speech sampling rate is 10 kHz and synthesizer parameters are updated every 5 ms.

III. THE SEMI-AUTOMATIC APPROACH :

Work over a complete French diphone dictionary has been accomplished in our laboratory; a professional speaker corpus of nonsense words was recorded by CNET-Lannion, and labeled by an expert phonetician. The diphones are extracted and then a first phase of signal processing is applied: A set of automatic analysis procedures inspired from the I.L.S. package compute pitch, voiced and unvoiced signal energy, and raw data for formant tracks with their frequency, amplitude and bandwidth computed from LPC parameters. A first operator intervention takes then place to roughly correct formant trajectories and other parameters depending on a priori acoustic expertise over sonagraphic representations over the complete utterances.

The second phase of the analysis method consists of an analysis by synthesis process applied on overlapped frames of about 25 ms in duration (shorter frames are used at signal transitions). Here we use a graphic editor: the natural and the synthetic signals are plotted in both time and frequency domain in addition to inverse filtering results and the synthetic voicing source waveform and the trajectories of all the parameters (see fig. 2). The operator adjusts the parameters by comparing all these information and by taking into account the sound perception of the natural and the synthetic utterances.

IV. THE AUTOMATIC APPROACH :

The methodology used consists on first computing vocal tract parameters and then using them to do inverse filtering and obtain the voicing source parameters.

1. Vocal Tract Parameter Computation :

A good deal of methods are found in the litterature based on spectral peak picking, tracking on LPC coefficients, zero crossings, stochastic models as dynamic time warping and HMM, etc [Markel & Gray 1976, Kopec 1985]. Stochastic methods seem to give the best results but context information is still needed to correct eventual errors.

Our choice consists of picking formant candidates on the smoothed LPC spectrum or its second derivative in case of difficult tracking (see fig.3). A score is computed for each peak which is the ratio of its amplitude to its bandwidth and then the number of formants to track and their research interval are chosen. The candidates with the best score are then considered to represent the spectrum of the current frame. LPC spectra for 51,2 ms of speech are computed every 5 ms.

For each diphone, a formant model is given for the first phoneme and then dynamic programming is applied over the whole diphone. There is the possibility to retrieve missed formants on the previous frame and to update the formant model on the phoneme transition when necessary. Once the formants are tracked their amplitude is computed on the spectrum and their bandwidth is obtained by parabolic interpolation; when interpolation gives values far from the predefined targets, default values derived from a priori knowledge are used.

2. Source Parameters Computation :

The formant parameters are then used to compute an inverse filter; the resulting waveform is the voicing source input for the synthesizer. Median followed by Hanning smoothing is used to obtain a more regular waveform before extracting the voicing source parameters. To model the voicing source waveform, [Fant 1979] four parameter model is used (see fig.4). This gives a compromise between the model complexity and the produced speech quality; The four parameters as seen on the figure are: F0 the pitch, U0 an image of the voicing energy, QD & QO the dissymmetry and the opening quotients of the waveform.

Pitch is calculated by AMDF followed by dynamic time warping [Bailly 1986]. Automatic markers are set at the minima of the waveform. The results of the AMDF help to choose automatically the markers corresponding to the glottal closure; dynamic programming is also used then to compute the other parameters of this source. In parallel signal energy is computed in order to correct U0; A priori information is also used to find out frontier and target values for the parameters and to correct them (see fig.5).

V. CONTEXTUAL INFORMATION : EXTRACTION AND COMMENTS

The above method is used for non noisy sounds; in the case of noisy sounds a priori and statistical knowledge are of great help to find out the proportion of voiced and unvoiced energies. For nasals, most produced with the pole-zero pair a six pole extraction can be applied as if we have six formants. The location and the caracterestics of the zero will be given by the contextual information.

The a-priori and context dependent knowledge are obtained from the dictionary discribed in III as follows: First of all, the parameter trajectories for each diphone have been weighted by Bezier polynomials [Newmann 1973] in order to smooth big trajectory discontinuities which often occur in diphones having a silent part due to the inherent heterogeniousness of a manual method . The smoothed diphones are not affected in their quality.

In parallel another smoothing by segments of 2d order functions can be used and help to confirm the hand-edited segmentation or to find out the phoneme boundaries and is also fundamental for the synthesis by rule approach [Itahashi 1978].

Parameter trajectories are then integrated in an DBMS (the Knowledge MAN package) which enables to access the diphone information in a DataBase query manner (close to SQL language), so we can have statistical computations and plot the parameter trajectory for diphones fulfilling the conditions we ask and hence, we can study the behaviours of the parameters depending on the adjacent phonemes - the so called context (see fig.6). The up mentioned conditions can be held on various parameters at a time when plotting one of them; for instance, we can look up the position of F2 when the command parameters of the pole-zero pair simulate nasality effects or find out the diphones where the difference F3-F2 is smaller than a chosen threshold...etc.

This approach shall help us to ennumerate the configuration of the parameter trajectories and their context dependency, the targets for each phoneme and finally to integrate these knowledge in the analysis system for the choice of thresholds, default values, research prototypes...etc, in order to yield a completely automatic and correct analysis.

VI. BIBLIOGRAPHY :

- Badin P. & Murillo G. 1983
An Analysis Method for High Quality Formant Synthesis.
Proceedings of the 10 th Int. Cong. of Phon. Sc.
- Bailly G. 1986
Détection du Fondamental par Pretraitement AMDF et Programmation Dynamique.
15 ème JEP Aix-en-Provence France.
- Itahashi S. 1978
Description of Speech Data Patterns by Several Functions.
STL-QPSR 2-3 1978.
- Markel J.D. & Gray A.H. 1976
Linear Prediction of Speech
Springer-Verlag New York.
- Kopec G.E. 1986
Formant Tracking using Hidden Markov Models and Vector Quantization.
IEEE ASSP-34 N° 4.
-Newmann W. & Sproul R 1973.
Principles of Computer Graphics.
Mc Graw - Hill, New York.

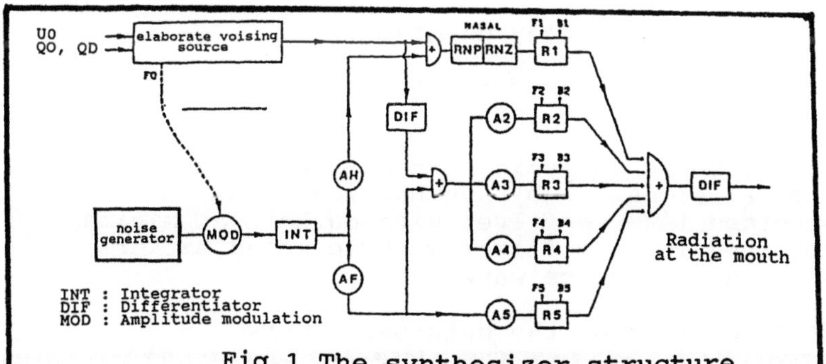

Fig.1 The synthesizer structure

2

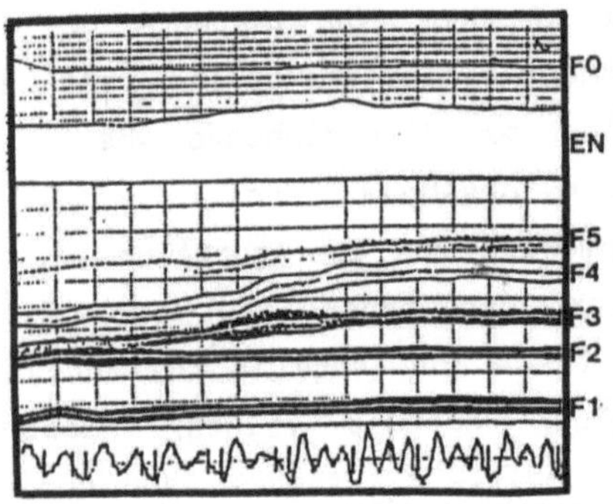

3

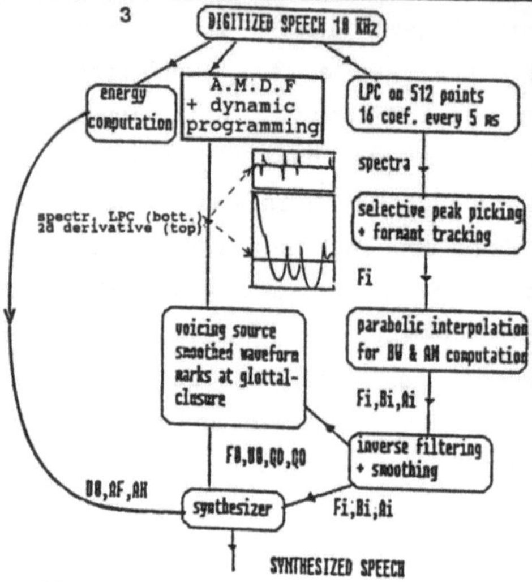

4

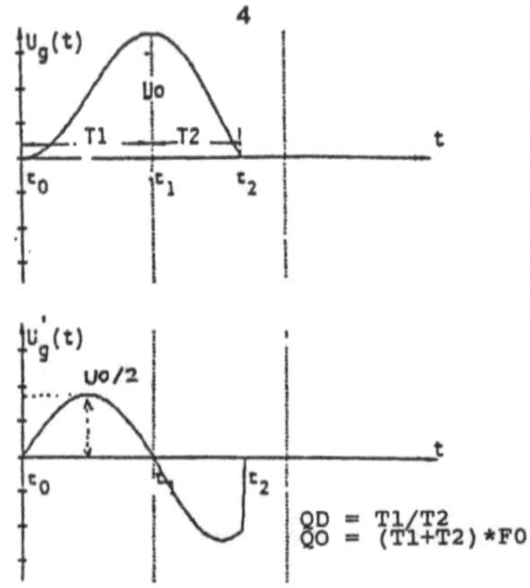

5

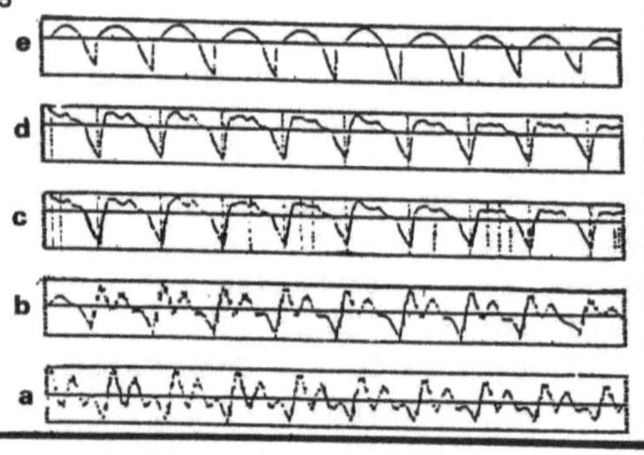

6

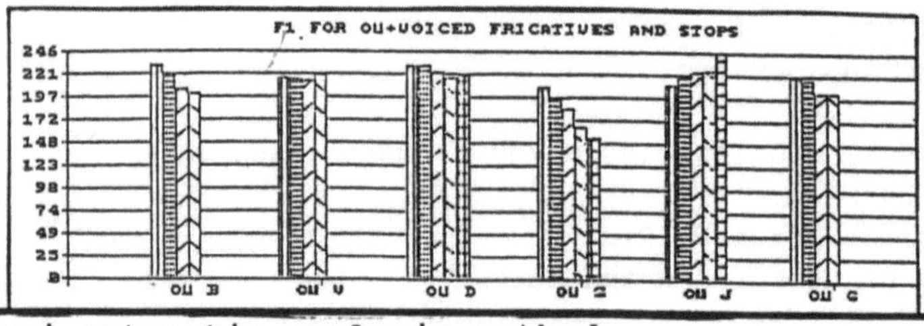

Fig.2 Semi-automatic analysis method

Fig.3 Analysis strategy diagram

Fig.4 The glottal waveform (top)
& its 1st derivative (down) FANT (1979)

Fig.5 Automatic analysis method -some results-
a) natural signal b) synthesized signal
c) smoothed inverse filter with markers at minima
d) smoothed inverse filter with selected markers
e) synthesized source waveform

Fig.6 An example of the data-base query

A SPEECH RECOGNITION STRATEGY BASED ON MAKING ACOUSTIC EVIDENCE AND PHONETIC KNOWLEDGE EXPLICIT

P D Green, M P Cooke, H H Lafferty and A J H Simons

Department of Computer Science
The University of Sheffield
Sheffield S10 2TN, South Yorkshire, England

Abstract: We describe a prototype implementation of a representational approach to acoustic-phonetics in knowledge-based speech recognition. Our scheme is based on the 'Speech Sketch', a structure which enables acoustic evidence and phonetic knowledge to be represented in similar ways, so that like can be compared with like. The process of building the Speech Sketch begins with spectrogram image processing and goes on to exploit elementary phonetic constraints. A multiscale approach is used throughout. The process of interpreting the Speech Sketch makes use of an object-oriented phonetic knowledge base. Objects in the knowledge base can be matched against objects in the Speech Sketch in a manner directed by the incoming evidence. This technique promises to avoid a combinatorial explosion.

1. INTRODUCTION

We have previously argued /GRE 86/ for an intermediate representation, the 'Speech Sketch' in the acoustic-phonetic signal-to-symbol transformation. The purpose of the Speech Sketch is to make acoustic parametric **behaviour**, rather than parameter **values**, explicit. The following sections outline the representational stages in a prototype acoustic-phonetics component for voiced speech based on this principle. Much of the software is implemented in SCOPE - a Small Common Object-based Programming Environment /JAC 87/.

2.1 Spectrogram Image Processing to Produce Spectral Objects

A conventional spectrographic representation of speech is converted into

NATO ASI Series, Vol. F46
Recent Advances in Speech Understanding and Dialog Systems
Edited by H. Niemann et al.

a list of 'Fragments' describing the time-evolution of spectral peaks, corresponding to formants or harmonics. First, a multiscale representation /WIT 84/ of spectral edges is created /LEU 86/. Next, a probabilistic relaxation algorithm, employing a spectral continuity constraint, seeks out the most likely labels for each spectral peak, (from the set: onset, offset, noise, part of a track and continuation at a finer scale) and identifies the most likely links between peaks in adjacent time-frames and scales. Finally, a deterministic procedure integrates information across scales, driving from onsets in the coarsest scale, continuing at a finer scale where necessary (seeking always to return to a coarser level) until an offset is reached. Figure 1 illustrates fragments for the first part of an utterance "Our lawyer will allow your rule", by a male speaker.

2.2 Characterising Spectral Objects to Produce the Raw Speech Sketch

Fragments, vectors of frequency, bandwidth and energy triples, are cartoonised to produce a multiscale piecewise linear description of frequency-variation in time. This characterisation scheme has been particularly influenced by /ALL 86/, /BAL 81/, /MAR 84/. Curvature extrema in the frequency track of a fragment are used to identify candidate segmentation points. Granularity is associated with the total error of a piecewise linear approximation of the segment by several sub-segments, using the candidate points. The characterisation algorithm builds a tree of segments where the successors of a segment represent its most economical description at the next-finest granularity level. Each node in the tree instantiates the SCOPE class 'Bar'; Bars constitute the discrete representation of fragment data in the Raw Speech Sketch. Figure 2 illustrates coarse-granularity Bars.

2.3 Utilising Common Sense Phonetic Constraints to Produce the Full Speech Sketch

Bars in the Raw Speech Sketch are interpreted as primitive phonetic objects, such that the most consistent global description is obtained using only weak local constraints /WAL 75/. An initial sub-set of labels, drawn from the set: harmonic or fine transition (H), formant-like resonances (F0...F4) and merged (unresolved) formant (F0F1, F1F2), is assigned to each bar, using gross frequency-region and bandwidth constraints. On each cycle, uniquely labelled bars broadcast to their neighbours in frequency-time, removing inconsistent labels, until no constraints remain to be propagated. This process degrades gracefully, such that any ambiguously labelled bars fairly reflect the data. Figure 3 illustrates.

2.4 A Strategy for Building Phonetic Hypotheses

Between the Speech Sketch (which makes **spectral objects** explicit) and hypotheses about phonetic identity, we envisage one or more stages of bottom-up hypothesis-refinement /LEV 84/ whose purpose is to make the **organisation of spectral objects** explicit: for instance we might form compound objects representing primitive objects which are roughly concurrent. Each object initiates a search for more complex objects that it could itself be a part of, until objects corresponding to phonemes are reached. In the prototype, this strategy is reduced to a single step. The coarse-granularity bars which have the F2 label are used to provide cues which drive the 'speech recognition' process of matching specific phonetic objects in the Speech Sketch. We distinguish between 'low F2 cues' (bars which start or end below 850 Hz), 'medium F2 cues' and 'high F2 cues', similarily defined. The low F2 cues trigger, and provide evidence for, a match for /w/, the high F2 cues for /j/, and so on.

2.5 Representing Phonetic Knowledge

Phonetic Knowledge is expressed in a SCOPE class hierarchy with PhoneticObject at its head. The classes in the hierarchy have slots called components, each of which describes some pattern which will match against a single object in the Full Speech Sketch (the 'filler'). Further slots express, in an algebraic formalism, the properties that fillers must possess and the relationships that must hold between them.

There is a weighted scoring mechanism which judges the quality of component fillers and the quality of the whole match. This scheme is used, in the prototype, to express the naive knowledge that any VowelLikeObject should, ideally, manifest itself as an initial transition, a steady state and a final transition in each of F1, F2 and F3, roughly concurrently. The SCOPE inheritance mechanism is used to fit particular vowels and semivowels into this pattern. In addition, we can make explicit the notions of a 'merged form', for instance that in the evidence for a semivowel F0 may be merged with F1, and 'counterevidence', for instance that a characteristic of /l/ is that there should be no object in the Speech Sketch around 2kHz.

2.6 Matching Phonetic Objects Against the Full Speech Sketch

The result of matching is to create instances of the given Phonetic Object. Each instance represents a collection of Speech Sketch descriptors which consistently match a subset of the PhoneticObject's components. As a consequence of having the Speech Sketch to examine, the state-space of partial instantiations is gratifyingly small. It can, in effect, be fully explored, using the given evidence first and then looking, among neighbouring objects, for support or contradiction. Figure 4 shows some matching results: the objects which contributed to the best matches for / /, /j/, /l/ and /w/ are displayed. Note that one object can contribute to several matches: there is no forced segmentation.

3. DISCUSSION

At the time of writing (May 1987), the prototype implementation is complete but has not been rigorously tested. Its performance on the few examples so far processed is exemplary: it is as if the Speech Sketch is asking to be recognised. Much work is required to put flesh on the bones. For instance, it remains to be seen whether our phonetic knowledge representation scheme is adequate, habitable to a phonetician and robust with respect to speaker variability. Our long term plans involve moving to an 'Auditory Speech Sketch' /COO 86/ and deploying 'Causal Phonetic Knowledge' /SIM 86/.

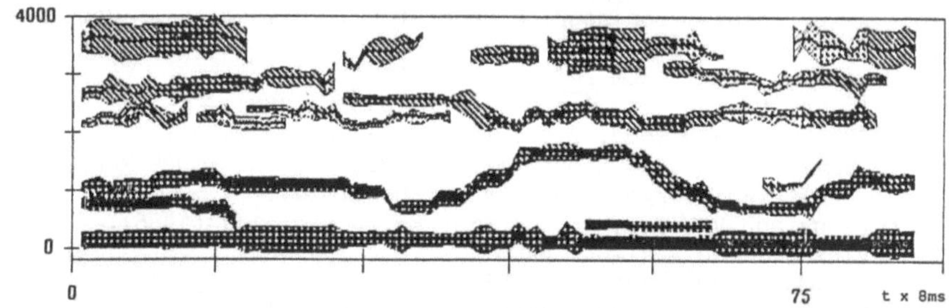

Figure 1: Fragments for "Our lawyer will.."

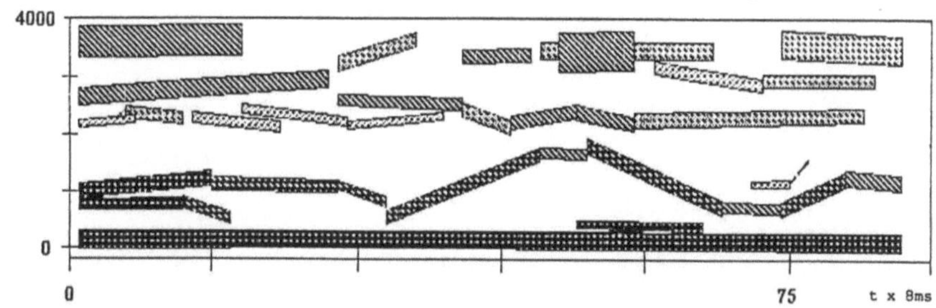

Figure 2: Raw Speech Sketch (coarse scale) for "Our lawyer will.."

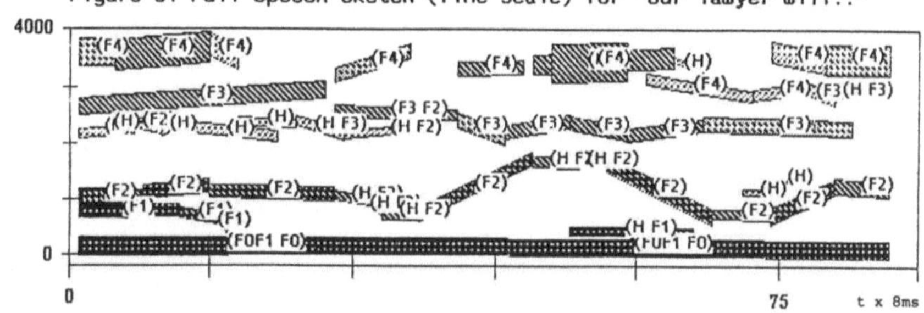

Figure 3: Full Speech Sketch (fine scale) for "Our lawyer will.."

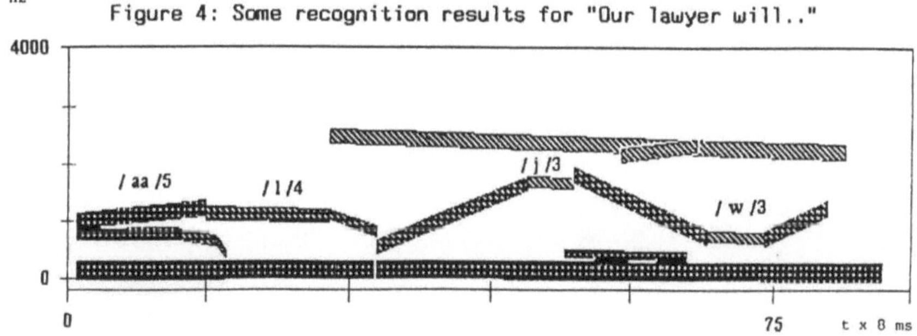

Figure 4: Some recognition results for "Our lawyer will.."

REFERENCES

/ALL 86/ M Allerhand, 'A Knowledge-based Approach to Speech Pattern Recognition', PhD Thesis, Engineering Laboratory, University of Cambridge, UK (1986).
/BAL 81/ D H Ballard, Comm. ACM 24, 5, p310 (1981).
/COO 86/ M P Cooke, Proc. Inst. Acous., 8, 7, p563 (1986).
/GRE 86/ P D Green and A R Wood, Proc. ICASSP-86, paper 23.4 (1986).
/JAC 87/ P Jackson, A J H Simons and G S Watson, The SCOPE Manual, (in preparation), EUSIP (Edinburgh) and SPLASH (Sheffield).
/LEU 86/ H C Leung and V W Zue, Proc ICASSP-86, paper 51.1 (1986).
/LEV 84/ R Levinson, Proc AAAI-84, p203.
/MAR 84/ D H Marimont, Proc AAAI-84 (1984).
/SIM 86/ A J H Simons, Proc. Inst. Acous., 8, 7, p499 (1986).
/WAL 75/ D Waltz, p19-92 in 'The Psychology of Computer vision', ed P H Winston, McGraw-Hill NY 1975.
/WIT 84/ / P Witkin, Proc ICASSP-84 paper 39A.1.

ON FINDING OBJECTS IN SPECTROGRAMS: A MULTISCALE RELAXATION LABELLING APPROACH

M P Cooke & P D Green

Department of Computer Science,
University of Sheffield
Sheffield S10 2TN, ENGLAND

Abstract: This paper describes a new technique for finding objects in spectrograms, and illustrates the idea with an application to the formant-tracking task. Starting with a multiscale representation of speech spectra, a probabilistic relaxation labelling algorithm is applied to determine primitive interpretations of the spectral components. Finally, a cross-scale integration procedure enables the scale space to be collapsed in a principled manner. The techniques are illustrated with an example of voiced speech.

1. MULTISCALE ANALYSIS OF SPEECH DATA

All conventional speech analysis techniques embody a scale constant in some form, which can lead to problems in deciding which scale to choose for the analysis. For instance, the performance of LPC depends on selecting a reasonable number of poles for the vocal tract model. Too few may cause formants to appear merged, whilst too many makes interpretation of the results difficult. A treatment of scale as a parameter leads to the construction of a so-called scale space. Events which are, in some sense, prominent appear at coarse levels of resolution, and may persist through to finer scales, whilst other events may only be represented at the finer levels. A scale space is typically produced by convolving data with a Gaussian kernel, where the standard deviation of the Gaussian is the scale parameter. Here, narrowband FFT spectra are convolved with the second derivative of a Gaussian, in a similar manner to that described in /LEU 86/.

Zero-crossings in this convolution correspond to extrema in spectral energy change as a function of frequency. Consecutive pairs of positive and negative going zero-crossings occur either side of a prominent peak (ie one whose bandwidth is greater than the scale parameter).

NATO ASI Series, Vol. F46
Recent Advances in Speech Understanding and Dialog Systems
Edited by H. Niemann et al.

Figure 1 illustrates this process applied to spectral data derived from the utterance "Why were you away a year, Roy". Lines are plotted where the convolution is positive. The rationale for using a multiscale approach is apparent from this figure. At the broad scale of analysis, only those spectral peaks of sufficient size remain after smoothing with the widest Gaussian. Formant-related stripes are manifest in this figure, whilst most other spectral detail is removed. However, there are situations where the close approach of two formants (in this example, F2 and F3 in /j/ and /r/) or the representation of F1 as merged lower harmonics requires greater spectral resolution. Clearly, a multiscale representation is sufficient to allow extraction of formant information, but how should cross-scale integration be achieved? Neutral techniques have been suggested /WIT 83/; here, we demonstrate the use of a relaxation labelling technique embodying low-level speech knowledge.

2. RELAXATION LABELLING OF MULTISCALE DATA

2.1 Background & Rationale

In accord with Marr's Principle of Least Commitment /MAR 82/, a formant-tracking technique which postpones decisions about tracks until sufficient disambiguating evidence has arrived will clearly outperform one which makes hard and fast decisions locally. A relaxation labelling framework is one mechanism which allows non-local evidence to affect decisions. The basic tasks are to

a) find a set of exclusive interpretations ("labels") for the primary data,

b) determine a neighbourhood relationship between primary data points, over which label probabilities will be updated, and

c) derive rules for updating label probabilities based on spectral constraints.

The algorithm then proceeds by iterating the application of the update rules until label probabilities have converged.

2.2 Spectral Labels

The multiscale data can be abstracted as a 3-dimensional graph structure where the vertices correspond to spectral peaks derived in scale-space production, and the edges are possible tracks through this set of points, both in time and in scale. Each edge is assigned a probability based on a metric which incorporates frequency, energy and bandwidth information. For the formant-tracking task, we look for interpretations of each vertex as one of the labels in the set [onset, offset, OnPath, noise]. Additionally, to enable cross scale connections to be formed, the label set [PrecFiner, SuccFiner] is added. Each label is assigned a probability based on edge weights in its neighbourhood.

2.3 Neighbourhood Relations and Update Rules

The neighbourhood of a vertex consists of other vertices in the adjacent pair of time frames, and vertices in neighbouring scales occurring in the same time frame. Initially, edges are formed between all pairs of vertices in the neighbourhood which satisfy broad continuity constraints on frequency, energy and bandwidth.

Vertex label probabilities are updated according to rules which reflect the compatibility between a vertex and its neighbours. For instance, evidence for an offset at a broad scale would support a similar label at a finer scale. Furthermore, edge weights can be brought into the calculation: the possibility of an onset should be placed in competition with the total likelihood of an incoming edge, for instance.

Edge weights are asymmetric. As a consequence, the likelihood of an edge viewed from one vertex may differ from that of its other vertex. The function used to update edge weights is designed to favour those edges for which there is good evidence from both vertices.

3. CROSS-SCALE INTEGRATION

Having allowed the iterative relaxation process to determine most likely labels for each element of the multiple scale description, it is a straightforward matter to collapse the three scales of description into a single set of time/frequency fragments. Starting from onsets at the coarsest scale, the process tracks along converged edges until either an offset is reached, in which case the process has found a complete fragment, or a SuccFiner label is encountered, in which case tracking continues at the finer scale until it is possible (via a PrecFiner label) to return to the coarser level. Figure 2 illustrates fragments discovered for the utterance of figure 1.

The rationale for driving the cross-scale integration process from the coarsest scale and providing a sustained upwards pressure is as follows: Those scraps of evidence at the coarsest level are likely to denote significant resonances as opposed to the finer level details which are more noisy. The fact that the coarser level entities may sometimes not appear resolved is overcome by the possibility of tracking to a finer level where required. The significant outcome of a multiscale analysis technique is that no matter how little evidence exists at a coarse scale, there is every possibility of tracking it fully at finer scales. Of course, this method breaks down when a pair of formants remain unresolved throughout their whole time evolution (as might occur in an isolated stable vowel, /i/, for instance). However, the method makes good use of any spectral nonstationarity.

4. CONCLUSION

The methodology described here is a first attempt at multiscale speech analysis and cross-scale integration. The performance of the system is currently being evaluated using a database which consists of voiced passages containing mainly vowels, diphthongs and semivowels. The time-frequency fragments produced by this method form the input to a knowledge-based acoustic-phonetic reasoning process, described in /GRE 87/. The advantages to be gained by employing a process operating at multiple resolutions are clear. One issue which remains is the nature of cross-scale integration. The solution presented here makes no use of knowledge about expected formant identities. This information could be used to search the multiscale representation for missing formants.

ACKNOWLEDGEMENT

This research was supported by ALVEY Grant MMI 052.

REFERENCES

/GRE 87/ P D Green, M P Cooke, H H Lafferty & A J H Simons: A Speech Recognition Strategy Based on Making Acoustic Evidence and Phonetic Knowledge Explicit, these proceedings (1987).
/LEU 86/ H C Leung, V W Zue: Visual Characterisation of Speech Spectrograms. Proc. ICASSP, paper 51.1, (1986).
/MAR 82/ D Marr: Vision, W H Freeman & Co, (1982).
/WIT 83/ A P Witkin: Scale-Space filtering. Proc. IJCAI, (1983), 1019-1022.

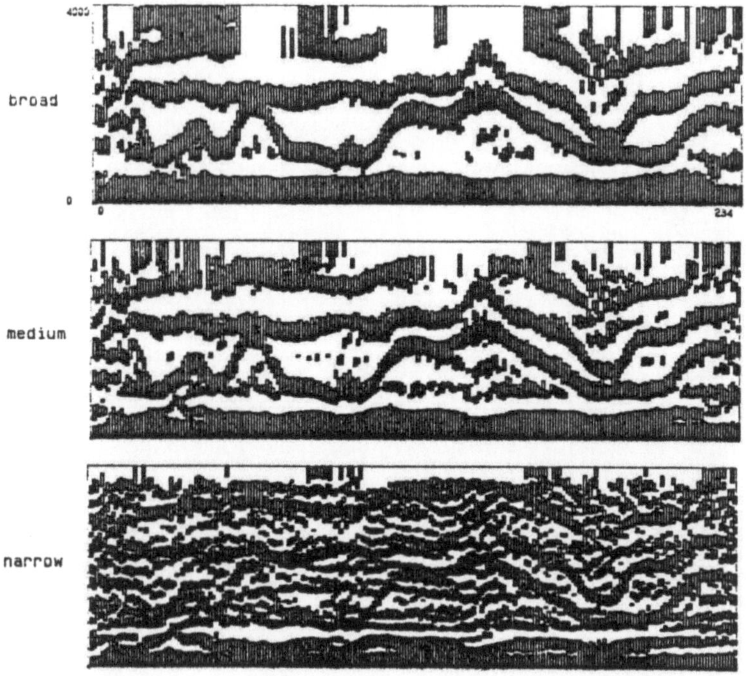

Figure 1

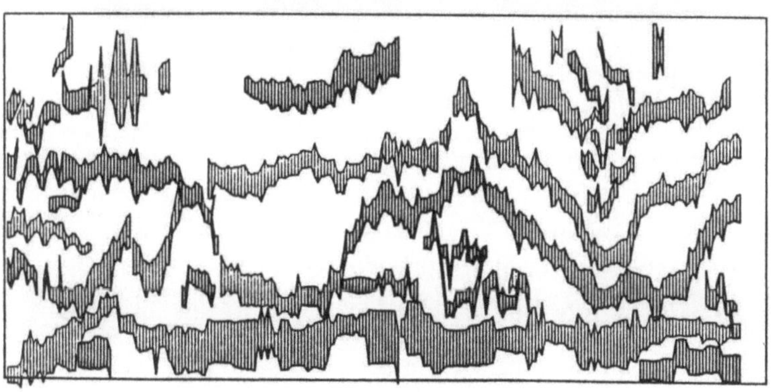

Figure 2

PHONETIC SEGMENTATION USING PSYCHOACOUSTIC SPEECH PARAMETERS

J.-P. Martens

Laboratorium voor Electronica en Meettechniek
St-Pietersnieuwstraat 41
9000 Gent, Belgium

Abstract: In this paper we describe a phonetic segmentation before classification algorithm. It is based on the inspection of temporal loudness patterns extracted by an acoustic front end incorporating knowledge about the human auditory system. In a speaker independent phonetic segmentation task more than 92.5 % of the phonetic boundaries were correctly detected, and no more than 10 % false alarms were counted.

1. INTRODUCTION

Although automatic speech recognizers don't operate the way humans do, we strongly believe they should employ acoustic features bearing perceptual meaning. I.e., they should incorporate knowledge about human auditory perception in their acoustic front end. Stimulated by the encouraging results obtained by others (DAS 86, DAV 80), we have developed a new acoustic front end incorporating a model of central as well as peripheral auditory processing of acoustic information. Its general outline is described in section 2.

Part of the information extracted by the acoustic front end is employed to achieve a phonetic segmentation of the speech signal. The purpose of that segmentation is not to produce the phoneme boundaries, but to locate the boundaries of the phone components. The recombination of phone components into phones will be accomplished according to phonological rules expressed in terms of a set of coarse phonetic classes (e.g. buzzbar+closure+burst⟶voiced stop). The segmentation algorithm we present here (section 3) is basically one of segmentation before classification.

NATO ASI Series, Vol. F46
Recent Advances in Speech Understanding and Dialog Systems
Edited by H. Niemann et al.

2. THE ACOUSTIC FRONT END

The general outline of the system is shown on fig. 1. Apart from the decimation units (2:1), we recognize a parallel analyzer.

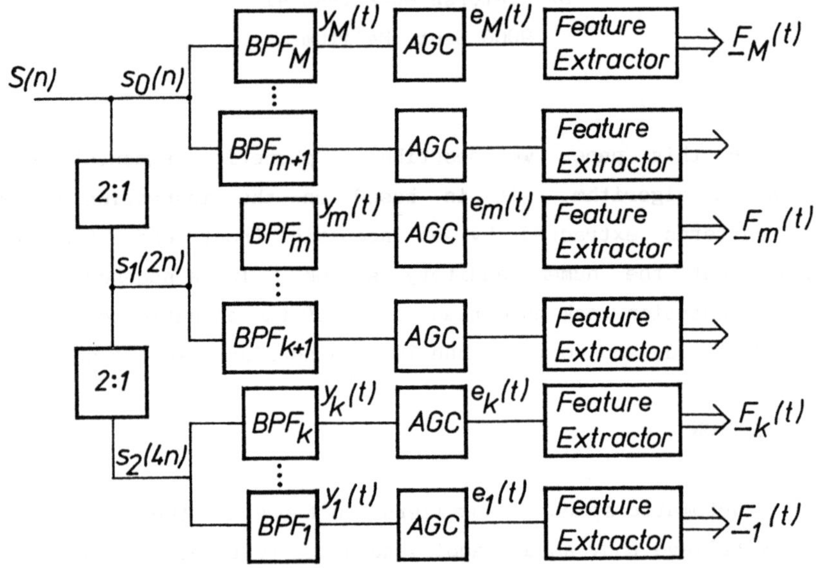

Fig.1: General outline of the acoustic front end

Each channel consists of a bandpass filter (BPF), an automatic gain control (AGC) device, and a feature extractor. The 'best' frequencies of the BPFs are uniformly spaced along a subjective pitch scale derived from physiological (GRE 61) and psychoacoustic (PLO 68) data. Using such a scale, 18 channels are needed to cover the 0.25-4 kHz frequency range. In combination with the proper decimation ratios, a good agreement between simultaneous masking curves and produced energy distributions can be obtained using 4th order BPFs.

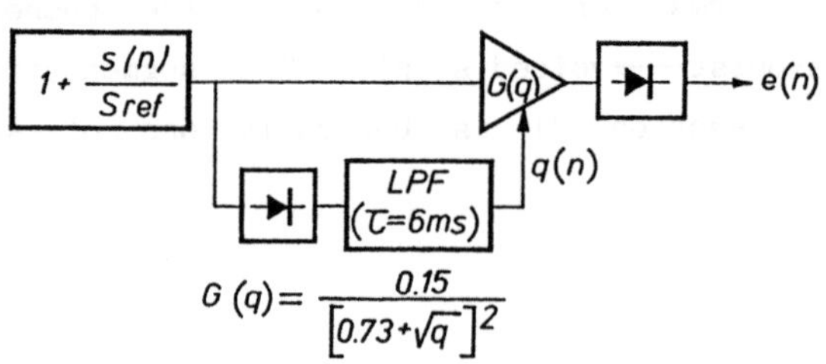

Fig.2 : AGC model for the haircell transduction

The forward driven AGC devices (fig. 2) model the mechanical to neural transduction in the haircells. Important properties of the haircell transduction are: a severe dynamic range compression, a fair temporal information encoding, and a considerable short time adaptation.

The feature extractors are based on the hypothesis that only the envelope of the neural spike pattern produced by the haircell conveys relevant information. In fact, an envelope analysis theory (MAR 82) was able to produce quantitative predictions of several psychoacoustic experiments. It must be emphasized that most auditory system based acoustic front ends proposed recently (SEN 85, COO 86) focuss on the dominant frequency rather than on the envelope. The envelope features extracted by our system are: the average level (=loudness), the magnitude of the low frequency modulations (<50 Hz)(=roughness), and the importance of dominant periodicities (50-300 Hz) (=synchrony). Details on the feature extraction process will be explained in a forthcoming paper.

3. THE SEGMENTATION ALGORITHM

The segmentation algorithm presented here is based on the detection of particular discontinuities in partial loudness functions. These partial loudness functions are obtained by summing loudness contributions of adjacent analysing channels. In the present algorithm we determine two such functions: Wlf representing the loudness contribution of the low frequency channels (0.25-1 kHz), and Whf representing the loudness contribution of the remaining channels. It has been established that phonetic boundaries tend to produce sharp positive peaks in the second derivative of these functions. However, in order to avoid local irregularities in the patterns to produce such peaks it is necessary to introduce smoothing and normalization in the second derivative computation. If W is a loudness function sampled at a rate of 10 ms, the following Q-function is computed:

$$Q(W,n) = \max[0, \arctan(dWr(n))-\arctan(dWl(n))]$$
$$dWl(n) = \max[W(n)-W(n-1), 0.5*(W(n)-W(n-2))]$$
$$dWr(n) = \min[W(n+1)-W(n), 0.5*(W(n+2)-W(n))]$$

The Q-functions derived from Whf and Wlf are then combined into a global Q-function

Q(n) = Q(Whf,n) + alfa*Q(Wlf,n)

The value of alfa is not very critical and can be chosen somewhere between 0.2 and 0.5. Any significant peak in the Q-function is assumed to correspond to a phonetic boundary, and the area under the peak is considered an estimate for the likelihood of that boundary. It turns out that most of the phonetic boundaries are correctly detected (less than 4 % deletions). However, one third of the boundary candidates are false alarms (insertions). That is why a candidate elimination stage is required.

The generation of Q(n) is based on very local properties of the loudness functions. In order to find out whether a boundary candidate is really relevant, it is necessary to take into account the properties of the segments surrounding the candidate. The candidate elimination is therefore based on the preliminary likelihood estimate of the boundary, and on suprasegmental features like:

- the loudness distributions in the surrounding segments
- the presence of a loudness dip
- ...

We need no more than a few rules to remove more than 60 % of the observed insertions without introducing too many deletion errors.

4. RESULTS

The segmentation algorithm was tested on a multi speaker database of speech bandlimited to 4 kHz and sampled at a rate of 10 kHz. The corpus consisted of 1500 isolated words uttered by two female speakers, and 100 sentences uttered by 17 different speakers (3 female and 14 male). If we don't take into account the bursts of voiced stops, we obtain the following results.

database	deletions (%)	insertions (%)
Isolated Words	2.5	12.4
Continuous Speech	7.3	10.2

The motivation for not taking into account the bursts of voiced stops is twofold: they are often shorter than 10 ms and cannot be detected using a 10 ms frame rate, and more importantly, they are not required because a buzzbar followed by a closure is already enough an indication for a voiced stop.

The most frequently occurring deletion errors are: the initial or final boundary of an intervocalic sonorant, and the initial point of a postvocalic sonorant in a non stressed syllable. It is highly unlikely that two vowels are merged, even if the intervocalic consonant is a sonorant (more than 98 % of the vowel nuclei were detected). A substantial amount of the insertions occur in fricative segments.

5. CONCLUSION

It was demonstrated that an auditory model based acoustic front end can produce partial loudness functions with very interesting temporal properties. In particular, a very simple and efficient phonetic segmentation algorithm can achieve results (7 % deletions, 10 % insertions) that are better or comparable to those obtained by much more sophisticated algorithms. At this moment we are examining how the coarse phonetic classification algorithm can discover and correct potential segmentation errors. Preliminary tests have already provided some encouraging results.

REFERENCES

/COO 86/ M. Cooke: A computer model of peripheral auditory processing incorporating phase-locking, suppression and adaptation effects. Speech Communication 5 (1986), 261-281.

/DAS 86/ S. Das: An approach to robust signal processing in isolated utterance recognition. IBM Europe Institute (Oberlech, 1986).

/DAV 80/ S. Davis and P. Mermelstein: Comparison of parametric representations for monosyllabic word recognition in continuously spoken sentences. IEEE Trans. ASSP 28 (1980), 357-366.

/GRE 61/ D. Greenwood: Critical bandwidth and the frequency coordinates of the Basilar Membrane. JASA 23 (1961), 1344-1356.

/MAR 82/ J. Martens: A new theory of multitone masking. JASA 72 (1982), 397-405.

/PLO 68/ R. Plomp and A. Mimpen: The ear as a frequency analyzer II. JASA 43 (1968), 764-767.

/SEN 85/ S. Seneff: Pitch and spectral analysis of speech based on an auditory synchrony model. PhD dissertation (1985), M.I.T.

Morphological Representation of Speech Knowledge for Automatic Speech Recognition Systems

Mathew J. Palakal

Computer Science Department
Concordia University
1455 de Maisonneuve Blvd. West
Montreal, Quebec CANADA H3G-1M8

Abstract

This work proposes a technique to capture speech knowledge which is available in spectrograms by considering it as a scene. A simple pattern analysis technique applied to these patterns reveals significant properties which are relevant to transitions of vocal tract as well as being speaker independent in nature. This process is labeled under Biological Vision since, Biological vision system uses a global recognition strategy by considering the image as a "whole". The recognition processor, the brain, uses symbols and symbolic relationships in image for image interpretation. Also, the knowledge base consists of symbols as well as symbolic relationship of objects in its long term memory. In order to give the machine a similar capability as that of biological vision systems, the pattern of a speech spectrogram is described as a morphology of symbols and symbolic relationships. Such symbols are then used for final hypothesis generation by statistical means.

1. Introduction

A robust vowel-diphthong detector is an integral part of any ASR system. The problem of vowel recognition is not new and extensive work has been done in the past in this area. Unfortunately, most of the vowel recognition algorithms use parameters extracted by various signal processing algorithms. These algorithms incorporate little speech knowledge and are not capable of adapting to variations in the speech signal.

Speech Spectrograms, a 3-dimensional time-frequency-energy representation of speech signals, has been in existence for the past four decades or so. Since then, speech spectrograms were the most valuable aid used by researchers for the Recognition and Understanding of human speech. Latest experiments by Zue and Cole further highlights the significance of using spectrograms in ASR research [1].

In our approach, the 3-dimensional speech spectrograms are treated as images, and standard image processing (pattern recognition) techniques are applied on these images. Contextual variations in speech images are somewhat similar to real world changes in scene analysis. Therefore, by considering speech pattern as images and applying image processing techniques to these patterns, one should be able to interpret and capture variations in a better way.

NATO ASI Series, Vol. F46
Recent Advances in Speech Understanding and Dialog Systems
Edited by H. Niemann et al.

The allowable degradations for any given scene, (a scene corresponding to a particular vowel or diphthong; each vowel or diphthong having a unique or similar scene appearance) are finite and caused by speaker variations and noise in the signal. The knowledge about a scene and its variations can be learned statistically or be represented by rules.

Property based prototypes of words of speech units may differ from real patterns not only because properties are distorted, but also because some properties are missed or some unexpected properties have been inserted. Insertions and deletions can be often characterized by deterministic rules reflecting basic coarticulation knowledge, but in many cases they cannot be fully explained and are better characterized by statistical methods.

Based on the above considerations, the system proposed in this work represents an attempt to integrate knowledge-based extraction of relevant speech properties and statistical modelling of their distortion.

2. Generating Speech Images (Speech Patterns)

For conceptual reasons, from now on we will designate speech images as speech patterns. The time-frequency-energy pattern of speech segments are obtained by considering the 0-4KHz portions of spectra computed with the Fast Fourier Transformation (FFT) algorithm applied to the preemphasized speech signal. Fig. 1.1 shows an example of such a pattern.

In Fig 1.1, frequency from 0 to 3.5 kHz is shown along the horizontal axis and each printed line corresponds to a centisencond interval. Also in Fig. 1.1, letters indicate the peak relative energy. Letter "B" represents twice the energy that is represented by letter "A"; digit "0" represents an energy that is twice than the one represented by letter "Z" and so on. Digit "9" is the strongest energy point.

Spectral lines are then extracted with a skeletonization algorithm from the time-frequency-energy patterns as shown in Fig. 1.2. Preprocessing on skeletonized patterns is then performed by a Line Tracing Algorithm (LTA) [2] for discarding all isolated, weak, and scattered points in the pattern. The LTA algorithm retains properites like, collinearity, curvelinearity, continuity etc. present in the pattern. Thinning and preprocessing surface all significant and non-significant lines in the pattern and discard all scattered points. Fig 1.3 shows the preprocessed pattern.

3. Perceptual Organization and Grouping of Lines

Description of grouped objects are carried out at various levels [3]. At the lowest level description, level-0, we use a morphology in the time_frequency domain for characterizing phonetic events. Level-1 consists of describing each line in terms of its time evolution and frequency range. At level-2, temporal relations between line descriptions are considered. Among these relations, there are relations which are perceptually significant, like, *downward shift in the first formant region*. Details of various such properties are shown in Table 1.1.

3.1 A Continuous Parameter and Frequency Domain Based Markov Model (CPMM)

So far, HMMs have been successfully used for modelling time varying processes representing spoken words and sentences. The advantages of such models when applied to ASR systems have been reported in the literature.

Recently, Kopec [4] has applied Markov models to formant frequency estimation showing new possible application of such a paradigm in aspects of speech processing other than time varying processes. In conjunction with this work we proposed [5] an application of HMM in another aspect in ASR, such as, characterization of the place-of-articulation of vowels for a large population of speakers and a large variety of contexts.

Instead of generating symbols of a finite alphabet, the parameters used are "spatial relations" and "locational informations" among spectral lines which were originally generated over frequency domain. Each spectral line is represented by continuous distribution of parameters. Switching from time domain to frequency domain drastically reduces the number of states on the Markov chain and the use of continuous parameters completely eliminates quantization error.

The input to the CPMM is a string of vectors of the form, $x = v1, v2, \ldots, vm$. The vectors are obtained from fixed length segments of pattern (40msec in this case). The fixed segments obtained are sonorant portions of the signal which are quasi-stationary. From these quasi-stationary segments, the vector x is obtained from some of the morphological properties which were already extracted at various levels in the hierarchy.

The process that is modelled can generate spectral lines and their energies. The output of the CPMM is a sequence of place of articulation symbols (PA) belonging to the set,

{(VB:back vowel), (VC:central vowel), (VF:front vowel)}

For example, the letter "U" can be characterized in terms of places of articulation of its vowel as, U = (VF) (VB). Since PA symbols are generated for every 40msec., in reality, for letter U, the sequence generated may be, U = (VF) (VB VB VB). The best probability for the hypothesis {(VF)(VB)} is computed by using a Markov Model in the time domain like the one given in Fig. 1.4.

4. Recognition of Diphthongs and Vowels Using Perceptual Components.

The classification and recognition procedures effectively use hierarchically organized perceptual components at various levels including the output from CPMM. The task is to characterize all vowels and diphthongs in a letter-digit vocabulary. A Procedural Network [6] as shown in Fig. 1.5 is used to solve this task. In the first level of the network, the PUSH action activates a markov model of the type shown Fig. 1.4. At this level, the probability, *P(data_seq|voc_seq$_i$)* is computed, where,

data_seq : sequence of PA symbols {eg. (VF VF) (VB VB VB)}

voc_seq : the actual PA symbol for each letter-digit (Table 1.2).

At the next level, the network computes for all *voc$_i$*,

$$a_k : \prod_{j=1}^{n} P(data_j \mid voc_i , voc\_seq_k)$$

where,

k : conflict set of PA symbols for letter-digit vocabulary (Table 1.2),

i : vowels and diphthongs in the letter-digit vocabulary (eg. a, ai,...),

j : set of perceptual properties (Table 1.1)

The candidate with the highest probability is now selected and in case of equal probabilities, special rules are used to resolve the conflict.

5. Conclusion

The idea of treating speech spectrograms as patterns, describing them in a symbolic way, and learning the variations statistically achieves the expected goals, namely, speaker-independency and robust recognition of vowels and diphthongs in any given context. An overall recognition rate of 90% was obtained for vowels and diphthongs.

References

[1] V. W. Zue and L. F. Lamel, "An Expert Spectrogram Reader: A Knowledgebased approach to Speech Recognition," IEEE International Conference on Acoustics, Speech and Signal Processing, Tokyo, pp. 1197-1200,1986.

[2] M. Palakal, "Morphological representation of Speech Knowledge, for Automatic Speech Recognition Systems," Ph.D. Thesis, Concordia University, Montreal, 1987.

[3] R. De Mori and M. Palakal, "On the use of a Taxonomy of Time-Frequency Morphologies for Aotomatic Speech Recognition," International Joint Conference on Artificial Intelligence, Los Angles, California, 1985.

[4] G. Kopec and M. Bush, "Network-based isolated digit recognition using vector quantization", IEEE Transactions on Acoustics, Speech and Signal Processing, Vol. ASSP-33, pp. 850-856, August 1986.

[5] E. Merlo, R. De Mori, M. Palakal, R. Rouat, and G. Mercier, "A Continuous Parameter and Frequency Domain based Markov Model," IEEE International Conference on Acoustics, Speech and Signal Processing, Tokyo, 1986.

[6] R. De Mori, E. Merlo, M. Palakal and J. Rouat, "Use of Procedural Knowledge for Automatic Speech Recognition", International Joint Conference on Artificial Intelligence, Milano, Italy, 1987.

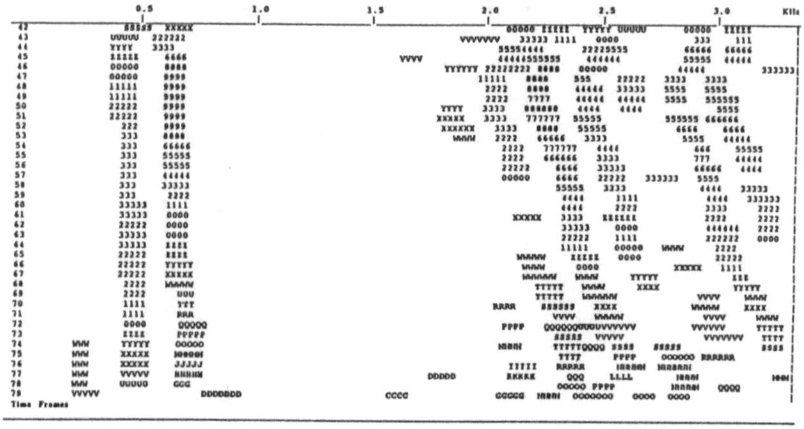

fig. 1.1 A sample Pattern of letter 'A'

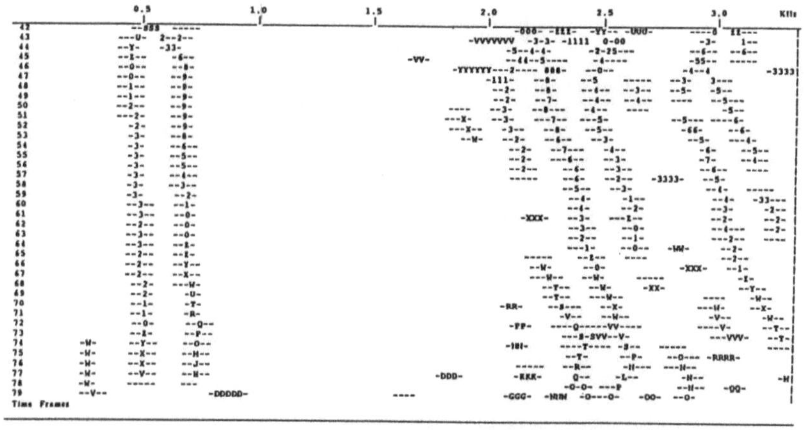

fig. 1.2 Skeletonized Pattern of Fig. 1.1

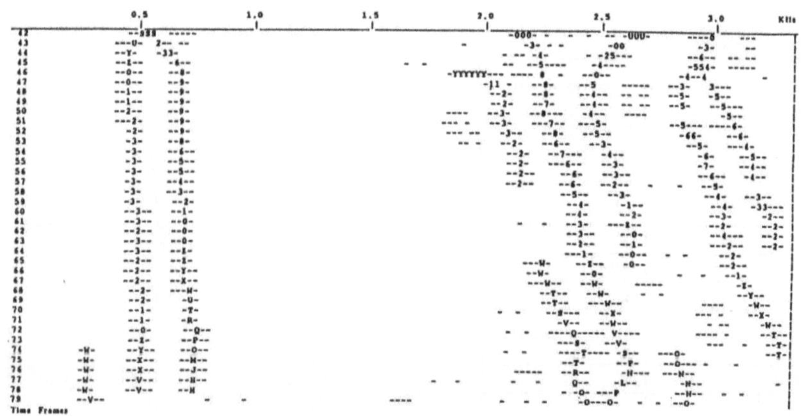

fig. 1.3 Preprocessed Pattern of Fig. 1.2

Table 1.1 Properties and descriptions of perceptual components

Components	comments	stylized patterns of properties
FDN	anchor line shifts downward along frequency	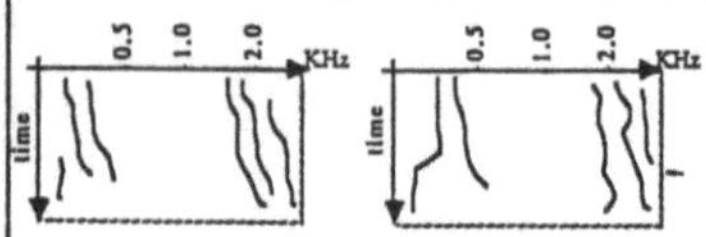
ASND	lines grow upward along frequency from low-to-mid or from mid-to-high frequency bands	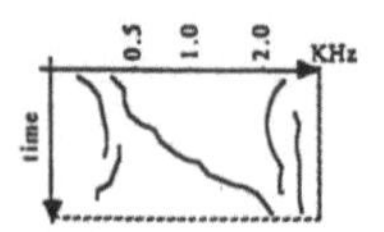
DSND	lines grow downward along frequency from mid-to-low or from high-to-mid frequency bands	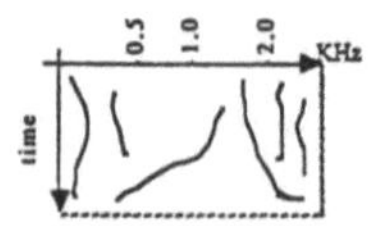
STCR	Ascending lines are not continuous and appear as stair cases	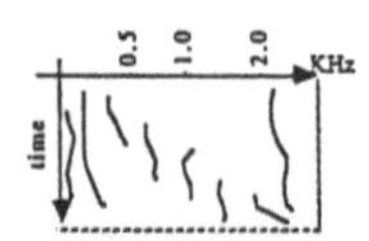
STCL	Descending lines are not continuous and appear as stair cases	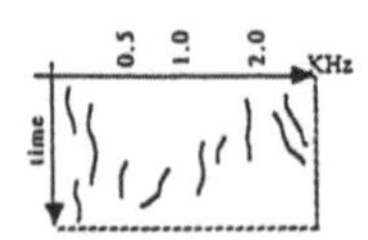

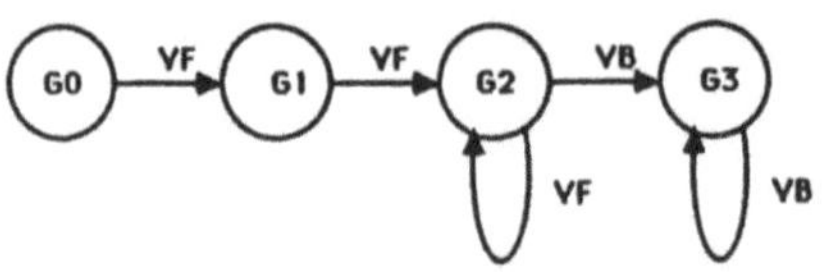

Fig. 1.4 HMM for PA sequences

TABLE 1.2	
Sequence of places of articulation	confusion set
VF	E,G,P,3,V,C,B,T,D L,M,N,S,F A,K,J X,H,8 6 Z,7
VC	R
VB	2,O,4
VF VB	0,Q,U
VC VF	I,5,9
VB VC	1
VB VC VF	Y
VC VF VB	W

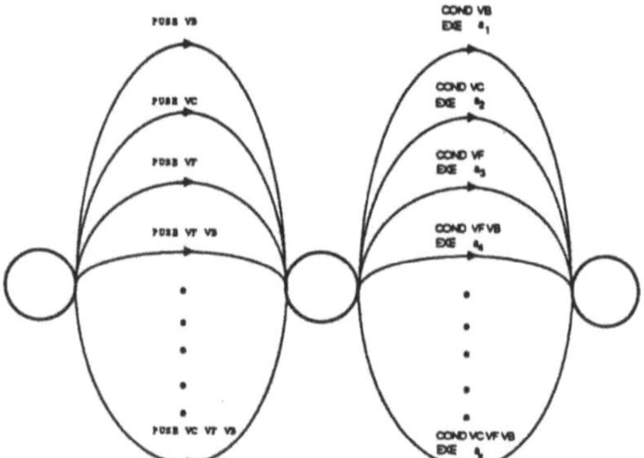

Fig 1.5 A Procedural Network for Vowel-Diphthong

SPEAKER-INDEPENDENT AUTOMATIC RECOGNITION OF PLOSIVE SOUND IN LETTERS AND DIGITS

Régis Cardin
Mc Gill University
School of Computer Science
805, Sherbrooke Street, West
Montréal, Québec, Canada
H3A 2K6

KEYWORD

Speech Recognition /Automatic Speech Recognition /Recognition Plosive sound

ABSTRACT

This paper reports an experiments on a speaker-independent automatic recognition system of plosive sound. Experimental results in the recognition of plosive sound for the set [bdev], which is the set that gives the worst result, on 20 speakers are presented.

INTRODUCTION

The recognition of plosive sounds is a difficult task. The way letters containing plosive sounds are generated depends on the mother tongue, physiology, speaking modes, habit and mood of the speaker. The result presented in this paper is for the set [bdev].

The test is based on a set of 20 speakers (10 male + 10 female) with 2 sequences each for the set [bdev]. The learning phase used a

NATO ASI Series, Vol. F46
Recent Advances in Speech Understanding
and Dialog Systems
Edited by H. Niemann et al.

set consisting of 60 speakers with 2 prononciation each for the entire alphabet including digits. There is a variety of speaking modes, accents and mother tongues. The data acquisition was done on an HP 9000-236 with 12 bits A/D converter at 20 000 Hz.

Modelling knowledge about speaking modes or speaking styles is one of the biggest problems in speaker independent recognition. Some sounds, for example, are characterized for some speakers by formant transitions. Our experience on the analysis and recognition of plosive sounds has shown that formants offer good discriminant cues in some cases but not always. In a speaking mode, for example, formant transitions, represented by transitions of spectral lines, have a high discrimination power for a class of sounds. In another speaking mode, broad-band energy concentrations may have a better discriminating power for the same class of sounds. Different speakers may use different speaking modes and styles because of their anatomy, education, and mood.

The speech signal is described in terms of sequences of sets of acoustic properties. Descriptions can be insufficient for decoding the speech waveform but cannot be wrong because they represent events of the signal and not interpretations of it.

Phonetic knowledge can be used in many ways. One way suggest algorithms to be incorporated into the procedures and the contextual constraints that have to be satisfied when the procedures are invoked. Phonetic knowledge can also help in setting initial conditions for learning algorithms requiring a preliminary alignment of the data to be learned.

Some descriptions can appear sufficient after a number of experiments involving a set of speakers or a set of speaking modes. These descriptions may become insufficient when new speaking modes are observed. In such a case, conditions for generating descriptions can be made more specific through a revised learning phase. Should this operation appear not feasible, new acoustic properties have to be extracted and discriminant descriptions become preconditions for refinement.

METHODOLOGY

The method used consist of 2 phases: The learning phase and a recognition phase. The learning phase which is fully automatic consists of the application of operators and to store the parameter result for the recognition phase. The recognition phase consists of the application of operators, then to take the parameter result and to apply the kernel method to the data collected in the learning phase and base the decision on the probability returned by the kernel method. Finally give a score for each possible candidate.

With such an approach, different researchers from different laboratories can provide suggestions for acoustic properties and operators together with constraints and, perhaps, performances. In this way, the system can be improved easily by just augmenting the number of operators and to adjust the markov models.

The probability is calculated with the kernel method. This method applies a Gaussian curve around all the parameters that were calculated which meet the operator precondition, in the learning phase.

Then in order to calculate the probability, we apply all the Gaussian curves calculated to the result just obtained, then divide the result by n which is the number of curves calculated. This returns the probability to be used in the Markov model.

The recognition phase consist in the application of the kernel method on parameter collected in the learning phase. The kernel method consist to put a gaussian curve around all parameter collected for a given class. Then the application of those gaussian curve to the property extracted and divide the result by N. So each node return a vector of probability. The decision to use the probability is based on parameter precondition.

CONCLUSION

The results are presented in Table I. The overall recognition on the set [BEVD] is 81%. There are some improvements necessary especially in the case of B which has the lowest recognition rate. The research is still undergoing some improvements and do not represent final results. The improvement can be made on the operators and also in the creation of new ones.

Those result represent a lower bound on the plosive sounds. This program also serve as a head detection and do not cause problems with letters which do not have plosive sounds.

REFERENCE

De Mori, R., Cardin, R., Merlo, E., Palakal, M. and Rouat, J. *A Network of Actions for Automatic Speech Recognition*, submitted for publication.

TABLE I

RECOGNIZED					
	B	D	V	E	other(ptg)
B	25	4	3	4	0
D	1	27	0	1	1
E	1	0	2	29	2
V	1	0	25	4	3

A REAL-TIME AUDITORY MODEL: DESCRIPTION AND APPLICATIONS IN AN ASR ACOUSTIC-PHONETIC FRONT END

Frank Gooding* Ian Shaw+ Husein Mahdi+

*Department of Linguistics

+School of Electronic Engineering Science

University College of North Wales

Bangor, Gwynedd LL57 2UW

U.K.

Abstract: A model of peripheral auditory processing is implemented using a Texas Instruments TMS 320C25 Digital Signal Processor mounted on an IBM PC-AT compatible microcomputer. The TMS 320C25, running at 40 MHz, performs both the spectral analysis of a sampled signal and the auditory transformation at a speed that allows for real-time presentation of an "auditory spectrogram" of any audio signal. Such a representation would serve as the basis for parameterization, feature extraction, etc., in an ASR system.

1. INTRODUCTION

1.1 MOTIVATION FOR AUDITORY PROCESSING IN ASR

It has frequently (though not universally) been claimed that it would be advantageous to incorporate a model of human auditory processing into the acoustic-to-phonetic stage of an automatic speech recognizer. The rationale for such a claim lies in the fact that the only successful real-time speaker-indepenedent continuous speech recognizer to date is the human one, and that the human recognizer is also the only benchmark for accuracy for any recognition system. It is therefore reasonable to assume that the performance of an artificial speech recognizer would be enhanced to the extent that it made identifications on the same basis as does the human. Central to this assumption is the notion that the defining characteristics of speech sounds must be quite robustly represented in actual human auditory representations in order for speech perception to proceed as rapidly and efficiently as it does. Traditional input to ASR systems such as

NATO ASI Series, Vol. F46
Recent Advances in Speech Understanding and Dialog Systems
Edited by H. Niemann et al.

FFT or LPC spectra may produce perceptually extraneous detail, enhance irrelevant features, and obscure or miss essential ones. Such loss is compounded by processes of data reduction.

More positively, there are a number of specific benefits that auditory modeling in an ASR system would provide. It should

1. HIGHLIGHT phonetically salient characteristics
2. minimize perceptually non-salient characteristics such as
   a) intrinsic coarticulation effects
   b) inter-speaker differences
   c) differences between phonetically similar but distinct sounds.

While it may be accepted in principle that it is desirable to capture such auditory robustness in an ASR system, nonetheless few if any working ASR systems actually attempt to do so. To become part of a successful and commercially viable ASR system, the auditory processing must meet three basic requirements:

1. It must be fast, opreating in real time or nearly so.

2. It must be flexible. Our knowledge of auditory function is not static, nor is our understanding of which aspects would prove most valuable in an ASR. Consequently the model should be easily modifiable to reflect changes in our understanding.

3. It should be relatively inexpensive.

One may implement the desired auditory processing either in hardware or software, but neither method fulfills all three requirements. Hardware implementations meet the speed requirement, but fail on flexibility and expense. Software implementations, on the other hand, meet the flexibility requirement, but fail on speed (and often also expense, when large mini- and mainframe computers are involved).

1.2 The DSP solution

Modern digital signal processor chips provide a very attractive solution to this quandry by providing the best of both worlds: virtually the speed of hardware but with felexiibilty of software, and at low cost. The auditory model described here is implemented on a DSP board from Loughborough Sound Images, based on the Texas Instruments TMS 320C25 DSP chip. This chip runs at

40 MHz and is capable of 10 MIPS performance and can be run without wait states on the LSI board. In addition to the obvious advantage of greatly increased processing speed for the computationally demanding tasks, the use of a separate DSP board also allows for parallel processing, since the host computer's CPU is freed to perform additional analysis of the transformed signal while the DSP is performing the transform operations.

2. AUDITORY MODEL

A complete model of human auditory function should include at least the following broad aspects:

1. Characteristics of the auditory FILTER
2. FREQUENCY SCALING
3. LOUDNESS LEVEL compensation
4. LOUDNESS SCALING
5. TEMPORAL aspects

The present psychoacoustic model incorporates the spectral aspects (1-4), and was chosen because it is well motivated and capable of being efficiently coded on a DSP. A more complete description of the auditory model can be found elsewhere (Gooding 1986, 1987). This model is based on that of Moore and Glasberg 1983, 1986), but with the addition of conversion of the ordinate to loudness level (phon conversion) and loudness scaling (sone conversion). Temporal aspects are omitted from the RT model partially because so little is known about them, and partly because it was deemed unlikely that additional computation could be included in RT even using a DSP. Post-processing on the host computer is envisioned for these aspects instead.

Briefly, the frequency spectrum of an input signal is converted to an auditory "excitation pattern" in three stages. First the energy in each Equivalent Rectangular Bandwidth (ERB) is integrated. Secondly, the integrated spectrum is convolved with the auditory filter shape (a rounded exponential -- Patterson _et al_. 1982) and the frequency axis scaled to ERB-rate.

3. REAL-TIME DSP IMPLEMENTATION

Computation of the auditory transform takes place in four

stages. The incoming signal is sampled at 10 KHz, and every 256 points first multiplied by a window function stored in program memory. This window consists of the combination of a Hamming window and the auditory filter shape which has been defined in the time domain via inverse FFT to avoid the more costly convolution required in the frequency domain. Next, a 256 point spectral transform (Fast Hartley Transform) of the resulting signal is computed (Bracewell 1984, Duhamel and Vetterli 1986). The ordinate values are then converted to dB by a rapid algorithm utiliizing the TMS 320C25's NORM instruction, and further converted to loudness level in phons, reflecting the frequency sensitivity of perceived loudness. Lastly, the abcissa in Hz is converted to the perceptually relevant ERB (equivalent rectangular bandwidth) scale, reflecting the frequency resolving properties of the peripheral auditory system (Moore and Glasberg 1983) and quantized to .1 ERB between about 3 and 30 ERB. Both of the phon and ERB conversions are done by table lookup. The final result is a dB versus ERB representation. The demand for speed of throughput for the present application has meant that some features, such as level-senitive filter shape and sone conversion, have been omitted for the present.

4. APPLICATIONS

This RT auditory model is envisioned as serving a research tool as well a a part of an in-place ASR. In its former role, variety of display modes are available to aid reseachers in examining and extracting information from the auditory representations. These include spectrogram, waterfall, or section. "Spectrogram" mode will display pitch versus time, with loudness shown by gray level (currently mapped onto a scale of 16 levels). Individual spectral sections (as on a traditional spectrograph) can be chosen for detailed display by a movable cursor. Various parameters can be extracted from such representations and simultaneously displayed. Since it is implemented in software, alterations of model characteristics are easily made.

5. CONCLUSION

The DSP-based auditory transform presented here aims significantly to improve the accuracy and efficiency of the acoustic-to-phonetic front end of an ASR system. Improvement in this area has been accorded a high priority by ASR researchers in recent years, as it is seen as essential to enhancing overall system performance. The basic rationale for an auditory conversion in an ASR front end is that it enhances the perceptually salient features of the speech signal thereby increasing efficiency and accuracy. Preliminary work towards extracting robust auditorily-based parameters including sonority, sharpness, and vowel features is in progress. More generally, the system described here should serve as a valuable and flexible tool for speech research. At relatively small expense, it allows speech scientists to investigate the auditory properties of speech sounds with an ease and rapidity previously unobtainable even on minicomputers.

REFERENCES

1. Bracewell, R.: The fast Hartley transform. Proc. IEEE 22.8, 1010-1018 (1984)
2. Duhamel, P. and Veterli, M.: Cyclic convolution of real sequences: Hartley versus Fourier and new schemes. Proc. IEEE ICASSP 1.229-232 (1986)
3. Gooding, F.: Formant amplitudes and vowel perception: a reappraisal, Bangor Working Papers in Linguistics 2.27-41 (1987)
4. ________.: Formantless vowels and theories of vowel perception, paper presented to the 112th meeting of the Acoustical Society of America, Anaheim, CA, DEC. 1986. Abstract in JASA 80:Suppl. 1, S126 (1986)
5. Moore, B.C.J and Glasberg, B.: The role of frequency selectivity in the perception of loudness, pitch, and time, in Moore, B.C.J., ed., Frequency Selectivity in Hearing, Academic Press (1986)
6. ________, and ________.: Suggested formulae for calculating auditory-filter bandwidths and excitation patterns. JASA 74.3, 750-753 (1983)
7. Patterson, R.D., Nimmo-Smith, I., Weber, D.L., and Milroy, R.: The deterioration of hearing with age: Frequency selectivity, the critical ratio, the audiogram and speech threshold. JASA 72.1788-1803 (1982)
8. Zwicker, E. and Scharf, B.: A model of loudness summation. Psychological Review 73.2-26 (1965)

A NEW PHONEMATIC APPROACH TO SPEECH RECOGNITION

A. J. Rubio-Ayuso and J. M. Herrera-Garrido

Departamento de Electrónica y Sistemas Informáticos
Universidad de Granada
18071 Granada, Spain

Abstract: A phonematic recognition system is presented. It works in only one step without precategorical classification nor segmentation. The system analyses a frame of 12.8 ms of voice and decides the phoneme to which it belongs. A piece of speech can be considered as a series of input symbols (phonemes-frames) transmitted through an information channel (recognition system) to give a series of outpout symbols. In this work the recognition system is characterized as an information channel in order to compute an error rate.

1. INTRODUCTION

A phonemic recognition system is presented in this paper. Although the utterance to recognize is a word belonging to a finite vocabulary, the system presented is very ambitious because the generality implied in the phonemic recognition.

We approach the phoneme recognition in only one step, without using precategorical classification as in others papers [4], [5]. This characteristic makes our system simpler and faster than other, the final results being comparable.

From the finite vocabulary the permissible phonemes are determined. Every utterance is sampled and segmented in frames of fixed length. An unknown frame must belong to one of the possible phonemes. To determine to which, a set of parameters are computed on each frame, which allows to assign to the frame an output symbol.

A word can be considered as a series of input symbols (phonemes-frames) transmitted through an information channel (recognition system) to give a series of output symbols.

In this paper the recognition system is also characterized as an information channel in order to compute an error rate.

2. INFORMATION SOURCES AND CHANNELS

An information source is a device that generates information [1]. Here are only considered the discrete information sources. This type of source emits symbols from an alphabet called source alphabet, which is supposed to be fixed and finite (q symbols): $S = \{s1, s2, ..., sq\}$, where si are the source symbols with fixed probabilities $P(s1), P(s2), ..., P(sq)$.

A channel is defined by an input alphabet $A = \{ai\}$, an output alphabet $B = \{bj\}$ and a set of conditional probabilities $P(bj/ai)$.

Decision rule d(bj) is a function that especifies the input

NATO ASI Series, Vol. F46
Recent Advances in Speech Understanding
and Dialog Systems
Edited by H. Niemann et al.

symbol associated to every output symbol.

The error probability EP is defined as EP = $\sum$ P(E/bj)P(bj), where P(E/bj) is the error probability when the output is bj. Evidently, it depends on the decision rule.

3. PARAMETERS

Each utterance is digitized and sampled at 10 kHz during 1.5 s. Segments of 128 consecutive samples will be considered as a frame. The frames are overlapped in 64 samples. The vocabulary is compounded of the followind spanish words and vowels: "Cero", "Uno", "Dos", "Tres", "Cuatro", "Cinco", "Seis", "Siete", "Ocho", "Nueve", "Màs", "Menos", "Igual", "A", "E", "I", "O", "U".

Every word was spoken three times by a male speaker (the system is mono-speaker).

Although it has no real importance in the system here presented, the first task is to find the ends of the words. This is done by an automatic algorithm [2] that allows a portion of silence before and after the word (about ten frames).

On each frame six parameters are computed then:

- First formant (F1)
- Second formant (F2)
- Parameter Rv (Rv)
- Zero crossing rate (ZC)
- Normalized energy (EN)
- Normalized error in LPC (ER)

The election of this six parameters corresponds to a trade-off between simplicity and effectivity. So, ZC and EN are computed in the ends delimitation phase. All the others parameters are computed in the LPC analysis [3]. This is carried out using the Durbin algorithm with a predictor order of 12.

The parameter Rv is here defined as

$$R_V = \frac{S(401, 1000)}{S(0, 400)} \quad , \quad S(k_1, k_2) = \sum_{k=k_1}^{k_2} \left(20 \log_{10} \left[H\left(e^{-j 2\pi \frac{5k}{FS}}\right)\right] - H_{min}\right)$$

where Fs is the Nyquist frequency (5000 Hz), H is the spectrum of the signal (obtained by LPC) and Hmin is the minimum value of 20logH. With this definition, the parameter Rv represents the ratio of the high energies to the low energies in the frame of signal.

The prediction error completes the information in those cases that the signal is not well represented by the all-pole model implicit in the LPC analysis (as in the case of plosive phonemes). It is supplied by the Durbin algorithm.

4. PHONEME CHARACTERIZATION

With the aid of these six parameters and the knowledge of the spoken word, the frames was labeled by hand with a phoneme (input symbol). All the frames corresponding to the same phoneme was edited together in a file. We consider in this paper the 18 spanish phonemes included in the vocabulary {A, D, E, G, H(Ch), I, E, L, M, N, O, R, S, T, U, V, Z, #(Silence)}.

Each frame can be considered as a point in an hexa-dimensional space and can be projected over the 15 main planes (F1-F2, F1-Rv, F1-EN, ...).

At every main plane an ellipse has been defined for each phoneme, in such a way that the ellipse contents the maximal number of points corresponding to their own phoneme, and the minimal from the others phonemes.

Thus a number of 270 ellipses are defined (15 main planes x 18 phonemes) and a phoneme is characterized by its 15 ellipses, which are determined by statistical considerations in such a way that the half-length of the main axis is proportional to the standard deviation of the data. ($L=\alpha\sigma$).

We noted that in the set of points corresponding to several phonemes there was some "strange" points very separated of the gravity center and clearly out of the ellipse. These points could correspond to bad classified frames in the segmentation stage, and they have too much importance in the obtaining of the ellipses. To avoid this problem, these "strange" point are removed and then, a new ellipse is computed. With this approach the final rate of recognition is improved in fact.

We have experimentaly found the best value for α, by varying the value of α and computing the corresponding recognition rate. With the maximum recognition rate we obtain the ellipses to be used in the system (Table 1).

α	Recognition rate (%)
1.3	55.2
1.4	55.4
1.5	60.5
1.6	64.5
1.7	64.9
1.75	65.1
1.79	65.9
1.795	66.3
1.8	66.1
1.9	65.4
2.0	63.2
2.1	62.1
2.2	61.5
2.3	56.6
2.4	53.8
2.5	50.1
2.6	48.2

Table 1:
Recognition rate versus α

5. PHONEME RECOGNITION

In this phase, an output symbol is assigned to each frame. This is done in the following way. The 270 ellipses are considered, and they are labelled with 1 if the frame is inside the ellipse and with 0 if the frame is outside. Thus, the matrix REALIZ(i,j) is formed. REALIZ(i,j)=1 if the frame is inside the ellipse j (phoneme j) in the plane i. Otherwise, REALIZ(i,j)=0.

Now, a number is obtained for each phoneme:

$$NR(j) = \sum_{i=1}^{15} REALIZ(i,j)$$

for j=1, 2, ..., 18.

The phoneme with the maximum value of NR(j) is considered as the output symbol. As it is possible that several phonemes have the same value of NR(j), (NR(j) goes from 0 to 15) actually the output symbol is a set of possible phonemes. In this way, the output alphabet consists on $S = \{ x \in \mathcal{P}(F) \ / \ Card(x) <= 5 \}$, where $\mathcal{P}(F)$ represents the set of the parts of F (set of the phonemes). The restriction

Card(x) <= 5 is enough since in practice the probability for Card(x) > 3 is nearly null.

In order to obtain the output symbol vocabulary of our information channel, we look at the results of the recognition process corresponding to the 18 phonemes and we look for all the symbols appearing in them. The output symbol vocabulary varies with the ellipses size and thus, with the recognition rate. For the maximum recognition rate the vocabulary has a minimum number of elements. In table 2 can be seen an example of phoneme (frame) recognition of part of the spanish word "Seis".

```
HHSHHHHHHHHHSSHSSSSSHSSSZZSTKEEEEEEEEEEEEEEEEEEEEEIIIIIIIIIININK
                             N                            NN
```

Table 2. Example of recognition of the spanish word "Seis"

The output symbols can be simplified in the following way:

Given an output symbol (x1 x2 x3 x4 x5), if a conditional probability $P(xi/xj)=0$, xi and xj appearing in the output symbol, we can remove xj, since if the output were xj, xi would have probability 0 of appearing in the output symbol.

In practice we consider $P(xi/xj) \simeq 0$ if it is less than 4.5%.

We can define a presence matrix PRE(i,j) in the way:

$$PRE(i,j) = \begin{cases} 0 & \text{if } P(xi/xj) <= 4.5\ \% \\ 1 & \text{if } P(xi/xj) > 4.5\ \% \end{cases}$$

The permanence of a phoneme xj in the output symbol is given by

$$PERM(xj) = \prod_i PRE(i,j)$$

Thus, if PERM(xj)=1 the phoneme remains in the output symbol and if PERM(xj)=0, the phoneme xj is deleted.

This procedure allows us to obtain a more simplified output symbol. In table 3 can be seen the same example as in table 2, after simplification.

```
HHSHHHHHHHHHSSHSSSSSHSSSZZSTKEEEEEEEEEEEEEEEEEEEEEIIIIIIIIIININK
                                                          NN
```

Table 3. Same as Table 2, after simplification

If we want an error for the channel, we are forced to determine a especific decision rule. This is not trivial and it has not been studied in this work. In order to compute EP we apply the fixed decision rule of minimum error [1]. With this fixed decision rule, the probability of the error in the channel is of 33.7%.

It must be pointed out that there is a probability of 66.3% of correctely assign a phoneme to an <u>isolated</u> <u>frame</u> of 128 samples (12.8 ms) of voice.

6. PARAMETERS CLASSIFICATION

In order to substitute the paramaters here used with others in future works, we have tried to classify the parameters according its importance in the success of the recognition system.

To carry out this classification one given parameter is eliminated and the process of computing the recognition rate is repeated with the resting five parameters. We may conclude that the most important parameter in our system is the first formant, while the less important one is prediction error, since its elimination almost does not affect the recognition rate.

7. CONCLUSIONS

A phonemic recognition system is presented and it is based on the analysis of one parametric representation for speech segments of 12.8 ms.

The system assigns to every speech segment an output symbol which is an element of the set $\mathcal{P}(F)$. F is the set of phonemes considered and included in the finite vocabulary. Not all the output symbols have not null probability and in the present application there is only 36 symbols.

The recognition is carried out by working with the main projections of the parametric representation, using a clustering technique with ellipses, one for phoneme and plane. To each voice segment one or several phonemes are assigned in such a way that their ellipses include the segment in the maximal number of planes.

The output symbols are simplified using relations on the conditional probability matrix. The system presented is characterized as an information channel.

The error of the channel under a fixed decision rule is computed. It is valued to 33.7 %. So, the recognition rate is of 66.3 % with that fixed decision rule.

We have classified the parameters according its importance in the recognition rate, being first formant the most important parameter and prediction error the less important one.

8. REFERENCES

[1] N. Abramson "Teoria de la información y de la codificación" Paraninfo 1974, Madrid.

[2] M. C. Carrión-Pérez and A. J. Rubio-Ayuso "Un detector explicito de principio y final para palabras aisladas" Revista de Informática y Automática, n 60, 1984, pp. 34-39.

[3] L. R. Rabiner and R. W. Schafer "Digital Processing of Speech Signals" Prentice-Hall, 1978

[4] P. Regel "A module for acoustic-phonetic transcription of fluently spoken german speech" IEEE Trans. on ASSP, vol ASSP-30, n 3, June 82, pp. 440-450.

[5] R. de Mori, P. Laface "Use of fuzzy algorithms for phonetic and phonemic labeling of continuous speech" IEEE Trans on PAMI, vo PAMI-2, n 2, March 80, pp. 136-147.

PRIMARY PERCEPTUAL UNITS IN WORD RECOGNITION

Walter F. Sendlmeier
Max-Planck-Institut für Psycholinguistik
Wundtlaan 1
NL-6525 XD Nijmegen

KEYWORDS / ABSTRACT : word recognition / speech perception / perceptual units / word similarities / mental representation / feature robustness / language acquisition / reading/writing proficiency / psychological reality

Results from different experiments concerning word similarity, word identification and manipulation of single sounds and findings from first language acquisition research are discussed as to their relevance for an understanding of which perceptual units are primary in word recognition. It is argued that units of different sizes may serve as primary perceptual units equally well depending on certain characteristics of the perceptual situation.

In human speech recognition meaning is extracted from acoustic stimuli. Since the recogniser cannot memorize the meanings of entire utterances to match them against an acoustic input, what is stored in the lexicon must be the meanings of the discrete units, i.e. words, of which utterances are composed. According to some word recognition models the code by which the listener has access to words is based on distinctive features or phonetic segments, according to others it is based on syllables, and according to again others words are held to be presented as holistic entities without regarding any segmentation within word boundaries necessary for the word recognition process.

In the fifties, experimental phoneticians, guided by the concept of minimal pairs and the ensuing distinctive feature theory developed by phonologists, focussed on the smallest isolated and reduced units in investigating the relation between the linguistic unit and its processing by the human listener. In criticizing the assumption of distinctive features as being psychologically real, in the beginning of the seventies, an explicit discussion on the nature of the primary perceptual unit began. A number of reaction time experiments were conducted which led to the result that the reaction times for short sentences, words, syllables and sounds are the same, if the search list consists of units of the same size as the target unit. Thus, it seems plausible to deduce that units of different sizes may serve as primary perceptual units. But, in spite of such results most authors still argue for certain units to be the exclusive representatives of primary perception. To my knowledge, no-one has raised the question whether differently sized units might serve as primary perceptual units equally well depending on certain characteristics of the perceptual situation. I think this is an approach which deserves closer

NATO ASI Series, Vol. F46
Recent Advances in Speech Understanding
and Dialog Systems
Edited by H. Niemann et al.

investigation. In order to present evidence for this understanding of the nature of speech recognition I would like to describe some experiments.

WORD SIMILARITIES

The first experiment concerns the question which dimensions are fundamental for perceived similarities between words (Sendlmeier 1987a). The general underlying assumption was that the judgements of similarity can satisfactorily be described by only few dimensions. Vocabularies were constructed of meaningless words. Meaningless material was chosen to avoid interference of semantic relations with phonetic similarity. The words were constructed in such a way that no minimal pair within a vocabulary ensued. Every word of the vocabulary appeared twice with every other word in varying sequence. The listeners had never received any phonetic-phonological training. They were asked to estimate the pairs of words which were acoustically presented as to their similarity on a graded scale. The similarity judgements were evaluated with the method of multi-dimensional scaling based on a four-dimensional solution.

The results show that the judgements of similarity do not vary in an unsystematic way, but that they are structured according to certain phonetic parameters. It is remarkable that in the judgements the quality of single consonants plays a subordinate role for the perceived degree of similarity. Only for one-syllable words - and here only for the explanation of the third and fourth dimensions - can single consonants, but only if occuring in the same exposed, that is initial, position, help to explain the dimension. Looking at the vowels, one finds that for one-syllable words their quality is of great importance. Yet, in more complex stimuli the relevance of vowel similarity is of less impact than properties which characterize the words as a whole, such as number of syllables, presence or absence of consonant clusters and position of word stress. This result can be seen as an indication to the fact that global properties are increasingly considered as criterium for similarity for more complex stimuli.

In this investigation listeners were asked to come to meta-phonetic judgements of similarity between words. This implies, however, that the results may only provide a first indication as to the relevant parameters in word recognition. However, it should be noted that these results are in line with those obtained in a number of other studies in which it could be shown that vowels, and especially stressed vowels, contribute more to a word's identity than consonants (e.g. Nooteboom & Doodeman 1984).

WORD IDENTIFICATION

There is also evidence from identification experiments that the single sound is not the only unit of primary importance in speech recognition. In an identification experiment, I presented 96 different words masked by noise to listeners in six steps with increasing signal/noise ratios from -9 dB S/N up to +6 dB S/N. The listeners were asked to write down on an answer sheet whatever words they could identify; in case they could not identify a word they were asked to write down in broad transcription including stress indicators whatever sound or sound combination they had heard. The number of syllables proved to be the most robust characteristic of words, followed - in decreasing order of robustness - by accent patterns, quality of stressed vowels, quality of vowels in unstressed position and quality of voiced consonants (especially liquids and nasals) in stressed syllables, voiced consonants in unstressed syllables and finally unvoiced consonants in stressed and unstressed syllables; in consonants the place of articulation cues caused special difficulties for discrimination. A similar hierarchy of robustness was found for hearing impaired subjects by Boothroyd (1984). Cutler (1984) could also show that errors in whole word recognition experiments with degraded speech quality invariably match the target word in terms of stress pattern.

MANIPULATION OF SINGLE SOUNDS

Another study (Sendlmeier 1987b) is based on the question whether the consciousness of speech as a sequence of single sounds is related to the degree of mastering an alphabetic writing system. If the ability to make a precise phonetic analysis is influenced by the degree of mastering a writing system, then adult functional illiterates - depending on their reading/ writing proficiency - must fail to a varying degree in word manipulation tasks which are based on such analytical processes. If, however, the ability to process speech in a phonetically analytic way is dependent on the process of general cognitive maturation, then literates as well as illiterates must be able to solve the presented tasks equally well. Functional adult illiterates were asked to add, delete or substitute single consonants in initial position in certain words. Half of the consonants to be manipulated occurred as single consonants, the other half occurred in consonant clusters. The subjects' teachers were asked to rate their pupils reading/writing proficiency on a graded scale.

The evaluation of the data revealed significant effects for the phonotactic characteristics, i.e. isolated consonants versus consonants in clusters. The mean of correct solutions in tasks involving isolated consonants proved to be significantly higher than the mean of correct solutions in those tasks in which consonants had to be linked together or in which a consonant cluster had to be seperated. This indicates that consonant clusters are regarded to a high degree as units which cannot be further dissolved or composed of smaller units. Correlations between reading/writing proficiency and the ability to manipulate single sounds revealed an almost linear relation. These data indicate that functional illiterates, depending on their degree of reading/writing proficiency, have a more or less distinct concept of single acoustic segments. Thus, the argument cannot be upheld that the single sound and the underlying concept of the phoneme is a natural category which is either genetically fixed or which appears universally in the course of cognitive development. Even though the concept of speech as a sequence of discrete single sounds has proved useful on a descriptive meta-level to set up general rules in modern linguistics - from the Young Grammarians to generative phonology - the result of the present experiment leads to the assumption that phonemes and the ensuing units are not necessarily psychologically real. This result seems to have the more impact since the types of tasks used were deliberately constructed to resemble the procedures of phoneme analysis by minimal pairs.

FIRST LANGUAGE ACQUISITION RESEARCH

Another possibility of gaining insight into the phonetic mental representation of words lies in looking at the early stages of the child's language acquisition process. In first language acquisition research, it has become quite an unquestioned fact that the child learns a word as bearing meaning corresponding to a certain object or class of objects. It seems plausible to assume that in this learning process the phonetic characteristics are globally perceived; in other words, the child learns, for example, the word 'ball' as one phonetic unit and not as a combination of the single sounds /b/+/ɔ:/+/l/ or even as a matrix of 3x9 distinctive features.

Empirical results support this view: For example, Liberman et al. (1974) carried out experiments with 4- and 5-year-olds and found that these children could segment words much more easily into syllables than into single sounds. In using rhyming tests Magnusson et al. (1983) found that preschool children were not able to give meta-linguistic judgments on the basis of the phonetic/phonological structure of the words they heard. School children, however, were well able to do this, which may be accounted for by their ability to read and write. These findings, among others, point to the fact that at first the child perceives words phonetically in a global, non-analytic manner. The development of the ability to recognize sound patterns within word boundaries seems closely related to the complexity of the speech signal. Here again we find that low-frequency/high-intensity simple patterns such as vowel or prosodic contrast are superior (i.e. here: earlier acquired) to high-frequency low-intensity complex patterns such as place of articulation contrasts (Hazan & Fourcin 1985).

MENTAL PHONETIC REPRESENTATION

These empirical results lead to the following model of phonetic mental representation (Sendlmeier 1987c). The grown-up speaker/listener has stored a variety of mental representations on the phonetic level, the most important being: words, syllables, single sounds and phonetic features. It should be noted that the different units are not localised on different levels of representation, but that they are different kinds of representation within one level, i.e. the phonetic level. These different kinds of representation are simultaneously at the disposal of the listener/speaker once he has established them. From which kind of representation the listener primarily takes the relevant information for solving a perception task is determined, for example, by the type of task, the context of perception, the speed and/or the complexity of the incoming stimuli etc. Such a type of model in which a simultaneous representation of stimuli within different systems of similarity and contexts is postulated, is successfully being used in other psychological fields; for example, in the cognitive psychological research on problem solving, it has amply been shown that the flexibility in problem solving is based on the ability to change perspective.

CONCLUSION

Word recognition models which assume only one kind of primary perceptual unit are confronted with a number of problems when trying to explain findings like the ones listed above. It seems that only such models will be of lasting importance which start from the assumption that the listener has active control over the process of auditory word recognition and that he can focus at will on any kind of representation that seems useful for successful word recognition.

From the presented results also some consequences for the basic concepts of automatic speech recognizers can be deduced. For example, the finding that more global characteristics like the number of syllables prove to be very robust in human speech recognition and, so, often function as important cues in pre-processing the signal could be adopted. If such principles were considered in constructing automatic speech recognizers, some drawbacks of mere pattern-matching procedures could be avoided such as the confusions of words due to the similarity of single sounds. This, however, is only one aspect. It seems even more important - if one tries to construct automatic speech recognizers so that they function similarly to a human recognizer - to construct them in such a way that several strategies are available and that a flexible switch between these strategies is possible.

REFERENCES

1. Boothroyd, A.: Auditory perception of speech contrasts by subjects with sensorineural hearing loss. Journal of Speech and Hearing Research 27, 134-144 (1984)
2. Cutler, A.: Stress and accent in language production and understanding. In: Intonation, accent and rhythm (D. Gibbon & H. Richter, eds.). pp. 77-90. Berlin: de Gruyter 1984
3. Hazan, V. & Fourcin, A.J.: Microprocessor-controlled speech pattern audiometry. Audiology 25, 647-657 (1985)
4. Liberman, I.Y., Shankweiler, D., Fischer, F.W. & Carter, B.: Explicit syllable and phoneme segmentation in the young child.Journal of Experimental Child Psychology 18, 201-212 (1974)
5. Magnusson, E., Naucler, K. & Söderpalm, E.: Form or substance? The linguistic awareness of preschool children and school children investigated by means of a rhyming test. Abstr. 10th Intern. Congress of Phonetic Sciences 1983, Utrecht. p. 633. Dordrecht: Foris 1983
6. Nooteboom, S.G. & Doodeman, G.J.N.: Speech quality and the gating paradigm. Proc. 10th Intern. Congress of Phonetic Sciences 1983, Utrecht. pp. 481-485. Dordrecht: Foris 1984
7. Sendlmeier, W.F.: Auditive judgements of word similarity. Zeitschrift für Phonetik, Sprachwissenschaft und Kommunikationsforschung 40, 538-547 (1987a)
8. Sendlmeier, W.F.: Die psychologische Realität von Einzellauten bei Analphabeten. Sprache und Kognition 6, 64-71 (1987b)
9. Sendlmeier, W.F.: A model for the phonetic mental representation of words. Proceedings of the 11th International Congress of Phonetic Sciences, Tallinn 1987. (in press) 1987c

CONTEXT-DEPENDENT PHONE MARKOV MODELS FOR SPEECH RECOGNITION.

Anne-Marie Derouault.
IBM France Scientific center
36 av Raymond Poincare, 75116 Paris, FRANCE

KEYWORDS: Markov phonetic models, coarticulation principles, right context dependant machines.

ABSTRACT: In our automatic dictation system, which accepts sentences pronounced in Isolated syllable mode, the acoustic decoder is classically based on 40 phonetic Markov machines. These models obviously do not account for coarticulatory effects.
In this paper, we deduce general principles about coarticulation and automatic phoneme recognition. This allows us to classify the right contexts of the consonants into relevant classes, and to keep the resulting number of models reasonable for training and robustness. The new contextual system achieves a significant improvement in phoneme recognition performance.

INTRODUCTION

For large vocabulary, speech recognizers based on phonetic Markov models have been successfully designed. The word models are obtained by concatenation of subword unit models.

Our group already designed an acoustic decoder based on 40 phonetic Markov machines. This decoder is part of an automatic dictation system, which accepts sentences pronounced in isolated syllable mode, i.e. with short pauses between syllables. The system vocabulary has been extended to the full French dictionary, which includes 200,000 words [5]. Since there is one machine per phoneme, these models are an average of the phoneme behaviour in different coarticulation situations.

We present the results obtained with this classical system and use the analysis of the errors to determine the most important negative effects of coarticulation. We then present our experiment with a system of contextual phonetic models for French.

NATO ASI Series, Vol. F46
Recent Advances in Speech Understanding and Dialog Systems
Edited by H. Niemann et al.

THE PRESENT SYSTEM

Phonetic sources

Each individual phoneme is represented by a Hidden Markov Model whose output symbols are the codewords from the vector quantizer. Our first system contained 40 Markov phonetic machines.

All these phonetic machines have the same number of states (7), except the machine for silence, which has only 2 states. The figure below shows the structure of these sources:

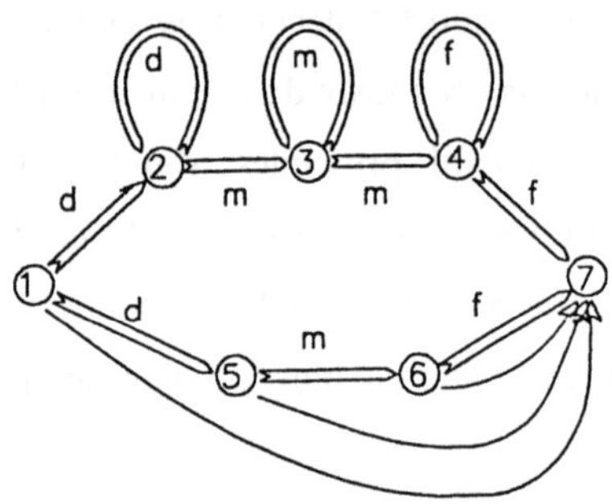

The double arrows represent 200 transitions, each of them emitting one of the 200 codewords. The simple arrows represent null transitions.

Training.

The transition probabilities, and output distributions, for each phonetic machine, are automatically adjusted from recorded data. The training is done on 410 known sentences, using the Baum-Welch algorithm [3].

Phonetic recognition.

Although the goal of our system is to recognize words, we can use the phonetic models alone, without language model, to recognize phonemes. This is a way to test the acoustic modeling. 80 test sentences are pronounced in isolated syllable mode, and a Viterbi decoding chooses the most likely sequence of phone machines. A first order model is used at the phone sequence level.

Results

With this set of context independant machines, the global recognition rate on phonemes is 80.5%, with a 12% insertion rate.

The vowels are generally well recognized:

a	u	e	ɛ	i	ɔ	y	o	oe	O	ã	ɛ̃	õ
91	88	96	89	99	58	95	63	79	96	97	92	94

The plosives have the worst rates:

p	t	k	b	d	g
55	70	57	25	64	43

The fricatives, nasals and liquids obtain the following scores:

s	ch	f	z	jj	v	m	n	l	r
89	100	85	89	86	75	52	88	76	74

ERROR ANALYSIS

The analysis of the phonetic errors with the classical context-independent models shows the different contexts that are most influent. The vowels are generally well recognized despite the coarticulation, because of the stable part. On the contrary, some classes of consonants, especially voiced plosives, unvoiced plosives, affricates, give rise to many intra-class confusions. A systematic analysis [1] suggests that the right vocalic contexts influence the consonant according to the place of the vowel articulation. For example, when a *p* (labial articulation), is misrecognized as a *k* (palatal), the following vowel was always a back vowel, conversely *k* is taken for a *p* by the system when the following vowel is a front vowel, and so on. This influence is summarized by the diagram below, where the hypothesis concerning the displacement of the consonant articulation place by the consecutive vowel are indicated by arrows. The consonant articulation places **P** = **palatal** (k, g), **D** = **dental** (t, d, n), and **L** = **labial** (p, b, m) are presented from left to right. The type of vocalic influence responsible for the migration from one place to another is indicated by the symbols: **F** = **front, M** = **middle, B** = **back**

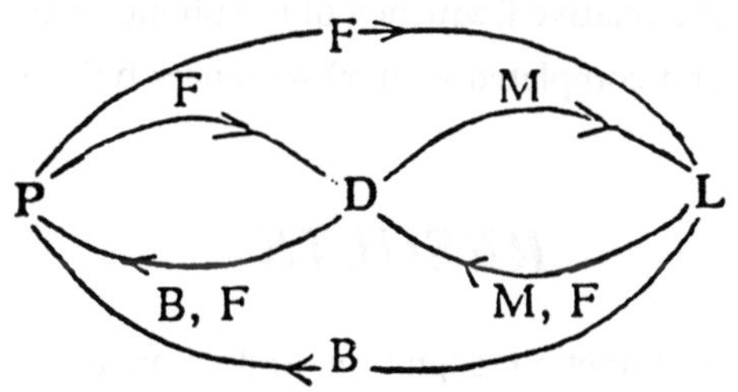

This agrees with what is known as the anticipatory vocalic influence in linguistic and phonological studies [6].

CHOICE OF A CONTEXT-DEPENDENT SYSTEM

Definition

First experiments with 10,000 words have shown the interest of a classification of the right contexts of voiceless plosives into 5 types: front, middle and back vowels, liquids, and silence. The introduction of context dependant models for these phonemes allowed to increase the phoneme recognition performance significantly [1].

The method has been generalized to other consonants, and all types of right contexts. Contextual machines are defined for voiced and unvoiced plosives, fricatives, semi-vowels, nasals, liquids. Since consonant clusters are rather frequent in French, consonantic contexts have to be accounted for. Ten types of contexts are defined for the consonants:

- Three vocalic contexts: front (e, o, i, y), middle (a, oe, a), back (o, u, o).
- Six consonantic right contexts: unvoiced plosives (p, t, k), voiced plosives (b, d, g), unvoiced fricatives (f, s, ch), voiced fricatives (v, z, j), nasals (m, n), liquids (l, r).
- silence

To each phoneme, correspond as many machines as relevant contexts. The new set has 130 markovian machines, which have the same structure as previously.

Training

These new machines are trained with the Baum algorithm, and smoothed with deleted interpolation [3]. However, a new corpus had to be designed, that would contain a minimum number of occurrences (20 in this experiment) of each contextual phoneme. This corpus has been chosen in a semi-automatic manner, from a large corpus of French texts. First, each sentence S was given a score representing its phonetic value, computed by $\sum_{\phi \in S} 1/f(\phi)$, where $f(\phi)$ is the relative frequency of the phoneme ϕ. The top 200 (richest) sentences were extracted, and completed with 50 sentences built by hand [2].

RESULTS

We test this new model on phonetic recognition, and compare it with the previous system. The recognition rates are presented below for the consonants.

Plosives

p	t	k	b	d	g	
55	70	57	25	64	43	(no context)
64	78	81	42	64	57	(contextual)

Others

s	ch	f	z	jj	v	m	n	l	r	
89	100	85	89	86	75	52	88	76	74	(no context)
94	100	91	81	90	80	67	81	80	87	(contextual)

The overall phoneme recognition rate (substitutions plus deletions) raised from 80.5% with the classical phonetic system, to 84.5% with the contextual one. The analysis of the results shows a significant improvement for most of the consonants: at least 10% better recognition performance on plosives, 5% better on fricatives, 8% on liquids.

In conclusion, we studied what coarticulation effects were most appropriate to take into account when defining phonetic models. We made hypothesis about the predominant effects, which allowed us to classify the right contexts into relevant classes, and to keep the resulting number of models reasonable for training and robustness. The new contextual system achieves a significant improvement in phoneme recognition performance.

1. A.M. Derouault, "Context-dependant phonetic Markov Models for large vocabulary speech recognition", Proceedings of the International Conference on Acoustics, Speech and Signal Processing, April 6-9 1987, Dallas, USA.

2. A.M. Derouault, Constitution d'un corpus d'apprentissage rendant compte des contextes phonétiques. Etude de service du Centre Scientique IBM France, (to appear).

3. F.Jelinek, R.L. Mercer "Interpolated Estimation of Markov Source Parameters from Sparse Data" Proceedings of the Workshop on Pattern Recognition in Practice, May 21-23, 1980, Amsterdam (Netherland), North Holland Publishing Company.

4. R.M. Schwartz and all, "Context dependent modeling for acoustic phonetic recognition od continuous speech", Proc. of ICASSP 85, Tampa, USA.

5. B. Merialdo "Speech Recognition with very large size dictionary". Proceedings of the International Conference on Acoustics, Speech and Signal Processing, April 6-9 1987, Dallas, USA.

6. J.P. Zerling: "Articulation et coarticulation dans des groupes occlusives-voyelles en français", 3rd cycle Thesis, University Nancy II.

SPEECH RECOGNITION BASED ON SPEECH UNITS

G. ZANELLATO
Faculté Polytechnique de Mons
31, Bvd DOLEZ, B-7000 MONS - BELGIUM

1. INTRODUCTION

In a classical quantization system, each vector is represented by the nearest centroïd; two vectors belonging to the same class are then indistinguishable. In order to mitigate this situation, we take into account the two nearest neighbours and define a "belonging degree" calculated from the distances between the vector and the two centroïds. In the case of speaker independent speech recognition system, this "fuzzy" quantization gives better results.

For the recognition of large vocabularies, it is usual to perform a phonemic segmentation and then to achieve the matching on the obtained sequence. But it is very hard to set up a good modeling for the phonemes. Nevertheless, we can take into account elementary components of the phonemes, for which simplest models may be used. We investigate a set of 100 "speech units" that have been defined from the centroïds of the fuzzy quantization. The results we obtained are very attractive.

2. FUZZY QUANTIZATION PRINCIPLE

Each spectral vector (SV) x_j is quantized by 4 numbers : the two nearest neighbours (C_1 and C_2) and the respective belonging degree :

$$a_1 = \frac{d(x_j,C_2)}{d(x_j,C_1) + d(x_j,C_2)} \quad \text{and} \quad a_2 = 1 - a_1$$

where d(.,.) is the ITAKURA distance between two SV .

Using this kind of quantization increases the recognition rate in the case of speaker-independent Hidden Markov Modeling recognizer : with a twenty-french words vocabulary (10 digits + 10 command words) uttered one time by 100 different male speakers, we use 50 versions for training the models and the left 50's for the tests. With a 100-classes classical quantization, we observed 36 errors for 1000 tests, but only 20 if we use the fuzzy quantization; the number of errors for the 1000 training utterances was 11 in both the cases.

NATO ASI Series, Vol. F46
Recent Advances in Speech Understanding and Dialog Systems
Edited by H. Niemann et al.

3. RECOGNITION USING SPEECH UNITS

When the size of the vocabulary increases, it is generally agreed to use a phonemic approach for the speech recognition. In this case, one can imagine a phoneme as being composed of a sequence of "elementary sounds", each of which being produced by a sequence of different articulatory configurations of the vocal tract. But it exists a one-to-one correspondence between a given position of the vocal tract and the position of a SV in the spectral space. Then, the sequence of SV representing an elementary sound draws a path in this space; this path may run across several classes. Different paths may correspond to the same elementary sound. Our objective is to model those paths; their set will be called a "speech unit" (SU).

The choice of the elementary components of a phoneme as base units for the segmentation and the recognition represents an attractive solution if they could be obtained automatically. To this end, we use, as base for the SU, the 100 centroïds obtained by the "fuzzy" quantization of the spectral space described above. In brief, this principle allows to segment a vocal signal into a sequence of speech units. Those units share the spectral space into "areas" characterized by centroïds obtained by vector quantization. Actually, each area may overlap others; they agree with a larger concept than the one of quantization class. In this case, the quantization technique takes a greater importance, in the assumption that it can be seen as a kind of preparation to the segmentation.

4. MODELING OF THE SPEECH UNITS

4.1. INITIALIZATION

The probabilistic model we retained for a SU is shown in figure 1. The first state characterizes in the best way the sound corresponding to the given SU , and the second one characterizes a sound as "far" as possible from the one represented by the first state; it is, in fact, the complementary area, with regard to the spectral space, of the one associated with the first state.

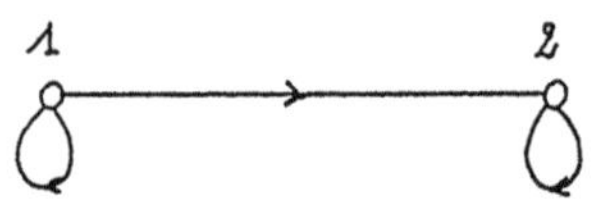

Figure 1 : Model of a speech unit.

In order to determine the production matrices, we proceed as follows :

1°) We use all the quantized SV for which the C_1 corresponds to the SU we want to model (for instance, the SU J).

2°) Each one of those vectors is regarded to be a part of the class J for an amount equal to its belonging degree a_1 to this class.

3°) The sum of all those a_1 represents the "amount" (real value) of SV allocated to class J .

4°) We also take into account the C_2 (class L) and a_2 of each one of the SV defined in 1°).

5°) For each class L , we sum the respective a_2 , what furnishes the "amount" of SV allocated to this class, for the model of SU J .

6°) The sum of all those "amounts" (for all the used classes) is equal to the number N of SV defined in 1°).

7°) The ratio between the "amount" Q_k attached to the class k and the number N gives the "production probability" of the class k in the first state of the model of the regarded SU.

8°) The value of the probability attached to the classes never "used" is half of the lowest probability determined in point 7°).

9°) We weight all those probabilities in order to assign a given value (e.g. 0.9) to the production probability of the class corresponding to the SU we have modelled (i.e. the class J for the SU J). In this case, the sum of the probabilities related to a given state is unitary anymore.

The initial values of the production probability vector $b_2(u_k)$ associated to the second state of the model is calculated from the first one : $b_2(u_k) = 1 - b_1(u_k) \qquad k = 1,2,\dots,100$.

4.2. TRAINING

4.2.1. RECOGNITION OF CONNECTED WORDS

The signal to be recognized is composed of a sequence of elements (words, phonemes, SU, ...) in any order. It is then necessary to match it with all the reference models, and that must be done from the beginning to the end of the signal. But, the use of the 100 centroïds as base for the SU presents an important advantage : the matching will be performed only with the models of the SU really presents in the signal ! (moreover, we process only about 15 frames at a time). For instance, if the signal has the following form (for the nearest neighbour only) :

17-34-34-31-34-34-34-34-34-52-17-58-58-61-14-32-14-14,

then the models to be used for the recognition will be those of the SU 14, 17, 31, 32, 34, 52, 58 et 61, i.e. eight models instead of 100 !

The first purpose is to determine the models of SU to be used, then we have to execute several times a kind of Viterbi algorithm (there is one for each retained SU (see figure 2)). In each "VITERBI", we have to determine the maximum probability with which we reach the second state. That means we have to execute a "back-tracking" <u>at each frame</u> of the signal (for each model). We consider that we are leaving the model when we are "looping" for at least three times in the second state.

In figure 2, the backtracking performed from the frame t_1 is such that we may consider still being in the model, but at the frame t2, we may consider we are leaving it (we have chosen 3 running points).

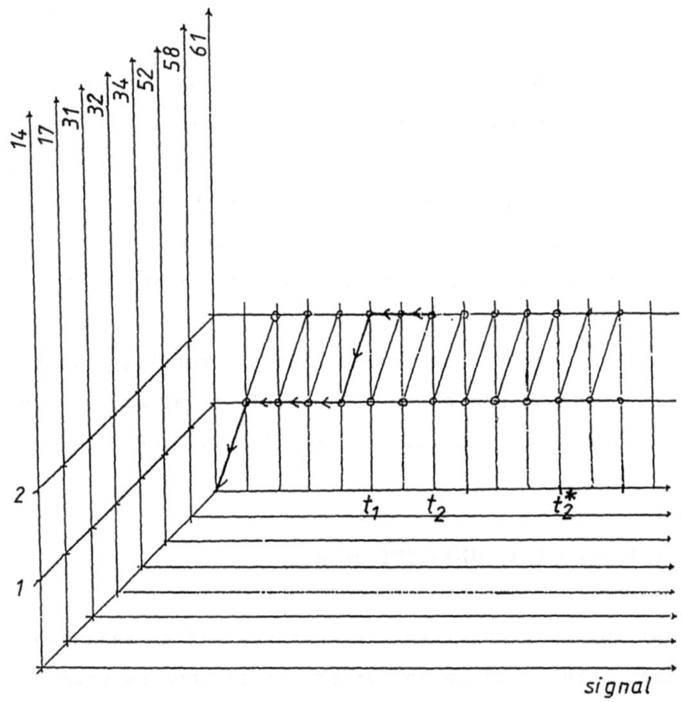

Figure 2 : Signal to speech units matching

We note the value of the maximum probability obtained in (t_2-3), i.e. at the moment we "leave" the model. We perform the same determination of optimal path for all the models of SU (the t_2's can be different) and we choose as "recognized" the one that in its own (t_2-3) gives the highest maximum probability. Let's suppose t_2^* being this frame. We cut out the frames 1 until (t_2^*-3), i.e. those that, in the determination of the optimal path, have been assigned to the first state of the "recognized" model. Then we start again the same processing on the fifteen frames following (t_2^*-3), in order to determine the next SU.

Finally, we obtain, for the whole signal, a sequence of SU (let's suppose 34 - 58 - 14 in our example) that represents the segmentation of the word into SU.

4.2.2. PARAMETERS CALCULATION

The speech unit models will be trained by a set of 1000 isolated words segmented into sequences of SU.

Marking the initial SV groups associated to each SU of each sequence, allows an easy determination of the production probabilities of the first state of each model. Nevertheless, we have to take into account that the contribution of each SV is equal to its "belonging probability" to the regarded class. For instance, if a SV assigned by the training to the first state of the SU model n° 30, is quantized in the following way :

C1 : 17 ; a1 : 0.8 and C2 : 21 ; a2 : 0.2 ,

then, the contribution of this vector is such that the "amount" of the class 17 is increased of 0.8 and the one of class 21 is increased of 0.2. We take care that any probability has a zero value and then we weight them as explained above. The probabilities of the second state are calculated from those ones.

5. FROM THE SU TO THE PHONEMES

The second part of the proposed method is related to the identification of the phonemes from the obtained sequences of speech units.

We can consider that a phoneme is composed of a sequence of SU drawing a path in the the spectral space. The coarticulation effect drives this path across several SU, in regard with the different pronunciations. Taking into account all the possible sequences allows to create a phoneme model. This one will be trained by a set of SU, as well as the SU models were trained by a set of SV.

In order to determine the sequence (or sequences) corresponding to a phoneme, we use again the words of our data base. Each word of the vocabulary is modelled by a probabilistic automaton composed of a number of states equal to the number of phonemes of the word. The training of those automatons will be performed using the words that have been segmented into SU, in order to determine, for each state, a SU production probability vector. We forecast that after this training, each state of a model will be specialized in the production of a phoneme (i.e. a sequence of SU). In the other hand, it seems that the principle of the Boltzmann Machines might be an interesting method in the determination of the phonemes from the SU, and eventually, in the determination of the SU themselves from the quantized signal.

In brief, the proposed methodology consists to forecast an intermediate stage before the segmentation of a word into phonemes. The main interest is a complete automatization of the processing.

The recognition of a word is now performed in the following way : the signal is at once segmented into speech units, performing a matching with the predefined SU models; then the sequence of obtained segments is processed by the automaton representing each of the vocabulary word. The recognition decision is taken at that point.

6. RESULTS

A set of 1000 words (50 versions) has been used for the training of the SU models *and* of the words models; the error rate is then :

1 % (10 errors) if we use the same words as tests

2 % (19 errors) if we use 1000 new words (50 new speakers).

7. BIBLIOGRAPHY

R.BOITE, H.Leich, G.Zanellato "Isolated Word Recognition by Hidden Markov Model", EUSIPCO-86, pp. 541-544.

R.M.GRAY, "Vector Quantization", IEEE ASSP Mag., April 1984, pp. 4-29.

F.ITAKURA, "Minimum Prediction Principle Applied to Speech Recognition", IEEE Trans., ASSP-23, February 1975, pp. 67-72.

F.JELINEK, "Continuous Speech Recognition by Statistical Methods", Proc. IEEE, Vol. 64 (April 1976), pp.532-556.

L.R.RABINER, S.E.Levinson, and M.M.Sondhi, "On the Application of Vector Quantization and Hidden Markov Models to Speaker-Independent Isolated Word Recognition", BSTJ, V62, N°4, April 1983, pp.10-1105.

G.ZANELLATO "Quantification vectorielle souple, base de la reconnaissance de la parole", 11 Colloque GRETSI, pp.455-458.

Mathematical Foundations of Hidden Markov Models

Lawrence R. Rabiner

AT&T Bell Laboratories
Murray Hill, New Jersey 07974

ABSTRACT: Stochastic methods of signal modeling have become increasingly popular. There are two strong reasons why this has occurred. First the models are very rich in mathematical structure and hence can form the theoretical basis for use in a wide range of applications. Second the models, when applied properly, work very well in practice for several important applications. In this paper we attempt to carefully and methodically review the theoretical aspects of one type of stochastic modelling, namely hidden Markov models (HMM's), and show how they have been applied to a couple of problems in machine recognition of speech.

I. INTRODUCTION

A problem of fundamental interest is characterizing real world signals in terms of signal models. Such signal models can provide the basis for a theoretical description of a signal processing system. Signal models are also potentially capable of teaching us a great deal about the signal source (i.e. the real world process which produced the signal) without having to have the source available. Finally, the most important reason why signal models are important is that they often work extremely well in practice, and enable us to realize important practical systems – e.g. prediction systems, recognition systems, identification systems, etc, in a very efficient manner.

Broadly one can dichotomize the types of signal models into the class of deterministic models, and the class of stochastic models. Deterministic models generally exploit some known specific properties of the signal, e.g. that the signal is a sine wave, or a sum of exponentials etc. In these cases, specification of the signal model is generally straightforward; and all that is required is to determine (estimate) values of the parameters of the signal model (e.g. amplitude, frequency, phase of a sine wave, amplitudes and rates of exponentials, etc). The second broad class of signal models is the set of stochastic models in which one tries to characterize only the statistical properties of the signal. Examples of such stochastic models include Gaussian processes, Poisson processes, Markov processes, and hidden Markov processes, among others. The underlying assumption of the stochastic model is that the physical process producing the signal can be well characterized as the output of a random process, and that the parameters of the stochastic process can be determined (estimated) in a precise, well defined manner.

For the applications of interest, namely speech processing, both deterministic and stochastic signal models have had good success. In this paper we will concern ourselves strictly with one type of stochastic signal model, namely the hidden Markov model (HMM). (These models are referred to as Markov sources in the communications literature.) We will first review the theory of Markov processes and then extend the ideas to the class of hidden Markov processes using several simple examples. We will then focus our attention on the three fundamental problems for HMM's, namely; the calculation of the probability (or likelihood) of a sequence of observations given a specific HMM; the determination of a best sequence of model states; and the adjustment of model parameters so as to best account for the observed signal. We will show that once these three fundamental problems are solved, we can apply HMM's to a wide variety of interesting and important problems. In particular, we will show how to apply the theory of HMM's to the problems of isolated word speech recognition, and to connected word speech recognition.

II. DISCRETE MARKOV PROCESSES

Consider a system which may be described at any time as being in one of a set of N distinct states, $S_1, S_2, \ldots, S_N$, as illustrated in Fig. 1 (where $N = 5$ for simplicity). At regularly spaced discrete times, the system undergoes a change of state (possibly back to the same state) according to a set of probabilities associated with the state. We denote the time instants associated with state changes as $t = 1, 2, \ldots,$ and we denote the actual state at time t as q_t. A full description of the above system would, in general, require specification of the current state (at time t), as well as all the predecessor states. For the special case of a discrete, first order, Markov process, this description is truncated to just

NATO ASI Series, Vol. F46
Recent Advances in Speech Understanding and Dialog Systems
Edited by H. Niemann et al.

the current and the predecessor state, i.e.

$$P\left[q_t = S_i \mid q_{t-1} = S_j, q_{t-2} = S_k, \dots\right] = P\left[q_t = S_i \mid q_{t-1} = S_j\right] \tag{1}$$

Furthermore we only consider those processes in which the right-hand side of Eq. (1) is independent of time, thereby leading to the set of state transition probabilities, a_{ji}, of the form

$$a_{ji} = P\left[q_t = S_i \mid q_{t-1} = S_j\right] \quad 1 \leqslant i,j \leqslant N \tag{2}$$

with the state transition coefficients having the properties:

$$a_{ji} \geqslant 0 \tag{3a}$$

$$\sum_{i=1}^{N} a_{ji} = 1 \tag{3b}$$

since they obey standard stochastic constraints.

II.1 Extension to Hidden Markov Models

So far we have considered Markov models in which each state corresponded to an observable (physical) event. This model is too restrictive to be applicable to many problems of interest. In this section we extend the concept of Markov models to include the case where the observation is a probabilistic function of the state – i.e. the resulting model (which is called a hidden Markov model) is a doubly stochastic process with an underlying stochastic process that is *not* observable (it is hidden), but can only be observed through another set of stochastic processes that produce the sequence of observations.

II.2 Elements of an HMM

We now formally define the elements of an HMM, and explain how the model generates observation sequences.

An HMM is characterized by the following:

1. N, the number of states in the model. Although the states are hidden, for most practical applications there is attached some physical significance to the states. Generally the states are interconnected in such a way that any state can be reached from any other state (e.g. an ergodic model); however we will see later in this paper that other possible interconnections of states are often of interest. We denote the individual states as $S = \{S_1, S_2, \dots, S_N\}$, and the state at time t as q_t.
2. M, the number of distinct observation symbols per state. The observation symbols correspond to the physical output of the system being modelled. We denote the individual symbols as $V = \{v_1, v_2, \dots, v_M\}$.
3. The state transition probability distribution, $A = \{a_{ij}\}$, where

$$a_{ij} = P\left[q_{t+1} = S_j \mid q_t = S_i\right], \quad 1 \leqslant i, j \leqslant N \tag{4}$$

For the special case where any state can reach any other state in a single step, we have $a_{ij} > 0$ for all i, j. For other types of HMM's, we would have $a_{ij} = 0$ for one or more (i, j) pairs.

4. The observation symbol probability distribution in state j, $B = \{b_j(k)\}$, where

$$b_j(k) = P\left[v_k \text{ at } t \mid q_t = S_j\right], \quad 1 \leqslant j \leqslant N, \quad 1 \leqslant k \leqslant M \tag{5}$$

5. The initial state distribution, $\pi = \{\pi_i\}$, where

$$\pi_i = P[q_1 = S_i], \quad 1 \leqslant i \leqslant N \tag{6}$$

Given appropriate values of N, M, A, B, and π, the HMM can be used as a generator to give an observation sequence

$$O = O_1 \, O_2 \cdots O_T \tag{7}$$

(where each observation O_t is one of the symbols from V, and T is the number of observations in the sequence) as follows:

1. Choose an initial state $q_1 = S_i$ according to the initial state distribution π

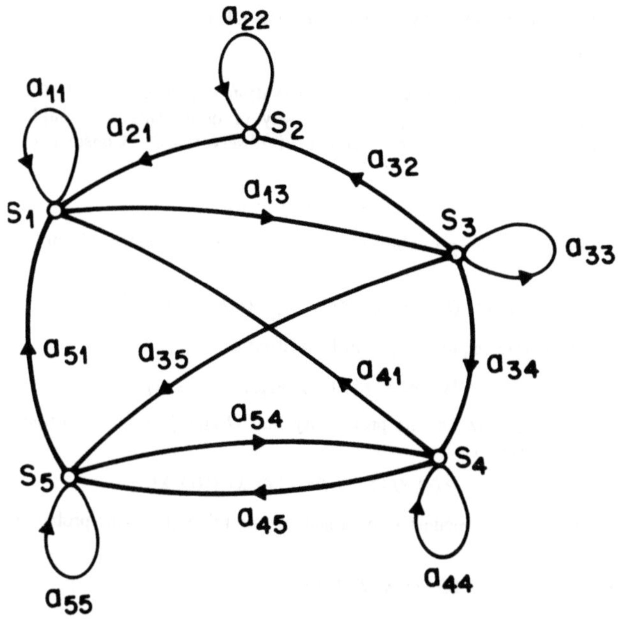

Fig. 1: A Markov chain with 5 states (labelled S_1 to S_5) with selected state transitions.

2. Set $t = 1$
3. Choose $O_t = v_k$ according to the symbol probability distribution in state S_i, i.e. $b_i(k)$
4. Transit to a new state $q_{t+1} = S_j$ according to the state transition probability distribution for state S_i, i.e. a_{ij}
5. Set $t = t+1$; return to step 3 if $t < T$; otherwise terminate the procedure.

The above procedure can be used as both a generator of observations, and as a model for how a given observation sequence was generated by an appropriate HMM.

It can be seen from the above discussion that a complete specification of an HMM requires specification of two parameters (N and M), some thought as to what observation symbols will be used, and the specification of the three probability densities A, B, and π. For convenience, we use the compact notation

$$\lambda = (A, B, \pi) \tag{8}$$

to indicate a completely specified model.

II.3 The Three Basic Problems for HMM's

Given the form of HMM of the previous section, there are three basic problems of interest that must be solved for the model to be useful in real world applications. These problems are the following:

Problem 1 – Given the observation sequence $O = O_1 \, O_2 \cdots O_T$, and a model $\lambda = (A, B, \pi)$, how do we (efficiently) compute $P(O \mid \lambda)$, the probability of the observation sequence, given the model.

Problem 2 – Given the observation sequence $O = O_1 \, O_2 \cdots O_T$, and the model, λ, how do we choose a state sequence $Q = q_1 \, q_2 \cdots q_T$ which is optimal in some meaningful sense.

Problem 3 – How do we adjust the model parameters $\lambda = (A, B, \pi)$ to maximize $P(O \mid \lambda)$.

In the next section we present formal mathematical solutions to each of the three fundamental problems for HMM's. We shall see that the three problems are linked together tightly under our probabilistic framework.

III. SOLUTIONS TO THE THREE BASIC PROBLEMS OF HMM's

III.1 Solution to Problem 1

We wish to calculate the probability of the observation sequence, $O = O_1 \, O_2 \cdots O_T$, given the model λ, i.e. $P(O \mid \lambda)$. The most straightforward way of doing this is through enumerating every possible state sequence of length T (the number of observations). Consider one such fixed state sequence

$$Q = q_1 \, q_2 \cdots q_T \tag{9}$$

where q_1 is the initial state. The probability of the observation sequence, O, for the state sequence of Eq. (9) is:

$$P(O \mid Q, \lambda) = b_{q_1}(O_1) \cdot b_{q_2}(O_2) \cdots b_{q_T}(O_T) \tag{10}$$

The probability of such a state sequence, Q, can be written as

$$P(Q \mid \lambda) = \pi_{q_1} \, a_{q_1 q_2} \, a_{q_2 q_3} \cdots a_{q_{T-1} q_T} \tag{11}$$

The joint probability of O and Q, i.e. the probability that O and Q occur simultaneously, is simply the product of the above two terms, i.e.

$$P(O, Q \mid \lambda) = P(O \mid Q, \lambda) \, P(Q, \lambda) \tag{12}$$

The probability of O (given the model) is obtained by summing this joint probability over all possible state sequences j giving

$$P(O \mid \lambda) = \sum_{\text{all } Q} P(O \mid Q, \lambda) \, P(Q \mid \lambda) \tag{13}$$

$$= \sum_{q_1, q_2, \ldots, q_T} \pi_{q_1} b_{q_1}(O_1) \, a_{q_1 q_2} b_{q_2}(O_2) \cdots a_{q_{T-1} q_T} b_{q_T}(O_T) \tag{14}$$

The interpretation of the computation in the above equation is the following. Initially (at time $t = 1$) we are in state q_1 with probability π_{q_1}, and generate the symbol O_1 (in this state) with probability $b_{q_1}(O_1)$. The clock changes to time $t = t+1$ ($t = 2$) and we make a transition to state q_2 from state q_1 with probability $a_{q_1 q_2}$, and generate symbol O_2 with probability $b_{q_2}(O_2)$. This process continues in this manner until we make the last transition (at time T) from state q_{T-1} to state q_T with probability $a_{q_{T-1} q_T}$ and generate symbol O_T with probability $b_{q_T}(O_T)$.

A little thought should convince the reader that the calculation of $P(O \mid \lambda)$, according to its direct definition (Eq. (14)), involves on the order of $2T \cdot N^T$ calculations, since at every $t = 1, 2, \ldots, T$, there are N possible states which can be reached, (i.e. there are N^T possible state sequences), and for each such state sequence about $2T$ calculations are required for the summed of Eq. (14). (To be precise, we need $(2T-1)N^T$ multiplications, and $N^T - 1$ additions.) This calculation is computationally unfeasible, even for small values of N and T; e.g. for $N = 5$ (states), $T = 100$ (observations), there are on the order of $2 \cdot 100 \cdot 5^{100} \approx 10^{72}$ computations! Clearly a more efficient procedure is required to solve Problem 1. Fortunately such a procedure exists and is called the forward-backward procedure.

The Forward-Backward Procedure

Consider the forward variable, $\alpha_t(i)$, defined as

$$\alpha_t(i) = P\left(O_1 \, O_2 \cdots O_t, \, q_t = S_i \mid \lambda\right) \tag{15}$$

i.e. the probability of the partial observation sequence (until time t) *and* state S_i at time t, given the model λ. We can solve for $\alpha_t(i)$ inductively, as follows:

1. Initialization;

$$\alpha_1(i) = \pi_i \, b_i(O_1), \quad 1 \leqslant i \leqslant N \tag{16}$$

2. Induction;

$$\alpha_{t+1}(j) = \left[\sum_{i=1}^{N} \alpha_t(i) \, a_{ij}\right] b_j(O_{t+1}), \quad 1 \leqslant t \leqslant T-1, \quad 1 \leqslant j \leqslant N \tag{17}$$

3. Termination;

$$P(O \mid \lambda) = \sum_{i=1}^{N} \alpha_T(i) \tag{18}$$

Step 1 initializes the forward probabilities as the joint probability of state S_i and initial observation O_1. The induction step, which is the heart of the forward calculation, shows how state S_j can be reached at time $t+1$ from the N possible states, S_i, $1 \leqslant i \leqslant N$, at time t. Since $\alpha_t(i)$ is the probability of the joint event that $O_1\ O_2 \cdots O_t$ are observed, and the state at time t is S_i, the product $\alpha_t(i)\, a_{ij}$ is then the probability of the joint event that $O_1\ O_2 \cdots O_t$ are observed, and state S_j is reached at time $t+1$ via state S_i at time t. Summing this product over all the N possible states S_i, $1 \leqslant i \leqslant N$ at time t results in the probability of S_j at time $t+1$ with all the accompanying previous partial observations. Once this is done and S_j is known, it is easy to see that $\alpha_{t+1}(j)$ is obtained by accounting for observation O_{t+1} in state j, i.e. by multiplying the summed quantity by the probability $b_j(O_{t+1})$. The computation of Eq. (17) is performed for all states j, $1 \leqslant j \leqslant N$, for a given t; the computation is then iterated for $t = 1, 2, \ldots, T-1$. Finally step 3 gives the desired calculation of $P(O \mid \lambda)$ as the sum of the terminal forward variables, $\alpha_T(i)$. This is the case since, by definition,

$$\alpha_T(i) = P\left[O_1\ O_2 \cdots O_T,\ q_T = S_i \mid \lambda\right] \tag{19}$$

and hence $P(O \mid \lambda)$ is just the sum of the $\alpha_T(i)$'s.

If we examine the computation involved in the calculation of $\alpha_t(j)$, $1 \leqslant t \leqslant T$, $1 \leqslant j \leqslant N$, we see that it requires on the order of N^2T calculations, rather than $2TN^T$, as required by the direct calculation (Eq. (14)). (Again, to be precise, we need $N(N+1)(T-1) + N$ multiplications and $N(N-1)(T-1)$ additions.) For $N = 5$, $T = 100$, we need about 3000 computations for the forward method, versus 10^{72} computations for the direct calculation, a savings of about 69 orders of magnitude.

The forward-backward procedure is, in effect, based upon a lattice structure. The key is that since there are only N states (nodes at each time slot in the lattice), all the possible state sequences will re-merge into these N nodes, no matter how long the observation sequence. At time $t = 1$ (the first time slot in the lattice), we need to calculate values of $\alpha_1(i)$, $1 \leqslant i \leqslant N$. At times $t = 2, 3, \ldots, T$, we only need to calculate values of $\alpha_t(j)$, $1 \leqslant j \leqslant N$, where each calculation involves only N previous values of $\alpha_{t-1}(i)$ because each of the N grid points is reached from the same N grid points at the previous time slot.

In a similar manner, we can consider a backward variable, $\beta_t(i)$, defined as:

$$\beta_t(i) = P\left[O_{t+1}\ O_{t+2} \cdots O_T \mid q_t = S_i, \lambda\right] \tag{20}$$

i.e. the probability of the partial observation sequence from $t+1$ to the end, given state S_i at time t and the model λ. Again we can solve for $\beta_t(i)$ inductively, as follows:

1. Initialization;

$$\beta_T(i) = 1, \quad 1 \leqslant i \leqslant N \tag{21}$$

2. Induction;

$$\beta_t(i) = \sum_{j=1}^{N} a_{ij}\, b_j\, (O_{t+1})\, \beta_{t+1}(j), \quad t = T-1, T-2, \ldots, 1, \quad 1 \leqslant i \leqslant N \tag{22}$$

The initialization step 1 arbitrarily defines $\beta_T(i)$ to be 1 for all i. Step 2, shows that in order to have been in state S_i at time t, and to account for the observation sequence from time $t+1$ on, you have to consider all possible states, S_j, at time $t+1$, accounting for the transition from S_i to S_j (the a_{ij} term), as well as the observation O_{t+1} in state j (the $b_j(O_{t+1})$ term), and then account for the remaining partial observation sequence from state j (the $\beta_{t+1}(j)$ term). We will see later how the backward, as well as the forward calculations are used extensively to help solve fundamental Problems 2 and 3 of HMM's.

Again, the computation of $\beta_t(i)$, $1 \leqslant t \leqslant T$, $1 \leqslant i \leqslant N$, requires on the order of N^2T calculations, and can be computed in a lattice structure.

III.2 Solution to Problem 2

Unlike Problem 1 for which an exact solution can be given, there are several possible ways of solving Problem 2, namely finding the "optimal" state sequence associated with the given observation sequence. The difficulty lies with the definition of the optimal state sequence; i.e. there are several possible optimality criteria. For example, one possible optimality criterion is to choose the states, q_t, which are *individually* most likely. This optimality criterion maximizes the expected number of correct individual states. To implement this solution to Problem 2, we define the variable

$$\gamma_t(i) = P\left[q_t = S_i \mid O, \lambda\right] \tag{23}$$

i.e. the probability of being in state S_i at time t, given the observation sequence, O, and the model, λ. Equation (23) can be expressed simply in terms of the forward-backward variables, i.e.

$$\gamma_t(i) = \frac{\alpha_t(i)\,\beta_t(i)}{P(O \mid \lambda)} \tag{24}$$

Since $\alpha_t(i)$ accounts for the partial observation sequence $O_1\, O_2 \cdots O_t$ and state S_i at t, while $\beta_t(i)$ accounts for the remainder of the observation sequence $O_{t+1}\, O_{t+2} \cdots O_T$, given state S_i at t. The normalization factor $P(O \mid \lambda)$ makes $\gamma_t(i)$ a probability measure so that

$$\sum_{i=1}^{N} \gamma_t(i) = 1 \tag{25}$$

Using $\gamma_t(i)$, we can solve for the individually most likely state, q_t, at time t, as:

$$q_t = \underset{1 \leqslant i \leqslant N}{\operatorname{argmax}} [\gamma_t(i)], \quad 1 \leqslant t \leqslant T \tag{26}$$

Although Eq. (26) maximizes the expected number of correct states, there could be some problems with the resulting state sequence. For example, when the HMM has state transitions which have zero probability ($a_{ij} = 0$ for some i and j), the "optimal" state sequence may, in fact, not even be a valid state sequence. This is due to the fact that the solution of Eq. (26) simply determines the most likely state at every instant, without regard to the probability of occurrence of *sequences* of states.

One possible solution to the above problem is to modify the optimality criterion. For example one could solve for the state sequence that maximized the expected number of correct pairs of states (q_t, q_{t+1}), or triples of states (q_t, q_{t+1}, q_{t+2}) etc. Although these criteria might be reasonable for some applications, the most widely used criterion is to find the *single* best state sequence (path), i.e. to maximize $P(Q \mid O, \lambda)$ which is equivalent to maximizing $P(Q, O \mid \lambda)$. A formal technique for finding this single best state sequence exists, based on dynamic programming methods, and is called the Viterbi algorithm.

Viterbi Algorithm

To find the single best state sequence, $Q = \{q_1\, q_2 \cdots q_T\}$, for the given observation sequence $O = \{O_1\, O_2 \cdots O_T\}$, we need to define the quantity:

$$\delta_t(i) = \max_{q_1, q_2, \ldots, q_{t-1}} P\left[q_1\, q_2 \cdots q_t = i,\ O_1\, O_2 \cdots O_t \mid \lambda\right] \tag{27}$$

i.e. $\delta_t(i)$ is the best score (highest probability) along a single path, at time t, which accounts for the first t observations and ends in state S_i. By induction we have:

$$\delta_{t+1}(j) = \left[\max_i \delta_t(i)\, a_{ij}\right] \cdot b_j(O_{t+1}) \tag{28}$$

To actually retrieve the state sequence, we need to keep track of the argument which maximized Eq. (28), for each t and j. We do this via the array $\psi_t(j)$. The complete procedure for finding the best state sequence can now be stated as follows:

1. Initialization;

$$\delta_1(i) = \pi_i\, b_i(O_1), \quad 1 \leqslant i \leqslant N \tag{29a}$$

$$\psi_1(i) = 0 \tag{29b}$$

2. Recursion;

$$\delta_t(j) = \max_{1 \leqslant i \leqslant N} [\delta_{t-1}(i)\, a_{ij}]\, b_j(O_t), \quad \begin{matrix} 2 \leqslant t \leqslant T \\ 1 \leqslant j \leqslant N \end{matrix} \tag{30a}$$

$$\psi_t(j) = \underset{1 \leqslant i \leqslant N}{\operatorname{argmax}} [\delta_{t-1}(i)\, a_{ij}], \quad \begin{matrix} 2 \leqslant t \leqslant T \\ 1 \leqslant j \leqslant N \end{matrix} \tag{30b}$$

3. Termination;

$$P^* = \max_{1 \leqslant i \leqslant N} [\delta_T(i)] \tag{31a}$$

$$q_T^* = \underset{1 \leqslant i \leqslant N}{\operatorname{argmax}} [\delta_T(i)] \tag{31b}$$

4. Path (state sequence) backtracking;

$$q_t^* = \psi_{t+1}(q_{t+1}^*), \quad t = T-1, T-2, \ldots, 1 \tag{32}$$

It should be noted that the Viterbi algorithm is similar (except for the backtracking step) in implementation to the forward-backward calculation. The major difference is the maximization in Eq. (30a) over previous states which is used in place of the summing procedure in Eq. (17). It also should be clear that a trellis structure efficiently implements the computation of the Viterbi procedure.

III.3 Solution to Problem 3

The third, and by far the most difficult, problem of HMM's is to determine a method to adjust the model parameters (A, B, π) to maximize the probability of the observation sequence given the model. There is no known way to analytically solve for the model which maximizes the probability of the observation sequence. In fact, given any finite observation sequence as training data, there is no optimal way of estimating the model parameters. We can, however, choose $\lambda = (A, B, \pi)$ such that $P(O \mid \lambda)$ is locally maximized using an iterative procedure such as the Baum-Welch method (or equivalently the EM method), or using gradient techniques. In this section we discuss one iterative procedure for choosing model parameters.

In order to describe the procedure for re-estimation of HMM parameters, we first define $\xi_t(i, j)$, the probability of being in state S_i at time t, and state S_j at time $t+1$, given the model and the observation sequence, i.e.

$$\xi_t(i, j) = P\left[q_t = S_i,\ q_{t+1} = S_j \mid O, \lambda\right] \tag{33}$$

It should be clear, from the definitions of the forward and backward variables, that we can write $\xi_t(i, j)$ in the form:

$$\xi_t(i, j) = \frac{\alpha_t(i)\, a_{ij}\, b_j(O_{t+1})\, \beta_{t+1}(j)}{P(O \mid \lambda)} \tag{34}$$

where the numerator term is just $P(q_t = S_i,\ q_{t+1} = S_j,\ O \mid \lambda)$ and the division by $P(O \mid \lambda)$ gives the desired probability measure.

We have previously defined $\gamma_t(i)$ as the probability of being in state S_i at time t, given the observation sequence and the model; hence we can relate $\gamma_t(i)$ to $\xi_t(i, j)$ by summing over j, giving

$$\gamma_t(i) = \sum_{j=1}^{N} \xi_t(i, j) \tag{35}$$

If we sum $\gamma_t(i)$ over the time index t, we get a quantity which can be interpreted as the expected (over time) number of times that state S_i is visited, or equivalently, the expected number of transitions made from state S_i (if we exclude the time slot $t = T$ from the summation). Similarly, summation of $\xi_t(i, j)$ over t (from $t = 1$ to $t = T-1$) can be interpreted as the expected number of transitions from state S_i to state S_j. That is

$$\sum_{t=1}^{T-1} \gamma_t(i) = \text{Expected number of transitions from } S_i \tag{36a}$$

$$\sum_{t=1}^{T-1} \xi_t(i, j) = \text{Expected number of transitions from } S_i \text{ to } S_j \tag{36b}$$

Using the above formulas (and the concept of counting event occurrences) we can give a method for reestimation of the parameters of an HMM. A set of reasonable reestimation formulas for π, A, and B are:

$$\bar{\pi}_i = \text{Expected number of times in state } S_i \text{ at time } 1 = \gamma_1(i) \tag{37a}$$

$$\bar{a}_{ij} = \frac{\text{Expected number of transitions from state } S_i \text{ to state } S_j}{\text{Expected number of transitions from state } S_i}$$

$$= \frac{\sum_{t=1}^{T-1} \xi_t(i, j)}{\sum_{t=1}^{T-1} \gamma_t(i)} \tag{37b}$$

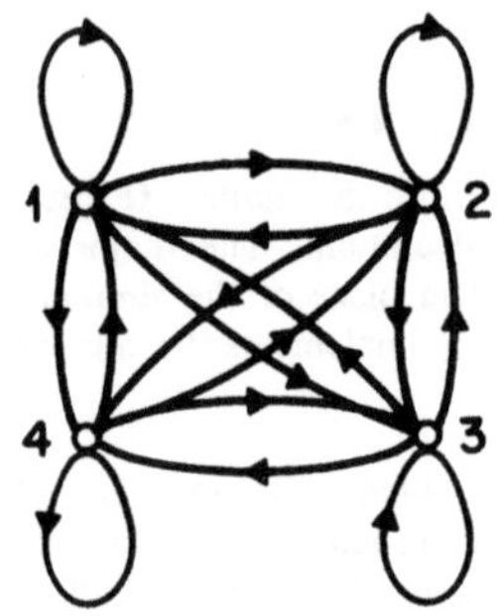

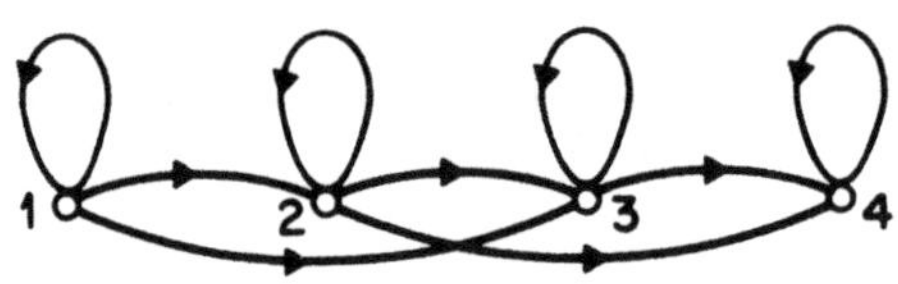

Fig. 2: Illustration of 3 distinct types of HMM's, including: (a) a 4-state ergodic model; and (b) a 4-state left-right model.

$$\bar{b}_j(k) = \frac{\text{Expected number of times in state } j \text{ and observing symbol } v_k}{\text{Expected number of times in state } j}$$

$$= \frac{\sum\limits_{\substack{t=1 \\ \text{s.t. } O_t = v_k}}^{T} \gamma_t(j)}{\sum\limits_{t=1}^{T} \gamma_t(j)} \tag{37c}$$

If we define the current model as $\lambda = (A, B, \pi)$, and use that to compute the right hand sides of Eqs. (37a-c), and we define the reestimated model as $\bar{\lambda} = (\bar{A}, \bar{B}, \bar{\pi})$, as determined from the left hand sides of Eqs. (37a-c), then it has been proven that either:

1. The initial model λ defines a critical point of the likelihood function, in which case $\bar{\lambda} = \lambda$,

or

2. Model $\bar{\lambda}$ is more likely than model λ in the sense that $P(O \mid \bar{\lambda}) > P(O \mid \lambda)$, i.e. we have found a new model $\bar{\lambda}$ from which the observation sequence is more likely to have been produced.

Based on the above procedure, if we iteratively use $\bar{\lambda}$ in place of λ and repeat the reestimation calculation, we then can improve the probability of O being observed from the model until some limiting point is reached. The final result of this reestimation procedure is called the maximum likelihood estimate of the HMM.

IV. TYPES OF HMM's

Until now, we have only considered the special case of ergodic or fully connected HMM's in which every state of the model could be reached (in a single step) from every other state of the model. (Strictly speaking, an ergodic model has the property that every state can be reached from every other state in a finite number of steps.) As shown in Fig. 2a, for an $N = 4$ state model, this type of model has the property that every a_{ij} coefficient is positive.

For some applications other types of HMM's have been found to account for observed properties of the signal being modelled better than the standard ergodic model. One such model is shown in Fig. 2b. We call this model a left-right model since the underlying state sequence associated with the model has the property that as time increases, the state index increases, i.e. the states proceed from left to right. Clearly the left-right type of HMM has the desirable property that it can readily model signals whose properties change over time – e.g. speech.

It should be clear that the imposition of the constraints of the left-right model, essentially have no effect on the reestimation procedure. This is the case because any HMM parameter set to zero initially, will remain at zero throughout the reestimation procedure.

IV.1 Continuous Observation Densities in HMM's

All of our discussion, to this point, has considered only the case when the observations were characterized as discrete symbols chosen from a finite alphabet, and therefore we could use a discrete probability density within each state of the model. The problem with this approach, at least for some applications, is that the observations are continuous signals (or vectors). Although it is possible to quantize such continuous signals via codebooks, etc., there is a serious degradation associated with such quantization. Hence it would be advantageous to be able to use HMM's with continuous observation densities.

In order to use a continuous observation density, some restrictions have to be placed on the form of the model probability density function (pdf) to insure that the parameters of the pdf can be reestimated in a consistent way. The most general representation of the pdf, for which a reestimation procedure has been formulated, is a finite mixture of the form:

$$b_j(\mathbf{x}) = \sum_{m=1}^{M} c_{jm}\, \mathcal{N}[\mathbf{x}, \boldsymbol{\mu}_{jm}, \mathbf{U}_{jm}], \quad 1 \leqslant j \leqslant N \tag{38}$$

where $\mathbf{x}$ is the vector being modelled, c_{jm} is the mixture gain for the mth mixture in state j and $\mathcal{N}$ is any log-concave or elliptically symmetric density (e.g. Gaussian), with mean vector $\boldsymbol{\mu}_{jm}$ and covariance matrix $\mathbf{U}_{jm}$ for the mth mixture component in state j. Usually a Gaussian density is used for $\mathcal{N}$. The mixture gains satisfy the stochastic constraint:

$$\sum_{m=1}^{M} c_{jm} = 1, \quad 1 \leqslant j \leqslant N \tag{39a}$$

$$c_{jm} \geqslant 0, \quad 1 \leqslant j \leqslant N, \ 1 \leqslant m \leqslant M \tag{39b}$$

so that the pdf is properly normalized, i.e.

$$\int_{-\infty}^{\infty} b_j(\mathbf{x})\, d\mathbf{x} = 1, \quad 1 \leqslant j \leqslant N \tag{40}$$

The pdf of Eq. (38) can be used to approximate, arbitrarily closely, any finite, continuous density function. Hence it can be applied to a wide range of problems.

It can be shown that reestimation formulas for the coefficients of the mixture density, i.e. c_{jm}, $\boldsymbol{\mu}_{jk}$, and $\mathbf{U}_{jk}$, are readily obtained.

IV.2 Inclusion of Explicit State Duration Density in HMM's

Perhaps the major weakness of conventional HMM's is the modelling of state duration. It is easily shown that the inherent duration density, $p_i(d)$, associated with state S_i, with self transition coefficient a_{ii} is of the form:

$$p_i(d) = (a_{ii})^{d-1}\,(1-a_{ii}) = \text{probability of } d \text{ observations produced while in state } S_i \tag{41}$$

For most physical signals, this exponential state duration density is inappropriate. Instead we would prefer to model duration density with an explicit duration density, $p_j(d)$.

The sequence of events of a variable duration HMM with state duration density $p_j(d)$ is as follows:

1. An initial state, $q_1 = S_i$, is chosen according to the initial state distribution π_i.
2. A duration d_1 is chosen according to the state duration density $p_{q_1}(d_1)$

3. Observations $O_1\, O_2 \cdots O_{d_1}$ are chosen according to the joint observation density, $b_{q_1}(O_1\, O_2 \cdots O_{d_1})$. Generally we assume independence of observations so that $b_{q_1}(O_1\, O_2 \cdots O_{d_1}) = \prod_{t=1}^{d_1} b_{q_1}(O_t)$.
4. The next state, $q_2 = S_j$, is chosen according to the state transition probabilities, $a_{q_1 q_2}$, with the constraint that $a_{q_1 q_1} = 0$, i.e. no transition back to the same state can occur. (Clearly this is a requirement since we assume that, in state q_1, exactly d_1 observations occur.)

A little thought should convince the reader that the variable duration HMM can be made equivalent to the standard HMM by setting $p_i(d)$ to be the exponential density of Eq. (41).

It is fairly straightforward to incorporate an explicit state duration density into the scoring and training algorithms. For some problems the quality of the modelling is significantly improved when explicit state duration densities are used. However, there are drawbacks to the use of the variable duration model discussed in this section. One is a greatly increased computational load associated with using variable durations. It can be shown that for densities defined over D frames (i.e. $p_j(d)$ for $1 \leqslant d \leqslant D$) about D times the storage and $D^2/2$ times the computation is required. For D on the order of 25 (as is reasonable for many speech processing problems), an increase in computation of 300 to 1 results. Another problem with the variable duration models is the large number of parameters (D), associated with each state, that must be estimated, in addition to the usual HMM parameters. Furthermore, for a fixed number of observations, T, in the training set, there are, on average, fewer state transitions and much less data to estimate $p_i(d)$ then would be used in a standard HMM. Thus the reestimation problem is more difficult for variable duration HMM's than for the standard HMM.

One proposal to alleviate some of these problems is to use a parametric state duration density instead of the non-parametric $p_i(d)$ used above. In particular, proposals include the Gaussian family with

$$p_i(d) = \mathcal{N}(d, \mu_i, \sigma_i^2) \tag{42}$$

with parameters μ_i and σ_i^2, or the Gamma family with

$$p_i(d) = \frac{\eta_i^{\nu_i}\, d^{\nu_i - 1}\, e^{-\eta_i d}}{\Gamma(\nu_i)} \tag{43}$$

with parameters ν_i and η_i and with mean $\nu_i \eta_i^{-1}$ and variance $\nu_i \eta_i^{-2}$. Reestimation formulas for η_i and ν_i have been derived and used with good results. Another possibility, which has been used with good success, is to assume a uniform duration distribution (over an appropriate range of durations) and use a path-constrained Viterbi decoding procedure.

V. IMPLEMENTATION ISSUES FOR HMM's

The discussion in the previous two sections has primarily dealt with the theory of HMM's and several variations on the form of the model. In this section we deal with several practical implementation issues including scaling, multiple observation sequences, initial parameter estimates, missing data, and choice of model size and type. For some of these implementation issues we can prescribe exact analytical solutions; for other issues we can only provide some seat-of-the-pants experience gained from working with HMM's over the last several years.

V.1 Scaling

In order to understand why scaling is required for implementing the reestimation procedure of HMM's, consider the definition of $\alpha_t(i)$ of Eq. (15). It can be seen that $\alpha_t(i)$ consists of the sum of a large number of terms, each of the form

$$\left[\prod_{s=1}^{t-1} a_{q_s q_{s+1}} \prod_{s=1}^{t} b_{q_s}(\mathbf{O}_s)\right]$$

with $q_t = S_i$. Since each a and b term is less than 1 (generally significantly less than 1), it can be seen that as t starts to get big (e.g. 10 or more), each term of $\alpha_t(i)$ starts to head exponentially to zero. For sufficiently large t (e.g. 100 or more) the dynamic range of the $\alpha_t(i)$ computation will exceed the precision range of essentially any machine (even in double precision). Hence the only reasonable way of performing the computation is by incorporating a scaling procedure.

The basic scaling procedure that is used is to multiply $\alpha_t(i)$ by a scaling coefficient that is independent of i (i.e. it depends only on t), with the goal of keeping the scaled $\alpha_t(i)$ within the dynamic range of the computer for $1 \leqslant t \leqslant T$. A similar scaling is done of the $\beta_t(i)$ coefficients (since these also tend to zero exponentially fast) and then, at the end of the computation, the scaling coefficients are cancelled out exactly.

V.2 Multiple Observation Sequences

In Section IV we discussed a form of HMM called the left-right model in which the state proceeds from state 1 at $t=1$ to state N at $t=T$ in a sequential manner. We have already discussed how a left-right model imposes constraints on the state transition matrix, and the initial state probabilities. However the major problem with left-right models is that one cannot use a single observation sequence to train the model (i.e. for reestimation of model parameters). This is because the transient nature of the states within the model only allow a small number of observations for any state (until a transition is made to a successor state). Hence, in order to have enough data to make reliable estimates of all model parameters, one has to use multiple observation sequences.

The modification of the reestimation procedure is straightforward and goes as follows. We denote the set of K observation sequences as:

$$\mathbf{O} = [\mathbf{O}^{(1)}, \mathbf{O}^{(2)}, \ldots, \mathbf{O}^{(k)}] \tag{44}$$

where $\mathbf{O}^{(k)} = \left[O_1^{(k)}\ O_2^{(k)} \cdots .O_{T_k}^{(k)}\right]$ is the kth observation sequence. We assume each observation sequence is independent of every other observation sequence, and our goal is to adjust the parameters of the model, λ, to maximize

$$P(O\,|\,\lambda) = \prod_{k=1}^{K} P(\mathbf{O}^{(k)}\,|\,\lambda) \tag{45}$$

$$= \prod_{k=1}^{K} P_k \tag{46}$$

Since the reestimation formulas are based on frequencies of occurrence of various events, the reestimation formulas for multiple observation sequences are modified by adding together the individual frequencies of occurrence for each sequence.

V.3 Initial Estimates of HMM Parameters

In theory, the reestimation equations should give values of the HMM parameters which correspond to a local maximum of the likelihood function. A key question is therefore how do we choose initial estimates of the HMM parameters so that the local maximum is the global maximum of the likelihood function.

There basically is no simple or straightforward answer to the above question. Instead, experience has shown that either random (subject to the stochastic and the non-zero value constraints) or uniform initial estimates of the π and A parameters is adequate for giving useful reestimates of these parameters in almost all cases. However, for the B parameters, experience has shown that good initial estimates are helpful in the discrete symbol case, and are mandatory in the continuous distribution case. Such initial estimates can be obtained in a number of ways, including manual segmentation of the observation sequence(s) into states with averaging of observations within states, maximum likelihood segmentation of observations with averaging, and segmental k-means segmentation with clustering etc.

V.4 Effects of Insufficient Training Data

Another problem associated with training HMM parameters via reestimation methods is that the observation sequence used for training is, of necessity, finite. Thus there is often an insufficient number of occurrences of different model events (e.g. symbol occurrences within states) to give good estimates of the model parameters. One solution to this problem is to increase the size of the training observation set. Often this is impractical. A second possible solution is to reduce the size of the model (e.g. number of states, number of symbols per state etc). Although this is always possible, often there are physical reasons why a given model is used and therefore the model size cannot be changed. A third possible solution is to add extra constraints to the model parameters to insure that no model parameter estimate falls below a specified level. Thus, for example, we might specify the constraint, for a discrete symbol model, that

$$b_j(k) \geqslant \epsilon \tag{47}$$

or, for a continuous distribution model, that

$$U_{jk}(r, r) \geqslant \delta \tag{48}$$

The constraints can be applied as a postprocessor to the reestimation equations such that if a constraint is violated, the relevant parameter is manually corrected, and all remaining parameters are rescaled so that the densities obey the required stochastic constraints. Such post-processor techniques have been applied to several problems in speech processing with good success.

V.5 Choice of Model

The remaining issue in implementing HMM's is the choice of type of model (ergodic or left-right or some other form), choice of model size (number of states), and choice of observation symbols (discrete or continuous, single or multi-mixture, choice of observation parameters). Unfortunately, these issues are not ones for which the theory guides the user as to his choices. These choices must be made depending on the signal being modelled. Thus we end our discussion of the theoretical aspects of hidden Markov models, and proceed to a discussion of how such models have been applied to problems in speech recognition.

VI. IMPLEMENTATION OF ISOLATED WORD RECOGNIZERS USING HMM's

The purpose of this, and the following sections, is to illustrate how the ideas of HMM's, as discussed in the first 5 sections of this paper, have been applied to selected problems in speech recognition. As such, we will not strive to be as thorough or as complete in our descriptions as to what was done as we were in describing the theory of HMM's. Our main goal is to show how specific aspects of HMM theory get applied, not to make the reader an expert in speech recognition technology.

As our first example, consider trying to use HMM's to build an isolated word recognizer. Assume we have a vocabulary of V words to be recognized. Further assume that for each word in the vocabulary we have a training set of K occurrences of each spoken word (spoken by 1 or more talkers) where each occurrence of the word is a distinct observation sequence, where the observations are some appropriate representation of the (spectral and/or temporal) characteristics of the word. (We will return to the question of what specific representation is used later in this section.) In order to do isolated word speech recognition we must perform the following:

1. For each word, v, in the vocabulary, we must build an HMM, λ^v, i.e. we must reestimate the model parameters (A, B, π) that optimize the likelihood of the training set observation vectors for the vth word.
2. For each unknown word which is to be recognized, the processing of Fig. 3 must be carried out, namely measurement of the observation sequence $O = \{O_1 \; O_2 \; \cdots \; O_T\}$, via a feature analysis of the speech corresponding to the word; followed by calculation of model likelihoods for all possible models, $P(O \mid \lambda^v)$, $1 \leqslant v \leqslant V$; followed by selection of the word whose model likelihood is highest, i.e.

$$v^* = \underset{1 \leqslant v \leqslant V}{\operatorname{argmax}} \, [P(O \mid \lambda^v)] \tag{49}$$

The probability computation step is generally performed using the Viterbi algorithm (i.e. the maximum likelihood path is used) and requires on the order of $V \cdot N^2 \cdot T$ computations. For modest vocabulary sizes, e.g. $V = 100$ words, with an $N = 5$ state model, and $T = 40$ observations for the unknown word, a total of 10^5 computations is required for recognition (where each computation is a multiply, and add, and a calculation of observation density, $b(O)$). Clearly this amount of computation is modest as compared to the capabilities of most modern signal processor chips.

VI.1 LPC Feature Analysis

One way to obtain observation vectors, O, from speech samples, s, is to perform a front end spectral analysis. (We assume that we are processing only the speech samples corresponding to the spoken word – i.e. all background before and after the spoken word has been eliminated by an appropriate word detection algorithm.) The type of spectral analysis that is often used, is called linear predictive coding (LPC), and a block diagram of the steps that are carried out is given in Fig. 4. The overall system is a block processing model in which a frame of N_A samples is processed and a vector of features, O_t, is computed.

VI.2 Vector Quantization

For the case in which we wish to use an HMM with a discrete observation symbol density, rather than the continuous vectors above, a vector quantizer (VQ) is required to map each continuous observation vector into a discrete codebook index. Once the codebook of vectors has been obtained, the mapping between continuous vectors and codebook indices becomes a simple nearest neighbor computation, i.e. the continuous vector is assigned the index of the nearest (in a spectral distance sense) codebook vector. Thus the major issue in VQ is the design of an appropriate codebook for quantization.

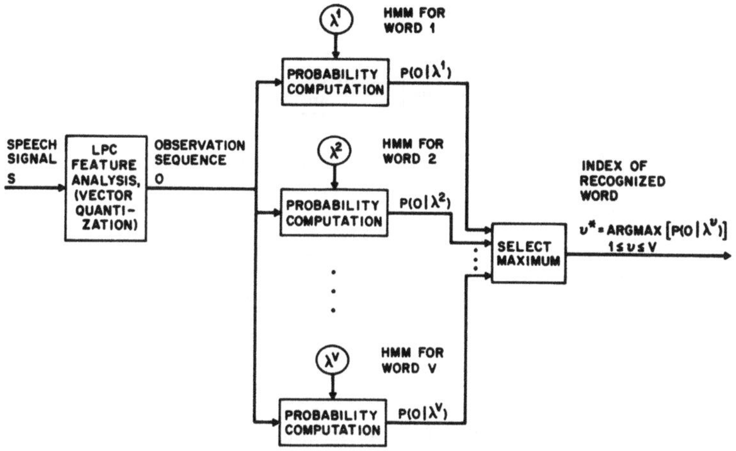

Fig. 3: Block diagram of an isolated word HMM recognizer.

Fortunately a great deal of work has gone into devising an excellent iterative procedure for designing codebooks based on having a representative training sequence of vectors. The procedure basically partitions the training vectors into M disjoint sets (where M is the size of the codebook), represents each such set by a single vector, $(v_m, 1 \leqslant m \leqslant M)$, which is generally the centroid of the vectors in the training set assigned to the mth region, and then iteratively optimizes the partition and the codebook (i.e. the centroids of each partition). Associated with VQ is a distortion penalty since we are representing an entire region of the vector space by a single vector. Clearly it is advantageous to keep the distortion penalty as small as possible. However this implies a large size codebook, and that leads to problems in implementing HMM's with a large number of parameters.

VI.3 Choice of Model Parameters

We now come to the issue of how do we select the type of model, and how do we choose the parameters of the selected model. For isolated word recognition with a distinct HMM designed for each word in the vocabulary, it should be clear that a left-right model is more appropriate than an ergodic model, since we can then associate time with model states in a fairly straightforward manner. Furthermore we can envision the physical meaning of the model states as distinct sounds (e.g. phonemes, syllables) of the word being modelled.

The issue of the number of states to use in each word model leads to two schools of thought. One idea is to let the number of states correspond roughly to the number of sounds (phonemes) within the word — hence models with from 2 to 10 states would be appropriate. The other idea is to let the number of states correspond roughly to the average number of observations in a spoken version of the word. In this manner each state corresponds to an observation interval — i.e. about 15 msec for the analysis we use. In the results to be described later in this section, we use the former approach. Furthermore we restrict each word model to have the same number of states.

The next issue is the choice of observation vector and the way it is represented. We use LPC derived cepstral coefficients as the observation vectors for continuous models; for discrete symbol models we use a codebook to generate the discrete symbols. For the continuous models we use as many as $M = 9$ mixtures; for the discrete symbol models we use codebooks with as many as $M = 256$ codewords. Also, for the continuous models, we have found that it is preferable to use diagonal covariance matrices with several mixtures, rather than fewer mixtures with full covariance matrices. The reason for this is simple, namely the difficulty in performing reliable reestimation of the off-diagonal components of the covariance matrix from the necessarily limited training data. To illustrate the need for using mixture densities for modelling LPC observation vectors (i.e. 8th order cepstral vectors with log energy appended as the ninth vector component), Fig. 5 shows a comparison of marginal distributions, $b_j(O)|_{O = \cdots O_n \cdots}$ against a histogram of the actual observations within a state (as determined by a maximum likelihood segmentation of all the training observations into states). The observation vectors are 9th order, and the model density uses $M = 5$ mixtures. The covariance matrices are constrained to be diagonal for each

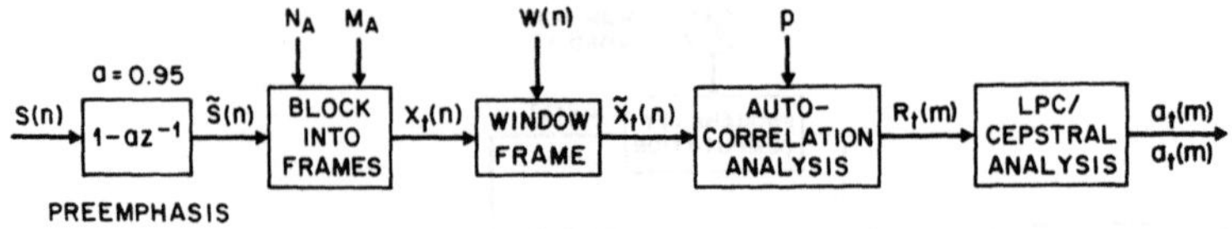

Fig. 4: Block diagram of the computations required in the front end feature analysis of the HMM recognizer.

individual mixture. The results of Fig. 5 are for the first model state of the word "zero". The need for values of $M > 1$ is clearly seen in the histogram of the first parameter (the first cepstral component) which is inherently multimodal; similarly the second, fourth, and eighth cepstral parameters show the need for more than a single Gaussian component to provide good fits to the empirical data. Many of the other parameters appear to be well fitted by a single Gaussian; in some cases, however, even $M = 5$ mixtures do not provide a sufficiently good fit.

Another experimentally verified fact about the HMM is that it is important to limit some of the parameter estimates in order to prevent them from becoming too small. For example, for the discrete symbol models, the constraint that $b_j(k)$ be greater than or equal to some minimum value, ϵ, is necessary to insure that even when the kth symbol never occurred in some state j in the training observation set, there is always a finite probability of its occurrence when scoring an unknown observation set. To illustrate this point, Fig. 6 shows a curve of average word error rate versus the parameter ϵ (on a log scale) for a standard word recognition experiment. It can be seen that over a very broad range ($10^{-10} \leqslant \epsilon \leqslant 10^{-3}$) the average error rate remains at about a constant value; however when ϵ is set to 0 (i.e. $10^{-\infty}$), then the error rate increases sharply. Similarly, for continuous densities it is important to constrain the mixture gains, c_{jm}, as well as the diagonal covariance coefficients $U_{jm}(r, r)$ to be greater than or equal to some minimum values (we use 10^{-4} in all cases).

VI.4 Segmental *k*-Means Segmentation into States

We stated earlier that good initial estimates of the parameters of the $b_j(O_t)$ densities were essential for rapid and proper convergence of the reestimation formulas. Hence a procedure for providing good initial estimates of these parameters was devised and is shown in Fig. 7. The training procedure is a variant on the well known K-means iterative procedure for clustering data.

We assume we have a training set of observations (the same as is required for parameter reestimation), and an initial estimate of all model parameters. However, unlike the one required for reestimation, the initial model estimate can be chosen randomly, or on the basis of any available model which is appropriate to the data.

Following model initialization, the set of training observation sequences is segmented into states, based on the current model, λ. This segmentation is achieved by finding the optimum state sequence, via the Viterbi algorithm, and then backtracking along the optimal path.

The result of segmenting each of the training sequences is, for each of the N states, a maximum likelihood estimate of the set of the observations that occur within each state, S_i, according to the current model. In the case where we are using discrete symbol densities, each of the observation vectors within a state is coded using the M-codeword codebook, and the updated estimate of the $b_j(k)$ parameters is:

$$\hat{b}_j(k) = \text{number of vectors with codebook index } k \text{ in state } j$$
$$\text{divided by the number of vectors in state } j$$

In the case where we are using continuous observation densities, a segmental K-means procedure is used to cluster the observation vectors within each state, S_j, into a set of M clusters (using a Euclidean distortion measure), where each cluster represents one of the M mixtures of the $b_j(O_t)$ density. From the clustering, an updated set of model parameters is derived as follows

$\hat{c}_{jm}$ = number of vectors classified in cluster m of state j divided by the number of vectors in state j

$\hat{\boldsymbol{\mu}}_{jm}$ = sample mean of the vectors classified in cluster m of state j

$\hat{\mathbf{U}}_{jm}$ = sample covariance matrix of the vectors classified in cluster m of state j.

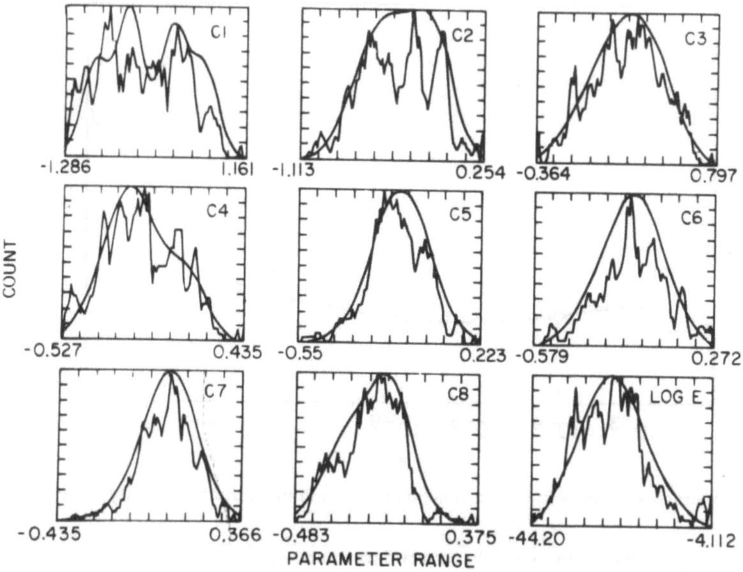

Fig. 5: Comparison of estimated density (jagged contour) and model density (smooth contour) for each of the nine components of the observation vector (eight cepstral components, one log energy component) for state 1 of the digit zero.

Based on this state segmentation, updated estimates of the a_{ij} coefficients can be obtained by counting the number of transitions from state i to j and dividing it by the number of transitions from state i to any state (including itself).

An updated model, $\hat{\lambda}$, is obtained from the new model parameters and the formal reestimation procedure is used to reestimate all model parameters. The resulting model is then compared to the previous model (by computing a distance score that reflects the statistical similarity of the HMM's). If the model distance score exceeds a threshold, then the old model, λ, is replaced by the new (reestimated) model $\bar{\lambda}$, and the overall training loop is repeated. If the model distance score falls below the threshold, then model convergence is assumed and the final model parameters are saved.

VI.5 Incorporation of State Duration into the HMM

In Section 4.2 we discussed the theoretically correct method of incorporating state duration information into the mechanics of the HMM. We also showed that the cost of including duration density was rather high; namely a D^2-fold increase in computation and storage. Using a value of $D = 25$ (as is required for word recognition), the cost of the increased computation tended to make the techniques not worth using. Thus an alternative procedure was formulated for incorporating state duration information into the HMM.

For this alternative procedure, the state duration probability, $p_j(d)$, was measured directly from the segmented training sequences used in the segmental K-means procedure of the previous section. Hence the estimates of $p_j(d)$ are strictly heuristic ones.

The way in which the heuristic duration densities were used in the recognizer was as follows. First the normal Viterbi algorithm is used to give the best segmentation of the observation sequence of the unknown word into states via a backtracking procedure. The duration of each state is then measured from the state segmentation. A post-processor then increments the log-likelihood score of the Viterbi algorithm, by the quantity:

$$\log \hat{P}(q, O \mid \lambda) = \log P(q, O \mid \lambda) + \alpha_d \sum_{j=1}^{N} \log [p_j(d_j)] \tag{50}$$

where α_d is a scaling multiplier on the state duration scores, and d_j is the duration of state j along the optimal path as determined by the Viterbi algorithm. The incremental cost of the post-processor for duration is essentially negligible, and experience has shown that recognition performance is essentially as

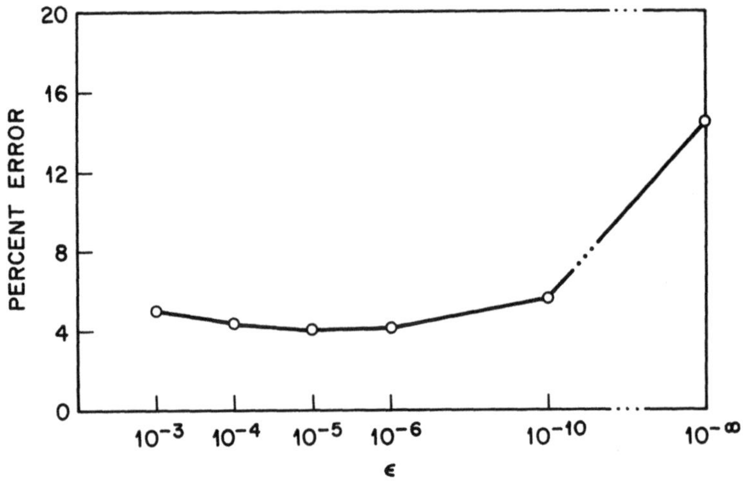

Fig. 6: Average word error rate as a function of the minimum discrete density value, ϵ.

good as that obtained using the theoretically correct duration model.

VI.6 HMM Performance on Isolated Word Recognition

We conclude this section on isolated word recognition using HMM's by giving a set of performance results (in terms of average word error rate) on the task of recognizing isolated digits in a speaker independent manner. For this task, a training set consisting of 100 occurrences of each digit by 100 talkers (i.e. a single occurrence of each digit per talker) was used. Half the talkers were male; half female. For testing the algorithm, we used the initial training set, as well as three other independent test sets with the following characteristics:

TS2 – the same 100 talkers as were used in the training; 100 occurrences of each digit

TS3 – a new set of 100 talkers (50 male, 50 female); 100 occurrences of each digit

TS4 – another new set of 100 talkers (50 male, 50 female); 100 occurrences of each digit.

The results of the recognition tests are given in the table below:

Recognizer Type	Evaluation Set			
	Original Training	TS2	TS3	TS4
LPC/DTW	0.1	0.2	2.0	1.1
LPC/DTW/VQ	–	3.5	–	–
HMM/VQ	–	3.7	–	–
HMM/CD	0	0.2	1.3	1.8

Average digit error rates for several recognizers and evaluation sets.

The recognizers were the following:

LPC/DTW – Conventional template-based recognizer using dynamic time warping (DTW) alignment

LPC/DTW/VQ – Conventional recognizer with vector quantization of the feature vectors ($M=64$)

HMM/VQ – HMM recognizer with $M=64$ codebook

HMM/CD – HMM recognizer using continuous density model with $M=5$ mixtures per state

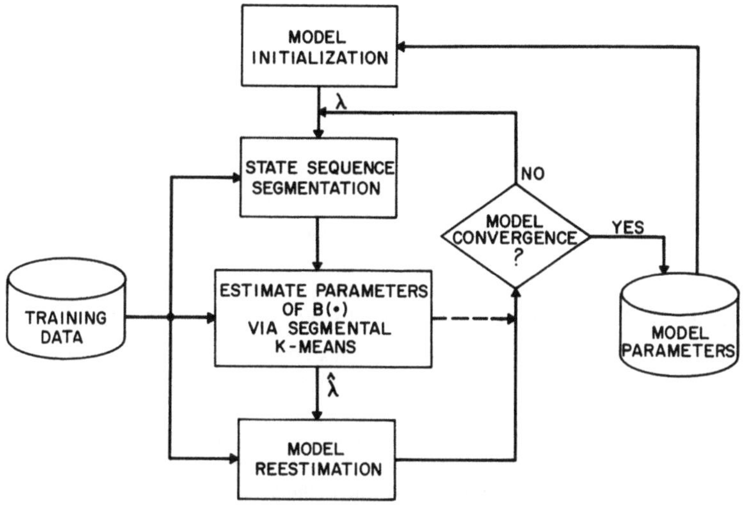

Fig. 7: The segmental *k*-means training procedure used to estimate parameter values for the optimal continuous mixture density fit to a finite number of observation sequences.

It can be seen that, when using a VQ, the performance of the isolated word recognizer degrades in both the conventional and HMM modes. It can also be seen that the performances of the conventional template-based recognizer, and the HMM recognizer with a continuous density model are comparable.

VII. CONNECTED WORD RECOGNITION USING HMM's

A somewhat more complicated problem of speech recognition, to which HMM's have been successfully applied, is the problem of connected word recognition. The basic premise of connected word recognition is that the recognition is based on individual word models (as opposed to models of speech units smaller than words which will be briefly discussed in the next section). Literally the recognition problem (once the appropriate word models have been derived) is to find the optimum sequence (concatenation) of word models that best matches (in a maximum likelihood sense) an unknown connected word string. In this section we discuss one method (called the level building approach) for solving for such optimum sequences of word models. For convenience, we restrict our discussion to the recognition of strings of connected digits.

VII.1 Connected Digit Recognition from Word HMM's Using Level Building

A block diagram of the overall level building connected digit recognizer is given in Fig. 8. There are essentially three steps in the recognition process, namely:

1. Spectral Analysis — the speech signal, $s(n)$, is converted to either a set of LPC vectors or a set of cepstral vectors. This defines the observation sequence, $\mathbf{O}$, of the unknown connected digit string.

2. Level Building Pattern Matching — The sequence of spectral vectors (the observations) of the unknown connected digit string is matched against the single word HMM's using a Viterbi scoring algorithm. The output of this process is a set of candidate digit strings, generally of different lengths (i.e. different number of digits per string), ordered by log probability scores.

3. Postprocessor — The candidate digit strings are subjected to further validity tests, e.g. duration, to eliminate unreasonable (unlikely) candidates. The postprocessor chooses the most likely digit string from the remaining (valid) candidate strings.

Individual digits are each characterized by an HMM of the type shown in Fig. 9. (Transitions between words are handled by a switch mode from the last state of one word model, to the first state of another word model, in the level building implementation.) The parameters of the HMM's used for characterizing digits are the following:

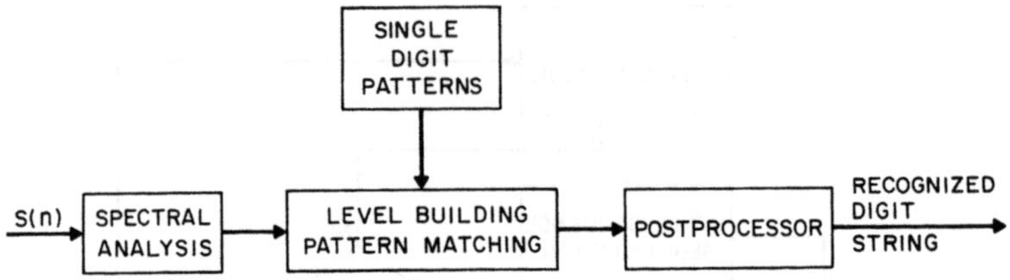

Fig. 8: Block diagram of level building, connected digit recognizer.

1. $N = 5$ or 8 states for digit models trained from observations of a single talker, and $N = 8$ or 10 states, for digit models trained from observations of several talkers.
2. Continuous mixture densities with $M = 3$ or 5 mixtures for single talker models and $M = 9$ mixtures for multiple talker models. (The observation vectors were cepstral coefficient vectors augmented by cepstral time derivatives of order 8 or 12.)
3. Energy probability, $p_j(\epsilon_t)$, where ϵ_t is the dynamically normalized log energy of the frame of speech used to give observation vector $\mathbf{O}_t$, and $p_j(\cdot)$ is a discrete density of log energy values in state j. The density is derived empirically from the training data.
4. State duration density, $p_j(d)$, $1 \leqslant d \leqslant D = 25$.

In addition to the observation density, log energy probability, and state duration density, each word HMM, λ^v, is also characterized by an overall word duration density, $p_v(D)$, of the form:

$$p_v(D) = \mathcal{N}(\overline{D}_v, \sigma_v^2) \tag{51}$$

where $\overline{D}_v$ is the average duration for word v, σ_v^2 is the variance in duration for word v, and $\mathcal{N}$ is the normal density.

VII.2 Level Building on HMM's

The way in which level building is used on HMM's is as follows. If we denote the set of V word HMM's as λ^v, $1 \leqslant v \leqslant V$, then to find the optimum sequence of HMM's that match $\mathbf{O}$ (i.e. maximize the likelihood), a sequence of Viterbi matches is performed. For each HMM, λ^v, and at each level, ℓ, we do a Viterbi match against $\mathbf{O}$, starting at frame (observation interval) 1 on level 1, and retain for each possible frame, t, the following:

1. $P_\ell^v(t)$, $1 \leqslant t \leqslant T$, the accumulated log probability to frame t, at level ℓ, for reference model λ^v, along the best path.
2. $F_\ell^v(t)$, $1 \leqslant t \leqslant T$, a backpointer indicating where the path started at the beginning of the level.

To compute $P_\ell^v(t)$, we need a local measure for the probability that observation $\mathbf{O}_t$, with log energy ϵ_t, occurred in state j of model λ^v. We use, as the observation density, the function:

$$\hat{b}_j^v(\mathbf{O}_t) = b_j^v(\mathbf{O}_t) \cdot [p_j^v(\epsilon_t)]^{\gamma_\epsilon} \cdot K_1 \tag{52}$$

where γ_ϵ (set to 0.375) is a log energy scaling coefficient and K_1 is a normalization constant. The state transition coefficients enter the calculation of $P_\ell^v(t)$ via the dynamic programming optimization in determining the Viterbi path.

At the end of each level, ℓ, (where the level corresponds to word position within the string), a maximization over v is performed to get the best model at each frame, t, as follows:

$$P_\ell^B(t) = \max_{1 \leqslant v \leqslant V} P_\ell^v(t), \qquad 1 \leqslant t \leqslant T \tag{53a}$$

$$W_\ell^B(t) = \operatorname*{argmax}_{1 \leqslant v \leqslant V} P_\ell^v(t), \qquad 1 \leqslant t \leqslant T \tag{53b}$$

$$F_\ell^B(t) = F_\ell^{W_\ell^B(t)}(t), \qquad 1 \leqslant t \leqslant T \tag{53c}$$

where $W_\ell^B(t)$ records the number of the word model which gave the best score at frame t, level ℓ, and $F_\ell^B(t)$ records the backpointer of the best word model.

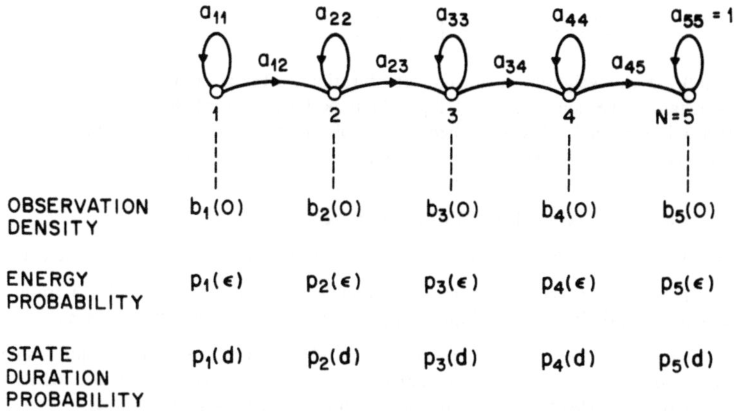

Fig. 9: HMM characterization of individual digits for connected digit recognition.

Each new level begins with the initial best probability at the preceding frame on the preceding level and increments the Viterbi score by matching the word models beginning at the new initial frame. This process is repeated through a number of levels equivalent to the maximum expected number of digits in any string (e.g. typically 7).

At the end of each level, a best string of size ℓ words ($1 \leqslant \ell \leqslant L$) with probability $P_\ell^B(T)$ is obtained by backtracking using the backpointer array $F_\ell^B(t)$ to give the words in the string. The overall best string is the maximum of $P_\ell^B(T)$ over all possible levels, ℓ.

VII.3 Training the Word Models

The key to success in connected word recognition is to derive word models from representative connected word strings. We have found that although the formal reestimation procedures developed in this paper work well, they are costly in terms of computation, and equivalently good parameter estimates can be obtained using a segmental K-means procedure of the type discussed in Section VI. The only difference in the procedure, from the one discussed earlier, is that the training connected word strings are first segmented into individual digits, via a Viterbi alignment procedure, then each set of digits is segmented into states, and the vectors within each state are clustered into the best M cluster solution. The segmental K-means reestimation of the HMM parameters is about an order of magnitude faster than the Baum-Welch reestimation procedure, and all our experimentation indicates that the resulting parameter estimates are essentially identical in that the resulting HMM's have essentially the same likelihood values. As such, the segmental K-means procedure was used to give all the results presented later in this section.

VII.4 Duration Modelling for Connected Digits

There are two forms of durational information used in scoring connected digit sequences, namely word duration and state duration. The way in which word duration information is incorporated into the model scoring is as follows. At the end of each level, for each frame, t, the accumulated probability $P_\ell^B(t)$ is modified by determining the word duration, $\tau_v(t)$, as

$$\tau_v(t) = t - F_\ell^B(t) + 1 \tag{54}$$

and then multiplying the accumulated probability by the word duration probability, i.e.

$$\hat{P}_\ell^v(t) = P_\ell^v(t) \cdot \left[\mathcal{N}(\tau_v(t), \bar{D}_v, \sigma_v^2)\right]^{\gamma_{wD}} \cdot K_2 \tag{55}$$

where γ_{wD} (set to 3.0) is a weighting factor on word durations and K_2 is a normalization constant.

State duration probabilities are incorporated in a postprocessor. The level building recognizer provides multiple candidates at each level (by tracking multiple best scores at each frame of each level). Hence overall probability scores are obtained for R^L strings of length L digits, where R is the number of candidates per level (typically $R = 2$). Each of the R^L strings is backtracked to give both individual words and individual states within the words. For an L-word string, if we denote the duration of state j at level ℓ as $\Delta_\ell(j)$, then, for each possible string, the postprocessor multiplies the overall accumulated probability, $P_L^b(T)$, by the state duration probabilities, giving

$$\hat{P}_L^B(T) = P_L^B(T) \cdot \prod_{\ell=1}^{L} \prod_{j=1}^{N} \left[p_j^{w(\ell)} \left(\Delta_\ell(j) \right) \right]^{\gamma_{sD}} \cdot K_3 \tag{56}$$

where γ_{sD} (set to 0.75) is a weighting factor on state durations, $w(\ell)$ is the word at level ℓ, and K_3 is a normalization constant. The computation of Eq. (56) is performed on all R^L strings, and a reordered list of best strings is obtained. The incremental cost of the postprocessor computation is negligible compared to the computation to give $P_L^B(T)$, and its performance has been shown to be comparable to the performance of the internal duration models.

VII.5 Performance of the Connected Digit HMM Recognizer

The HMM-based connected digit recognizer has been trained and tested in 3 modes, namely;

1. Speaker trained using 50 talkers (25 male, 25 female) each of whom provided a training set of about 500 connected digit strings and an independent testing set of 500 digit strings
2. Multispeaker in which the training sets from the 50 talkers above were merged into a single large training set, and the testing sets were similarly merged. In this case a set of 6 HMM's per digit was used, where each HMM was derived from a subset of the training utterances.
3. Speaker independent based on the TI training and testing databases. Both the training and testing sets had about 113 talkers (different ones were used in each set) and the talkers were divided into 10 dialectal groups. In this case a set of 4 HMM's per digit was used.

In each of the above databases there were variable length digit strings with from 1 to 7 digits per string.

The performance of the HMM connected digit recognizer, in these modes, is given in the following table:

	Training Set		Testing Set	
Mode	UL	KL	UL	KL
Speaker Trained (50 talkers)	0.4	0.16	0.8	0.35
Multispeaker (50 talkers)	1.7	1.0	2.85	1.65
Speaker Independent (225 talkers)	1.2	0.4	2.9	1.7

where the entries in the table are average string error rates for cases in which the string length was unknown apriori (UL), and for cases in which the string length was known apriori (KL). Results are given both for the training set (from which the word models) were derived), and for the independent test set.

VIII. HMM's FOR CONTINUOUS SPEECH RECOGNITION

Although HMM's have been successfully applied to problems in isolated and connected word recognition, the anticipated payoff of the theory, to problems in speech recognition, is in its application to continuous speech recognition — i.e. recognition of speech from basic speech units smaller than words. In this section we briefly outline the ideas of how HMM's can be applied to such a problem.

A block diagram of one type of a continuous speech recognition system is shown in Fig. 10. There are four key choices, in the recognition system, that must be made before we can see how HMM's can be applied to the problem. These choices include the following

1. Choice of sub-word unit — possibilities include acoustic-phonetic units (phoneme-like units), diphone or demi-syllable units, or syllable-like units. The less complex the unit (e.g. phoneme), the fewer of them there are in the language, and the more complicated (variable) their structure in continuous speech.
2. Choice of word model — possibilities include deterministic networks (state diagrams) with explicit representations of each word (and all variations on the word) in terms of the chosen sub-word unit; statistical networks (state diagrams) based on the chosen sub-word units; lexical access approaches (look-up of words in terms of standard phonetic units) from a stored dictionary.
3. Choice of syntax — possibilities include explicit state diagram of all word combinations; stochastic grammars (e.g. tri-gram word statistics); formal grammars with text parsing.

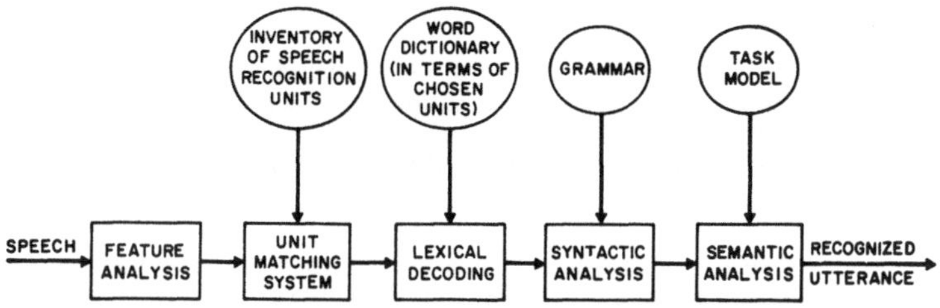

Fig. 10: Block diagram of a continuous speech recognizer based on sub-word speech units.

4. Choice of semantics — description of the task of the recognizer.

In the most advanced of systems, the theory of HMM's has been applied to each of the first three choices above, namely representation of phoneme-like sub-words as HMM's; representation of words as HMM's; and representation of syntax as an HMM. To solve the speech recognition problem, a triply embedded network of HMM's must be used. This leads to an expanded network with an astronomical number of equivalent states; hence an alternative to the complete, exhaustive search procedure is required. Such an alternative, called the stack algorithm, was devised and shown to be capable of handling such large networks in an efficient and reliable manner. Details of this approach are way beyond the scope of this paper.

In another attempt to apply HMM's to continuous speech recognition, an ergodic HMM was used in which each state represented an acoustic-phonetic unit. Hence about 40-50 states are required to represent all sounds of English. The model incorporated the variable duration feature in each state to account for the fact that vowel-like sounds have vastly different durational characteristics than consonant-like sounds. In this approach, lexical access was used in conjunction with a standard pronouncing dictionary to determine the best matching word sequence from the output of the sub-word HMM. Again the details of this recognition system are beyond the scope of this paper. The purpose of this brief discussion is to point out the vast potential of HMM's for characterizing the basic processes of speech production; hence their applicability to problems in continuous speech recognition.

IX. SUMMARY

In this paper we have attempted to present the theory of hidden Markov models from the simplest concepts (discrete Markov chains) to the most sophisticated models (variable duration, continuous density models). It has been our purpose to focus on physical explanations of the basic mathematics; hence we have avoided long, drawn out proofs and/or derivations of the key results, and concentrated primarily on trying to interpret the meaning of the math, and how it could be implemented in practice in real world systems. We have also attempted to illustrate some applications of the theory of HMM's to simple problems in speech recognition, and pointed out how the techniques could be (and have been) applied to more advanced speech recognition problems.

Acknowledgements:

The author gratefully acknowledges the major contributions of several colleagues to the theory of HMM's in general, and to the presentation of this paper, in particular. A great debt is owed to Drs. Jack Ferguson, Alan Poritz, Lou Liporice, Alan Richter, and to Fred Jelinek and the various members of the IBM group for introducing the speech world to the ideas behind HMM's. In addition Drs. Steve Levinson, Mohan Sondhi, Fred Juang, Amir Dembo and Yariv Ephraim have contributed significantly to both the theory of HMM's as well as the author's perspective and knowledge as to how the theory is best applied to problems of speech recognition.

BIBLIOGRAPHY ON HMM's

Markov Processes

1. A. W. Drake, "Discrete – State Markov Processes," Chapter 5 in *Fundamentals of Applied Probability Theory*, McGraw Hill Book Co, 1967.

Hidden Markov Model Theory

1. L. E. Baum, T. Petrie, G. Soules, and N. Weiss, "A Maximization Technique Occurring in the Statistical Analysis of Probabilistic Functions of Markov Chains," *Ann. Math. Stat.*, Vol. 41, No. 1, pp. 164-171, 1970.
2. L. E. Baum and J. A. Egon, "An Inequality with Applications to Statistical Estimation for Probabilistic Functions of a Markov Process and to a Model for Ecology," *Bull. AMS*, Vol. 73, pp. 360-363, 1967.
3. L. E. Baum and T. Petrie, "Statistical Inference for Probabilistic Functions of Finite State Markov Chains," *Ann. Math. Stat.*, Vol. 37, pp. 1554-1563, 1966.
4. L. E. Baum and G. R. Sell, "Growth Functions for Transformations on Manifolds," *Pac. J. Math.*, Vol. 27, No. 2, pp. 211-227, 1968.
5. L. E. Baum, "An Inequality and Associated Maximization Technique in Statistical Estimation for Probabilistic Functions of Markov Processes," *Inequalities*, Vol. 3, pp. 1-8, 1972.
6. A. P. Dempster, N. M. Laird, and D. B. Rubin, "Maximum Likelihood from Incomplete Data Via the EM Algorithm," *J. Royal Stat. Soc.*, Vol. 39, No. 1, pp. 1-38, 1977.
7. L. R. Rabiner and B. H. Juang, "An Introduction to Hidden Markov Models," *IEEE ASSP Magazine*, Vol. 3, No. 1, pp. 4-16, Jan. 1986.
8. S. E. Levinson, L. R. Rabiner, and M. M. Sondhi, "An Introduction to the Application of the Theory of Probabilistic Functions of a Markov Process to Automatic Speech Recognition," *Bell System Tech. J.*, Vol. 62, No. 4, pp. 1035-1074, April 1983.
9. L. A. Liporice, "Maximum Likelihood Estimation for Multivariate Observations of Markov Sources," *IEEE Trans. on Information Theory*, Vol./ IT-28, No. 5, pp. 729-734, 1982.
10. B. H. Juang, "On the Hidden Markov Model and Dynamic Time Warping for Speech Recognition – A Unified View," *AT&T Tech. J.*, Vol. 63, No. 7, pp. 1213-1243, September 1984.
11. B. H. Juang, S. E. Levinson, and M. M. Sondhi, "Maximum Likelihood Estimation for Multivariate Mixture Observations of Markov Chains," *IEEE Trans. on Information Theory*, Vol. IT-32, No. 2, pp. 307-309, March 1986.
12. B. H. Juang, "Maximum Likelihood Estimation for Mixture Multivariate Stochastic Observations of Markov Chains," *AT&T Tech. J.*, Vol. 64, No. 6, pp. 1235-1249, July-Aug. 1985.
13. L. R. Rabiner, B. H. Juang, S. E. Levinson, and M. M. Sondhi, "Some Properties of Continuous Hidden Markov Model Representations," *AT&T Tech. J.*, Vol. 64, No. 6, pp. 1251-1270, July-Aug. 1985.
14. A. B. Poritz, "Linear Predictive Hidden Markov Models and the Speech Signal," *Proc. ICASSP '82*, Paris, France, pp. 1291-1294, May 1982.
15. B. H. Juang and L. R. Rabiner, "Mixture Autoregressive Hidden Markov Models for Speech Signals," *IEEE Trans. on Acoustics, Speech, and Signal Proc.*, Vol. ASSP-33, No. 6, pp. 1404-1413, Dec. 1985.
16. S. E. Levinson, "Continuously Variable Duration Hidden Markov Models for Automatic Speech Recognition," *Computer, Speech and Language*, Vol. 1, No. 1, pp. 29-45, March 1986.
17. M. J. Russell and R. K. Moore, "Explicit Modeling of State Occupancy in Hidden Markov Models for Automatic Speech Recognition," *Proc. ICASSP-85*, Tampa, Florida, pp. 5-8, March 1985.
18. L. R. Bahl, P. F. Brown, P. V. de Souza, and R. L. Mercer, "Maximum Mutual Information Estimation of Hidden Markov Model Parameters for Speech Recognition," *Proc. ICASSP-86*, Tokyo, Japan, pp. 49-52, April 1986.
19. Y. Ephraim, A. Dembo, and L. R. Rabiner, "A Minimum Discrimination Information Approach for Hidden Markov Modeling," *Proc. ICASSP-87*, Dallas, Texas, April 1987.
20. F. Jelinek and R. L. Mercer, "Interpolated Estimation of Markov Source Parameters from Sparse Data," in *Pattern Recognition in Practice*, E. S. Gelesma and L. N. Kanal, Eds., North Holland, pp. 381-402, 1980.
21. B. H. Juang and L. R. Rabiner, "A Probabilistic Distance Measure for Hidden Markov Models," *AT&T Tech. J.*, Vol. 64, No. 2, pp. 391-408, Feb. 1985.

General Speech Recognition with VQ and HMM's

1. S. E. Levinson, "Structural Methods in Automatic Speech Recognition," *Proc. IEEE*, Vol. 73, No. 11, pp. 1625-1650, Nov. 1985.
2. J. Makhoul, S. Roucos, and H. Gish, "Vector Quantization in Speech Coding," *Proc. IEEE*, Vol. 73, No. 11, pp. 1551-1588, Nov. 1985.
3. J. S. Bridle, "Stochastic Models and Template Matching: Some Important Relationships Between Two Apparently Different Techniques for Automatic Speech Recognition," *Proc. Inst. of Acoustics*, Autum Conf., pp. 1-8, Nov. 1984.

Isolated Word Recognition Using HMM's

1. L. R. Rabiner, S. E. Levinsion, and M. M. Sondhi, "On the Application of Vector Quantization and Hidden Markov Models to Speaker-Independent Isolated Word Recognition," *Bell System Tech. J.*, Vol. 62, No. 4, pp. 1075-1105, April 1983.
2. L. R. Rabiner, S. E. Levinson, and M. M. Sondhi, "On the Use of Hidden Markov Models for Speaker-Independent Recognition of Isolated Words from a Medium-Size Vocabulary," *AT&T Tech. Journ.*, Vol. 63, No. 4, pp. 627-642, April 1984.
3. R. Billi, "Vector Quantization and Markov Source Models Applied to Speech Recognition," *Proc. ICASSP-82*, Paris, France, pp. 574-577, May 1982.
4. L. R. Rabiner, B. H. Juang, S. E. Levinson, and M. M. Sondhi, "Recognition of Isolated Digits Using Hidden Markov Models with Continuous Mixture Densities," *AT&T Tech. J.*, Vol. 64, No. 6, pp. 1211-1222, July-Aug. 1986.
5. A. B. Poritz and A. G. Richter, "Isolated Word Recognition," *Proc. ICASSP-86*, Tokyo, Japan, pp. 705-708, April 1986.

Connected Word Recognition Using HMM's

1. L. R. Rabiner, J. G. Wilpon, and B. H. Juang, "A Segmental *k*-Means Training Procedure for Connected Word Recognition," *AT&T Tech. J.*, Vol. 65, No. 3, pp. 21-31, May-June 1986.
2. L. R. Rabiner and S. E. Levinson, "A Speaker-Independent, Syntax-Directed, Connected Word Recognition System Based on Hidden Markov Models and Level Building," *IEEE Trans. on Acoustics, Speech, and Signal Processing*, Vol. ASSP-33, No. 3, pp. 561-573, June 1985.
3. L. R. Rabiner, J. G. Wilpon, and B. H. Juang, "A Model-Based Connected Digit Recognition System Using Either Hidden Markov Models or Templates," *Computer, Speech, and Language*, 1986.
4. H. Bourlard, Y. Kamp, H. Ney, and C. J. Wellekens, "Speaker-Dependent Connected Speech Recognition via Dynamic Programming and Statistical Methods," in *Speech and Speaker Recognition*, M. R. Schroeder, Ed., Karger, pp. 115-148, 1985.
5. C. J. Wellekens, "Global Connected Digit Recognition Using Baum-Welch Algorithm," *Proc. ICASSP-86*, Tokyo, Japan, pp. 1081-1084, April 1986.

Continuous Speech Recognition Using HMM's

1. L. R. Bahl, F. Jelinek, and R. L. Mercer, "A Maximum Likelihood Approach to Continuous Speech Recongition," *IEEE Trans. on Pattern Anal. and Machine Intell.*, Vol. PAMI-5, pp. 179-190, 1983.
2. F. Jelink, "Continuous Speech Recognition by Statistical Methods," *Proc. IEEE*, Vol. 64, pp. 532-536, April 1976.
3. J. K. Baker, "The Dragon System – An Overview," *IEEE Trans. on Acoustics, Speech, and Signal Processing*, Vol. ASSP-23, No. 1, pp. 24-29, Feb. 1975.
4. L. R. Bahl and F. Jelinek, "Decoding for Channels with Insertions, Deletions, and Substitutions with Applications to Speech Recognition," *IEEE Trans. Information Theory*, Vol. IT-21, pp. 404-411, 1975.
5. F. Jelinek, "A Fast Sequential Decoding Algorithm Using a Stack," *IBM J. Res. and Devel.*, Vol. 13, pp. 675-685, 1969.
6. F. Jelinek, L. R. Bahl, and R. L. Mercer, "Continuous Speech Recognition: Statistical Methods," in *Handbook of Statistics, II*, P. R. Krishnaiad, Ed., North Holland, 1982.
7. F. Jelinek, L. R. Bahl, and R. L. Mercer, "Design of a Linguistic Statistical Decoder for the Recognition of Continuous Speech," *IEEE Trans. on Information Theory*, Vol. IT-21, pp. 250-256, 1975.
8. S. E. Levinson, "Continuous Speech Recognition by Means of Acoustic-Phonetic Classification Obtained from a Hidden Markov Model," *Proc. ICASSP-87*, Dallas, Texas, April 1987.

COMPUTER RECOGNITION OF SPOKEN LETTERS AND DIGITS

Renato De Mori

McGill University, School of Computer Science
Centre de recherche informatique de Montréal, inc.
Montréal (Québec) Canada

1. INTRODUCTION

Recent results on *Automatic Speech Recognition* (ASR) and Speech Analysis suggest that progress in designing recognition devices and in advancing speech science knowledge may arise from an integration of the so called *cognitive* and *information-theoretic* approaches/LEVINSON 85/.

The cognitive approach attempts to infer analytic knowledge about possible speech invariants and their relations. Work by Zue /ZUE 85/, Klatt /KLATT 77/, Stevens /STEVENS 80/ and De Mori et al./DEMORI 79, 83/ are along this line.

The information theoretic approach is based on a performance model containing states and transitions between any pair of states /BAHL 83/. Probabilities can be learned that the system is in any of the model states or is changing state through any of the allowed transitions. Furthermore, the model generates in each state or in each transition, observable system parameters or descriptors according to some statistical distribution.

This chapter proposes an attempt to integrate the two above mentioned approaches.

The idea is that of extracting speech properties using *knowledge* about acoustic correlates of linguistic units. For an abstract linguistic unit, the corresponding acoustic correlates have attributes which may differ from an instantiation to another due to the fact that different speakers produce different signals even if they intend to pronounce the same sound. Attribute statistics of sound properties collected on a large variety of pronounciations of the same sound from different speakers are probably the best knowledge we can gather today for characterizing different speaking styles. Furthermore, some expected acoustic properties can be missed in some cases and some unexpected properties can be detected in some other cases. These aspects can also be characterized by stochastic performance models.

An important problem arising when large vocabularies have to be recognized is that of identifying a possibly small set of *Speech Units* (SU) with which all the possible words and word concatenations can be obtained by *compilation*. The learning problem is then reconducted to the conception of a performance model for each SU.

The model proposed in this paper has a *data-driven* component that identifies *Acoustic Segments* (AS) based only on acoustic evidence and knowledge of the information bearing

NATO ASI Series, Vol. F46
Recent Advances in Speech Understanding
and Dialog Systems
Edited by H. Niemann et al.

properties corresponding to different spectral structures. An Acoustic Segment usualy contains at least a "vocalic" part identifed by resonancies reprensented by narrow band spectral lines in a time-frequency-energy representation of speech. An AS may contain one or more vowels with one or more consonants in the "vocalic" part. An AS may also have a *head* and a *tail.*. Heads and tails may contain low energy sonorant consonants or consonants characterized by frication noise or by a transition between a deep dip in the signal energy curve and an energy peak.

The coarse acoustic properties that characterie ASs and are used for delimiting them are by no means *interpretations,* they are just elements for *focusing the attention* of the property extractors. Relations between ASs and SUs like phonemes, diphones of syllables are established by *performance models* representing, for each SU of interest, insertions, deletions, substitutions and their statistics.

As unambiguous segmentation of continuous speech into ASs is very useful for reducing the complexity of word hypotheses generation and verification because word hypotheses can start only a specific time instants of the head, vocalic part or tail of an AS.

For the head, vocalic part and tail of each AS, plans of property extraction *operators* (procedures) are executed. These plans produce descriptions of speech segments. These descriptions may apply to segments of *variable duration.* Ferguson /FERGUSON 80/ has shown how performance models can be build under the assumption that properties generated by a model have variable duration. Plans producing descriptions perform a sort of *Variable Depth Analysis* (VDA) because they may generate different types of properties for different segments.

The results of VDA can be *descriptors* obtained by a sort of "Knowledge-based vector quantizer". They can also be Speech Unit hypotheses affected by a certain score. These scores that are generated by procedures are used by performance models consisting in stochastic automata relating words and SUs.

Unfortunately there is not a suitable theory for the conception of performance models in such a case, but an interesting research is in progress /HARALICK/. Such research is motivated by the existence of a similar problem in different application areas /SHAPIRO 86, BAIRD 86/. While waiting for a probabilistic theory of hetereogeneous pattern descriptions, a pseudo solution can be adopted where word hypotheses scores are obtained by just multiplying probabilities or scores of each segment even if the type of acoustic properties may vary from segment to segment.

The validity of this approach has been tested on a multispeaker task consisting in the recognition of sequences of letter and digits with a short pause between any pair of them. This vocabulary is defined in Table I.

2. A MODEL FOR COMPUTER PERCEPTION OF SPEECH

The speech signal $x_1(t)$ is *generated* by a discreted and finite sequence of actions

$$A = a_1(t_1)\, a_2(t_2)\, a_3(t_3) \ldots\ldots a_t(t_k) \ldots\ldots a_K(t_K) \qquad (1)$$

where $a_k(t_k)$ denotes an action ending at time t_k ; $a_1(t_1)$ represents the silence preceding the beginning of a sentence.

When a person reads a sentence S, a relation

$$R_1(S, A) \qquad (2)$$

is applied which produces A. The relation R_1 may depend on the speaker, his/her mood, state of health and history. As R_1 may produce several As for the same S, probability distributions for all the possible As can be derived using a generative model.

The speech signal $x_1(t)$ is generated by the sequence of actions A using another relation

$$R_2(A, x_1(t)) \qquad (3)$$

R_2 depends on the anatomy of the speaker. Again, the same actions may produce different signals, because the speech production system is soft and its behavior is affected to some extent by the environment.

If the speaker does not read but generates a sentence from a set C of concetps, then a third relation is applied :

$$R_3(C, S) \qquad (4).$$

R_3 may depend on the speaker and his/her culture. Statistical models can also be used for characterizing this relation.

The generation of $x_1(t)$ can be seen as the application of the following composite relation :

$$G = R_3 \, o R_1 \, o R_2 \tag{5}$$

according to the scheme shown in Figure 1.

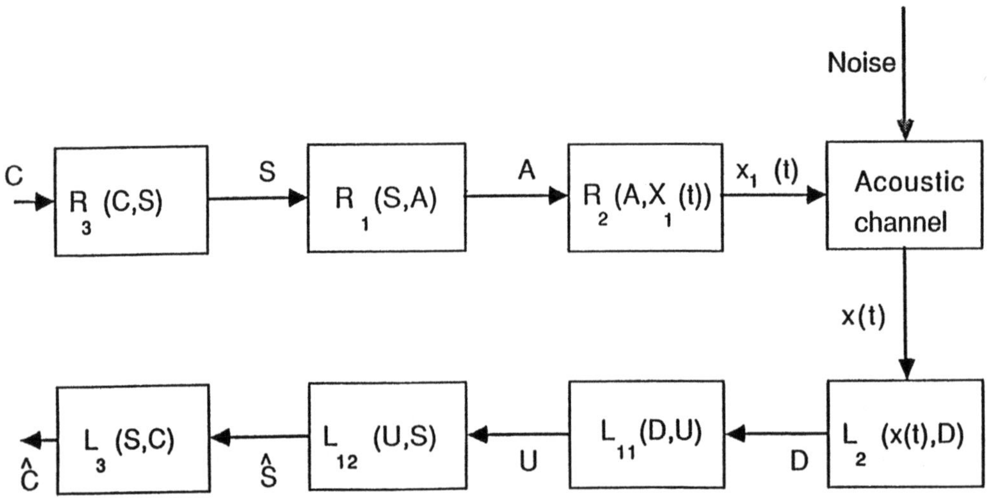

Fig. 1 Speech Communication Channel

Recognition consists in applying the relations in the opposite direction. Unfortunateley we have only a limited knowledge of these relations. We have used it for building speech synthesizers. We do not even know the alphabet $\Sigma_A \{a_k\}$for the elements of A, although we know alphabets Σ_c and Σ_s for the elements of C and S respectively. Furthermore, signal $x_1(t)$ is affected by noise and is transformed into another signal $x(t)$ through the acoustic channel.

As we do not know Σ_A , nor we know R_2 , we can characterize actions by *descriptions* of what they produce. According to this approach, the *perception* of $x(t)$ consists in extracting a sequence of descriptions :

$$D = d_1(\tau_1)\, d_2(\tau_2) \ldots d_i(\tau_i) \ldots d_I(\tau_I) \tag{6}$$

where $d_1(\tau_1)$ describes the silence preceeding the beginning of the speech signal and $d_i(\tau_i)$

describes the segment of *x(t)* between the time instants τ_{i-1} and τ_i .

Segments of *D* can be 10 msecs. frames or intervals of variable duration obtained by a segmentation algorithm like the one proposed in /DE MORI 85/.

The descriptions *D* can be obtained by *perceptual actions* in analogy with the generative scheme. Perceptual actions, as well as generative actions have to be defined and used according to a creterion of economy. That is, there must be a limited number of actions (operators) based on which a variety of networks of actions can be built.

Recognition can be seen as a combination of a relation

$$L_2 (D,S) \tag{7}$$

that is the perceptual counterpart of relation R_1 used for speech generation, and a relation :

$$L_2\left(x\left(t\right),D\right) \tag{8}$$

that is the perceptual counterpart of $R_2\left(A,x,\left(t\right)\right)$

The relation $L_2\left(x\left(t\right),D\right)$ is *deterministic* in the sense that it can produce only one description of *D* for a signal *x(t)*. Description *D* is a sequence of descriptive phrases. Each phrase can be of *fixed duration,* i.e. generated at constant time intervals, or of *variable duration,* i.e. generated for intervals of different length. If we want to maintain the analogy with the production model just outlined, *D* should be of variable duration because the articulatory actions (gestures) are of variable duration.

Descriptions must refer to paramemers, morphologies and properties that are characteristic for a sound and exhibit low variances when many speakers, different microphones and environments are considered.

In practice, fixed duration models have been developed and tested with a considerable degree of success mostly in speaker-dependent systems. In one of the most successful systems developed so far /JELINEK 84/, *D* is a sequence of symbols obtained every 10 msecs. by *vector-quantization* with a process that is speaker-dependent and context-independent.

Relation L_1 *(D,S)* has to capture two different types of knowledge. The first type of knowledge is a relation :

$$L_{11}\left(D,U\right) \tag{9}$$

between a sequence U of *Speech Units* (SU) and corresponding description D. There are speech units like the plosive soud /b/ for which a large variety of different descriptions D are perceived as the *same sound.* Relation L_{11} is many-to-one and it could be interesting to collect statistics of the elements of the universe of acoustic descriptions that produce the perception of the same linguistic sound. These statistics may represent distribution of acoustic patterns produced by a single or many speakers having the intention of producing the same sound. Statistics may also take into account characteristics of background noise.

The choice of SUs, for our purpose, has to be based on practical considerations as well as on theoretical ones. For example, for some purposes, units can be just phone classes or syllable classes.

The introduction of SUs is important because once a vocabulary Σ_U of speech units has been chosen and effective relations between each $SU \in \Sigma_U$ and descriptions of acoustic properties have been established, large varieties of word and sentence models can be built by *compiling* networks of SU models.

A second type of knowledge is a relation :

$$L_{12}(U,S) \tag{10}$$

where S is a linguistic entity like a sentence and U is a sequence of Speech Units. L_{12} can also contain statistics. L_{12} may represent how *different* speakers may have different pronounciations of the *same* word. A stochastic model representing a word W in terms of SUs can be built.

An interesting possibility, we would like to explore in this paper, is that of designing L_2 and L_1 *procedurally*, through actions to be performed on $x(t)$ in order to obtain D,U and S.

Knowledge-based extraction and interpretation of signal properties has proven to be very effective when interpretation can benefit from contextual relations /NI 82/.

Descriptions D of different level of detail (depth) can be obtained depending on model expectations or the already available context. Feedback is also possible between relations, although it has not been implemented in the application described in this paper.

It seems that *variable depth descriptions* can be very useful in complex tasks where a preliminary selection of hypotheses has to be done based on robust but simple descriptions and then a more detailed analysis has to be performed involving levels of depth depending on the competing hypotheses or on acoustic evidence.

The entire perception model can be represented by *procedural networks* which invoke subnetworks at several levels.

Building procedural networks is an activity of *conditional planning*. Waldinger /WALDINGER 77/ discusses elementary planning techniques and conditional planning. An introduction to the use of planning techniques for ASR is described in /DE MORI 87/.

The most general procedural network has to operate along *two* dimensions using acoustic properties extracted in different time intervals and at different levels of detail. It will be shown in the following Sections how these capabilities can be implemented.

In order to perform variable depth analysis, a context in which the analysis is performed has to be defined. Algorithms were proposed in the past for segmenting continuous speech into Pseudo-Syllabic-Segments /DE MORI 85/. Although these algorithms have shown good performances in different tasks and for varieties of speakers, they were not error free in segmenting the speech signal into syllables. The principal reason for these errors was that segmentation was based only on *acoustic evidence. Acoustic Segments* (AS), obtained by segmentation algorithms based on acoustic properties, have to be treated as data rather than interpretations. Being based on acoustic evidences, ASs can be used for driving and delimiting the extraction of more detailed acoustic properties or as anchors for lexical access in continuous speech.

Once an AS has been delimited, a *Procedural Network* (PN) is invoked to further segment it into *intervals* and to generate scored SU hypotheses on each interval. Scored SU hypotheses are used by word models that consider possible distortions, insertions and deletions.

Figure 2 shows a short *performance model* for the word W.

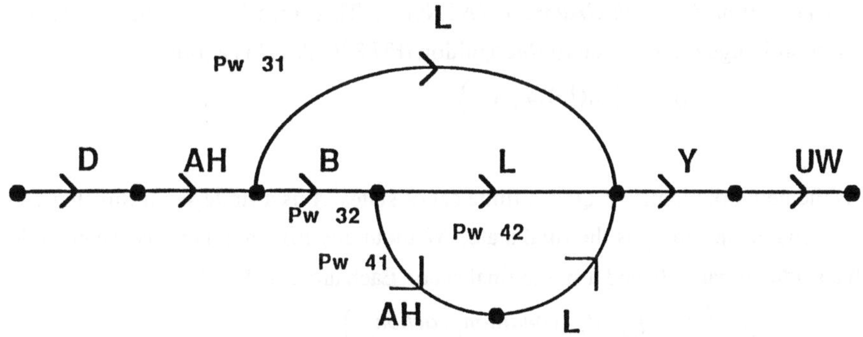

Fig. 2

For the sake of simplicity, the alphabet Σ_U is made equal to the ARPABET (see./KLATT 77/).

In practice less detailed models suffice for recognizing the vocabulary defined in Table I.

Table I The 36 word vocabulary

Zero	One	Two	Three
Four	Five	Six	Seven
Eight	Nine	A	B
C	D	E	F
G	H	I	J
K	L	M	N
O	P	Q	R
S	T	U	V
W	X	Y	Z

3. PROCEDURAL NETWORKS

A Procedural Network (*PN*) can be described with a formalism similar to that used for an *Augmented Transition Network Grammar* (ATNG). This formalism has been successfully used for Natural Language and Pattern Recognition /FU 82/. A PN is a 5-tuple

$$\mathrm{PN} = \left\{ j, Q, A, q_0, q_f \right\} \tag{11}$$

where j is the network identifier, Q is a finite set of states, A is a finite set of directed arcs, $q_0 \in Q$ is the initial state and q_f is the final state. Without any loss of generality we consider on PNs with a single initial state and a single final state. Each arc $a_i \in A$ is a 5-tuple :

$$a_i = \left(q_{bi}, q_{ei}, P_i, condition_i, action_i \right) \tag{12}$$

where $q_{bi} \in Q$ is the starting state of a_i, $q_{ei} \in Q$ is the terminal state of a_i, P_i is a measure associated to the arc (it can be a weight or a probability according to the scoring method used by the PN supervisor described later on), $condition_i$ is a condition and $action_i$ is an action; both of them are associated to the arc.

More details on Procedural Networks can be found in the chapter by E. Merlo in this volume.

Each *PN* is associated a Working Memory (WM). Actions associated with the arcs of a subnetwork produce descriptions or evaluate scores that are stored into the subnetwork WM. When a push to a subnetwork is made, the supervisor may link the subnetwork WM with other WM, thus establishing the *viewpoint* within which conditions are tested. Data are transferred between PNs through WMs.

Most of the actions associated with arc include plans, *Hidden-Markov-Models* (HMM), Local parsers , rule-based inference units. All these tools are used for extracting an unambiguous description D of a speech pattern and for computing an a-priori probability for an hypothesis H :

$$P\,(D\,/\,H) \tag{13}$$

The *PN* supervisor keeps up to date a search space where each node is represented by the following four-tuple :

$$(\,q\,,\,context\,,T\,,\ score\ ) \tag{14}$$

where :

-q is a state of the *PN* , with a buffer containing the information propagated by the actions executed before reaching it,

- *context* is the context (viewpoint) in which the conditions and actions of the arcs starting at q have to be executed,

- T is the starting time of the speech signal for the execution of sensory procedures invoked by the actions associated withe the arcs starting at q ,

- *score* is the score of the hypothesis contained in or implied by *context* in a time interval ending at T ; score could be $P(D(t_\phi T)\,/\,H)$ where t_ϕ is the beginning of the sentence. T could also be a set of possible time references; in this case, *score* will be a set of scores $\{s(t)\,/ \in T\}$. Composite scores can be evaluated as likelihoods :

$$L\,(D\,,H\,) = Pr\,(D\,/\,H\,)Pr\,(H\,) \tag{15}$$

where $Pr\,(H\,)$ is obtained by a language model.

The size of the search space can be kept small in spite of a large number of states in the *PN* if conditions and actions are properly chosen and placed in the network.

4. AN EXAMPLE OF APPLICATION

Lets assume we want to characterize sequences of letters and digits according to the lexicon defined in Table I with a little pause between them. Let us also assume we want to represent knowledge that is speaker-independent.

The *PN* conceived for this purpose is based on a *data-driven* approach (action execution is decided based on data) and has several levels.

The highest level, is represented in Fig. 3. It consists of a "push" arc to a subnetwork LEX representing the lexicon. The arc following state $S\,\phi\,1$ in Figure 4 is associated with a PUSH

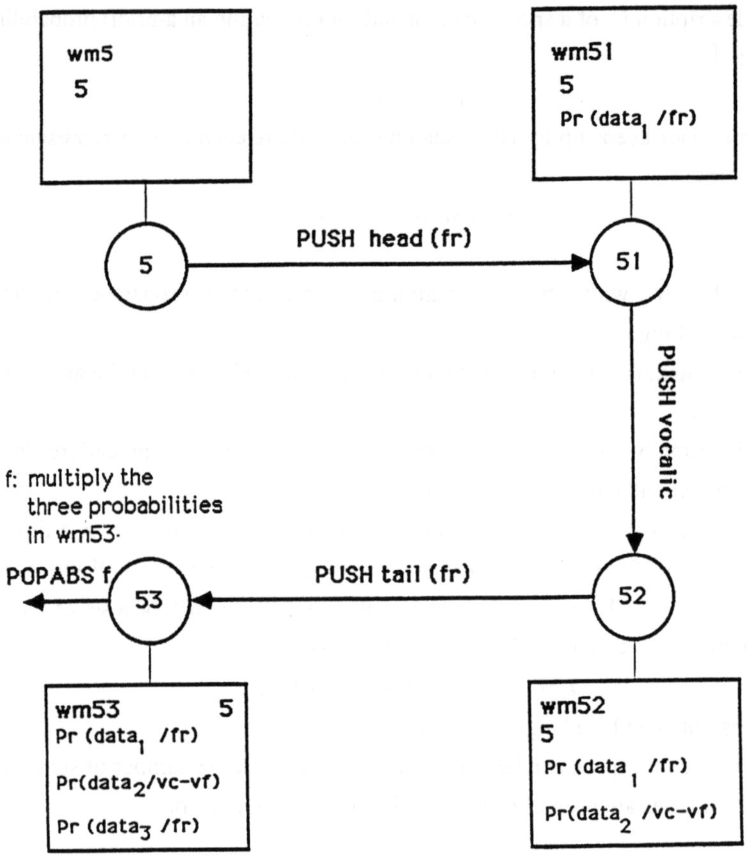

Fig. 3

action to a subnetworks that returns the probability of having a PAUSE after the just analyzed AS. From state $S\ \phi\ 2$ an iterative jump to state $S\ \phi$ under the condition "not-end" represents the fact that there is still a part of the input signal to be analyzed; otherwise the recognition process will stop on the execution of a POBABS arc with a stop function associated to it.

The subnetwork LEX, is shown in Figure 4.

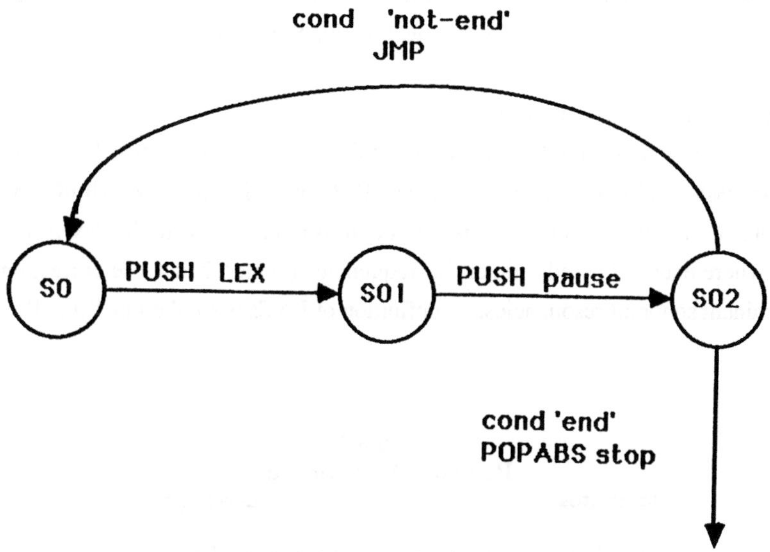

Fig. 4

It is subdivided into three subnetworks depending on the number of ASs detected per word. A subnetwork ASH for generating SU hypotheses for each AS is shown in Fig. 5. Two subnetworks similar to the one in Fig. 5 are available for words with 2 ASs. Three subnetworks are used for words with three ASs.

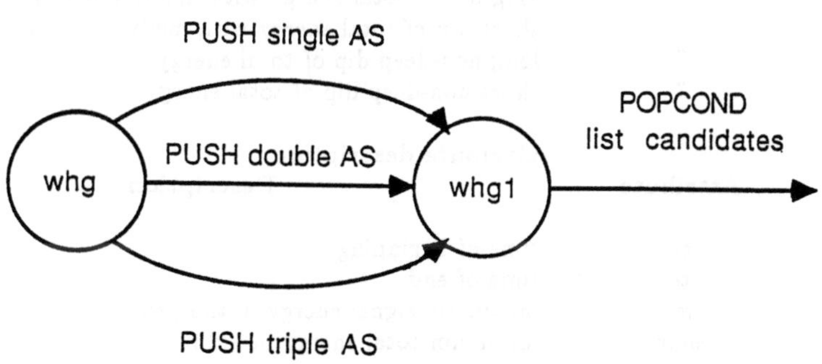

Fig. 5

ASH subnetwork uses actions for analyzing the "head", the "vocalic part" and the "tail" of each AS. The AS head is analyzed by *attached procedures* (actions) performing an *Elaboration-Decision* (ED) paradigm. Let us call these types of procedures *ED-actions*. Ed-actions perform *variable-depth analysis* on intervals of AS and will be described in the next Section. There are two possible ED-actions for the head of an AS, namely :

- plosive head
- fricative (including afficate) head

The choice of ED action is made by disjoint conditions associated to arcs. These conditions are regular expressions of *Primary Acoustic Cues* (PAC) intruduced in /DE MORI 85/. PACs are descriptions of the time evolution of speech loudness combined with the description of speech intervals where energy is predominant in frequencies greater than those corresponding to the most prominent sonorant resonancies. A definition of PACs is recalled in Table II.

Table II
Primary Acoustic Cues

Symbol	**Attributes**	**Description**
LPK	tb,te,ml,zx,	long peak of total energy (TE)
SPK	"	short peak of TE
MPK	"	peak of TE of medium duration
LOWP	"	low energy peak of TE
LNS	tb,te,zx	long nonsonorant tract
MNS	"	medium nonsonorant tract
LVI	tb,te,ml,zx	long vocalic tract adjacent to a LNS or a MNS in a TE peak
MVI	tb,te,ml,zx	medium vocalic tract adjacent to a LNS or a MNS in a TE peak
LDD	emin,tb,te,zx	short deep dip of total energy
LMD	"	long dip of total energy with medium depth
SMD	"	short dip of total energy with medium depth
LHD	"	long non-deep dip of total energy
SHD	"	short non-deep dip of total energy

Attribute description

Attribute	**Description**
tb	time of beginning
te	time of end
ml	maximum signal energy in the peak
emin	minimum total energy in a dip
zx	maximum zero-crossing density of the signal derivative in the tract

A *data-driven* process DDP1 performs signal acquisition, *Fast-Fourier Transformation* (FFT), signal description in terms of PACs and segmentation of the speech signal into ASs. For each AS a process is created that instantiates ASH.

For the AS for which an ASH instantiation has been created, the signal, its FFT and the PAC description are stored into the WM associated to the ASH instantiation.

Condition "pl-head" is a regular expression of PACs corresponding to acoustic morphologies that are cues for plosive sounds.

The condition "fr-head" is analogous but it contains morphologies that are cues for fricative sounds. If none of the two above mentioned conditions is verified, there the *default* condition is satisfied. State M1 in Fig. 6 will be reached by only one arc. As it will be seen later, the ED action for the AS head identifies the AS head as a possible acoustic subsegment and extracts some acoustic properties. Using techniques partially described elsewhere /DE MORI 87/,

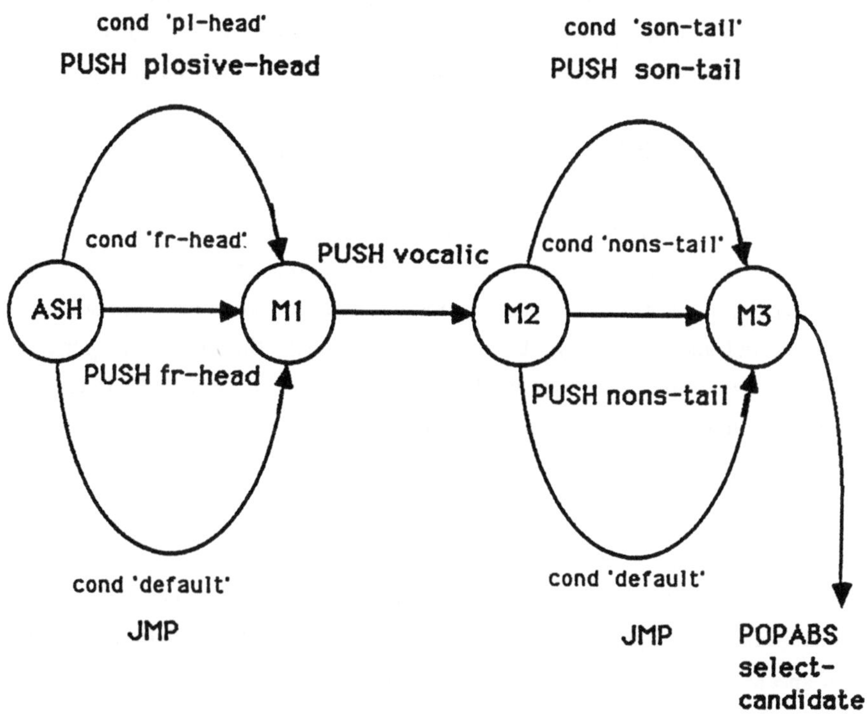

Fig. 6

hypotheses about the place and manner of articulation for the speech unit in the head subsegment are generated and scored by the following a-priori probability :

$$Prh = Pr \{data (h) / place \cap manner \} \tag{16}$$

"place is a variable that takes values in the following set :

$$PLset = \{labial, front, central back\} \quad (17)$$

"manner" is a variable that take values in the following set :

MNset = {high-vowel, low-vowel, oral, nasal, unvoiced, voiced-nonsonorant }
(18).

The description data(h) contains acoustic properties the system knowledge considers worth to be extracted given the suprasegmental characteristics of the head subsegment. These properties can be broad-band spectral energies for a fricative head or transient descriptors for a plosive head.

In the case of letters and digits, the place and manner of articulation are not identified separately. Speech Units hypothesized by head actions are phoneme symbols, when they are important for recognizing the letter or the digit. For example, only the head actions can distinguish between P,B,T,G and all the letters beginning by a consonant and ending with the same wvowel. In this case the consonants are SU hypothesized by the head process. For the letters or the digits beginning with a vowel, it is not the head action that has the proper knowledge for distinguishing among vowels, thus a generic "vocalic" SU is hypothesized for all these words.

For each head action, suitable acoustic properties are extracted and a-priori probabilities are collected in a learning phase for concatenations of acoustic properties corresponding to each SU symbol that can be hypothesized as an AS head.

For example, "plosive head" executes a network of actions described in /DE MORI 87/. These actions extract a number of acoustic properties and produce hypotheses not only about plosive sounds but also about any SU (including "vocalic") that may have generated the observed properties. After state M1, the ED-action "vocalic" is executed. It segments the vocalic part of AS into stationary and transient units.

Let

$$v_1 \, v_2 \, ...v_x \, ...v_X$$

be such subsegments. For each segment v_x spectral lines are considered as data (see/MERLO 86/ for details) and a-priori probabilities about place and manner of articulation are obtained by HMMs of spectral lines in the segment v_x . For each subsegment and for each consistent "place-manner" pair, the following probability is computed.

$$Pr\left(v_x\right) = Pr\left(data\left(v_x\right) / place \cap manner\right) \quad (19)$$

From state M2 to state M3, ED-actions for the tail of AS are executed similar to those used for the head.

5. ACOUSTIC PROPERTIES, PHONETIC FEATURES AND PLANS

This section describes how relations of phonetic features to acoustic properties are embedded in *plans* which are executed by the expert system. With this approach a phoneme PH_i is expressed by a set of phonetic features, i.e.

$$PH_i = \left(pf_{i1}, pf_{i2}, \ldots, pf_{ij}, \ldots pf_{iJ}\right)$$

Each phonetic feature pf_x is represented by a relation R_x to a set of acoustic properties ap_x, i.e.

$$pf_x = R_x\left(ap_{x1}, ap_{x2}, \ldots ap_{xk}, \ldots ap_{xK}\right)$$

For example, the phoneme / p / is represented as follows :
/ p / = (nonsonorant-interrupted-consonant,tense,labial) = (nit,labial).

The phonetic feature "labial" in the context of "nit" features is represented by the following relation R_k :

(*relation* R_k
(*left-side*
(*feature* (labial))
    (*feature context* (nit))
    (*temporal context* (*followed-by* front vowel)))
(*right-side*
(suprasegmental and time-domain properties)
(formant-transition properties)
(burst--spectra properties)))

The rule for "labial" takes into account different types of *contextual dependencies* . One contextual dependency is represented by the other features that appear with "labial" in a plosive phoneme. The other contextual dependences are represented by the class of phonemes that can follow or precede the plosive phoneme under consideration. Relations are used by *plans* executed by the expert system. In many cases, acoustic property extraction is context dependent; for example, we may be forced to impose precedence relations on the extraction processes. For more on the latter, we refer the reader to/DEMICHELIS 83/ and /KOPEC 84/.

A *plan* is a sequence of items. Each item may contain a *precondition expression* for applying rules of the type R_k, *operators* containing sensory procedures, for extracting the properties used by R_k, and an *algorithm* for evaluating the evidence of the hypothesis generated by R_k.

The operators of plans are signal processing and property extraction algorithms. Property extraction can be organized as a hierarchy of actions. Important material on hierarchical planning and networks of action hierarchical planning and networks of action hierarchies may be found in STEFIK 80/ and /SACERDOTI 75/. Actions can be associated with *constrains* that have to be verified in order for an action to be executable. For example, an action may consist in the extraction of buzz descriptors can be extracted only in time intervals where the speech loudness curve has deep dips. Once a network of actions has been conceived, constraints of actions are propagated backward and upward and used for setting *preconditions* . Action hierarchies are executed through *elaboration-decision* cycles. During the *elaboration phase* a set of executable actions is performed. Actions may result in the generation of *objects* or in the updating of existing objects. Objects are data structures containing structured descriptions of segments of signal to be interpreted. During the *decision phase* all the actions that can be executed in the next elaboration phase are considered.

6. THE ELABORATION-DECISION PARADIGM

This section discusses how the objective of producing accurate descriptions of essential properties of speech segments can be achieved through a Network of Action Hierarchies /SACERDOTI 75/. Actions to be performed for recognition are selected using the *elaboration-decision* paradigm /LAIRD 84/. Elaboration may involve the execution of sensory procedures or of inferences that will provide information about the signal to be interpreted.

Actions can consist of the generation of phonemic hypotheses based on decision table or of the execution of other elaboration-decision cycles.

Decisions are controlled by rules obtained during a planning phase with *inductive learning*.

The execution of an action of the hierarchy may be conditioned by the verification of some events called *precondition* and may consist in the application of a terminal decision-making *operator* or in the activation of a more detailed sequence of actions belonging to a lower level of the hierarchy. In such a case, the node of the hierarchy that will be expanded into a more detailed plan is considered to represent an *abstract action*.

The hierarchy of actions is executed according to the following algorithm :

```
action hierarchy execution algorithm
      begin
         next-action :=spontaneous activities;
         elaboration-decision (next-action)
      end
procedure elaboration-decision (next-action)
      begin
         elaboration-phase (next-action)
         decision-phase (rule set (next-action), result)
            ration-decision (new-action)
      else the most detailed descriptions or hypotheses
         are generated
      end
```

During the *elaboration phase* , a sequence of operators corresponding to the action chosen in the previous decision cycle is applied in a specific context. The execution of such a subplan (action) may result in the generation of structured descriptions of acoustic properties called *objects* or in the updating of existing objects.

Objects are part of a network of data descriptions called the *Data Description Network* (DDN).

7. DEVELOPMENT OF PERCEPTUAL PLANS

This section describes methodologies and tools that have been developed in order to build in a semiautomatic manner the Network.

The design of a Network for ASR is a planing activity where refinements are decided based on recognition confusions that are considered unacceptable. Refinement is seen as the expansion of an action into a more detailed plan. In such a case the action that is expanded will be seen as an abstract one.

Interesting planning systems are proposed in recent literature. A report by Stefik /STEFIK 80/ critically compares existing systems and discusses the differences between HEARSAY II /ERMAN 80/, one of the most popular knowledge-based speech understanding systems developed so far, and hierarchical systems as the one proposed in this paper.

A paper by Wilkins /WILKINS 83/ discusses the major problems in automatic planning and points out the advantages of an evolutionary approach to planning especially in large real-world problems. Such an evolutionary approach allows interaction with users throughout the planning and plan execution processes. Our approach belongs to this category as, indeed, it has to deal with a real-world problem. Reasoning about actions, a core problem in planning, is rather peculiar in our case. In fact, actions produce *descriptions of speech signals* that are expected to *discriminate* among segments corresponding to different sounds. The discrimination power of a description cannot be predicted; it has to be evaluated by experiements.

The evolution of a plan goes through the following cycle :

```
plan evolution cycle
begin
        definition of spontaneous activities for extracting
            descriptions for precondition #1
    repeat
            perform experiments;
            learning and generalization;
            elimination of actions producing descriptions
                ruled out by generalization;
            refinement for discriminating cases that remain
```

confused after learning;

until discrimination is satisfactory for a large population of speakers

end

The new actions are actually decided and implemented by a human expert who uses the planning and the learning programs. He bases his decision on his knowledge, the type of patterns that require better discriminant descriptions and the statistics of the ambiguous descriptions of these patterns as obtained by the available system.

A *Plan Generation Expert System* (PGES), written in OPS5 /BROWNSTON 85/ contributes to producing the Network of Actions. It uses speech knowledge for suggesting acoustic properties that can solve a problem in a given context (for example {b, d} distinction in the absence of burst evidence). PGES uses also Speech Knowledge and proposes signal processing algorithms (operators) for extracting suggested acoustic properties. Constraints are associated by PGES to operators. A final phase of *constraint satisfaction* is performed by PGES which produces a plan as an acceptable sequence of operators useful for refining a plan which produced descriptions with unsatisfactory discrimination power.

8. SOME DETAILS OF THE RECOGNITION PROCESS

The speech signal is first analyzed on the basis of loudness, zero-crossing rates and broad-band energies as described in /DE MORI 85/. The result of this analysis is a string of symbols and attributes. Symbol belong to an alphabet of Primary Acoustic Cues.

The use of coarse acoustic properties (PAC) for segmenting continuous speech into acoustic segments has been described in a previous paper /DE MORI 85/. The segmentation algorithm based on an attributed grammar has been simplified, in such a way that a preliminary segmentation is performed first based only on signal energy deep dips and frication intervals. Each *acoustic segment* obtained in this way may contain one or more syllables but it never contains less than one vowel. Each acoustic segment could be further described following the scheme shown in Fig. 7.

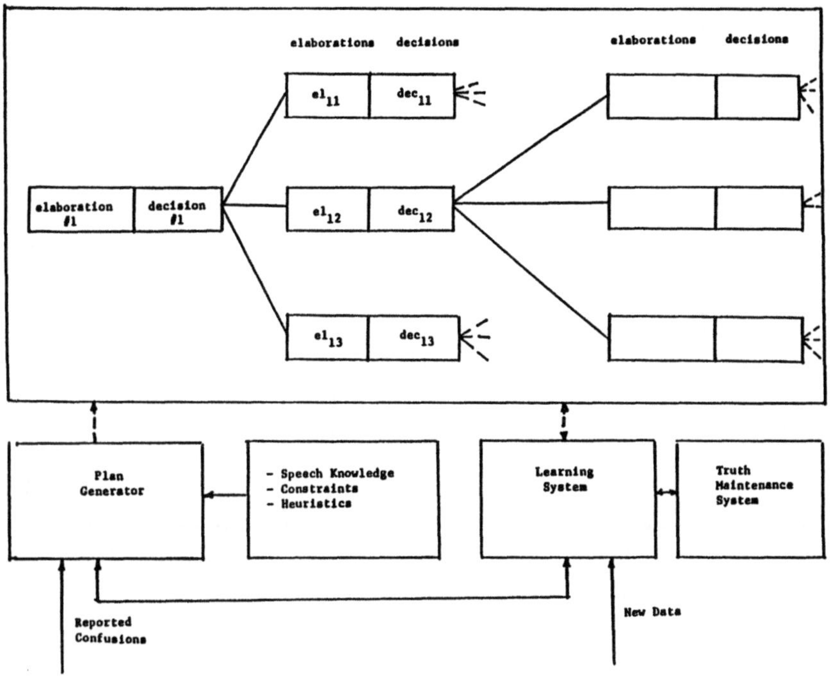

FIG. 7

Fig. 8A shows the loudness curve (thick line) and the zero crossing rate of the first derivative of the signal (dashed line) for the sequence of elements of the E1 set EDTBP. The speaker is an anglophone female student. This example will be the running example of this Section. Fig. 8B shows the ratio between low (0.2-0.6 kHz) and high (5-7 kHz) frequency energy for this particular utterance. Deep dips in the ratio are burst indicators for D,T, and P. This parameter is used for describing frication noise (LNS, MNS) together with peaks of the zero crossing rate.

The three curves in Figs. 8A and 8B are processed by a linguistic descriptor that produces the following PAC description :

LDD	LPK		(12, 30)
LDD	LPK		(40, 65)
LDD	MNS	LVI	(104, 122)
LDD	LPK		(132, 146)
LDD	LPK		(165, 196)

Time references are in centiseconds and are reported only for the vocalic tracts.

An action hierarchy is then applied for interpreting the consonantal segment of every syllable.

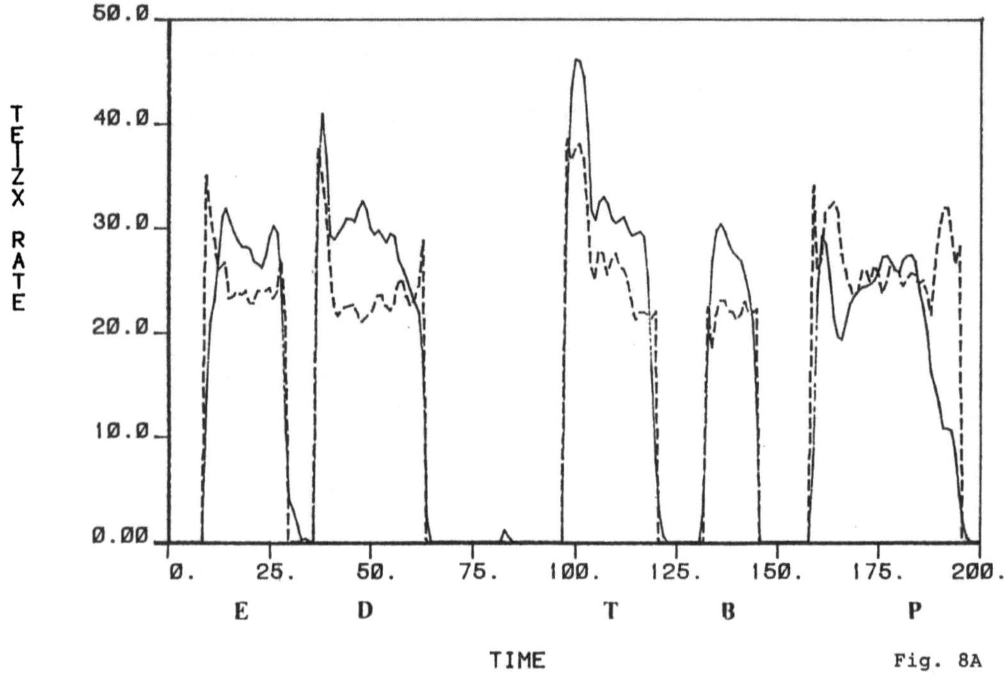
50.0
40.0
30.0
20.0
10.0
0.00
TEIZX RATE
0.
25.
50.
75.
100.
125.
150.
175.
200.
E
D
T
B
P
TIME

Fig. 8A

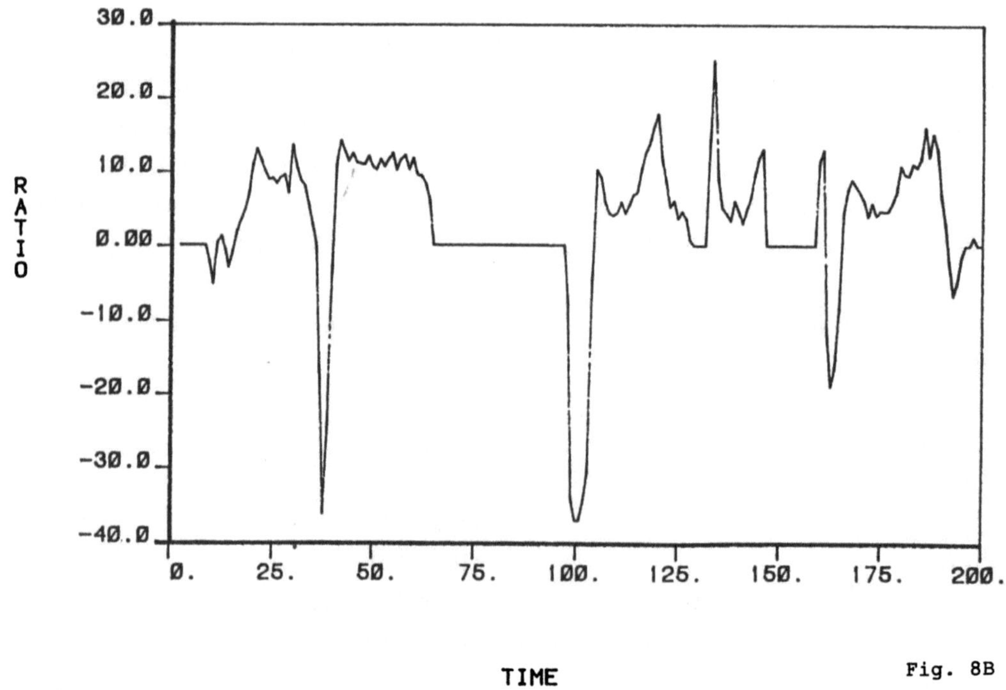
30.0
20.0
10.0
0.00
-10.0
-20.0
-30.0
-40.0
RATIO
0.
25.
50.
75.
100.
125.
150.
175.
200.
TIME

Fig. 8B

Fig. 9 shows the more abstract part of the action hierarchy. PAC extraction and segmentation is a preliminary spontaneous activity that is followed by a decision phase where a rule-set is applied. Rules are made of preconditions and actions. Preconditions are sequences of PAC's. Actions describe what acoustic properties are worth to be extracted given the suprasegmental morphology described by the PAC expression.

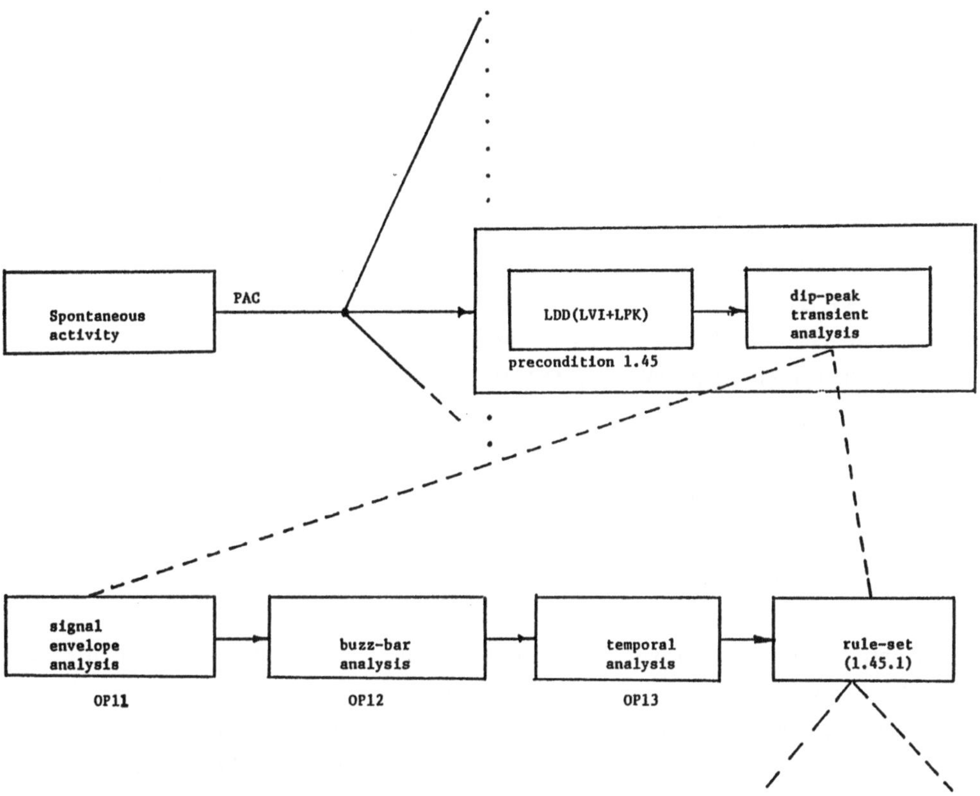

FIG. 9

For the sake of simplicity only the action corresponding to rule (1.45.1) is shown in Fig. 9. The precondition for this rule is (LDD) (LPK + LVI). The symbol + represents here logical disjunction. This AC morphology may correspond to a vowel after a pause, to the consonants |v| or |g| or to plosive consonants for which burst is not evident in the loudness curve. This precondition represents a speaking mode that is rather frequent for |b| and is one of the most difficult to analyze. The action to be executed in this case is the analysis of the (deep dip) | (peak) transition. Useful operators are those that detect voicing, the existence of burst and some temporal relations among the onset of the energies in various bands because delays in these onset times are cues for the presence of plosive sounds.

The approach is that of extracting a *redundant set* of cues so that the final decision about the acoustic properties that describes them is reliable.

According to Fig. 9, the activity "dip peak analysis" is refined by a more detailed subplan which is produced by the planning system introduced in the previous section. As broad-band energies have to be analyzed at the end of the buzz-bar and when the signal envelope starts rising, the chaining order shown in Fig. 9 is obtained.

If there is enough evidence for burst and if there is still a need of discriminating among classes, then a rule of rule-set (1.45) will invoque the execution of a burst analysis action.

OP11 in Fig. 9 produces an envelope description by analyzing the signal amplitude before and after preemphasis. Envelope samples are obtained every millisecond (ms) by taking the absolute value of the difference between the absolute maximum and the absolute minimum of the signal in a 3 ms interval. The envelope description is based on the following alphabets :

A111 = {SHORT--STEP (ST1),
LONG--STEP (ST2),
NO--STE (STO)/

A112 = {HIGH LOW FREQUENCY ENERGY (BZ1),
ABSENCE OF BUZZ INDICATOR IN THE
ENVELOPE (BZ0)}

A113 = {POSSIBLE BURST (PB1),
ABSENCE OF BURST EVIDENCE (PBO)}

A114 = {STRONG BURST EVIDENCE (BU1),
NO STRONG BURST EVIDENCE (BU0)}.

(26)

The description produced by Op11 as well as those produced by OP12 and OP13 are attached to the DDN describing the segment under analysis.

Fig. 10 shows the envelope curve in the energy dip preceding the onset of |b|. The time reference 0 in Fig. 10 corresponds to frame 27 in Fig. 8A the unit of time axis is number of samples divided by 10. There are 20 000 samples per second. Because of the shape of the envelope, the 10 ms segment between 500 and 700 is described as (ST0, BZ1, PB1, BU0). The peak in the signal envelope is described by PB1 (possible burst). As there is no evidence of burst in the waveform in the peak envelope (long zero-crossing intervals) BU0 expresses no burst evidence. The bar in the envelope before the peak is described by BZ1. As there is no step in the envelope before the peak, a descriptor STO is produced. Descriptors are represented in Fig. 10

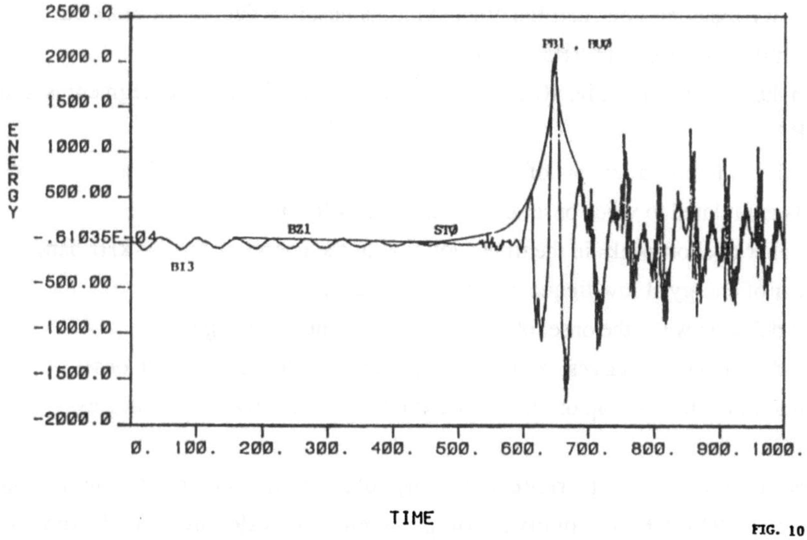

FIG. 10

OP12 describes the buzz-bar by analyzing the shape of the time waveform and of the spectra before the voice onset. The alphabets of the descriptions it produces are :

BZA1 = {BI1,BI2, BI3, BI4, BI5}

for the time waveform and

BZA2 = {BR1,BR2,BR3,BR4,BR5}

for the spectra.

Fig. 11 shows the LPC (continuous line) and the FFT (dashed line) spectra computed before the TE peak onset. The consistent low frequency peak in the FFT spectrum is the cue for buzz-bar. The low frequency oscillations in Fig. 10 are other buzz cues.

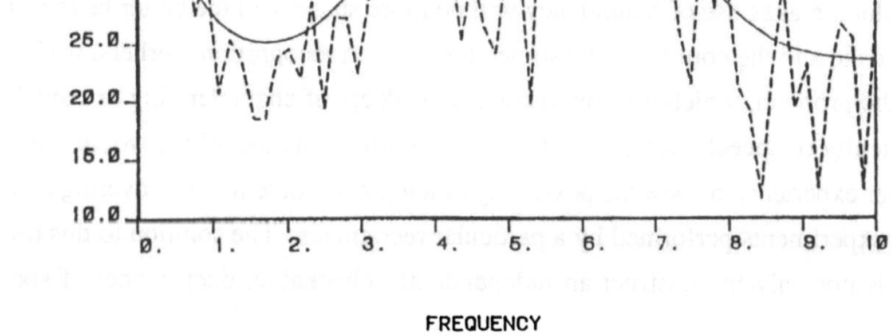

FIG. 11

BI1 and BR1 mean no buzz and the other symbols describe degrees of buzz-bar evidence : (BI2,BR2 : little evidence; BI5,BR5 : strong evidence).

Based on the waveform of Fig. 10 and the spectra shown in Fig. 11 the segment is described as (BI3, BR5).

Op13 analyzes temporal events of the energy in some frequency bands at the voice onset. These events are related to voice onset time. They are as follows.

NP Number of short peaks in the time evolution of the energy in the 2-4 kHz band

RE A bar of energy at low frequency before the peak.

DL The delay between the onset of low and high frequency energies

ZQ The duration of the largest zero-crossing interval of the signal at the onset.

DR Minimum value in a dip of ratio between low and high frequency energies.

The first two cues in (i) represent morphologies described by the alphabets : {NP0,...,NP5}, {RE0,RE1}. Intervals of parameters in (29) are coded with symbols {DL1,...,DL5}. {ZQ1, ... , ZQ5}, {DR1, ..., DR5}. From a dip-peak transition, a vector of values of (NP,RE,DL,ZQ,DR) is extracted and represented by a conjunction of symbols according to the intervals the parameters fall into. Intervals are determined after clustering vectors corresponding to the same letter and intersecting culsters of different letters.

The description obtained by OP11, OP12, and OP13 for the |b| in the interval (0.27-0.35 s) is the following :

Descr.	1.45 :	{PB1	ST0	BZ1	BU0	RE0	NP1
		DR4	DL2	ZQ4	BI3	BR5 }	

9. CONCLUSION

The proposed paradigm has been tested on the vocabulary defined in Tab. I. A correct recognition rate of 90 % was achieved on 40 speakers (20 male and 20 female) whose voice were not used for learning 50 models.

This consideration of redundancies leads to a parenthetical remark that we should like to make in the guise of a conclusion. It is fairly clear that, in the presence of noise, a recognizer of a language which makes use of redundancy will be more successful the better he (or it) knows both the language and the context. Like some other speech recognition workers, we have been attracted to the problem, which we now recognize as deep, of characterizing or modelling the intrinsic difficulty of speech recognition tasks. In building this model we would like to learn from computer experience but see the possibility of a logical problem in discovering an intrinsic model using experiments performed by a particular recognizer. The solution to this difficulty, we suggest, is not only to construct an independently checkable, deep model of speech for hierarchically modelling the intrinsic complexity of speech recognition tasks, but also to build this model into the recognizer for doing computer experiments.

Modelling the complexity of speech recognition tasks, designing computer systems for continous speech recognition, learning more about speech ourselves, designing computer systems for machine learning about speech -- all these, we suggest, require large amounts of prior deep knowledge about speech. And yet, how should this knowledge be organized ? We suspect that a remark by Moses /MOSES 82/ concerning the relatively low overall complexity of an organizational structure disigned as a pyramid or tower of linguistic abstractions has not yet been fully assimilated by the designers of knowledge-based computer systems for continous speech recognition or, indeed, for other computer tasks.

REFERENCES

/BAHL 83/ Bahl L.R., Jelinek F., Mercer R. L., A Maximum Likelihood Approach to Continous Speech Recognition, IEEE Trans. on Pattern Analysis and Machine Intelligence, Vol. PAMI-5, No. 2, pp. 179 - 190, March 1983.

/BAHL 84/ Bahl L. R., Das S. K., de Souza P. V., Jelinek F., Katz S., Mercer R. L., Picheny M.A., Some experiments with Large-Vocabulary Isolated Word Sentence Recognition, Proc. of the IEEE Conference on Acoustic, Speech, and Signal Processing, San Diego, CA., pp. 2651 - 2653, March 1984.

/BAIRD 86/ Baird H. S., Applications of Multidimensional Search to Structural Feature Identification, Proc. Nato Advanced Research Workshop on Syntactic and Structural Pattern Recognition, Sitges, Spain, October 1986.

/BROWNSTON 85/ Brownston L, Farrel R., Kant E., Martin N., Programming Expert Systems in OPS5, Reading, MA : Addison-Wesley, 1985.

/CHURCH 83/ Church K. W., Phrase-Structure Parsing : A Method for Taking Advantage of Allophonic Constraints, MIT/LCS/TR-296, Cambridge, MA, January 13, 1983. (MIT Ph.D. thesis).

/DEMICHELIS 83/ Demichelis P., De Mori R., Laface P., O'Kane M., Computer Recognition of Plosive Sounds Using Contextual Information, IEEE TRANS. ACOUST., SPEECH, SIGNAL PROCESSING VOL. ASSP-31, PP. 359 - 377, 1983.

/DE MORI 79/ De Mori R., Gubrynowicz R., Laface P., Inference of a Knowledge Source for the Recognition of Nasals in Continous Speech, IEEE Trans. on Acoust., Speech, Signal Processing, vol. ASSP-27, no. 5, pp. 538 - 549, October 1979.

/DE MORI 85/ De Mori R., Laface P., Mong Y., Parallel Algorithms for Syllable Recognition in Continous Speech, IEEE Trans. Pattern Anal. Machine Intell., vol. 39, pp. 1 - 88, 1985.

/DE MORI 85/ De Mori R., Laface P., Mong Y., Parallel Algorithms for Syllable Recognition in Continous Speech, IEEE Trans. Pattern Anal. Machine Intell., vol. PAMI-6, pp. 56 - 69, January 1985

/DE MORI 87/ De Mori R., Lam L., Gilloux M., Learning and Plan Refinement in a Knowledge-based System for Automatic Speech Recognition, IEEE Trans. Pattern Anal. Machine Intell., vol. PAMI-9, No. 2, pp. 289 - 305, 1987.

/ERMAN 80/ Erman L. D., Hayes-Roth F., Lesser V. R., Reddy D. R., The HEARSAY-II Speech Understanding System, Integrating Knowledge to Resolve Uncertainty, ACM Comput. Serveys, vol. 12, pp. 213 - 253, 1980.

/FERGUSON 80/ Ferguson J. D., Variable Duration Models for Speech, Proc. Symp. on Application of Hidden Markov Models to Text and Speech, J. D. Ferguson, Ed., Princeton, NJ, pp. 143 - 179, 1980.

/FU 82/ Fu K. S., Syntactic Pattern Recognition and Applications, Prentice Hall, 1982.

/HARALIK/ Haralick R. M., Personal Communication

/JELINEK 84/ Jelinek F., The Development of an Experimental Discrete Dictation Recognizer, IEEE Proceedings, pp. 1616 - 1624, November 1984.

/KLATT 77/ Klatt, D. H., Review of the ARPA Speech Understanding Project, J. Acoust. Soc. Amer., vol. 62, pp. 1345 - 1366, 1977.

/KOPEC 84/ Kopec G. E., Voceless Stop Consonant Identification Using LPC Spectra, Proc. of the IEEE Conference on Acoustics, Speech, and Signal Processing, San Diego CA., pp. 4211 - 4214, March 1984.

/LAIRD 84/ Laird J. E., Universal Subgoaling, Dep. Comput. Sci. Carnegie-Mellon Univ., Pittsburgh, PA, Rep. CMU-CS-84-129, May 1984.

/LEVINSON 81/ Levinson S., Rabiner L. R., Isolated and Connected word Recognition : Theory and Selected Applications, IEEE Trans. on Communications, Vol. COM-29, No. 5, pp.621 - 659, May 1981.

/LEVINSON 85/ Levinson S. E., Structural Methods in Automatic Speech Recognition, IEEE Proceedings, pp. 1625 - 1650, November 1985.

/MERLO 86/ Merlo E., De Mori R., Palakal M., Mercier G., A Continous Parameter and Frequency Domain Based Markov Model, in Proc. Inter. Conf. on Acoust., Speech, Signal Processing, pp. 1597 - 1600, Tokyo, Japan, 1986

/MOSES 82/ Moses J., Computer Science as the Science of Discrete Man-made Systems, Knowledge : Creation, Diffusion, Utilization, Vol. 4, No. 2, pp. 219 - 226, December 1982, reprinted in the Study of Information : Interdisciplinary Messages, F. Machlup and U. Mansfield, eds., John Wiley and Sons, New York, NY, 1983.

/NI 82/ Ni H. P., Feigeinbau E. A., Anton J. J., Rockmore A. J., Signal-to-symbol Transformation. HASP/SIAP Case Study, The Artificial Intelligence Magazine, vol. 3, No. 2, pp. 23 - 35, 1982.

/RABINER 84/ Rabiner L. R., Wiopon J. G., Terrace S. G., A Directory Listing Retrieval System Based on Connected Letter Recognition, Proc. of the IEEE Conference on Acoustics, Speech, and Signal Processing, San Diego, CA, pp. 3541 - 3544, March 1984.

/SACERDOTI 75/ Sacerdoti E. D., The Nonlinear Nature of Plans, IJCAI-4, International Joint Conference on Artificial Intelligence, Tbilisi, Georgia, USSR, September 1975, pp. 115 - 135.

/SHAPIRO 86/ Shapiro L. G., McDonald R. M, Sternberg S. R., Shape Recognition with Mathematical Morphology, Proc. 8th Inter. Conf. on Pattern Recognition, IEEE E.C. 86 CH 2342 - 4, Paris, France, pp. 416 - 418, 1986.

/STEFIK 80/ Stefik, M. J. : Planning with Constraints, Stanford Heuristic Programming Project, Memo HPP-80-2, Computer Science Department, Report no. STAN-CS-80-784, January 1980.

/STEVENS 80/ Stevens K. N., Acoustic Correlates of Some Phonetic Categories, J. Acoust. Soc. Amer., vol. 68, pp. 836 - 842, 1980.

/WALDINGER 77/ Waldinger R., Achieving Several Goals Simultaneously , Machine Intelligence, E. Elcock and D. Michie eds., Ellis Horwood, pp. 8, 94 - 136, 1977.

/WILKINS 84/ Wilkins D. E., Domain-independent Planning : Representation and Plan Generation, Artificial Intell., vol. 22, no. 3, pp. 269 - 302, April 1984.

/ZUE 85/ Zue V. W., The Use of Speech Knowledge in Automatic Speech Recognition, IEEE Proceedings, pp. 1602 - 1615, November 1985.

RECOGNITION OF WORDS IN VERY LARGE VOCABULARY

P. Laface
Politecnico di Torino
Corso Duca degli Abruzzi 24, 10129 Torino, Italy

G. Micca and R. Pieraccini
CSELT - Via G. Reiss Romoli 274, 10148 Torino, Italy

Abstract: Word pre-selection by means of partial phonetic descriptions is a method of lexical access in speech recognition systems for very large vocabularies that is being receiving particular attention. It can be effective provided that segmentation errors are taken into account within the lexical access procedure, and that the resulting candidate word set is reasonably sized. As errors in the segmentation of input utterances are unavoidable, even if a limited number of phonetic categories must be discriminated, a lattice of segmentation hypotheses is generated. Word pre-selection is obtained, therefore, by matching a lattice of phonetic hypotheses against a graph structure that represents a generic word. A Dynamic Programming procedure is introduced that solves this problem. A sub-optimal solution and heuristic constraints have been investigated that improve the algorithm efficiency. In the second step, word verification, a detailed representation of the phonemic structure of word candidates is used for estimating the most likely words. Words are modeled by sequences of sub-word units represented by Hidden Markov Models and a beam-search Viterbi algorithm estimates their likelihood. Experimental results on large vocabularies demonstrate the effectiveness of the method.

1. INTRODUCTION

Increasing interest is being devoted to automatic recognition of isolated words from very large vocabularies, but efficiency issues pose strong constraints on the strategies to be used

NATO ASI Series, Vol. F46
Recent Advances in Speech Understanding and Dialog Systems
Edited by H. Niemann et al.

[1,4,5,6,7,8,9,12]. Even if a recognition method used for small vocabularies such as template matching or stochastic modeling could be in principle extended to larger ones, it becomes impracticable when the vocabulary size is of the order of thousands. As the number of words to be discriminated is large, it is not practically feasible to collect thousands of templates, thus it is mandatory that lexical knowledge is built from a phonetic transcription of the orthographic form of the words. To this aim, sub-word recognition units must be defined, that can be trained from a limited size learning vocabulary and used as building blocks for the words of any lexicon. Furthermore, in order to reduce the computational complexity of the pattern matching process, the search for the best matching words must be as far as possible focused. The reduction of the searching space can be obtained by carefully exploiting the structural constraints that a lexicon imposes at the phonologic level [5] by using the hypothesize and test paradigm. First, a vocabulary subset to which the utterance is estimated to belong to is hypothesized on the basis of a description that allows a fast search to be performed. Second, a more detailed and time consuming verification process is activated only for words belonging to that subset [6].

Perceptive studies [11] and recent experiments [3,5,9,12] demonstrate that a convenient representation of the words of a lexicon can be made in terms of broad phonetic classes. From the automatic recognition point of view this is important because broad classes can be hypothesized more reliably than detailed phonetic segments. The effectiveness of the latter approach, in terms of pre-selection capability, has been investigated by considering the statistical properties of large vocabularies under the assumption of a correct partial description of the words. For instance, as far as Italian language is concerned, by using only six broad phonetic classes for the description of a 13747 word vocabulary, 7225 words can be uniquely identified, while the maximum and average size of the subset of words identically described is 34 and 1.5 respectively [3]. The results of these statistical analyses, however, do not take into account segmentation and classification errors. These errors depend on the inherent variability in speech and occur even if the acoustic-phonetic module must discriminate among a limited number of gross phonetic categories. Moreover, lexicon specifications made on the basis of a reduced set of symbols can lead to low redundancy, this means that a small distortion occurring on a string of symbols that corresponds to a set of words is likely to perfectly fit the representation of a different set of words. Hence, lexical access must be performed through error correcting procedures that tackle the problem of high confusability of partial descriptions of words by generating a suitable set of likely candidates. Although word subsets larger than those predicted by an error free analysis are hypothesized, nevertheless, the results of several experiments, referring to different languages [9,12] show the substantial pre-selection capability of the method even in presence of classification errors.

This paper is devoted to the description of an isolated word recognition system based on this hypothesize and test paradigm. Word pre-selection is achieved by segmenting and classifying the input signal in terms of broad phonetic classes. To achieve high performances, rather than a single sequence of hypotheses, a lattice of phonetic segments is generated. It can be organized as a graph in a structure referred to in this paper as "micro-segmentation". Word hypothesization is obtained by matching the micro-segmentation graph against the models of all vocabulary words. A model is a phonetic representation of a word in terms of a graph accounting for deletion, substitution, and insertion errors. A modified Dynamic Programming (DP) matching procedure gives an efficient solution to this graph to graph matching problem.

Hidden Markov Models (HMMs) of sub-word units are used as a more detailed knowledge in the verification step. The word candidates generated by the previous step are represented as sequences of diphone-like sub-word units, and the Viterbi algorithm is used for evaluating their likelihood.

2. SYSTEM OVERVIEW

The architecture of the system (Fig.1) relies on several modules that are briefly described in the following.

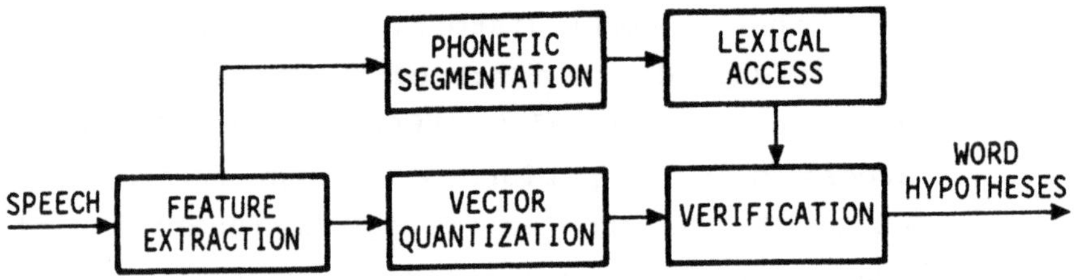

Fig.1 - System Architecture.

1. The feature extraction module performs a critical-band frequency analysis of the signal (sampled at 12 KHz) followed by a discrete cosine transform. Its output is a set of 18 cepstral coefficients computed each 10 msec frame.

2. the vector quantization module associates to every speech frame a label belonging to an alphabet of 128 acoustic symbols.

3. the phonetic segmentation module performs a transcription of the input utterance in terms of broad phonetic classes.

4. the lexical module uses the coarse phonetic description produced by the phonetic segmentation module to select the set of word candidates that must be verified.

5. the verification module determines the likelihood that a candidate word has been uttered.

3. PHONETIC SEGMENTATION

The phonetic segmentation is performed by two modules that work in sequence: a frame-by frame phonetic classifier and a phonetic segmenter. The frame by frame labeler estimates, by means of a hierarchical cubic polynomial classifier, the likelihood that a cepstral vector belongs to the phonetic classes described by the following symbols:

$$\begin{aligned} k1 &= pl : \text{silence or plosive consonant} \\ k2 &= fr : \text{fricative consonant} \\ k3 &= ln : \text{liquid or nasal consonant} \\ k4 &= fv : \text{front vowel} \\ k5 &= cv : \text{central vowel} \\ k6 &= bv : \text{back vowel} \end{aligned} \quad 1)$$

This alphabet has been chosen as a result of a preliminary study on the discrimination of words in a large Italian lexicon by partial descriptions [3]. These phonetic features are simple enough to be extracted reliably, but, at the same time, they carry sufficient information to reduce the set of word that are described by the same sequence of symbols to a reasonable size. For each 10 msec speech frame 18 Mel based cepstral parameters (c0, c1, ... c17) are computed; c1 to c9 and total frame energy form the pattern vector $\underline{x}$ of a given frame. The classification task consists in deciding to which class a given frame belongs. The ideal classification of a generic frame can be described by a target vector:

$$\underline{z} = | z_1, z_2, \dots z6 | \quad 2)$$

where the i-th component is 1 if that frame belongs to the i-th class and 0 otherwise. An estimation

$$\underline{d} = | d_1, d_2, \dots d_6 | \quad 3)$$

of target vector $\underline{z}$ is given by the classifier that consists of a cubic function of vector $\underline{x}$:

$$\underline{d} = K(\underline{x}) \quad 4)$$

The estimation is optimized for minimum mean-squared error S, defined as:

$$S = E[(\underline{z} - \underline{d})^T(\underline{z} - \underline{d})] \quad 5)$$

where E[.] is the expected value. The optimization is carried out as described in [13] using a database of more than 10000 isolated utterances recorded by 9 different speakers and phonetically labeled using an automatic procedure [2].

For each input frame, the highest value component dj of the estimation vector $\underline{d}$ selects the corresponding class kj to be associated to the frame. Furthermore, uncertainty and reject regions are considered in the $\underline{d}$ space. If the estimation $\underline{d}$ falls into an uncertainty region, two labels are assigned to that frame, while no decision is drawn in correspondence of reject regions. Two strings of symbols belonging to the classification alphabet (with an additional symbol for reject or no decision) are associated to an utterance. The first string corresponds to the sequence of unique and best first frame by frame labels, the second one is composed of the sequence of alternative decisions corresponding to uncertainty regions. The two strings are smoothed by means of a majority voting filter whose window length and quorum has been experimentally designed in order to minimize the number of deletions and insertions of spurious segments. Additionally, simple heuristics is used to improve the segment accuracy, taking into account acoustic cues that can be easily extracted from the signal energy.

A micro-segment is defined as a portion of the phonetic lattice in which homogeneous labeled frames appear both at first and at second level of the lattice. Micro-segmentation can be represented, therefore, by a list of elements:

$$MSEG^j = (t_i^j,\ t_e^j,\ s_1^j,\ a_1^j,\ s_2^j,\ a_2^j) \qquad j=1,2...,N \qquad 6)$$

where ti and te are the beginning and ending time of the micro-segment, s1 and s2 are their first and the second phonetic label and a1 and a2 are their classification reliability; of course, s2 and a2 are missing whenever a single hypothesis is produced. In the present system, a1 and a2 are obtained by adding the values, within the segment, of the components of the estimation vector $\underline{d}$ corresponding to the labels s1 and s2. An example of micro-segmentation and its corresponding graph is shown in Fig.2.

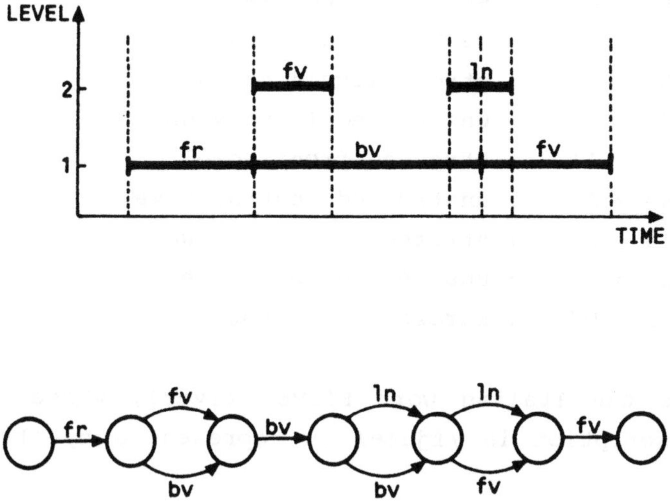

Fig.2 - Micro-segmentation lattice of the word /fjume/.

4. WORD REPRESENTATION

Each word of the lexicon is represented by its detailed standard phonemic transcription that is automatically derived from the orthographic form through a set of rules. This transcription could be directly matched against the micro-segmentation, but large matrices of substitution, insertion, and deletion costs should be estimated that would require a large amount of training data for a good accuracy. On the other hand, a coarse description of the words does not take into account the behavior of the classifier for different sounds. For instance, the classifier accuracy varies for phonemes /s/ and /v/ even though they belong to the same class (fricative); /s/ is very likely to be classified as fricative, while /v/ is quite often classified as liquid/nasal. These considerations lead us to select an intermediate alphabet as representation alphabet. It is described by the following classes of phonemes:

h1	= Spl	: short plosive	
h2	= Lpl	: long plosive or silence	
h3	= Wfr	: weak fricative	
h4	= Sfr	: strong fricative	
h5	= Wln	: weak liquid or nasal	
h6	= Sln	: strong liquid or nasal	7)
h7	= I	: unstressed front vowel	
h8	= II	: stressed front vowel	
h9	= A	: unstressed central vowel	
h10	= AA	: stressed central vowel	
h11	= U	: unstressed back vowel	
h12	= UU	: stressed back vowel	

As an example the Italian word FIUME (river), whose standard phonetic transcription is /fjume/ is represented by the following string:

Wfr I UU Wln I 8)

The compiled representation of a word will be referred to in the following as:

$$W = [\ w^r\ ] \qquad r=1,2,\ldots,M \tag{9}$$

where M is the length of the representation.

5. GRAPH TO GRAPH MATCHING

A representation of the words which takes into account misclassifications can be modeled by a graph such that shown in Fig.3 where each link is associated to the following set of costs:

SUB(hi, kj) = - Log (Prob[substitution of kj for hi])
INS(hi, kj) = - Log (Prob[insertion of kj after hi]) 10)
DEL(hi) = - Log (Prob[deletion of hi])

The costs can be estimated in a training phase that will be illustrated in the next Section.

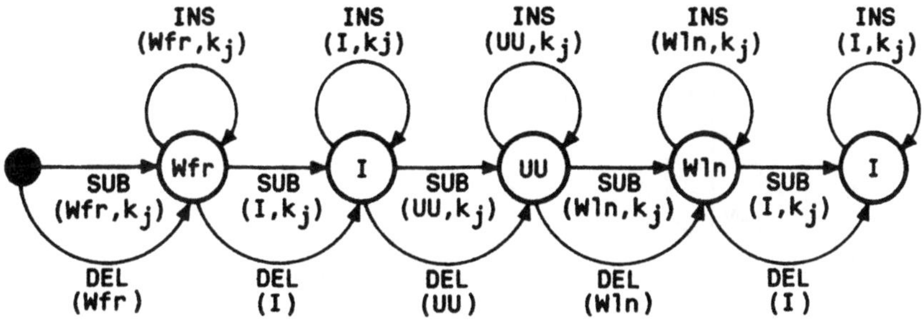

Fig.3 - An example of the model for the word /fjume/.

The problem of finding the best matching of a reference word model against a test micro-segmentation can be stated as follows:

- Select one path in word description and one in micro-segmentation; each path corresponds to a string of symbols belonging to the representation and to the classification alphabet respectively.

- Compute the alignment cost between these strings using the costs defined in 10).

- Repeat this procedure for all path pairs.

- Select the minimum cost path pair.

Two optimization must be carried out: the innermost computes the alignment cost between two strings, the outermost finds the minimum cost path pair.
These optimization can be carried out by the one pass Dynamic Programming procedure (3DP or 3-dimensional DP) that is illustrated in Fig.4.

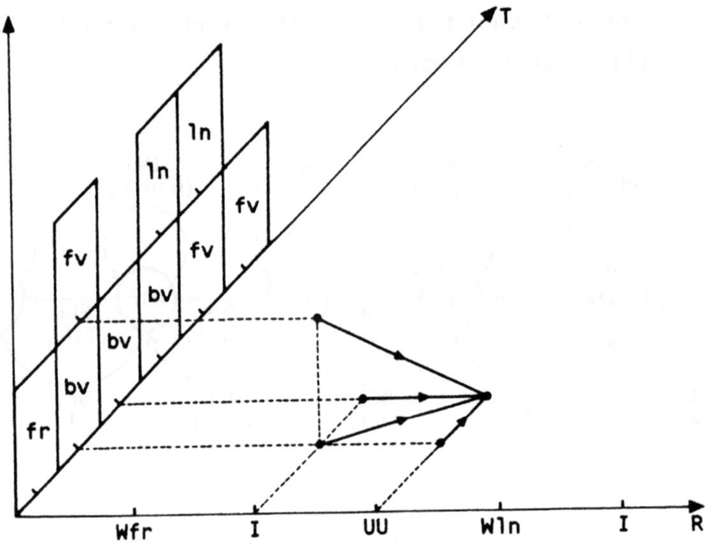

Fig.4 - Three dimensional dynamic programming.

The three dimensions in which an alignment path evolves represent the nodes of the reference word model (dimension R), the sequence of the test micro-segments (dimension T), and the levels of the micro-segmentation lattice (dimension L). Each point of the RTL space has associated a local cost function G(r,t,l), where r is a state of the word model corresponding to a symbol of the representation alphabet, t is the index of a micro-segment, and l, the lattice level, assumes the values 1 or 2 referring to the best and second best segmentation labels respectively.

The DP equations take the following form when applied to the above stated problem:

$$G(r,t,n) = \min_{k=1,2} \left| \begin{array}{ll} G(r-1,\ t-1,\ k) + SUB(w^r,\ s^t_n) & 11) \\ G(r,\ t-1,\ k) + IC(w^r,\ s^t_n) & 12) \\ G(r-1\ \ t,\ k) + DEL(w^r) & 13) \end{array} \right.$$

where:

$$IC(w^r,\ s^t_n) = \left| \begin{array}{l} INS(w^r,\ s^t_1) \quad \text{if} \quad s^t_1 <> s^{t-1}_k \\ \\ 0 \ \text{otherwise} \end{array} \right. \qquad 14)$$

where n and k assume the value 2 only if the t-th micro-segment has associated two classification symbols. Equation 11), 12), and 13) account for symbol substitution, insertion, and deletion respectively. It is worth noting that this structure can lead to "false insertion" situations whenever the same symbol appears in time adjacent micro-segments. Equation 14) solves this case by letting a micro-segment be the continuation of the preceding one if it has the same symbol.

In the above formulation, for each value of r and t, 10 equations must be evaluated (equation 13 does not depend on n). A sub-optimal solution that reduces the number of equations to 4 is used that, given the statistical characteristics of the segmentation process, does not substantially affect the performance of the system. In fact, the system of equations 11-13) carries on all warping paths that are locally optimal. For any given t and r, therefore, two optimal paths are considered that correspond to the optimal alignment up to t-th micro-segment and considering both its first and alternative label. It must be considered, however, that if the t-th micro-segment has associated a single label, optimal partial paths passing through the point (r,t-1,1) and through the point (r,t-1,2) in the RTL space are forced to converge, in the next step, to the same point (r,t,1) and the Dynamic Programming algorithm is forced to select the best path. As 65% of the micro-segments, on the average, has associated, a single decision, even if the selection is made at each step t, the results of the matching procedure should not be appreciably affected. In addition, as insertion of a segment at second level of the micro-segmentation lattice (equation 12 with n=2) does not carry any physical meaning, the insertion of segments can be considered only for best first labels. These hypotheses have been confirmed by the experimental results given in Section 9. Thus the dynamic programming equations are modified as follows:

$$H(r, t) = \min_{k=1,2} \begin{cases} H(r-1, t-1) + SUB(w^r, s_k^t) & 15) \\ H(r, t-1) + IC(w^r, s_1^t) & 16) \\ H(r-1, t) + DEL(w^r) & 17) \end{cases}$$

As the decision about the lattice level is made at each step t, the cost function H depends only on the variables r and t.
Further improvements have been obtained including the duration and the reliability of the micro-segments in the metric involved in the dynamic alignment. The duration is an important cue for the hypothesization of words, while reliability avoids matching unlikely labels within the micro-segmentation. Moreover, three heuristics can be exploited to further reduce both the computation cost and the average number of hypothesized words:

H1. The search is limited to the N best candidates.

H2. A threshold on label reliability can be estimated in order to detect highly reliable segments that constrain the warping path.

H3. Very reliable cues can be used to exclude unlikely substitutions for a given class; for instance a high energy segment cannot be substituted for a plosive.

6. ESTIMATION OF THE ERROR MODEL

The costs SUB(hi,kj), INS(hi,kj), and DEL(hi) are estimated using as training samples 1105 words pronounced once by 6 speakers (4 males and 2 females). The estimation procedure is based on the detection of the number of substitutions, insertions and deletions of symbols that occur when the training word is aligned to its phonetic description by means of the 3DP algorithm. The initial costs are set as:

$$\mathrm{SUB}(hi,\ kj) = \begin{cases} 0 & \text{if } hi \text{ is a subset of } kj \\ 2 & \text{otherwise} \end{cases} \qquad 18)$$

$$\mathrm{INS}(hi,\ kj) = 1$$
$$\mathrm{DEL}(hi) = 1$$

This initial setting corresponds to performing a 3DP matching using a modified Levensthein distance.

The error costs are reestimated by iterating the training procedure until it converges to a stable solution.
The error rates of the segmentation module for different speakers are shown in following table. These statistics were collected during the training phase.

speaker	1	2	3	4	5	6
sex	M	F	M	M	F	M
% of deletions	8.1	6.1	5.6	7.2	10.6	8
% of substitutions	2.3	4	3.8	3.1	2.4	2.6
% of insertions	2.6	10	4.8	5.6	4.3	3.5
% total	13.0	20.1	14.2	15.9	17.3	14.1

7. THE LEXICAL ACCESS ALGORITHM

Even if the number of phonetic micro-segments in a word is about an order of magnitude less than the number of centisecond frames, the complexity of the lexical access by the 3DP matching of the input string against every lexicon item would be impractical when the vocabulary size is of the order of thousands. Hence the set of word descriptions is organized in a tree structure where each node is a phoneme represented by the coarse phonetic class to which it belongs to. All words which share the same coarse phonetic transcription are associated, therefore, with the same node, and constitute a set of phonetically indistinguishable lexical items.

The lexical access problem can be stated as follows: given the micro-segmentation of an uttered word belonging to a lexicon represented by a tree SN, detect the sequences of phonetic nodes SN(i), and hence the corresponding words, whose scores computed by means of the 3DP lie in a given range.
The algorithm is based on the dynamic expansion of the tree SN [8]. For each input micro-segment MSEG(j) a set of dynamic nodes activated by the previous micro-segment MSEG(j-1) is created for representing the current local values of the 3DP optimization procedure.

In order to limit the number of active nodes a beam search strategy stops the expansion of any path whose score exceeds the best one of a fixed threshold. When all micro-segments are processed, the words corresponding to the active terminal nodes constitute the hypothesized set. The value of the beam search threshold controls the average dimension of that set.

8. VERIFICATION MODULE

This module applies a more refined phonetic knowledge than the phonetic classification module. Words are described by means of sequences of sub-word units represented by HMMs. These phonetic units have been chosen according to a tradeoff between phonemes, which do not take into account coarticulation effects, and diphones, whose number is practically too large. The resulting recognition unit system is based on context independent models of the stationary parts of the signal (22 units) and on context dependent models of the transitions between adjacent sounds (101 units). The transcription of an utterance into recognition units relies on a detailed representation of the phonemic structure of words [2].

Each unit is modeled by a HMM whose structure (number of states and allowed transition among them) depends on the kind of unit it represents.

The efficiency of the verification algorithm can be greatly increased by compiling on-line a tree of graphs, where each graph stores the different phonetic transcriptions of each candidate word. The evaluation of the most likely words is carried out by means of a beam-search Viterbi algorithm.

The estimation of the model parameters can be performed by the Forward-Backward algorithm using as observation symbols a particular sequence of codewords obtained from the signal corresponding to the utterance of a unit. As it is often impossible to pronounce an isolated sub-word unit (such as a phoneme or a diphone), the training procedure must rely on the observation of larger units such as words or sentences. The required observation subsequences can be obtained by hand segmentation and labeling of the utterances, a time consuming and error prone process. It is possible, instead, to estimate the parameters of a set of sub-word units, with a procedure that does not require human interaction. From the orthographic form of each word in a training vocabulary, various phonemic transcriptions are generated according to their possible pronunciations and taking also care of the ambiguity arising in the translation process. One of these alternative, possibly chosen by an operator, is automatically converted into the unit sequence. The training corpus is the set of words of a predefined vocabulary pronounced once by a speaker and represented as sequence of Vector Quantization codewords. Starting with untrained HMMs (equiprobable transition and emission matrices), for each word forward and backward matrices are computed [10]. For every unit appearing in the word a partial factor of the reestimation formulae is computed and accumulated. When all training words have been analyzed, reestimation formulae are computed for transition and emission probabilities of each unit. This procedure is repeated until convergence is reached.

9. EXPERIMENTAL RESULTS

Results in Fig.5 refer to a set of experiments performed on a corpus of 1011 words of a test vocabulary (different from the training vocabulary) pronounced by a male speaker. The average inclusion rate of the uttered word in the hypothesized set is plotted versus the average cardinality of the set.
Curve A and B refer to the results achieved by using the optimal and sub-optimal matching procedures respectively, while curve C shows the performance improvements due to the application of the heuristics on the reliability of segments. Finally, curve D demonstrates that alignment of the word models using only the best first segmentation and a straightforward dynamic programming algorithm give worse results. This results refer to a dynamic

alignment that does not include in its metric information about the duration and the reliability of micro-segments. Fig.6 shows the recognition rates obtained by using the duration and the reliability information (curve A).

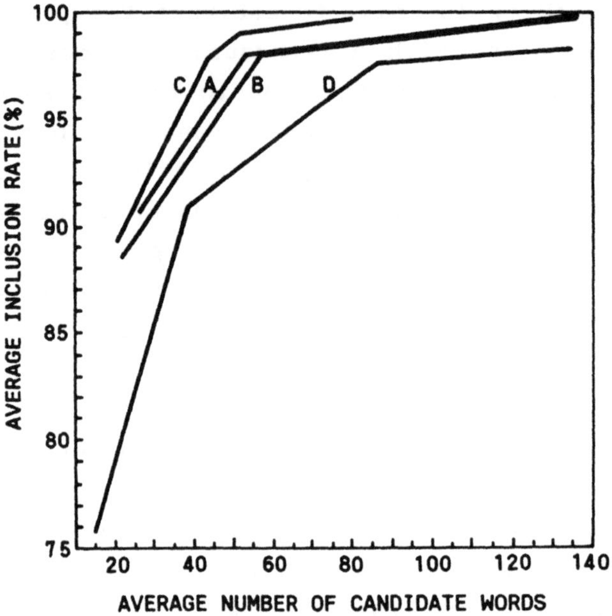

Fig. 5

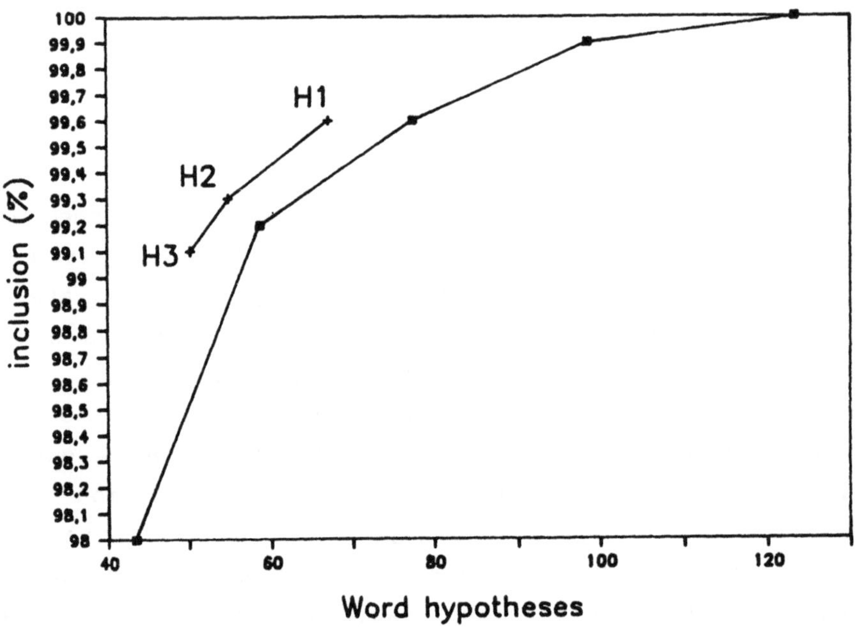

Fig. 6

Curve B points out the reduction on the average number of word candidates achieved by using the heuristics introduced in Section 5. In Fig.7 and Fig.8 the variation of the inclusion rate and of the average number of candidates is plotted as a function of the vocabulary size.

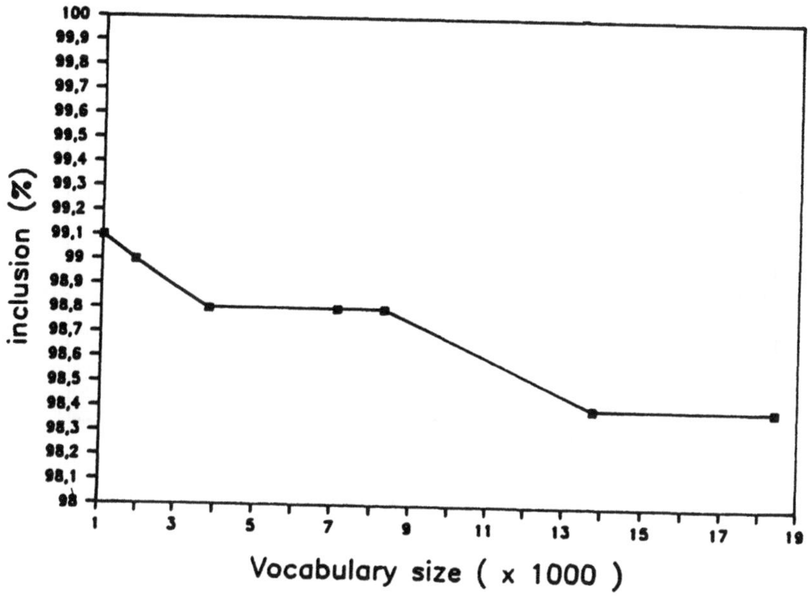

Fig. 7

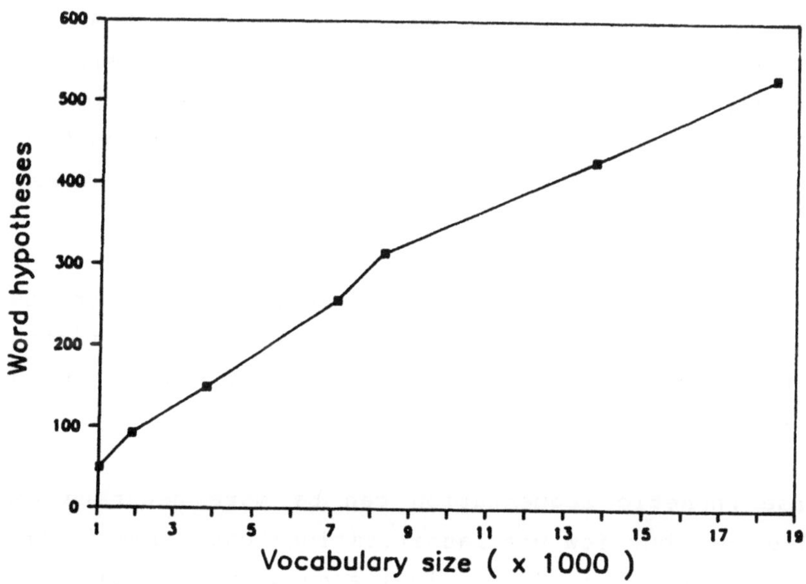

Fig. 8

The recognition rates of the verification module are shown in Fig.9, as a cumulative function of the n-best likelihoods obtained by using a speaker dependent (A) and a speaker independent (B) vector quantizer.

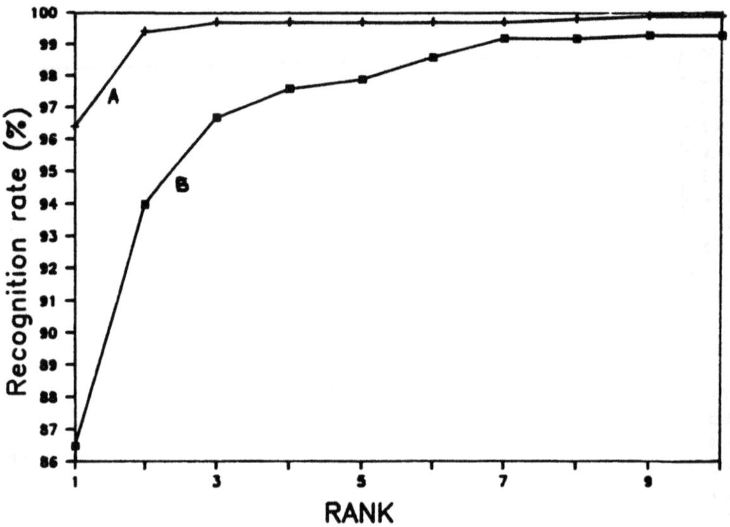

Fig. 9

10. CONCLUSIONS

A large vocabulary isolated word recognition system has been presented. It is based on a two pass approach that relies on an efficient graph to graph matching algorithm for candidate word generation, and on HMM modeling for their verification. The main suggestions deriving from this work can be summarized as follows:

1. It is very easy obtaining about 90% inclusion rate in the set of candidate words, but the real problem in large vocabulary lexical access is to obtain almost 100% inclusion rate and a reasonably small number of word candidate.

2. A coarse phonetic segmentation can be more accurate than a detailed one, but few misclassifications can dramatically reduce the performance of a lexical access due to the small redundancy of the code.

3. Robust phonetic segmentation can be achieved by generating rather than a sequence of segments, a lattice of phonetic hypotheses to be matched against the vocabulary words which can be represented by a graph model including statistics about possible segmentation errors.

4. An efficient structure for lexical representation is in terms of a tree, of phonetic nodes in the hypothesize step, and of HMM sub-word units in the verification step.

5. A three dimensional DP matching algorithm has been introduced that performs better than other conventional algorithms.

6. A sub-optimal version of the matching procedure can be used without appreciable performance degradations.

The experimental results show the capability of the statistical models and of the lexical constraints to cope with the errors of the segmentation module and the accuracy of the HMMs of the sub-word phonetic units used in the verification phase.
A robust hypothesization system leads to interesting applications in the field of isolated and continuous speech recognition/understanding tasks.

11. REFERENCES

[1] Billi R., Massia G., Nesti F.,'Word Preselection for Large Vocabulary Speech Recognition', Int. Conf. on Acoustics, Speech and Signal Processing, pp.23.6.1-23.6.4, (1986).

[2] Cravero M., Pieraccini R., Raineri F.,'Definition and Evaluation of Phonetic Units for Speech Recognition by Hidden Markov Models', Int. Conf. on Acoustics, Speech and Signal Processing, Tokyo, pp.42.3.1-42.3.4 (1986).

[3] Giordana A., Laface P., Saitta L.,'Discrimination of Words in a Large Vocabulary using Phonetic Descriptions', Int. Journal of Man-Machine Studies, n.24,pp.453-473 (1986).

[4] Gupta V.N., Lenning M., Mermelstein P.'Integration of Acoustic Information in a Large Vocabulary Word Recognizer', Int. Conf. on Acoustics, Speech and Signal Processing, Dallas pp.17.2.1-17.2.4, (1987).

[5] Huttenlocher D.P., Zue V.W.,'A Model of Lexical Access from Partial Phonetic Information', Int. Conf. on Acoustics, Speech and Signal Processing, pp.26.4.1-26.4.4, (1984).

[6] Kaneko T., Dixon N.R.,'A Hierarchical Decision Approach to Large-Vocabulary Discrete Utterance Recognition', IEEE Trans. on Acoustic Speech and Signal Processing, Vol. ASSP-31, n.5, pp.1061,1066, (1983).

[7] Koonen T. et al.,'On-Line Recognition of Spoken Words from a Large Vocabulary', Information Sciences, n.22, pp. 3-30, (1984).

[8] Laface P., Micca G., Pieraccini R., 'Experimental Results on a Large Lexicon Access Task', Int. Conf. on Acoustics, Speech and Signal Processing, Dallas pp.20.4.1-20.4.4 (1987).

[9] Lagger H., Waibel A.,'A Coarse Phonetic Knowledge Source for Template Independent Large Vocabulary Word Recognition', Int. Conf. on Acoustics, Speech and Signal Processing, pp.2.7.1-2.7.4, (1985).

[10] Levinson S.E, Rabiner L.R., Sondhi M.M.,'Introduction to the Application of the Theory of Probabilistic Functions of a Markov Process to Automatic Speech Recognition', Bell System Technical Journal,Vol.62, n.4, Part 1, pp.1035-1074, (1983).

[11] Pisoni D.B., Nusbaum H.C., Luce P.A., Slowiaczek L.M., 'Speech Perception, Word Recognition and the Structure of the Lexicon', Speech Communication, Vol.4, n.1-3, pp.75-96 (1985).

[12] Schukat-Talamazzini G., Niemann H.'Generating Word Hypotheses in Continuous Speech',Int. Conf. on Acoustics, Speech and Signal Processing, Tokyo pp.30.2.1-30.2.4 (1986).

[13] Zelinsky R., Class F., 'A Segmentation Algorithm for Connetted Word Recognition Based on Estimation Principles', IEEE Trans. on ASSP, Vol.31, No.4 (1983).

ISOLATED WORD RECOGNITION USING HIDDEN MARKOV MODELS

S. Euler and D. Wolf

Institut für Angewandte Physik der Universität Frankfurt a.M.
D-6000 Frankfurt a. M., Robert-Mayer-Straße 2-4, FRG

Abstract: An automatic speaker independent isolated word recognition system based on continuous hidden Markov models is presented using multidimensional spherically invariant density functions which describe the statistical properties of words. Different types of density functions are applied to represent the observed data. In simulations the recognition performance depending on these density functions is evaluated.

1. INTRODUCTION

In automatic speech recognition systems hidden Markov models (HMM) have been introduced successfully for modeling speech waveforms. The speech signals are segmented into frames of equal lengths. For each frame a k-dimensional vector $\underline{\eta}$ of characteristic features is measured. The vectors $\underline{\eta}$ are considered to be output symbols of a N-states Markov chain. The probability of a given value $\underline{y}$ of $\underline{\eta}$ in a specific state q_n, $1 \le n \le N$, is described by a k-dimensional density function $b_{\underline{\eta}}(\underline{y})$. The N density functions together with the transition probabilities of the Markov chain define the model of a specific word. The state densities as well as the transition probabilities for each word of the vocabulary have to be estimated in a training procedure examining the utterances of a large variety of different speakers. In order to classify a word to be recognized, the probabilities of the corresponding sequence of feature vectors are calculated for each model. The model yielding the highest probability is chosen. [1]

2. SPHERICALLY INVARIANT DENSITY FUNCTIONS

The density functions $b_{\underline{\eta}}(\underline{y})$ are assumed to be spherically invariant. Then $b_{\underline{\eta}}(\underline{y})$ can be expressed by a certain function f in the form

NATO ASI Series, Vol. F46
Recent Advances in Speech Understanding and Dialog Systems
Edited by H. Niemann et al.

$$b_{\underline{\eta}}(\underline{y}) = M^{-\frac{1}{2}} \cdot f((\underline{y}-\underline{m})^T \underline{\underline{M}}^{-1}(\underline{y}-\underline{m})) \quad , \tag{1}$$

with the mean $\underline{m}=E\{\underline{\eta}\}$, the covariance matrix $\underline{\underline{M}}=\{E\{\eta_i\eta_k\}\}$, and $M=\det\underline{\underline{M}}$. While, in general, higher dimensional density functions cannot be measured directly, in the case of spherical symmetry the k-dimensional density $b_{\underline{\eta}}(\underline{y})$ can be deduced from the onedimensional density of the random variable

$$\zeta = \sqrt{\frac{1}{k} \cdot (\underline{\eta}-\underline{m})^T \underline{\underline{M}}^{-1}(\underline{\eta}-\underline{m})} \quad . \tag{2}$$

The distribution function $P_\zeta(s)$ of ζ is given by

$$P_\zeta(s) = \int_G b_{\underline{\eta}}(\underline{y})\, d\underline{y} \;, \qquad G = \{\underline{y} \mid \zeta \le s\} \;. \tag{3}$$

By transformation Eq. (3) is reduced to

$$P_\zeta(s) = C \int_0^{s\sqrt{k}} dr\; f(r) r^{k-1}, \quad C = \left(\int_0^{\infty} dr\; f(r) r^{k-1} \right)^{-1} . \tag{4}$$

Differentiation leads to the density

$$p_\zeta(s) = \frac{d}{ds} P_\zeta(s) = C\sqrt{k}^k \cdot s^{k-1} f(s\sqrt{k}) \quad . \tag{5}$$

From Eq. (5) the function f and thus the k-dimensional density $b_{\underline{\eta}}(\underline{y})$ can be derived from the onedimensional density $p_\zeta(s)$.

3. SIMULATION SYSTEM

A speaker independent recognition system for isolated German words based on HMM was implemented on a MicroVax II minicomputer. The vocabulary consisted of the ten digits plus the words 'anfang', 'ende', 'ja', and 'nein'. All speech signals were recorded at a sampling rate of 8 kHz and logarithmically quantized with 8 bit per sample.

Within the continuous speech recordings start- and endpoints of the isolated words were detected by application of an algorithm which employs blockwise measured energies and correlation coefficients. For each frame of 20 msec duration the normalized energy value and the first nine log-area-ratio coefficients were calculated, constituting a 10-dimensional feature vector. The parameters $\underline{m}$ and $\underline{\underline{M}}$ for each of the states of the word models were evaluated by a generalized Baum-Welch algorithm [2,3] using the utterances of 100 different male and female German speakers. For a given set of parameters and a sequence of vectors the corresponding maximum likelihood state sequence and the conditional probability were computed simultaneously by means of the Viterbi algorithm [4].

4. EXPERIMENTAL RESULTS

4.1 DENSITY FUNCTIONS

At first the parameters of the word models based on the normal density function were calculated. From the training data of each word the corresponding maximum likelihood state sequences were evaluated and applied to divide the data into segments, each corresponding to a specific state of the Markov chain. For these segments the histograms of $p_\zeta(s)$ were measured with respect to each state and to each word. Typical results are demonstrated in Figure 1 concerning the example of the word 'drei' using a 5-states model. For comparison the density function $p_\zeta^!(s)$ derived from the normal density function is

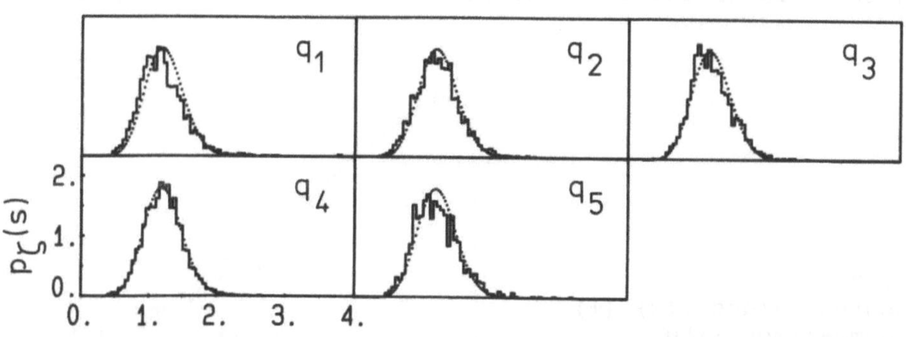

Fig. 1 Measured density function $p_\zeta(s)$ for five states of the word 'drei' compared with the density $p_\zeta^!(s)$ (...)

included. The histograms of different states show similar shapes; all of them can be approximated by $p_\varsigma^!(s)$ fairly well. However, in the range of large values of s the more detailed examination of the measured shapes of the functions f(s) related to $p_\varsigma(s)$ revealed significant deviations from the normal density. Therefore, two other types of functions f(s), namely the 10-dimensional K_0-density [5]

$$f_K(s) = \frac{e^{-s}}{32\cdot\pi^5}\cdot(105s^{-11}+105s^{-10}+45s^{-9}+10s^{-8}+s^{-7} \qquad (6)$$

and the 'Laplacian' density

$$f_L(s) = \frac{1}{(k-1)!!}\cdot\left(\frac{k+1}{2\pi}\right)^{\frac{1}{2}}\cdot e^{-s\sqrt{k+1}} \qquad (7)$$

were considered. Figure 2 illustrates the good approximation of the measured average values f(s) achieved by $f_L(s)$.

4.2 RECOGNITION TESTS

With HMMs using spherically invariant probability density functions recognition rates were determined for a set of 100 test speakers. Figure 3 shows results for various model configurations. In general, the recognition rates increase with the number of states and the results for different densities converge. For small numbers of states the normal density yields best results, but with increasing number of states, the recognition rates for the 'Laplacian' density become superior.

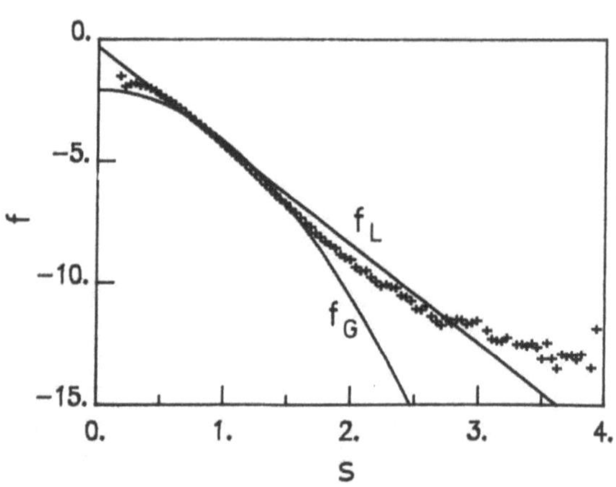

Fig. 2
Measured values f(s) (+) in comparison with Gaussian (f_G) and 'Laplacian' (f_L) densities (logarithmic scale)

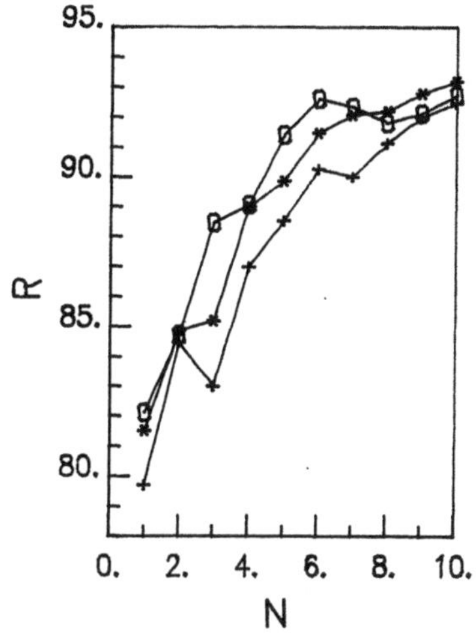

Fig. 3 Recognition rates R obtained with Gaussian (O), 'Laplacian' (*), and K_0 (+) model

5. CONCLUSION

The investigations have shown that spherically invariant density functions can successfully be used for the representation of feature vectors related to the states of a HMM. In particular these functions offer the possibility to determine experimentally the higher dimensional density functions. Among the density functions considered here - Gaussian, Laplacian, and K_0-type - best results were achieved by the Laplacian model.

REFERENCES

[1] Euler, S. und Wolf, D., Sprecherunabhängige Einzelworterkennung mit Hilfe stochastischer Wortmodelle, Informatik-Fachberichte 149, Springer, Berlin 1987, pp.91-95

[2] Baum L.E., An Inequality and Associated Maximization Technique in Statistical Estimation for Probabilistic Functions of a Markov Process, Inequalities 3, 1972, pp.1-8

[3] Liporace L.A., Maximum Likelihood Estimation for Multivariate Observations of Markov Sources, IEEE Trans. Inf., Vol. IT-28, 1982, pp.729-734

[4] Viterbi A. J., Error Bounds for Convolutional Codes and an Asymptotically Optimum Decoding Alorithm, IEEE Trans. Inf., Vol. IT-13, 1967, pp.260-269

[5] Wolf D., Statistical Models of Speech Signals, NTG-Fachberichte 65, 1978, pp.1-9

ISOLATED DIGIT RECOGNITION USING THE MULTI-LAYER PERCEPTRON

S.M. Peeling, R.K. Moore and A.P. Varga

Speech Research Unit,
Royal Signals and Radar Establishment,
Malvern, Worcs, UK

Abstract: This paper introduces the *multi-layer perceptron* (MLP) as a new approach to isolated digit recognition. A comparison is made with hidden Markov modelling (HMM) techniques applied to the same data. The experimental results show that the performance of the *multi-layer perceptron* is comparable with that of hidden Markov modelling.

1. INTRODUCTION

A pressing problem in speech pattern processing is the construction of stochastic models which have appropriate internal *hidden* structures [MOO 86a]. Normally, the structure of a model is defined using a-priori constraints based on some understanding of the nature of the relevant patterns; for example in hidden Markov modelling the number of states in a model may be defined by the expected number of roughly stationary spectrum regions in a spoken word [MOO 86b]. The stochastic parameters of such a model are then estimated using information extracted from a set of training examples of actual speech patterns; in hidden Markov modelling the state transition probabilities and the state output probabilities are derived in this way.

Recent work in this laboratory [BRI 84] and elsewhere has been concerned with model building strategies which are capable of learning structural as well as stochastic information. This paper introduces the *multi-layer perceptron* [RUM 86] as a new approach to speech pattern processing and, in particular, to the problem of isolated digit recognition.

2. THE MULTI-LAYER PERCEPTRON

The MLP is a member of the class of self-organising machines known as *adaptive parallel distributed processing networks* [MCC 86]. In this formalism, a-priori speech knowledge is expressed in the pattern of weighted connections in a network of very simple processing units. Input data is presented to the network as a pattern of activity on the input units, and the interpretation of the input data is represented by the resulting activity on the output units. The information embedded in the network is refined by adjusting the weights in order to produce the required input-output relationship.

2.1 Two-Layer Networks

As its name suggests, the MLP is related to work done in the 1960's on simple two-layer associative networks known as *perceptrons* [MIN 69]. In the perceptron, a

NATO ASI Series, Vol. F46
Recent Advances in Speech Understanding and Dialog Systems
Edited by H. Niemann et al.
Springer-Verlag Berlin Heidelberg 1988

set of input patterns is mapped directly to a set of output patterns and a learning algorithm is used to adjust the weights on the input-output connections in order to optimise the accuracy of the mapping. However, it was found that two-layer networks cannot compute many important functions (for example, it is impossible to perform an exclusive-or operation without at least one intermediate or hidden unit) and there was no known learning algorithm for networks with hidden units. Such a learning algorithm has recently been reported; Rumelhart et al. [RUM 86] have shown that it is possible to generalise the original perceptron learning algorithm to handle *multi-layer* feed-forward networks.

2.2 Multi-Layer Networks

A multi-layer perceptron is configured with a layer of input units, any number of intermediate layers of hidden units, and a layer of output units. Connections within a layer or from higher to lower layers are not permitted. Each unit has a real-valued output (between 0 and 1) which is a non-linear function of its total input:—

$$y_j = \frac{1}{1 + e^{-\sum_i y_i w_{ij}}}$$

where y_j is the output of unit j, and w_{ij} is the value of the weighted connection between unit i and unit j. Thus, given an input pattern, the output pattern can be computed in a single *forward pass* through the network.

2.3 Training The Network

If a unit j is an output unit then, for a given target value t_j, the total error, E, at the output is defined by the following expression:—

$$E = \frac{1}{2} \sum_c \sum_j (t_{jc} - y_{jc})^2$$

where c is an index over input-output pairs. The learning algorithm minimises E by gradient descent. This involves changing the weights according to the following rule:—

$$w_{ji}(n+1) = \epsilon \delta_j y_i + \alpha w_{ji}(n)$$

where ϵ is the learning rate, α is a 'momentum' term and δ is a measure of the local error at unit j. For an output unit, the error term is given by the expression:—

$$\delta_j = (t_j - y_j)\, y_j\, (1 - y_j)$$

and for an internal (hidden) unit the expression is:—

$$\delta_j = \sum_k \delta_k w_{kj}\, y_j\, (1 - y_j)$$

From the foregoing it can be seen that the learning algorithm changes the weights by apportioning the error at the output using a *backward pass* from the output layer to the input layer. This process is termed '*error back-propagation*'.

The effect of the learning algorithm is thus to 'discover' a set of weights which produce an appropriate non-linear transformation between input and output. The MLP is thus a powerful technique for deriving high-order internal representations and its computational requirements are quite modest.

2.4 Application To Speech Pattern Processing

The MLP has been applied to a range of problems in speech pattern processing. These include the recognition of single vowel spectra, whole-word patterns and visual speech information based on lip shape [PEE 86]. The technique has also been applied to the automatic derivation of orthographic-to-phonetic conversion rules for text-to-speech synthesis [SEJ 87].

The rest of this paper is devoted to comparing the most recent results obtained using the MLP for the recognition of isolated digits with those obtained using more traditional methods.

3. ISOLATED DIGIT RECOGNITION EXPERIMENTS

The data consisted of four sets of speech patterns each containing ten examples of the digits "zero" to "nine". Each data set was available from forty different speakers [SMI 86]. One of the four sets was used for testing purposes in all the experiments. The data were obtained from a 19 channel filter-bank analyser with a 20ms frame rate [HOL 80]. The words varied in length between 35 and 60 frames.

Two different recognition experiments were conducted: speaker dependent and multiple speaker. The first was performed on data taken from each of the twenty 'least consistent' speakers in the forty speaker database. The second experiment used data from all forty speakers.

For all the experiments reported here each MLP had a 19 x 60 array of inputs and 10 output units but varying numbers of hidden units. In some cases there were no hidden units, i.e. the input and output units were directly connected as in the original *perceptron*. Other experiments involved either 1 or 2 layers of hidden units, e.g. "1 x 8" refers to a single layer containing 8 hidden units and "2 x 8" refers to two hidden layers each containing 8 units. (Words shorter than 60 frames were padded with silence (zeros) and randomly positioned within the input array.)

In the speaker dependent experiments the MLP was trained using either 10 or 30 examples of each digit. In the multiple speaker experiments between one and three examples of each digit from each speaker were used. Further details of these experiments can be found in [PEE 87].

The same data were also processed using hidden Markov modelling (HMM). In this case the speaker dependent tests used an 8 state HMM with Gaussian state output probability density functions, trained on 10 examples of each digit [RUS 86]. For the multiple speaker experiments, a 16 state hidden semi-Markov model (HSMM) with Gaussian state output probability density functions and non-parametric (Ferguson) state duration probability distribution functions [RUS 87] was trained on one example of each digit from each speaker.

Training the MLP required considerably more computation time than either the HMM or HSMM, and more parameters needed to be estimated for the MLP. However, during the testing/recognition phase the situation was reversed and the MLPs ran up to 30 times faster than the HMMs.

4. RESULTS

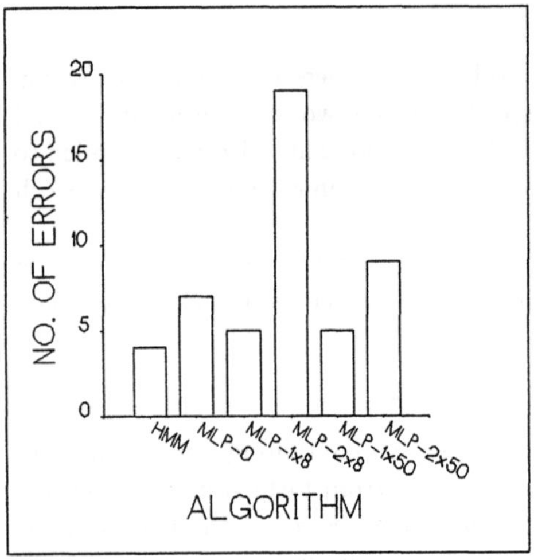

Figure 1: Results of speaker dependent experiment (errors out of 2000)

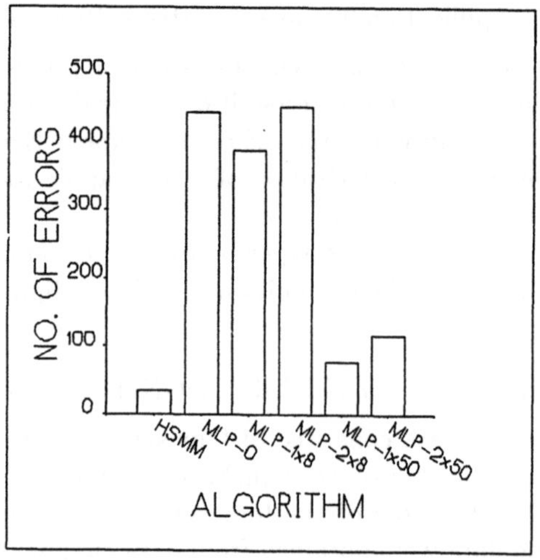

Figure 2: Results of multiple speaker experiment (errors out of 4000)

Figure 1 shows a comparison of the total errors from the speaker dependent isolated word recognition experiments on 2000 digits spoken by 20 speakers (100 digits per speaker). The best performance (99.8% correct) was obtained from the HMM, but both the single hidden layer MLP's gave almost identical results (99.75% correct). The worst performance was obtained from the MLP with 2 layers of 8 hidden units (99.05%).

Figure 2 shows a comparison of the total errors from the multiple speaker isolated word recognition experiments on 4000 digits spoken by 40 speakers. The best performance (99.175%) came from the HSMM and the best MLP performance (98.1%) from an MLP with a single layer of 50 hidden units. The worst performance came from an MLP with no hidden layer.

It can be seen from the two figures that the pattern of behaviour is similar in the speaker dependent and the multiple speaker experiments; the performance of an MLP with a single hidden layer is better than that obtained from a system with either 2 hidden layers or no hidden layers at all. (The 2 layer system probably performed less well because the large number of parameters involved allowed the system to characterise the training data completely giving only limited generalisation to the test data.)

In general the MLPs with 50 hidden units per layer performed better than those with 8, especially in the multiple speaker case. Overall, the best MLP results were obtained from the 1 x 50 system.

5. CONCLUSION

It is clear that in both speaker dependent and multiple speaker recognition of isolated digits the multi-layer perceptron is capable of a level of performance comparable to that obtained using hidden Markov modelling.

REFERENCES

[BRI 84] J.S. Bridle and R.K. Moore, 'Boltzmann Machines for Speech Pattern Processing', Proc. IoA, Vol.6, Part 4, 315–322, (1984).

[HOL 80] J.N. Holmes, 'The JSRU Channel Vocoder', Proc. IEE, Vol.127, Pt.F, No.1, 53–60, (1980).

[MCC 86] J.L. McClelland, D.E. Rumelhart and the PDP Research Group, *Parallel Distributed Processing: Explorations in the Microstructure of Cognition. Vol. 1: Foundations*, MIT Press (1986).

[MIN 69] M.L. Minsky and S. Papert, *Perceptrons*, MIT Press, (1969).

[MOO 86a] R.K. Moore and J.S. Bridle, 'Speech Research at RSRE', Proc. IoA Autumn Conf. on Speech and Hearing, Vol.8, No.7, 257–264, (1986).

[MOO 86b] R.K. Moore, 'Computational Techniques', *Electronic Speech Recognition*, G. Bristow (ed.), Collins, 130–157, (1986).

[PEE 86] S.M. Peeling, R.K. Moore and M.J. Tomlinson, 'The Multi-layer Perceptron as a Tool for Speech Pattern Processing Research', Proc. IoA Autumn Conf. on Speech and Hearing, Vol.8, No.7, 307–314, (1986).

[PEE 87] S.M. Peeling and R.K. Moore, 'Experiments in Isolated Digit Recognition Using the Multi-layer Perceptron', RSRE Memo. No.4073, (1987).

[RUM 86] D.E. Rumelhart, G.E. Hinton and R.J. Williams, 'Learning Internal Representations by Error Propagation', *Parallel Distributed Processing: Explorations in the Microstructure of Cognition. Vol. 1: Foundations*, D.E. Rumelhart and J.L. McClelland (eds.), MIT Press, (1986).

[RUS 86] M.J. Russell and A.E. Cook, 'Experiments in Speaker-Dependent Isolated Digit Recognition using Hidden Markov Models', Proc. IoA Autumn Conf. on Speech and Hearing, Vol.8, No.7, 291–298, (1986).

[RUS 87] M.J Russell and A.E. Cook, 'Experimental Evaluation of Duration Modelling Techniques for Automatic Speech Recognition', Proc. ICASSP 87, (1987).

[SEJ 87] T.J. Sejnowski and C.R. Rosenberg, 'Parallel Networks That Learn to Pronounce English Text', Complex Systems 1, 145–168, (1987).

[SMI 86] D.C. Smith, M.J. Russell and M.J. Tomlinson, 'Rank-ordering of Subjects Involved in the Evaluation of Automatic Speech Recognisers', RSRE Memo. No.3926, (1986).

USE OF PROCEDURAL KNOWLEDGE FOR SPOKEN LETTERS AND DIGITS RECOGNITION

Ettore MERLO
School of Computer Science
805 Sherbrooke St. W.
McGill University
Montreal, Quebec, Canada
H3A 2K6

1. PROCEDURAL NETWORKS

A Procedural Network (PN) can be described with a formalism similar to that used for an Augmented Transition Network Grammar ($ATNG$). This formalism has been successfully used for Natural Language and Pattern Recognition [8]. A PN is a 5-tuple

$$\mathrm{PN} = \{ j, Q, A, q_0, q_f \} \tag{1}$$

where j is the network identifier, Q is a finite set of states, A is a finite set of directed arcs, $q_0 \in Q$ is the initial state and q_f is the final state. Without any loss of generality we consider only PNs with a single initial state and a single final state.

Each arc $a_i \in$A is a 5 - tuple:

$$a_i = (q_{bi}, q_{ei}, P_i, condition_i, action_i) \tag{2}$$

where $q_{bi} \in Q$ is the starting state of a_i, $q_{ei} \in Q$ is the terminal state of a_i, P_i is a measure associated to the arc (it can be a weight or a probability according to the scoring method used by the PN supervisor described later on), $condition_i$ is a condition and $action_i$ is an action; both of them are associated to the arc. The conditions can be categorized in two classes:

COND n

refers to a user defined condition n.

DEFAULT r

refers to a default condition (it is satisfied only if no other condition of any arc whose starting state is q_{bi} returns a score greater than r).

The actions are executed by the PN supervisor and can be categorized in five classes:

EXE n

executes a user defined action; such an action is usually a "matcher" which

NATO ASI Series, Vol. F46
Recent Advances in Speech Understanding
and Dialog Systems
Edited by H. Niemann et al.

performs some computations on the input data and returns a result.

PUSH i

is defined as follows. Let's assume that PN_j has an arc that contains PUSH i. Let π_j be the process that executes PN_j. When the arc is reached whose associated action is PUSH i, the execution of π_j is suspended. The state of π_j is pushed on the top of the stack of the PN supervisor. A new process π_i that executes PN_i is created and executed. When the final state of PN_i is reached, the last arc of PN_i is considered. It has associated either a POPABS f or a POPCOND f action. This action is executed. It returns scores computed by PN_i. These scores are passed to π_j whose execution is resumed while π_i terminates.

POPABS f

is associated to the final state of a PN. It stops the execution of the current network process as soon as the final state is reached. The result of the execution of the user defined function f is returned.

POPCOND f

This action is also associated to the final state of a PN. It stops the execution of the current network if all the actions associated to the paths in the network leading to the final state have been executed. If the condition is reached, then the result of the execution of the user defined function f is returned.

JMP

makes the score associated to q_{bi} propagate to q_{ei} without any change.

A procedural network is a formalism for implementing knowledge representations by compiling concatenations of a limited number of basic actions. These actions produce scored interpretations of segments of the speech signal that have to be combined with scored expectations represented in data structures attached to network actions.

Each *PN* is associated a Working Memory (WM). Actions associated with the arcs of a subnetwork produce descriptions or evaluate scores that are stored into the subnetwork WM. When a push to a subnetwork is made, the supervisor may link the subnetwork WM with other WM, thus establishing the viewpoint within which conditions are tested. Data are transferred between PNs through WMs.

Most of the actions associated with arcs include plans, Hidden-Markov-Models (HMM), local parsers, rule-based inference units. All these tools are used for extracting an unambiguous description D of a speech pattern and for computing an a-priori probability for an hypothesis H:

$$P(D/H) \tag{3}$$

The *PN* supervisor keeps up to date a search space where each node is represented by the following four-tuple:

$$(q, context, T, score) \tag{4}$$

where:

-q is a state of the PN, with a buffer containing the information propagated by the actions executed before reaching it,
-"context" is the context (viewpoint) in which the conditions and actions of the arcs starting at q have to be executed,
-T is the starting time of the speech signal for the execution of sensory procedures invoked by the actions associated with the arcs starting at q,
-"score" is the score of the hypothesis contained in or implied by "context" in a time interval ending at T; score could be $P(D(t_\phi T)/H)$ where t_ϕ is the beginning of the sentence. T could also be a set of possible time references; in this case, score will be a set of scores $\{s(t)/t \in T\}$. Composite scores can be evaluated as likelihoods:

$$L(D,H) = Pr(D/H)Pr(H) \quad (5)$$

where $Pr(H)$ is obtained by a language model.

The size of the search space can be kept small in spite of a large number of states in the *PN* if conditions and actions are properly chosen and placed in the network.

2. THE SUPERVISOR

Several strategies can be applied in order to build a state space of hypotheses and to find the most plausible one. A Dynamic Programming approach has been used to design the PN supervisor for the application described in [10].

Let a_i be an arc of the j-th PN. Let s_k be the k-th segment of the input speech signal. The contribution of such an arc is

$$c_i = f_i(p_i, g_i(cond_i), h_i(act_i)) \quad (6)$$

where:

p_i is the score associated to a_i, g_i is a function which returns the evidence of satisfaction of condition i, h_i is the function which returns the value computed by the action i and f_i is the function which combines the values of its arguements in order to give the contribution of the arc.

According to the definition of p_i, g_i, h_i, and f_i several interpretations of the contribution of an arc are possible.

The assumption made for the experiment described in this paper is summarized in the following. Score p_i is the a priori probability of an arc; g_i is the probability that the condition is satisfied; h_i is the probability that the segment s_k matches with the knowledge used by action act_i; f_i is a multiplication operator, The contribution c_i can be rewritten as:

$$c_i = p_i\, g_i(cond_i)h_i(act_i) \quad (7)$$

Let $s = s_1, s_2, \ldots, s_n$ be an input sequence of speech segments, $PN_k = \{K, Q, A, q_o, q_f\}$ be the k-th PN and $a = a_1, a_2, \ldots, a_n$ be a sequence of arcs in the network PN_k such that the initial point of a_1 is q_ϕ and the terminal point of a_n is q_f.

We would like to find the sequence of arcs "a" which maximizes the conditional probability

$$P(a/s) = P(s/a)/P(s) \tag{8}$$

for a given s. That is to find the sequence "a" which maximizes:

$$P(s/a) = \prod_{i=1}^{n} \left[P_i \, g_i(cond_i) h_i(act_i) \right] \tag{9}$$

Given a fixed value of $k, k \in \{1, 2 \_\_\_, n-1\}$

$$\max_a P(s/a) = \max_{q \in Q} \left[\max_{q_k} P(s/a^k) \right] \tag{10}$$

where $a_k = a_1, a_2, \ldots, a_k, a_{k+1}, \ldots, a_n$ is a sequence of arcs such that the terminal point of a_k and the initial point of a_{k+1} is q ($i.e. a_k$ is the sequence of arcs such that the corresponding sequence of states contains q as the k-th state of the sequence). The DP algorithm computes the second term of (10).

Several other strategies, including forward and backward chaining, hierarchical planning, markov models, syntactic models, hypothesize and and test paradigm and son on, can be implemented by setting the proper procedural network parameters: probabilities, conditions and actions.

REFERENCES

1. S.E. Levinson, "Structural methods in automatic speech recognition", IEEE Proceedings, pp. 1625-1650, November 1985.
2. V. W. Zue, "The use of speech knowledge in automatic speech recognition", IEEE Proceedings, pp. 1602-1615, November 1985.
3. D. H. Klatt, "Review of the ARPA Speech Understanding Project", J. Acoust. Soc. Amer., vol. 62, pp. 1345-1366, 1977.
4. K. N. Stevens, "Acoustic correlates of some phonetic categories", J. Acoust. Soc. Amer., vol. 68, pp. 836-842, 1980.
5. R. De Mori, P. Laface, and Y. Mong, "Parallel algorithms for syllable recognition in continuous speech", IEEE Trans. Pattern Anal. Machine Intell., vol. 39, pp. 1-88, 1985.
6. R. De Mori,L. Lam, M. Gilloux, "Learning and plan refinement in a knowledge-based system for automatic speech recognition" IEEE Trans. Pattern Anal. Machine Intell., vol. 41, pp. , 1987.

7. L. R. Bahl, F. Jelinek, and R. L. Mercer, "A maximum likelihood approach to continuous speech recognition", IEEE Trans. Pattern Anal. Machine Intell., vol. PAMI-5, pp. 179-190, 1983.

8. K. S. Fu, "Syntactic pattern recognition and applications", Prentice Hall, 1982.

9. E. Merlo, R. De Mori, M. Palakal and G. Mercier, "A continuous parameter and frequency domain based Markov model", in Proc. Inter. Conf. on Acoust., Speech, Signal Processing, pp. 1597-1600, Tokyo, Japan, 1986.

10. R. De Mori, "Computer Recognition of Spoken Letters and Digits", this volume

REAL–TIME LARGE VOCABULARY WORD RECOGNITION VIA DIPHONE SPOTTING AND MULTIPROCESSOR IMPLEMENTATION

C. Scagliola – A. Carossino – A.M. Colla – C. Favareto
P. Pedrazzi – D. Sciarra – C. Vicenzi

RRL Dept. – Elettronica San Giorgio – Elsag S.p.A.
Via Puccini 2 – 16154 Genova (ITALY)

Abstract: This paper describes Elsag's Large Vocabulary Isolated Word Recognition system *DSPELL*. The system makes use of a diphone–based speech model and an extremely efficient word decoding algorithm, and is implemented on Elsag's multiprocessor *EMMA-2* [1] . *DSPELL* requires a very convenient training session and features a high recognition performance and real–time response on lexicons of up to 2,000 words.

1. INTRODUCTION

This paper presents a Large Vocabulary Isolated Word Recognition (*LVIWR*) system implemented at the *RRL* Laboratory of Elsag, beginning in 1986. This recognition system will be referred to by means of the acronym *DSPELL* (**D***iphone* **Sp***otting on* **E***MMA-2 for* **L***arge* **L***exicons*).

The main problem with a LVIWR task is related to computing resources, in the form of both the memory necessary to store the word representations and the huge amount of computation involved for word decoding. Therefore fast matching algorithms and a compact and discriminating word representation are required in order to achieve satisfactory results and *real–time* response.

In implementing *DSPELL*, we followed the general philosophy adopted in our former recognition systems, that is, we chose a word representation based on *diphone–like sub-word units* [COL 85b], a *template–matching* strategy [SCA 82] and a *speaker–trained* mode in order to achieve better performance. An automatic, quick and robust training procedure [COL 85a] extracts the templates for each new prospective user of the system.

DSPELL is implemented on *EMMA-2*, a very powerful general–purpose multiprocessing computer, designed and manifactured by Elsag [APP 85]. The hardware characteristics of the system cooperated to lead us to some implementation choices. For instance, in order to exploit *EMMA-2* 's capabilities, completely parallelizable matching and decoding algorithms have been adopted; namely, a *diphone spotting* approach for distance computation [SCA 82] and a *whole–word matching strategy*, which corresponds to a regular search [VIC 86]. The real–time response requirement pushed us to operate some further simplifications on both language representation and search strategy. This led to considerable savings both in memory requirements and in the computational load, without affecting significantly the recognition performance achieved by the system.

[1]patent pending

NATO ASI Series, Vol. F46
Recent Advances in Speech Understanding and Dialog Systems
Edited by H. Niemann et al.

In the following, after spending few words about the diphone–like units and the word models, we will present the recognition system *DSPELL*, with some details about its modules. Then we will briefly describe the hardware/software configuration of *DSPELL*. Finally some experimental results will be presented.

2. SPEECH AND LANGUAGE MODEL

2.1. The diphone–like units

The units we have defined and successfully adopted for the Italian language [COL 85a] [COL 85b] supply a compact and discriminative representation of any large lexicon. The diphone–like units, or, briefly, diphones, differ from the classical definition of diphones in that they are shorter, composite units, representative of both the steady–state and the transient portions of the speech signal. Their theoretical number, as defined according to Italian phonology, is slightly inferior to 300; however, a smaller number of units (about 240) are actually used.

Each diphone–like unit is represented by one or more templates; in particular, each steady–state unit is represented by multiple one–frame templates, out of various prosodic contexts (word–initial/final, stressed/unstressed, and so on), while transitions are represented by multi–frame templates, ranging from 4 up to 7 frames each (that is, 50 up to 90 msec), according to the kind of transition.

The training session is completely automatic [COL 85a]. It has to be performed only once for each talker in order to obtain diphone templates representative of the whole Italian language. The training material consists of a short meaningful passage, composed of 36 sentences (less than 5 minutes of speech). For each talker the diphone template set for the whole Italian language contains about 500 templates, corresponding to less than 1,500 speech frames.

2.2. Word models

The representation of the words of the lexicon is automatically generated starting from their regular spelling [COL 85a]. The representation of each word consists of one or more symbolic templates, each one built as a sequence of phonetic events named *classes*. Each node in a symbolic word template bears also information about its minimum and maximum permitted durations, which are context–dependent features.

Each class can correspond to one or more diphones. Currently almost every class contains only one diphone, with few exceptions related to common ambiguities in Italian pronunciation, such as for instance the possible realization of intervocalic **s** as either /s/ or /z/. In the last case, a class $< \& >$, containing both diphones **S** (/s/) and $\$$ (/z/), is defined along with classes $<$ **S** $>$ and $< \$ >$, which are proper in other definite cases.

Due to the use of classes, the word templates have the regular structure of a sequence, which is quite convenient for decoding: neither parallel branches, apt to represent possible phonological variations, nor skips, used to take into account allowable omissions, are present. Phonological variations are represented, when possible, by classes in which two or more diphones are merged. For instance, in the network representing any word containing an intervocalic s, class < & > is used to avoid a double branch. Other types of alternative pronunciations are dealt with by separate symbolic templates. Possible omissions are accounted for by imposing a minimum duration equal to one frame for the events that may be skipped.

Each reference template is embedded in silence, in order to take into account a possible imprecise end-pointing of the input word.

3. THE RECOGNITION SYSTEM *DSPELL*

3.1. Scheme of the system

The recognition system *DSPELL* consists of 6 modules, performing respectively acoustic analysis, end-point detection, diphone spotting, classification, word decoding and reliability evaluation. The input speech, picked up by a close-talking microphone, is analyzed by an acoustic front-end [CAV 85] and end-pointed. The distances between each input frame and the whole set of diphone templates are computed by the spotting module; in the classification phase these distances are replaced with distances from the *classes*. Word decoding is performed by using the frame-to-class distances according to the word models. Finally, a reliability score can be computed. In the following paragraphs the modules are presented in more details.

3.2. Acoustic analysis and end-point detection

The input signal is sampled at 10 KHz and pre-emphasized. Sixteen MEL-based Cepstrum parameters are computed on 256-point Hamming windows shifted every 12.8 msec; each parameter is then subjected to *liftering* [ITA 87]. Also the logarithm of the energy is stored for each frame.

End-point detection of words has been devised for very noisy environments. It is a 2-step procedure. In the first step the analyzed signal is grossly end-pointed by taking into account the energy contour on 100 msec windows; thresholds on energy levels, which are continuously updated, determine candidate speech segments out of the background noise and further thresholds on time separation of these segments cause the detection of prospective word boundaries. The second step consists of some local refinements applied at the candidate word boundaries.

3.3. Diphone spotting and classification

The distance of each input frame to each diphone template is evaluated by adopting a *diphone spotting* technique [SCA 82]: a N-frame-long diphone template is matched against all the N-frame windows in the signal containing the given frame, and the minimum distance value, over all these windows, is taken as the distance of the frame from the template. The distance is simply computed as the average frame-to-frame distance between the template and the portion of the signal in the window. The *Chebyshev* distance measure between liftered cepstral vectors, augmented by a penalty for energy difference, is adopted as frame-to-frame distance.

The classification module relates the acoustic distance measures from the diphone templates to the set of *classes*. The distance of an input frame to a given class is defined as the minimum distance over all the templates of the diphones belonging to that class.

3.4. Word decoding

Word decoding is performed by matching the output of the classification module against synthetic templates of all the words in the lexicon [VIC 86]. Adopting a *whole-word matching strategy* has several advantages: a fast, regular dynamic programming algorithm can be used; the memory requirements are constant and, finally, an ordered list of word candidates can be issued. A synthetic whole-word template is automatically generated, by expanding each node in the symbolic word representation into a sequence of as many states as the minimum duration associated with the node. Actually each state is a pointer used for retrieving the frame-to-class distance.

The dynamic programming algorithm adopted is slightly different from those proposed in [VIC 86]. All the states of each node but the last one, which corresponds to the *stretchable* portion of the node, must be traversed diagonally, while the last state can also be reached along horizontal paths. The pre-computed frame-to-class distances are used to calculate the distance score between input signal and reference word templates. The distance score is obtained by updating at each frame the distance cumulated along each permitted time warping path traversing that frame by adding the relevant pre-stored frame-to-class distance.

Given the execution speed of the decoding algorithm, there is no need for pre-pruning the lexicon even for fairly large vocabularies, but the symbolic templates of all the words in the vocabulary are matched against the input signal. The distance scores from all the words in the lexicon are re-arranged, and an ordered list of candidates is issued. A real-time response can be obtained even for a 2,000-word lexicon, by using a small hardware configuration (see Section 4).

3.5. Reliability evaluation

The aim of the reliability evaluation module is to produce the shortest list of candidate words including the correct one. This module is activated if *DSPELL* is used as part of an interactive system. If the top candidate is reliably recognized, no list is issued; otherwise a list of candidate words is presented to the user for confirmation.

The criterion for *cutting* the output list is based on the comparison of the distance scores of the first K candidate words: the list is cut after the k-th candidate if the ratio of the distance of the top candidate to the distance of candidate number $(k+1)$ is less than a given value, which is a statistically determined function of the candidate order k.

4. HARDWARE CONFIGURATION

DSPELL runs on a multiprocessor *EMMA-2* [APP 85] controlled by a main frame host computer. The configuration used for the implementation of *DSPELL* is rather small. It is composed of three kinds of boards: one *P1* board, featuring only one processing element (PE), which acts as the *master*; six *PN* boards, each featuring 3 PE's, which are the *slaves*, and a high capacity memory board (*HCSM*) for storing large data structures, such as the word representations and the frame-to-class distance matrices. The host computer adopted for *DSPELL* is a *VAX* 11/785. A Front-End (FE) unit [CAV 85] supplies a real-time acoustic analysis of the input signal.

The *P1* processor performs the following tasks: communication with the host, collection of the output from the FE, end-point detection, activation of the recognition processes in the slaves, ordering of the recognition results from the slaves, and off-line supervision. The *PN* boards perform the diphone spotting and classification and the word decoding. Two *PN*'s constitute the spotting group and four the decoding group. Each PE in the spotting group computes the frame-to-class distances for a part of the input frames and all the diphone classes, while each PE in the decoding group matches the whole input signal with a sub-lexicon and returns to the master the ordered list of the top candidates within the sub-lexicon. The master merges all the partial lists from the slaves, performs the reliability evaluation and sends the final list to the host for the interaction with the user.

5. EXPERIMENTAL RESULTS

		Speaker 1		Speaker 2	
Vocabulary	Test Set	% WRR	% ≤ 5 Top	% WRR	% ≤ 5 Top
V1 686 entries	1372 words	93.1	99.0	88.6	97.4
V2 1392 entries	1372 words	90.6	96.3	87.5	96.2
V3 1976 entries	500 words	93.0	98.3	—	—

Table 1: ***Results of three recognition experiments.***

Several on-line recognition experiments have been carried out, on different talkers and lexicons. In Table 1 the results of an experiment on two speakers with three different vocabularies, made up of proper nouns, are summarized. Speaker 1 is a male and Speaker 2 a female. Vocabulary *V1* is a highly confusable subset of *V2*, while vocabulary *V3* is completely different. The average number of symbolic templates per word is approximately 1.2 for vocabularies *V2* and *V1*, and 1.3 for *V3*. In the first two experiments, the test set, consisting of two utterances by each speaker of all the words in *V1*, was matched against *V1* itself and the whole *V2* respectively. In the third experiment Speaker 1 performed a one-hour on-line test uttering words randomly generated out of vocabulary *V3*.

Table 1 shows the performance in terms of the Word Recognition Rate and the recognition rate within the 5 top candidates. These results are satisfactory, especially considering that all the tests were performed in an environment affected by a strong, highly variable background noise (more than 80 dB on the average).

6. CONCLUSIONS

In this paper we have presented the LVIWR system *DSPELL*, designed and implemented by the *RRL* Department of Elsag S.p.A. The system features a high recognition performance and real-time response on lexicons of up to 2,000 Italian words, mainly due to the accurate but economical diphone-based speech model, the efficient word decoding algorithm and the implementation on a powerful multiprocessor architecture (*EMMA-2*). Other characteristics of the system are a very convenient training session, to be performed for each talker once for the whole Italian language, and a quick and easy adaptation to different lexicons.

Bibliography

[APP 85] E. Appiani, G. Barbagelata, F. Cavagnaro, B. Conterno & R. Manara, *EMMA-2 : An Industry-Developed Hierarchical Multiprocessor for Very High Performance Signal Processing Applications*, Proc. 1st Int. Conf. on Supercomputing Systems, St. Petersburg, Florida, pp. 310—319 (Dec. 1985)

[CAV 85] M. Cavazza, A. Ciaramella & R. Pacifici, *Implementation of an Acoustic Front-End for Speech Recognition*, in R. DeMori & C.Y. Suen (Editors), *"New Systems and Architectures for Automatic Speech Recognition and Synthesis"*, NATO ASI Series, vol. F16, Springer-Verlag, pp. 215—223 (1985)

[COL 85a] A.M. Colla & D. Sciarra, *Automatic Generation of Linguistic, Phonetic and Acoustic Knowledge for a Diphone-Based Continuous Speech Recognition System*, in R. DeMori & C.Y. Suen (Editors), *"New Systems and Architectures for Automatic Speech Recognition and Synthesis"*, NATO ASI Series, vol. F16, Springer-Verlag, pp. 361—387 (1985)

[COL 85b] A.M. Colla, C. Scagliola & D. Sciarra, *A Continuous Speech Recognition System using a Diphone-Based Language Model*, Proc. ICASSP 1985 (31.9), Tampa (Mar. 1985)

[ITA 87] F. Itakura & T. Umezaki, *Distance Measure for Speech Recognition based on the Smoothed Group Delay Spectrum*, Proc. ICASSP 1987 (29.1), vol. 3, pp. 1257—1260, Dallas (Apr. 1987)

[SCA 82] C. Scagliola & L. Marmi, *Continuous Speech Recognition via Diphone Spotting: a Preliminary Implementation*, Proc. ICASSP 1982, vol. 3, pp. 2008—2011, Paris (May 1982)

[VIC 86] C. Vicenzi & D. Sciarra, *Using Diphones in Large Vocabulary Word Recognition*, Proc. Montreal Symposium on Speech Recognition, pp. 47—48, Montreal (July 1986)

SPEECH RECOGNITION
WITH
DIFFICULT DICTIONARIES
(+)

F. Casacuberta and E. Vidal
Dpto. Sistemas Informáticos y Computación
Universidad Politécnica de Valencia
46071 Valencia, Spain

Abstract: In this paper we introduce a new generalization of the Generalized Linear Discriminant Function, in which the dimension of the representation space depends on the class. This generalization is applied to Speech Recognition with Difficult Dictionaries, leading to a (preliminary) error rate reduction over 50% with respect to the standard approach.

1. INTRODUCTION

Dynamic Time Warping methods have been found to be not sufficiently adequate to deal with dictionaries of very similar words. This is due to the fact that the difference between such words comes usually from few frames, and this difference can be confused, in many cases, with the intrinsic variability of the speech signal. Some heuristic approaches to this problem have already been proposed in the literature /RAB 81/ /MOO 82/ /MOO 83/ /BOC 86/.

In this paper, another approach dealing with this kind of difficult dictionaries is proposed, in which the actual interword distance is computed by using a sequence of production weights which can vary along the dynamic time warping path. This method is, in a certain sense, similar to that proposed in /RAB 81/ and also shares certain ideas with /MOO 82/ and /MOO 83/, but in this case: 1) we allow each individual production to have associated a different and variable weight, thus accounting simlutaneously for the variablility both in the time and in the spectral domain, and 2) they are automatically learnt from speech samples, using a non-parametric approach; i.e. no assumption is made about the (possibly) underlying statistical nature of the data involved.

The proposed approach comes from the well known classical non-parametric learning methods of Pattern Recognition /DUD 73/; in particular,

---

(+) Work partially suported by grant No. PA85-0086 of the Spanish CAICYT.

NATO ASI Series, Vol. F46
Recent Advances in Speech Understanding and Dialog Systems
Edited by H. Niemann et al.

those corresponding to the (generalized) Linear Discriminant Function (GLDF). However, since the set of word representatives can not be assumed to constitute a vector space /VID 85/, a new type of GLDF has to be previously introduced.

2. A GENERALIZATION OF THE LINEAR DISCRIMINANT FUNCTION

In this section, we introduce a new generalization of the Generalized Discriminant Function /DUD 73/ as:

$$g_i(X) = \sum_{j=1}^{d_i} a_{ij}\, y_{ij}(X) = \mathbf{a}_i\, \mathbf{y}_i(X) \qquad 1 < i < m$$

where for each category i, we have the standard weight vector $\mathbf{a}_i$ as well as a vector function $\mathbf{y}_i$ different for each category, both of d_i-dimension.

With this generalization of GLDF, we can define a decision rule for classification, and the concepts of "linear" separability in the usual way /DUD 73/.

Most of the learning methods, based on Gradient Descendent Procedures can be easily extended to this formulation in order to obtain $\mathbf{a}_i$ such that correctly classifies the samples of some training set. The procedure chosen here is a modification of the procedure of Mimimization of the Perceptron Criterion Function, which builds a sequence of weight vectors $\mathbf{a}_i(k)$, k=1,2,... in the following way:

$\mathbf{a}_i(1)$ = arbitrary

IF X_k M belongs to category i AND $g_j(X_k) > g_i(X_k) \quad i \neq j$

THEN $\mathbf{a}_i(k+1) \leftarrow \mathbf{a}_i(k) + r_k\, \mathbf{y}_i(X_k)$

$\mathbf{a}_j(k+1) \leftarrow \mathbf{a}_j(k) - r_k\, \mathbf{y}_i(X_k)$

$\mathbf{a}_l(k+1) \leftarrow \mathbf{a}_l(k) \qquad l \neq i$ and $l \neq j$

FI

where r_k is, in general, a function of k called increment, and determines the size of each correction step.

The classical Kesler construction /DUD 73/ can be easily modified so as to acomodate this variable dimension formulation /VID 87/. This allows to reduce the variable dimension multicategory case to one of single dimension two categories, and hence, to use the existing convergence proofs /DUD 73/ to guarantee the convergence of the proposed approach /VID 87/.

3. ISOLATED WORD RECOGNITION AND GLDF

Given two words X and P, an optimal time warping path is obtained using a

Dynamic Time Warping procedure with a symmetric set of productions (Fig.1):

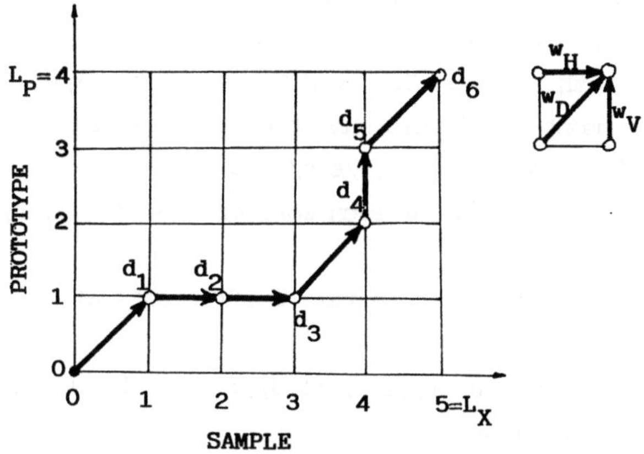

FIGURE 1: Example of a Dynamic Time Warping path with local distances attached.

The distance between P and X is, in the example:

$$D(P,X) = w_D\, d_1 + w_H\, d_2 + w_H\, d_3 + w_D\, d_4 + w_V\, d_5 + w_D\, d_6$$

where w_D , w_H and w_V are the corresponding weights associated to the production used.

Associated to the class represented by the word P, we define a vector function $\mathbf{y}_P(X)$ as:

$$\mathbf{y}_P(X) = (d_1,\ d_4,\ 0,\ d_6,\ d_2{+}d_3,\ 0,\ 0,\ 0,\ 0,\ 0,\ d_5,\ 0)$$

that is, a component for each frame of P and for each production, which represents the total distance in which the frame is used with the corresponding production.

Obviously, in the multicategory case, a vector for each class P_i can be obtained from the optimal time warping path between P_i and X.

From a set of m prototypes (P_i $1 \leqslant i \leqslant m$), and a given training set, we can apply the learning method presented in section 2, using the vector function introduced in this section, to obtain a variable weight vector set $\mathbf{a}_i$.

Given a test word X, the recognition procedure consists of two steps. In the first step, classical DTW is computed for X and each prototype P_i, and an optimal time warping path is obtained. In the second step, a distance between X and each P_i is recomputed by using the variable weight vector instead of the conventional weights of the productions in the optimal time warping path. Finaly, a minimun distance criterium is used for classification purposes.

4. PRELIMINARY EXPERIMENTS AND RESULTS

Some very preliminar experiments were carried out in order to test the method proposed in this paper. The conditions of the experiments were:

Vocabulary: the most difficult subset of the Spanish alpha set: /efe/, /ele/, /eme/, /eλe/, /ene/, /eɲe/, /ere/ and /ese/.

Speech Data: 21 repetitions of each word of the vocabulary from a single female speaker.

Parameters: vectors of 11 cepstral coefficients at a rate of 66.66 vectors/second.

DTW: a) productions = ((0,1),(1,1),(1,0)); b) weights = (1,2,1) and c) local distance = euclidean norm.

In the folowing experiments, Varaible Increment Rule was used for training.

Experiment 1 The first 12 repetitions were used as a training set, and the remaining 9 repetitions as a testing set. The prototype of each word was chosen arbitrarily among the repetitions of the training set. For a value of r of 0.5 an error rate of 23% was obtained, and 19% for a value of 0.05. The classical error rate, using the same prototype and conventional DTW was 39%.

Experiment 2 This experiment was identical to experiment 1, but the prototype of each word was the centroid of the repetitions of this word in the training set. For a value of r of 0.05 an error rate of 11% was obtained, and 6% for a value of 0.01. The classical error rate, using the same prototype and conventional DTW was 14%.

In both experiments, for the adequate values of the correction step, recognition improvements of more than 50% with respect to conventional DTW based methods are achieved.

It is easy to see that extra computation in the recognition step of the method proposed is not significant as compared to DTW procedures.

5. CONCLUSIONS

A new approach has been proposed for dealing with discrimination between very similar words. It is based on a new formulation of Generalized Linear Discriminant Functions, which allows the introduction of variable production weights in the computation of DTW-based interword distances. Also, the new formulation permits one to automatically learn an "optimal" set of weights through a Percetron-like Gradient Descendent procedure.

Preliminary experimental results have shown that this approach leads to significant reduction in error rates with respect to the classical approach. These results corroborates earlier studies reported by other authors /RAB 81/.

More exhaustive experiments are needed to test the method introduced here, and other learning procedures can be tried, such as the Minimum Squared Error procedures.

6. REFERENCES

/BOC 86/ E.L. Bocchieri; G.R. Doddington: "Frame-Specific Statistical Features for Speaker Independent Speech Recognition" IEEE Trans. on Acoust. Speech and Signal Proc. Vol. 34 (4), pp. 755-764 (1986)

/COR 87/ F.J. Corell; J.C. Tabarés; E. Vidal; F. Casacuberta: "Utilización de Funciones Discriminantes Lineales Generalizadas en el Reconocimiento de Palabras Aisladas con Ciertos Diccionarios Difíciles" To appear in Qüestió.

/DUD 73/ R.O. Duda; P.E. Hart: "Pattern Classification and Scene Analysis". J. Wiley. (1973)

/FER 87/ A. Fernandez; P. Rodriguez; E. Vidal; H. Rulot: "Reconocimiento de Palabras muy Semejantes basado en la Minimización del Criterio Perceptron" To be appear in Revista de Informática y Automática.

/MOO 82/ R.K. Moore; M.J. Russell; M.J. Tomlinson: "Locally Constrained Dynamic Programming in Automatic Speech Recognition" Proc. of the ICASSP-82, pp. 1270-1273 (1982)

/MOO 83/ R.K. Moore; M.J. Russell; M.J. Tomlinson: "The Discriminative Network: A Mechanism for focusing Recognition in Whole-Word Pattern Recognition" Proc. of the ICASSP-83, pp. 1041-1044 (1983)

/RAB 81/ L.R. Rabiner; J.G. Wilpon: "Isolated Word Recognition using a Two-Pass Pattern Recognition Approach". Proc. of the ICASSP-81, pp. 724-727. (1981)

/VID 85/ E. Vidal; F. Casacuberta; H. Rulot: "Is the DTW "Distance" really a Metric?: An Algorithm reducing the Number of DTW comparisons in Isolated Word Recognition". Speech Communication. Vol (4), pp. 333-344 (1985)

/VID 87/ E.Vidal; F.Casacuberta: "Variable Dimension Generalized Linear Discriminant Functions and Applications". To be published.

ACKNOWLEDGEMENTS

Thanks are due to A. Fernandez, P. Rodriguez, F. Corell and J. Tabarés for their help in programming and experimentation.

RECENT RESULTS ON THE APPLICATION OF A METRIC-SPACE SEARCH ALGORITHM (AESA) TO MULTISPEAKER DATA

Enrique Vidal, M.José Lloret
Dpto.Sist.Informáticos y Computación.
Univ.Politécnica de Valencia

1. INTRODUCTION

Isolated Word Recognition (IWR) is usually approached by Minimum Distance classifiers [3] which rely on Dynamic Time Warping (DTW) procedures to compute appropriate Dissimilarity Measures between the uttered test words and the reference utterances (prototypes) stored in a dictionary [6] [1]. As the time complexity of these methods is linear with the size of the dictionary, they are often considered **"efficient"** in the literature. However, even linear time is, in practice, fairly inadequate for the problem in hand; first, because of the relatively large time complexity of the DTW procedures, and second, because it is quite **"unnatural"** (and also undesirable) that the time response of a speech recognition device be proportional to the number of words of its vocabulary.

To reduce the time complexity of DTW-based IWR, a number of (heuristic) techniques have been introduced during the last few years. Specifically with regard to reducing the number of DTW computations, some new and promessing methods have recently been proposed which are based on search algorithms (formerly) designed for finding Nearest Neighbours in Metrics Spaces [4] [5]. In particular, we have recently introduced the so called **"Approximating and Eliminating Search Algorithm" (AESA)** which, in simulation experiments with abstract Metric Spaces, has proved to have an asymptotical **constant average time complexity** ; i.e., for sufficiently large data sets, the number of required distance computations tends to be a constant which depends **only** on the actual distances from the test samples to their nearest prototypes [7] [9].

The possibility of applying the AESA to IWR was first investigated in [8] in which preliminary average DTW computation savings over 70% were achieved for rather small dictionaries using a specific DTW procedure and speech parameterization. The next step was then devoted to systematically test the performance of the algorithm with wider choices in speech parameters and DTW procedures, as well as using larger dictionaries in order to verify whether the asymptotical constant-time behaviour found in the simulation experiments [7] also holds for real speech. The main results of that work,

(*) Work supported in part by the Spanish CAICYT under grant PA85-86.

NATO ASI Series, Vol. F46
Recent Advances in Speech Understanding
and Dialog Systems
Edited by H. Niemann et al.

in fact, showed that the same main features reflected in the former simulation experiments are also true for real speech samples; to be more specific, with dictionaries **up to 200 words** and for most of the different speech parameters, local metrics and DTW productions taken into account, the AESA proved able to find the Nearest Neighbour (NN) prototype of a given speech sample through an average of **7 to 12 DTW computations** (94% to 96% computation savings for 200 words), with a strong (exponential) tendency to need less computations if the samples are close to their corresponding prototypes ("well uttered" words) [9] [10].

This strong tendency, along with the small dependence of the number of DTW computations on the size of the dictionary, give rise to an important implication in the application of the AESA to **multispeaker tasks.** In fact, in a dictionary with multi−represented words (e.g. one set of prototypes for each speaker), it is well known that the (NN−rule) error rate tends to be smaller as the number of word representatives is increased; but, unfortunately, the classical search time is increased correspondingly. By searching with the AESA, instead, a **simultaneous** reduction in both the error rate and the search time can be expected. This follows from the fact that, as the number of representatives is increased, a greater probability exists that the test utterances fall **nearer** to some of them, leading to an (exponential) tendency to reduce the required number of DTW computations which compensate more than sufficiently for the little dependency of this number on the increasing size. This paper is mainly devoted to present some empirical evidence which seems to confirm the above expectations.

2. THE APPROXIMATING AND ELIMINATING SEARCH ALGORITHM (AESA)

The main idea is to use a precomputed array of distances between prototypes for two main purposes: 1)Fast dynamic search through successive "**approximations**" towards the NN prototype of the given test sample; and 2)Look ahead "**elimination**" from the searching of those prototypes which, by using the Triangle Inequality (TI), can be shown that they can not be nearer to the test sample then the current NN found so far. Formal descriptions and details of the AESA have been given elsewhere [7] [10] and we will not insist in such topics. We shell only mention here that the AESA achieves exact NN searching results whenever the Dissimilarity Measure adopted fulfill "exactly" the metric properties (the TI in particular). In other cases the algorithm can use a "TI Looseness Constant", H, in order to tailor its elimination rules to the degree of TI verification observed in the given data, and so to control the exactness of the NN search [8] [10]. This "optimal" value of H can be estimated from the empirical distributions (histograms) of the "TI Looseness function", (defined as: $H(x,y,z) = D(x,y) + D(y,z) - D(x,z)$ [2] [11] for every triplet (x,y,z) of utterances) or, alternatively, by running prospective recognition experiments.

3. MULTISPEAKER EXPERIMENTS

The speech data consisted of 10 repetitions of the 10−word Spanish digit vocabulary, which where uttered by 10 different speakers (5 male and 5 female). This makes a total of 1000 utterances. Each speaker uttered his data in two or more sessions which spread over a period ranging from one day to one month. The acquisition and end−point detection procedures were rather standard and the signal was sampled at 8533 Hz. with a twelve bits A/D converter. The acquired speech data were then converted into strings of 10−dimensional parameter vectors of Cepstrum Coefficients, which where obtained from a 16 channel Mel Frequency Scale filter bank at a rate of 66.66 vectors per second. DTW consisted of a symmetric slope−constraining procedure (productions = {(2,1),(1,1),(1,2)}, and weights = {2,1,2}) and the Local Distance was the Euclidean Norm.

The main results are summarized in Table 1. Following these results it seems clear that, with AESA searching, very accurate recognition can be achieved with a dramatical computation reduction with respect to the classical exhaustive search procedure. Furthermore, as this applies for a wide range of values of the Looseness Constant, no optimization procedure is strictly required to estimate an appropriate value of this constant.

Table 1: *Avg. Number of DTW computations/ Error rate, for several data sets and search conditions ("m" = male,"f" = female)*

TEST TYPE		Speakers / Utterances REFER.SET	TEST SET	EXHS. SEARCH	AESA H=40%	H=50%	H=60%
Multspk.		10(5m−5f)/200	10(5m−5f)/800	200/0.1	5.4/0	4.5/0.5	3.9/1.3
Spk.	m&f	6(3m−3f)/180	4(2m−2f)/400	180/0.3	8.2/0.3	5.7/0.8	4.5/1
	m	3(m)/180	2(m)/200	180/0.5	7.7/0	4.9/0.5	3.8/0.5
Ind.	f	3(f)/180	2(f)/200	180/0	6.4/0	4.3/0	3.5/0.5

Also, from these results and other (not reported) results, it turns out that the errors produced with AESA searching decrease as the Looseness Constant is smaller. Since another, obvious, general way of reducing errors in dictionaries with multirepresented words is by increasing the number of tokens included in the dictionary, it would be most interesting to take both factors into account and to see how many DTW computations are **actually** needed on the average to achieve a **given** constant error rate. This is explicitly shown in fig. 1 and 2, where families of equal-error curves have been drown as a function of the number of word representatives. It seems clear in these figures that, for a pre-specified error rate, our algorithm can run faster as the number of word representatives is increased; more specifically, by increasing this number, a simultaneous reduction in both the error rate and the search time can be achieved (cf. Section-1).

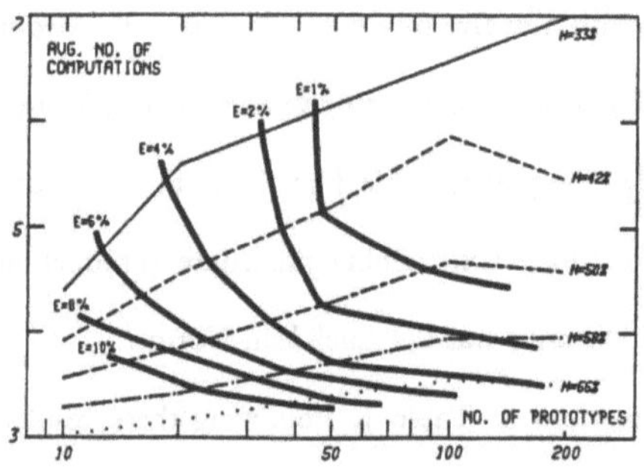

Fig.1. Equal-error curves for a multispeaker test (10 speakers: 5 male, 5 female).

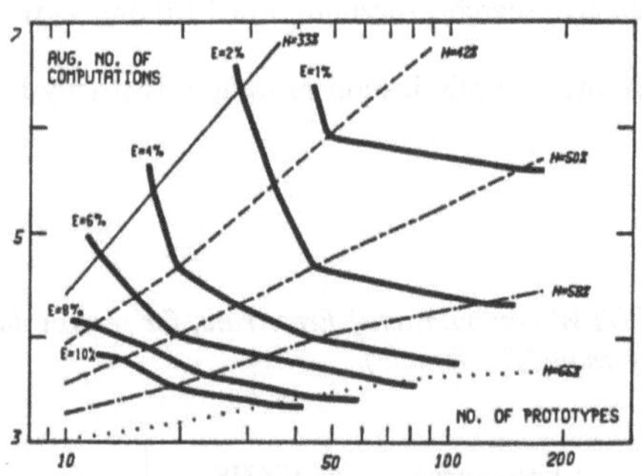

Fig.2. Equal-error curves for a speaker-independent test (ref.-set: 3 male, 3 female; test-set: 2 male, 2 female).

4. CONCLUDING REMARKS

From the above results we can conclude that, by using the Approximating and Eliminating Search Algorithm, very accurate (>99%) speaker independent recognition of the Spanish digits is possible while requiring only about 5 Dynamic Time Warping computations on the average. On the other hand, it should be emphasized that these results were obtained without using any clustering procedure for selecting the prototypes. This was made possible thanks the above discussed AESA property that, increasing the number of word representatives results in a simultaneous reduction in both the error rate and the number of distance computations. Consequently, instead of looking for possible clusters of utterances, and representing each cluster by a limited number of its members, (so as to keep the number of prototypes as low as possible, in an attempt to render exhaustive searching tractable), the best strategy for AESA searching should consist of representing each word by as many utterances as possible. However, this strategy is unfortunately limited by the quadratic preprocessing time and memory which are required for computing and storing the interprototype distances needed by the AESA. Taking also this into account, it turns out that practical reasonable limits correspond to dictionaries with approximatly 500 prototypes [8]. For the digits vocabulary, this represents the possibility of having each word represented by about 50 utterances, which seems more than sufficient, at least for the Spanish digits. Obviously, for other (larger) vocabularies, clustering can in fact result in being necessary to keep the total number of prototypes within manageable values.

REFERENCES

[1] F.Casacuberta, E.Vidal: "Reconocimiento Automático del Habla". Ed. Marcombo. 1987.

[2] F.Casacuberta, H.Rulot, E.Vidal: "On the metric Properties of Dynamic Time Warping. To appear in IEEE Trans. ASSP.

[3] R.O.Duda, P.E.Hart: "Pattern Classification and Scene Analysis". J.Wiley & Sons, 1973.

[4] V.N.Gupta, M.Lenning, P.Mermelstein: "Decision Rules for Speaker−Independent Isolated Word Recognition". Proc. of ICASSP. pp. 9.2.1−9.2.4, 1984.

[5] P.Lockwood: "A Low Cost DTW−Based Discrete Utterance Recognizer" ICPR. Paris, 1986.

[6] H.Sakoe, S.Chiba: "Dynamic Programming Algorithm Optimization for Spoken Words Recognition". IEEE Trans. ASSP, Vol.ASSP−26, pp.43−49 Feb. 1978.

[7] E. Vidal: "An algorithm for finding Nearest Neighbors in (approximately) constant average time complexity". Pattern Recognition Letters. 4, pp. 145−157, 1986.

[8] E.Vidal, F.Casacuberta, H.Rulot: "Is the DTW "distance" really a metric ? − An algorithm reducing the number of DTW comparisons in Isolated Word Recognition". Speech Communication. N.4, pp. 333−344, 1985.

[9] E.Vidal, H.Rulot, F.Casacuberta, J.M.Benedí: "Searching for Nearest Neighbors in Constant Average Time with Applications to Discrete Utterance Speech Recognition". 8th. Int. Conf. Patt. Recogn. (ICPR), Vol.2, pp. 808−810. Paris. Oct. 1986.

[10] E.Vidal, H.Rulot, F.Casacuberta, J.M.Benedí: "On the use of a Metric Space Search Algorithm for fast DTW−based recognition of isolated words. To appear in IEEE Trans. ASSP.

[11] E.Vidal, F.Casacuberta, H.Rulot, J.M.Benedí, M.J.Lloret: "On the verification of the Triangle Inequality by DTW dissimilarity measures". To appear in Speech communication.

Robust Features for Word Recognition

E. Günter Schukat-Talamazzini

Lehrstuhl für Informatik 5 (Mustererkennung)
Universität Erlangen-Nürnberg
Martensstraße 3
D-8520 Erlangen, F.R. Germany

Abstract : This paper presents a new approach to automatic recognition of spoken words. After discussing the demands upon appropriate subword units and reporting some experiments in using phone superclasses for word recognition we will develop techniques of robust classification, segmentation, and lexical access, utilizing binary phonetic features as processing units.

1. Subword units

Except for problems such as speaker-dependent isolated word recognition using a small vocabulary, automatic speech recognition requires the use of appropriate processing units below the word level for providing contact between acoustic input and word lexicon. Especially large vocabulary speaker-independent systems as the Erlangen dialog system EVAR [Niemann 85] already need such units for alleviating acquisition of word pronunciations. For the definition of these speech units at least three dimensions have to be fixed: their temporal duration (e.g. phones, syllables), their abstraction level (e.g. articulatory, acoustical, auditory) and their granulation (fine or coarse classes). The subword units have to obey two requirements:

- The units should posess a material correlate in the speech signal, i.e. classification and segmentation should be possible with sufficient success.
- The units should operate phonologically distinctive, i.e. they should be suited for characterizing the pronunciation of vocabulary words just like a phonetic transcription.

Given the mentioned provisions, one may hope for a successful word recognition by connecting in series speech input classification and lexical access both using the chosen subword units.

NATO ASI Series, Vol. F46
Recent Advances in Speech Understanding
and Dialog Systems
Edited by H. Niemann et al.

2. Critical remarks concerning previous approaches

Some facts have to be noted concerning the traditional speech units and their use in speech recognition. The large amount of distinguished classes of the usual inventories in connection with the mutual disjointness of their elements first of all cause a rather low recognition rate of automatic phonetic classification [Goldberg 75, Mariani 82]. This situation is sharpened by arising errors of segmentation, a processing step, which seems to be conceptually questionable at least in the case of phone-like units. Both phenomena together usually enforce treating the phonetical variability of word pronunciation during the word level pattern matching process. So compensation of classificational as well as segmentational flaws is left to common mathematical techniques like *Dynamic Time Warping* or *Hidden Markov Modeling*. Due to their geometrical resp. statistical settings and their view of global similarity in terms of cumulated local similarities, these techniques are not able to keep apart patterns that merely differ for a short time period [Moore 83], and to take into account phone structure and syllable structure simultaneously when matching word patterns.

3. Using phone superclasses for word recognition

In [Shipman 82], a reduction of the phoneme inventory of american english to five superclasses was proposed. Clearly, these coarse classes are more robust against classification errors of acoustic-phonetic modules in ASR systems as compared to, for instance, allophonic classes. At the same time, it could be shown that the phonetic transcription of words in terms of these superclasses provides sufficient discrimination between the items of large vocabularies. An even larger degree of word representation uniqueness (e.g. for 60 % instead of 44 % of the entries of a 1222 word lexicon) using the same number of classes could be achieved by automatically optimizing superclasses due to a transinformation criterion [Schukat 86]. Phone superclasses were applied for large vocabulary IWR [Lagger 85, Laface 87] and for word hypothesizing in continuous speech [Schukat 85]. In the latter case, word candidates were retrieved from an associatively organized pronunciation lexicon using consecutive superclass triplets as addressing units. The approach operated remarkably fast but showed a slightly lower recognition rate in comparison with an HMM method. We argue that these unsatisfactory results are due to the segmentation problem, i.e., we cannot expect to reliably draw segment boundaries between phones that we have merged to a superclass before in order to obtain robust classification. Indeed, the (by far too optimistic) *expected cohort size* of 3.2 words in a 3918 word vocabulary using five superclasses dramatically raised to about 11.0 when regarding intraclass segmentation as impossible.

4. Using binary phonetic features for word recognition

The basic idea behind the following approach is to accomplish very coarse but reliable categorial labelings of the input signal. Consequently, the adjacent lexical access may be based upon pattern matching techniques providing only little tolerance of errors.

As a starting point for classification we employ an inventory containing a large amount of coarse phone superclasses. Clearly, the intersection between two classes is allowed to be non-empty, and, for each class, the inventory includes the set-theoretical complement, too. From an intensional point of view, these superclasses may be viewed as phonetic features. Instead of prefixing a set of units to be used for labeling the speech signal (and being surprised by the recognition rate), we now, on the contrary, fix a lower threshold (e.g. 95 %) for classification reliability. Presently, we compute 10 mel frequency cepstral coefficients and energy for consecutive 12.8 msec frames of the incoming speech. For each frame, a posteriori probabilities of 49 allophonic classes are calculated using a Bayes classifier under normal density assumption [Regel 87]. The score of a binary feature (at the present time we use forty of them, e.g. $\pm$*consonant*, $\pm$*fricative*, $\pm$*labial*, etc.) is determined by summing up the probabilities of all allophonic labels contributing to that feature. After that, for each time frame we will be interested only in superclass labelings with scores exceeding the given threshold. We observed that because of the large amount of very coarse features practically in each time frame one or more features exceeded the threshold. For instance, the percentage of frames leading to at least *one* decision is about 86.6 % (98.8 %) when applying a feature acceptance threshold of 99 % (90 %).

Segmentation of the signal proceeds in tiers with respect to every single phonetic feature. Besides the fact, that we do not need any explicit segmentation of the input in terms of subword units for the lexical access stage, this autosegmental procedure offers a number of advantages. On one hand, it allows for the phenomenon of articulatory control, leading to transitions between the components of adjacent feature bundles, which do not happen parallel in time according to an idealized conception of phone boundaries. On the other hand, our analysis is not restricted to units of equal temporal duration. As an example we mention the features $\pm$SN, $\pm$CC *(may/not occur in syllable nuclei resp. consonant clusters)*, which cause a syllable structured segmentation of the speech signal. With respect to the consequent word matching stage, this will assure the rejection of candidates with deviating syllable structure.

Using the fact, that there are certain limitations on the temporal duration of feature presence and absence, segmentation is done by applying an iterated third order median filter to the time series of categorial yes/no decisions of each separate feature.

Pattern matching for the word decision is done, as is customary, by looking for an acceptable time alignment connecting the representations of a reference word and the acoustical input. Equipped with a rather certain although coarse segmentation of the signal in terms of features, we abandon tolerant matching strategies (and the incidental drawbacks). Instead we reject alignments exhibiting local incompatibilities in the sense, that there is a feature of the reference pattern with its complementary feature showing up in the robust classification of the corresponding time frame of the input (cf. Fig. 1).

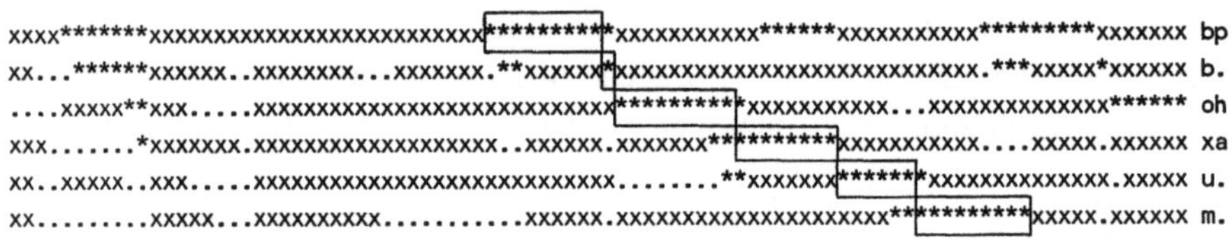

Fig. 1 For each phone component of the german word *Bochum* (closure and burst of /b/, /o/, [χ]-allophone of /x/, /u/, and /m/) we calculated the *refutation* vector by labeling a frame by **x** if the complement feature of at least one of the reference features has been robustly detected (in the above sense). As can be seen, there is a possible time registration path for the actually uttered word *Bochum*.

As in the example, the simplest way to construct word reference patterns is to map an allophonic word transcription into a sequence of binary feature bundles. Additionally, we will make conservative use of phonological assimilation rules to relax the feature constraints on a given vocabulary word. That means that if the application of an optional rule to a segment would change a feature absence into presence or vice versa, this feature is entirely deleted from this segment. Finally, each reference segment will be equipped with a fuzzy temporal duration, that is computed due to intrinsic phoneme durations, segmental context, accent pattern, and estimated speech rate. This inclusion of temporal information is important to model *voice onset time* and vowel quantities.

5. Conclusion

We presented an approach using very coarse phonetic classes (binary features) for large vocabulary word hypothesization. The approach includes the creation of robust frame labels, independent segmentation of binary features and a word matching scheme that incorporates segmental duration, simultaneously compares segmental as well as syllabic word structure, and makes economic use of coarticulation rules. Due to its refutation strategy, word pattern matching is sensitive to even short local incompatibilities, but, at the same time, there will be no false rejections because of frames lacking any reliable categorial information.

Bibliography

[Goldberg 75]
H.G. Goldberg: Segmentation and Labeling of Speech: a comparative Performance Evaluation, Techn. Rep. Computer Science, CMU, Pittsburgh, PA, 1975.

[Laface 87]
P. Laface, R. Pieraccini: Recognition of Words in Very Large Vocabulary, this Volume, 1987.

[Lagger 85]
H. Lagger, A. Waibel: A Coarse Phonetic Knowledge Source for Template Independent Large Vocabulary Word Recognition, ICASSP-85, 862-865, 1985.

[Mariani 82]
J.J. Mariani: The AESOP Continuous Speech Understanding System, ICASSP-82, 1637-40, 1982.

[Moore 83]
R.K. Moore, M.J. Russell, M.J. Tomlinson: The Discriminative Network: a Mechanism for Focusing Recognition in Whole-Word Pattern Matching, ICASSP-83, 1041-44, 1983.

[Niemann 85]
H. Niemann, A. Brietzmann, R. Mühlfeld, P. Regel, G. Schukat: The Speech Understanding and Dialog System EVAR, in: R. DeMori, C.Y. Suen: New Systems and Architectures for Automatic Speech Recognition and Synthesis, NATO ASI Series F, Springer Verlag, 271-302, 1985.

[Regel 87]
P. Regel: Akustisch-phonetische Transkription für die automatische Spracherkennung, Dissertation, IMMD 5 (Pattern Recognition), Univ. Erlangen-Nürnberg, 1987.

[Schukat 85]
E.G. Schukat-Talamazzini, S. Heunisch: Schnelle Präselektion von Wörtern aus kontinuierlich gesprochener Sprache, Proc. 7. DAGM Symposium, Informatik FB 107, Springer Verlag, 170-174, 1985.

[Schukat 86]
E.G. Schukat-Talamazzini: Automatic Generation and Evaluation of Phone Superclasses for Continuous Speech Recognition, EUSIPCO-86, 537-540, 1986.

[Shipman 82]
D.W. Shipman, V.W. Zue: Properties of Large Lexicons: Implications for Advanced Isolated Word Recognition Systems, ICASSP-82, 546-549, 1982.

STATISTICAL ANALYSIS OF LEFT-TO-RIGHT PARSER FOR WORD-HYPOTHESING

H. Höge, E. Marschall

Siemens AG, Zentrale Aufgaben Informationstechnik, München
Otto-Hahn-Ring 6
8000 München 83, F.R. Germany

Abstract: The recognition rate for fluently spoken speech achieved with beam search algorithms depend on factors as the perplexity and the recombination structure of the language model, the difficulty of the vocabulary, the quality of the acoustic phonetic decoder, and the chosen pruning strategy. In this paper a statistical model taking these factors in account is develloped. An iterative algorithm to calculate the score distribution of beam search paths and the resulting sentence error rate is presented.

1. INTRODUCTION

In order to recognize fluently spoken speech beam search algorithms are used successfully to map the acoustic signal of an utterance on a chain of words, the recognized utterance /1, 2, 3, 4/. The recognition rate achieved with beam search algorithms depends on many factors. Some of these are the perplexity of the language model, the difficulty of vocabulary with respect to acoustic similar words etc. Consequently recognition rates of different recognition systems are hardly to be compared.

The aim of the paper is to clarify quantitatively the role of these factors using a statistical model. With this framework for a given recognition task, the achievable recognition rate together with the complexity of the algorithm can be roughly estimated.

Generally beam search is implemented as a left to right search where speech segments are mapped on states (e.g. phonemes) of sequences of word hypotheses. Each mapped sequence of states is called a path, which is weighted by a score s(t), a measure for the quality of the acoustic match between the speech segments and the states. At the end of the speech signal the path with best score is decided to represent the recognized utterance.

2. THE STATISTICAL MODEL

For the mapping of the speech segments on states mainly two methods are used. In the first method the states of a word are represented by a set of acoustic parameters (parametric word model). Examples are template match algorithms

NATO ASI Series, Vol. F46
Recent Advances in Speech Understanding
and Dialog Systems
Edited by H. Niemann et al.

/2/ and HMM /5/. In the second method the speech signal is segmented and classified according to phonetic units /4, 6, 7/.

In both methods the states of a word can be represented by nodes in a directed network (see fig. 1).

Fig. 1: a) HMM-word network
b) Phonetic-unit-word network of a word with different pronunciations

The word networks can be chained in order to create word sequences. Depending on the organization of the chained networks their structure can be globally characterized by a branching factor and a recombination factor. The branching factor bf represents the average number of nodes, which follow a node in the network.

Recombination occurs, if the paths of different word pronunciations are combined to a single path or if the paths of different words are continued by the same word networks (see fig. 2). The recombination factor α is defined as the

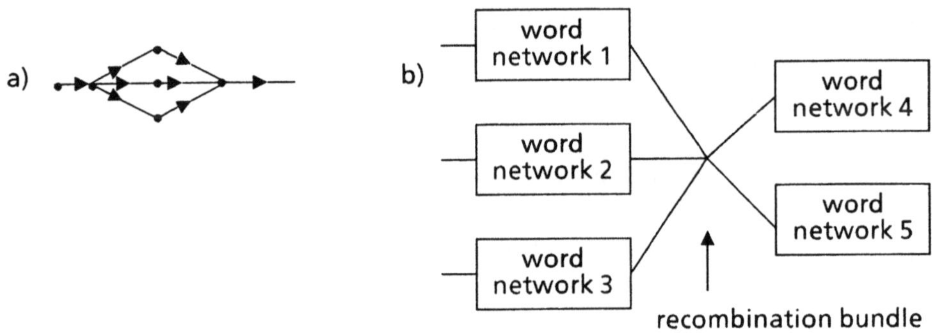

Fig. 2: a) recombination for different pronunciation
b) recombination due to a language model

probability , the path of a node is recombined. At a given time difference recombination bundles may be observed. The average number of recombination bundles at a given time is called μ. For recognition the scores of different paths are compared. The scores are calculated by accumulating local distances d.

In the following the difficulty of a recognition task will be described more precisely.

As "right" nodes we define such nodes, which represent the chain of nodes of the path of the spoken utterance, the "right" path. Other paths of word hypotheses may contain some nodes which are equal to those of the right path. If during the search the same speech segment is mapped on these equal nodes, all these nodes are called "right" nodes. The other nodes are called "wrong" nodes. At a given time the corresponding nodes of all paths are regarded. The average of the ratio of wrong nodes and all nodes is defined as the confusibility factor v with the range $0 < v < 1$. If v approaches 1 highly confusable utterances have to be considerd.

Whenever a speech segment is matched on a node a local distance d is produced. In the following it is assumed that distances with high values are optained on "right" nodes and low values on "wrong" nodes. The distribution of the distances of the right nodes and of the wrong nodes is called $P_r(d)$ and $P_w(d)$, respectively.

It is assumed that the speech segments are statistically independent. Consequently the score s(t) can be modelled as the sum of statistically independent local scores. All local distances of the right path obey the distribution P_r. The local distances of the wrong paths obey partly the distribution P_w and partly on P_r depending on the confusibility factor v. The average distribution $P_{wr}(d)$ of the wrong nodes is assumed to be

$$P_{wr}(d) = (1 - v)\, P_w(d) + v\, P_r(d) \qquad (1)$$

Besides the recognition rate the computational load plays an important role in recognition. A high branching factor combined with a low recombination factor leads to an exponential growing number n(t) of paths in time. In order to limit n, pruning techniques are applied. The pruning strategy is based on the best score $s_T(t)$ of the scores of all paths. Paths whose scores are less than the value of a pruning-function $g(s_T)$ are pruned. A pruning factor pf(t) is defined which is specified by the ratio of pruned nodes compared to all nodes. The probability of pruning the right path is called pruning probability prp(t).

3. THE PATH STATISTICS

In the following formulas to calculate the recognition rate er(t), the pruning rate prp(t) and the number of paths n(t) as a function of time are given.

The beam search can be described as an iterative three step procedure. In the first step paths are recombined and all successor nodes of the actual ending-nodes are determined. In the second step all successor nodes are matched with the next speech segment. In the last step pruning occurs. The equal sign in the formulas is in the spirit of assignment of variables in computer programs.

3.1 Step 1

We assume that at a time t the number of paths is n(t) with given score distributions $P_0(s, t)$, $P_c(s, t)$ of the correct and the wrong paths. From these paths $\alpha\, n(t)$ are recombined in bundles of μ different paths. Two cases have to be considered. In the first case, the correct path is contained in one of the recombined bundles with a certain probability β, the correct path recombining factor. In the second case (probability 1-β) the correct path is not recombined.

In the first case the not pruned, bf·α·n(t) new paths have an unchanged score distribution $P_0(s,t)$. Each of the μ bundles is recombined and assumed to have in the average n_R successor nodes. The resulting $(\mu-1)\cdot n_R$ new paths possess a distribution $P_{R0}(s,t)$ which will be calculated later. The n_R paths of the successor nodes of the bundle with the correct path have a different distribution $P_{Rc}(s,t)$.

In the second case additionally to the bf(1-α) n(t) incorrect paths with distribution $P_0(s,t)$ the correct path creates (bf-1) incorrect paths with distribution $P_c(s,t)$. The paths of the $n_R\cdot\mu$ successor nodes are distributed with $P_{R0}(s,t)$.

The resulting average distribution of the recombined and not recombined paths and the number is given by

$$P_0(s,t) = \left[bf(1-\alpha)\, n(t) + (1-\beta)(bf-1) + \mu\, n_R - \beta \right]^{-1} \tag{2}$$

$$\left[bf(1-\alpha)\, n(t)\, P_0(s,t) + (1-\beta)\,(bf-1)\, P_c(s,t) + (\mu-\beta)\, n_R\, P_{R0}(s,t) + \beta\,(n_R-1)\, P_{Rc}(s,t) \right]$$

$$n(t+1) = bf(1-\alpha)\, n(t) + (1-\beta)\,(bf-1) + \mu\, n_R - \beta \tag{3}$$

Next the calculation of the P_{R0} and P_{Rc} is given. Each bundle contains $l = \alpha\cdot n(t)/\mu$ paths. The recombined path inherits the highest score of one of the l paths. The probability that the score s_k of a given incorrect path is the highest is given by

$$P(s_k > s_i,\ i=1,\dots,l;\ i \neq k) = \left[\int_{-\infty}^{s_k} P_0(s',t)\, ds' \right]^{l-1},\ l = \alpha\, n(t)/\mu$$

Each of the l paths may have the highest score leading to

$$P_{R0}(s,t) = l\, P_0(s,t) \left[\int_{-\infty}^{s_k} P_0(s',t)\, ds' \right]^{l-1} \tag{4}$$

If the correct path is contained in the bundle either the correct path or an incorrect path may have the highest score. The probability that the score s_c of the correct path is the highest is given by

$$P(s_k > s_i,\, s_k > s_c,\ k \neq i,\, k \neq c,\, i=1,\dots,l) = \left[\int_{-\infty}^{s_k} P_0(s',t)\, ds' \right]^{l-2} \int_{-\infty}^{s_k} P_0(s',t)\, ds'$$

As a result P_{Rc} is calculated by

$$P_{Rc}(s,t) = P_c(s,t) \left[\int_{-\infty}^{s} P_0(s',t)\, ds' \right]^{l-1} + P_0(s,t)\,(l-1) \left[\int_{-\infty}^{s} P_0(s,t)\, ds' \right]^{l-2} \int_{-\infty}^{s} P_c(s,t)\, ds$$

3.2 Step 2

The nodes of the n(t + 1) paths are matched against a speech segment and the resulting local distance is added to the scores of the paths:

$s(t+1) = s(t) + d(t)$

With distribution $P_s(s)$ of the scores and $P_d(d)$ of the local distances distribution of the resulting scores is derived by

$$P_0(s, t+1) = P_0(s, t) \bigstar P_{wr}(d) \qquad P_c(s, t+1) = P_c(s, t) \bigstar P_r(d) \qquad (\bigstar = convolution) \tag{5}$$

3.3 Step 3

Each of the n paths is pruned if its score is less than the value of the pruning function $g(s_T)$ of the highest score s_T of all paths. A wrong path with score s_k is not pruned with the probability

$$P\left(s_k > g(s_i) \;\; \forall\, i, k \neq i\right) = \prod_{i=1;\, k \neq i}^{n} P\left(s_i < f(s_k)\right), \quad f(s) = g^{-1}(s)$$

$$= \left[\int_{-\infty}^{f(s_k)} P_0(s', t+1)\, ds'\right]^{n-2} \int_{-\infty}^{f(s_k)} P_c(s', t+1)\, ds' \tag{6}$$

With the distribution $P_0(s_k, t+1)$ of the k-th path the probability of not pruning this wrong path is given by

$$pf(t+1) = \int_{-\infty}^{+\infty} P_0(s, t+1) \left[\int_{-\infty}^{f(s)} P_0(s', t+1)\, ds'\right]^{n-2} P_c(s', t+1)\, ds'\, ds \;, \tag{7}$$

which represents the pruning factor.

Similar to the probability pr(t + 1) of pruning the right path is given by

$$pr(t+1) = 1 - \int_{-\infty}^{+\infty} P_c(s, t+1) \left[\int_{-\infty}^{f(s)} P_0(s', t+1)\, ds'\right]^{n-1} ds \tag{8}$$

$$prp\,(t+1) = prp\,(t)\;\; pr\,(t+1) \tag{9}$$

Due to the pruning process the distributions $P_0(s)$ and $P_c(s)$ are changed.

$$P_0(s, t+1) = pf(t+1)^{-1}\, P_0(s, t+1) \left[\int_{-\infty}^{f(s)} P_0(s', t+1)\, ds'\right]^{n-2} \int_{-\infty}^{f(s)} P_c(s', t+1)\, ds' \tag{10}$$

$$P_c(s, t+1) = \left(1 - pr(t+1)\right)^{-1} P_c(s, t+1) \left[\int_{-\infty}^{f(s)} P_0(s', t+1)\, ds'\right]^{n-1} \tag{11}$$

The remaining number of paths is calculated by

$$n(t+1) = n(t)\;\; pf(t+1) \tag{12}$$

The recognition rate er(t + 1) is defined as the probability, the score s_c of the correct state is greater than the wrong paths:

$$er(t+1) = \int_{-\infty}^{+\infty} P_c(s,t+1) \left[\int_{-\infty}^{s} P_0(s',t+1)\, ds' \right]^{n-1} ds \qquad (13)$$

4. RESULTS

Several simulations were carried out in order to investigate the influence of the model parameters on the recognition rate. A syllable oriented recognition scheme, where the phonetic units are assumed to be initial consonant clusters ICC, syllabic nuclei SN and final consonant clusters FCC /4/, has been chosen.

The words of the correct path are assumed to be built out of two syllables. As a consequence the factors α, β and μ are timevariable (see tab. 1).

Speechsegment	ICC	SN	FCC	ICC	SN	FCC
3 nodes	syllable			syllable		
6 nodes	word					
α	0	0	α_0	0	0	α_0
β	0	0	0	0	0	β_0
μ	0	0	μ_0	0	0	μ_0

Tab. 1

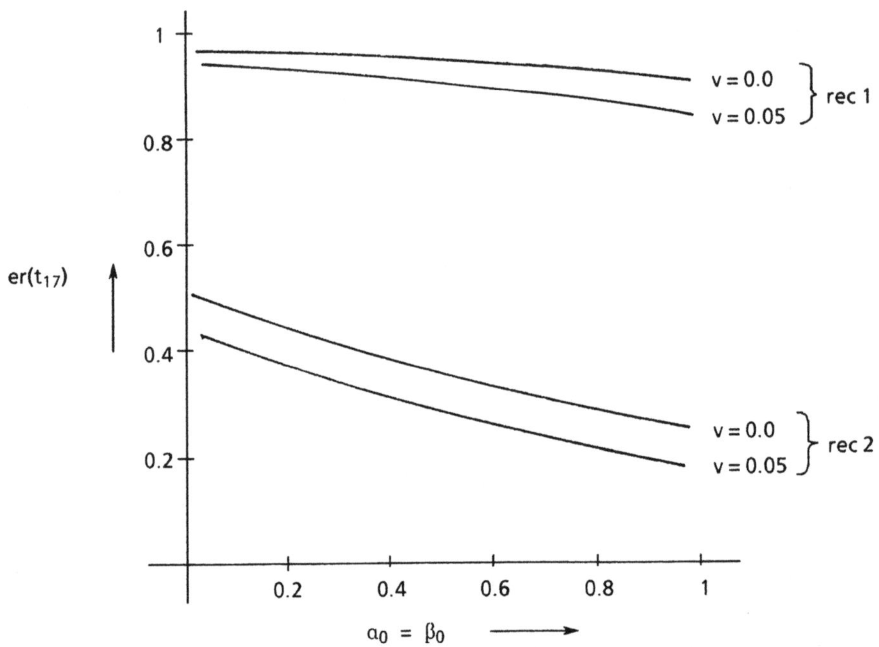

Fig. 3: Recognition rates for a two word chain (6 syllables)
bf = 4 $\mu_0 = 2$ nR = 18
rec 1: $\langle d \rangle_r = 3$ $\sigma^2_r = 3.5$ $\langle d \rangle_w = 0$ $\sigma^2_w = 4.5$
rec 2: $\langle d \rangle_r = 5$ $\sigma^2_r = 1.5$ $\langle d \rangle_w = 0$ $\sigma^2_w = 4.5$

For Pr(d) and Pw(d) Gaussian distributions were chosen. In fig. 3 two different recognizers of phonetic units rec1, rec2 were simulated.

The most dominant factor on the word chain recognition rate er is given by the recognition rate on the phonetic units and the confusibility factor v.

REFERENCES

/1/ B. Lowere, R. Reddy: "The Harpy Speech Understanding System", in: Trends in Speech Recognition, Prentice Hall (1980), pp. 340-360.

/2/ J. Bridle et al.: "An Algorithm for Connected Word Recognition", Proc. IEEE ASSP, Paris (1982), pp. 892-902.

/3/ H. Ney: "The Use of a One-Stage Dynamic Programming Algorithm for Connected Word Recognition", IEEE ICASSP-32 (1984), pp. 263-271.

/4/ H. Höge et al.: "Syllable-based Acoustic-Phonetic Decoding and Word Hypotheses Generation in Fluently Spoken Speech", Proc. ICASSP-86, pp. 1561-1564.

/5/ S.E. Levinson et al.: "An Introduction to the Application of the Theory of Probabilitic Functions of a Markov Process to Automatic Speech Recognition" BSTJ Vol. 62 (1983), pp. 1035-1074.

/6/ A. Adams, R. Bisiani: "The Carnegie-Mellon University Distributed Speech Recognition System", Speech Technology (1986), pp. 14-23.

/7/ H. Niemann et al.: "A System for Understanding German Speech", Information Sciences, Vol. 3 (1984), pp. 87.

OVERVIEW OF SPEECH RECOGNITION IN THE 'SPICOS' SYSTEM

H. Ney, D. Mergel, A. Noll, A. Paeseler

Philips GmbH Forschungslaboratorium Hamburg
2000 Hamburg 54, West Germany

ABSTRACT: In this paper, a recognition technique used in the 'SPICOS' project is described. It is based on an integrated approach that combines the various knowledge sources, such as inventory of subword unit, pronunciation lexicon and language model, during the process of decision making in order to improve the reliability of the acoustic recognition. The recognition decision amounts to a search through a large state space with delayed decisions. The speaker dependent recognition tests are performed on a speech data base comprising 3 sessions of each of 5 speakers. A session consists of 200 sentences and amounts to 1391 word samples.

1. INTRODUCTION

The word 'SPICOS' stands for 'Siemens-Philips-Ipo COntinuous Speech recognition and understanding'. The goal of this project is a man-machine dialogue system that is able to understand fluently spoken German sentences and thus to provide voice access to a data base.

The data base has been defined to contain information about the 'SPICOS' project itself. It can be considered as a personal documentation system about the activities within and the communication between the research teams involved in the 'SPICOS' project. 200 example sentences were chosen to capture the range of queries and commands to be handled by the system. To simplify the linguistic structures, certain restrictions were introduced: no relative clauses, no passive voice, no pronouns, no coordinate conjunctions. The vocabulary comprises 917 complete word forms that are made up of 420 word stems.

This paper gives an overview over the recognition component in the system. The recognition principle is referred to as the integrated approach and attempts to find the best interpretation of the input speech data in terms of knowledge sources such as language model, pronunciation lexicon and inventory of subword units.

2. STATISTICAL DECISION THEORY

Continuous speech recognition is more complex than isolated word recognition for several reasons: the vocabulary is larger, the words are pronounced less carefully, and the sentences have a syntactic-semantic structure that must be taken account of by the recognition system. As a consequence, the recognition process has to deal with a larger state space, i.e. with a larger number of hypotheses to be formed about words and sentences, and to take account of high level constraints as given by syntax, semantics and pragmatics.

NATO ASI Series, Vol. F46
Recent Advances in Speech Understanding and Dialog Systems
Edited by H. Niemann et al.

From the viewpoint of the statistical decision theory, the problem looks as follows. In order to minimize the probability of error according to the Bayes' decision rule [Jelinek 1976], the task of a speech recognizer must be to determine that sequence of words $w(1),\ldots,w(n),\ldots,w(n) := w[1:N]$ (of unknown length N) that has most probably caused the observed sequence of measurements $x(1),\ldots,x(i),\ldots,x(I) := x\ [1:I]$. Using the Bayes' theorem, we can cast it into the form:

Determine that sequence of words $w[1:N]$ that maximizes

$$Pr(w[1:N]) * Pr(x[1:I] | w[1:N]).$$

This important equation highlights the interaction between the observed data and the knowledge sources of the system: the decision must lead to the best compromise between the observed data and the knowledge sources. At the same time, the equation allows a clear border line to be defined between the acoustic-phonetic knowledge sources and the higher level knowledge sources. The first term, $Pr(w[1:N])$, is the a-priori probability of the word sequence $w[1:N]$. It is independent of the acoustic observations and completely specified by the higher level knowledge sources. In other words, the high level knowledge sources syntax, semantics and pragmatics are equivalent to the knowledge of the a-priori probabilities $Pr(w[1:N])$ of all word sequences $w[1:N]$. These knowledge sources are usually referred to as language model. The second term, $Pr(x[1:I]|w[1:N])$, is the conditional probability of observing the sequence $x[1:I]$ when the word sequence $w[1:N]$ has been uttered. It must reflect the acoustic-phonetic and lexical knowledge sources. Once the probability functions of the language and of the acoustic-phonetics are known, it is in principle possible for a given sequence of measurements $x[1:I]$ to evaluate $Pr(w[1:N])*Pr(w[1:N]|x[1:I])$ for each word sequence $w[1:N]$ and to determine the most likely word sequence directly. Thus from the point of view of the statistical decision theory, the distinction between 'top-down' and 'bottom-up' approaches is irrelevant. What matters is the search procedure for finding the most likely word sequence. In the following, the language model, the acoustic word models and the search will be considered in more detail.

3. THE LANGUAGE MODEL

The language model is closely related to the complexity of a recognition task which is not necessarily correlated with the size of the vocabulary. In the following, we simplify the language model by assuming that all sentences of the model are equiprobable. By generalizing the 200 example sentences, production rules are set up by hand in the form of a context-free grammar [Mergel, Paeseler 1987]. These rules are then automatically converted to a finite-state network. The transitions in the network are identified with spoken words such that each path through the network results in an acceptable sentence. Although the vocabulary comprises 917 words, the number of word choices at each language node is much smaller and typically between 10 and 100. The perplexity of the 'SPICOS' network defined as the geometric mean over the word choices is 58.

The network conists of 368 language nodes and 3481 word transitions and is completely defined by specifying for each word transition k its beginning node b(k) and its end node e(k). Several transitions representing the same acoustic word are typically required to capture the various linguistic environments in which the word can occur. The average number of copies is 3481/917 = 3.8.

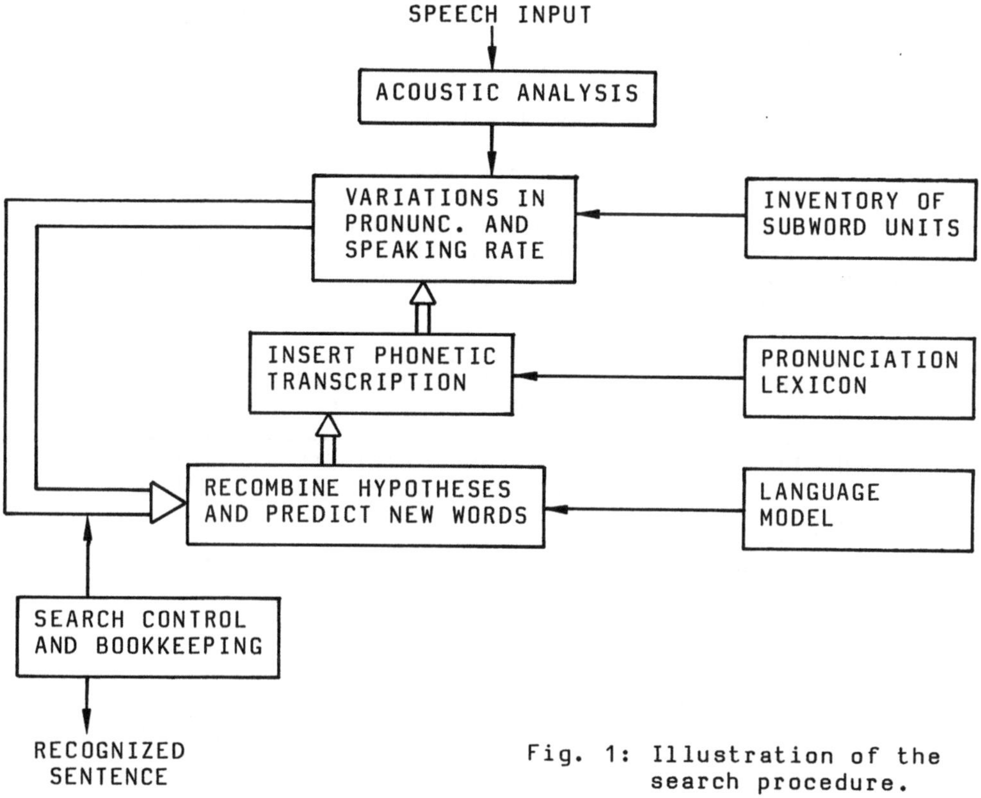

Fig. 1: Illustration of the search procedure.

4. SEARCH PROCEDURE OF THE INTEGRATED APPROACH

The search procedure is an extension of the one-pass dynamic programming algorithm for connected word recognition that presents a closed-form solution for handling the interdependence of nonlinear time alignment, word boundary detection and word identification in continuous speech recognition [Ney 1984]. By approximating the 'most likely word sequence' by the 'most likely state sequence' [Baker 1975, Jelinek 1976], this algorithm allows us to compute the conditional probabilities as introduced in Section 2 and to carry out the optimization at the same time. The incorporation of the language model into the dynamic programming algorithm leads to two conflicting effects. On one hand, the number of word transitions and thus the overall state space is much higher than without language constraints. On the other hand, the language model imposes heavy constraints on the 'acceptable' word sequences. Therefore, the full-search dynamic programming procedure must be modified in order to focus the search on the 'relevant' regions of the state space.

Fig. 1 depicts an organization of the search procedure. There is a three-level hierarchy consisting of the language model, the pronunciation lexicon and the inventory of subword units which are modelled as finite state machines [Baker 1975]. These three levels are kept separately and interact only via the search procedure. Conceptually, the search is a left-to-right time-synchronous beam search where the evaluation of the dynamic programming recursion is limited to the most likely hypotheses. The overall state space is given by the product of the average number of states per word and the number of word transitions. Due to such a space of about 100000 or more states, a special organization is required to reduce the overhead and the storage requirements [Ney et al. 1987]. Since all knowledge sources are exploited by the search procedure, we call this technique an integrated approach.

SPEECH CORPUS	'SPICOS' WORDS	SOTSCHECK SENTENCES	'SPICOS' SENTENCES
FUNCTION	RECOGNITION VOCABULARY	TRAINING SENTENCES	TEST SENTENCES
SENTENCES	-	100	200
VOCABULARY	917	341	351
- OVERLAP -	43		43
WORD SAMPLES	917	524	1391
PHONEME SAMPLES	7773	2240	7826
RECORD. SESSIONS	-	2	3
SPEAKING MODE	-	CONTIN.	CONTIN.

Fig. 2: Table of speech corpora.

5. RECOGNITION TESTS

In evaluating a continuous speech recognition system, it is helpful to distinguish three various types of vocabularies and sentences as summarized in Fig. 2 for the 'SPICOS' task.

1.) The recognition vocabulary is the set of words from which the search procedure can choose. There is no need for the recognition system to have 'heard' all these words acoustically before. By using suitable subword units and a pronunciation lexicon, the recognition vocabulary can be built up synthetically.

2.) The acoustic models representing the subword units are trained on what is referred to as training sentences. In 'SPICOS', these training sentences are made up from a 341-word vocabulary which is essentially different from the recognition vocabulary. The overlap of 43 words is mainly due to functional

words such as prepositions and articles. The training sentences as a whole are representative of the phoneme distribution of the German language. More details on one type of acoustic models are given in [Noll, Ney 1987].
3.) Finally, the test sentences, i.e. the 'SPICOS' sentences, are made from a 351-word subset of the 917-word recognition vocabulary and are used to test the performance of the recognition system.

Experimental tests were run for five speakers each of whom had 2 recording sessions for the 100 Sotscheck training sentences and 3 recording sessions for the 200 'SPICOS' test sentences. The sentences were spoken in a continuous manner, i.e. with no deliberate pauses between the words. The word error rate depends very much on the speaker. For the present version of the system, the word error rate varies between 5 % and 20 % for the different speakers. The word errors are not uniformly distributed over the sentences, but tend to form clusters or correlate with short words. In these recognition experiments, it turned out that it was sufficient to search only 2-5% of the overall potential state space, which amounts to a computational cost of 50-200 MIPSS (=Million of Instructions per Second of Speech).

ACKNOWLEDGMENT

The work described was carried out in a joint Siemens-Philips-IPO(Eindhoven) project and sponsored by the German Federal Ministery for Research and Technology (BMFT) under grant No. 413-5839-ITM 8401. Only the authors are responsible for the contents of this publication.

REFERENCES

J.K. BAKER (1975): "Stochastic Modeling for Automatic Speech Understanding", in D.R. REDDY (ed.): 'Speech Recognition', Academic Press, New York, pp.512-542, 1975.
F. JELINEK (1976): "Continuous Speech Recognition by Statistical Methods", Proc. of the IEEE, Vol. 64, No. 10, pp.532-556, April 1976.
D. MERGEL, A. PAESELER (1987): "Construction of Language Models for Spoken Data Base Queries", Proc. 1987 IEEE Int. Conf. on Acoustics, Speech and Signal Processing, Dallas, Texas, pp.20.13.1-4, April 1987.
H. NEY (1984): "The Use of a One-Stage Dynamic Programming Algorithm for Connected Word Recognition", IEEE Trans. on Acoustics, Speech and Signal, Vol. ASSP-32, No. 2, pp.263-271, April 1984.
H. NEY, D. MERGEL, A. NOLL, P. PAESELER (1987): "A Data-Driven Organization of the Dynamic Programming Beam Search for Continuous Speech Recognition", Proc. 1987 IEEE Int. Conf. on Acoustics, Speech and Signal Processing, Dallas, Texas, pp.20.10.1-4, April 1987.
A. NOLL, H. NEY (1987): "Training of Phoneme Models in a Sentence Recognition System", Proc. 1987 IEEE Int. Conf. on Acoustics, Speech and Signal Processing, Dallas, Texas, pp.29.6.1-4, April 1987.

An Experimental Environment for Generating Word Hypotheses in Continuous Speech

S. Kunzmann, T. Kuhn, H. Niemann

Friedrich-Alexander University Erlangen-Nürnberg
Lehrstuhl für Informatik 5 (Mustererkennung)
Martensstraße 3
8520 Erlangen, F.R. Germany

Abstract: We present a flexible environment for the generation of word hypotheses in continuous speech. After describing the interface to the other modules of our speech understanding system a word spotting technique based on HMM will be discussed. The generation of reference models for the matching procedure is done automatically using the standard pronunciation of a word and a set of phonological rules about intra word assimilation. These alternative pronunciations are represented by graphs with labeled edges. Some preliminary results for parameter training and the matching procedure are also given.

1. Environment of the word recognition unit

The word recognition unit (WRU) is embedded in the speech understanding system EVAR /NIE 84a/. The application field of our system is information retrieval about Intercity trains. Some topics of the system are speaker independence, the recognition of continuous spoken German utterances and the use of large lexica (about 4000 words).

The acoustic phonetic unit /REG 87a/ computes the input data for the matching procedure. For example:

- 10 mel-frequency-cepstral-coefficients and a normalized loundness parameter for each frame,
- classification of each frame in at most 5 phone component classes,
- segmentation and classification of several frames in at most 5 phone classes (no alternative segmentation).

Frames are consecutive, not overlapping and have a duration of 12.8 msec.

The modules for syntatic, semantic, pragmatic analysis /EHR 88a/ and dialog handling interact with the WRU by requests for a set of words or word chain hypotheses. This way it is easy to realize a bottom up system structure as well as a top down oriented architecture. During the analysis these

NATO ASI Series, Vol. F46
Recent Advances in Speech Understanding and Dialog Systems
Edited by H. Niemann et al.

modules are able to predict word classes and to restrict the search domain. For example: The semantic unit assumes that source and goal hypotheses exist in the utterance. The request would be to generate hypotheses for all entries in the lexicon with the syntatic class verb and the semantic class movement. The search domain can be restricted by excluding the locations of the source and goal hypotheses.

2. Structure of the word recognition unit

The WRU is divided into a lexical unit and search strategies for generation and verification of hypotheses (see figure 1). The tasks of the lexical unit are the resolution of complex requests for word hypotheses from other units into simple requests and the generation of the corresponding reference models (see section 3). The seperation is done to allow a flexible adaption of the search strategies to other kinds of subword units. We distinguish two types of search strategies:

- Verification of hypotheses: Hypotheses are matched with a given part of the speech signal using the corresponding frame data. The results are new scores computed out of detailed acoustic information. The techniques used are dynamic time warping /Müh 86a/, /MYE 81a/ or HMM algorithms as described in /Rab 88a/.
- Generation of hypotheses: We have to position words in a given interval of the speech signal. To resolve this kind of requests we use a word spotting technique, explained in section 4. At the moment we use the segment classification of the acoustic phonetic unit as input data.

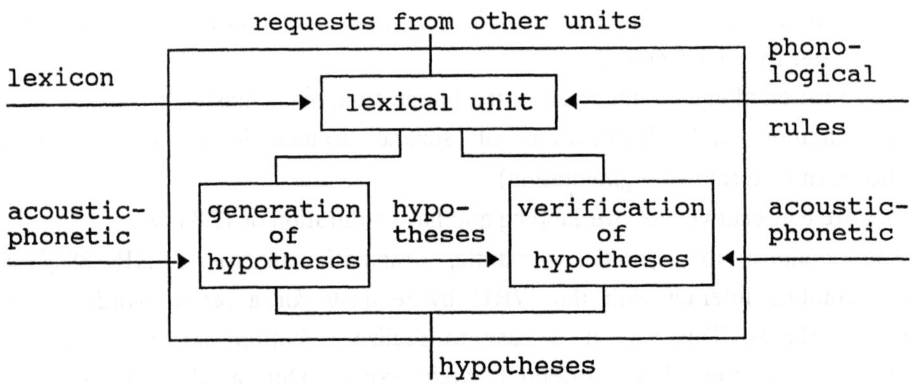

Fig. 1: Structure of the word recognition unit

3. The lexical unit

The lexical unit uses a lexicon that contains bit-vectors describing syntatic classes, semantic classes, and pragmatic concepts, the standard pronunciation of a word and a unique word identification number. Every class or concept has a logical name assigned. For the definition of a subset of the lexicon the use of the logical operators AND, OR and NOT is allowed. To override the operator precedence parentheses can be used. A sequence of expressions allows the definition of a set of word chains. A sample request without restriction of the search domain may be given as:

(AND (AND (pragmatic ic_city) (semantic location))
(OR (syntactic npr) (syntactic adv))

The bit-vectors of each entry in the lexicon will be matched against this logical expression. For each valid match a reference model will be generated.

A reference model is an edge oriented, labelled graph. This allows an efficient representation of alternative pronunciations besides the standard pronunciation. The initialization of the graph is done with the standard pronunciation from the lexicon. A number of rewriting rules /Müh 86a/ are applied to it one by one. As one rule can generate the context for another rule, the application order is significant. One can distinguish two types of rewriting rules:

- Generation of the pronunciation graph. This will be done by including alternative paths in the graph to model i.e. the elision of a sound or the assimilation of [g] and [n].
- Transcription of a pronunciation graph to another level of abstraction. That is, a phone component graph will be generated out of a phone graph. In this case the input and output alphabet of the graph differ.

To simplify the design of a set of rewriting rules the definition of superclasses is allowed. The rules are given in the following form:

Superclasses: superclass=subword_unit$_1$/subword_unit$_2$/.../subword_unit$_n$/
Rules: /left_side/ = = = > /left_context/substitution/right_context/

The application of the rules can be interpreted as: Look in the graph for the pattern 'left_side' with the context pattern 'left_context' and 'right_context'. If found, introduce a path consisting of 'left_context', 'substitution' and 'right_context'.

4. Generation of hypotheses

The reference models define the global structure of a Markov Model. Each edge will be substituted by a 2-state Markov Model. The edges model the insertion, substitution and deletion of an output symbol. The parameters $P_X{}^m$ and $P^m(O_t|X)$ for the submodels are estimated with the Forward-Backward-Algorithm. $P_X{}^m$ denotes the probabiltiy to follow edge X in model m. $P^m(O_t|X)$ is the conditional probabiltiy to emit O_t following edge X in model m. Descriptions of the algorithm may be found in /LIP 82a/ or /Rab 88a/. If more than one edge leaves a node (alternative pronunciation), these transmissions are weighted by the relative number of outgoing edges. The computation of the α -matrix provides us with a similarity measure between a reference model and a given part of the speech signal. For the generation of hypotheses we have to find good matching regions $O_i...O_t$ in the output pattern $O = O_1...O_T$ for a reference model $R = R_1...R_N$. An efficient computation can be done by a word spotting technique called 'vertical summation' /Schuk 87a/. The idea is to compute the profile vector $P_{N,t}(O_1...O_t|R)$, $t = 1,...,T$ which is the probability that the reference model R matches the region $O_1...O_t$ or $O_2...O_t$ ... or O_t (figure 2).

$$P_{s,t}(O_1...O_t|R_1...R_s) = \Sigma_{j=1,t} P_{s,j,t}(O_j...O_t|R_1...R_s) = \Sigma_{j=1,t} \alpha_{j,t}(s)$$

$P_{s,t}$ is the probability of emitting the symbols O_1 to O_t and being in state s of a reference model. Applying the definition of α gives the computation scheme for the calculation of the summation matrice $M_{P_{.,.}}$. A proof is given in /KUH 87a/.

$$P_{0,t} = \begin{cases} 1 & t = 0 \\ P_I^{(0,1)} * P^{(0,1)}(O_t \mid INS) * P_{0,t-1} + 1 & 0 < t < T \\ P_I^{(0,1)} * P^{(0,1)}(O_t \mid INS) * P_{0,t-1} & t = T \end{cases}$$

The recursion for $P_{s,t}$ is calculated as:

$$P_{s,t} = \sum_{r \in V(s)} P_S{}^{(r,s)} * P^{(r,s)}(O_t|SUB) * P_{r,t-1} + \sum_{r \in V(s)} P_D{}^{(r,s)} * P_{r,t} + P_I{}^{(s,succ(s))} * P^{(i,succ(s))}(O_t|INS) * P_{s,t-1}$$

with

(r,s)	=	model between node r and node s
V(s)	=	set of predecessors of node s
succ(s)	=	successor of node s
INS, SUB, DEL	=	edges of the 2 state model

High values of the profile vector $P_{N,t}(O_1...O_t|R)$ indicate end points for good matches. Hypotheses are generated for a given number of maxima in the profile vector. An estimate for the corresponding starting point is received by back tracking. As the logarithm of the scores of the hypotheses and the length of the reference model are linearly correlated, a normalisation is done by substraction of the regression line. The parameters are estimated out of a test set of correct hypotheses. Because of the different number of factors in the transitions substitute, insert and delete we introduced some weighting factors C_S, C_I and C_D. A very rough adaptation increased the recognition results significantly.

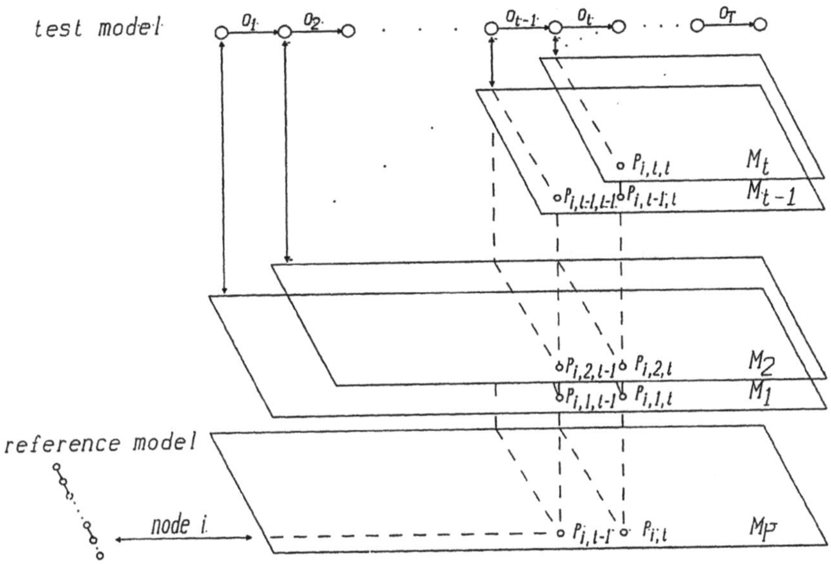

Fig. 2: Principle of vertical summation

5. Experimental results

The experiments were done with about 10 minutes of read German utterances (6 male and 6 female speakers). In order to use the utterances both for training and testing we used the leave-one-out method. The hypotheses were generated for all entries of the lexicon. For the experiments no alternative pronunciation was used. The weighting factors were set to: $C_S = 1.0$, $C_I = 10.0$, $C_D = 0.08$. The slope of the regression line is 2.57.

lexicon	hypotheses per segment							
	1	2	5	10	20	30	40	50
klexs	34%	45%	62%	73%	84%	86%	87%	88%
glexs	16%	24%	36%	46%	58%	65%	70%	75%

Table 1: Recognition rates for two lexica

Table 1 shows the recognition rate in percent for two lexica with about 500 (klexs) and 4000 (glexs) entries. As optimization criterion we use the rank normalized by the number of segments per utterance.

6. Conclusion

We presented a word recognition unit which works in a bottom up structured system as well as in a top down approach. The requirements for complex requests to a search strategy can be processed by the lexical unit. Using phonological information reference models are generated which reflect alternative pronuncations in continuous speech. Better recognition results can be expected as the deletion of sounds does not have to be modelled by the 2 state Markov Model alone. The use of verification algorithms gives us the possibility of a detailed but time consuming match aimed to reduce the number of wrong hypotheses.

7. Bibliography

/EHR 88a/ Ehrlich U., Niemann H.: "Using Semantic and Pragmatic Knowledge for the Interpretation of Syntatic Constituents". In this volume.

/KUH 87a/ Kuhn T.: "Implementation von Algorithmen zum Vergleich von eindimensionalen Mustern". Studienarbeit. Lehrstuhl für Informatik 5 (Mustererkennung), Universität Erlangen, 1987.

/LIP 82a/ Liporace S.E.: "Maximum Liklihood Estimation for Multivariate Observations of Markov Sources". IEEE Trans. Inf., IT-28, 1982, pp 729-734.

/MÜH 86a/ Mühlfeld R.:"Verifikation von Worthypothesen". Dissertation. Lehrstuhl für Informatik 5 (Mustererkennung), Universität Erlangen, 1986.

/MYE 81a/ Myers C.S., Rabiner L.R.: "A Level Building Dynamic Time Warping Algorithm For Connected Word Recognition". IEEE Trans. ASSP-29, 1981, pp 284-296.

/NIE 84a/ Niemann H., Brietzmann A., Mühlfeld R., Regel P., Schukat G.: "The Speech Understanding and Dialog System EVAR". in De Mori R., Suen C.: "New Systems and Architectures for Automatic Speech Recognition and Synthesis", Springer-Verlag, Berlin 1985.

/RAB 88a/ Rabiner L.R.:"Theory of Hidden Markov Models and its Application to Speech Recognition". In this volume.

/REG 87a/ Regel P.:"Akustisch-phonetische Transkription für die automatische Spracherkennung". Dissertation. Lehrstuhl für Informatik 5 (Mustererkennung), Universität Erlangen, 1987.

/SCHUK 87a/ Schukat-Talamazzini E.G.: "Generieren von Worthypothesen in kontinuierlicher Sprache". Springer-Verlag, Berlin, 1987.

APPLICATION OF THE ERROR CORRECTING GRAMMATICAL INFERENCE METHOD (ECGI) TO MULTI-SPEAKER ISOLATED WORD RECOGNITION (+)

E. Vidal (*), N. Prieto (*), E. Sanchis (*) and H. Rulot (**)

(*) Dpto. de Sis. Inform. y Comput. Univ. Pol. de Valencia (Spain).

(**) Centro de Informática de la Universidad de Valencia.

1. INTRODUCTION

It is well known that speech signals constitute highly structured objects which are composed of different kinds of subobjects such as words, phonemes, etc. This fact has motivated several researchers to propose different models which more or less explicitly assume the structural nature of speech. Notable examples of these models are Markov models /Bak 75/, /Jel 76/; the famous Harpy /Low 76/; Scriber and Lafs /Kla 80/; and many others works in which the convenience of some structural model of the speech objects considered is explicitly claimed /Gup 82/, /Lev 83/, /Cra 84/, /Sca 85/, /Kam 85/, /Sau 85/, /Rab 85/, /Kop 85/, /Sch 85/, /Der 86/, /Tan 86/.

Despite this, only very few attempts have been made so far in order to automatically learn these models directly from speech samples; rather, the models are usually established by hand on the basis of a priori heuristic knowledge presumably belonging to human speech experts, and only certain numerical parameters (e.g. probabilities) of the resulting systems are left for automatic optimization on the basis of speech data. However, the importance of the model structures themselves can by no means be neglected, as is shown, for example, by the fact that no HMM canonical structure is yet commonly accepted, even for the simple task of recognizing Isolated Words.

Recently, the importance of the stated problem seems to start being recognized, and a number of authors have in fact investigated different methods for automatically learning different structural models of speech, from samples of the speech objects considered /Smi 85/, /Tho 86/, /Ven 86/, /Koh 86/, /Lee 86/, /Eng 86/, /Vid 87/. One of the methods in this direction is that proposed in /Rul 87/ which consists of a Grammatical Inference (GI) "heuristic" /Ang 83/, /Fu 75/ that incorporates certain speech knowledge in its inference algorithm.

We call this algorithm the Error Correcting Grammatical Inference algorithm (ECGI). It was specifically designed in order to achieve an "abstraction ability" which captures all the relevant variability exhibited

---

(+) Work partially suported by grant N. PA85-0086 of the Spanish CAICYT.

NATO ASI Series, Vol. F46
Recent Advances in Speech Understanding and Dialog Systems
Edited by H. Niemann et al.

by the local substructures of the patterns being considered, and by their concatenation, as well as by the length of these substructures. Therefore, it can be considered as specially appropiate for the inference of the structural models (automata) required in Automatic Speech Recognition (ASR).

The appropiatness of the ECGI algorithm for ASR was investigated through a preliminary series of experiments, involving recognition of the 10 spanish digits, uttered by a single speaker, and (very roughly) represented as strings of broad microphonetic categories /Rul 87/. The results of these experiments were encouraging, and now a new series of more realistic experiments have been carried out with a more difficult ASR task and a finer string representation of the speech data. A report of these experiments is the main topic of this paper.

2. ECGI ALGORITHM AND PROPERTIES OF THE INFERRED AUTOMATA.

The ECGI algorithm constructs a finite state automaton in an incremental way which considers the training strings one after the other and with no repetitions. Initially, a trivial automaton is built from the first training string. Then, for every new string which can not be recognized by the current automaton, the automaton is updated by adding those states and transitions required for the new string to be accepted. In order to determine such states and transitions, a Dynamic Programming procedure is used to find the best alignement of the input string with its closest string in the language accepted by the current automaton (Error Correcting Parsing -ECP-). Once the ECP is obtained, the current automaton is updated so as to take advantage of as much of this automaton as possible; that is, only the (sequences of) error transitions in the ECP lead to the addition of new states and/or transitions.

On the other hand, since the normalized number of error transitions in the ECP can be considered as a measure of the distance from the input string to the language of the current automaton, this distance can be used for classification in the usual way. Consequently, the ECGI method achieves the essential feature required by any proper learning methodology; that is, performing both learning and recognition in an integrated and simultaneous way. More detailed descriptions of ECGI can be found in /Rul 87/.

Several interesting properties of the learnt automata can be derived from this inference procedure. First, the automaton is free of loops and circuits. This has been explicitly imposed on the inference procedure in order to achieve a purely syntactic modelling of the concatenation of the substrings and the lengths of these substrings. Secondly, each inferred automaton contains the canonical automaton; furthermore, its language is in fact a generalization of the training set, which also includes strings composed of adequate concatenations of those substrings commonly found in the training set. Although this language is finite, it grows exponentially with the number of states (fig. 1). On the other hand, since only those substrings which are not already modelled by the current automaton lead to the addition of new states and transitions, the average growth of the automaton for each new training sample is directly related to the variability of the data considered. Consequently, the size of the inferred automaton exhibits an asymptotical tendency towards a constant when all the relevant variations in the data have already appeared in the sequence of training strings. This is shown in figure 2, where the average Leveinshtein distance from the new training strings to the automaton inferred at each step is also presented. The decrease of this curve shows how the inferred automaton became more and more "adapted" to the learning samples.

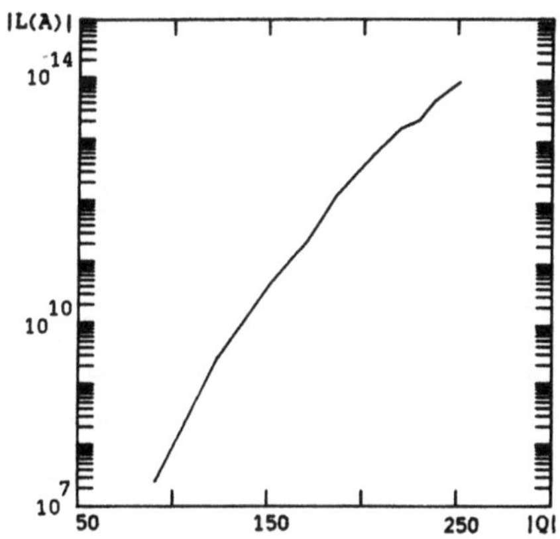

Fig.1. Size of the language as a function of the number of states for the spanish digit /oco/.

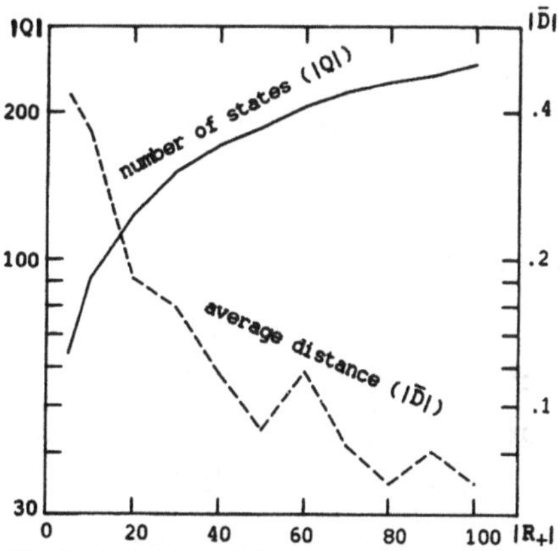

Fig.2. Evolution of the automaton complexity and average Leveinshtein distance for the spanish digit /oco/.

3. EXPERIMENTS

All the experimental work was based on the same corpus of 1000 multispeaker utterances of the Spanish digits as that used in /Vid 87/; also, identical parametrization and (string) representation were adopted.

This data were partitioned in several ways into training and test sets (see Table 1). For each partition, in the learning phase, ten automata were inferred from each of the 10 training sets (one per word) using the ECGI, with 0/1 values for the error correcting weights of either substitution, insertion and deletion. In the recognition phase each string in the test set was submited to 0/1 error correcting recognition by the ten automata learnt with the corresponding training set (based on earlier results /Rul 87/ only substitution errors were allowed for recognition). The decision rule was to classify the input string into the class in which the total normalized error correcting weight is minimun.

The results of the experiments are summarized in Table 1. The best results were obtained, as expected, in experiment 1 which is essentially speaker-dependent test. Experiments 2 and 3 represent truely speaker-independent tasks, and the results were correspondingly worse. It is worth noting that the addition of three new speakers in the learning phase from experiment 2 to experiment 3 led to a significant recognition improvement, despite that the size of the training set was maintained essentially unchanged.

TABLE 1: Results

	Training set	Test set	Recognition rate (%)	Average num. of states
Exp1	10 speakers 500 samples	The same 10 spk.; different utterances; 500 samples	99.5	210
Exp2	5 speakers 500 samples	5 different speakers 500 samples	95.5	180
Exp3	8 speakers 480 samples	2 different speakers 200 samples	97.5	196

4. CONCLUSIONS

We have shown in this paper how the ECGI algorithm can be conveniently used to automatically learn structural models of isolated words. Using these (purely structural) models, acceptable recognition rates have been achieved for speaker-independent recognition of the Spanish digits. Furthermore, these results are only orientative, and they can be improved in several ways (using finer speech representation, adding probabilities to the inferred automata and using the Maximun Likelihood criterion for recognition, etc.).

Finally, it should be pointed out that the actual target of ECGI is not IWR; rather, it was conceived from the begining, as a method for automatically learning (integrated) task-oriented structural models, directly from samples of the corresponding task languages. In fact, for many task-oriented applications, continuous speech can be conveniently represented by finite-state automata. However, if the task semantics is rather complex, the recognition output can by no means consist of a single classification result; rather, it should also consist of some type of structured information. Most generally, the recognition process should be now considered in terms of a traslation from a microphonetic string input language to a task-dependent semantic output language.

The ECGI method can be fairly naturally extended in order to achieve such traslation ability. For doing so, rather than associating with each training input string a simple label, specifying its correct classification, we have to associate an output string specifying the semantics of each segment of the input strings. Using this information, the inference procedure can be easily modified so as to disallow the merger of those sequences of states and transitions which correspond to input segments with different output symbols, regardless of the eventual equality of the corresponding input symbols. This issue is currently under investigation, and some preliminary results have already shown the feasibility of the proposed alternative for actually learning (integrated) structural models of task-oriented (pseudo-) natural languages.

5. REFERENCES

Angluin D. "On the complexity of minimun inference of regular sets". Information and Control (39), 1978.

Baker J. "Stochastic modeling for automatic speech understanding". Speech recognition, R. Reddy Ed. Ac. Press, 1975.

Cravero M. et al. "Syntax driven recognition of connected words by Markov models". ICASSP, 1984.

Derouault A., Merialdo B. "Natural modeling for phoneme-to-text transcription". PAMI-8 (6), 1986.

English T., Boggess L. "A grammatical approach to reducing the statistical sparsity of languages models in natural domains". ICASSP, 1986.

Fu K.S., Booth T.L. "Grammatical Inference: Introduction and Survey". Parts 1 and 2. IEEE Trans. Syst. Man Cybern. SMC-5, 1975.

Gupta V. Mermelstein P. "Effects of speaker accent on the performance of a speaker-independent IWR". Ac. Soc. of America (71, 6), 1982.

Jelinek F. "Continuous speech rec. by statistical methods". IEEE (64,4),1976

Kamp Y. "State reduction in Hidden Markov chains used for speech recognition". IEEE, ASSP-33, (4), 1985.

Klatt D. "Scriber and Lafs: Two new approach to speech analysis". W.A. Lee, Ed. Trends in speech recog. Prentice-Hall, 1980.

Kohonen T. "Dinamically expanding context, with application ...". 8 th. ICPR, 1986.

Kopec G., Bush M. "Network-Based isolated digit recognition using vector quantization". IEEE Trans. ASSP-33 (4), 1985.

Lee K. "Incremental network generation in word recognition". ICASSP, 1986.

Levinson S. "Some experiments with a linguistic processor for continuous speech rec.". IEEE, ASSP-31 (6), 1983.

Lowerre B.T. "The Harpy speech recognition system". Intern report, Carnegie- Mellon University, 1976.

Rabiner L., Levinson S. "A speaker-indep., syntax-directed, CWR system based on HMM and level building". IEEE Trans. ASSP-33 (3), 1985.

Rulot H., Vidal E. "Modelling (sub)string-length-based constraints through a Grammatical Inference method". Devijver, Kittler eds. Springer, 1987.

Sauter L. "Isolated word rec. using a segmental approach". ICASSP, 1985.

Scagliola C. "Language models and search algorithms for real-time speech recognition". Int. J. Man-machine studies, (22), 1985.

Schwartz R. et al. "Context dependent modeling for acoustic-phonetic recognition of continuous speech". ICASSP, 1985.

Smith A.R. et al. "Application of sequential pattern learning system to connected speech recognition". ICASSP, 1985.

Tanaka K. et al. "A demiphoneme network representation of speech ...". ICASSP, 1986.

Thomason M. et al. "Experiments in dynamic programming inference of Markov networks with string representing speech data". Patt. rec. (19, 5), 1986.

Venta O., Kohonen T. "A non-stochastic method for the correction of sentences". 8 th. ICPR, 1986.

Vidal E. et al. "On the use of the Morphic Generator Grammatical Inference (MGGI) methodology in ASR". Also in this book, 1987.

MULTI-SPEAKER EXPERIMENTS WITH THE MORPHIC GENERATOR GRAMMATICAL INFERENCE METHODOLOGY*

E.Vidal, E.Segarra, P.García, I.Galiano.
Departamento de Sistemas Informáticos y Computación.
Universidad Politécnica de Valencia (SPAIN).

1.-INTRODUCTION

Grammatical Inference (GI) is the learning or model estimation phase required by any Syntactic approach to Pattern Recognition (PR). Some fundamental results on GI have been known since the 60's through the works by Gold (1967) and Feldman (1972), which stablished that the decidability of any (even regular) GI problem depends largely upon the avaibility of both an adequate positive sample R+ of strings known to have been generated by the unknown Grammar, and an equally adequate negative sample R- of strings not generated by that Grammar. Despite these results being commonly recognized, taking into account negative samples, lead, in general to intractable GI problems (see /Angluin,78/) and, consequently, most recent works on GI only use positive samples, an aim just at giving practical solutions to specific PR problems (see eg. /Angluin,83/ /Fu,75/). Clearly, this paradigm is not a very appealing one, and some general methodology seems to be strongly required.

Recently, a step towards such methodology has been proposed /García,87/. It is mainly based on the generative mechanism associated to Local Languages (LL), which allows us to obtain arbitrary regular languages by applying morphic operators to LL's /Eilemberg,74/. The actual inference procedure of this methodology, which is refered to as the "Local Language Inference Algorithm" (LLIA) /García,87b/, consists of obtaining the smallest LL which contains the given positive sample. This procedure, which is very simple, is always the same, regardless of the problem considered, while the task-dependent features that are desired for the inferred languages are specified through the definition of certain task-appropiate symbol renaming functions (morphisms). Fig.1 shows a diagram of MGGI, where R+ c E* is the given positive sample; g: R+ → E'* is a renaming function (g(R)=R'); E'is a new ("renamed") alphabet; $l_{R'+}$ is the smallest LL containing R'+; h: E'* ⟶ E* is a letter-to-letter morphism such that h(g(R+))=R+, and L is the target MGGI-inferred language.

(*) Work supported in part by the Spanish CAICYT under grant PA85-86.

NATO ASI Series, Vol. F46
Recent Advances in Speech Understanding and Dialog Systems
Edited by H. Niemann et al.

In /García,87/ the use of this methodology was illustrated through a number of simple examples, in which the functions g and h were chosen on the basis of the features which were desired for the target inferred languages. Nevertheless, these functions must obviously be left to be actually defined for each PR task. We propose here two definitions of the morphic operators h and g which, on the basis of a-priori knowledge about the structure of speech, allow for the inference of structural models (grammars and/or automata) of spoken words, from positive samples of these words.

It is well known that speech is composed of a succession (in time) of acoustic events which can at its turn be characterized by their spectral features and their duration. Therefore if the speech signals are assumed to be represented as strings of "microphonetic labels", each of which corresponding to a spectral shape, then two important features which characterize different speech units (words) are the relative position of the different labels whithin the strings, and the lengths of the substrings which represent the corresponding acoustic events. One can take advantage of this knowledge to define the morphic operators of the MGGI methodology so as to obtain, from a sample of utterances of a given word, an structural model of this word which is a generalization of the given sample, while being as well consistent with the a-priori knowledge-based characteristics stated above. This has lead us to the definition of both the "Relative Position" (RP) and "Length Constraining" (LC) renaming schemes. For the RP, each training string x is divided into a fixed number (d) of intervals, and then each symbol of x is renamed by afixing to it a supraindex specifying to what interval it belongs. For the LC, each symbol of each homogeneous substring of x (a substring in which all the symbols are the same), is renamed by afixing to it a subindex specifying the absolute position within the substring /García,87b/.

2.-EXPERIMENTS AND RESULTS.

The speech data consisted of 10 repetitions of the 10-word Spanish digits vocabulary, which were uttered by 10 different speakers (5 male and 5 female). These data were processed as in /Vidal,87/ resulting in 1000 strings of 10-dimensional vectors of Cepstrum coefficients. Each vector (frame) was then given a name from a set of 11 broad microphonetic categories /García,87b/. The labelling procedure consisted simply of a

Nearest-Neighbour Classification of each frame with respect to a set of 11 prototypes, which were derived by averaging the corresponding frames from a training corpus of 2206 hand-labeled frames. This corpus corresponded to single-speaker utterances which were borrowed from another Speech Recognition project with different vocabulary as that considered here. Obviously, this labelling process can be greatly improved by using more speakers, and more prototypes per phonetic category. The above data where partitioned into several combinations of training sets for learning (GI) and test sets for classification (recognition).

In the learning phase, we apply a given renaming function g (RP and/or LC) over the strings in R+, so as to obtain R'+. From R'+, and using the LLIA, ten stochastic automata Ai, i=1..10, corresponding to the ten classes (Spanish digits) are generated. Finallly, we apply the morphism h (the inverse of g) to the terminal symbols of the obtained automata. In the recognition phase the test strings are submited to recognition by each Ai, and then, they are classified following the criterion of maximum likelihood.

Note that the stochastic automata Ai obtained in the learning phase after the application of the morphism h, can be non-deterministic and even ambiguous. Therefore, we use the Viterbi algorithm /Forney,73/ for recognition. On the other hand, an error correcting trick has been used in order to allow for the acceptance of strings not exactly in L(Ai).

The results are summarized in Table 1. The best results are achieved, as could be expected, from the position-constraining renaming scheme (RP), though useful results are also obtained by only imposing length constraining (LC). In all the experiments involving RP, d=8 intervals have been used. This value was obtained from a previous optimization experiment involving the same data as in exp-1.

The incremental learning ability of the MGGI was investigated in another experiment with the same data as those of exp-3'. The results are shown in Fig.3. It is seen in this figure that the error rate drops to 3.5% for 30 training samples per class and, for greater number of samples, stabilizes at ~2.5% with same fluctuations. On the other hand, both the average number of states and the average branching factor increase rather slowly with the number of training samples, with clear asymptotical tendency towards a constant as the training set size is increased.

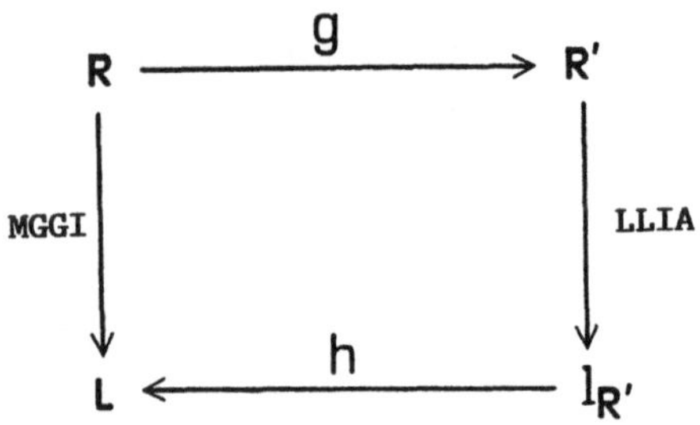

Fig.1. Morphic Generator Grammatical Inference methodology.

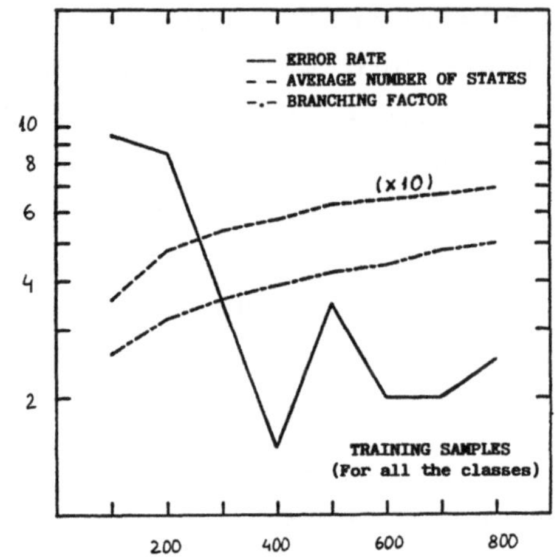

Fig.3. The error-rate and the average number of states, and branching factor, are represented as a function of size of the training set.

FFFIIIIIRRRRRRUUUUT	/θero/	GGNTFFFIIIUUUUUIIIIB?T?T
?UUUU?NNGGUUUUT	/uno/	UUUUGU?UULGGGGRRAAUUUUUUU?
BGUUUUUUUUUSSSSSSSF	/dos/	BITTTTUUUUTSSSSSSSSSF
BBIIRIIIIIIIIIFSSSSSSSB	/tres/	SBRRRIIIIIIRIFFFSFFT
GUUUUUAAAAAIRTTTTFBUIBBRUUUUUUU	/kuatro/	UUUUUUAAAURTTTBIRR?RRR?RT
FFFIIIIIINNNNNBNGTTB?GUUUUUUUUUUUT	/θinko/	SSSSSFNLLLLLG?UUGRTTTBAUUUUUUUUUT
FSSSSSSSIIIIIIIIIIIIIIFSSSSSSSSSS	/seis/	FSSSFFGRAAUIIIIIIIINFSSSFFFFTT
FSSSSSSIIIIIIIIIITTTTTBBIIIIIIF?TFT	/siete/	SSSSSSLIIIIIIIGTTTTTBB?UUUNNNN
UUUUUUUUAGGTTTTTSSSSFFFIIIUUUUUUUU	/oco/	UUUUGIGGTTTTFASSFIIGIGRRRT
NNUUUUAAIIGGGGGIIIIIIFFFF	/nueβe/	GIIIIIAUUUAAABFBAIIRRRRRIIIIIAAALNNNN?

Fig.2. A subsample of the training set used for the inference of the automata of the SPANISH DIGITS. The symbols are : I, A, U = Front, Central and Back vowels resp.; N = Nasal; L = Liquid; R = Vibrant; S, Z = Strong and Week fricatives resp.; T = Voiceless stop or silence; G = Voiced stop; B = Burst.

TABLE 1. RESULTS

		Training set	Test set	% Classification error RP	% Classification error LC	Averag number states RP	Averag number states LC	Branching factor RP	Branching factor LC
SPEAKER DEPENDENT	EXP1	10 SPEAKERS 5 REPETITIONS 500 SAMPLES	10 SPEAKERS 2 REPETITIONS 200 SAMPLES	0.0	5.5	65.7	63.9	4.3	3.9
SPEAKER INDEPENDENT	EXP2	5 SPEAKERS 10 REPETITIONS 500 SAMPLES	5 SPEAKERS 4 REPETITIONS 200 SAMPLES	6.5	10.5	64.0	63.8	4.2	3.8
SPEAKER INDEPENDENT	EXP3	8 SPEAKERS 6 REPETITIONS 480 SAMPLES	2 SPEAKERS 10 REPETITIONS 200 SAMPLES	3.5	16.0	64.6	61.8	4.2	3.9
SPEAKER INDEPENDENT	EXP3'	8 SPEAKERS 10 REPETITIONS 800 SAMPLES	2 SPEAKERS 10 REPETITIONS 200 SAMPLES	2.5	10.5	69.1	67.5	5.0	4.4

3.-CONCLUSIONS

We have shown throughought this paper the possibility and appropiateness of using GI for the automatic learning of the <u>structure</u> of speech models. This has been achieved by using the MGGI methodology, which enables:

-The incorporation of arbitrary a-priori problem-domain knowledge into the the learning device.

-The learning of structural models that are a generalization of the training samples, and well-consistent with the incorporated knowledge.

Reasonable recognition rates have been obtained using this methodology in the task of Spanish digits recognition, involving multiple speakers. Moreover, these results can be easily improved in several ways /García,87b/.

Finally, let us emphasize that the <u>long-term target</u> of the proposed methods is to achieve fully automatic learning of task-oriented integrated models for <u>Continuos Speech</u>. For doing so, the framework of Recognition must be changed to that of Traslation /Vidal,87b/. The MGGI methodology can be easily extended formally to this framework, and preliminary empirical results have already shown the posibility of applying this extension to real (continuous) speech problems.

4.-REFERENCES.

Angluin D.: "On the complexity of minumun inference of regular sets". Information and Control, Vol.39, pp.337-350, 1978.

Angluin D., Smith C.H.: "Inductive Inference: Theory and methods". Computing Surveys. Vol.15, N.3, Sept. 1983.

Eilemberg S.: "Automata Languages and Machines". Academic Press, 1974.

Feldman J.: "Some Decidability Results on Grammatical Inference and Complexity". Information and Control, Vol.29, pp.244-262, 1972

Forney G.D.: "The Viterbi Algorithm". Proc. IEEE 61(3), pp.268-278, 1973.

Fu K.S., Booth T.L.: "Grammatical Inference: Introduction and Survey". Parts 1 and 2. IEEE Trans. Syst. Man Cybern. SMC-5, 95-111, 409-423, 1975.

García P., Vidal E., Casacuberta F.: "Local Language, the Succesor Method and a step towards a general methodology for the inference of Regular Grammars". IEEE Trans. on PAMI. Vol.6, N.6, 1987.

García P., Segarra E., Vidal E., Galiano I.: "On the use of the Morphic Generator Grammatical Inference (MGGI) methodology in Automatic Speech Recognition". Unpublished manuscript. 1987.

Gold M.: "Language Identification in the Limit". Information and Control, Vol.10, pp.447-474, 1967.

Vidal E., Lloret M.J.: "Recent results on the application of a metric space search algorithm to multi-speaker data". Also in this book (1987).

Vidal E., Prieto N., Sanchís E, Rulot, H. "Application of the Error-Correcting Grammatical Inference Algorithm to mutispeaker IWR". Also in this book.

A NEW APPROACH TO TEMPLATE SELECTION FOR SPEAKER INDEPENDENT WORD RECOGNITION

N. Yalabık, F.Yarman-Vural, A.Mansur*
Middle East Technical University
Ankara, Turkey

Abstract: This study explores the possibility of using Condensed Nearest Neighbor (CNN) rule for classification in various word recognition problems. A modified version of "Condensing" combined with "Editing" algorithm is implemented to select the reference templates for a speaker independent isolated word recognition problem. It is shown that these algorithms improve the recognition rate in comparison to using clustering techniques for template selection.

1. INTRODUCTION

The problem of selecting a few representative samples from a large sample set may appear in various levels in speech recognition, such as selection of word reference templates in a speaker independent isolated word recognition system which employs whole word matching, or selection of a codebook for linear predictive coding (LPC) coefficient vectors in Vector Quantization. The most common approach to solve this problem is to employ clustering. For the word recognition problem clustering makes use of the assumption that the learning samples from a category form a few natural clusters. However, it does not make any use of the relative position of the samples from the different categories.

In this study, an alternative approach is taken, which mainly involves the selection of reference templates by "Editing" and "Condensing" algorithms. These methods when used together, result in a much lower computational load without significant

---

* Drexel University, Philadelphia, PA, USA

NATO ASI Series, Vol. F46
Recent Advances in Speech Understanding and Dialog Systems
Edited by H. Niemann et al.

performance degredation in comparison to the Nearest Neighbor (NN) classification with all learning samples used as the reference set /DEV 82/. Conceptually, editing eliminates samples that fall in the Bayes rejection regions and Condensing selects the samples near NN-rule decision boundaries. In the following sections we describe these methods as applied to speaker independent isolated word recognition.

2. EDITED AND CONDENSED NEAREST NEIGHBOR RULE

It is known that the storage space and computational complexity requirements of the NN rule with a large sample set makes it impractical for most applications. Many attempts have been made to reduce the number of samples and to select a representative subset without significantly degrading the performance. Editing /WIL 72/ algorithm can be summarized as follows: Partition the sample set into two independent sets S_1 and S_2. Use S_1 to classify all samples in S_2 using NN rule. Discard all samples that are misclassified in S_2 and use the rest of S_2 as the representative subset. This procedure has later been modified as the Multiedit /DEV 80/ algorithm, which initially starts with N subsets and discards the misclassified samples in an iterative manner. It was shown /DEV 82/ that the Multiedit algorithm even improves the recognition rate while reducing the sample set size. However, to obtain a minimal, representative subset, further processing is needed, which is provided by the Condensing algorithm /HAR 68/. Condensing basically results with a subset that will classify all the remaining correctly. This can be achieved by the following algorithm, which is called the Condensed Nearest Neighbor (CNN) rule:

1. Set two bins called S_o and S_n, by placing all samples (that passed editing) initially in S_n.

2. Move samples from S_n to S_o one by one if they are incorrectly classified by the samples that are already in S_n. First sample always moves to S_o.

3. Iterate (2) until no samples can be transferred. Use final set in S_o for classification.

It can be observed that the final set is not unique and it may change depending on how the samples are ordered in S_n. As a remedy, some initial ordering algorithms were proposed /CH1 79/. In these, the samples are ordered in a way that the ones to the NN decision boundaries are considered first. These algorithms are generally called Modified CNN (MCNN).

3. SPEAKER INDEPENDENT ISOLATED WORD RECOGNITION

We applied above algorithms to a speaker independent, 18-word isolated word recognition system developed earlier /UNA 83/. Here, Dynamic Time Warping based whole word matching is employed with LPC vectors as frame features. The distance between two words is given as the output of DTW algorithm, where frame by frame distance in found using a symmetric version of Itakura distance measure. Editing and Condensing are applied with modifications as will be discussed below.

3.1. Editing

The multiedit algorithm requires a very large sample set to start with to be effective. In this study, the following algorithm is used to obtain a similar effect with a relatively smaller sample set size:

1. Find a "Cluster center" for each category and call the collection of all samples that are at a certain range to their own center S_c. The range is chosen such that at least half of the total number of samples are in S_c.
2. Use S_c to classify all the rest using the NN rule. Call correctly classified samples S_{cor}.
3. Use $S_c \cup S_{cor}$ as the sample set for the next stage.

3.2. Multicategory MCNN

Modified CNN for a multicategory problem becomes computationally prohibitive especially when the number of categories is large, since all distances between all distinct pairs of samples should be calculated. In this study, we use the following algorithm:

1. Generate a "minimum spanning tree" of the word cluster centers, as shown in Figure 1. The edge lengths are proportional to the distance between cluster centers in the figure.

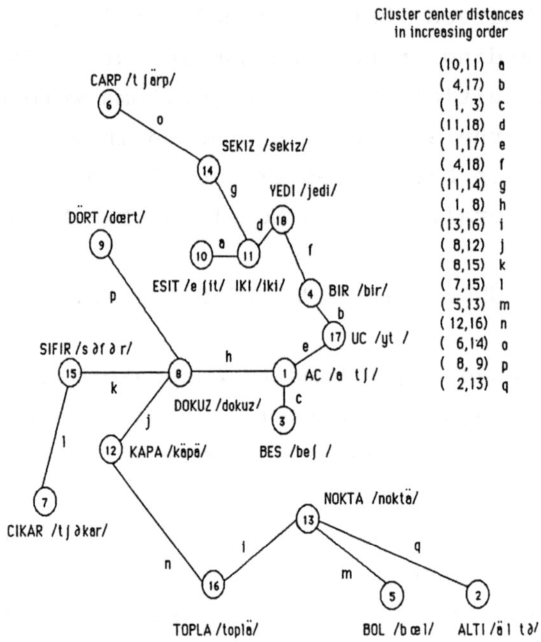

Figure 1. Minimum spanning tree for Turkish word cluster centers.

2. For each category, apply MCNN to it and all others that are connected to it by an edge. For example, UC,AC and BIR in Figure 1. Repeat for all categories.

3. Find a union of all samples selected in 2, call it S_{un}.

4. Use S_{un} to classify the eliminated samples. If a sample is misclassified, add it to S_{un}. Iterate until all samples are tested.

3.3. Experimental results

333 samples collected from 5 male and 5 female speakers were used as the learning sample set. 100 samples collected from 6 different male and female speakers are used for testing. The classification results obtained are shown in Table 1.

4. CONCLUSION

As can be observed in Table 1, CNN when used together with Editing increased the correct classification ratio compared to clustering. One disadvantage of above algorithms compared to

template selection criterion	average number of templates/word retained	correct classification ratio
Editing + CNN	6	91%
CNN only	8	77
Clustering	6	85

Table 1. Classification results

clustering is that they are computationally a few times more costly. However, since they are used in the learning phase, this is not a significant restriction.

The results show that Editing and MCNN can be used as an alternative to clustering in speech recognition problems.

REFERENCES

/CHl 79/ K.Chidananda Gowda, G.Krishna "The condensed nearest neighbor rule using the concept of mutual nearest neighborhood" IEEE Trans. Inform. Th. Vol.125 (1979) 488-490.

/DEV 80/ P.A.Devijver and J.Kittler: "On the edited nearest neighbor rule" Proc.Fifth Int.Conf.on Pattern Recognition, Miami Beach, Fl. (1980), 72-80.

/DEV 82/ P.A.Devijver and J.Kittler: "Pattern Recognition: A statistical Approach". Prentice-Hall, London (1982), 109-119.

/HAR 68/ P.E. Hart: "The Condensed Nearest Neighbor Rule" IEEE Trans. on Info. Theory, Vol.14, (1968), 515-516.

/UNA 83/ A.F.Unal: "A Speaker Independent Isolated Turkish Word Recognition System" M.S. Thesis, Middle East Technical U. (1983)

/WIL 85/ J.G. Wilpon, L.R.Rabiner: "A Modified K.Means Algorithm for use in Isolated Word Recognition" IEEE Trans. ASSP. Vol. ASSP-33, no.3 (1985),587-594.

/WIL 72/ D.L. Wilson: "Asymptotic properties of nearest neighbor rules using edited data", IEEE Trans. Systems Man Cybernet.Vol 2, (1972), 408-420.

DYNAMIC SPECTRAL ADAPTATION OF AUTOMATIC SPEECH RECOGNIZERS TO NEW SPEAKERS

Gérard CHOLLET , Khalid CHOUKRI

ENST Dept. SIG, CNRS UA 820
46 rue Barrault, F-75013 Paris, France

Abstract: This is an overview of approaches to automatically reduce the intra and inter speaker variability in the speech signal. Attention is focussed on particular methods to adapt standard Automatic Speech Recognizers (ASR) to new users, taking into account their specific acoustical characteristics. Speaker normalization and adaptation techniques for a template-based recognizers are described. They are based on spectral normalization, on the learning of spectral transformations and on code book substitution for VQ front end.

1. INTRODUCTION

The large inter-speaker variability of speech creates difficulties in Automatic Speech Recognition. Best performances are achieved with a time consuming training for each new speaker. To avoid this training, multireference templates have been used with some success /RAB 79/. But storage and recognition time become rapidly prohibitive with increasing vocabulary size. The techniques described in this paper are complementary. References are being adapted using a limited set of words of the new speaker. This adaptation consists of a transformation of the spectral space. If that space is vector quantized, specific techniques are used. If not, more general transformations are applied. A detailed review of the literature is given in /CHO 87a/.

2. SPEAKER ADAPTATION USING VECTOR QUANTIZATION

Vector Quantization (V.Q.) reduces both computation and space requirements. Therefore many isolated word recognizers use this coding technique.

Speaker adaptation algorithms using VQ have been proposed by Shikano and his colleagues /SHI 86/, and other authors referenced in /CHO 87a/. The speaker adaptation is carried out by substituting vectors of the reference codebook by new vectors obtained from the adaptation vocabulary.

Several strategies have been reported previously /CHO 87b/. Our contribution consists in a combination of these with the Canonical correlation analysis, introduced in the next paragraph.

NATO ASI Series, Vol. F46
Recent Advances in Speech Understanding and Dialog Systems
Edited by H. Niemann et al.

3. SPECTRAL TRANSFORMATIONS

The size of the adaptation vocabulary should be reduced to a minimum. Its purpose is the association of corresponding spectra for the reference and new speaker.

3.1 Linear Multivariate Regression

A linear transformation Φ, can be estimated and used to modify the reference dictionary into an adapted dictionary. **Linear Multivariate Regression (LMR),** applied to the available spectra of both speakers, can be used to compute the matrix Φ. For all available spectra, one may write $[\ Y_1\ Y_2\ ....\ Y_J\ ] = \Phi\ [\ X_1\ X_2\ ....\ X_J\ ] + E$ where E is the prediction error. A minimisation of E leads to an estimation of Φ in a least mean-square sense. In this case, the new spectral parameters are $[\ Y_1\ Y_2\ ....\ Y_J\ ] = \Phi\ [\ X_1\ X_2\ ....\ X_J\ ]$ where X_i are the reference spectral parameters.

3.2 Canonical Correlation Analysis

Let us imagine a new parametric space **U** (an "interpretation" space) /CHO 86/,where the representations of the same sounds, uttered by speakers **S** (standard) and **N** (new), are supposed to be identical. This can be represented by the diagram shown below:

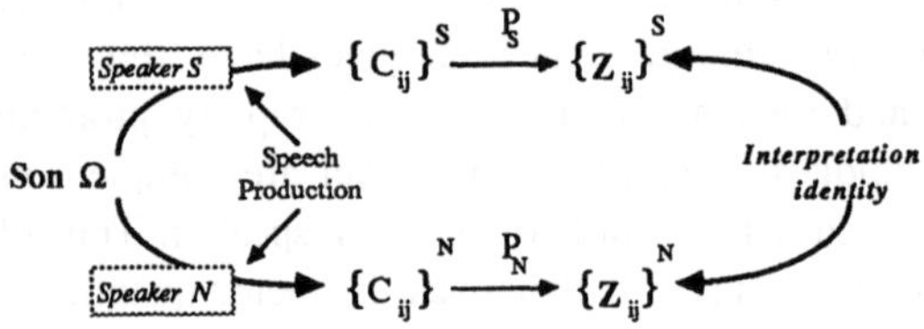

Figure 3-1. Interpretation space

The identity can be represented, using a distance measure, by the equation: $d(Z_{ij}^{s}, Z_{ij}^{n}) = 0$.

An ideal transformation would be found by solving the equation. Unfortunately, the matrices of parameters $(C_{ij})^s, (C_{ij})^n$ are needed for the entire vocabulary, so this computation requires acquiring all utterances for speaker N, which contradicts our intent.

Therefore, the best linear estimates of the transformations P_s and P_n can be defined from the available information samples about the spectral space of speaker N. P_s and P_n respectively project the reference and new speaker spectra into the space U so that corresponding spectra coincide in a least mean square sense ($d(Z_{ij}^{s}, Z_{ij}^{n})$ **is minimized).**

Canonical correlation analysis (CCA) is a technique which (as applied to our problem) allows the construction of the interpretation space U and the computation of the two projection operators P_s and P_n /CHO 86/.

3.3 Dynamic aspects

Some linear algebraic developments allow the updating of the transition function Φ in LMR or the two projection operators P_S and P_N in CCA, as new data become available and make the dynamic adaptation process possible /CHO 86/. This means that it can be performed interactively during the recognition session (with a feedback conditionned by the result of the recognition). It can take place under user supervision and on his decision. This permit to improve the representative sample of the spectral space, particulary if these utterances are badly recognized (by concatenation of the former words and the new ones).

3.4 Local canonical correlation analysis

Canonical correlation analysis is a linear approach. It transforms all spectra in the same way using one projection operator without any care about speech diversity. Refering to spectral representation for different speech segments, it is clear that segment class-specific and speaker-specific transformations will be better than the simple speaker-specific one. Instead of computing only one projection, several homogenous speech classes (as voiced/unvoiced) are defined and CCA is performed separately on each class. In the same way, it is possible to introduce a Local Linear Multivariate Regression.

4. EXPERIMENTS AND RESULTS

For the evaluation of these approaches, a data base of french digits, repeated one time by 98 speakers has been used. Each digit is represented by a set of MFCC coefficients (6 for each 10ms window). In order to compute the transition function Φ or the two projection operators P_S and P_N, we use the dynamique procedure with an adaptation vocabulary containing one digit, two digits (new one is concatenated to the former one), or more. The DTW algorithm realises the one-to-one correspondance between spectra. The recognition score before adaptation is 70% for the first position and 84% for the first two positions. For LMR experiments, we consider 27 new speakers and 4 standard ones (other than the 27 for tests), the results are given by the next figure.

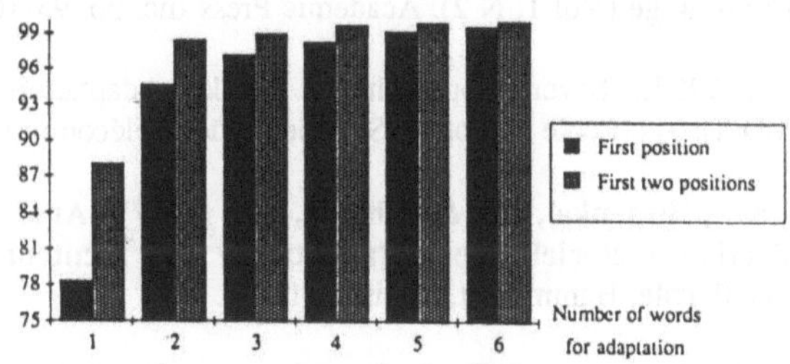

Figure 4-1. Recognition score with multivariate regression

For validation purpose, in case of Canonical correlation procedure, a second experiment is conducted in the same conditions as above, but with 87 new speakers instead of 27 and about 15 standard ones. The results are given by the next figure.

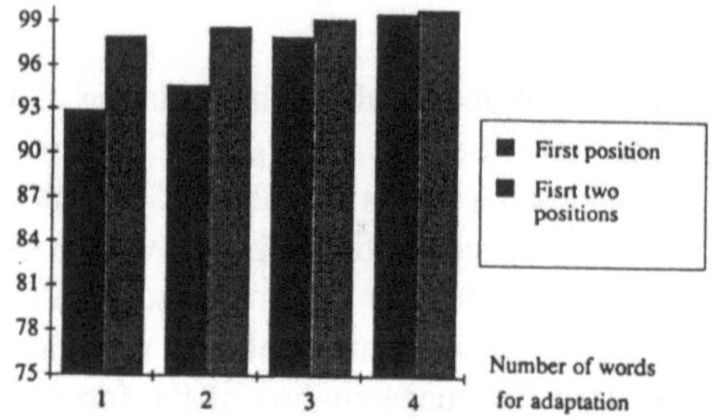

Figure 4-2. Recognition score with Canonical correlation analysis

Applied to an isolated digit recognition these techniques improves recognition scores significantly (CCA improved a 70% correct score to 87%, when the utterance providing a representative sample of the spectral space is one word). Meanwhile recognition of a large vocabulary should show more significant improvement.

5. CONCLUSION

This paper describes different learning techniques of spectral transformations which allows to adapt dictionaries to new speakers in Automatic Speech Recognition.

A dynamic but supervised technique has also been introduced and evaluated in case of an isolated word recognition system with a single reference dictionary.

This paper describes a local canonical correlation analysis (LCCA), which is introduced to take into account the speech diversity (voiced/unvoiced frames, ...).

Acknowledgement: *This work was partly supported by the CEE ESPRIT SPIN project (contract N° 64).*

REFERENCES:

/CHO 86/ **Choukri, K. , Chollet, G. (1986)**, Unsupervised and Dynamic learning of Spectral transformations using canonical correlation analysis for adaptation of ASR to new speakers. **Computer and Speech Language** (Vol 1, N 2). Academic Press Inc. pp. 95-107.

/CHO 87a/ **Choukri, K. , (1987)**, Several approaches to Speaker Adaptation in Automatic Speech Recognition Systems. PhD Thesis, Ecole Nationale Supérieure des Télécommunications, Paris.

/CHO 87b/ **Choukri, K. , Fraenkel, S. & Chollet, G. (1987)**, **Analyse des corrélations canoniques et quantification vectorielle pour l'adaptation aux locuteurs**. in Proc. **XVIème Journées d'Etudes sur la Parole**, Hammamet, Tunisie, (1987).

/RAB 79/ **Rabiner, L.R., Levinson, S.E. & Rosenberg, A.E. (1979)**, Speaker-independent Recognition of isolated words Using Clustering Techniques. in IEEE ASSP, August, ASSP-27, no 4, pp 336-349.

/SHI 86/ **Shikano, K., Lee, K.F. & Reddy, R. (1986)**, Speaker adaptation through vector quantization. **IEEE-ICASSP**, Tokyo, pp. 2643-2646.

Towards Speaker-Independent Continuous Speech Recognition

Kai-Fu Lee
Computer Science Department
Carnegie-Mellon University
Pittsburgh, PA 15213 U.S.A

ABSTRACT: Speaker-independent continuous speech recognition is an extremely difficult task. In this paper, we analyze the nature of its difficulty. Moreover, we propose a new approach to speaker-independent continuous speech recognition through the use of hidden Markov models, context-dependent phonetic units, perceptually motivated parameters, and two speaker-adaptation algorithms. Finally, we present some preliminary results, and outline future plans.

1 INTRODUCTION

Humans recognize continuous speech from many speakers remarkably well; however, automatic recognition of speaker-independent continuous speech is still in an infantile stage. There are four major obstacles impeding its progress:

1. Need of a sophisticated yet tractable model of speech.
2. Need of a unit of speech that is trainable, well-understood, and relatively insensitive to context.
3. Need to incorporate speaker-independent acoustic/phonetic information.
4. Need to normalize between-speaker spectral differences, and to learn speaker-specific characteristics.

In this paper, we propose a new approach to speaker-independent speech recognition that focuses on these four problems. We will first describe our solution for each of the four problems. We will then present an initial system that used some of these ideas. This system achieved 85% word accuracy on a 1000-word task, which is very encouraging. Finally, we will outline our plans for future work.

2 MODEL OF SPEECH: Hidden Markov Models

Hidden Markov models (HMM) are a powerful new technique that is capable of robust modeling of speech. HMM's are a parametric model that is particularly suitable for describing speech events. Their doubly stochastic processes enable modeling of not only acoustic phenomena, but also timescale distortions. Furthermore, efficient algorithms exist for accurate estimation of HMM parameters. Unlike other non-parametric and ad-hoc approaches, the Forward-Backward re-estimation algorithm for hidden Markov models arose from the E-M algorithm [Baum 72], which guarantees a finite improvement every iteration. Unlike gradient-descent procedures, the Forward-Backward Algorithm converges after only a few iterations. Hidden Markov models are a succinct representation of speech events, and require considerably less storage than other strategies. Finally, efficient heuristic search algorithms are more easily implemented using HMM. In fact, it has been shown that an optimal stochastic search is not infeasible for moderately difficult tasks [Baker 75].

Hidden Markov models were first used independently by Baker [Baker 75] and Jelinek *et al.* [Jelinek 76] in speech recognition. Recently, researchers have successfully applied these HMM techniques to model and recognize various units of speech [Bahl 83, Chow 87]. We will use hidden Markov models to represent all knowledge sources, from phonemes to words to sentences. At the lowest level, HMM's will be used to model speaker independent phonemes.

NATO ASI Series, Vol. F46
Recent Advances in Speech Understanding
and Dialog Systems
Edited by H. Niemann et al.

3 UNIT OF SPEECH: Context-Dependent Phonetic Units

In order to model continuous speech, we need a good unit of speech that is not only trainable and well-defined, but also relatively insensitive to context. The most natural units for humans are words and phonemes. Words are not a practical choice for large vocabulary recognition because of the great amount of storage and training data required. Phonemes are well-understood and easily trainable; however, they are highly dependent on context [Schwartz 85].

Schwartz *et al.* [Schwartz 85] of BBN applied *context-dependent* modeling of phonemes by creating a phoneme model for each left/right phonemic context. However, this leads to a large number of models which dissipates the training data and complicates the search. They dealt with the first problem by combining the context-dependent models with context-independent ones. The recognition results using this approach were very good.

Our context-dependent modeling will be based on the BBN approach. However, we believe that it is possible to generalize further by merging similar contexts together. If successful, this will result in substantially fewer context-dependent units. In addition, we will experiment with automatic learning to generalize phonetic contexts.

4 INCORPORATING KNOWLEDGE: Adding Perceptually Motivated Parameters

Although HMM's have been used to represent units of speech, they were almost always speaker dependent models. We hope to extend HMM's to speaker independent modeling by adding perceptually motivated parameters.

Most speech recognition systems, including HMM-based systems, rely on relatively simple speech parameters, such as FFT or LPC coefficients. It has been shown that many other parameters are useful for speech recognition [Shikano 86a, Furui 86]. We will use these additional parameters by vector quantizing them into separate codebooks, and training multiple sets of output pdf's simultaneously. We will also add phoneme and word duration modeling to our recognizer.

5 SPEAKER LEARNING AND ADAPTATION: Two Algorithms

While the above representations will improve recognition, they do not account for vocal tract differences between different speakers, nor do they capture speaker specific characteristics. We propose two learning algorithms that adapt the HMM system to the speaker.

The first algorithm is based on *codebook normalization* [Shikano 86b]. This learning algorithm assumes that the set of all speakers can be divided into *speaker clusters*, and all speakers in each cluster are similar. During the training stage, the training speakers are split into clusters. A cluster-dependent codebook and a set of HMM's are generated for each cluster. Also, a speaker-independent codebook is created from all speakers. Then, a probabilistic mapping from the speaker-independent codebook to each cluster codebook obtained using the Forward-Backward algorithm [Schwartz 87]. Finally, the cluster-dependent output pdf's are replaced by multiplying the speaker-independent pdf's by the mapping. During recognition, the testing speaker is first classified into the speaker cluster that best characterizes the speaker's spectral properties. Then, the adapted parameters for that cluster are selected and used for recognition. This adaptation algorithm is illustrated in Figure 1-a.

The second algorithm, *dynamic interpolation*, begins with a speaker independent

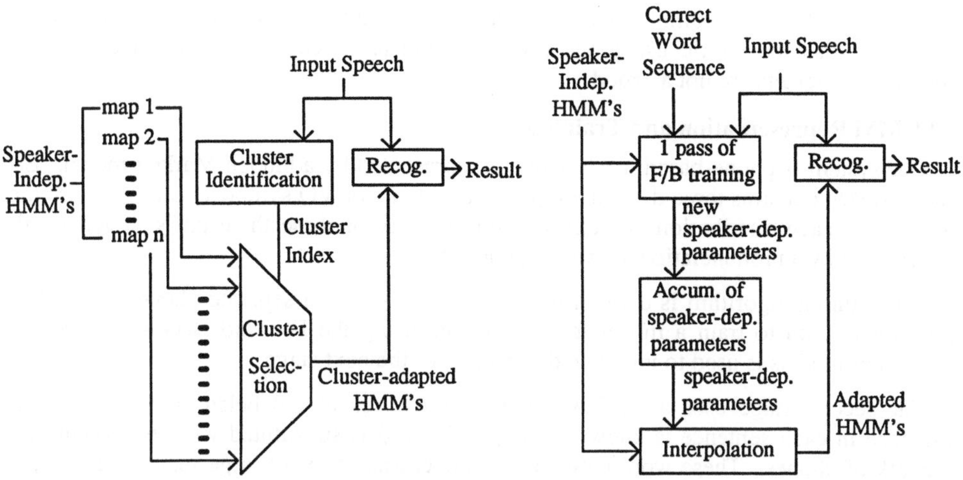

(a) Codebook normalization adaptation (b) Dynamic interpolation adaptation

Figure 1: Two speaker adaptation algorithms

codebook and HMM's. After each recognition trial, the correct word sequence is provided. One iteration of the Forward-backward algorithm is run with the correct word sequence on the input speech, and a set of speaker-dependent parameters is updated. Then, the parameters of the HMM's are dynamically re-estimated as a linear combination of the speaker-independent and speaker-dependent parameters in order to learn and incorporate the characteristics of the speaker. The *dynamic interpolation* algorithm is illustrated in Figure 1-b.

Both learning algorithms are virtually transparent to the user, and require little additional training data and time. We will implement and evaluate these algorithms individually as well as simultaneously.

6 IMPLEMENTATION AND RESULTS

In this section, we will describe the implementation of a preliminary system that uses some of the ideas discussed in this paper.

6.1 Speech Representation

The speech is sampled at 16 KHz, and pre-emphasized with a filter of $1 - 0.97z^{-1}$. Then, a Hamming widow with a width of 20 msec is applied every 10 msec. Autocorrelation analysis with order 14 is followed by LPC analysis with order 14. Finally, a set of 12 LPC-derived cepstral coefficients are computed from the LPC coefficients, and these LPC cepstral coefficients are transformed to a mel-scale using a bilinear transform [Shikano 85].

These 12 coefficients are vector quantized into a codebook of 256 prototype vectors. In order to incorporate additional speech parameters, we created two additional codebooks. One codebook is vector quantized from *differential coefficients*. The differential coefficient of frame n is the difference between the coefficient of frame n+2 and frame n–2. This 40 msec. difference captures the slope of the spectral envelope. The other codebook is vector quantized from *energy* and *differential energy* values.

The use of multiple codebooks was first proposed by Gupta, *et al.* [Gupta 87]. There are other ways of incorporating additional knowledge, and we have experimented with a composite distance metric using one codebook and all three sets of parameters [Shikano 86b], but the results are not as good.

6.2 HMM Representation and Training

Our system is phone-based; each phone is represented by a hidden Markov model. Each phone HMM contains three discrete output distributions of VQ symbols. Since we use three codebooks, each distribution is really the joint density of these three pdf's. Each word is represented by a pronunciation network of phones.

Our training algorithm is divided into two stages. First, a separate phonetically labeled database is used to train a model for each phone using the Forward Backward algorithm. This set of models is used to initialize the training of the next stage.

The second stage uses a database of 3200 sentences of unlabeled speech. The word sequence in each sentence is known. First, each word is substituted with its pronunciation network of phones. These word networks are concatenated into a large sentence HMM, and trained with the corresponding speech using the Forward Backward algorithm.

Because the initial estimates for the second stage are already quite good, only two iterations of the Forward Backward algorithm are needed. The output probabilities are then smoothed by deleted interpolation [Bahl 83] with a uniform distribution. This set of phone models is used for recognition.

6.3 HMM Recognition and Results

The recognition stage is a Viterbi search for the optimal state sequence in a large HMM network. At the highest level, this HMM is a network with all word HMM's in parallel. Each word is instantiated with its phonetic pronunciation network, and each phone is instantiated with the corresponding phone model. Beam search is used to reduce the amount of computation.

We applied the above system to the 1000-word resource management task of the DARPA project. We used 3200 sentences produced by 80 speakers to train the recognizer, and 100 sentences produced by 10 other speakers to test it. Using a bigram language model, we obtain a top choice word recognition rate of 85%. We expect that with a more restrictive finite state grammar, recognition rate would be about 95%. This is more accurate than any previous speaker-independent continuous recognizer on similar tasks.

7 CONCLUSION

While there are many successful speech recognition systems, no successful recognizer for speaker-independent continuous speech has emerged. We believe the difficulty of recognizing speaker-independent continuous speech is primarily caused by poor modeling of speech, lack of trainable yet relatively context-insensitive unit, lack of acoustic/phonetic information, and need to learn speaker characteristics and adapt to them.

In this paper, we discussed our remedies for each of the above problems. By using hidden Markov models to model speech, we will be able to train and recognize efficiently and accurately. By finding a good unit of speech, we will be able to deal with coarticulation. By adding acoustic/phonetic knowledge to our parameters, we will have a more robust representation of speaker-independent speech. Finally, by adding a learning stage, our system can adapt to an input speaker rapidly and non-intrusively.

We presented some preliminary results on speaker-independent continuous speech recognition of a 1000-word vocabulary. Although only some of the ideas have been implemented, the results are quite encouraging. A full implementation and results will be forthcoming [Lee 88].

Our future work will involve improving the existing system, and incorporation of context-dependent modeling, adaptation, and learning. We hope that through knowledge and learning, our system will bridge the gap between speaker dependent and speaker independent systems.

ACKNOWLEDGEMENTS

The author wishes to thank H. W. Hon for his contributions in the implementation of this system, and D. R. Reddy and R. M. Stern for their suggestions and discussions.

REFERENCES

[Bahl 83] Bahl, L. R., Jelinek, F., Mercer, R. A Maximum Likelihood Approach to Continuous Speech Recognition. *IEEE Transactions on Pattern Analysis and Machine Intelligence* PAMI-5(2):179-190, March, 1983.

[Baker 75] Baker, J. K. The DRAGON System -- An Overview. *IEEE Transactions on Acoustics, Speech, and Signal Processing* ASSP-23(1):24-29, February, 1975.

[Baum 72] Baum, L. E. An Inequality and Associated Maximization Technique in Statistical Estimation of Probabilistic Functions of Markov Processes. *Inequalities* 3:1-8, 1972.

[Chow 87] Chow, Y.L., Dunham, M.O., Kimball, O.A., Krasner, M.A., Kubala, G.F., Makhoul, J., Roucos, S., Schwartz, R.M. BYBLOS: The BBN Continuous Speech Recognition System. In *IEEE International Conference on Acoustics, Speech, and Signal Processing*, pages 89-92. April, 1987.

[Furui 86] Furui, S. Speaker-Independent Isolated Word Recognition Using Dynamic Features of Speech Spectrum. *IEEE Transactions on Acoustics, Speech, and Signal Processing* ASSP-34(1):52-59, February, 1986.

[Gupta 87] Gupta, V.N., Lennig, M., Mermelstein, P. Integration of Acoustic Information in a Large Vocabulary Word Recognizer. In *IEEE International Conference on Acoustics, Speech, and Signal Processing*, pages 697-700. April, 1987.

[Jelinek 76] Jelinek, F. Continuous Speech Recognition by Statistical Methods. *Proceedings of the IEEE* 64(4):532-556, April, 1976.

[Lee 88] Lee, K.F. *Speaker-Independent Continuous Speech Recognition Using Hidden Markov Models*. PhD thesis, Carnegie-Mellon University, 1988.

[Schwartz 85] Schwartz, R., Chow, Y., Kimball, O., Roucos, S., Krasner, M., Makhoul, J. Context-Dependent Modeling for Acoustic-Phonetic Recognition of Continuous Speech. In *IEEE International Conference on Acoustics, Speech, and Signal Processing*. April, 1985.

[Schwartz 87] Schwartz, R., Chow, Y., Kubala, F. Rapid Speaker Adaptation Using a Probabilistic Spectral Mapping. In *IEEE International Conference on Acoustics, Speech, and Signal Processing*. April, 1987.

[Shikano 85] Shikano, K. *Evaluation of LPC Spectral Matching Measures for Phonetic Unit Recognition*. Technical Report, Carnegie-Mellon University, May, 1985.

[Shikano 86a] Shikano, K., Lee, K. Reddy, D. R. *Speaker Adaptation through Vector Quantization*. Technical Report CMU-CS-86-102, Carnegie-Mellon University, December, 1986.

[Shikano 86b] Shikano, K., Lee. K, Reddy, D. R. Speaker Adaptation through Vector Quantization. In *IEEE International Conference on Acoustics, Speech, and Signal Processing*. April, 1986.

EVALUATING SPEECH RECOGNIZERS AND DATA BASES

Gérard CHOLLET, Claude MONTACIE
ENST Dept. SIGNAL, CNRS UA-820
46 rue Barrault, 75634 PARIS cédex 13, FRANCE.

Abstract: The problems of evaluating speech recognizers are considered from several points of view. The value of making large data bases available to the research and development community is acknowledged. Some recommandations are made about the size and content of data bases distributed for test purpose. A test workstation implemented on a PC is described. Reference speech recognition algorithms are available on this workstation. Examples of several applications are given.

1. INTRODUCTION

The value of speech recognition technology needs to be assessed in order to gain acceptance. Predicting performance is one of the most important need. We must distinguish the point of view of the designers from the one of the buyers.

- Designers need to efficiently test the degree of success they are attaining, and to reliably measure the impact of each algorithm change.
- buyers need reliable and comprehensive information about how each device will perform in the specific conditions of their practical applications.

A recognition rate depends of numerous parameters /LEA82/PAL85/, some of them cannot be easily quantized. Among many elements we can retain : the vocabulary (complexity, syntax, size...), recording conditions (bandwidth, varied types of noise and level, distorsion ...), speakers (stressed/relaxed, trained/untrained).

The European speech community is activily involved in evaluation. This effort is primarily funded by the CEE ESPRIT SAM project. This paper reflects some of the work under completion.

2. SPEECH DATA BASES

Most manufacturers claim performance over 99% on their laboratory data bases. This sole number is not sufficient to predict performance of speech recognizers. It should be at least, supported by vocabulary and test description, types of errors, confidence interval, confidence level.

2.1. Which data bases

Large data bases are necessary to evaluate the performance of speech recognizers. Application vocabularies (digits, letters of the alphabet ...) are available. Minimal series could also be used to measure the phonetic sensitivity /CHO81/.

NATO ASI Series, Vol. F46
Recent Advances in Speech Understanding and Dialog Systems
Edited by H. Niemann et al.

The intra and inter-speaker variability should be measured and the corresponding stastistical distribution should be controlled for every data base.

Speech coding and synthesis techniques could be used to simulate differents environmental conditions, test the limits of the recognizers, control an acceptable variability, and hopefully reduce the size of data bases.

2.2. Types of errors and statistical validity

Three types of errors are common : substitution (a word of the vocabulary is recognized for an other one), false alarm (a word is chosen on the detection of noise or out of vocabulary word), miss (a vocabulary word is not detected).

Confidence interval and level must be estimated for each type of error.

In order to calculate the confidence interval, several methods /BAK82/LEB73/ give similar results. One such method considers that the probability distribution for the number of errors is binomial . It is characterized by 2 parameters:

- N = Bernouilli trials (nb of items in test set)
- P = probability that an individual test is an error

In this particular case the confidence interval p with a confidence level of x% is /LEB73/ :

$$p = \frac{P + \frac{z_x^2}{2N} \pm z_x \sqrt{\frac{P(1-P)}{N} + \frac{z_x^2}{4N^2}}}{1 + \frac{z_x^2}{N}}$$

with $z_{95\%} = 1.96$
$z_{99\%} = 2.48$

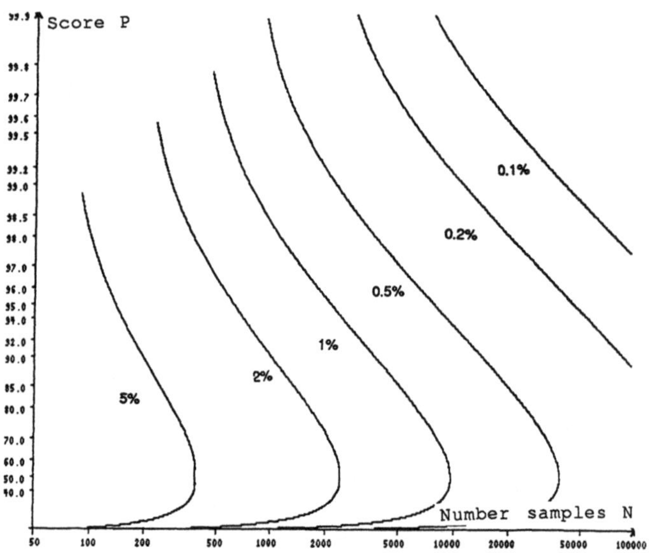

Interval confidence p at 95%

example: A manufacturer does 200 tests and gets 199 successes and one failure, the recognition rate is 99.5% and the confidence interval is [97.2%,99.9%] with confidence level of 95%. In order to get a precision of 0.2%, 8000 tests would be necessary.

3. EVALUATION WORKSTATIONS

Two evaluation workstations have been defined, the cheapest (PC/XT with CD-ROM) could be used to test recognizers on standard data bases. The other one is more powerful (PC/AT with signal processing board). It allows real time implementation of reference systems to evaluate new applications.

3.1. Evaluating recognition equipments

In the SAM Protocol, the equipement under test is connected to the PC which monitors access to data bases available on optical disks.

3.2. Evaluating data bases

From our knowledge of human perception, an intrinsic measure of complexity of speech data bases can be used. The Human Equivalent Noise Ratio (HENR) has been proposed by Moore /MOO77/.

An another solution is the use of reference systems /CHO82/ to evaluate intra-class variability and the inter-class distance.

3.3. Evaluating new applications

On the SAM workstation, state of the art recognition algorithms should be available as reference systems. The feasibility of a particular application could therefore be assessed rapidly.

4. A CONNECTED-WORD RECOGNITION REFERENCE SYSTEM

4.1. Description

A connected-word recognition reference system using one pass dynamic time warping algorithm has been implemented /CHO82/BAK82/MON87/. An utterance is coded as a sequence of vectors of Weighted Mel Frequency Cepstral Coefficients (WMFCC) /TOH86/, every 20 ms. The window width is 41 ms. Silence is considered to be a particular instance of word which needs to be trained as another word.

4.2. Experiments and results

To evaluate the performance of this reference system, the TI isolated word data base was used. It consists of 20 isolated words repeated 26 times by 16 speakers /DOD81/. This vocabulary is not very difficult (reduced noise and excellent pronunciation).

The first elocution in the data base was taken as the reference. Word "silence" has been created from the three vectors WMFCC of the first utterance of the first word.

6000 tests were performed with 109 failures, this gives a recognition rate of 98% (± 0.5%). The confusion between the second and the sixth word (no-go) is the main cause of errors.

5. CONCLUSION

Evaluating speech recognition technology is necessary for gaining acceptance. The European community is putting some effort in this direction. Data bases and reference systems are made available on test workstations. Preliminary results are promissing.

ACKNOWLEDGMENTS

This work is partly supported by the ESPRIT "SAM" project. It also reflects opinions within the IEEE-WG on speech assessement.

REFERENCES

/BAK82/ BAKER J.M (1982) **The performing arts - how to measure up.** Workshop on Standardization for Speech I-O Technology, Washington, pp 25-33

/BAK82/ BAKER K. (1982) **Assessment of using a reference system for the evaluation of speech and data bases.** Report to National bureau of standard, Wash, USA

/CHO81/ CHOLLET G., ASTIER A., ROSSI M. (1981) **Evaluating the performance of speech recognizers at the accoustic-phonetic level** IEEE-ICASSP, Denver.

/CHO82/ CHOLLET G., GAGNOULET C. (1982) **Evaluating speech recognizers and data bases using a reference system.** IEEE-ICASSP, Paris.

/DOD81/ DODDINGTON G., SCHALK T. (1981) **Speech recognition: turning theory to practice.** IEEE-SPECTRUM

/LEA82/ LEA W. (1982) **Available speech databases for evaluating speech recognizers.** Workshop on Standardization for Speech I-O Technology, Washington

/LEB73/ LEBART L., FENELON J.P. (1973) **Stastistiques et informatiques appliquées** Dunod, Paris.

/PAL85/ PALETT D.S. (1985), **Automatic Speech recognition performance assessements** National bureau of standard, Wash, USA.

/MON87/ MONTACIE C.,CHOLLET G. (1987) **Systemes de reference pour l'evaluation d'applications et la caracterisation de bases de donnees en reconnaissance automatique de la parole.** 16eme JEP, Hammamet.

/MOO77/ MOORE R. (Fev 1977) **Evaluting speech recognizers.** IEEE-ASSP, pp 178-185

/TOH86/ THOHKURA Y. (1986) **A weighted cepstral measure for speech recognition** IEEE-ICASSP, Tokyo.

On-line Interpretation in Speech Understanding and Dialogue Systems

Harry Bunt
Institute for Language Technology and Artificial Intelligence
Tilburg University, The Netherlands

Abstract

This paper addresses syntactic, semantic and pragmatic aspects of central concern in the design of on-line language understanding systems.

In the area of syntax, the paper focuses on the phenomenon of discontinuous constituents. A form of syntactic representation is defined, called *discontinuous trees*, which allows the constituent structure of sentences with discontinuous constituents to be represented without changing the word order in the sentence. A kind of phrase-structure grammar is defined which can generate such representations, and an on-line parsing algorithm is presented which parses sentences into these representations.

In the area of semantics, the paper focuses on the effective resolution of ambiguity and vagueness, and on the on-line interpretation of anaphora. For dealing with ambiguous and vague expressions in an effective, on-line manner a cascaded model-theoretic approach is developed which makes use of intermediate semantic representations in a formal language that preserves some of the ambiguity and vagueness in natural language. For the interpretation of anaphora, an approach is outlined that has recently been suggested by Groenendijk and Stokhof, based on the use of dynamic logic.

In the area of pragmatics, the paper focuses on the analysis of information-exchange dialogues as consisting of communicative actions. The notion *function of a communicative action* is defined in terms of the flow of information between speaker and addressee. It is argued that Groenendijk and Stokhof's dynamic approach to semantic interpretation can be elegantly combined with this 'functional' approach to communicative action into in an integrated theory of utterance meaning. The resulting *'dynamic interpretation theory'* is outlined, which offers exciting perspectives for a full-fledged, on-line utterance interpretation process.

1 Introduction

This paper is concerned with syntactic, semantic and pragmatic aspects of language understanding which are essential to the design of speech understanding and dialogue systems.

A central issue in speech understanding is *on-line* interpretation, i.e. dealing with linguistic information which is relevant to its interpretation as it becomes available,

NATO ASI Series, Vol. F46
Recent Advances in Speech Understanding
and Dialog Systems
Edited by H. Niemann et al.

rather than waiting until all the input has been received. The relevant linguistic information includes morphosyntactic, semantic, and pragmatic aspects. In each of these areas one or more crucial problems and some new ideas for their solution will be discussed. Since the syntactic, semantic and pragmatic analysis should go hand in hand in an effective interpretation system, their integration is of the greatest importance. Separate attention will therefore be given to the consequences of the individual problems and solutions discussed for the integration of syntactic processing with semantic and pragmatic processing, and of the integration of semantic and pragmatic processing.

A fundamental problem in on-line processing is that of syntactic (and semantic) *discontinuity*: s syntactic unit may consist of non-adjacent parts. This has the effect that, when the first part of a discontinuous unit is encountered, its contribution to the syntactic (and semantic) interpretation cannot fully be taken into account until the other parts have been encountered. If the material following the first part of the discontinuous unit is to be processed on-line, it follows that we should construct intermediate syntactic representations of a different kind than the familiar constituent-structure trees used in linguistics. I will provide precise definitions of the required syntactic representations, describe a kind of phrase-structure grammar to generate them, and present an algorithm to parse them in an on-line fashion.

Two fundamental semantic problems in on-line processing, which are separated by a somewhat fuzzy boundary, are *ambiguity* and *vagueness*. In the case of an ambiguity, the semantic interpretation process can go several ways to construct semantic representations; in cases of vagueness, the interpretation process lacks sufficient information to go anywhwere at all (or, to put it differently, it can go in a virtually infinite number of directions) in constructing a precise formal representation.

Both ambiguity and vagueness can often be resolved using semantic information that becomes available later in the input. But in an on-line process we want to deal with ambiguous and vague elements as they come along. This means that we should construct intermediate semantic representations with a certain amount of ambiguity and vagueness, which get resolved at a later stage. I will describe a cascaded model-theoretic method designed to deal with these problems, which has been used in the PHLIQA question-answering system (Bronnenberg et al., 1980), in the TENDUM dialogue system (Bunt et al., 1985), and in the SPICOS speech communication system (Niedermair et al., 1986; van Deemter et al., 1986).

A quite different semantic problem concerns the interpretation of anaphoric expressions, which occur very frequently in natural spoken dialogues. The best developed framework for handling anaphora is Kamp's Discourse Representation Theory, in which semantic representations are built up in an on-line fashion as a stretch of dicourse is interpreted. This approach is indeed on-line, but it violates the basic principle of semantics, the principle of compositionality. Recently, a new approach to the interpretation of anaphora has been suggested by Groenendijk and Stokhof in terms of dynamic models, borrowing concepts from the theory of programming languages (Groenendijk & Stokhof,

1987). I will describe and discuss this approach, which is claimed to be both on-line and compositional.

Where semantics is the study of those aspects of meaning that concern the relation between linguistic elements and concepts in the universe of discourse, other aspects of meaning which are of particular importance for language understanding in dialogue systems concern the relations between linguistic elements and the beliefs, intentions, expectations, etc. of the speaker. The study of these aspects belongs to the area of pragmatics.

For dealing with these aspects of meaning in the setting of information-exchange dialogues, I have developed an approach where the meaning of an utterance is viewed as the way in which a listener's state of beliefs and intentions is changed as the result of interpreting the utterance (Bunt, 1988a). I will describe this approach, formalizing the concept of the *communicative function* of an utterance as a mathematical function operating on knowledge representation structures.

By combining the pragmatic theory where the 'functional' meaning of utterances is treated in terms of state changes in an interpreter, and Groenendijk & Stokhof's semantic theory where sentence meaning is approached in terms of dynamic models of the universe of discourse, a new, integrated approach to language understanding emerges where all aspects of meaning are accounted for as changing in complex dynamic models. The models in this 'dynamic interpretation theory' are rich and modular knowledge representation structures, describing the states of both participants in the communication.

I will describe this new, integrated approach to language understanding and discuss its perspectives for the possibilities of on-line interpretation in speech understanding and dialogue systems.

Before embarking, let us briefly consider what is meant by an 'on-line' process. A process can have the property of being 'on- line' if it operates on sequential inputs. It has that property if it processes each element in an input sequence immediately, i.e. without waiting for further input elements; the only input information which the process uses is the last input element and the result of processing the preceding input elements. We can express this formally as follows:

(1) A process F is *on-line* if for every input sequence $< i_1, i_2, .., i_k >$:
$$F(< i_1, i_2, .., i_k >) \;=\; f(F(< i_1, i_2, .., i_{k-1}>, i_k)$$

Note that, if $< i_1, i_2, .., i_k >$ is a sequence of inputs which forms part of a complete input sequence $< i_1, i_2, .., i_n >$, according to this definition the processing of that part indeed takes place immediately, as it does not depend on later inputs.

2 On-line parsing and the problem of discontinuous constituents

In English, German, French, Dutch and many other languages it happens quite often that the parts of a constituent are not adjacent. In such a case we speak of a ***discontinuous constituent.*** This phenomenon occurs in a wide variety of constituent types: noun phrases, verb phrases, adjective phrases, adverb phrases, etc. The examples (2) - (9) illustrate this: in (2) we see a discontinuous verb phrase: ('talked about politics'); in (3) a discontinuous preposition phrase ('from wchich children'), in (4) a discontinuous adjective phrase ('better than I expected'); in (5) a split verb; in (6) a split negation ('ne ... pas') and a discontinuous noun phrase with "extraposed" relative clause; in (7) a discontinuous adverb phrase ('harder dan ooit tevoren'); in (8) a discontinuous noun phrases with "extraposed" prepositional phrase, and in (9) an example of the famous "cross-serial dependency" construction in Dutch.

(2) John *talked*, of course, *about politics*
(3) *Which children* did Anne expect to get a present *from*?
(4) This was a *better* movie *than I expected*
(5) *Wake* me *up* at seven thirty
(6) Tu *ne* crois sûrement *pas* qu'*un de tes cousins* viendra *qui demeure à Bruxelles*?
(= Surely you don't think that one of your cousins will come who lives in Brussels?)
(7) Leo is *harder* gegaan *dan ooit tevoren*
(= Leo has been going faster than ever before)
(8) Ich habe *ein Auto* gekauft *mit 5 Türe*
(= I have bought a car with 5 doors)
(9) Ik hoor dat Jan Marie de kinderen de hond heeft helpen leren uitlaten
(= I hear that John has helped Mary to teach the kids to walk the dog)

These examples do not represent a single class of linguistic phenomena, and it is doubtful whether they should all be handled by means of the same techniques.

Sentence (2), which has been discussed extensively in the literature, presents a problem for any analysis in terms of adjacent constituents, since the parenthetical clause 'of course' divides the verb phrase 'talked about politics' into two nonadjacent parts. This means that we are forced to either consider the parenthetical as part of the VP, as Ross (1973) has suggested, or as a constituent at sentence level, as has been suggested by Emonds (1976; 1979). In the latter case, the sentence is analysed as consisting of the embedded sentence 'John talked', with 'of course' and 'about politics' both as specifiers at sentence level. McCawley (1982) provides detailed arguments showing that both suggestions are inadequate (which seems intuitively obvious, from a semantic point of view), and suggests, instead, the syntactic representation (10).

(10)

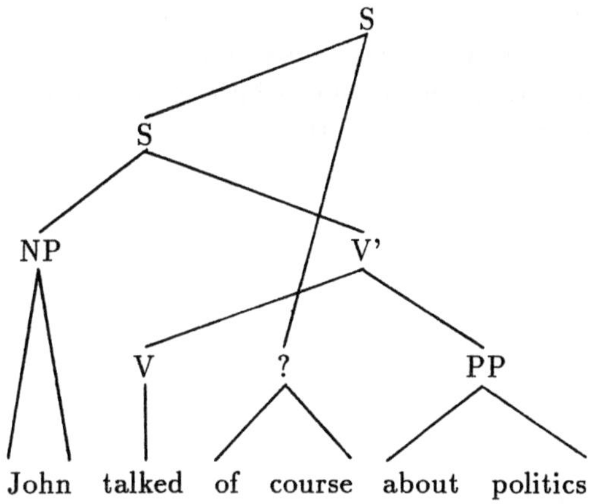

This is of course no longer an ordinary tree structure, but McCawley suggests that we there is no reason to be afraid of constituent structures like (10). We will return to this suggestion below.

Example (3) represents a different class of phenomena, which are conveniently thought of in terms of movements of parts of phrases. In this example, the NP 'which children' can be thought of as having moved out of the PP 'from which children', of which only the preposition has been left behind. The use of transformations, such as movements, is computationally unattractive, however. In order to deal with such cases without transformations, in GPSG a special type of syntactic categories have been introduced, called "slash categories". For instance, the category PP/NP is assigned to a prepositional phrase which "misses" an NP. In the present example, this category would be assigned to 'from'. The assumption that an NP is missing, propagates to higher nodes in the syntactic tree which the phrase-structure rules construct for the sentence, until it is acknowledged at the top level. Diagram (11) illustrates this.

(11)

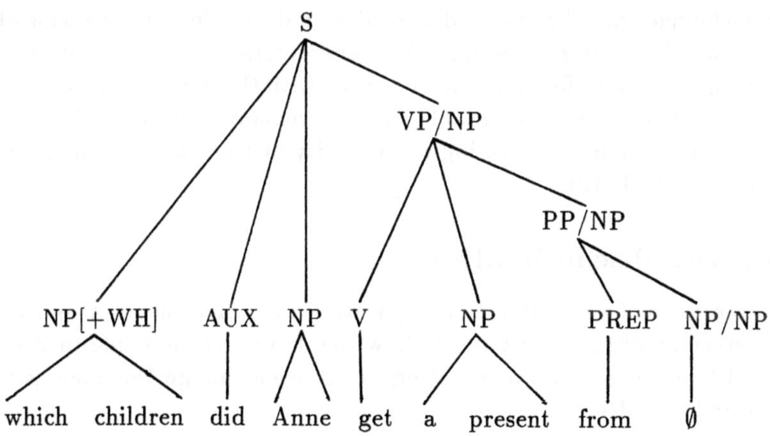

The technique of using phrases that miss some constituent cannot be used for at least some of the examples (4) - (9), such as (6) and (8). In both sentences the discontinuous NP contains a fullfledged NP, which cannot sensibly be said to "miss" the relative clause or prepositional phrase that occurs later in the sentence.

The most straightforward way of dealing with these cases would be to allow syntactic structures with crossing branches as in (10), representing discontinuous constituents as they occur in a sentence, and to formulate grammar rules which describe the discontinuities, producing a structure like (12) for the example (8).

(12)

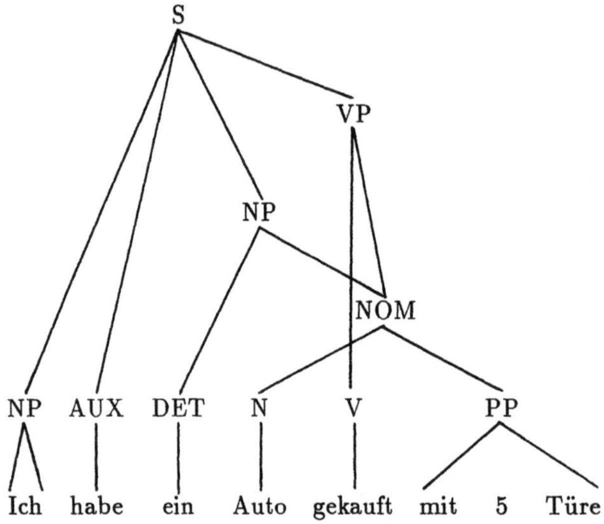

The generation of a representation like (12) seems computationally more attractive than the application of a movement transformation, for the latter approach requires 3 steps: 1. the identification of a discontinuity; 2. the aplication of the transformation to resolve the discontinuity; 3. the generation of the tree structure for the transformed expression. The generation of (12), on the other hand, can simply be done without the second of these steps.

Whatever techniques may be invented to deal with discontinuities, it seems obvious that a grammar which recognizes discontinuities and describes them in syntactic representations is the most straightforward way of dealing with them, and produces syntactic representations which are the most suitable basis for semantic interpretation.

It therefore seems worth investigating the viability of tree-like structures with discontinuities, like (10) and (12).

2.1 Trees with discontinuities

If we want to represent the situation that a phrase P has constituents A and C, while there is an intervening phrase B, we must allow the node corresponding to P to dominate the A and C nodes without dominating the B, even though this node is located between the A and C nodes:

(13)

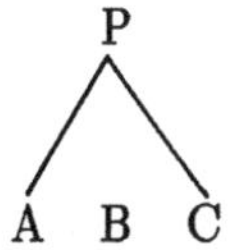

This whill have the consequence that our structures will get crossing branches, if we still want all nodes to be connected to the top node. The above structures (11) and (12) illustrate this. In what respects exactly do these structures differ from ordinary trees? McCawley (1982) has tried to answer this question, suggesting a formal definition for trees with discontinuities by amending the definition of an ordinary tree.

A tree is often defined as a set of elements, called "nodes", on which two relations are defined, *immediate dominance* (D) and *linear precedence*, or left-right order ($\prec$), which are required to have certain properties to the effect that a tree has exactly one root node, which dominates every other node (immediately or indirectly); that every node in a tree has exactly one "mother" node, etc. (see e.g. Wall, 1972).

Given the relations of immediate dominance and linear precedence, *dominance* is defined as the reflexive and transitive closure D' of D, and *adjacency* as linear precedence without intervening nodes.

A node in a tree is called *terminal* if it does not dominate any other node; the terminal nodes in a tree are totally ordered by the $\prec$ relation. For nonterminal nodes the precedence relation satisfies the requirement that x $\prec$ y if and only if every node dominated by x precedes every node dominated by y. Formally:

(14) for any two nodes x and y in the node set of a tree, $x \prec y$ if and only if for all nodes u and v, if x dominates u and y dominates v, then $u \prec v$.

Part of the definition of a tree is also the stipulation that any two nodes either dominate or precede one another:

(15) for any two nodes x and y in the node set of a tree, either $xD'y$, or $yD'x$, or $x \prec y$, or $y \prec x$.

This stipulation has the effect of excluding discontinuities in a tree, for suppose a node x would dominate nodes y and z without having a dominance relation with node w, where $y \prec w \prec z$. Since neither x dominates w nor w dominates x, by (15) either $x \prec w$ or $w \prec x$. But x dominates a node to the right of w, so by (14) x does not precede w; and w is to the right of a node dominated by x, so w does not precede x either.

McCawley's definition of trees with discontinuities comes down to dropping the condition that any two nodes should either dominate one another or have a left-right relation. Instead, he proposes the weaker condition that a node has no precedence relation to any node that it dominates:

(16) for any two nodes x and y in the node set of a tree, if x D' y then neither $x \prec y$ nor $y \prec x$.

We shall call any node u, situated between daughters of a node x without being dominated by x, *internal context* of x. McCawley's definition of trees with discontinuities is inaccurate in some respects; however, his general idea is correct: trees with discontinuities can be defined essentially by relaxing condition (15) in the definition of a tree.

This is only the beginning of what needs to be done, however. The next question is how discontinuous trees can be produced by phrase-structure rules. This question, not addressed by McCawley, is far from trivial and turns out to have interesting consequences for the notion of adjacency in discontinuous trees.

2.2 Adjacency in phrase-structure rules for discontinuous constituents

A phrase-structure rule rewrites a constituent into a sequence of pairwise adjacent constituents. The formulation of phrase- structure rules for discontinuous trees thus requires a notion of adjacency in discontinuous trees. Since we already have precedence relation for discontinuous trees, the obvious definition would seem to be that two nodes are adjacent if one precedes the other, and there are no intervening nodes. This is expressed in (17):

(17) two nodes x and y in the node set of a tree are adjacent if and only if $\prec y$ and there is no z such that $x \prec z \prec y$.

We shall write '$x + y$' to indicate that x and y are adjacent (or 'neighbours'). Unfortunately, this notion of adjacency is of no help for formulating rules that could do anything with internal context constituents. The following example illustrates this. Suppose we are to generate the discontinuous tree structure (18):

(18)

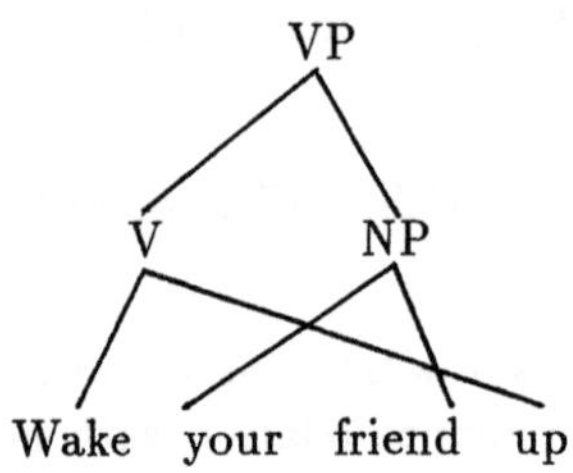

To generate the top node, we need a rule combining the V and the NP, like (19):

(19) $VP \rightarrow V + NP$

Since the NP dominates nodes at either side of the VP, however, there is no precedence relation between the NP and V nodes, leave alone an adjacency relation.

This can be remedied by replacing clause (15) in the definition of a tree by the more general clause (20):

(20) for any two nodes x, y in the node set of a tree, $x \prec y$ if and only if x's leftmost daughter precedes y's leftmost daughter.

(We refrain here from a formal definition of "leftmost daughter" node, which is intuitively obvious; a terminal node should be understood to be its own leftmost daughter.)

Note that (20) is indeed a generalization of the usual notion of precedence in trees, which is a special case of (20). The recursion in the definition (20) always comes to an end for any finite tree, since the terminal nodes are totally ordered.

Note also that (20) is not consistent with clause (15); by (20), we do get the possibility of a precedence relation between a node and some of its daughter nodes. This is not unreasonable, though. In (21), for example, we do want that $X \prec Y$, and since $Y \prec C$ and the precedence relation

(21)

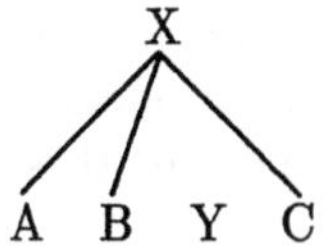

is transitive, we get that $X \prec C$. On the other hand we do *not* want that $X \prec B$, however. We should therefore modify clause (15) to the effect that a mother node does not precede daughter nodes which have no internal context nodes to their left. Formally:

(22) for any nodes x and z in the node set N of a tree, if $x\ D\ z$ and there are no nodes u, v in N such that $x\ D\ u$, not $x\ D\ v$, and $u \prec v \prec z$, then neither $x \prec z$ nor $z \prec x$.

With the modifications (17) and (22), we have a consistent definition of "discontinuous trees" which allows us to write phrase-structure rules containing discontinuous constituents as follows:

(23) $X \rightarrow A + B + [Y] + C$

where the square brackets indicate that the NP is not dominated by the X node, but is only internal context. The '+' symbol represents the notion of adjacency, defined as before but now on the basis of the revised precedence relation '$\prec$'.

(24) two nodes x and y in a tree are adjacent if and only if $x \prec y$ and there is no node z in the tree such that $x \prec z \prec y$.

Upon closer inspection, the neighbour relation defined in this way is unsatisfactory, however, as the following example illustrates.

Suppose we want to generate the following (part of a) tree structure:

(25)

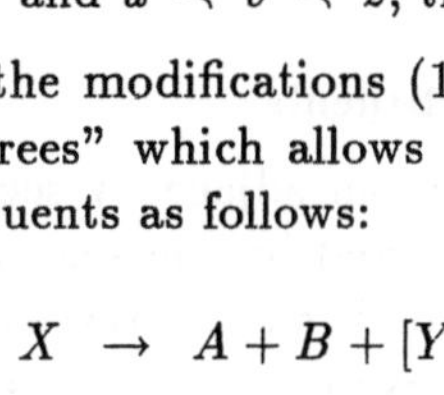

To generate the S node, we would like to write a phrase-structure rule that rewrites S into its constituents, like (26):

(26) $S \rightarrow P + Q + E$

However, this rule would not apply here, since P, Q and E do not form a sequence of adjacency pairs, as Q and E are not adjacent. According to our definitions, Q has C as its right neighbour, not E. Therefore, the correct rule for generating (25) would be (27):

(27) $S \rightarrow P + Q + [C] + [D] + E$

This is ugly, and even uglier rules are required in more complex trees with discontinuities at different levels. Moreover, there seems to be something fundamentally wrong, since the C and D nodes are on the one hand internal context for the S node, according to rule (27), while on the other hand they are also dominated by S. That is, these nodes are *both* "real" constituents of S and internal context of S.

To remedy this, we introduce a new concept of *adjacency sequence*, which generalizes the traditional notion of (sequence of) adjacency pairs. The definition goes as follows:

(28) A sequence $< a, b, ..., n >$ is an adjacency sequence if and only if:
1. every pair $< i, j >$ in the sequence is either an adjacency pair or is connected by a sequence of adjacency pairs of which all members are a constituent of some element in the subsequence $< a, b, ..., i >$;
2. the elements in the sequence do not share any constituents.

For example, in the structure (25) the triple $< P, Q, E >$ is an adjacency sequence since $< P, Q >$ is an adjacency pair and Q and E are connected by the sequence of adjacency pairs $Q - C - D - E$, with C and D constituents of P and Q, respectively. Moreover, P, Q, and E do not share any material. Another example of an adjacency sequence in (25) is the triple $< P, B, D >$. The triple $< P, B, C >$, on the other hand, is not an adjacency sequence since P and C share the constituent C.

This notion of adjacency sequence can now be used to define a phrase-structure rule for discontinuous trees as a prescription to rewrite a nonterminal into sequence of constituents which forms an adjacency sequence, where some (but not the first and not the last) of the elements may be marked as internal context. A phrase-structure grammar consisting of rules of this kind we call **Discontinuous Phrase-Structure Grammar**, or **DPSG**.

It is worth emphasizing that this notion of phrase-structure rule is a generalization of the usual notion, since an adjacency sequence as defined by (28) subsumes the usual notion of sequence of adjacency pairs. We have also seen that trees with discontinuities are a generalization of the traditional tree concept. Therefore, phrase-structure rules of the familiar sort coincide with DPSG rules without discontinuous constituents, and they produce the familiar sort of trees without discontinuities. In other words, DPSG-rules can simply be *added* to an ordinary PSG (including a generalized or augmented PSG), with the result that the grammar generates trees with discontinuities for sentences with discontinuous constituents, while doing everything else as before.

2.3 DPSG and parsing

A parser for DPSG meets certain complications which do not arise in parsing with an ordinary context-free grammar. To see these complications, we consider what would happen when we apply an ordinary chart parser (see Winograd, 1983) to DPSG.

Context-free chart parsing is a matter of fitting adjoining pieces together in a chart. For example, consider the grammar:

(29)
$$\begin{array}{lll} S & \rightarrow & VP\, NP \\ NP & \rightarrow & DET\, N \\ VP & \rightarrow & V \end{array}$$

For the input 'V DET N', a chart parser begins by initializing the chart as follows:

(30)

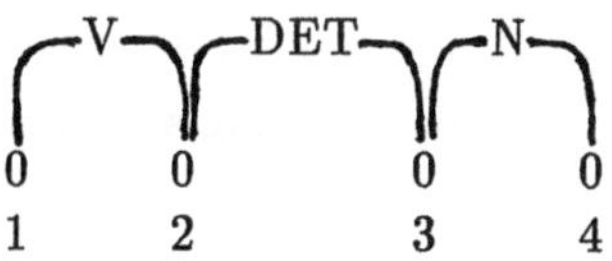

These pieces fit together because the begin- and end vertex numbers of adjoining elements are equal. Given the arc V(1,2) in the chart, we look up all those rules which have a 'free' V as the first constituent. These rules are placed in a separate list, the 'active rule list'. We 'bind' the V's in these rules to the V(1,2) arc, i.e. we establish links between these rules and that arc. When all constituents in a rule are bound, the rule is applied. In this case, the VP(1,2) will be built, taking over the begin vertex number of its first constituent and the end vertex number of the last. This procedure is repeated for the new VP node. When nothing more can be done, as in this case, we move on in the chart. The final result is the chart (31).

(31)

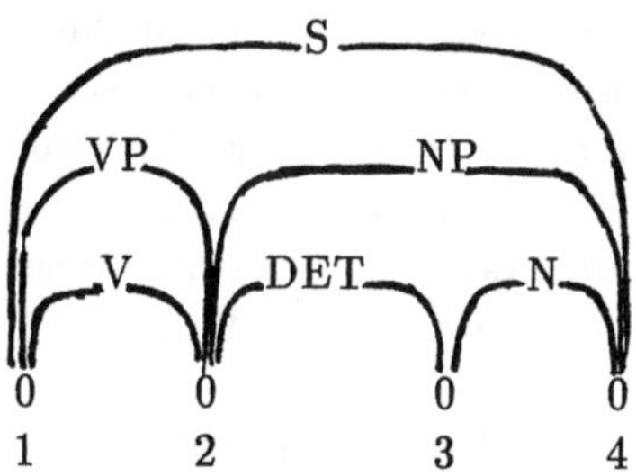

When we use DPSG rules and follow the same procedure, we run into difficulties. Consider the example grammar (32).

(32)
$$\begin{array}{lll} S & \rightarrow & VP + NP \\ NP & \rightarrow & DET + N \end{array}$$

For the input 'V DET N PART' the first constituent that can be built is NP(2,4); the second is VP(1,5). The VP will activate the S rule, but this rule will not be applied since the NP does not have a binding. And even if it had, the rule would not be applicable as the VP(1,5) and the NP(2,4) are not adjoining in the traditional sense.

To make sure that the parser finds all applicable rules of a DPSG, the following following providion may be added to the parsing algorithm.

Whena rule with internal context is applied, we first follow the standard procedure; subsequently we go through all those rules that appear on the active-rule list as the result of applying the standard procedure and give bindings to those free constituents that correspond in category to the context-element(s) in the rule that was applied.

In the case of (32), this means that just before application of the VP rule (after the PART has been bound), we have the active-rule list (33). (Underlining indicates that a constituent is bound.)

(33)
$$\begin{aligned} VP &\rightarrow \underline{V} + [NP] + PART \\ VP &\rightarrow \underline{V} + [\underline{NP}] + PART \\ VP &\rightarrow \underline{V} + [\underline{NP}] + \underline{PART} \end{aligned}$$

We now apply the VP rule. The standard procedure will add one rule to this list, namely $S \rightarrow VP + NP$. The VP is given a binding, so we obtain the following active-rule list:

(34)
$$\begin{aligned} S &\rightarrow \underline{VP} + NP \\ VP &\rightarrow \underline{V} + [NP] + PART \\ VP &\rightarrow \underline{V} + [\underline{NP}] + PART \\ VP &\rightarrow \underline{V} + [\underline{NP}] + \underline{PART} \end{aligned}$$

Since the VP rule contained an internal context element, the additional procedure mentioned above is now applied; a binding is given to the NP in (a copy of) the S rule. The S arc is now built in the chart, which does not cause any new active rules. There are no free S's in the old active-rule list either, which would have to be bound, so we look for other rules with a free NP. There is one such rule, the second in (34), but this one will be skipped because it was already present in the rule list before application of the rule; see (33). Skipping of this rule is essential, as there is already a version of the VP rule on the active-rule list containing an NP with the same binding as the context element.

Note that, when applying the rule $S \rightarrow VP(1,5) + NP(2,4)$, we have combined constituents that are not adjacent in the traditional sense, as reflected in successive vertex numbers. In such a case, where the vertex numbers indicate that the constituents in a rule are overlapping, we must perform an additional test whether these constituents form an adjacency sequence.

In order to make sure that only consituents are combined that form an adjacency sequence, the parser keeps track of daughter nodes and internal context in a so-called 'construction list', which is added to each arc in the chart; internal context nodes are marked as such in these lists. With the help of these lists, it is easily detected whether two (or more) nodes share a constituent, in the sense of commonly domination. Moreover, by organizing these lists in a particular way they can also be used to determine whether a sequence of constituents is an adjacency sequence in the sense of definition (28). The reader is referred to Bunt et al. (1987) for a description of the use of construction lists in DPSG parsing.

The important conclusion at this point is that discontinuous syntactic-tree representations of discontinuous constituents can effectively be constructed in an on-line fashion by a slightly modified algorithm for context-free parsing. The importance of this conclusion lies in the fact that such an on-line process produces syntactic representations that are particularly suitable for semantic interpretation. Methods for systematic semantic interpretation assume the *principle of compositionality*, which is the thesis that the meaning of a sentence is determined by the combination of (a) the meanings of its constituents; (b) the constituent structure. This entails, for a grammar which associates meanings with the expressions of the language, that the syntactic rules should characterize the constituent structure of every expression in a 'meaningful' way, using only constituents that are semantically meaningful. Since discontinuous constituents by their very nature form meaningful parts of a sentence, they should be treated as such in syntactic representations. Discontinuous trees offer this possibility, while at the same time representing the linear order of the words in the sentence. Indeed, the use of DPSG allows on-line syntactic parsing integrated with semantic interpretation with the effect that discontinuous constituents are interpreted as they are syntactically recognized. Such an integration has been implemented in the TENDUM system.

3 Semantics: Ambiguity and Vagueness

3.1 On-line interpretation, ambiguity and vagueness

In this section we consider two difficulties in the formal semantic interpretation of natural-language expressions, which pose a particular challenge for on-line interpretation: ambiguity and vagueness.

Ambiguity is the phenomenon that an expression has several clearly distinct interpretations; vagueness is the phenomenon that an expression has a wide variety of readings, often without clear demarcations. Both ambiguity and vagueness arise at the level of words, as well as at the level of sentences and texts, and they also have in common that their resolution often requires information that becomes available at a later moment in the sentence or text than where they occur. This is the reason why they pose a particular challenge to an on-line interpretation process: an ambiguous or vague expression can often not be interpreted adequately at the moment that it is encountered. Therefore, an on-line process should record the relevant information at that moment, and proceed in such a way that this information can be used at a later stage when more information becomes available.

The latter approach is quite common in the case of *syntactic* ambiguities. For instance, as we have seen in the previous section, a breadth-first chart parser records the relevant syntactic information in a chart (and, in a sense, in the active rule list), where it is available for further processing at a later stage. Such a parser is in fact facing local syntactic ambiguities all the time. But *semantic* ambiguities, such as lexical ones, are not the business of such a parser. If lexical ambiguities are represented as alternative lexical insertion rules, as linguistic theories have it, the parser has to duplicate all the syntactic work.

For dealing with lexical items which are vague, rather than ambiguous, the situation is in fact still worse. Linguistic semantic theory tells us that vague lexical items are not properly viewed as homonymous words, and hence cannot be handled adequately by means of alternative lexical insertion rules. Instead, a vague lexical item should be treated as a single item whose precise meaning is determined by the surrounding context. But, as long as no methods are provided for how surrounding context determines meaning, this only tells us what a language understanding system should *not* do.

3.2 Vagueness and language-understanding systems

Vagueness in natural language comes primarily from the indeterminacy of lexical items. Consider, for instance, the following ways of using the verb 'have':

(36) Mary has blue eyes
(37) KLM has an office in Frankfurt
(38) Harald has 4 children
(39) Rosemary is having a baby
(40) Fidel is having a smoke
(41) Peter has a cold
(42) Let me have a look
(43) They mostly have good weather there
(44) I had Latin and greek at school

'To have', like 'to do', is one of those verbs that has a large number of possible interpretations, and in fact represents a case where one may doubt whether it should be viewed as ambiguity or as vagueness. Many prepositions, like 'from', 'of', 'in' and 'for' can be used in so many ways, which all have something to do with each other, that it seems hopeless to try and list all the possible interpretations; they represent obvious, problematic cases of vagueness.

The general problem of dealing with vagueness in a semantic theory poses itself very strongly in the context of language- understanding computer systems, due to the fact that such systems mostly require an unusual precision in the interpretation. The following example illustrates this. Webster's dictionary tells us that the word 'Canadian' means: "pertaining to Canada". Let us look at some sentences with this word:

(45) This is a Canadian song.
(46) I have a Canadian friend.
(47) Kakabekafalls is a Canadian town.
(48) The Canadian oak differs from the European oak.
(49) That's the Canadian flag.
(50) The Canadian ice hockey team was defeated by the Swedes.
(51) A Canadian airplane crashed last night.

Clearly, in each of these examples 'Canadian' means something more specific than "pertaining to Canada"; it means such things as 'made in Canada', 'of Canadian nationality', 'situated in Canada', 'representing Canada', etc. Lexicographers can certainly be excused for not spelling out all cases, however; it seems in fact quite doubtful whether this would at all be feasible.

Now in the case of a language-understanding system, such as a question-answering system, it is necessary to assign very detailed interpretations to such a word. For example, a system which contains information about air planes, like TENDUM, will have to distinguish several interpretations of an expression like 'Canadian air plane':

(52) air plane manufactured in Canada
(53) air plane owned by a Canada-based company
(54) air plane which departed from a city in Canada

The necessity of distinguishing these interpretations can be seen from the following sentences, where in each case at least one of the possibilities should be excluded in view of the surrounding context:

(55) Does Canadian Pacific only use Canadian air planes?
(56) Is there a Canadian air plane leaving from Toronto tonight?

In order to determine the intended interpretations of these questions, it is necessary to distinguish between the meanings of 'Canadian' in these sentences. In particular, in order to answer these questions appropriately, a question-answering system will have to be able to figure out how the word 'Canadian' is to be interpreted in terms of the objects and relations in its data base.

It may be noted that in the three questions (52) - (54) the adjective 'Canadian' could roughly be paraphrased by the prepositional phrase 'from Canada'. The preposition 'from' presents a particularly striking example of the unusual precision in semantic interpretation required by a question-answering system. Consider the questions (57) and (58):

(57) Does the KL402 come from Canada?
(58) Does the KL402 come from Calgary?

Given a data base where flights have a city of departure, and where cities are known to be located in a country, (57) has to be interpreted as something like (59), and (58) as (60):

(59) $Country(Departureplace(kl402)) = canada$
(60) $Departureplace(kl402) = calgary$

where *Country* and *Departureplace* are data base attributes of cities and flights, respectively. This shows that we are forced to make a distinction between an interpretation of 'from' as "from a country" and as "from a city". In fact, for any two types of objects A and B where we can say 'A from B', we have to distinguish a separate interpretation.

In question-answering systems and other language-understanding systems which require precise semantic interpretation, the commonly found approach is that vagueness is treated as ambiguity, distinguishing a number of alternative interpretations as distinct lexical items. For instance, in one of the early language-processing systems, Raphael (1965) treats 'have' as ambiguous between 'have-as-part', 'have-as-property' and 'own'. This is reasonable form a linguistic point of view, as it may be argued that, generally, 'to have' allows these interpretations. One can see from the examples (36) - (44) that this is clearly not an adequate solution, however, and for application-dependent cases like the precise interpretations of 'from' (and similarly of 'to have') such an approach is obviously not feasible for a nontrivial domain of application. The commonly found "solution" here is to distinguish those interpretations which the application requires, and treat the word in the lexicon as ambiguous between those interpretations. This is most unsatisfactory, of course, as it introduces a high degree of application-dependence in the lexicon, presents an ambiguity explosion for the parser, for which separate solutions have to be found, and, from a linguistic point of view, it does exactly what the theory says one should *not* do.

From a theoretical point of view, inherent to the phenomenon of semantic vagueness is that it is impossible to list all the precise interpretations of a vague item. The above example of 'from' confirms this. Therefore, the "resolution" of the vagueness of such an item should be accomplished by combining semantic information from the context with the general interpretation of the item, which should be vague. However, this presents a fundamental problem both for modern semantic theories, like Montague Grammar or Discourse Representation Theory, and for language-understanding systems, since in both cases the semantic interpretation of natural language takes the form of translating sentences into representation structures, whose semantics is defined relative to a model of the discourse domain. These representation structures aim explicitly at *avoiding* the vagueness and ambiguity of natural language; therefore, these approaches have no place for representations that reflect unresolved vagueness.

A solution to this dilemma has been found by the designers of the PHLIQA system (Bronnenberg et al., 1980), which consists of allowing ambiguous constants in formal semantic representations. Instead of assigning a single denotation to each constant, a set of alternative denotations is assigned. How this works is outlined in the next subsection.

3.3 Vagueness in two-level semantics

The use of ambiguous terms in formal representations to represent lexical vagueness immediately raises the question as to why this would be any better than treating vague words as ambiguous in the lexicon. The answer lies in the use of two (or more) levels of semantic representation. We describe the method in the form in which it has been implemented in the TENDUM dialogue system (Bunt et al., 1985).

Natural-language expressions are interpreted in two steps, each of which result in a representation in a formal language. The formal languages used for this purpose are two members of the same family, that of Ensemble Languages (the EL family). These languages are based in their semantics on *ensemble theory*, an extension of classical set theory designed for the purpose of natural language interpretation (Bunt, 1985). The languages of the family all have the same syntactic constructions, but differ in their constants. The language used in the first stage, called *EL/F ("Ensemble Language, Formal")* has constants that have a one-to-one correspondence with content words (lexemes) in the natural language; one might as well say that the semantic representations constructed at this level are *in terms of the content words*. What the formal language does is making the *formal*, or "logical" semantic aspects of a sentence explicit - hence the name "Ensemble Language, *Formal*". The language used in the second stage has constants standing in a one-to-one relation to the elements in a model of the discourse domain. The semantic representations constructed at this level are elaborations of those constructed in EL/F, the elaborations consisting in the replacement of the content words by expressions made up of terms that refer to elements in the discourse domain; this language is therefore called *"Ensemble Language, Referential"*, or *EL/R*.

The following example illustrates tthe working of the two levels. Consider the question:

(61) Does the KL402 come from the U.S.?

At the first level of analysis, a formal semantic structure is assigned to the sentence, expressed in EL/F:

(62) $COMEFROM(< kl402, usa >)$

Here, 'COMEFROM' is a 2-place predicate of EL/F, corresponding to the verb "come from"; 'kl402' and 'usa' are individual constants corresponding to the proper names "KL402" and "U.S.", respectively. The second stage of analysis is extremely simple in this case, since the flight "KL402" and the country "USA" are simple concepts in the domain of discourse; only "come from" is not such a concept. Therefore, all that needs to be done is to express the latter relation in terms of EL/R concepts, and to replace the EL/F constants 'kl402' and 'canada' by their EL/R counterparts (which are written in capitals, for clarity). The result is:

(63) $Country(Departureplace(KL402)) = USA$

Here, 'Country' and 'Departureplace' are EL/F function constants relating a city to its country and a flight to its city of departure, respectively. The second stage of analysis, that of EL/F - EL/R translation, consists simply of looking up the EL/F constants in the EL/F - EL/R lexicon, making appropriate replacements, and simplifying the resulting expression if possible. For the present example, the following part of the lexicon would be relevant:

(64)	**EL/F:**	**EL/R:**
	kl402	KL402
	usa	USA
	COMEFROM	$(\lambda x : Departureplace(elem_1(x)) = elem_2(x))$
		$(\lambda x : Country(Departureplace(elem_1(x))) = elem_2(x))$

The variable x in the translations of COMEFROM ranges over pairs of individuals, $elem_1(x)$ denoting the first element of such a pair, $elem_2(x)$ the second.

Since the EL/F constants are in fact simply lexical items of the natural language, they carry the same ambiguity and vagueness. As a consequence of this ambiguity, not all combinations of their EL/R interpretations are meaningful. The combinations which are not meaningful are filtered out by means of an articulate type system, which forms part of the EL/R definition. In the example, the first possible translation of

COMEFROM would violate the EL/R type restrictions since the type of Departure-place requires the right-hand side of the equality to be an expression of type CITY, whereas USA is of type COUNTRY. Formula (63) is obtained by replacing the EL/F constants in (62) by their translations (for COMEFROM: the second), and simplifying the result by applying lambda conversion.

Having seen, very briefly, how the two-level technique works, we return to the question why the use of ambiguous terms in EL/F for dealing with lexical vagueness would be any better than treating vague words as ambiguous in the lexicon. The answer is that, as we have seen, is it not possible to specify in general all the precise interpretations that a vague word may have. Lexical vagueness can be treated effectively as a case of ambiguity only in connection with a certain domain of discourse. Well, this is precisely what happens in the two-level approach: a vague lexical item of the natural language corresponds with a single term in EL/F; the vagueness gets resolved in the EL/F - EL/R translation, which is the domain-of-discourse specific part of the semantic analysis. The natural language - EL/F translation, on the other hand, uses only general linguistic information, and a domain-of-discourse independent lexicon.

Clearly, this approach is eminently suited to on-line interpretation. For the natural language - EL/F stage of interpretation, the occurrence of a vague lexical item is nothing special. The entire interpretation process, which translates natural language into EL/R and evaluates EL/R expressions, need not be a sequential two-stage process, but can be designed in such a way that each time a constant is introduced in the EL/F representation under construction, its possible EL/R translations are looked up in the EL/F - EL/R lexicon and attached to the EL/F representation. Information about the types of the EL/R expressions attached to the various constants in the EL/F representation under construction may be used on the fly to rule out some of those expressions. When a complete input sentence has been processed in this way, the possible end results of precise semantic interpretation, i.e. the EL/R representations, can be read from the attachments to the EL/F representations, taking the type constraints into account. (Note that the syntactic structure of the EL/F representations remains unaffected; it is only *expanded* by the EL/F - EL/R translation, if an EL/F constant is translated into a complex expression of EL/R.)

3.4 Ambiguity in two-level semantics

Lexical ambiguity, as opposed to vagueness, can be handled by treating ambiguous words as corresponding to several lexical items; so, for instance, the English noun 'plant' can be represented in the lexicon as plant1: vegetation; plant2: factory; plant3: conspiracy. But if we treat lexical vagueness by means of ambiguous terms in an intermediate level of semantic representation, lexical ambiguity may as well be treated in the same way. This in fact comes down to moving the ambiguity from the natural-language level to the EL/F level and postponing its resolution. This relieves the natural-language parser of the task of ambiguity resolution, and gives rise to a more efficient on-line interpretation process than lexical resolution at an earlier stage would do. Of course, this only applies to *within-category* ambiguity; 'plant' as a verb will have to be distinguished from 'plant' as a noun in the lexicon. More generally, only those cases of lexical ambiguity which have no syntactic repercussions may be postponed.

Where vagueness in natural language has its origins virtually exclusively in the vagueness of lexical items, ambiguity may have different sources. Besides lexical ambiguity, we have syntactic ambiguity and "logical" ambiguity. Syntactic ambiguities, i.e. different possible interpretations of a phrase as the result of different possibilities to view the phrase as being structured grammatically, are handled in a parser which constructs several alternative syntactic structures in such cases, each of which is interpreted separately by the application of semantic rules. Another type of ambiguity, which we may call *logical*, occurs in the following example:

(65) The boats carried 400 passengers

The ambiguity is whether *each* of the boats under consideration carried 400 passengers, or whether they carried 400 passengers in total. This ambiguity concerns the way the predicate 'carried 400 passengers' "distributes" over the set of boats concerned. Such ambiguities may *also* be handled by using ambiguous terms in intermediate EL/F expressions, by introducing special constants for representing distributions (Bunt, 1984). This extended approach to ambiguity procrastination has been implemented in the TENDUM system and taken over in the SPICOS system.

The construction of semantic representations in EL/F is integrated in TENDUM with the use of DPSG, described in the previous section. The complete syntactic/semantic grammar used in TENDUM consists of rules with a syntactic component and a semantic component. The syntactic components are DPSG rules with syntactic categories as complex feature bundles, like in GPSG; the semantic components specify the translation of each syntactic unit into EL/F (see also Thurmair, this volume.)

We thus see that, through the coupling of natural language - EL/F translation rules to DPSG syntax rules, we obtain a parser-interpreter which is able to deal with lexical ambiguity and vagueness as well as with cases of logical ambiguity (and, of course, also with syntactic ambiguity) in an on-line fashion.

4 On-line interpretation and the problem of anaphora

Anaphora are expressions in a discourse (text, dialog, or other) that refer to something that is mentioned elsewhere in the discourse, called its *antecedent*. The antecedent usually precedes the anaphora, sometimes within the sentence, but often in another sentence. The interpretation of an anaphora thus means that the antecedent be found and in some way be substitued for the anaphora; this is an almost unsurmountable problem for sematic theories that operate within the boundaries of a sentence, as most semantic theories do. But there is an additional problem with anaphora in relation to on-line interpretation. For consider the following two-sentence discourse:

(66) Pedro owns a donkey. He loves it.

The second sentence contains the anaphora 'he' and 'it', referring to Pedro and his donkey, respectively. Now suppose an on-line interpretation process first processes the first sentence, generating a formal representation like (67):

(67) $(\exists x : DONKEY(x)\ \&\ OWN(pedro, x))$

Subsequently the second sentence is processed; assuming that somehow the correct antecedents of the anaphora are chosen, we would expects this sentence to be represented as (68):

(68) $LOVE(pedro, x)$

Since the discourse (66) states that both Pedro owns a donkey and he loves it, we would expect the representation of the discourse to be the conjunction of the representations (67) and (68):

(69) $(\exists x : DONKEY(x)\ \&\ OWN(pedro, x))\ \&\ LOVE(pedro, x)$

Unfortunately, (69) is not an adequate representation, however, since the variable x in the second conjunct occurs outside the scope of the existential quantifier in the first conjunct; therefore, for the semantics of this formula that second x has nothing to do with the first x; it is merely an optical illusion that the anaphora 'it' is interpreted as Pedro's donkey. Instead, a correct representation would be (70):

(70) $(\exists x : DONKEY(x)\ \&\ OWN(pedro, x)\ \&\ LOVE(pedro, x))$

To construct this representation, however, we have to break into the representation of the first sentence. This could be done fairly simply for the present example, but for an anaphora whose antecedent is several sentences away, and perhaps hiding in a quantifier within a complex formula, this can be extremely difficult. And even within a single sentence, the correct interpretation of an anaphoric expression may require representations constructed for earlier parts to be revised. This happens in particular in case of reference into a relative clause, or into the if-part of a conditional sentence. The following example illustrates the difficulties.

(71) Every man who loves a woman, admires her.

Here, the problem is that an on-line interpretation process would construct, for the sentence part up to the comma, the representation:

(72) $(\forall x : (\exists y : WOMAN(y)\ \&\ LOVES(x, y))...)$

Normally, the sentential predicate would be put on the place of the dots, but if we do that here something strange happens:

(73) $(\forall x : (\exists y : WOMAN(y) \,\&\, LOVES(x,y)) \;\rightarrow\; ADMIRE(x,y))$

The problem is similar to that in (69): the variable y in the $ADMIRE(x,y)$ clause is outside the scope of the quantifier $(\exists y : ..)$, so the anaphoric reference doesn't really succeed. Moreover, the existential quantification is in fact wrong: sentence (71) makes a statement about *any* woman loved by a man, so we should have a universal quantifier instead! We thus see that an expression like 'a woman' should be interpreted as universally quantified in some context, while it should be interpreted as existentially quantified in others.

The severeness of the anaphora problem is brought out by the following figures about the frequency of intersentential anaphora. In a corpus of 960 utterances in human - (simulated) computer dialogues, recorded at the Institute for Perception Research in Eindhoven in a joint project with the Computational Linguistics Unit at Tilburg University, 302 intersentential anaphora were identified, with the following distribution over three major categories:

definite determiner + noun	146	(15%)
definite pronoun	122	(13%)
other	34	(3%)
total	302	(30%)

Keeping in mind that among the 960 utterances is a large number (roughy 50%) of semantically trivial ones, like 'Yes', 'O.K.', 'Good morning', 'Thank you' and 'Goodbye', we see that intersentential anaphora occur more often than not in those sentences that require semantic analysis.

In the early eighties, a breakthrough has been accomplished by Kamp's Discourse Representation Theory (DRT), designed especially to handle anaphora and other intersentential semantic phenomena (Kamp, 1981). DRT interprets texts consisting of more than one sentence in a two-stage process. In the first stage, a semantic representation is constructed in an incremental, 'on-line' fashion. The representation structure which is built for the first sentence in a text is expanded to incorporate the semantic analysis of the second sentence. For a text consisting of several sentences, the end result is one large structure which represents the semantics of the text as a whole; the structure in general does not fall apart into substructures corresponding to the individual sentences. The following examples illustrate the representation structures of DRT, called 'Discourse Representation Structures' (DRSs).

A DRS consists, in the simplest case, of a set of variables, called reference markers, and a set of 'conditions', simple predicate logic formulas. For instance, the sentence (74) has the semantic representation (75), where a predicate constant 'WITP' is used for simplicity to represent the verb phrase 'walks in the park':

(74) A man walks in the park
(75) $< \{x\}, \{MAN(x),\; WITP(x)\} >$

The definition of DRSs is such that (75) is true, given a model M of the domain of discourse, if there is a value assignment to the reference marker x which makes all the conditions true. Therefore, the reference marker is in fact treated as an existentially quantified variable.

When we have a two-sentence text beginning with (74), like (76), the resulting DRS is the one constructed for the first sentence with some additions, depending on the second sentence:

(76) A man walks in the park. He sees Mary.
(77) $< \{x,y\}, \{MAN(x), WITP(x), y = Mary, SEE(x,y)\} >$

Here we see the use of reference markers for the treatment of anaphora. For more complex cases, the additions to a DRS constructed earlier may include logical connectives linking one (sub-)DRS to another one, and the definition of these structures ensures that reference markers are treated as existentially or universally quantified. The end result of DRS building is always a structure that is formally equivalent to a predicate logic formula; the distinguishing feature of DRT is thus not the kind of semantic representation that is built, but *the way* it is built.

DRT is the first explicit, formal semantic theory that goes beyond sentence boundaries. Recently, another such theory has been suggested by Groenendijk and Stokhof(1987), which looks particularly attractive from a computational point of view. They propose to use a form of Dynamic Logic, a formalism developed in theoretical computer science for defining the semantics of programming languages (see Harel, 1984).

The starting point of Dynamic Logic is that the meaning of a computer program can be viewed as the way in which the state of a machine changes as the result of executing the program. Of course, the state of a machine after executing program P does not only depend on P but also on the state prior to the execution of P. But we have captured the meaning of P if we specify for every possible initial state the state which results after executing P. Thus, formally, the meaning of a program is a set of machine state pairs $< \textit{initial state}, \textit{final state} >$; 'state transitions', we might say.

This idea relates to the classical way of defining the semantics of formal languages as follows. In the classical approach, interpretation is defined relative to a model M and a function g assigning values to variables. In the simplest case, a model is a pair $< D, F >$ where D is the set of individual objects in the domain of discourse and F an assigment of values to the constants of the language. Sometimes it is more convenient to include the variable assignment function g also in the model. We will do so in this paper, and thus consider models of the form (78):

(78) $M = < D, F, g >$

The functions F and g, assigning values to constants and variables, are called the *constant-* and *variable interpretation*, respectively. A formula of the language in question is now true if the values assigned to its constants and variables by F and g are such that the corresponding entities in the domain of discourse have such properties and relations as stated in the formula.

In the Dynamic Logic approach, a computer program is treated as a formal-language expression which contains certain variables, whose values characterize the state of a machine. Execution of the program changes the state of the machine as the values of the variables change. Thus, if g is the function describing the values of the variables before execution of the program, and h the function describing this afterwards, then the pair $< g, h >$ represents a state transition that forms part of the meaning of the program.

For example, consider the semantic definition of an assignment statement '$x := a$', where 'a' may be a complex expression. Its meaning is that, whatever the initial state is, after executing the assignment x has the value of a. This is expressed in (79), where $||.||$ stands for "the meaning of".

(79) $||x := a|| = \{< g,h > \mid$ h is equal to g except, possibly, for the value assigned to x, and $h(x) = ||a||\}$

Groenendijk & Stokhof (1987), henceforth referred to as "G & S", have suggested the possibility of approaching the semantics of formal logical language, like predicate logic, in the same spirit. The meaning of a predicate logic sentence would be described by the set of state transitions taking place in system (human or electronic) interpreting that formula. For example, the meaning of an existentially quantified statement '$\exists x : P(x)$' would be expressed by (80), where the notation h[x]g is used to indicate that h is equal to g except, possibly, for the value assigned to x:

(80) $||\exists x : P(x)|| = \{< g,h > \mid h[x]g \ \& \ h(x) \in F(P)\}$

(with F as in (78)). Accordingly, the meaning of a predicate-logic sentence is no longer the conditions for its truth or falsity; we are thus leaving the classical idea of truth-conditional semantics here. Instead, on this approach the truth value of a formula is derived from its meaning as follows:

(81) X is true in model $M = < D, F, g >$ if and only if there is a value assignment h such that $< g, h > \in ||X||$

The following example may help to clarify this. Consider a model $M_1 = < D_1, F_1, g_1 >$ with a domain of 4 individuals: $D_1 = \{a, e, j, m\}$, denoted in DPL as 'adam', 'eve', 'john' and 'mary', two of which are sleeping. In terms of the constant interpretation:

(82) $F_1 = \{< adam, a >, < eve, e >, < john, j >, < mary, m >, < SLEEP, \{< j, m >\}\}$

Let a state of the model be described by the following assignment of values to variables:

(83) $g_1 = \{< x, e >, < y, a >, < w, j >, < z, m >\}$

We consider the meaning of the expression '$\exists x : SLEEP(x)$' and its truth value in the model M_1. By (80), the meaning of the expression is the set $\{< g, h > \mid h[x]g \ \& \ h(x) \in F(SLEEP)\}$ of state transitions where in the final state the variable x belongs to the extension of the SLEEP predicate. By (81), the expression is true in M_1 if the set

(84) $\{< g_1, h > | h[x]g_1 \ \& \ h(x) \ \in F_1(SLEEP)\}$

is not empty. Indeed, it is not, for the pairs $< g_1, h_1 >$ and $< g_1, h_2 >$ belong to this set:

(85) $h_1 = \{< x, j >, < y, a >, < w, j >, < z, m >\}$
$h_2 = \{< x, m >, < y, a >, < w, j >, < z, m >\}$

What this in effect comes down to is that $\exists x : P(x)$ is true in a model M if it is possible to assign to x a value in the extension of P; this is possible exactly if P has a non-empty extension, which is the traditional condition for this formula to be true. So from the concept of meaning we obtain the traditional truth condition through the definition (81).

By means of rules like (80), G & S present a definition of the semantics of predicate logic; the resulting system they call Dynamic Predicate Logic (DPL). They subsequently propose to use DPL for semantic representation of natural-language sentences, instead of Discourse Representation Structures, and argue that there are significant advantages in doing so. In the next subsection we consider some of the advantages and limitations of their proposal.

4.1 Dynamic Logic and natural language

G & S claim that the use of DPL is fundamentally better than DRT, since the semantic interpretation process in DRT is not compositional, whereas the use of DPL does give rise to a compositional process. To assess this claim, let us first recall what compositionality means.

A process K is *compositional* if the processing by K of a complex input is a function of (1) the way in which the input is composed of parts; (2) the results of processing the parts. In a compositional interpretation process, each input element is processed separately ("context-free", if it were) and the final result is obtained from these partial results.

We have seen that both DRT and the DPL approach use a two-stage interpretation process 'Int' which can be represented in terms of a process 'R', of constructing formal representations, and a process 'E' of evaluating the representations:

(86) $Int(< i_1, .., i_n >) = E(R(< i_1, .., i_n >)$

The inputs to R are sequences of linguistic units (words, phrases, sentences,..), from which R constructs representations with a well-defined structuring into parts and specification of the relations between them (like: one is a predicate, another one the first argument of that predicate, etc.) The output of R can thus indeeed serve as input to a compositional evaluation process E. Now DRT can be accused of not being compositional, since the DRS-construction stage R is not compositional. The above example (46)-(47) illustrates this: the DRS for the text 'A man walks in the park. He sees Mary.' is not obtained from separate DRSs, constructed for the individual sentences.

To make the comparison with G & S's proposal, let us consider the treatment of anaphora in the DPL-framework. For the text (87a) we would get the DPL-representation (87b):

(87a) A man walks in the park. He whistles.
(87b) $(\exists x: MAN(x)\ \&\ WITP(x))\ \&\ WHISTLE(x)$

Viewed as a formula in ordinary predicate logic, this would be an inadequate representation since the variable x in WHISTLE(x) is outside the scope of the existential quantifier. Viewed as a formula in DPL, however, (87) *is* adequate, since G & S define a DPL-conjunction in an order-dependent way as denoting those state transitions which can be obtained by a succession of two transitions, corresponding to the first and second conjunct, respectively. In formula:

(88) $||p\ \&\ q|| \quad = \quad \{< g,h > \mid \exists k : < g,k > \in ||p||\ \&\ < k,h > \in ||q||\}$

Combining this with the definition (80) of existential quantification, we see that interpretation of (87) in an initial state g gives rise to an intermediate state k, where an individual is assigned to x that is a man and walks in the park; subsequently, we move to a final state where WHISTLE(x) is true for the same x. The remarkable thing is that the dynamic semantics of DPL has the effect that free variables in a formula get a value as the result of interpreting some other part of the formula where that variable has a bound occurrence. Intuitively, this is precisely how anaphora seem to work in natural language! This is indeed a very attractive point of DPL.

As DPL, like DRT, offers the possibility of semantic interpretation over sentence boundaries, it is an attractive candidate for use in the interpretation of utterances in a dialogue. However, the DPL framework as proposed by G & S still has some important limitations, which will have to be overcome before it can actually be used for this purpose.

First, an inherent feature of dynamic logic as used in the theory of computer programming, is that the semantic values of the constants of the language are constant; only those of the variables are variable. Consider a computer program consisting of the single statement: GREATERTHAN(5,4). In dynamic-logic terms, the meaning of this program is the set of those state transitions where nothing happens, but where in the final states the pair $< 5,4 >$ belongs to the extension of the predicate GREATERTHAN. Assuming that this predicate has been defined in the way the name suggests, this is the set of all state chaanges where indeed nothing happens. (If the predicate has not been defined in such a way that 5 is greater than 4, the meaning of the program is the empty set.) Therefore, the program has the same meaning as, for instance, GREATERTHAN(4,3) and as EQUALS((2+2),4). This is clearly undesirable, but rather harmless since programs without any variables are usually uninteresting anyway. Applied to a natural-language sentence like 'John walks' we get a similar result: given a model where it is the case that John walks, the meaning of the sentence is the set of changes in the model where nothing changes. If, on the other hand, we start with a model where it is not the case that John sleeps, then the meaning of the sentence is the empty set. From the point of view that meaning is the way an interpreter's information changes, this is most unsatisfactory. Also, as in the case of computer programs without variables, no difference in meaning is obtained between sentences whose interpretation does not involve anaphoric or quantified variables, such as 'John walks' and 'Peter sleeps'. In sum, the G & S proposal does not offer a satisfactory way of interpreting expressions made up of constants only.

Second, and closely related to the previous point, is the impossibility of accomodating new information. The dynamic-logic approach to program semantics is in terms of changes in the state of a machine. The state of a machine is considered as always completely determined (although not by the values of the variables in a program alone); in this framework, there is no such thing as a partially determined state. At this point, the parallel between the state of a machine and the information state of a natural-language user goes wrong: one of the main purposes of saying something in natural language is *for informing*, that is, for supplying new information. We will have to consider incomplete information states in order to take this into account.

A third, more technical limitation of the DPL-framework is that the interpretation of bound variables is not quite satisfactory, which creates a problem for the application to natural language (see Bunt, 1988b).

Fourth, and finally, a fundamental limitation has to do with the difference in nature between natural language and formal languages like predicate logic or Prolog. In the DPL-approach, a sentence is interpreted as the set of those changes in the state of an interpreter that make the sentence true. However, a declarative sentence can be used with different functions, such as informing, answering, or asking. If the sentence is used as a question, it should of course be interpreted as a different set of state changes, with final states involving such things as the interpreter knowing that the speaker wants to know whether the sentence is true. The DPL-approach only covers the case where something is asserted, which is in accordance with the use of "sentences" in languages of logic, but which does not do justice to the use of sentences in natural language. G & S state explicitly as their philosophy that

> "the meaning of a sentence does not lie in its truth conditions, but rather in the way it changes the (representation of the) information of the interpreter. The utterance of a sentence brings us from a certain state of information to another. The meaning of a sentence lies in the way it brings about such a transition." (G & S, 1987, p. 1)

Where the shoe pinches is in the distinction between *sentence* and *utterance*. Sentence is a grammatical notion, a string of words with certain syntactic properties. A sentence cannot bring about a change in information state, only an utterance can. It follows, that the state-change approach to meaning should be applied to utterances, rather than to sentences. This means that, rather than considering state changes in an interpreter caused by interpreting a sentence, we should consider state changes caused by a sentence *used as an assertion* or *used as a question*. It also means that we should consider changes in states of much greater complexity than those considered by G & S, who treat the state of an interpreter as simply the set of things he knows (and which are supposed to be true). However, the state of a participant in a dialogue involves at least weak and strong beliefs, goals, and mutual beliefs, as we shall see in the next section. These are the things that change as the result of interpreting an utterance.

5 Pragmatic interpretation: utterance meaning in dialogue

5.1 Information dialogues

By analogy with the notion of an "informative question" as a pure request for information, an "informative dialogue" or "information dialogue" is defined as a case of linguistic interaction in which two partners participate with the sole purpose of accomplishing the transfer of certain information. In its simplest form, such a dialogue consists of an informative question followed by an answer. In real-life situations, an informative dialogue never consists of a question and an answer only; what natural information dialogues look like can be seen in the examples (89) and (90).

Example (89) is a transcription of a telephone conversation with the information service at Schiphol, Amsterdam Airport, simulated in an experiment at the Institute for Perception Research IPO in Eindhoven in the context of a joint project with the Computational Linguistics Unit at Tilburg University.

(89) S = subject, I = information service

1.	I:	Schiphol information
2.	S:	Good afternoon. This is Van I. in Eindhoven. I would like to have some information about flights to Munich. When can I fly there between now and ... next Sunday
3.	I:	Let me have a look. Just a moment
4.	S:	Yes
5.	I:	O.K., there are ... three flights every day, one at nine fifty
6.	S:	Yes
7.	I:	one at one forty ... and one at six twenty-five
8.	S:	Six twenty-five ... These all go to Munich
9.	I:	These all go to Munich
10.	S:	And that's on Saturday too
11.	I:	That's on Saturday too, yes
12.	S:	Right ... Do you also have information about the connections to Schiphol by train?
13.	I:	Yes, I do
14.	S :	Do you know how long the train ride takes to Schiphol?
15.	I:	You are travelling from Eindhoven?
16.	S:	That's right
17.	I:	It's nearly two hours to Amsterdam ... You change there and then it's another fifteen minutes, so you should count on some two and a half hours

18. S: O.K. ... Thank you
19. I: You're welcome
20. S: Bye
21. I: Bye

Dialogue (90) was conducted via computer terminals, it was also recorded at IPO in a joint project with Tilburg University. Of the two participants, one has been trained to act in spoken dialogues like the employees at the telephone information service at Schiphol airport. The other participant (the "subject") has no experience in the use of computer terminals, and has been told that she participates in an experiment to study the influence of modern technology on information services. The subject has read a little story about a person who plans a holiday trip to Spain and want to know certain details about the possibillities of travellling; the subject was asked to act as being in theposition of that person. This story was based on the recording of a actual dialogue over the telephone with the information service at Schiphol. (The English text given here is a translation from the Dutch original, which is available from the author.)

(90) (S = subject, I = information service)

1. I: Schiphol information.
2. S: I have booked for flight IB 885 next Saturday to Alicante. What time should I be at Schiphol?
3. I: You should check in half an hour before departure at the latest.
4. S: So between what time and what time?
5. I: Between twelve and one-thirty.
6. S: Do you also have information about departure and arrival times of trains?
7. I: In Holland?
8. S: Yes.
9. I: I do.
10. S: What is the last train from Breda I cantake to be there in time for flight next IB 885?
11. I: The train of 12:06.
12. S: What is the arrival time in Alicante?
13. I: 17 hours.
14. S: What is the duration of the bus travel Alicante Benidorm?
15. I: We don't have information about that.
16. S: Thank you.
17. I: You're welcome.

Rather than going into the differences between the spoken and the terminal dialogue (see Beun & Bunt, 1988), we will concentrate here on a few important properties of natural information dialogues in general, which are illustrated in both examples.

First, an information dialogue is much more complex than a sequence of question-answer pairs. In dialogue (90), only 5 of the subject's 9 utterances and 4 of the informant's 9 utterances are factual questions and answers, respectively. In the telephone dialogue (89), there are only 2 factual questions ('When can I fly there between now and next Sunday?' and 'Can you tell me how long the train ride to Schiphol takes?') and two factual answers ('There are three flights every day ..', 'It's nearly two hours to Amsterdam ...'). The other 13 utterances (the exact number depending a little on the way of counting) have to do with verification, acknowledgement, introducing a new topic, or opening and closing the dialogue. We call the latter kind of communicative actions, which, roughly speaking, serve to make sure that the communication proceeds smoothly and stays on the right track, *dialogue control acts.*

Second, it is worth noting that when reading a dialogue text like (89) or (90), one has little problem in identifying the communicative functions of the utterances, be it in informal terms. Exactly how we do this is not immediately clear, but it seems intuitively obvious that the functional interpretation of utterances involves a combination of linguistic features (such as syntactic structure, use of special lexical items, intonation/punctuation) and of the semantic content in relation to the preceding dialogue. There are two points here which deserve further investigation. On the one hand the way in which functions of utterances are recognized, on the other the clarification of the very concept of the (communicative) function of an utterance. The characterization with labels like 'question', 'answer', 'inform', 'verification', 'acknowledgement' is too informal to be immediately useful. For instance, a reply like 'Let me have a look. Just a moment' should perhaps not be called an 'answer', as it does not answer a question. Also, the common intuition is that a verification is a kind of question; we will have to make clear in what sense this is the case. These matters will be taken up in the next subsection.

5.2 Contexts in information dialogues

The study of the functions of natural-language utterances in communication has mostly been undertaken in the borderland of linguistic pragmatics and philosophy. Unfortunately, even the best developed theories of linguistic communicative action, or "speech acts", such as those of Searle (1969), Allwood (1976), or Gazdar (1979), do not have the explicitness and formality required for use in building computer dialogues systems. Levinson (1983) argues that the most promising approach for arriving at such a theory would be one where speech acts are characterized in terms of their context- changing effects, as has for instance been proposed by Gazdar (1979), and Bunt (1977). But as the notion of context in general is an extremely broad and vague one, this does not seem to be a feasible approach. I believe, however, that by limiting ourselves to pure information dialogues, we can obtain a notion of context which is sufficiently clear and manageable to provide the basis for an explicit formal characterization of linguistic communicative action. In this subsection I will indicate the structure of these contexts.

Inherent to the very notion of an information dialogue is that we have two partners A and B with the purpose of obtaining or providing factual information. The communicative actions that A and B perform will obviously have effects on their information. So, basic to the notion of context we are looking for, must be what A and B know and in what respects they want to expand their knowledge. However, we must be careful using the term "knowledge", for two reasons. First, it would perhaps be better to speak of "belief" rather than "knowledge", since we do not want to exclude the possibility that a participant has incorrect information. What is meant here by saying that A knows that p, is just that A has the information p available, without implying the actual truth of p. This corresponds to one of the uses of the verb 'to know'; there is another use according to which something which is known must be true. It is the former use which is relevant here, since the course of the dialogue between A and B does not depend on what is actually true, but on what A and B believe to be true.

Second, beliefs can be uncertain. Natural information dialogues contain a substantial amount of verification, as example 2 illustrates. Apparently, participants in information dialogues often have uncertain knowledge about something and a desire to resolve their uncertainties. The effects of communicative actions in information dialogues thus include effects on the uncertain knowledge of the participants. I shall describe the situation where a participant A has some information p available, without fully trusting it, as "A suspects that p". So in describing the context of an informative dialogue, two important types of elements we must take into account are:

(91) A knows that p
(92) A suspects that p

with the interpretation of "knows" and "suspects" discussed above. What "p" may stand for will be discussed below.

In an information dialogue, not only the information available to the partners is important but also the information which is not available, and in particular the information they want to become available. There are two ways in which one may want information to become available: one may want it to become available to oneself or one may want it to become available to the partner. In other words, one may want to know something or one may want to make something known. These are the only kinds of goal that can underly an information dialogue. As ingredients of the context that gives rise to an information dialogue we must therefore also take into account elements of the form

(93) A wants to know whether p
(94) A wants to make known that p.

The things that A and B may want to know or to become known are, in the first place, specific facts about the domain of dicourse; that is what the dialogue is all about. However, sometimes a participant may want to know or to make known certain information about oneself or the other. We see examples of this in dialogue (89), where participant S wants to know, in line 6, what information is available to the other; where participant I wants to know for certain in line 7 that the other refers to trains in Holland, and where participant I wants to make known in 15 that she does not have information about buses in Spain. Apparently, we should allow the "p" in (91) - (94) to be information about the discourse domain as well as about what the speaker knows or what the other knows. Moreover, when we look at line 14 in dialogue (89), we see that a participant may want to know something which cannot be expressed in the form of (93); this form only allows for the case where one wants to know the truth of a proposition. We therefore need a more general form than (93), namely:

(95) A wants to know the value of x

where x may be a proposition, in which case the value is either TRUE or FALSE, but may also be something else, such as the duration of a train ride, or the time. This generalization is also required for the "know" attitude and the "suspect" attitude: one may know (or suspect) that a plane has flight number KL402, but one may for example also suspect that the partner knows what the flight number is. Apparently, we must distinguish between the following two cases:

(96) A knows the value of x
(97) A knows that the value of x is y

Similarly for the "suspect" attitude. (Although in English one doesn't say 'I suspect the value of ...', it is clearly possible to have information which is not fully trusted about the value of something.) In combination with the observation that the objects of the various attitudes, indicated by "p" and "x" in these formulae, may be aspects of the discourse domain as well as aspects of the dialogue partner, this means that we should allow context elements with nested speaker/attitude references, such as:

(98) A knows that B knows the arrival time of flight KL402
(99) A knows that B wants to know the arrival time of flight KL402
(100) A knows that B suspects that the arrival time of flight KL402 is 12:45
(101) A knows that B suspects that A knows the arrival time of flight KL402

and so on. In sum, what we find as key elements of the context can be described by the following recursive rules:

(102)
1. [A, B] [knows, suspects, wants to know, wants to make known] the value of x, where x is information about the discourse domain.
2. [A, B] [knows, suspects, want to make known] that p, where p is a proposition expressing information about the discourse domain.
3. [A, B] [knows, suspects, wants to know, wants to make known] the value of p, where p is a proposition of the form described by 1, 2, 3 or 4.
4. [A, B] [knows, suspects, want to make known] that p, where p is a proposition of the form described by 1, 2, 3 or 4.

These rules then describe the types of beliefs and intentions that are hypothesized to make up the "context" that gives rise to and is affected by the utterances in an information dialogue. Schematically, we can represent such a context as a pair:

(103) $K = < K_A, K_B >$

where K_A and K_B are the respective sets of beliefs and intentions of A and B, as characterized by the rules (102). (Note: in Bunt (1988a) contexts are represented as unordered pairs; it turns out to be technically advantageous to order these pairs.)

5.3 Communicative acts and context change

The idea behind exploring the notion of context in the preceding subsection was that different types of communicative action can be distinguished in terms of their effects on the context. Clearly, the effects on a context as defined above consist primarily in additions to the addressee's information. For instance, if speaker A asks speaker B whether flight KL402 comes from Montreal, B is provided with at least the following information:

(104a) A wants to know whether flight KL402 comes from Montreal
(104b) A suspects that B knows whether flight KL402 comes from Montreal

And if B answers that this is indeed the case, A is provided with at least the following information:

(105) B knows that flight KL402 comes from Montreal

But this is not all, for the performance of a communicative act does not only influence the information of the addressee, but also that of the speaker. For one normally assumes, unless there is evidence to the contrary, that the action one performs does transmit the information which it conveys when correctly understood. For instance, asking whether flight KL402 comes from Montreal not only has the effects (104), on B, but also the effects (106), on A:

(106a) A suspects that B knows that A wants to know whether flight KL402 comes from Montreal
(106b) A suspects that B knows that A suspects that B knows whether flight KL402 comes from Montreal

Schematically, the effects of a communicative action CA can thus be represented as follows:

(107) $K = < K_A, K_B > \quad = CA => \quad K' = < K'_A, K'_B >$

where K'_A and K'_B are A's and B's respective beliefs and intentions, 'updated' as the result of the action. There is a simple relationship between the effects on the addressee and those on the speaker, as (104) and (106) illustrate, namely that for every effect E_j on the addressee there is a corresponding effect on the speaker of the form

(108) A suspects that E_j

This expresses simply that the speaker (A) 'suspects" his action to be correctly understood. It should be emphasized that the effects considered here are only those which are indissolubly connected to the action. In speech act theory, these effects are often called illocutionary. Of course, an action like answering that the KL402 is leaving in 20 minutes may have other effects than that the addressee knows the speaker to know that, such as the addressee starting running to the gate. Such "indirect" effects, which are often called perlocutionary, obviously play no part in the characterization of communicative action and are therefore not considered here, important though they are. Note that the "direct" effects E_j on an addressee B, resulting from the understanding of the communicative act, are always of the general form (109):

(109) E_j = B knows that C_j

where C_j is some condition on the state of the speaker. The above examples illustrate this. The conditions C_j are in fact those conditions that the speaker's state should satisfy in order for him to act in accordance which the implicit rules of the information dialogue game, which include certain general principles concerning cooperativeness, honesty, rationality, etc. (see Allwood, 1976). These are sometimes called the ***appropriateness conditions*** of the action in question. For a communicative action with appropriateness conditions $\{C_1, ..., C_k\}$, performed by speaker A and addressed to B, we thus get the following direct effects, inherent to the recognition of the action:

(110) 1. B knows that C_j
2. A suspects that B knows that C_j
for j = 1, ..., k.

And this is only the tip of an iceberg. For the participants A and B surely both know, in principle, that these effects occur. Therefore, B also knows that A suspects B to know that C_j:

(111) 3. B knows that A suspects that B knows that C_j

By the same token, A knows, at least in principle, that B knows this:

(112) 4. A knows that B knows that A suspects that B knows that C_j

And by the same token, B knows, at least in principle, that this is the case:

(113) 5. B knows that A knows that B knows that A suspects that
B knows that C_j

And so on. More of this infinite iceberg is shown in (114), where we use the notation '$A \models p$' for 'A knows that p' and '$A \mid\doteq p$ for 'A suspects that p':

(114)

$$
\begin{array}{r}
B \models C_j \\
A \mid\doteq B \models C_j \\
B \models A \mid\doteq B \models C_j \\
A \models B \models A \mid\doteq B \models C_j \\
B \models A \models B \models A \mid\doteq B \models C_j \\
A \models B \models A \models B \models A \mid\doteq B \models C_j \\
B \models A \models B \models A \models B \models A \mid\doteq B \models C_j \\
A \models B \models A \models B \models A \models B \models A \mid\doteq B \models C_j \\
B \models A \models B \models A \models B \models A \models B \models A \mid\doteq B \models C_j \\
A \models B \models A \models B \models A \models B \models A \models B \models A \mid\doteq B \models C_j
\end{array}
$$

It seems that, in principle, there is no end to the iteration of speaker/hearer pairs (cf. Clark & Marshall, 1982 for a discussion of this phenomenon), though for practical purposes it may of course be reasonable to impose a limit on the recursion somewhere. This means that we should extend (110) with (111), (112), (113), and ever deeper nestings of alternate participant/attitude pairs. It is instructive to separate the context effects that thus arise into the effects on A and those on B. The effects on B are:

(115) 1. B knows that C_j
2. B knows that A suspects that B knows that C_j
3. B knows that A knows that B knows that A suspects that B knows that C_j
etc.

The effects on A are:

(116) 1. A suspects that B knows that C_j
2. A knows that B knows that A suspects that B knows that C_j
3. A knows that B knows that A knows that B knows that A suspects that B knows that C_j
etc.

These effects can be represented in a finite form by introducing a 'one-sided mutual knowledge operator'. By *mutual knowledge* of a certain fact f is meant that both A and B know that f, they both know that the other knows that f, they both know that the other knows that the other knows that f, and so on (see e.g. Clark & Marshall, 1981; Perrault & Cohen, 1981). One-sided mutual knowledge is one half of mutual knowledge, so to speak, namely the set of those pieces of mutual knowledge that constitute the knowledge of one speaker. Using such a one-sided mutual knowledge operator KMK, for *'know to be mutually known'*, we can represent the effects (115) and (116) on A and B in finite form:

(117a) KMK(A, B, A suspects that B knows that C_j)
(117b) B knows that C_j &
KMK(B, A, A suspects that B knows that C_j)

Mutual knowledge operators can be given a direct interpretation in finite form (Halpern & Moses, 1984) which means that they can be treated as finite primitive concepts rather than as mere abbreviations of infinite notions. This makes their use acceptable from a psycholinguistic point of view, and feasible from a computational point of view.

For the present discussion, the important conclusion is that the direct effects of a communicative act, represented schematically as (107) above, can be represented as follows:

$$\begin{array}{lll} (118) & < K_A, K_B > & = CA => \\ & < \mathit{updt}(K_A, & \{\text{KMK(A, B, A suspects that B knows that } C_j(c))\}), \\ & \mathit{updt}(K_B, & \{\text{B knows that } C_j(c)\} \cap \\ & & \{\text{KMK(B, A, A suspects that B knows that } C_j(c))\})> \end{array}$$

Here we have introduced a function *updt* of two arguments: (1) a set of beliefs and intentions, constituting the "state" of a dialogue participant, and (2) a set of beliefs with which this state has to be "updated". In the simplest case these beliefs can be added to those already present in that state, but in general the update has to take the revision of beliefs and intentions into account. We will return to this function in section 6.

In (118) we have written C_j(c), rather than just C_j, in order to indicate that the appropriateness conditions C_j depend on the semantic content c of the communicative act. From (118) we obtain a definition of the concept of communicative function as a context-changing function in the mathematical sense, by performing lambda abstraction over the semantic content and the context. This gives us the following function CF, where A and B are the "owners" of the states K_A and K_B that make up a context K:

$$\begin{array}{lll} (119) & \text{CF} = (\lambda z, K: & \\ & < \mathit{updt}(K_A, & \{\text{KMK(A, B, A suspects that B knows that } C_j(z))\}), \\ & \mathit{updt}(K_B, & \{\text{B knows that } C_j(z)\} \cap \\ & & \{\text{KMK(B, A, A suspects that B knows that } C_j(z))\}) > \end{array}$$

The agent whose state is changed in the way indicated at the first use of the *updt* function in (119) plays the role of the speaker, the other that of the addressee. Application of this function to a certain content c gives us the communicative act CA = CF(c), construed as a function with the context-changing effect described in (117). This is in line with the classical view of the concept of illocutionary force as a function that can be applied to a propositional content to yield an illocutionary act (Searle, 1969; Gazdar, 1979b). An interesting point to note is that the effects which are characteristic for a communicative act can be derived systematically from its appropriateness conditions. This means that the simplest way of distinguishing one communicative function from another is, after all, by the set of appropriateness conditions.

5.4 Communicative functions in information dialogues

Let us now consider the application of the approach to communicative action, outlined in the previous subsection, to information dialogues. In information dialogues, contexts consist of beliefs and intentions as described by (102), and so do appropriateness conditions and the possible packages of them that corespond to communicative functions.

In the above discussion we have come across three different types of motivation that may underly a dialogue act: (1) the speaker wants to know something; (2) the speaker wants to make something known; (3) the speaker knows that the hearer wants to know something. This trichotomy can be used as a starting point for a taxonomy of communicative functions as falling into three categories: question, inform, and answer functions. For each of the three categories a class of functions by means of the corresponding package of appropriateness conditions has been characterized in Bunt (1988a). Some of these functions are more specific than others, by which we mean that the set of appropriateness conditions of one includes that of another. This is conveniently represented in a hierarchical diagram, like (120), which shows the class of yes/no questions and its instances.

The appropriateness conditions of the various functions contain, of course, the semantic content to which the function is applied, according to (119), to form a dialogue act. For yes/no-questions (as well as for informing functions) the semantic content is always a proposition, designated in (120) by 'p'.

(120)

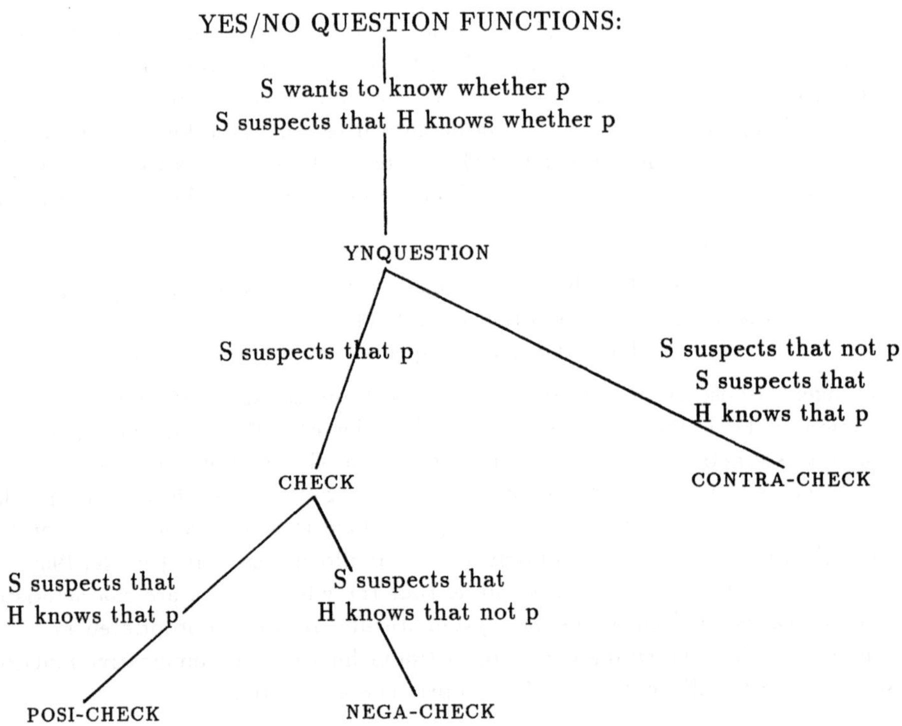

A point of interest to consider is the logical independence of the appropriateness conditions within a package corresponding to a communicative function. In the speech act literature it is usually assumed that one of the appropriateness conditions of a question is that the speaker does not possess the infor- mation he asks for (a "sincerity condition"). Such a condition has not been included in (120), in view of the fact that wanting something to be the case is usually understood as implying that this something is not already the case. Therefore, if S wants to know whether p, it is logically implied that S does not know whether p. Logically redundant appropriateness conditions have been left out in (120).

It may also be observed that the appropriateness conditions for a CONTRA-CHECK with content p are identical to those of a NEGA-CHECK with content not p. The reason for nonetheless distinguishing the two is that p in both cases stands for the semantic content of the utterance, and that a CONTRA-CHECK can be expressed by a positive sentence, as in (121):

(121) Does he come from *Montreal*?

with heavy stress on the last word. Now this sentence would normally be assigned the semantic content *He comes from Montreal.* So in order to interpret the utterance as a NEGA-CHECK with content *He does not come from Montreal*, we would have to use the intonation to change the semantic content. Basically, we can interpret intonation in two ways: semantically or pragmatically. Since intonation in general is one of the major sources of information for determining the commmunicative function of an utterance, and is therefore interpreted pragmatically, we think it is preferable to interpret the intonation pragmatically here as well. This means that we have the semantic content *He comes from Montreal*, and we assign the utterance a different communicative function: *contra-check.*

Interestingly, in Dutch and in several other languages it does not seem possible to express the verification of the falsity of a certain proposition, or the verification of suspected agreement concerning the falsity of a certain proposition, without using an explicit negation. This is the cause of the asymmetry in the tree structure dominated by the YN-QUESTION in (120). Note that this is a purely empirical matter.

Other types of questions, such as WH-questions, multiple-choice questions, examination questions and requests, as well as informing and answering functions are defined and discussed in Bunt (1988a).

6 Towards an integrated dynamic interpretation theory

6.1 Extending the dynamic-logic approach

In this section I will indicate how the dynamic-logic approach to semantics and the context-change approach to pragmatics may be combined into an integrated theory of natural-language interpretation.

Pragmatic interpretation according to the context-change approach described in the previous section is based on the transfer of information between speaker and hearer, including cases where previous beliefs are changed and where gaps in an incomplete state of information are filled. We have seen earlier that two severe limitations of the dynamic-logic approach are precisely its failure to deal with these cases. To overcome these limitations we have to consider extending the dynamic-logic approach in two respects:

- allow not only value assignments to variables to change, but assignments of values to constants as well;
- allow DPL-models to be partial; in particular, allow the assignments of values to variables and constants to be partial functions.

In this subsection we consider such extensions. We first consider the case of changing beliefs.

An obvious consquence of allowing both constant and variable interpretations to change, is that a *state in a model* $M = < D, F, g >$ is no longer just a specification of g, but a specification of both F and g: a pair $< F, g >$. We consider the example of an interpreter whose information is represented by the state $< F, g >$ of a model. For this interpreter we consider the semantic interpretation of the DPL-sentence:

(122) SLEEP(adam)

If we take the meaning of this formula to be the way it changes an interpreter's information, the interpretation of (122) should bring our interpreter in a state $< G, h >$ where it becomes (or remains) true that Adam sleeps. This can be accomplished by extending the extension F(SLEEP) of the predicate SLEEP so as to include the individual denoted by 'adam', if it didn't already do so. The meaning of (122) is the set of all such state changes, for any initial state $< F, g >$, so we obtain as the meaning of (122):

(123) $$||SLEEP(adam)|| = \{<< F,g >, < G,h >> \mid h = f \ \& \ \text{G[SLEEP]=F} \ \& \ \text{G(adam)} \in \text{G(SLEEP)}\}$$

If the information of an interpreter consists not only of the contents of a model but also of postulates which are external to the model, the consequences of the changes in G required by these postulates have to be taken into account as well; see Bunt (1988b). In the rest of this paper, I only consider the case where an interpreter's information is represented in a model without additional constraints.

Next we consider the accomodation of new information to an incomplete state of information. If an incomplete state is to be modelled by pairs $< F, g >$, as before, then the functions F and g should be partial, i.e. they should not necessarily assign a value to each of the constants and variables of the DPL language.

The most interesting form of incompleteness concerns the interpretation of predicate constants, in case the extension of a predicate is not completely known. If P is such a predicate constant, F(P) is undefined. However, the extension of P being partly known, we would of course like to say that F(P) is *not completely defined*, rather than undefined. In realistic situations, it will often be the case that certain individuals are known to belong to the extension of a predicate, certain individuals are known not to belong to it, and of certain individuals it is not known whether they belong to it. This cannot be represented in the traditional way by means of a single function F; instead, we need two functions, say F and F', where F(P) is the set of individuals known to belong to the extension of P, and F'(P) the set of individuals known not to belong to the extension of P.

This interpretation of F, plus the introduction of the function F', specifying known "negative extensions" of predicate constants, has the consequence that F (and F') can be a total function, after all. Where in the traditional approach F would, for instance, be undefined if nothing is known about the extension of a predicate P, we now represent this by F(P) = F'(P) = $\emptyset$.

Partial models are thus not simply models with partial functions, but 4-tuples:

$$(124) \quad M \;=< D,\, F,\, F',\, g >$$

where F and F' are total functions, F having the set of all constants of the DPL language as its domain; F' only the set of predicate constants. Consequently, a state will now be a triple $< F,\, F',\, g >$ rather than a pair $< F,\, g >$.

As an example, we consider a partial model $M \;=< D,\, F,\, F',\, g >$, with a domain consisting of four individuals: $D \;=\; \{a,\, e,\, j,\, m\}$, and the following state $< F,\, F',\, g >$:

$$(125) \quad \begin{array}{l} F = \{< adam, a >, < eve, e >, < john, j >, < mary, m >, \\ \qquad < MAN, \{a, \supset\} >, < WOMAN, \{e, m\} >, < SLEEP, \{m\} >\} \\ F' = \{< MAN, \{e, m\} >, < WOMAN, \{a, j\} >, < SLEEP, \{e, j\} >\} \\ g \;= \{< x, a >, < y, e >, < z, j >, < w, m >\} \end{array}$$

There is complete information in this state as to who is a man and who is a woman, but there is incomplete information about who is sleeping and who is not. Mary is known to sleep and Eve and John and known not to sleep, but whether Adam sleeps is not known. We consider once again the interpretation of the DPL statement (122): SLEEP(adam). As the result of interpreting this statement, an interpreter whose state of information is described by (125) will add the individual a to the extension of SLEEP and remove it from the "negative extension" F'(SLEEP), if necessary. The meaning of SLEEP(adam) as expressed in (123) in fact already covers this; we only have to adapt (123) to partial models in order to cover the case that Adam was known not to sleep. We thus get:

$$(126) \quad ||SLEEP(adam)|| \;=\; \begin{array}{l} \{<< F, F', g >, < G, G', h > | h = f\& \\ G[SLEEP]F \;\&\; G(adam) \,\in\, G(SLEEP) \;\& \\ G'[SLEEP]F' \;\&\; G(adam) \,\notin\, G'(SLEEP)\} \end{array}$$

Let us now consider the introduction of new information by a quantified DPL-sentence, such as $\exists x \,:\, MAN(x) \;\&\; SLEEP(x)$. Note that, in state (125), no man is sleeping. Straightforward adaptation of the G & S interpretation of existential quantification to partial models would give us the following:

$$(127) \quad \begin{array}{l} ||\exists x : MAN(x) \;\&\; SLEEP(x)|| = \\ = \{<< F,\, F',\, g >,\; < G,\, G',\, h >> |\; F = G \;\&\; F' = G' \;\&\; \exists k :\, k[x]g \;\& \\ \qquad\qquad < k,\, h > \subset\; ||MAN(x) \;\&\; SLEEP(x)||\} \\ = \{<< F,\, F',\, g >,\; < G,\, G',\, h >> |\, F = G \;\&\; F' = G' \;\&\; h[x]g \;\& \\ \qquad\qquad h(x) \,\in\, F(MAN) \;\&\; h(x) \,\in\, F(SLEEP)\} \end{array}$$

This is inadequate, however, since the constant interpretation functions F and F' are such that no man is in the extension of SLEEP; therefore, it is not possible that h(x) ∈ F(MAN) and h(x) ∈ F(SLEEP). To accomodate the new information that a man is sleeping, F and F' have to change as well. There are several possibilities: Adam or John can be brought into the extension of SLEEP, or Eve or Mary, if they are also moved from the extension of WOMAN to that of MAN. And of course any combination of these changes would do as well.

We thus obtain the following interpretation:

$$(128) \quad ||\exists x : MAN(x) \,\&\, SLEEP(x)|| = \\ = \{<< F, F', g>, < G, G', h >> \mid G[SLEEP, MAN]F \,\& \\ G'[SLEEP, MAN]F' \,\&\, h[x]g \,\& \\ h(x) \in G(MAN) \,\&\, h(x) \in G(SLEEP) \\ h(x) \notin G'(MAN) \,\&\, h(x) \notin G'(SLEEP)\}$$

This still does not seem quite satisfactory, due an unsatisfactory point which is inherited from DPL. According to (128), an interpreter who processes the DPL-sentence asserting that a man sleeps, would get into a state where either he knows that Adam sleeps or that John sleeps (or both, or Eve or Mary, assumed to be a man). But shouldn't the new state rather be that it is known that one of them sleeps, whithout knowing which one? This requires more complex models. This complication is due to the fact that we now look at states of a model as representing *an interpreter's knowledge*, where states in DPL-models represent states of affairs in a domain of discourse. This shift in the view on states and models closely relates to the shift we want to make from a state-change semantics approach to a changestate approach to the interpretation of utterances.

6.2 Dynamic logic and utterance meaning

As a point of fundamental criticism on the DPL-approach, we have mentioned in section 4 that G & S consider sentence meaning in terms of changes in an interpreter's state of information, but such changes are not accomplished by sentences (either in DPL or in natural language), but by communicative actions: sentences uttered with a certain communicative function.

So let us look at the state-change interpretation of the utterance 'Adam sleeps', for example, addressed to hearer H by speaker S in order to inform H that Adam sleeps. The immediate suggestion would be to use (57) as the interpretation of this utterance rather than of its semantic content. Describing the utterance as a quadruple $< communicative\ function,\ semantic\ content,\ speaker,\ addressee >$ this would give us (129):

$$(129) \quad || < inform, SLEEP(adam), S, H > || = \\ \{<< F, F', g>, < G, G', h >> \mid \; h = f \,\& \\ G[SLEEP]F \,\&\, G'[SLEEP]F' \,\& \\ a \in G(SLEEP) \,\&\, a \notin G'(SLEEP)\}$$

But according to the pragmatic theory outlined in the previous section, this communicative act would have considerably more complex effects than (129) suggests. The effects on the interpreter H would be (130):

(130) H knows that S wants to make known that Adam sleeps
H knows that S knows that Adam sleeps
H knows that H and S mutually know that S suspects that H knows that S wants to make known that Adam sleeps
H knows that H and S mutually know that S suspects that H does not know that Adam sleeps

There would be effects on the state of S too (see (32a)), but we will leave those out of consideration for the moment. The effects (130) should be contrasted with the effect assumed in the DPL approach reflected in (129), which is simply that H knows that Adam sleeps. To take (130) into account, we need more complex state descriptions than the triples $< F, F', g >$. Since we have to take two agents into account and various attitudes toward the information that Adam sleeps, we can no longer get by with a single function F, describing a constant's extension as far as known, and its negative counterpart F'. We need to make the description of extensions relative to speaker and hearer and to their attitudes. It is beyond the scope of the present paper to discuss the structure of the more complex models to which this leads (Bunt, in prep.), but we will indicate here what we get by assuming that our models M contain sets of interpretation functions which assign (partial) extensions to predicate constants relative to S's knowledge, to H's knowledge, to S's knowledge of H's knowledge, to S's suspicions, etc. The various F functions will be distinguished by indices which reflect the speaker-hearer-attitude combinations involved, as follows:

(131) $F_{hs}(P)$ = the extension H knows S knows P to have
$F_{hsm}(P)$ = the extension H knows S wants to make known P to have
$F_{hMK_{swhs}}(P)$ = the extension H knows H and S mutually know that S suspects ('w': 'weakly believes') that H knows that S knows P to have
$F_{hMK_{swhsm}}(P)$ = the extension H knows H and S mutually know that S suspects that H knows S wants to make P known to have

It becomes quite cumbersome to represent these more complex states and state changes in terms of n-tuples of functions, many of which will be unaffected by the changes. Instead, we will describe changes in the format (132):

(132) $\{< M, M' > \mid M'[...]M \ \& \ ...\}$

where M'[...]M means that M and M' are identical except for the M-components mentioned in '[...]'; the way these components are different in M' is stipulated in the clause '& ...'. Instead of (129) we then obtain (133), which is more complicated than (129) not only because we acknowledge the more complex effects (130), but also because the constant-interpretation functions mentioned in (131) have more than one negative counterpart, corresponding with different scope of negations. For instance, F_{hsm} has the negative counterparts $F_{h'sm}$ and $F_{hsm'}$; $F'_{hsm}(P)$ describes the extension of P as far as H knows that S does not want it to make known, and $F_{hsm'}(P)$ represents those individuals that H knows S wants to make known not to belong to the extension of P.

(133) $||<inform, SLEEP(adam),\ S,\ H>||$
$\{<M, M'> \mid M'[F_{hsm}, F_{hs}, F_{hMKswhsm}, F_{hMKswhs}$, and their
negative counterparts$]M$ &
$G_{hsm}[SLEEP]F_{hsm}$ & $a \in G_{hsm}(SLEEP)$ &
$G_{hs}[SLEEP]F_{hs}$ & $a \in G_{hs}(SLEEP)$&
$G_{hMKswhsm}[SLEEP]F_{hMKswhsm}$ & $a \in G_{hMKswhsm}(SLEEP)$&
$G_{hMKswhs}[SLEEP]F_{hmkswhs}$ & $a \in G_{hMKswhs}(SLEEP)$&
$G_{h'sm}[SLEEP]F_{h'sm}$ & $a \in G_{h'sm}(SLEEP)$&
$G_{hsm'}[SLEEP]F_{hsm'}$ & $a \in G_{hsm'}(SLEEP)$&
$G_{h's}[SLEEP]F_{h's}$ & $a \in G_{h's}(SLEEP)$&
$G_{hs'}[SLEEP]F_{hs'}$ & $a \in G_{hs'}(SLEEP)$&
negative counterparts of $G_{hMKswhsm}, G_{sMKswhs}\}$

An interesting question is how this analysis of utterance meaning compares to the one that is implicit in the pragmatic theory outlined in the previous section. There, we analysed communicative functions as mathematical functions, applicable to a semantic content plus a context, consisting of the knowledge states of speaker and addressee, respectively. The meaning of an utterance is than obtained by applying its communicative function CF to its semantic content p, while maintaining the abstraction over the context $< K_S,\ K_H >$:

(134) $||<CF,\ p,\ S,\ H>|| \ = \ CF(p) \ =$
$(\lambda K_S,\ K_H: \quad < updt(K_S, \{z|\ z\ =$ KMK(S, H, S suspects that
H knows that $C_j(p)$
for some appropriateness
condition $C_j(p)\})$,
$updt(K_H, \{z|\ z =$ H knows
that $C_j(p)$ or
$z\ =$ KMK(H, S, H knows that S
suspects that H knows that $Cj(p)$
for some appropriateness
condition $C_j(p)\}) >)$

Applying this to the example of the informing utterance 'Adam sleeps', (133) and (134) are almost the same, if we disregard the effects on the speaker in (134), even though they may seem quite different at first sight. The *updt* function in (134) changes the hearer's state K_H in such a way that it becomes the case that (1) H knows that $C_j(p)$ for every appropriateness condition for informs, where p = SLEEP(adam), and (2) H knows that the two participants mutually know that the speaker suspects this to be the case. Representing the knowledge state of H as a state of the kind considered in this section, the *updt* function makes precisely the changes described in (133).

Two differences remain, between (133) and (134). First, (134) takes also changes in the speaker's state into account. Second, (133) is of the general form of a set of pairs (135a), and (134) of the general form of a function (135b):

$$(135a) \quad ||u|| = \{< M_H, M'_H > | \ldots\}$$
$$(135b) \quad ||u|| = (\lambda M_S,\ M_H : < updt(M_S,\ \ldots),\ updt(M_H,\ \ldots) >$$

where M_S and M_H represent the states of S and H, respectively.

We think the form (135b) is to be preferred, if the meaning of an utterance is viewed as the way it changes the state(s) of the hearer (and speaker). For the function in (135b) indeed tells us exactly how this (these) state(s) change, whereas the set of changes (135a) only indicates a set of possible ways of changing state(s). This point is closely related to the closing remark in the previous subsection, where we mentioned as a shortcoming of the G & S-approach that the semantic interpretation of a sentence like 'A man sleeps' is the set of all those changes which result either in a state where Adam sleeps, or one where John sleeps, or ...; in short, in a state where a specific man sleeps. Instead of considering all those states, it seems preferable to consider only the change which results in the state where it is known that some man sleeps, without having to choose a particular man.

In fact, we think a state-change approach to meaning should be required to use such models that the state-changing effect of an utterance can always be a single state transition, rather than a set of possible transitions, so that the meaning of an utterance is indeed described as the way it changes an interpreter's (and a speaker's) state of information.

7 Conclusion

The on-line interpretation of natural-language utterances in a (human-computer) dialogue meets with many obstacles. In this paper we have looked at obstacles of a syntactic, of a semantic, and of a pragmatic nature. In each case we have discussed some recently developed tools that seem useful for removing those obstacles, and we have paid separate attention to the possible combination of tools.

As an obstacle of a syntactic nature we have considered the phenomenon of discontinuous constituents. We have defined tree- like structures with discontinuities ("discontinuous trees") which allow us to represent the constituent structure of sentences with discontinuous constituents without using transformations or artifacts like slash categories. On the basis of the notion "adjacency sequence", which generalizes the notion of a sequence of adjacency pairs, we have developed a kind of phrase-structure grammar, called DPSG ("Discontinuous Phrase- Structure Grammar") which is able to generate discontinuous trees.

Discontinuous trees are a generalization of ordinary trees, and DPSG rules are generalizations of ordinary rewrite rules. Both concepts can therefore be added to an ordinary (generalized) phrase-structure grammar, with the effect that such a grammar generates syntactic representations with discontinuities for sentences with discontinuous constituents, while doing everything else as before.

DPSG rules can also be handled by a parser for ordinary phrase- structure grammars, such as a chart parser, by adding some bookkeeping to make sure that no rules are overlooked and that the adjacency sequence relations are satisfied. Such a parser handles sentences with discontinuous constituents in the same on- line fashion as other sentences.

As obstacles of a semantic nature we have looked at (lexical) vagueness and ambiguity. We have outlined a two-level model-theoretic semantic approach which uses intermediate formal representations that preserve the vagueness and (within-category) lexical ambiguity of natural language. This allows us to postpone the resolution of such ambiguity and vagueness, which in general cannot be resolved in a domain-of-discourse-independent way, until we have the information that is required for this purpose. We indicated that some cases of structural, "logical" ambiguity can also be handled in that way. This approach can be combined with DPSG (or other syntactic formalisms) in a syntactic-semantic grammar where the semantic components of the rules translate syntactic constituents into these intermediate semantic representations. A parser-interpreter which applies the rules of such a grammar can deal with virtually all kinds of ambiguity and vagueness in an on-line manner.

Another obstacle of a semantic nature is formed by anaphora. We have described a suggestion by Groenendijk and Stokhof to handle anaphora using predicate-logic representations that are interpreted as in dynamic logic. In that approach, the meaning of a representation is conceived as the way a model of the domain of discourse would have to change in order to make the representation true. This leads to a particularly elegant treatment of anaphora by means of free variables. However, the approach has serious deficiencies for its application to natural language. We have indicated some of these deficiencies, and directions for removing them.

As an obstacle of a pragmatic nature, we have considered the interpretation of the communicative function of an utterance in an information-exchange dialogue. We argued that utterance meaning is appropriately defined in terms of the way the interpretation of the utterance changes the states of information of the speaker and addressee, and that this can be viewed as an extension of the dynamic logic idea of Groenendijk and Stokhof. We indicated how a pragmatic theory of utterance function and the dynamic logic approach may be combined into a unified theory of utterance interpretation, which we tentatively called "dynamic interpretation theory".

Groenendijk and Stokhof's approach gives rise to an on-line interpretation process for sentences in a text. This can be seen as an instance of the more general phenomenon that the use of semantic representations whose interpretation is defined in terms of state changes, is a suitable basis for on-line interpretation. "Dynamic interpretation theory" is another instance, where instead of predicate-logic representations of sentences we use meaning representations of utterances, which include, besides the semantic representation, the indication of communicative function, speaker and hearer. These more complex representations are interpreted dynamically in terms of changes in the states of speaker and hearer. Although many details still have to be worked out, this approach offers the exciting prospect of a full- fledged, on-line semantic and pragmatic interpetation of utterances in dialogue.

References

Allwood, J. (1976) Linguistic communication as action and coope- ration. Gothenburg Monographs in Linguistics 1.

Beun, R.-J. (1986) The function of repetitions in spoken infor- mation dialogues. IPO Annual Progress Report 20, 91-98.

Beun, R.-J. (1988) Declarative question acts. In M.M. Taylor, F. Neel & D.G. Bouwhuis (eds.) The Structure of Multimodal Dialogues. North-Holland, Amsterdam.

Beun, R.-J. & Bunt, H.C. (1988) Investigating linguistic behaviour in human-computer dialogues. In IPO Annual Progress Report 22.

Bronnenberg, W.J. Bunt, H.C., Landsbergen, S.P.J., Scha, R.J.H., Schoenmakers, W.J. & Utteren, E.P.C. van (1980) The question- answering system PHLIQA1. In L. Bolc (ed.) Natural language communication with computers. Hauser, München.

Bunt, H.C. (1977) Towards an analysis of dialogue organization principles. IPO Annual Progress Report 12, 105-114.

Bunt, H.C. (1984) The resolution of quantificational ambiguity in the TENDUM system. COLING'84 preprints, 130 - 133.

Bunt, H.C. (1985) Mass terms and model-theoretic semantics. Cambridge University Press, Cambridge, England.

Bunt, H.C. (1988a) Information dialogues as communicative action in relation to partner modeling and information processing. In M.M. Taylor, F. Neel & D.G. Bouwhuis (eds.) The Structure of Multimodal Dialogues. North-Holland, Amsterdam.

Bunt, H.C. (1988b) Information dialogues and the dynamics of language understanding. In B. Elsendoorn (ed.) Working models of human perception. North-Holland, Amsterdam.

Bunt, H.C. (forthc.) A multiple-data base knowledge representation formalism. Unpublished paper.

Bunt, H.C., Beun, R.J., Dols, F.J.H., Linden, J.A. van der, & Schwartzenberg, G.O. thoe (1985) The TENDUM dialogue system and its theoretical basis. IPO Annual Progress Report 19, 105- 113

Clark, H.H. & Marshall, C.R. (1981) Definite reference and mutual knowledge. In: A.K. Joshi, I. Sag & B.L. Webber (eds.) Elements of discourse understanding. Cambridge University Press, Cambridge.

Cohen, P.R. & Levesque, H.J. (1985) Speech Acts and Rationality. In: Proceedings of the 23rd Annual Meeting of the Assoc. for Computational Linguistics, 49-59.

Emonds, J.E. (1976) A transformational approach to English syntax. Academic Press, New York.

Emonds, J.E. (1979) Appositive relatives have no properties. Linguistics Inquiry 10, 211-243.

Gazdar, G. (1979a) Pragmatics: Implicature, Presupposition, and Logical Form. Academic Press, London & New York.

Gazdar, G. (1979b) Speech act assignment. In: A.K. Joshi, I. Sag & B.L. Webber (eds.) Elements of discourse understanding. Cambridge University Press, Cambridge.

Gazdar, G., Klein. E., Pullum, G.K. & Sag, I.A. (1985) Genera- lized Phrase-Structure Grammar. Harvard University Press, Cambridge, MA.

Groenendijk, J. & Stokhof, M. (1987) Dynamic Predicate Logic. Unpublished paper, ITLI, Amsterdam, March 1987

Halpern, J.Y. & Moses, Y.(1984) Knowledge and common knowledge in a distributed environment. In: Proceedings of the Third ACM Conference on Principles of Distributed Computing, 50-61.

Harel, David (1984) Dynamic Logic. In D. Gabbay & F. Guenthner (eds.) Handbook of Philospohical Logic, vol II. Reidel, Dordrecht 1984

Joshi, A.K. (1982) Mutual Beliefs in Question-Answer Systems. In: N.V. Smith (ed.) Mutual Knowledge, 181-197. Academic Press, London & New York.

Kamp, J.A.W. (1981) A theory of truth and semantic representation. In" J. Groenendijk & M. Stokhof (eds.) Formal methods in the study of language. Mathematisch Centrum, Amsterdam.

Levinson, S. (1983) Pragmatics. Cambridge University Press.

Lewis, D. (1969) Convention. Harvard University Press, Cambridge, MA.

McCawley, J.D. (1982) Parentheticals and Discontinuous Constituent Structure. Linguistic Inquiry 13 (1), 91-106

Perrault, C.R. & Cohen, P.R. (1981) Inaccurate reference. In: A.K. Joshi, I. Sag & B.L. Webber (eds.) Elements of discourse understanding. Cambridge University Press, Cambridge.

Raphael, B. (1965) A computer program which 'understands'. In AFIPS Conference Proceedings 26, 577-589.

Ross, J.R. (1973) Slifting. In M. Gross, M. Halle & M.P. Schützenberger (eds.) The formal analysis of natural language. Mouton, The Hague.

Searle, J.R. (1969) Speech Acts. Cambridge University Press.

Wall, R.E. (1972) Introduction to Mathematical Linguistics. Prentice-Hall, Englewood Cliffs.

Winograd, T. (1983) Language as a cognitive process. Addison- Wesley, Reading, MA.

SEMANTIC PROCESSING IN SPEECH UNDERSTANDING

G. Thurmair

Siemens AG
D AP 323
Otto Hahn Ring 6
D-8 Munich 83

Abstract: This paper will try to evaluate the state of the art in semantic representation techniques as far as they are used in speech understanding systems. It will not deal with knowledge representation techniques in general, because only some of them are used and are even usable in speech environment. First, a scetch of the problem domain will be given: Recognition levels, search spaces and system design decisions are outlined, and from this, the task of linguistic analysis procedures is derived. Second, existing techniques to incorporate semantic information into the Speech Understanding task are presented and discussed, like statistics, semantic markers, semantic grammars etc. Third, two approaches for Speech Understanding are discussed: predicate logic as representation as used in the SPICOS system, and semantic frames as used in the CMU-DARPA project. At the end, two proposals of possible system architectures are presented.

1. THE PROBLEM DOMAIN

1.1. Levels of Representation

Usually, the standard view of the analysis of speech is as follows:

- acoustic-phonetic decoding of the speech signal is performed, and subword unit candidates are extracted (phonemes, syllables etc.)
- a word verification component tries to match these units with possible words and finds word candidates
- these word candidates are combined into sentences, using syntactic information; the result is a list of sentence hypotheses
- the syntactic structures are interpreted semantically in order to find meaningful concepts and are further embedded into the pragmatic context of the ongoing discourse.

This strategy seems to be the most natural one, and there are several systems which try to implement this analysis strategy in a straight-forward manner.

But, first of all, human perception does not seem to work like this:

- we know that we "hear" units which were not produced: they are derived from the context (cf. /FUJ 86/)
- we vary acoustic phenomena according to semantic intentions

NATO ASI Series, Vol. F46
Recent Advances in Speech Understanding
and Dialog Systems
Edited by H. Niemann et al.

(/COO 76/): acoustic decoding has to take higher level information into accout
- the observation of speech errors indicates that such errors do not follow the steps outlined above (/HAR 84/)

Second, systems which are built in this straight bottom up manner tend to run into serious problems, if they use dictionaries of realistic sizes (1000 and more words); the reason is that the search space increases dramatically, and the search explodes.

1.2 Complexity of search processes

The following figures give an impression of the kinds of search processes which are involved if a sequential bottom up system design is chosen:

- recognition of subword units:
  the worst case would be that every unit at every place will be proposed; the number of units by experience ranges from 30 (phonemes) to several hundred (syllables). The state of the art is as follows:
  - 75% of the phonemes among the top 5 hypotheses (/HEA 77/) (i.e. 25% of the spoken phonemes below that level!)
  - 80% of the syllables among the top 10 (/SHI 86/)
  - 65% of the demisyllables on top position (/MUD 84/)

  This means that even if the top 10 to 15 subword units are searched, the word verification component must deal with 20% units in addition. It has to eliminate what it has recognised, and at the same time, it has to propose units it did not find.

- recognition of words
  the word verification has to match possible words with subword units and take into account assimilation phenomena. The worst case here is that every word at every place is found. The search space is given by the number of subword units, the dictionary size, and the amount of insertions / deletions etc. which are allowed.
  Some figures reported in the literature show that the search in this stage is extremely problematic:
  - 80% of the correct words are found among the top 10 word candidates (/WOO 80/)
  - 13000 words were derived from a 600 word dictionary; 33% of the spoken words were missing, the correct words were at 12th position on avg. (/HEA 77/)
  - 1700 words were hypothesised for 45 words spoken; a 200 word lexicon was used (/MUD 84/)

  The average sentence length here was between four and ten. This means that thousands of words would have to be searched for a small sentence, and 20% of the words which were needed to find the correct sentence would be missing.

- syntactic analysis
  Here, the search space is given by the number of word

hypotheses and the syntactic complexity of the grammar.

- For 9 sentences, between 1200 and 2900 syntactic constituents were built (/MUD 84/)
- Using the top five word candidates, about 200 case frames for one sentence were instantiated (EVAR)
- Using the top fifty candidates, 30000 syntactic constituents were instantiated, from which several thousand were well-formed (SPICOS)

These figures indicate that the complexity of search processes cannot be reduced by a linear architecture: On the one side, each step reduces the ambiguities of its predecessor (and has to take into accout missing elements); on the other side, each step itself creates an enormous amount of uncertainty; as a result, the whole search process tends to explode. Therefore, from the beginning, systems tried to incorporate as much knowledge as available as early as possible in the analysis process.

1.3 System Design Decisions

If we consider the architectural proposals to overcome these difficulties, we can see that some systems try to avoid certain levels of analysis by collapsing the recognition procedures somehow.

Some systems use a straigth-forward bottom-up architecture, where acoustic-phonetic decoding is done, resulting in subword units; then, word verification is performed, resulting in a word lattice; then syntactic analysis is performed, resulting in a sentence. Systems like these are ALVEY or IKARUS or MYRTILLE 2.

Systems like HWIM or HEARSAY try to use feedback from the sentence level down to the word verification level. HEARSAY e.g. is completely bottom up in the acoustic and word verfification part and just restricts the search of the word candidates (which all are generated!).

Other systems try to avoid certain representation levels. Either they use whole word templates and do not generate the subword level complexity, or they avoid the word level and try to generate sentences directly from subword lattices (/HTZ 86/).

If all intermediate levels are avoided, an architecture like HARPY is produced, where all information is used at once in order to restrict the search space as effectively as possible.

The choice of certain archtitectural features depends on the purpose of a system:

Systems with more levels are more interesting (from a linguistic point of view) as they are able to model the different knowledge sources independently and explicitly, but they certainly are less effective as they do not reduce the search space sufficiently. Systems which are designed from a practical or efficiency point of view, however, try to restrict the search space as early as possible, and tend to integrate all the knowledge available into one big searching procedure.

The study of the interaction of knowledge sources is an effort of its own, as methods have to be found to analyse their contribution to the speech understanding process independently, but then, to integrate them into the most efficient cooperation, using a "compiling" technique. In order to do this, a complete running system is an absolute prerequisite.

There is another feature which nearly all the systems mentioned have in common: Besides phonology, syntax is the only kind of linguistic knowledge source which is used. Semantic information, if at all, is used in a very implicit way, e.g. semantic grammars. "Real" semantic components mostly are just interpretive, on the basis of a syntactically wellformed string; so they cannot contribute to the recognition process.

1.4 Tasks of a linguistic analysis component

Depending on the kind of system architecture, a linguistic component has to deal with two kinds of input. Its input is either an erroneous "best path" word string (without alternative readings), or a word lattice. Examples of a word string (taken from the SPICOS project) are:

(1a) Gib aller Autoren
(1b) Gib alle Autoren (print all authors)
(2a) Drucke aller Reports vom Juni auf
(2b) Drucke Reports vom Juni aus (print reports of June)
(3a) Wer bearbeitet am Thema Linguistik
(3b) Wer arbeitet am Thema Linguistik (who works on Linguistics)
(4a) Wer schrieb im Juli 84
(4b) Wer schrieb im Juni 84 (who wrote in June 84)
(5a) Wer hat Langs Briefe fuer Schilz angeschrieben
(5b) Wen hat Lang bezueglich Philips angeschrieben (to whom wrote Lang concerning Philips)

(The "a" sentences were recognised, the "b" sentences were spoken)

These cases show that linguistic analysis has to deal with many kinds of errors in the "best path" analysis: Many sentences are ungrammatical. The errors result from diferent sources and can be eliminated using different techniques.

Some errors (like (1)) are purely morphological; they are very frequent in languages like German. They can be covered by relaxing morphological tests (like agreement) in the grammar (as substitutional information, in SPICOS we used semantic features). Some others are syntactical: Example (3b) has to be blocked because of verb framing- but unfortunately, there are two possible readings ("arbeiten... am Thema" vs. "bearbeiten... das Thema"), both of which are syntactically possible. Here, methods have to be found to find the most plausible reading. Sentences like (4) or (2) (insertion of a quantifier) are syntactically correct but end up in a wrong database query and answer: All reports - not just some - are printed; or letters of July - instead of June - are presented.

Here, we could think of means of dialogue to disambiguate these sequences: An approach for a limited domain is presented in /FIB 86/. But it is unclear how sequences of dialogue steps can be modelled within a "best path" framework.

If a linguistic analysis uses a "best path" input, without alternatives, it must be able to cope with erroneous input, which requires weak linguistic techniques, together with special strategies to be applied to discover what a wrong sentence could have looked like.

On the other hand, if the input of a linguistic component is a word lattice, the analysis has to be as sharp as possible in order to get rid of all the wrong possible word candidates which the word verification produces. Therefore, the problem of missing word candidates is nearly unsolvable. In (6), an example of such a lattice (also from SPICOS) is given:

(6)

```
1    2    3    4    5      6    7    8    9     10
SIND IM   KANN WELCHER--   BRIEF     VOR  HERR  DREI
     DER  IN   WELCHE---   BRIEFE--- VOM  HAT   DA
     IRGENDWELCHE-------             VON  EIN   BEI
     EIN                        VIER EIN  AM
     DEN                        FUER      EIBL
     AN                                   HERR
```

(The lattice in fact is a net if inter-word assimilation phenomena are taken into account - and of course, it is much bigger).

All kinds of syntactic restriction have to be applied to get rid of wrong words and even constituents (e.g. "ein Herr", "welcher Brief"), and to find the correct sentence ("Sind irgendwelche Briefe von Eibl da"). Many hypotheses are well-formed but not possible in a given context. Linguistic analysis has to eliminate them, and to detect missing words at the same time. This can only be done if very strong top down hypotheses are applied - which have to be located above the syntactic level!

In SPICOS, both kinds of input could be handled: We started out modelling restrictions for word lattices, and when we took the best path analysis we just removed or substituted certain morphological-syntactic-semantic tests. This was due to a very flexible kind of syntactic rules (see below).

2. TECHNIQUES TO INCORPORATE SEMANTIC INFORMATION

As it is very plausible to use the meaning of words for recognition, semantic information is used in speech understanding and recognition systems. But it is used very differently and integrated into the system in different ways.

2.1 Statistics

The technique here is simple: To each word, store its possible successors. These successors are found by means of statistic techniques. The success of this approach is due to the fact that the surface of the language of course does mirror its underlying regularities; in this respect, they also do deal with semantic phenomena; and therefore, these approaches are in fact successful.

On the other hand, no real "knowledge" is used; and this is the reason for some serious drawbacks of these approaches:

- they depend on the text corpus on which the statistical analysis ran: office document successors cannot be used for patent abstracts. They cannot be used in other domains; instead, they have to be rebuilt for every new application.
- they cause big maintenance problems: Not only big data collections are needed for a new application area and big processing times have to be spent; also, maintenance of existing domains is difficult: What if the name of a new customer has to be added to an office letter environment?
- what they can find can be expressed very easily by linguistic rules: a standard noun phrase consists of a determiner, an adjective, a noun and attached prepositional phrases, relative clauses etc., some of which are optional. It is not necessary to search several million surface words to find this fact. And in addition, special rules for special cases can be written, but it is very difficult to insert such single phenomena into statistical analyses.
- sometimes, they produce surprising results: The successors on "vice" are "president", "director" and "versa".
- as they are restricted to pairs or triplets of words (for practical reasons), the analysis may end with a completely ungrammatical sentence, although all the transitions were possible and correct.

The consequence is to use the semantic knowledge in an explicit and clearly defined way, and to think of ways how to integrate it into the recognition procedure.

2.2 Word based semantics

The approach here is: To each word, store its possible dependency relations. The progress consists in using semantic relations (dependency) instead of just word sequence. Usually the dependencies are stored in a dictionary, resulting in a kind of "word expert" analysis: The recognition evaluates the dictionary entry, e.g. in (7) (example from /HAT 82/).

(7)
```
    IF you  find a possible  adjective within  a noun group
    THEN search for the head noun
        check its entry whether or not its entry is a
           possible dependency
    ELSE reject the hypothesis
```

But this approach also has some serious drawbacks:

- it cannot be generalised; each word added to the dictionary has to be compared with all the existing entries to find possible dependencies: recoding of the dictionary is needed.
- the maintenance is nearly as problematic as in the

statistical approach: new application areas, new entries etc. lead to serious adaptation tasks.
- the search direction usually is fixed: pointers lead from the head to its dependent constituents, not the other way round. If the inverse pointers are added, dictionary maintenance becomes even worse.
- syntactic analysis and dictionary are mixed up: dependency relations have also syntactic implications. If they are stored in the dictionary, parts of the syntax have also to be covered. This will lead to redundancies in the whole analysis process.
- there is a problem of redundancy: A new adjective has to be added to all possible nouns, for each noun all the possible modifiers have to be stored; no generalisation (e.g. that you can add an adjective to a noun) can be expressed.

The reason for this disadvantages is that the semantic information is based on words, and not used for classes of words. Again, significant linguistic generalisations cannot be expressed and result in unnecessary efforts for system development and maintenance.

2.3 Semantic grammars

Many systems do not store semantic information in the lexicon but in the grammar. The basic idea is to split the syntactic categories (like NPs) into categories for semantic subclasses: NP <ship> is replaced by <SHIPNP>, NP <fuel> is replaced by <FUELNP> etc. This seems to be just a notational variant of an augmented phrase structure grammar, where subcategories are used for categorial distinctions. The advantage is that only subsets of linguistic units are considered (e.g. not all NP-words but just the SHIP-NP-words); so the analysis can be much more restrictive; and this is the reason why systems like HERASAY, HWIM or HARPY used this representation technique.

In practice, however, things are quite different:
- semantic grammars are also not able to express linguistic generalisations: If an adjective can modify a noun, this information has to be repeated for all semantic classes (SHIPNP-> SHIPADJ SHIPN, FUELNP-> FUELADJ FUELN etc.). This will enlarge the syntax dramatically.
- as a consequence, the linguistic coverage of a system becomes quite unclear: as a syntactic phenomenon has to be repeated for all semantic classes, it is sometimes forgotten; and the users become completely uncertain about the real abilities of the system: Some words can have adjectives attached, others cannot. This was a serious drawback e.g. of the LIFER system in practice.

  As a result, incorrect sentences are allowed, and correct ones are blocked. E.g. the HERASAY grammar AIX15 has the following rules (cf. /HEA 77/):

```
(8)
<SS>             ::= <$ARE> <$ANY.PAPERS> <$ABOUT.TOPIC>
<$ARE>           ::= ARE ¦ ARE NOT ¦ AREN'T
<$ANY.PAPERS>    ::= <ANY ¦ MANY ¦ SOME> <$PAPERS>
<$PAPERS>        ::= <PAPERS> ¦<PAPERS> ON AI ¦
                     <ADJ.PAPER> <PAPERS>
<ADJ.PAPER>      ::= TECHNICAL ¦ COMPUTING SURVEY ¦
                     RECENT
<PAPERS>         ::= ABSTRACTS ¦ BOOKS ¦ SURVEYS
```

This grammar allows for sentences like (9) but blocks NPs like (10):

(9) Are not some computing survey surveys

(10) any recent papers on AI

- semantic grammars also run into maintenance problems: if the application area is changed, not only the "specific" semantic domain but also the general syntax has to be rewritten.

The reason for these shortcomings is that syntactic and semantic levels are mixed up if syntactic-semantic categories are used. Therefore, syntactic phenomena have to be reconsidered every time semantic information is used.

In order to keep the strength of this approach (reduction of search space), a kind of compiler should be written which takes some (semantic) subclassifications and produces the more restrictive semantic grammar automatically. In order to be able to do this, semantic information must be used in an explicit way, e.g. using semantic features.

2.4 Semantic features

The notion of semantic markers is well known in linguistic theory. /KAF 64/ tried to distinguish lexical entries using markers, and they presented a method for deriving the meaning of a sentence according to the set of markers involved in it (amalgamation).

But it is obvious that this theory cannot be used as a real theory of meaning:

- the markers themselves are semantic units: what status do they have? Is there a set of semantic primitives? Or is the definition just circular (on word's markers are "explained" using other words which use the original word as marker)?
- the marker theory cannot explain conflicts due to higher level information like in

  (11) I dreamed I was a spoon

  Here, the amalgamation of "I" (animate) and "spoon" (inanimate) would be blocked.
- The sentence meaning is destroyed if as a result, just a set of features is left at the top node. No difference between (12) and (13) can be found:

  (12) The man kills the tiger

  (13) The tiger kills the man

For these reasons, the marker theory cannot be used as the representation of sentence meaning. But it can be used for the

following purposes:
- elimination of "impossible" readings / combinations of words
- disambiguation of competing readings
- determination of valency slots.

Often, pure syntactic information leads to very many structures which all are possible but do not "make sense". If all of them are generated the system performance goes down rapidly. Semantic markers can make the syntactic analysis more precise and more performant.

There are several criteria for the comparison of the use of features: How they are selected, how they are used for disambiguation of readings, what information a new node obtains, how the feature checking mechanism is integrated into the system. Three examples are considered: SPICOS, EVAR and EUROTRA.

In SPICOS (cf. /MEY 86/), the semantic features are just an unordered set covering the office filing system domain SPICOS deals with. There is a conceptual hierarchy but it is not used in the system. The disambiguation of readings - and the check of combination of possible words - is done by looking up a table where possible combinations are stored, e.g.

```
(14)    <benefactory>       <person>, <organisation>
        <theme>             <area>, <abstract>, <object>
        <source-temporal>   <date>, <event>
```

Such lists exist for certain syntactic combinations, like adjective-noun, noun-noun, NP-PP combinations. If a certain feature of the head can be matched against a corresponding feature of a modifier, this head feature is propagated up to the new node, e.g.

```
(15)               NP
                <person>
                 /     \
              ADJ        N
      <benefactory>  <person>
                     <event>
```

(This might be incorrect if the new node changes its meaning radically. But this did not happen in the SPICOS domain).

The feature check was used within syntactic analysis. The semantic tests were treated just as morphological tests but in a special section of the rules; they could easily be switched on or off. Constructions which were syntactically possible but which were blocked for semantic reasons did not pass the syntactic analysis. This technique turned out to be very efficient; especially with the "best path" input, the semantic tests completely substituted the morphological and agreement tests, even in German.

In EVAR (cf. /BRE 86/), the features are organised in a tree structure according to their conceptual dependencies, as in (16).

Disambiguation and blocking of readings is done according to the criterion that two nodes which are semantically compatible must lay on the same path in the tree: <thing> matches with <concrete> but not with <abstract>. The problem here is that the features do not behave like trees but rather like nets; this complicates the analysis considerably. The feature attached to the new node is formed according to the amalgamation principle (cf. /BRI 84/).

```
(16)                      <nouns>
                         /       \
          <concrete>              <abstract>
           /      \                /  ¦   \
   <animate>    <inanim.>       ...   ¦    ...
    /     \      /      \             ¦
  ...    ... <location> <thing>       ¦
                         /  ¦  \      ¦
                       ...  ... <result>
```

The features are used after the syntactic analysis to the general principle of EVAR, which consists of clearly distinct according layers of analysis. Therefore, they behave like filters for certain syntactic trees (which unfortunately, are all produced).

In EUROTRA-D (which is a machine translation project of the EC), semantic features are used in the following way (cf. /ZEW 86/): The features are built up as a conceptual hierarchy which is supposed to be application-independent. Disambiguation, blocking of rules and attachment of features to the new nodes is done by a special attributed grammar, where rules over features are applied, as in (17).

```
(17)    COUNTABLE  ::=  CATEG1 * CATEG2 * DEFINITION
        DEFINITION ::=  MEASURE / SOCIAL
        CATEG2     ::=  CAUSE / RESULT
        CATEG1     ::=  INDIVIDUATIVE / COMPLEX /
                        PARTITIVE / COLLECTIVE
```

For a node to be countable, at least one of each category CATEG1, CATEG2 and DEFINITION must be present. This technique is more flexible than the SPICOS or EVAR approaches, because the formalism does not force the features into one single kind of treatment.

The feature grammar is used after the syntactic analysis in a special semantic component, which means that first many syntactic trees are produced which do not "make sense".

The three systems just mentioned make additional use of features when trying to build a sentence hypothesis: They try to fill certain slots of verbs with arguments, and these arguments - thematic roles of a verb - are identified using morphological (case), syntactic (position) but also semantic information. Here, semantic features are the strongest sources of restriction of hypotheses. Thematic roles like "agent", "object", "instrument" were introduced into linguistic theory by /FIL 68/ and further developed since - although no valid proposal exists which roles really should be used, and how many there are.

In SPICOS, the assignment of complements for a given set of roles is done using a special verb frame dictionary. For each verb, number and shape of possible complements is stored: NP with a certain case, PP with a certain preposition, presence or absence of semantic features etc. (see /NIE 86/). This information was strong enough to filter the correct sentence out of a word lattice of the top 10 candidates for a given utterance.

Nevertheless, in practical use, many problems have to be solved to make this dictionary useful: What are obligatory, optional and peripheral complements? How to determine which complement fills which role? What about imperatives, where obligatory roles are missing? What about the discontinuous verbs in German (a separate prefix on a legal path must be found in the acoustic input, before the verb frame can be opened)? What about elliptical expressions? What about syntactic ambiguities, e.g. in

(18) He saw a man with a telescope,

where the PP could be attached to the S-node if it were a verb complement (and marked as such in the dictionary, although it might not be even optional in a strict sense. And, when can be decided that a frame has been filled sufficiently?

To give an example of the interaction between features an verb frames, in (19) the frame for "write" is given:

(19)

```
   Role:   Agent                              Role: Benefactory
   Syntax: Subject                            Syntax: PP-to/Indir.Obj
   Sem.Feature: <human>                       Sem. Feature: <human>
   Status: obligatory              /          Status: optional
                                /
              \              /                Role: Object
               \          /                   Syntax: Dir.Object
                  WRITE  ------               Sem. Feature:<document>
                /        \                     Status: optional
   Role: Time                \
   Syntax: PP-on + <day>        \          Role: Topic
           PP-in + <month>                 Syntax: PP-about
   Sem.Feature: <date>                     Sem.Feature: <abstract>
   Status: optional                        Status: optional
```

Even in this small example, set up to cover sentences like

(20) Peter wrote to Paul

(21) Peter wrote Paul a letter about Syntax

for each role a counterexample can be given (e.g. "Topic": How to express that if "computers" (surely <concrete>) become a topic, they are something "abstract"? In imperatives, the only obligatory role is missing. How to express this fact? How to make sure that it is "on" 15th but "in" May? etc.

To sum up this overview, the following conclusions can be drawn:

1. If semantic information is to be added to a recognition system, it should be done in an explicit way, not just implicitly (in dictionary or in semantic grammars). The system becomes much more flexible, and many maintenance problems are avoided. The use of semantic features seems to be the best alternative. (They can be compiled into more effectice structures at runtime).

2. Semantic features are no representation of sentence meaning, but they are good means to block incorrect readings and to determine possible complements for verb frames.

3. They should model the problem domain as well as possible. Insofar, they are application-dependent. But this is a clearly defined part of a system which can be handled in a clear way. No other component (syntax, dictionary structure) is involved in a change. Tools for building up these domain models semi-automatically have recently been proposed (/GRI 86/).

4. The combination of features, determination of readings etc. should be done explicitly, using a context-free (or even finite-state) grammar as in EUROTA-D. This allows a clear modelling of their behaviour, without the restrictions of a formalism which is conceptually inadequate.

5. The application of the filter of semantic features should be done within the syntactic analysis in order to make the processing more compact and to avoid the production of senseless syntactic structures. This requires a clear structure of syntactic rules, where additional tests can easily be added or removed.

3. FORMAL SEMANTIC THEORIES USED IN SPEECH UNDERSTANDING

There are many approaches for knowledge representation, most of which deal with natural language structures (see /BLO 86/). From the point of view of Speech Understanding, all of them have in common that they are not used for recognition (except valency theories, cf. /SHI 86/), and that they operate on syntactic trees which they interpret. This means that they are syntax-based.

The representation techniques which were used in Speech Understanding were originally ad-hoc-representations, like in HEARSAY or HWIM, with an unclear theoretical status. Later, knowledge representation techniques became more formal.

In the following section, two possible approaches which are used in Speech Understanding are presented: predicate logic (SPICOS) and case frames (EVAR, DARPA). A third possibility, semantic networks, is presented by Sagerer (in this volume).

3.1 Predicate logic in the SPICOS system

SPICOS is a speech understanding system with continuous speech, 1000 word vocabulary, speaker-dependent, 20 times realtime. It is a database query system on an office task (personal filing systems); the queries are recognised acoustically, interpreted linguistically and given to the database. The result of the query is used to generate a natural language output which is given to a speech synthesis component and transformed into voice output. The first system was successfully demonstrated in June 86. (see Ney, Hoege, Paeseler, Niedermair in this volume).

The architecture of the linguistic component is as follows (see /DRE 86/ for further description of the syntactic components):

(22)

```
      input:                                          input:
      word lattice                                    best path
                   \                                /
                     \                            /
   morpho-syntactic        step 1:                    syntactic
   dictionary, incl. ->  constituent         <--      constituent
   semant. features        parsing                    rules
                   \          |
                     \        |
     verb frame            step 2:                    syntactic
     dictionary    -->    sentence           <--      sentence
                           parsing                    rules
                              |
                              |
     surface    -->    surface semantic      <--      semantic
    semantic            interpretation                rules
    dictionary
```

Parsing of a sentence is done in two steps. First, constituents are built (NP, PP etc.): they have a rather stable internal structure and their words are adjacent to each other (i.e. they can be searched from left to right). Every time there is an indication for a possible NP or PP, the analysis starts and tries to process it from left to right; it is a combination of island and left-to-right parsing. An active chart structure is used for control; it is an adapted version of /WIN 82/.

When the nominal constituents are built, the chart is cleaned up (which turns out to be very necessary in Speech Understanding) and initiated with the NPs / PPs found so far. Then possible verbal and sentential elements are searched and also tried to be parsed left-to-right. Here, the analysis has to cope with discontinuous verbs or structures (see Bunt in this volume), with verb frames, problems of variable constituent order (German!) etc.

In this stage, the verb frame dictionary is used. For each verb (and also noun), the following information ist stored: thematic role, its syntactic realisation, its case, its preposition, the semantic type of its filler, and its status (see /NIE 86/). It is used to attach arguments to verbs properly and to restrict possible readings, as desrcibed above. This dictionary is application-dependent in its content, but not in its structure; and to switch the application is a clearly defined operation over this dictionary.

SPICOS uses an augmented phrase structure grammar with more than 200 rules which are grouped according to common features. There are tests for sets of rules and tests for single rules. These tests include morphological (agreement), syntactic and semantic (feature, verb frame) tests. If a rule can fire, a formal description of the node to be built is given. To each syntactic rule, a semantic rule part is attached which determines the semantic representation of the constituent.

As tests can be switched on and off, the analysis can work with both best-path and word lattice input. But it cannot cover the problem of missing words.

A SPICOS rule looks as in (23):

(23)

```
   Phrase Structure:
                             a:ADJECTIVE  b:NOUN  -->  r:NOUN
   Common syntactic restrictions:
                             {a.morphol.} + {b.morphol.}  <>  0
   Common semantic  restrictions:
                             {a.sem-cat} FITS {b.sem-cat}
   Subrule 1:
   Example:                  new letters
   additional condition:     b.sem-cat <> abstract
   carry-over:               b.ALL; b.sem-cat
   semantic rule:            {x e b' ¦ a' (x)}
   Subrule 2:
   Example:                  semantic nets
   additional condition:     b.sem-cat + abstract <> 0
   carry-over:               b.ALL; b.sem-cat
   semantic-rule:            CONCAT (<a', b'>)
```

This means that an adjective and a noun forms a noun if the intersection of the morphological features (gender, number, case, inflection) is not empty (i.e. there is agreement), and if the semantic categories can be combined (FITS is an operator that triggers the table lookup for the semantic features). If the noun is not abstract, then subrule 1 is successful: The new node obtains all the features of the old noun node, and also its semantic features; and a semantic representation is built according to the semantic rule part (in this case, a set expression). If the noun is abstract, the same carry-over is performed, but the semantic rule will not build a set expression (it does not make sense to speak of "the elements of a set of nets which are semantic") but a concatenated expression (which will be a constant again).

If a sentence hypothesis has been found, the syntactic tree is transformed into a semantic tree according to the rules described below. To do this, a semantic lexicon is used.

The semantics used in SPICOS is based on representations developed in /BUN 85/: It is a type oriented predicate calculus using lambda abstraction. It was first tried out in the TENDUM system but had to be extended for the SPICOS application (cf. /BRO 86/), e.g. to cover imperatives. It is also able to cover dialogue phenomena (see Bunt in this volume). This representation language is called "Ensemble Language" in /BUN 85/.

To each syntactic rule, a semantic counterpart is given which specifies how the meaning of the constituent is built from the meanings of its dependent node. This process starts out from a semantic dictionary and is continued recursively up to the top node.

The semantic dictionary contains the representations of the single words, some of which are more complex (e.g.

determiners, quantifiers), some are just constants (like most of the "content" words).

For the string "new red books", the dictionary would contain the constants "new", "red", and "books", and the rule given in (23) would first produce the set expression (24), and in a second application (note that it is recursive!), the set expression (25) would be produced (because in the second rule application, the "b'" correspondes to the first set).

(24) {x e books ¦ red (x)}

(25) {y e {x e books ¦ red (x)} ¦ new (y)}

An example grammar is given in /BUN 85/, and an early version of the semantic parts of the SPICOS rules is presented in /MEY 86/. The application of the semantic parts of the rules is done after the syntactic analysis (in order to avoid calculating semantic representations for constituents which are not used at the end); and it is simply a recursive conversion of the syntactic tree into a semantic tree by applying the semantic rule part at the respective tree node. The result is a surface semantic representation of a given sentence.

The next steps of the analysis are performed as described in (26):

(26)

```
                              surface semantic
                              representation
                                    ¦        <--  application dependent
                                    ¦             dictionary
 semantic type                 deep semantic
 dictionary    -->            representations
                                    ¦
                                    ¦
 domain database <-->   dialogue        <-- user model
 (office filing)        interpretation      update
                        and planning          ¦
                              ¦               ¦
                              ¦               ¦
                           answer        <---
                         generation
                              ¦                  synthesis
                     speech synthesis  <---  dictionary
```

The surface semantic represenation is application-independent and mirrors the logical relations of the constituents of the sentence. But given a certain application (e.g. a specific database), it might be still ambiguous. This is not due to the fact that the language is ambiguous; but its constants have to be disambiguated. In (27)

(27) {x e letters ¦ of (x, Paul)} (letters of Paul)

the constants "letters", "of" and "Paul" might be ambiguous, given a certain database application. "Letters" might mean a document_type but also a "topic", "of" might mean authorship but also membership (as in "members OF Siemens"), and "Paul" might be an author but also a sender_of_document and a recipient_of_document, etc. This depends on the kind of organisation of the database.

The disambiguation of the surface semantic structure is done by a context-free replacement of its constants by application-dependent expressions of the same formal language. This is done by means of a dictionary which translates surface semantic constants into deep/application-semantic expressions with constants which refer to the database.

As ambiguities exist in the surface semantic representation, some expressions will have more than one translation. The incorrect readings are ruled out by means of a semantic type checking procedure, which uses a type dictionary where compatibilities of semantic types are stored.

The expression in (27) would be translated into the expression (29) which could be interpreted by the database; the following dictionary would be used (28). The interpretion "person_lab" for "OF" is blocked by the type checking mechanism.

```
   (28) LETTERS:    {x e documents ¦ doc_type (x) = letter}
        OF:         doc_author (x1) = x2
                    person_lab (x1) = x2
   (29) {x e {y e documents ¦ doc_type(y) = letter} ¦
                                  doc_author (x) = PAUL}
```

This means in a recursive evaluation: Search in the "documents" file for fields named "doc_type" containing the value "letter"; of these, search in the "author" field for the value "PAUL". (The variable x is bound to the key numbers).

The expression (29) uses the same formal language than (27), but its constants are not ambiguous any more; they can be interpreted by the database evaluation component. This also means that they are application- specific, whereas the formal language as a whole is not.

The result of the sentence interpretation is a deep semantic structure. This structure is passed to the dialogue planning component. This component was taken over from the TENDUM system (cf /BEU 85/) and performs the following steps:

First, it tries to interpret the dialogue acts. It uses syntactic clues (word order), lexical clues (special particles), and prosodic information (if available; not in SPICOS I), to determine what kind of dialogue act was performed. Possible acts are "Yes-No-Question", "WH-Question", "Check", "Imperative" etc. If the kind of dialogue act is recognised, the system's user model is updated by using special epistemic operators (see Bunt in this volume).

If the system recognises that a database query has to be performed, the recursive database evaluation is triggered, resulting in different kinds of expressions (e.g. a set of items for WH-questions, a truth value for YN-questions etc.) (Imperatives are a tricky problem here, see /BRO 86/).

When the database query is evaluated, the system has to plan the answer. This is performed by interpreting the user model and the result of the database query. E.g. if a WH-question was performed, the dialogue planning component recognises that a WH-inform speech act has to be performed, containing the items found from the database query. The PLANNER takes this information and produces a natural language answer. To do this, some transformations on the input string are carried out (changing the word order etc.). The dialogue and planning component and also the answer generation will be improved considerably in the following SPICOS versions.

At the end, the output string is given to the speech synthesis component; it is transformed into a sequence of sounds by means of a synthesis dictionary (including word accent), constituent boundaries are added, and then, the answer is synthesised.

If the SPICOS approach as a whole is considered, the following conclusions can be drawn:

The semantic component of SPICOS is domain-independent (this can be seen from the fact that it was transformed from an airplane application in TENDUM to an office filing application in SPICOS without problems). It allows a clear and well-defined distinction between general and domain-specific knowledge, using an explicit surface-to-deep-structure conversion procedure. It allows representation of quantifiers, questions, declarative and imperative sentences in a very natural way; and it is usable for the generation of answers and for dialogue acts.

On the other hand, there are several features which make this approach problematic in a speech environment: The main problem is that this approach is bottom-up, compositional, and interpretive: It builds its semantic representations according to a syntactic tree. Therefore, it presupposes that the input is syntactically well-formed - which is not always the case in speech. Second, it depends strongly on function words like prepositions, determiners etc.; but these words are very difficult to recognise. Third, no top-down prediction is possible with this kind of semantics, which means that no top down support for recognition can be given from this kind of representations.

In SPICOS, these disadvantages were compensated by several other semantic components (features, verb frames etc.) to make the formal language work properly. This leads to certain redundancy phenomena (e.g. compatibility checks), but in the end, the system performes as it is supposed to do: Wrong readings are blocked, correct readings are interpreted and answered.

3.2 Frame semantics (DARPA)

In the new DARPA Speech project, a different kind of representation has been selected: Here, frames are the basic objects of interpretation (cf /HAY 86/). Frames have names, instances (which can be other frames), types, syntactic and semantic cases, as in (30) (the application here is a mailing system). "MsgObj" (message-object) is itself a frame like in (31).

These structures are similar to the verb frames in SPICOS, but they add lexical material to their slots, and they are immediately used to build up semantic representations (whereas in SPICOS, they are just used for proper syntactic analysis).

```
(30) #S
       Name:    Forward_action
       Type:    Verb                                      FORWARDS
       Semantic_Cases (
               #S
                       Name:         Agent               PROF. NEY
                       InstanceOf:   MailAdrDescr
                       SyntCase:     Subject
               #S
                       Name:         MsgObj
                       InstanceOf:   MsgObjDesc (!)  A MESSAGE
                       SyntCase:     DirectObject
               #S
                       Name:         MsgRecipientObj   TO  HIM
                       InstanceOf:   MailAdrDescr
                       SyntCase:     IndirectObject
                       CaseMarker:   to
               )
       Headforms: forward resend

(31) #S
       Name:     MsgObjDesc
       Type:     noun
       Semantic_Cases (
               #S
                       Name:          Descriptors
                       Pattern:       new recent old examined
                       SyntCase:      prenominal
               #S
                       Name:          Determiners
                       Pattern:       the this a any every
                       SyntCase:      prenominal
               #S
                       Name:          MsgOriginObj
                       InstanceOf:    MailAdrDescr
                       CaseMarker:    from
                       SyntCase:      PP-O
               )
       Headforms: message mail
```

The idea is to support a top down search where certain frames are instantiated whenever certain clue words are found. If a frame is instantiated, the system tries to fill it by recursively instantiating its dependent frames, or by filling its slots with lexical material ("patterns").

The advantages of this approach are the following: This representation supports predictions (lexical material at certain places in the input); it performs its search via the heads of constituents, which are easier to recognise than function words; and it is able to deal with incomplete or ill-formed input to a certain extent.

Nevertheless, there are serious drawbacks from this approach: The search problems have been clearly neglected: All the examples given use imperative constructions where the first word opens the top frame which is used to control the rest of the input. But if we think of declarative sentences or questions, with discontinuous verb elements (which have to be found first in order to instantiate a frame) and with ambiguous case markers (not just evaluating word order), then the search gets very difficult, and it will end up with a lot of frames instantiated and partly filled with input, and the control of these chains of frames still seems to be an open question.

Moreover, there are several linguistic problems which are unsolved: Like the systems mentioned above (see 2.2 and 2.3), linguistic regularities cannot be expressed: For every frame like "Message-Object-Description", the information has to be stored that a determiner or an adfjective can be added. This leads to a repetitive action if a new determiner or adjective is added to the system. Also, things like quantifier scope cannot be handled properly within this approach: A basic item for every database query system! In general, the formal status of these frame representations is quite unclear.

Third, all the maintenance problems mentioned above (2.2 and 2.3) come up again: The whole analysis is application dependent, dictionary and syntax are merged in an unclear way, etc.

The consequence is that a method has to be found to keep the advantages of this apporach (top down prediction capability) without taking over its disadvantages.

4. TWO PROPOSALS FOR POSSIBLE STRATEGIES

If we consider all the effort carried out in semantics for speech understanding, two possible strategies can be concluded: Either linguistic techniques try to support the restriction of search space for acoustic analysis, or they take the leading part and perform a top down control of the search process. The first way is safer to end up with a running system, the second way might be more interesting for longer term research.

4.1 Support for Search Restriction

This approach tries to integrate all linguistic knowledge into an effective search strategy (e.g. beam search) for the acoustic component. The system architecture will look similar to HARPY, but the network to be searched will be produced according to clear procedures which integrate all the knowledge sources needed. This system would look like the following:

First, all the possible word sequences are produced as input for the acoustic search. This means to write compilers which transform a grammar together with its semantic features and tests into a network (this can be done before runtime, which will end in a very big net, or just at runtime, using a predictive parsing). The nonterminal nodes of the grammar would be replaced by their terminals, the terminals would be replaced by their lexical entries; and all the morphological, syntactic and semantic restrictions would be propagated down the tree to narrow the selection of the lexical material. The network compiled that way would contain only grammatical sentences (which could be analysed by the grammar and interpreted by a semantic component). The compilation could be carried out by using a modified Earley algorithm (cf Paeseler, in this volume). The result would be a language model like generated automatically from a grammar.

The second step will be to do a best-path search which seems to be the most eficient kind of search available at present.

Then, the output of the search will have to be reconstucted somehow. Linguistic techniques can be used for error-correction; here, semantic means and dialogue information will be needed.

Finally, the reconstructed sentence can be given to a semantic interpretation component, transformed into a representation language, and evaluated; on this basis, an answer can be generated.

This approach (which will be tried out in SPICOS, cf. Niedermair, in this volume) will come up with an effective state-of-the-art system, but several problems will remain (besides of the technical problem of the size of the network): What about missing words or uncertain parts of the input? Something will always be hypothesised, but it might be incorrect: How can these parts of the input be detected? What about dialogue acts? How can the system react on dialogue sequences? Do we provide different nets for different dialogue acts (e.g. if just digits or a yes/no answer is expected)? All these problems are far from being solved.

4.2 Top down control of search

The only possible alternative I can see is to control the analysis from the very top of all the knowledge and search just for the events the system is interested in. This fits to experiences with "real life" dialogues in EVAR: A train scheduling system, above all, is interested in the target station (just as a human is) and will search for it whatever the input might be; a lot of the input is simply skipped (like "Hello my name is..."). This would mean that the system needs a clear imagination of what to search for, derived form a discourse model; and that its search is guided by this model. Up to now, no system uses discourse or even semantic information to control search; the usual "top level" is syntactic analysis, certainly ot the best level as the problem of ill-formed input shows.

A system which consequently works top down could look like the following:

First, a model of the application or discourse has to be built, where all the topics of interest, strategies to ask for them, dialogue steps etc. are laid down. (For techniques of discourse representation, see Hoeppner, in this volume).

Second, this model is instantiated with likely hypotheses; they are linguistically based. E.g. in an office filing context it is likely that the user wants to search for files. Possible hypotheses (document names or types etc.) could be derived from this assumption. (If later on, no such things are found in the input, the basic assumptions have to be revised according to fall-back routines in the discourse model).

These hypotheses then are searched in the acoustic input. In order to be able to do this, a gross acoustic analysis has to be performed, as propposed in /SHI 86/ or Haton (in this volume). If a match is found, a more extensive acoustic verification can be done. Also, prosodic information can be used as topics of interest in the discourse mostly are marked by prosodic means (see /NOE 87/). The result of this step are "islands" which are based on discourse relevance, not just acoustic recognition scores.

Once these clues have been found, these islands can be extended by searching for possible contexts or complements. Here, frame representations could be used. The problem of frame instantiation could be reduced by using appropriate dialogue steps: The system can ask back for certain fillers of frames to make sure it is on the right path (see /HAT 80/ for a possible solution). If all the information needed has been collected, the next dialogue step can be performed (e.g. a database query).

There are many problems in this approach, like prediction of search clues from a discourse model, searching using frames, formal interpretation of the search results etc.; but it is worth investigating it as up to now, no approach has been made to really use discourse and semantic information consequently to do a top down search in Speech Understanding, just as the human beings do.

ACKNOWLEDGEMENTS

The work of the linguistic component of SPICOS reported here was done by G.Brockhoff, G.Dreckschmidt, M.Meya, G.Niedermair, M.Streit, G.Thurmair (all Siemens Munich), K. van Deemter, J. de Vet (IPO Eindhoven) and H. Bunt (Tilburg Univ.).

LITERATURE

/BEU 85/ R.J.Beun: PLANNER: ontwerp en implementatie van een systeem voor hat genereren vam dialooghandelingen. IPO-Report 472, Eindhoven 1985
/BLO 86/ U.Block, M.Gehrke, H.Haugeneder, R.Hunze: Wissensrepraesentationen im natuerlichsprachlichen Beratungssystem WISBER. Siemens Report 1986
/BRI 84/ A.Brietzmann: Semantische und pragmatische Analyse im Erlanger Spracherkennungsprojekt. Erlangen 1984
/BRE 86/ A.Brietzmann, U.Ehrlich:The Role of Semantic Processing in an Automatic Speech Understanding System. Proc. COLING Bonn 1986
/BRO 86/ C.J. van Deemter, G.Brockhoff, H.Bunt, M.Meya, J. de Vet: From TENDUM to SPICOS. IPO Annual Progress Report 1985.
/BUN 85/ H. Bunt: Mass Nouns and Model Theoretic Semantics. Cambridge Univ. Press 1985
/COO 76/ W. Cooper: Speech Timing of Coreference. Proc. IEEE Philadelphia 76
/DRE 87/ G. Dreckschmidt: The Linguistic Component in the Speech Understanding System SPICOS. Proc GLDV 1987 Bonn (in: H.Tillmann, G.Willee: Analyse und Synthese gesprochener Sprache. Hildesheim 1987).
/FIL 68/ Ch. Filmore: A Case for Case. 1968
/FIB 86/ P. Fink, A. Biermann: The correction of ill-formed input using History based Expectation with Applications to Speech Understanding. Computational Linguistics 12/1986
/FUJ 86/ H.Fujisaki, K.Hirose, H.Udagawa, N.Kanedera: A new approach to continuous Speech Recognition based on Considerations on Human Process of Speech Perception. Proc. ICASSP 86 Tokyo
/GRI 86/ R. Grishman, L.Hirshman, N. Thanh Nanh: Discovery Procedures of Sublanguage Selectional Patterns. Computational Linguistics 12/86
/HAR 84/ T.Harley: A Critique of top-down levels of speech production. Cognitive Science 8/1984
/HAT 86/ K.Hatazaki, T.Watanabe: A Linguistic Processor for Japanese Speech Recognition. Proc. ICASSP 1986 Tokyo
/HAT 82/ J.Haton, J.Pierrel, S.Sabbagh: Semantic and Pragmatic Processing in Continuous Speech Understanding. in: J.Haton, ed.: Automatic Speech Analysis and Recognition. Reidel 1982
/HAY 86/ Ph. Hayes, A.Hauptmann, J. Carbonell, J.Tomita: Parsing Spoken Language, A Semantic Caseframe Approach. Proc COLING 1986 Bonn
/HEA 77/ HEARSAY-Report 1976: Speech Understanding Systems. Summary of Results
/KAF 64/ J.Katz, J.Fodor: The structure of a semantic theory. Language 1963
/MEY 86/ M.Meya: The Semantics of SPICOS. Siemens Report 1986
/MUD 84/ J.Mudler, E.Paulus: Entwicklung und Erprobung der erwartungsorientierten Analyse fuer die automatische Spracherkennung. Sprache und Datenverarbeitung 8,1984
/NIE 86/ G.Niedermair: Divided and Valency-oriented Parsing in Speech Understanding. Proc. COLING 1986 Bonn
/NOE 87/ E.Noeth, A.Batliner, R.Lang, W.Oppenrieder: Automatische Grundfrequenzanalysen und Satzmodusdifferen-

zierung. Proc. GLDV Bonn 1987
/SHI 86/ M.Shigenaga et al.: A Speech Recognition System for Continuously spoken Japanese Sentences - Speech Yamanashi. Japan IECE Transactions, 69, 1986
/WIN 82/ T.Winograd: Language as a Cognitive Process. 1982
/WOO 80/ J. Wolf, W.Woods: The HWIM Speech Understanding System. in: W. Lea, ed: Automatic Speech Recognition. London 1980
/ZEW 86/ C.Zelinski-Wibbelt: An Empririically based Approach towards a system of Semantic Features. Proc. COLING 1986 Bonn

KNOWLEDGE BASED SYSTEMS FOR SPEECH UNDERSTANDING

G. Sagerer, F. Kummert
Lehrstuhl für Informatik 5 (Mustererkennung)
Universität Erlangen-Nürnberg
Martensstrasse 3
8520 Erlangen, F.R. Germany

Abstract: Based on a detailled discussion of system architectures for knowledge based speech understanding and knowledge representation techniques, criteria for both a knowledge representation scheme and system architectures are developed. Upon this background a system is introduced which is organized around a homogenuous knowledge base. Both the knowledge representation language and the content of the knowledge base are described. The knowledge representation language do not only cover declarative but also procedural knowledge. Analysis processes are guided by a flexibel bottom-up top-down strategy. Besides the procedural semantics of the language the A^*-Algorithm is used for this purpose. Search graph nodes are judged by a vector which reflects knowledge dependent and acoustic scores and which is admissable for the A^*-Algorithm.

1. INTRODUCTION

The term "knowledge based speech understanding" is strongly related to the first ARPA Speech Understanding Reseach Project /LEA 80a/. A number of different system architectures were developed and applied to speech understanding tasks. Architectures like the blackboard model of Hearsay-II /ERM 80a/ were also adopted to other problems like Computer Vision /KIM 84a/. But independent of speech applications, knowledge based systems were studied with great effort in the last years. Especially the technology of Expert Systems /HAY 82a, WAT 86a/ influenced the development of systems in the speech recognition /DEM 83a, MER 85a/ and understanding area /MCC 81a, NIE 86a/. The progress in knowledge representation resulted in different powerful approaches /MCC 83a/. Schemes and languages developed in this area are of increasing influence on natural language and speech understanding systems /THU 88a/. Besides these successful mutual effects between speech understanding systems and knowledge based

NATO ASI Series, Vol. F46
Recent Advances in Speech Understanding
and Dialog Systems
Edited by H. Niemann et al.

systems in general, a gap arose during the last years inside the speech understanding community. Perhaps based on the success of the Harpy /LOW 80a/ and the IBM /BAH 83a/ systems concerning the recognition rate of spoken texts, the recognition and the understanding of speech were more and more treated as two sequential, not cooperating and not interacting tasks /RAB 88a, SCH 88a/.

All these systems are based on a left to right analysis of the input signal. Linguistic knowledge is precompiled and implicitly used during the recognition process. If we change from spoken texts to dialog oriented systems, analysis becomes more complicated. Background of the following investigations to this problem is the system EVAR. EVAR is the abbreviation of the German words for recognition, understanding, answering, asking back. It is designed as speech understanding and dialog system with IC-train schedule information as discourse domain. Additionally, EVAR shall satisfy the following requirements: speaker independence, use of continuous speech, about 4000 words in the lexicon, use of linguistic knowledge. The different modules of this system together with a bottom-up control strategy are described in /NIE 85a/. The results generated by various modules and the experiences with the system initiated and strongly effected the considerations of this paper. The main points can be summarized as follows:

- A 100% recognition rate is not achievable at the word level with an acceptable number of word hypothesis.
- The "optimum" with respect to the recognition rate for words, word chains, or complete utterances is not necessarily the "optimum" with respect to the understanding task, if there is no feed back.
- If a grammar for conversational speech exists, it is different from the grammar of the corresponding natural language.
- Even if an utterance is syntactically wrong and/or uncomplete, it is understandable. That means, semantic and pragmatic knowledge is more important than syntactical one.
- Linguistic knowledge can constrain the complexity of the recognition process by giving restrictions and priorities for hypothesis. This capability is not sufficiently used in a bottom-up process.

Therefore, I agree with the following statements given in /GOO 80a/:

"We know that all the available **sources of knowledge must communicate** in the presence of error and uncertainty. ... The problem of **control** in a speech understanding system refers to **how knowledge is organized, activated and focused** to constrain the search. ... The **direction of knowledge flow** is not necessarily from a lower level to a higher level. ... some common representation is necessary if knowledge sources are to interact cooperatively." Contrary to the recognition of spoken texts, cooperation between signal related recognition processes and symbol related understanding processes is necessary to understand spoken utterances in a dialog situation. Therefore, we have to look for system architectures and knowledge representation schemes which **support the integration and flexible cooperation of knowledge and algorithms** developed in both, the speech recognition and the natural language understanding field. Since knowledge and algorithms are well described in other papers of this volume, e.g. /SCH 88a, THU 88a/ this paper will be mainly concerned with the problems of organization, activation, and focusing of the knowledge and the algorithms, in order to develop an architecture for a speech understanding system which fulfils the required properties.

In Section 2 different aspects of knowledge based systems will be discussed with respect to the speech understanding problem. Considering the integration and cooperation of algorithms and different kinds of knowledge, schemes for knowledge representation will be examined in Section 3. Based on the criteria evaluated in both sections **an active homogenuous knowledge base** will be developed in Section 4. This knowledge base is the kernel of the speech understanding system described in Section 5. Some remarks on the computer realization and a first test will conclude the paper.

2. SOME ASPECTS OF KNOWLEDGE BASED SYSTEMS

Generally spoken, the goal of speech understanding is to compute a symbolic description of those contents of a speech signal which are relevant for a given application. Therefore, for information dialogs it is not necessary to interpret the complete signal, but it is sufficient to extract a symbolic description which allows to continue the dialog in an appropriate way. Besides general linguistic knowledge like acoustic-phonetic, syntax, and semantics, the system has to cover pragmatical knowledge about the discourse domain, knowledge about dialog strategies, and about the former utterances of the actual dialog. The speech understanding task in this situation therefore requires an **explicit representation and an efficient use** of all this **knowledge** by the system. If we try to organize the declarative and procedural (algorithmic) knowledge, we can attack these problems under different viewpoints. First of all, we can seperate different modules from a processing oriented point of view. Contrary, system activities can be grouped around the different kinds of knowledge stored in or created by the system. Both organization principles are independent of speech specific knowledge. The third way is a problem dependent organization. The system is divided into several modules, and each module is related to one level of knowledge like syntax or semantics.

2.1 Organization with Processing Oriented Modules

Fig. 2-1 shows a system architecture which is quite common to most knowledge based systems /NIE 81a/. It is basically built up of the following four modules:

METHODS for doing low level processing like feature extraction, preprocessing, and segmentation. It can also cover more complex algorithms e.g. to calculate distance or similarity measures between a hypothesis and the signal.

KNOWLEDGE to support the understanding process by facts and algorithms (declarative and procedural knowledge).

CONTROL for determining a processing strategy by activating the appropriate algorithms at the proper time using a relevant subset of declarative knowledge and intermediate results.

RESULT DATA BASE for storing the results of processing and making them available to processing algoritms as necessary.

There are several schemes for **knowledge representation** (rules, formal grammars, ATNs, semantic networks, logic), and several **control** strategies and algorithms (backtracking, A^*, heuristics, rules, resolution). The organization of the **result data base** usually depends on the knowledge representation scheme. Some special **methods** may be required by the control algorithm which is used. But in principle,

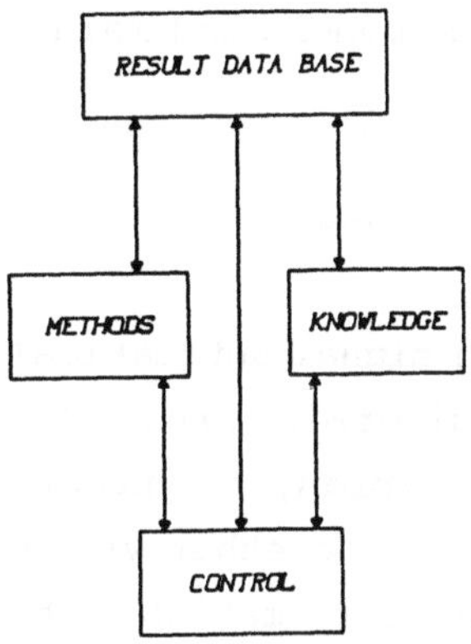

Fig.2-1: Architecture for Pattern Analysis Systems

declarative knowledge	procedural knowledge	a posteriori knowledge
conceptions	inferences	instances
features	extraction,combination	feature values
scheme for judgements	calculation and combination scheme and functions	values
constraints	propagation	restrictions

Fig.2-2: Components of Knowledge

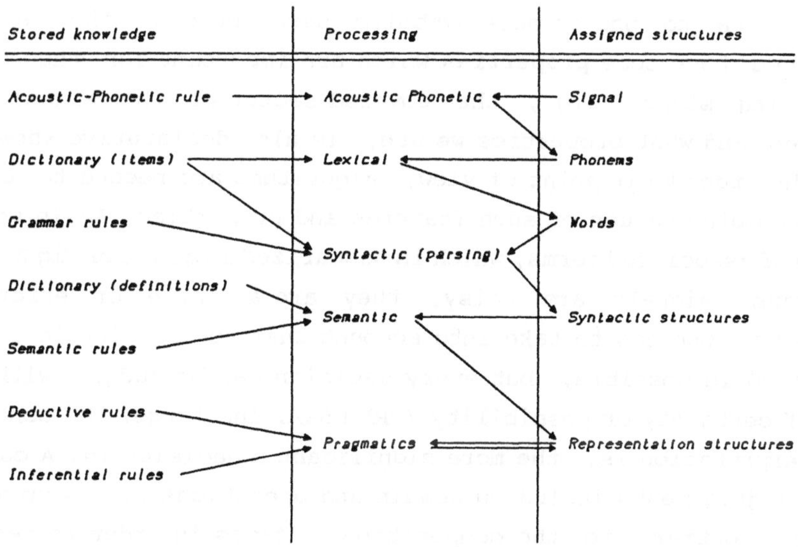

Fig.2-3: Stratified Linguistic Model

the four modules are independent of each other. Nevertheless, the behaviour of the complete system depends on each module and mainly on their cooperative interaction.

2.2 Organization along Different Aspects of Knowledge

In order to achieve descriptions of a speech signal automatically, different aspects of knowledge have to be considered. First of all, there are linguistic **conceptions** like words, syntactical constituents, verb frames, semantic classes etc. Together with task specific conceptions like train schedule information, these conceptions have to be modelled. For an analysis process, **inference processes** are needed to use this knowledge. Based on the a priori known conceptions and on the input signal, **instances** of conceptions are created by these processes. Thus we obtain a triple of associated knowledge aspects: **declarative knowledge** (conceptions), **procedural knowledge** (inferences), and **a posteriori knowledge** (instances). Furthermore, signals have to be transformed into a symbolic description (e.g. words) to initiate the inference processes. For this task **features** are needed. Additionally, if we associate some signal area to one or more symbolic descriptions, the resulting instances have some **properties** which are important for the further processing steps; e.g., the covered sector of the signal. What features and what properties we use, is also declarative knowledge. From the procedural point of view, algorithms are needed to extract and to combine values of such features and properties. Again we get a triple of associated terms, which is summarized in a line of Fig 2-2.

Because signals are noisy, they are a source of errors and ambiguity. One has to take into account that no decision in terms of YES or NO is possible, but every decision can be judged with some kind of certainty or possibility /PRA 85a/. The larger the context of an interpretation is, the more significant a decision is. A calculus for such **judgements** including domain and operations builds up a third triple. Contrary to the composition of facts in order to get more complex interpretations, there are **constraints** which are propagated by such interpretations. E.g., it is a priori known that a noun group can be built up of a noun and adjectives. If additionally the noun is known, the adjectives of the group can be restricted to those ones which are compatible with the detected noun. Therefore, a constraint can be propagated and this process results in a situation dependend **restriction** on the adjectives.

The described aspects are grouped in Fig.2-2. The a priori knowledge of a system consists of the declarative and procedural components mentioned in this figure. If a module KNOWLEDGE is able to cover and connect these aspects, the module CONTROL is reduced to a monitor, which just activates some processes dependending on the actual situation of the analysis process. Furthermore, most of the METHODS are integrated into the module KNOWLEDGE, and the organization of the RESULT DATA BASE strongly depends on the knowledge representation scheme. Because the system is centered around the module KNOWLEDGE, we extend the demand for "some common representation" (compare section 1.) to the following statement:

> A knowledge representation scheme must cover and connect all the knowledge components shown in Fig.2-2 to support an efficient cooperative interaction between the different components.

The main advantage of this organization principle is, that the communication problem is reduced to the **interactions within the module KNOWLEDGE.** If one knowledge representation language is able to fulfil this statement, most of the problems concerning a cooperative interaction are solved.

2.3 Organization along Levels of Knowledge

A **stratified model of language comprehension** is described in /WIN 83a/. According to this model, the knowledge for speech understanding is made up of levels of procedural and declarative knowledge, that transform the speech signal stepwise into a final interpretation. Fig.2-3 shows such a model with the levels Acoustic-Phonetic, Lexical Retrieval, Syntax, Semantics, and Pragmatics. The advantage of such a model is the modularity in order to get a flexible and expandable system architecture. But in /WIN 83a/ it is pointed out also: "What is needed for effective integration of the levels is a **uniform definition for the structures** that the components accept as input and produce as output", and furthermore that the processing sequence should be separated from the structural levels. The reason for the second point is also given: "Many experiments have demonstrated that in listening to speech we often **use knowledge of the expected meaning** as an aid in analyzing the sounds in order to decipher the words of the message." There are different possibilities for the required uniform definition for the structures and for a flexible processing sequence.

In Hearsay-II the **blackboard architecture** was introduced. All the modules (also called components or knowledge sources) communicate with each other only via the blackboard. All processing results are written on this structured memory. For the further processing they can be read by other modules. Also, all other kind of communication between modules can only be done via the blackboard. Therefore, the structure of the input and the output of all modules have to be unified. The advantage of this architecture is the modularity. The main disadvantage is that the problem of errors and ambiguity are more or less neglected. There is no explicit CONTROL module, which is able to regulate the activities of the different modules towards a given goal and therefore to manage the search process. Contrary, the **HWIM-architecture** /WOL 80a/ groups the system around a central CONTROL strategy. Only three modules are separated to cover the components of the stratified model. A uniform structure is used to represent the syntactical, the semantic, and the pragmatic knowledge. All these components are integrated into one augmented transition network (ATN) /WOO 70a/. The modules for acoustic-phonetic processing and lexical retrieval are sequentially ordered. The CONTROL module communicates with both the lexical retrieval and the integrated ATN module. Additionally, it is supported by a verification module. This module calculates judgements for hypothesis based on a match between a hypothesis and the signal. The disadvantage here is, that most of the linguistic knowledge is not explicitly stored, because it is not separated from the ATN. E.g., there is no conception for a noun group, for a semantic class, or for a verb frame. Contrary to the stratified model in /WIN 83a/, all such facts are only implicitly used to build up the ATN. The main advantages are the capability of a controlled but flexible processing, the use of uniform and therefore comparable judgements for hypotheses, and the use of predictions based on the ATN.

The two examples show that even system archtitectures for the stratified linguistic model are grouped around one centralized module: the RESULT DATA BASE at Hearsay-II, respectively the CONTROL module at HWIM. Other potential architectures like a strictly hierarchical or a strictly goal directed architecture are of minor interest /GOO 80a/. Because of the exponential number of data paths, also the complete heterarchical architecture was not realized.

In the previous subsection, the advantages of a system architecture around the module KNOWLEDGE were shown. So far, only requirements concerning different aspects of knowledge were stated for this architecture. The different levels of knowledge were neglected. But this **KNOWLEDGE centered architecture** can also support one main point of the blackboard architecture. If an uniform knowledge representation language is given for all aspects and levels, a uniform µtructure of the RESULT DATA BASE is the consequence. Then the remaining question is, whether one knowledge represenation language is able to integrate at least most of the levels, which are seperated into different modules at Hearsay-II, in an adequate manner. The ATN in the HWIM system does the job of integration. But we have to look for a scheme, which also reflects the different levels of knowledge, in order to keep all the knowledge explicit and to guarantee the modularity of the knowledge base. It was also pointed out, that the judgement calculus should be integrated into the knowledge base. Therefore, the four modules besides the CONTROL strategy of HWIM form the knowledge base, also including the verification. Because of this, the interaction between CONTROL and KNOWLEDGE becomes easier.

3. KNOWLEDGE REPRESENTATION

For a knowledge representation scheme (and language) it was required in section 2, that it should be able

(R1) to integrate the different aspects of knowledge,

(R2) to integrate the different levels of knowledge,

(R3) to make the different levels of knowledge explicit, and

(R4) to build up a modular knowledge base.

Because the intended system strongly depends on the organization of the knowledge base, the question, how adequate is a scheme or language, is of importance. Therefore, adequacy criteria will be presented, before different knowledge representation schemes are discussed with respect to these **criteria** and to the four **requisitions**, which are summarized above.

3.1 Criteria for Knowledge Representation Languages

In /MCC 69a, BRA 79a, SCH 86a/ the **epistemological adequacy** is accentuated as main criterion for knowledge representation languages. A compact definition for this criterion is given in /MCC 69a/: "A representation is called epistemologically adequate for a person or a machine if it can be used practically to express the facts that one actually has about the aspects of the world." /BRA 79a/ pointed out that an epistemologically adequate scheme must be neutral with respect to a conceptional level of a knowledge base. This level is built up of those conceptions and the relationships between them, which are relevant for a given context of problems. Therefore, a representation scheme should be independent from applications. Further criteria are summarized in /SCH 86a/:

Logical Adequacy: Is the system (language and interpreter) correct, logically complete, and decidable?

Psychological Adequacy: Are the structures used for knowledge representation a model of psychical structures and also the inference processes? Are the errors of the system, comparable to those of a man? Does the system permit contradictions?

Algorithmic Adequacy: Are the algorithms for knowledge utilization of acceptable complexity, and do algorithms exist to monitor the analysis with acceptable complexity?

Ergonomic Adequacy: Is the language manageable and comprehensible?

These criteria do not only ask questions concerning the declarative components of a knowledge representation scheme, but also questions concerning a complete system in the sense of section 2.1 excluding problem specific knowledge. This emphasizes that at least the components pointed out in the first two lines of Fig.2-2 must be judged as one unit with different facets. If a knowledge representation scheme is used to interprete sensor signals one should take a further criteria into account: the handling of uncertain data, and therefore uncertain decisions. In our oppinion it is impossible to extract an unique symbolic description out of speech signals, take them as being correct, and finally running an understanding process as it is done in systems for natural language understanding. Contrary, it is necessary to describe, how results can be judged in the knowledge representation language itself. Examples for such kinds of knowledge bases are given for example in /DEM 83a, TSO 80a, SAG 85a/. Because of these reasons, the criterion **adequate for sensor data interpretation** is introduced.

It is evident that one system can hardly fulfill all these criteria. Additionally, there is no effective test to decide whether a system realizes these criteria. For the task of pattern understanding psychological adequacy is of less interest compared to the epistemological, the algorithmic, and sensor data adequacy.

If these adequacy criteria are compared with the **requisitions** summarized as R1,..,R4 at the top of this section, it is evident, that both groups have common properties. At one point, those requisitions, which demand the integration of different aspects and levels of knowledge (R1,R2), supply the criterion "epistemological adequacy". Because the "facts ... about the aspects of the world" (see /MCC 69a/) are divided into a number of more special terms, they become more concrete. The most important subcriterion, which results from this division, treats this partial view on epistemological adequacy which concerns the representation of conceptions and their interrelations. If a knowledge representation scheme allows the integration of a judgement calculus (R1) this fact supports the sensor data adequacy. The algorithmic adequacy has references to the procedural aspects of knowledge shown in Fig.2-2. The question on logical adequacy asks for the declarative <u>and</u> the procedural aspects. By the requisition R1 both have to be integrated into one scheme. As a consequence, it is also stated that they are not independent from each other and that they cannot be exchanged individually. Therefore, R1 and the logical adequacy criterion are in correlation. Last not least, the manageableness, which was pointed out as one fact of ergonomic adequacy, is also reflected by the requisitions R1 and R3. Because an integrated knowledge base for speech understanding will be of large complexity, also the manageableness of a large knowledge base in the representation language is an important criterion.

Based on these considerations the following criteria are presented for knowledge representation languages:

(C1) Does the language support the manageableness of large knowledge bases?

(C2) Is the represenation of conceptions and their interrelations epistemologically adequate?

(C3) Does the language support the handling of uncertain data and uncertain decisions?

(C4) Do algorithms exist which monitor analysis processes efficiently?

Together with the requisitions R1,..,R4 these criteria subsume those adequacy criteria which are most relevant for the speech understanding task. Therefore, the requisitions and the criteria C1,..,C4 are used in the following subsection to examine knowledge representation languages.

3.2 Examples and Classification of Knowledge Representation Languages

Following /MYL 83a/ knowledge representation schemes can be classified into the categories **semantic networks**, **logical**, and **procedural schemes**, whereas most knowledge representation languages subsume more than one of these categories. The problems with such a classification are described in /MYL 83a/: "When trying to classify representation schemes we consider the world as a collection of individuals and as a collection of relationships that exist between them. The collection of all individuals and relationships at any time in any one world constitutes a state, and there can be state transformations that cause the creation/destruction of individuals or that can change the relationship among them."

One example to illustrate this is the language PROLOG /KOW 74a/. At one point of view PROLOG is a **logical representation scheme**. Therefore it employs the notations of constant, variable, function, predicate, logical connective and quantifier in order to represent elementary facts. A knowledge base is a collection of terms and formulas. But besides the traditional Tarskian semantics

"B_1 and B_2 and ... and B_m implies A"

the **procedural semantics**

"if you want to establish A,
try to establish B_1 and B_2 and ... and B_m"

is used. This procedural point of view establishes how knowledge can be used and is therefore comparable to calculus for proving theorems, like the Gentzen calculus or the resolution method /MAN 74a/. Because the use of knowledge is the crucial point for the procedural semantics, we prefer the notation that a **pragmatics** is defined **for the language**, respectively for logical schemes.

Procedural schemes view a knowledge base as a collection of active processes and agents. Most procedural schemes have been influenced by LISP and LISP itself was a favourite represenation language. Schemes like **production systems** /HAY 82a/ and PLANNER /HEW 71a/ offer activation mechanisms for processes. In both schemes a knowledge base is built up of pairs. Each pair consist of a pattern and one or more actions which manipulate the result data base. If the pattern of a pair can be successfully matched to the data base the corresponding theorem in PLANNER respectively the action of the rule is executed. One difference is, that a theorem can directly call another one, while the action of a rule can only modify the result data base. The PLANNER control module uses the backtracking algorithm. This is also used in many applications based on production systems. Nevertheless, numerous other algorithms are used to monitor such systems. Contrary, the ACTOR formalism /HEW 77a/ places the control structures into the foreground. All objects of a knowledge base are viewed as active agents, called actors. They have the capability to send and to receive messages. The messages themselves are actors. An object is specified by the kinds of messages it can receive and all the actions, including the sending of messages, it takes. The actions depend on the message the object received. One of the main points of **semantic networks** is the information retrieval. Although the languages based on such networks are of large diversity, there exists a most basic form. A priori and a posteriori knowledge is expressed by nodes and directed labeled links. The former stand for conceptions or classes of conceptions (mainly a priori) and individuals (mainly a posteriori), the latter for binary relations over these. The main problem of the scheme was that most of the early languages had little or no semantics for the types of nodes and links they used. The nessecity for a semantics and an epistemological adequacy was pointed out in /WOO 75a, BRA 79a/. In order to define a unique interpretation of the different types of nodes and links in a language, this set must be restricted. On the other hand, to get an epistemological adequate language, this set must be sufficient to build up knowledge bases for all possible or at least a large number of applications. Most network languages offer different organizational axes for structuring a knowledge base /FIN 79a/. The most common axes are:

Classification: A real world object is associated with its generic type(s): This axis forces a distinction between a concept, which is the intensional description or a prototype of a conception, and an instance, which is a member of the extensional set of a concept.

Aggregation: A concept or an instance is related to other concepts or instances respectively, which describe their components or parts.

Generalization: It relates a concept to more generic ones. Generalization, often called is_a, defines a hierarchy in the network due to a partial order. In most approaches properties associated with a general concept are inherited to the more special ones, unless they are not explicitely modified.

Semantic network languages like KL-ONE /BRA 85a/ and PSN /LEV 79a/ are influenced by the notation of **frames** /MIN 75a/. Such frames are complex data structures for representing stereotypical informations for a field of problems. A frame has slots for the objects which play a role in the situation as well as conditions between the slots. Furthermore, processes and facts are attached to the slots of a frame, like "if added", "if needed". In KL-ONE and PSN frame like data structures are used to build up the nodes of the semantic network. Links are described inside such a data structure by slots of different types, one for each link type. The interpretation of the slots and their facets is defined with respect to the semantics of the semantic network. While KL-ONE only uses procedural attachment associated with the slots, in PSN also a pragmatics (procedural semantics) is defined. Besides others, procedures to build up or to delete instances are associated with each concept. The slots in a concept are divided into prerequisites and consequences with respect to the instantiation procedure of the concept.

3.3 Discussion of Knowledge Representation Languages

For each class of knowledge representation schemes one language is choosen for the following discussion:

PROLOG for logical schemes

EMYCIN /BUC 85a/ for rule based system shells

PSN for semantic networks

As mentioned above the inference process of PROLOG is given by the definition of the procedural semantics. Therefore, PROLOG covers declarative and procedural aspects (R1). Vice versa, the rules in EMYCIN also allow a declarative description of facts. But both do not integrate the handling of numerical features (R1). Because it is a logical language, PROLOG offers no help to operate with uncertain data and uncertain decisions (C3). On the contrary, EMYCIN allows scores for rules. The main problem at this point is that both, PROLOG and EMYCIN, have to decide whether the premise of a rule is true or false. As a consequence, if uncertain data and judgements on interpretations are used, there is a need for thresholds. Because rules and formulas can be formulated independent of each other, both languages are modular (R4). They can also integrate different levels of knowledge (R2). But these facts imply that such levels cannot be made explicit (R3). Whereas identical conceptions are identified in PROLOG and EMYCIN implicitly by utilization of an identical name, each conception is representad exactly once in a semantic network. All relationships, the conception is associated with, are centered in the node standing for the conception. Therefore, semantic networks are more suited for large knowledge bases (C1). But this kind of organization is also helpful to keep a knowledge base modular (R4) in the following sense: If one conception has to be changed, it is known in a semantic network, where and how often it occurs in the knowledge base. Applications of PSN, e.g. /TSO 80a/, show that it is possible to integrate different aspects and levels of knowledge into one knowledge base (R1,R2), and that PSN supports the handling of uncertain data (C3). Contrary to PROLOG, EMYCIN and PSN do not include a complete monitor. But as it is shown by examples, there exist monitors which satisfy criterion C4. By their built in pragmatics, all these three languages prefer one direction, goal-directed or data-driven, for analysis processes. Thus, a flexible propagation of constraints (R1) and flexibility of processing sequences are limited.

The **epistemological adequacy** (C2) is one of the most serious problems concerning a knowledge representation language. For semantic networks, this adequacy strongly depend on the built in links and the distinction of different types of properties /BRA 79a/. The set of epistemological primitives is defined in KL-ONE and PSN by the link-types, which were presented in the last subsection, **attributes**, which describe further properties and relationships, and **structural relations** to describe and test relations, which must hold between referred conceptions and attributes. In PROLOG and EMYCIN it is not possible to distinguish such different classes of relationships and properties in an explicit way. All of them and the conceptions are represented uniformly by predicates and formulas. Additionally, there is no way to describe an inheritence between a class of conceptions and a corresponding superclass. In order to motivate the need for an additional link type in a semantic network language, we present an example given by /MYL 83a/: "for example the parts of John Smith, viewed as a physical object are his head, arms etc. When viewing as a social object, they are its address, social insurance number, etc." Two "worlds" or **conceptional systems** are distinguished in this example. A concept modelling a person has different parts within each of these systems. Parts in the social system are social conceptions, parts in the physical system are physical conceptions. In speech understanding conceptional systems like syntax, semantics, pragmatics build up the knowledge base. Therefore, links between conceptions have to be distinguished, whether they connect conceptions inside one or conceptions belonging to different conceptional systems. In /SCH 86a/ it is pointed out, that within one conceptional system parts of concepts may exist, which can only be described adequately inside the context of those conceptions they are part from. As an example, social structures like family, father, mother, and married couple are given. It is worked out, that an adequate description of these conceptions requires a definition by sets, and that a definition by atoms is not adequate. A **context dependent** definition like husband in /SCH 86a/

husband(x) := u (u=<x,y> married_couple(u))

could be established by defining "husband" to be an aggregation of "married couple" but also to depend on the context of "married couple".

4. A HOMOGENUOUS KNOWLEDGE BASE FOR SPEECH UNDERSTANDING

After the discussion of knowledge representation languages we now turn to the presentation of a particular semantic network language. this language is the kernel of the system shell ERNEST /KUM 87a/. There is a clear distinction between the syntax, semantics, and pragmatics of this language. In order to explain the interpretations, i.e. the semantics, of the ERNEST structures, the knowledge base designed for the system EVAR will also be presented in this section. The knowledge base is called homogenuous, because it integrates the different aspects and levels of knowledge discussed above.

4.1 The Declarative Aspects of the Knowledge Base

First of all the ERNEST network language distinguishes three types of nodes. A **concept** represent the model of a conception. According to classification (see 3.2), **instances** are associated with concepts. The connection between instance nodes, concept nodes and signal areas is shown in Fig.4-1. In this figure the three word hypothesis "train", "time", and "Hamburg" stand for the signal. Three concepts "noun", "source", and "goal" are given. Instances are denoted by circles. Each instance establishes a connection between exactly one concept and an unique signal area (word hypothesis). Such an area can be

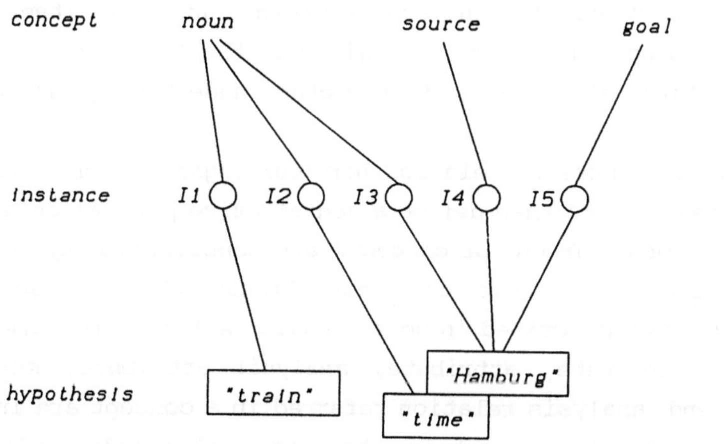

Fig.4-1: Relations between Concepts, Instances and Hypothesis

connected to more than one concept via instances and one concept to more than one area. It is obvious, that there are instances which compete each other: I4 and I5 because "source" and "goal" is a contradiction, and I2 and I3 because the signal areas overlap. Contrary, I3 and I4 are compatible, because "noun" and "source" belong to the different levels (conceptional systems) syntax respectively semantics. As illustrated by its name **modified concept**, the third node type is similar to a concept, but it is restricted with respect to a given situation of an analysis process. For example, in German adjectives and nouns have to agree in genus, number, and casus inside a noun group. A priori these attributes are unknown for the group or one member. If an adjective is yet instantiated, modified concepts for noun group and noun can be built up. This is done by restricting the attributes mentioned above with respect to the detected adjective. With the interpretation of the three node types also the link types **instance** and **instance of** are fixed according to the links between concepts and instances in Fig.4-1.

Similar to PSN, all node types are syntactically described by frame like structures. Fig.4-2 shows those parts of the data structures building up an ERNEST concept, which are relevant for the speech understanding application. Besides internal properties, the structures subsume all the links to and from other concepts. The structures for modified concepts and for instances differ only slightly from those for concepts. Therefore, the interpretation of the structure "concept" the substructures and the items, which together build up a concepts, are given in the following. If there are substantial differences to the other node types, it will be mentioned.

Besides the instance relationship four organizational axes are distinguished. All of them define a nonreflexive partial order on the set of concepts. Trees of concepts are constructed by the link **specialization**. This link type establishes the inverse of the generalization as described in section 3.2. All substructures of the groups part, concrete, attribute, analysis attribute, structural relation, and analysis relation referred in a concept are inhereted to its specialization, unless they are explicitely modified by marking this fact in the item **modified** of the superimposing *concept*

name of concept	→ text
degree	→ 4 integer
priorities	→ 5 integer
information	→ text
specialization of	→ link to concept
specialization	→ list of links to concepts
context of	→ list of concepts
part of	→ list of links to concepts
part	→ list of link descriptions
modality	→ list of modality descriptions
attribute	→ list of attribute descriptions
local attribute	→ liste of attribute descriptions
structural relation	→ list of relations
concrete of	→ list of links to concepts
concrete	→ list of link descriptions
analysis parameter	→ list of attribute descriptions
analysis relation	→ list of relations
identification	→ list of identifications
judgement	→ procedure
instance	→ list of instances

modality description

obligatory	→ list of roles
optional	→ list of roles
inherent	→ list of roles
adjacency	→ adjacency
coherent	→ YES or NO

value

type	→ type
meaning	→ meaning
value	→ value array

procedure

name	→ text
argument	→ list of arguments
inverse procedure	→ name of procedure

adjacency

dimension	→ integer
roles	→ list of roles
diagonal	→ integer vector
matrix	→ bitmatrix

attribute description

role	→ text
domain	→ type
selection	→ range
modifies	→ YES or NO or role
dimension	→ 2x2 integer
computation of value	→ procedure
adjacency dependent	→ YES or NO
restriction	→ procedure
preference	→ list of ranges
active graphic	→ procedure

link description

role	→ text
domain	→ list of concepts
context depending	→ YES or NO
modifies	→ YES or NO or role
dimension	→ 2 integer
restriction	→ procedure
transformation	→ value
preference	→ list of ranges

relation

role	→ text
test of relation	→ procedure
adjacency dependent	→ YES or NO

range

kind	→ kind
type of values	→ type
complement	→ YES or NO
values	→ list of values

identification

path1	→ list of roles
path2	→ list of roles

Fig.4-2: Data Structure Building up a Concept in ERNEST

substructure in the specialized concept. Aggregation is notified by the link **part**. Part and specialization relationships are restricted in the way, that they are only allowed inside the same conceptional system. If a concept is referred by the inverse link **part of** and in the item **context of**, this indicates that the concept itself is context dependent from that twice referred concept. (see 3.2). Links between different conceptional systems are established by the **concrete** relationship.

Fig.4-3 shows a snapshot on the network of the knowledge base. In order to simplify the following explanations, each concept in this figure has a prefix, which illustrates its membership to one of the conceptional systems **pragmatics** (P), **pragmatic classification** (PC), **semantics** (S), **semantic classes** (SC), or **syntax** (SY). At the very bottom, the concept WORD build up one interface of this network to the signal oriented analysis modules /SCH 87a/. At the top level, pragmatical conceptions like P_TRAIN_CONNECTION, with parts P_VF_FAHREN or P_FROM_TIME are shown. They build up the application oriented conceptions. E.g., P_VF_FAHREN relates the corresponding verbframe for "fahren" (to go, to drive) to the application. The concept S_VF_FAHREN itself is indepedent from the application. From the applications point of view, to ask for a train connection using the verb "fahren" requires time information (P_FROM_TIME). Contrary, S_TIME is not referred by S_VF_FAHREN. Concepts of the conceptional system describing the pragmatic level are connected via concrete links to concepts of the PC and the S levels. E.g., P_VF_FAHREN is concretized by S_VF_FAHREN, and P_FROM_TIME by both PC_TIME_INTERVAL and S_TIME. From the concept S_VF_FAHREN, deep cases like S_INSTRUMENT, or S_SOURCE are referred. They are concretized by both semantic classes and syntactical constituents. Syntactical conceptions like nominal phrase complex (SY_NPC) have other syntactical concepts like preposition phrase (SY_PP) as parts, which itself is built up of SY_NP (nominal phrase) and SY_PREP (preposition). While Fig.4-3 was restricted to a few concepts and links, Fig.4-4 gives a condensed view on the complete network. Here the part links are omitted. They connect only concepts, which are members of one conceptional system. Arrows between blocks and/or single concepts (capital letters) stand for bundles of links of the desired type. The membership of a block or a concept to a

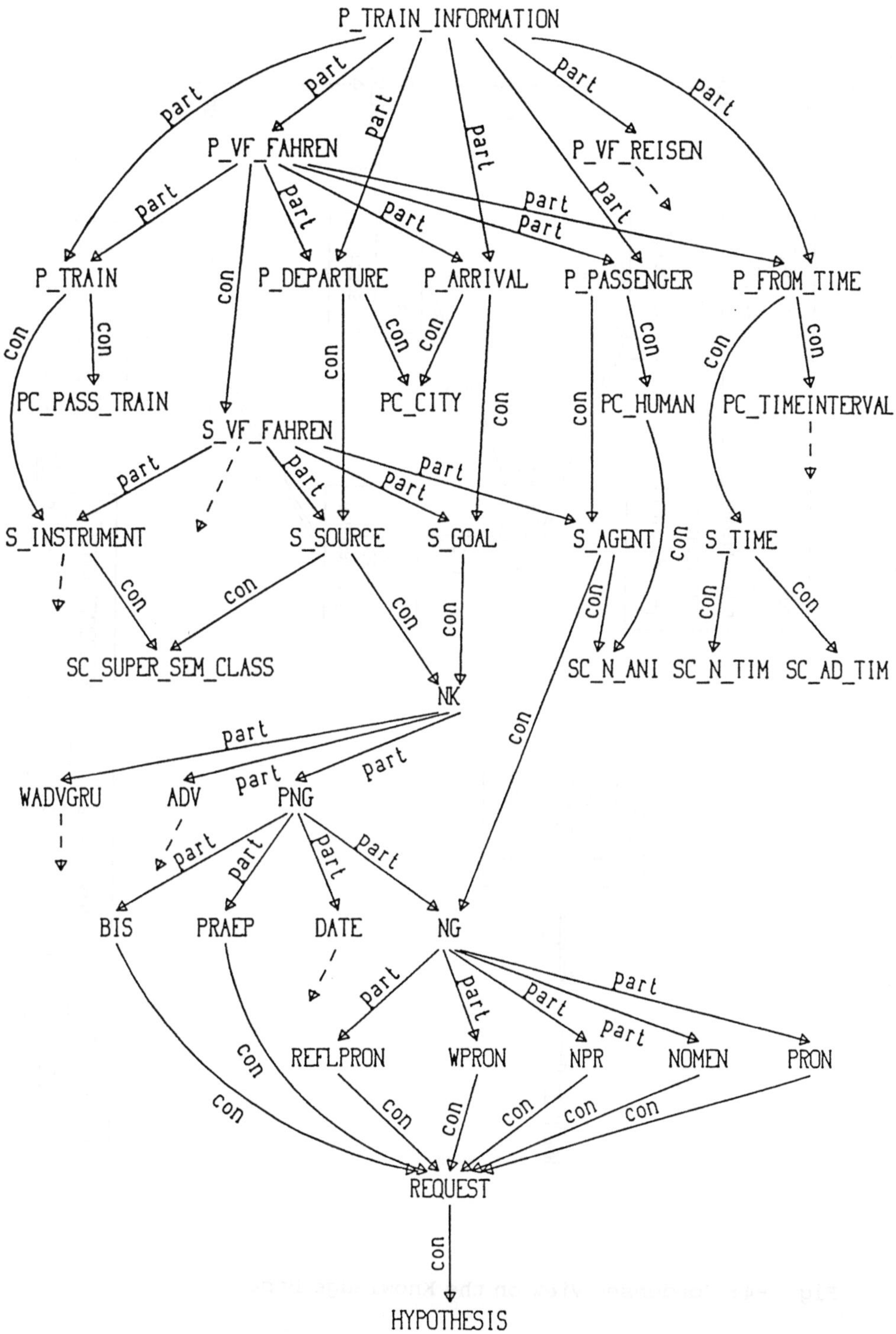

Fig.4-3: Snapshot on the Knowledge Base

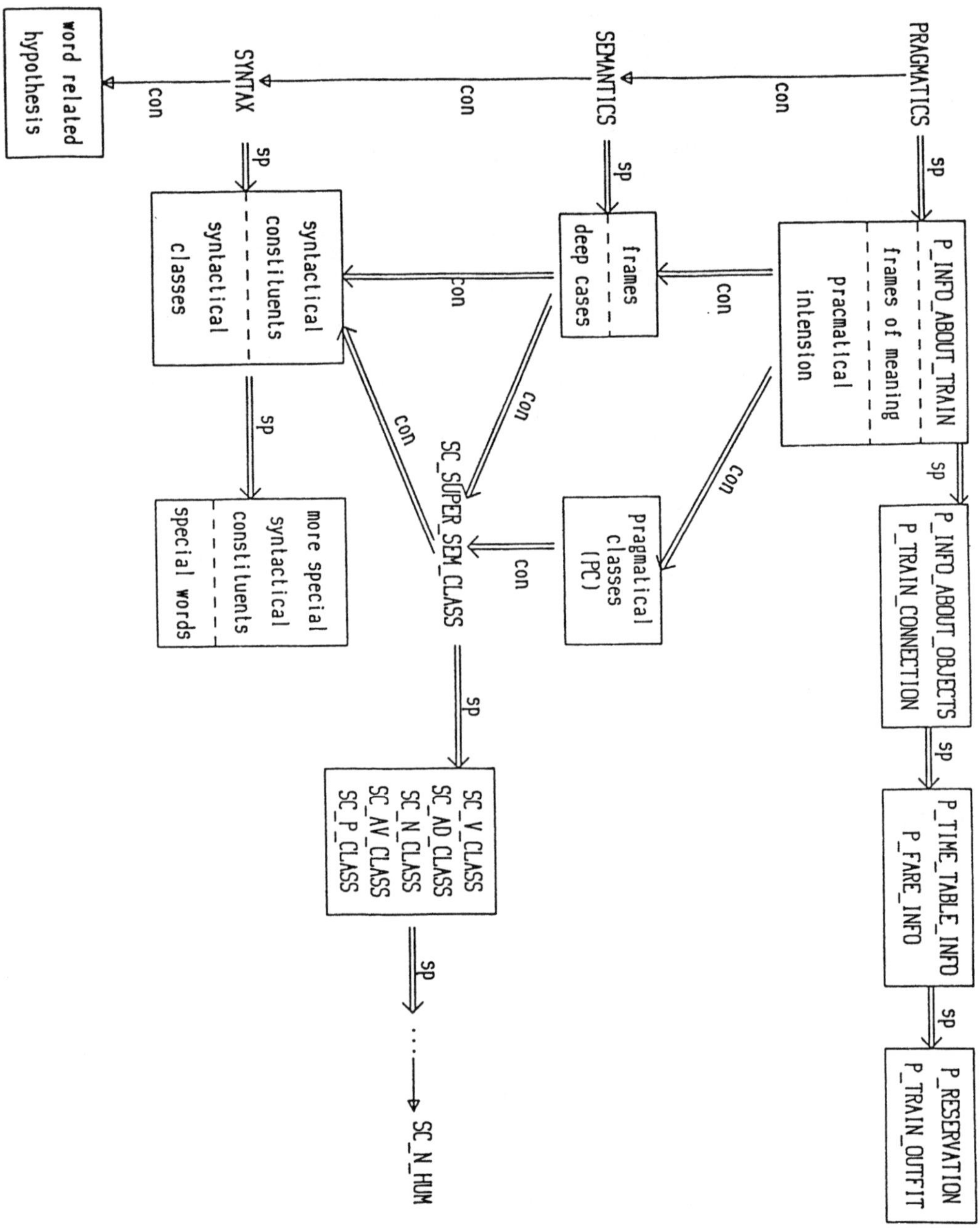

Fig.4-4: Condensed View on the Knowledge Base

conceptional system is denoted by the prefixis also used in Fig.4-3.

The complete definition of each part and concrete relationship is done by the substructure **link description.** Different from most similar knowledge representation languages, the **dimension** item inside a link description causes no differentiation for the correponding **role** in the instances. However, the role in an instance has to be filled with just as much instances the dimension intervall requests. Parts and concretes defined in a concept or inherited to the concept may be grouped into different **modality descriptions.** Each such substructure establishes one admissable combination of **obligatory**, **optional**, and **inherent** links, whereas one link can be inherent and optional or inherent and obligatory in the same modality. The substructure is completed by an **adjacency description** which allows a compact notation of required time neighbourhoods of parts. If no gaps are allowed between adjacent parts, this fact is notified by the term YES in the item **coherent.** An example of modality and adjacency descriptions is given in Fig.4-5. Fig.4-5a shows the graphical ATN representation of the concept SY_NP of Fig.4-3. This results in the modality description in Fig.4-5b. For simplicity, the roles of the parts are represented by the name of the corresponding concept but written in small letters. The adjacency description, i.e. the matrix, for first modality set of SY_NP is shown in Fig.4-5c. Because it is possible to describe the facts of a modality description also by specialized concepts and the adjacency in the substructures relation, both are not epistemological primitive. But they give compacter knowledge bases and therefore aids the ergonomic adequacy.

The intensional description of a concept is completed by its **attributes** and **structural relations.** E.g., the CNG features of nouns, adjectives, noun phrase are attributes. That they shall agree inside one noun phrase are structural relations. The main items in the substructures defining an attribute description respectively a relation are the **computation of value** for an attribute and the **test of relation** when building up an instance. A **procedure** defintion in the ERNEST-network includes the explicit notation of the **arguments**, and it is possible to refer also the inverse of the procedure. While the activation of the procedure itself results in concrete values if all arguments are known, the inverse is able to restrict the domain set, especially the **selection** of attributes in modified concepts. In

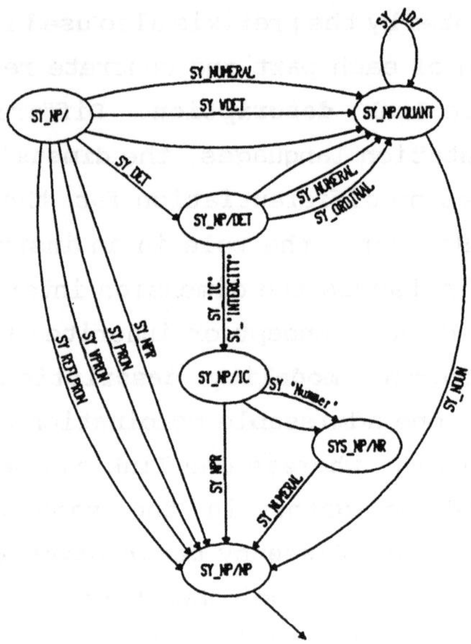

Fig.4-5a: Graphical Representation of an ATN

```
MODALITY_DESCRIPTIONS:

   MODALITY:
      OBLIGATORY: noun
      OPTIONAL:   det, wdet, numeral, ordinal, adj
   MODALITY:
      OBLIGATORY: ic, npr
      OPTIONAL:   ---
   MODALITY:
      OBLIGATORY: intercity, npr
      OPTIONAL:   ---
   MODALITY:
      OBLIGATORY: ic, numeral
      OPTIONAL:   nummer
   MODALITY:
      OBLIGATORY: intercity, numeral
      OPTIONAL:   nummer
   MODALITY:
      OBLIGATORY: npr
      OPTIONAL:   ---
   MODALITY:
      OBLIGATORY: pron
      OPTIONAL:   ---
   MODALITY:
      OBLIGATORY: wpron
      OPTIONAL:   ---
   MODALITY:
      OBLIGATORY: reflpron
      OPTIONAL:   ---
```

Fig.4-5b: Modality Description

	noun	det	wdet	numeral	ordinal	adj
noun	0	1	1	1	1	1
det	0	0	0	1	1	0
wdet	0	0	0	0	0	0
numeral	0	1	0	0	0	0
ordinal	0	1	0	0	0	0
adj	1	1	1	1	1	4

Fig.4-5c: Adjacency Description

a similar way the selection of an attribute may be restricted, if not all the argument values are known. The complete domain set of an attribute is described by the three items **domain, selection**, and **dimension**. The domain item refer the type, e.g. integer or casus. By the selection this type can be constraint to certain valus, e.g. to the numbers 1 to 10 or to the subset nominative, accusative. The dimension item gives the number of values which are necessary to fill the property in an instance, e.g. at least 1 at most 10. Arguments are described by a role or a pair of roles, respectively. If only one role is referred, the argument is taken from the instance or modified concept itself. By two roles attributes of parts or concretes are referred to by the role in the corresponding link description and the role of an attribut in this part or concrete. As þdditional argument the adjacency matrix is allowed. This is notified by the content of the item **ajancency dependent**. While the attributes show the features of a concept, **analysis attributes** accept quantitative parameters, which are necessary for the analysis process but do not contribute the intensional description. One example of such an attribute, is a data structure which is called "mask". It is analysis attribute of each concept of the network (see 4.2). Quite the same situation differs structural relations from **analysis relations**. All the attribute and relation groups described so fare are implicitely inhereted to more special concepts. Contrary, **local attributes** are not inhereted, they describe local properties.

The function to judge an instance with respect to the conception modelled by the corresponding concept is referred in the item **judgement** of the concept. Arguments of this function are the judgements of the parts and concretes, the restrictions of link and attribute descriptions, and the results of both kinds of relations. All arguments are ·eferred by the role of the corresponding substructure. The calculus for judgements is not fixed by the ERNEST network language. In section 5 the use of judgement vectors, which reflect quality, certainty, and priority of a (modified) concept, or an instance, for speech understanding will be discussed.

4.2 Procedural Aspects of the Knowledge Base

Besides the procedures and their inverse, which are attached to substructures of a concept, a **pragmatics** is defined for the ERNEST network language. Different from PSN and analogous to PROLOG, this procedural semantics is independent from the content of a knowledge base. It is build up of **five rules**, which only look for concepts, modified concepts, and instances in the premise. Starting with a few goal concepts, recursive applications of these rules results in a search tree, which is the skeleton of the search tree of the analysis process. Out of the skeleton, the search tree is generated because of procedures, which do not produce an unique result but competing values. For example, one noun may result in more than one instance of the concept noun, because there are different values for the attribute casus, which compete each other.

In order to illustrate the five rules, an example of an analysis process is chosen in Fig.4-6a. It is assumed that up to this situation the instances are yet created. Three of them are shown in the figure. They are denoted by $in_i(A)$, where A is a concept and i the index for the instance. The words, which are assumed to be the major content for the instances are also shown. Additionally, the instances are placed at those positions, which are established by the corresponding concepts. The snapshot on the knowledge is chosen with respect to Fig.4-4.

The most basic rule is

RULE 1: IF **for a concept A or a modified concept mod(A)** with respect to one obligatory set of a modality of A, **instances** for those concepts **exist**, which are referred to by the following slots in A or slots inherited to A without modification:

- **concrete** AND
- **part**, if the item **context dependent** in the link description is equal to NO
- one of **context of**, if this slot is not equal to NO

THEN build up a **partial instance inp_j(A)** as follows

- construct an empty instance of A
- connect the instance with those referred to by the premise
- activate the attached procedures in the sequence: restrictions of links, calculation of attributes, restrictions of attributes, tests of relations, judgement

Because of context depending parts and optional links, values do not exist for all arguments of the activated procedures. Nevertheless the knowledge of existing values of arguments and the procedure itself can be used, if the following strategy is applied. The selection values are also transferred to the procedures. The procedures themselves decide whether the existing values and the selections are sufficient for the **estimation of results**. In the case of attributes, this estimation is a new, more restrictive selection. For the other cases, which all are tests, the estimation must be optistic. Except the creation of an empty instance the same action takes place for the second and the third rule.

RULE 2: IF a **partial instance** $\mathbf{inp_j(A)}$ of a concept A exists AND
instances for all those concepts exist, which are refferd to as **part** with item **context depending** is equal to **YES** in the link description and are members of the **obligatory** set which was used for the construction of $inp_j(A)$
THEN build up new **instances** $\mathbf{in_k(A)}$ out of $inp_j(A)$

RULE 3: IF an **instance** $\mathbf{in_j(A)}$ of a concept A exist AND
at least one instance of a concept exist, which is **optional** due to the modality used for constructing $in_j(A)$
THEN build up **extended instances** $\mathbf{in_k(A)}$ out of $in_j(A)$

In the situation of Fig.4-6a, the premise of RULE1 is satisfied for the concept S_SOURCE. Because no context dependent parts are referred, RULE2 can be applied immediatelly after RULE1. The result is the instance iv_m(S_SOURCE) which is partially shown in Fig.4-6b together with the most relevant definitions of the concept S_SOURCE. The analysis attribute "mask" is a vector, where every position stands for one frame of the input signal. By "-" free positions are marked. The "x"-es represent positions of words which build up the instance.

The information represented by the instances iv_m(S_SOURCE) and in_l(VG) is able to restrict the concept S_VF_FAHREN. Based on such a modification it would be also possible to restrict the concepts S_OBJECT and/or S_GOAL. For the modifications of concepts the following rules are introduced:

RULE 4: IF for a **concept A** or a **modified concept** $\mathbf{mod_j(A)}$,
a new modified concept or a new instance were created for a concept, which is referred to as
part, or **concrete**, or **context_of**
by the concept A

THEN create a new **modified concept mod_k(A)** out of A or mod_j(A), respectively, as follows

- construct an empty modified concept of A
- connect this modified with all instances referred to by the premise and those, which are already referred to by mod_j(A)
- activate the procedures like in RULE1

RULE 5: IF for a **concept A** or a **modified concept mod_j(A)**,

a new modified concept or a new partial instance were created for a concept B, which is referred to as

part_of, or **concrete_of**

by the concept A

THEN create a new **modified concept mod_k(A)** out of A or mod_j(A), respectively, as follows

- construct an empty modified concept of A
- connect this modified with all instances referred to by the premise and those, which are already referred to by mod_j(A)
- activate the following procedures in the sequence: inverse restriction of link descriptions of B, inverse calculation of attributes of B, inverse tests of relations of B, restictions of limks of A, calculation of attributes of A, restrictions of attributes of A, tests of relations of A, judgement of A

The premise of RULE4 is satisfied for the concept S_VF_FAHREN. The differences between this concept and the resulting modified concept mod_i(S_VF_FAHREN) are illustrated by Fig.4-6c. Notice, that no value but only a new selection is calculated for the attribute "mask". With mod_i(S_VF_FAHREN) the premise of RULE5 holds for the concept S_GOAL. The modified concept mod_n(S_GOAL) can be created, Fig.4-6d. Besides the new selection for "mask", the domain of the two concret descriptions is restricted. The verbframe "fahren" requires special semantic classes for S_GOAL and a special syntactic realization. These are notified as restrictions in the corresponding link descriptions in the concept S_VF_FAHREN. The inverse procedures of these restrictions modify the corresponding domains in mod_n(S_GOAL).

The first three rules are suffient to create and to extend instances with respect to optional links. RULE4 and RUL5 make it

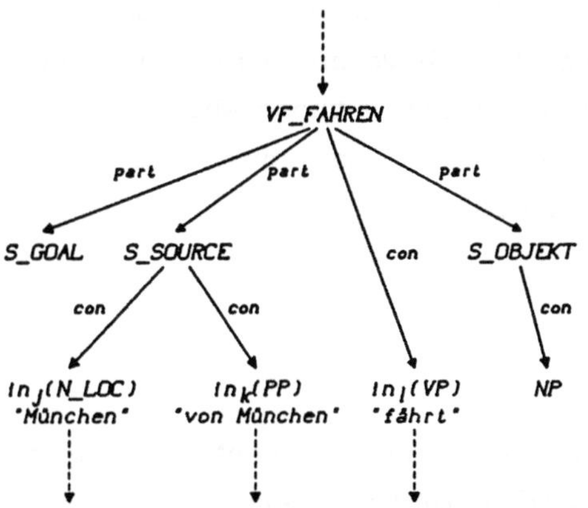

Fig.4-6a: Snapshot of a Search Graph Node

```
S_SOURCE:

   CONCRETE: sem_class
      DOMAIN:N_LOC
   CONCRETE: synt_realization
      DOMAIN:PP
   ANALYSESPARAMETER: mask
      ARGUMENT:  sem_class.mask,
                 synt_realization.mask
      SELECTION: [---------------------------]
      VALUE:     [---------------------------]
   RELATION: partial_identity
      ARGUMENT: sem_class.mask,
                synt_realization.mask
      VALUE:    ----

In_m(S_SOURCE)

   CONCRETE: sem_class
      DOMAIN:In_j(N_LOC)
   CONCRETE: synt_realization
      DOMAIN:In_k(PP)
   ANALYSESPARAMETER: mask
      ARGUMENT:  sem_class.mask,
                 synt_realization.mask
      SELECTION: [--------------xxxxxxx------]
      VALUE:     [--------------xxxxxxx------]
   RELATION: partial_identity
      ARGUMENT: sem_class.mask,
                synt_realization.mask
      VALUE:    0.9
```

Fig.4-6b: The Concept S_SOURCE and an Instance

```
S_VF_FAHREN

   PART: source
      DOMAIN:S_SOURCE
   PART: goal
      DOMAIN:S_GOAL
   PART: object
      DOMAIN:S_OBJECT
   CONCRETE: verbal_phrase
      DOMAIN:VP
   ANALYSESPARAMETER: mask
      ARGUMENT:  goal.mask,
                 source.mask,
                 object.mask,
                 verbal_phrase.mask
      SELECTION: [---------------------------]
      VALUE:     [---------------------------]
   RELATION: adjacency
      ARGUMENT: goal.mask,
                source.mask

mod_l(S_VF_FAHREN)

   PART: source
      DOMAIN:In_m(S_SOURCE)
   PART: verbal_phrase
      DOMAIN:In_l(VP)
   ANALYSESPARAMETER: mask
      ARGUMENT:  goal.mask,
                 source.mask,
                 object.mask,
                 verbal_phrase.mask
      SELECTION: [xxxxx---------xxxxxxx------]
      VALUE:     [---------------------------]
   RELATION: adjacency
      ARGUMENT: goal.mask,
                source.mask
      VALUE:    ---
```

Fig.4-6c: The Concept S_VF_FAHREN and a Modified Concept

```
S_GOAL:

   CONCRETE: sem_class
      DOMAIN:SUPER_SEM_CLASS
   CONCRETE: synt_realization
      DOMAIN:PP, NP
   ANALYSESPARAMETER: mask
      ARGUMENT:  sem_class.mask
                 synt_realization.mask
      SELECTION: [---------------------------]
      VALUE:     [---------------------------]
   RELATION: partial_identity
      ARGUMENT: sem_class.mask
                synt_realization.mask
      VALUE:    ---

mod_n(S_GOAL)

   CONCRETE: sem_class
      DOMAIN:N_LOC, A_LOC
   CONCRETE: synt_realization
      DOMAIN:PP
   ANALYSESPARAMETER: mask
      ARGUMENT:  sem_class.mask
                 synt_realization.mask
      SELEKTION: [####o---------o#####o------]
      WERT:      [---------------------------]
   RELATION: partial_identity
      ARGUMENT: sem_class.mask
                synt_realization.mask
      VALUE:    ---
```

Fig.4-6d: The Concept S_GOAL and a Modified Concept

feasible to adjust and therefore to restrict a complete knowledge base to every new instance by creating modified concepts. RULE5 can be applied recursively until concepts which have an empty premise with respect to RULE1. These concepts are exactly those which build up the interface between the declarative part of the knowledge base and the module which generates word hypotheses.

5. ANALYSIS STRATEGY AND JUDGEMENTS

In the last subsection the inference rules were presented. Their recursive application build up the skeleton of the search space of the analysis process. Competing word or word chain hypotheses together with competing intermediate results split up this skeleton into the complete search space. The A^*-Algorithm /NIL 82a/ in combination with judgement vectors, which scores both instances and search space nodes, is used to guide the analysis process. This process itself can be divided into the following major subprocesses. First of all, based on a few word hypotheses so called "goal concepts" are selected out of the knowledge base. For these concepts it is required, that they are located at the conceptional sub-system "pragmatics" of the knowledge base. Each of the selected word hypotheses forms a successor of the start node in the search space. By the second subprocess, nodes of this space have to be judged with respect to the required properties of judgements for the A^*-Algorithm. We use judgement functions, which are based on the content of the node. This subsumes all the instances and modified concepts which were created on the path from the start node to the node to be judged and the a priori knowledge base. The third kind of subprocesses expands search space nodes by applying rules of the rule set, which was described in the last subsection. Depending on the applied rule and the underlying concept, one or more new instances or modified concepts are created. If the application of a rule results in exactly one new modified concept, no successor is generated for the actual search space node. In all other cases one successor node is constructed for each created instance or modified concept. All the three subprocess types use judgements on search space nodes, instances, modified concepts, or concepts. Before we give an outline of the complete analysis process, the different scoring values which build up the judgements of the different objects are explained.

5.1 Knowledge Based Priority Scores

A priori for each concept of the network the **concept priority vector** is defined. These vectors can be calculated automatically only based on the different links of the network but independent of the special content of the concepts. They give answers to the following questions:

- What is the maximal distance via concrete links to the very bottom level? Concepts which have such a maximal distance belong to the conceptional system "pragmatics", of the network. ($prio_1$)
- What is the minimal distance via concrete links to one concept at the very bottom level, i.e. the conceptional system "word related hypothesis", of the network? ($prio_2$)
- What is the minimal distance via concrete and/or part links to one concept at the very bottom level of the network? ($prio_3$)
- How special is the concept? ($prio_4$)
- How complex is the concept with respect to the part relationship ($prio_5$)

A concept A is of higher priority compared to a concept B, if in lexical order for bottom-up rules the vector ($prio_1$,$prio_2$,$prio_3$,$prio_4$,$prio_5$) of A is greater than that of B and for top-down rules the vector ($-prio_2$,$-prio_3$,$prio_4$,$-prio_5$) of A is greater than that of B. Modified concepts inherit their priority vector from the corresponding concept.

Besides this static priority measurement two dynamic priority scores are defined for modified concepts and for instances. The first one is called the **pragmatic priority** pP /EHR 87a/. For many words in the dictionary a possible set of pragmatic conceptions can be determined. With this property for each word a pragmatic bit vector pbv(w) is defined. Each bit represents a conception. The conceptions themselves are organized in a tree structure with the most general one as root. The pragmatic bitvector is defined as an attribute or an analysis attribute in each concept of the network. For a word w the pragmatic bitvector has "1" for those conceptions that could be realized by the word or that can realize the domain of a part. If the word is a pronoun or a determiner, it gets the "1" with respect to its semantic class. For this there exist a mapping function from semantic classes to pragmatic conceptions. The **pragmatic bit vector of a group of words** $w_1, \ldots, w_n$ is defined by

$$pbv(w_1 \ldots w_n) := pbv(w_1) \text{ AND } \ldots \text{ AND } pbv(w_n)$$

The **pragmatic priority** $pP(w_1 \ldots w_n)$ is defined as the number of "1" in the pragmatic bitvector and has the following properties:

- If the pragmatic priority of a group of words is equal to 0, then the group is pragmatically inconsistent.
- The smaller the priority the better the hypothesis with these words

For instances and modified concepts the pragmatic bitvector is calculated respectively estimated on the basis of the underlying word hypotheses and the selections of the attribute "pragmatic bitvector" which are a priori notified in the concepts.

Additionally, also for modified concepts and instances a **semantic priority** /EHR 87a/ is defined. This priority measurement is only calculated for modified concepts and instances which represent verb, noun or adjective frames. But it is also transferred to other modified concepts and instances by the application of the rules. If a concept A represents such a frame, the semantic priority is defined as a fuzzy membership function which depends on the number of realized parts in relation to the obligatory and optional parts for one modality description. This function takes into account that a hypothesis, i.e. an instance or a modified concept, does not become always more probable the more parts of a frame or a sentence are realized.

5.2 Statistical Modelling of Hypotheses Scores

The acoustic dissimilarity scores for word or word chain hypotheses provided by Dynamic Time Warping or Viterbi algorithms usually do not merely reflect the goodness-of-fit of the hypothesized unit but, moreover, the temporal duration of its acustical evidence. This can be seen by the fact that DTW distances or negative logs of HMM probabilities are in essence being built by summing up local, segmental distances, whatever subword unit these segments may represent (e.g. phonemes or centisecond labels).

A simple but useful model for this would be to neglect segmentation errors, or time registration effects resp. at all and to assume the **acoustic score** as the sum of independent random variables, identically distributed by (μ_t, σ_t^2) in case of correct hypotheses, or by (μ_f, σ_f^2) in case of failing hypotheses. If the duration of the acoustical evidence covered by the hypothesis is L (taken as the number of segments involved), the quality score q of correct hypotheses is distributed with

$\mu_t(L)=E(q_t|L,correct)=L\mu_t$

and

$\sigma_t^2(L)=Var(q_t|L,correct)=L\sigma_t^2$,

and the analoguous formula holds for the incorrect ones.

This linear dependence of quality score means and variances on the duration (if duration is measured in terms of the units used by the word matching process) as forecasted by our model has been empirically verified by statistical evaluation of word hypotheses scores generated by the EVAR word recognition module /SCH 87a/. In addition, the quality model means and variances have been estimated for this recognizer by a regression analysis.

Note that a scoring spread decreasing with L as stated above gives a good explanation to the frequent observation that reliability of word recognition seems to rise with their temporal duration. This fact is used to attach a **certainty score** to each hypothesis. The duration dependent Bhattacharyya distance between the quality distributions of correct and incorrect hypotheses reflects such a certainty. Under normal density assumption, the respective distributions are given with the above means and variances.

The judgement of a hypothesis is meant to help the overall system strategy to focus on promising partial solutions. Its value is usually computed on the basis of the quality score and it should reflect the hypothesis' chance of being part of the/a correct interpretation covering the whole utterance. In order to fullfill the admissibility requirements /NIL 82a/ of the A* graph search strategy that we use, judgement should always be an optimistic estimate of the optimal quality achievable by extending the partial interpretation in question.

Provided that the qualities are additive, this estimate is usually given as the sum of the hypothesis quality and an upper (lower in case of dissimilarities) bound on the qualities of interpretations covering the remaining part of the utterance. If analysis is proceeding strictly from left to right, the shortfall method which estimates the remainder by the sum of segmentwise optimal qualities proves to be optimistic and therefore leads to an admissible search /WOO 82a/. If we make allowance for the by far larger search space using an island-driven strategy, admissibility can be achieved by the density method, i.e. by extrapolating the average within-hypothesis quality to the remaining utterance.

Our approach is to enforce a more goal-directed search as is possible with the "hypercautious" shortfall score by retaining the (relatively) small search space connected with the left-to-right conditions. For that, we include our knowledge concerning the statistical behaviour of the quality scores into the estimates mentioned above.

Let us assume the qualities of correct hypotheses to be distributed with $\mu(L)$, $\sigma^2(L)$, depending on their duration. Expectation and variance for the quality of an interpretation covering the by now uninterpreted part (of N segments duration) with correct hypotheses in general strongly depends on the assumptions of the statistical distribution of hypothesis duration. We are treating the three most simplifying cases:

Fine model: the remainder consists entirely of single-segment hypotheses, implying $\mu_{rem}(N)=N\mu(1)$ and $\sigma_{rem}^2(N)=N\sigma^2(1)$.

Coarse model: the remainder consists of exactly one N-segment hypothesis, implying $\mu_{rem}(N)=\mu(N)$ and $\sigma_{rem}^2(N)=\sigma^2(N)$.

Uniform block model: the remainder consists of N/B hypotheses of duration B each, implying $\mu_{rem}(N)=N/B\mu(B)$ and $\sigma_{rem}^2(N)=N/B\sigma^2(B)$.

Now we are able to loosen the requirement for an optimistic estimate in a reasonable fashion. As a **lower quality bound** for the not yet covered acoustic input we choose $s(N,c)=\mu_{rem}(N)-c\sigma_{rem}(N)$. The constant factor c is adjusted to satisfy a given probability of this bound being optimistic /SCH 87b, SAG 87a/.

Recalling our finding that the dependence of quality means and variances on hypothesis duration can be viewed as linear, the quality statistics of the remainder utterance reads as $\mu_{rem}(N)=\mu N$ and $\sigma_{rem}^2(N)=\sigma^2 N$, regardless of the duration model involved. With that, the quality bound reduces to $s(N,c)=\mu N-c\sigma N^{1/2}$, which guarantees a rather deep search especially in the initial phase of analysis, when N is relatively large.

5.3 Outline of the Analysis Stratagy

As mentioned before, the analysis process starts with the selection of a few goal concepts out of the knowledge base. Beginning at the word level, modified concepts are constructed bottom-up by applying RULE4. This iterative process is based on the best few word hypotheses with respect to the acoustic score and the pragmatic priority. After the word hypotheses are chosen the process that modifies concepts up to the pragmatic level starts. It is guided by the concept priority vectors. This results in one successor node in the search graph for each selected word hypotheses and in further successors if a word hypothesis forms more than one potential goal concept.

The further expansion of nodes is done by applying the rules which build up the procedural semantics of the network language. If in one node more than one rule is applyable, the rules which create instances are prefered. The second selection criteria is the concept priority vectors of those concepts for which the rules can be applied. Note that there are instantiation processes which activate word hypothesing. The described recursive procedure leads to a search tree. The process is finished if a goal concept is instantiated and if the signal is mostly covered by the resulting interpretation.

The search strategy inside this tree is the A^*-Algorithm. Each node in an intermediate state of search is judged with respect to the actual modification of the goal concept which is associated with this node. In detail, for search tree nodes the following judgement vector is used

(structural consistency, acoustic score + quality bound,
certainty, pragmatic priority, semantic priority)

The first decision is whether in all the modified concepts and instances, which were created at the path to the actual node, satisfy the structural conditions. The second and third component are based on the statistical modelling of hypotheses scores. But in both cases not the exact value but only intervals are used. The comparison between two nodes is defined by the lexical order of their judgement vectors. Exept the semantic priority all the components and therefore the lexical order of the vectors themselves fulfill the requirements of the A^*-Algorithm for scoring functions.

6. CONCLUSION

After a detailled discussion of system architectures for knowledge based speech understanding, a homogenuous architecture based on semantic networks was develloped. The problem independent procedural semantics of this network language allows a flexible control of analysis processes. The A^*-Algorithm builds the overall monitor of the system. Special judgement vectors reflect knowledge based and acoustic scores and they are admissible for the graph search procedure. So fare, the system was successfully tested in a prototype version. An efficient realization is presently under progress.

Acknowledgement: The work reported in this paper is supported by the German Research Foundation (DFG)

REFERENCES

/BAH 83a/ L.R. Bahl, F. Jelinek, R.L. Mercer: A Maximum Likelihood approach to Continuous Speech Recognition. IEEE Trans. PAMI 5 (1983) 179-190
/BRA 79a/ R.J. Brachman: On the Epistemological Status of Semantic Networks. In /FIN 79a/ 3-50
/BRA 85a/ R.J. Brachman, I.A. Schmolze: An Overview of the KL-ONE Knowldge Representation Language. Cognitive Science, Vol.9 (1985) 171-216
/BUC 85a/ B.G. Buchanan, E. Shortliffe: Rule Based Expert Systems. Addison-Wesley, Reading, Mass., 1985
/DEM 83a/ R. De Mori: Computer Models of Speech Using Fuzzy Algorithms. Plenum Press, New York, London, 1983
/EHR 87a/ U. Ehrlich: Multilevel Semantic Analysis in an Automatic Speech Understanding and Dialog System, Proc. Third Conference of the European Chapter of the Association for Computational Linguistics, Copenhagen, 1987
/ERM 80a/ L.D. Erman, V.R. Lesser: The Hearsay-II Speech Understanding System: A Tutorial. In /LEA 80a/ 361-381
/FIN 79a/ N.V. Findler (ed): Associative Networks. Academic Press, New York, 1979
/GOO 80a/ G. Goodman, R. Reddy: Alternative Control Structures for Speech Understanding Systems. In /LEA 80a/ 234-246
/HAY 82a/ F. Hayes-Roth, D.A. Waterman, D.B. Lenat (eds): Building Expert Systems. McGraw Hill, 1982
/HEW 71a/ C. Hewitt: PLANNER: A Language for Proving Theorems in

Robots. Proc. IJCAI 2 (1971)
/HEW 77a/ Viewing Control Structures as Patterns of Passing Messages. In: Artificial Intelligence 8 (1977) 323-364
/KIM 84a/ J.H. Kim, D.W. Payton, K.E. Olin: An Expert System for Object Recognition in Natural Scenes. Proc. IEEE 1st CAIA, Denver (1984) 170-175
/KOW 74a/ R. Kowalski: Predicate Logic as a Programming Language. Information Processing 74, North Holland, Amsterdam (1974) 569-574
/KUM 87a/ F. Kummert, H. Niemann, G. Sagerer, S. Schröder: Werkzeuge zur modellgesteuerten Bildanalyse und Wissensakqusition - Das System ERNEST. In M. Paul (Hrsg.): GI - 17. Jahrestagung Computerintegrierter Arbeitsplatz im Büro. Springer-Verlag, Berlin, Heidelberg, New York, Tokyo, 1987, 556-570
/LEA 80a/ W.A. Lea (ed): Trends in Speech Recognition. Prentice-Hall, Englewood Cliffs, N.J., 1980
/LEV 79a/ H. Levesque, J. Mylopoulos: A Procedural Semantics for Semantic Networks. In /FIN 79a/ 93-121
/LOW 80a/ B. Lowerre, R. Reddy: The Harpy Speech Understanding System. In /LEA 80a/ 340-360
/MAN 74a/ Z. Manna: Mathematical Theory of Computation. McGraw-Hill, New York, 1974
/MCC 69a/ J. McCarthy, P.J. Hayes: Some Philosophical Problems from the Standpoint of Artificial Intelligence. In B. Melzer, D. Ritchie (eds): Machine Intelligence 4. Edinburgh Univ. Press, Edinburgh, 1969, 463-502
/MCC 81a/ D.L. McCracken: A Production System Version of the Hearsay-II Speech Understanding System. UMI Research Press, Ann Arbor, Michigan, 1981
/MCC 83a/ G. McCalla, N. Cercone (eds): Knowledge Representation. IEEE Computer Magazine (1983)
/MER 85a/ G. Mercier: Expert Systems Approach to Acoustic-Phonetic Decoding and Word Recognition. In H. Niemann (ed): Mustererkennung 85. Springer-Verlag, Berlin, Heidelberg, New York, Tokyo, 1985, 290-312
/MIN 75a/ M. Minsky: A Framework for Representing Knowledge. In P.H. Winston (ed): The Psychology of Computer Vision. Mcgraw-Hill, New York, 1975, 211-277
/MYL 83a/ J. Mylopoulos, H. Levesque: An Overview of Knowledge Representation. In M. Brodie, J. Mylopoulos, J.V. Schmidt (eds): On Coceptual Modelling: Perspectives from Artificial Intelligence, Databases, and Programming Languages. Springer-Verlag, New York, Berlin, Heidelberg, Tokyo, 1983
/NIE 81a/ H. Niemann: Pattern Analysis. Springer-Verlag, Berlin, Heidelberg, New York, Tokyo, 1981
/NIE 85a/ H. Niemann, A. Brietzmann, R. Mühlfeld, P.Regel, G. Schukat: Th Speech Understanding and Dialog System EVAR. In R. De Mori, S.Y. Sun (eds): New Systems and Architectures for Automatic Speech Recognition and Synthsis. NATO Series F 16. Springer-Verlag, Berlin, Heidelberg, New York, Tokyo, 1985, 271-302
/NIE 86a/ G. Niedermair: Divided and Valency-Oriented Parsing in Speech Understanding. Proc of the 11th International conference on Computational Linguistics, Bonn (1986) 593-595
/NIL 82a/ N.J. Nilsson: Principles of Artificial Intelligence. Springer-Verlag, Berlin, Heidelberg, New York, Tokyo, 1982
/PRA 85a/ H. Prade: A Computational Approach to Approximate and Plausilble Resoning with Applications to Expert Sytems. IEEE Transactions on Pattern Analysisand Machine Intelligence PAMI-7

(1985) 260-283
/RAB 88a/ L.R. Rabiner: Mathematical Foundations and Applications of HMM. This volume
/SAG 85a/ G. Sagerer: Darstellung und Nutzung von Expertenwissen für ein Bildanalysesystem. Springer-Verlag, Berlin, Heidelberg, New York, Tokyo, 1985
/SAG 87a/ G. Sagerer, F. Kummert, E.G. Schukat-Talamazzini: Flexible Steuerung eines sprachverstehenden Systems mit Hilfe mehrkomponentiger Bewertungen. In E. Paulus (Hrsg.) Mustererkennung 1987. Springer-Verlag, Berlin, Heidelberg, New York, Tokyo, 1987, 123-127
/SCH 86a/ P. Schefe: Künstliche Intelligenz - Überblick und Grundlagen. Bibliographisches Institut, Mannheim, Wien, Zürich, 1986
/SCH 87a/ E.G. Schukat-Talamazzini: Generierung von Worthypothesen in kontinuierlicher Sprache. Springer-Verlag, Berlin, Heidelberg, New York, Tokyo, 1987
/SCH 87b/ E.G. Schukat-Talamazzini: Private Communication
/SCH 88a/ R.M. Schwartz: Acoustic Phonetic Decoding of Speech. This volume
/THU 88a/ G. Thurmair: Semantic Analysis of Continuous Speech. This volume
/TSO 80a/ J.K. Tsotsos, J. Mylopoulos, H.D. Covvey, S.W. Zucker: A Framework for Visual Motion Understanding. IEEE Transactions on Pattern Analysis and Machine Intelligence Pami-2 (1980) 563-573
/WIN 83a/ T. Winograd: Language as a Cognitive Process. Volume 1: Syntax. Addison-Wesley, Reading, Mass., 1983
/WOL 80a/ J.J. Wolf, W.A. Woods: The HWIM Speech Understanding System. In /LEA 80a/ 316-339
/WOO 70a/ W.A. Woods: Transition Network Grammars for Natural Language Analysis. Comm. ACM 13 (1970) 591-606
/WOO 75a/ W.A. Woods: What's in a Link? Foundations for Semantic Networks. In D.G. Bobrow, A. Collins (eds): Representation and Understanding. Academic Press, New York, 1975
/WOO 82a/ W.A. Woods: Optimal Search Strategies for Speech Understanding Control, Artificial Intelligence 18 (1982) 295-326
/WAT 86a/ D.A. Waterman: A Guide to Expert Systems. Addison-Wesley, Reading, Mass., 1986

RECOGNITION OF SPEAKER-DEPENDENT CONTINUOUS SPEECH WITH KEAL-NEVEZH

G. MERCIER - A. COZANNET - J. VAISSIERE
CNET LAA/TSS/RCP
BP 40 22301 LANNION FRANCE

KEYWORDS.

speech recognition/ acoustic/ phonetic/ segmentation/ syntax/ semantic parsing / sentence recognition

ABSTRACT.

A description of the speaker-dependent continuous speech understanding system KEAL-NEVEZH is given. An unknown utterance is recognized by means of the following procedures: Acoustic analysis, phonetic segmentation and identification, word and sentence analysis. This new system is an extension of the KEAL system, connected to ALOEMDA, an active chart parser modifying its strategy and linguistic capabilities.

A speaker adaptation module allows to adjust some of the system parameters by matching known utterances with their acoustical representation.

The task to be performed, described by its vocabulary and its grammar, is given as a parameter of the system. The new configuration is under test and first results are given. Continuously spoken sentences extracted from a "pseudo-LOGO" language are analysed with two different linguistic modules and recognition figures are presented.

0. INTRODUCTION.

The continuous speech recognition system KEAL [SIR & al,83] is to be modified to become the recognition component of a natural language dialog system able to provide voice access to data bases.

The paper relates results reached by KEAL, and extension in KEAL-NEVEZH ("nevezh" means new in britton language) when connected to a new linguistic module, ALOEMDA [COZ,87], designed to control speech recognition steps and to interface with a dialog module.

Roughly speaking, Keal is a hierarchical bottom-up knowledge-based speech recognition system [LEA,80], able to recognize continuous utterances. Sentence recognition is currently achieved by use of a CFG sentence recognizer. The new linguistic module modifies the control, extends the linguistic capability and changes the global strategy.

Four experimental tasks are currently under investigation: Recognition of french numbers, recognition of italian numbers [MER & al,87], recognition of pseudo-Logo commands and recognition of spoken requests to a small subset of an electronic yellow pages data base (with ALOEMDA).

NATO ASI Series, Vol. F46
Recent Advances in Speech Understanding and Dialog Systems
Edited by H. Niemann et al.

In this paper, we describe recognition experiments of spoken sentences extracted from the "Logo" task domain. "Logo" is a well-known natural programming language used to teach computer science to children.

In section 1, the main components of Keal are recalled and ALOEMDA is briefly described. In section 2, the vocabulary and the grammar of the application are described. In section 3, the experimental conditions and the training and test sets are presented. In section 4, recognition results and conclusions are discussed.

1. MAIN COMPONENTS OF KEAL-NEVEZH

Keal processing of input data integrates different knowledge sources.

ACOUSTIC ANALYSIS is carried out by an n-channel,mel-scaled vocoder (Usual values for the system parameter 'n' are 14,16 or 29); the acoustic spectrum is computed every 13.3ms or 10ms.

PHONETIC RECOGNITION is decomposed into a sequence of step activations: sentence onset detection, centisecond labelling, segmentation into pseudo-syllables and phones, primary phonetic feature recognition and phone recognition. A speaker-independent set of rules and speaker-dependent linear decision functions are used for this acoustic-phonetic decoding.

The phonetic module output is a sequence of segments (called a phonetic spectrum or lattice). Among the segment attributes, a probability weighting factor and a list of phonemes, ordered with decreasing likelihood are given.

LEXICAL ANALYSIS operates by matching whole word templates against the phonetic spectrum . The dictionary entries contain various phonetic transcriptions of each word of the application. Dynamic programming is used to compute the word distance to the unknown input. The ouput of the module is a lexical lattice. The lattice elements arec n-uplets describing the detected words, their limits and similarity index.

This dynamic programming algorithm can be optionally associated with a word verification module, using a set of phonetic and prosodic rules in order to optimize the word matching.

SENTENCE RECOGNITION . A sentence recognizer and a linguistic analyser are presently available to analyse the LOGO utterances.

The words forming the sentence must satisfy different types of constraints such as grammaticality, adjacency (two consecutive words must be not too far each from other and the overlapping, if any, must be short) and acoustic evidence (true detections show higher evaluations than false detections).

- The sentence recognizer is derived from the EARLEY's algorithm [QUI,80], and uses the context-free grammar formalism. It's a left to right parser, using a beam search strategy to reduce the search space. Syntactic guidance is available and only the best partial solutions are kept, at each step. The result of the parsing, if any, is the recognized sentence associated with a score and a parse-tree.

- ALOEMDA is an active chart parser, and is an extension of the algorithm described by WINOGRAD [WIN,83] to the ATN (Augmented transition networks) grammar formalism and lattice input.

  It is mainly top-down, left to right, and designed to control the lexical retrieval module, reducing the number of lexicon calls. Main modifications from WINOGRAD concern the use of ATN grammar and scoring of partial parses in order to realize a best first choice. Length, position and acoustic evidence are the main selection criteria, as in the previous parser. Semantic and syntactic parts in the condition set for transitions allow to use these pieces of information as soon as they are needed. Prosodic features could be used directly in the procedural part of the parsing mechanism. According to the grammar description, ALOEMDA allows to deal with natural language utterances, and can be used as an understanding module, to prepare the dialog process.

  With LOGO utterances, ALOEMDA has only been provided with a recursive transition network, in order to check the performances against the first sentence recognizer. Each application has its own grammar and internal representation schemes, but they are not to be detailed here.

The SPEAKER-ADAPTATION module is composed of two modules:

- a semi-automatic alignment program which maps an ideal phonemic transcription of words or sentences composing the reference data set onto the acoustic-phonetic spectrum given by the system;
- a stochastic approximation program which provides the optimal set of coefficients of the linear discriminant functions, obtained after computing the optimal hyperplanes dividing the reference data set of phones.

2. TASK DESCRIPTION.

Each word of the vocabulary is described by means of a sequence of basic units. At the lexical level, the basic units of the Keal system are the phonemes. Each word has usually a standard phonemic form and eventually one, two or more phonemic variants. Some sequences of phonemes, like the diphone /w a/, being difficult to separate into two different sounds, are considered as basic units. In this case, this particular diphone is named /oi/ like in the word /s ois an t/ ("soixante" or "60").

The lexicon is composed of 123 basic words, from which each sentence can be generated by means of a context-free grammar. A transcription in RTN formalism is automically provided for the use of ALOEMDA. This dictionnary is speaker-independent.

At the phonetic level, the set of phonemes is divided into two main classes: vowels and consonants (some phonemes like /r/ can belong to both classes.

Within each class, some allophonic units are introduced in order to have homogeneous classes of phonemes; for instance, the following phonemes /r/, /l/, /a/ and /o/ have two allophones. Each stop consonant is itself divided into two allophones corresponding respectively to the occlusion part and to the burst part; these allophones correspond to the following set: /p/, /p1/; /t/, /t1/; /k/, /k1/; /b/, /b1/; /d/, /d1/; /g/, /g1/.

The context-free grammar of Logo sentences is composed of 72 non-terminal or syntactic categories, 105 terminal or lexical categories and 100 rules. The perplexity figure of the corpus is around 18.

3. EXPERIMENTS.

3.1 Speech data.

Speech collected from nine speakers (4 female and 5 male speakers) has been recorded and digitized at a sampling rate of 12.8khz and F.F.T. is carried out each 13.3ms. The log-energy in each of 14 critical bands is computed. This speech data has been divided into two sets:

- The TRAINING set is composed of 73 short task-independent sentences uttered once by each speaker.
- The TEST set is composed of 39 logo sentences per speaker.

3.2 Speaker training experiment.

For each speaker, a reference set of phones is automatically extracted from the TRAINING set by means of the automatic alignment program which maps each phonetic lattice given by the phonetic analyser on the ideal phonetic transcription of each training sentence.

This phonetic reference set is then checked or improved by hand, in case of mapping errors. From this set, two new sets of coefficients (corresponding respectively to vowels and consonants), representing the optimal hyper-planes separating the phones in each of these two classes are computed. Accordingly for each speaker, at the end of this training time, the system is provided with these two sets of speaker-dependent coefficients used to refine the first phonetic recognition given by the rule-based part of the acoustic-phonetic decoding module.

4. RESULTS.

The percentage of correct sentence recognition obtained by KEAL, on the test set is 81.5% (264 sentences out of 324). At the word level the recognition percentage is 91% (1172 out of 1287). Detailed results obtained with the sentence recognizer are shown in table 1. At the phonetic level, more than 80% of the phonemes are identified within the first four candidates, without using phonotactic or lexical or syntactic constraints.

ALOEMDA has only been tested with two speakers (one male and one female) from the preceeding set, on another machine as it is written in common LISP.

As augmentations are not used in the transcribed grammar, slight differences are observed, due to the valuation functions, used to control the partial parses extension. The results are similar for these 2x39 sentences, and the process is more time-consuming (around 60 cpu s. for 5 word utterances).

Speakers	Female AB	MG	DD	JN	Male CG	JM	RV	GU	JS
Word Recognition percentage	89	91	94	94	94	86	83	93	98
Sentence Recognition percentage	80	87	93	80	80	77	67	88	88

Table 1: Speaker-dependent correct word and sentence recognition for 9 speakers

5. CONCLUSIONS.

These results show that reasonable continuous speech recognition performance can be obtained, even with a partially rule-based, bottom-up approach. Of course, different ways are possible to improve these results.

The phonetic lattice will be refined by adding new contextual rules and by improving the set of basic allophones. We hope also to improve the word recognition level by including a statistical error model for phonetic errors (confusions, deletions and omissions) which are automatically estimated by the alignment module.

Results obtained with ALOEMDA show that the program debugging is almost completed. This new parser has still to be fully integrated on the same machine to provide KEAL-NEVEZH with dialog facilities.

Acknowledgements

We wish to thank M. CLOATRE, D. BIGORGNE, L. LE GUENNEC, L. MICLET, J. MONNE, M. QUERRE for their collaboration in this work.

REFERENCES

[COZ 87] A. COZANNET. ALOEMDA, analyseur linguistique pour l'oral et l'ecrit. to appear in the Proceedings of the 6th RFIA Conference, 1987. Palabre Rome meeting, report IM22010, 1986.

[LEA 80] W. A. LEA. Trends in Automatic Speech Recognition. Englewoods Cliffs, Prentice-Hall, New York, 1980.

[MER & al 87] G. MERCIER, L. LE GUENNEC, P. LAFACE. Recognition of italian numbers and connected digits. Deliverable of P P1015 ESPRIT project, 1987.

[SIR & al 85] J. SIROUX, D. GILLET. A system for man-machine communication using speech. Speech communication 1985, Vol 4, No 4, 289-315.

[WIN 83] T. WINOGRAD. Language as a cognitive process. Part 1: Syntax. 1983, Addison Wesley.

MODIFICATION OF EARLEY'S ALGORITHM FOR SPEECH RECOGNITION

Annedore Paeseler

Philips GmbH Forschungslaboratorium Hamburg,
Vogt-Koelln-Str. 30, D-2000 Hamburg 54, FRG

Abstract: This paper describes an adaptation of Earley's algorithm for the recognition of spoken sentences. Earley's algorithm is one of the most efficient parsing algorithms for written sentences. The modifications and extensions of Earley's algorithm required by the variability and ambiguity of the speech signal concern the scoring of word and sentence hypotheses and the application of a beam search or pruning technique.

1. INTRODUCTION

The main problems of continuous-speech recognition are due to the unreliable recognition of both the word boundaries and the spoken words. To improve the recognition rate of a speech recogniton system, it is useful to define a grammar which is used to restrict the search for the best matching sequence of words for a spoken sentence to those that are grammatically correct.

Earley's algorithm /Ear 70/ is one of the most efficient parsing algorithms for general context-free grammars. It was one of the first parsing methods that used a central data structure, usually called chart, for storing all intermediate results during the parsing process of a sentence. Subsequently chart parsers were widely used in natural language systems for written input. Moreover Earley's algorithm was extended for error-correcting parsing /Lyo 74/, /Fu 82/ and spoken sentence recognition /Nak 87/. In /Ney 87/ a similar method is described that uses a context-free grammar for speech recognition, which is based on the Cocke-Younger-Kasami algorithm /Hop 79/.

NATO ASI Series, Vol. F46
Recent Advances in Speech Understanding
and Dialog Systems
Edited by H. Niemann et al.

2. THE MODIFIED ALGORITHM

The modified algorithm for speech recognition has to determine the grammatically correct sequence of words that yielded the best score. Scores can be computed by probabilistic methods or as geometric distance between acoustic vectors.

The modified algorithm comprises two levels. At the 'acoustic' level, the reference patterns of hypothesized words are compared with the string of input symbols into which the speech signal is converted by an acoustic analysis module (e.g. acoustic vectors or phoneme symbols). Scores for the hypothesized words are computed by dynamic programming /Ney 82/ which provides an optimal nonlinear time alignment of reference pattern and spoken sentence. Each time the end of a word reference-pattern is reached, a 'scanner' operation gives the corresponding word and the score to the 'grammar' level.

At the grammar level, recognized words and their scores are used by the 'completer' to extend already found sequences of words or, more precisely, to extend partial derivations. According to the grammar rules those words are determined by a 'predictor' and given to the acoustic level, which can follow the found word sequences.

As in the original version of Earley's algorithm we use item lists or state sets to store the intermediate results while processing the string of input symbols from left to right. All possible derivations of grammar rules are expanded simultaneously. Item list j contains all partial derivations and for each of them the best matching sequence of words that has been found while processing the input symbols along the time axis 1 to j.

Let G = {S, N, T, R} be a context-free grammar where $S \in N$ is the start symbol, N a set of nonterminal symbols, T a set of terminal symbols and R a set of context-free rules A --> w. The following notation is used:

A, B, C	: $\in N$;	a, b, c	: $\in T$;
u, w, x, y, z:	$\in (N \cup T)^*$;	g, h	: $\in T^*$;
i, j, k :	: number of item lists;	Ø	: the empty string.
U, V, W, X	: scores;		

An item represents the 'state' of the application of a grammar rule. An item [A, x, y, i, j, U, V, abc] has the following interpretation (cf. Fig. 1): in R exists a rule A --> u. The right-hand side of this rule is split into two parts x and y. x has already been compared to the input string, whereas y has still to be considered. i and j are positions within the string of input symbols. i points back to that input symbol after which the application of this rule was started. j indicates the position at which x has been completed and after which the verification of y begins. j also serves as the identifier of the item list in which this item is stored. abc is that specific sequence of terminal symbols (i. e. words of the vocabulary) of all sequences of terminal symbols derivable from x, that yielded the minimal score in the comparison between the input symbols from i+1 until j and their reference patterns. In other words abc is the 'best explanation' for that sequence of input symbols. V is the 'initialisation score' (IS), i.e. the minimal score value of all derivations that span the input symbols 1 to i and request the application of rule A → u for finding a grammatically correct continuation. The 'accumulated score' (AS) U is the sum of V and the minimal score for the words that have already been derived and compared to the input symbols (in the example: the score for abc).

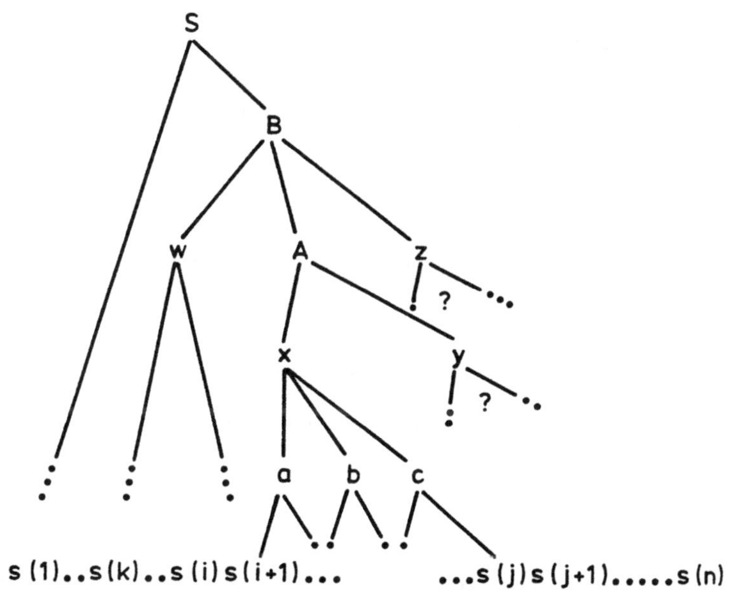

Fig. 1: Partial derivation tree after processing input symbols s(1)..s(j).

2.1 Scoring of Hypotheses

Using the two scores IS and AS is essential, if a beam search or pruning strategy shall be applied, because this requires normalized and thus comparable scores for all hypotheses. The AS of an item I in list j is the best score that can be achieved applying the grammar rule I stands for by taking into account (as IS) the best score of all rules that started the application of this rule and that are still waiting for its completion. It is a characteristic feature of Earley's algorithm that (in using the predictor operation) it is guaranteed that for each item such a predecessor exists /Gra 76/ and has already been matched to the beginning of the input string.

The IS V of an item $I = [A, x, y, i, j, U, V, g]$ is the minimal AS of all items in list i, which have A as next expandable symbol:

$$IS(I) = \min \{ W \mid [B, w, Az, k, i, W, X, h], k \le i \}.$$

The AS is defined as:

$$AS([S, \emptyset, x, 0, 0, 0, 0, \emptyset]) = 0,$$

$$AS(I) = INI(I) + CS(x, i, j).$$

$CS(x, i, j)$ is the best score of the acoustic match of the input symbols $i+1$ to j and the reference patterns of the words derived from the already processed part of the right hand side of the rule:

$$CS(x, i, i) = 0,$$

$$CS(a, i, j) = \text{Score for matching the reference pattern of word a to the input symbols } i+1 \text{ until } j.$$

$$CS(A, i, j) = \min_{I} (AS(I) - INI(I)), \quad \text{where } I = [A, w, \emptyset, i, j, U, V, g],$$

$$CS(yz, i, j) = \min_{k} (CS(y, i, k) + CS(z, k, j)), \quad \text{with } i \le k \le j.$$

2.2 Formal Description

As in the original algorithm each item list is defined as a set of items, i.e. duplicates of items are not allowed. Two items [A, y, x, k, l, U, V, g] and [B, w, z, i, j, W, X, h] are identical, if A = B, y = w, x = z, k = i and l = j. If an operation tries to create an item I2 that is identical to an already existing item I1, depending on which one has the lower accumulated score either I1 or I2 is retained. This dynamic programming minimization is correct, since I1 and I2 represent the same state of the application of one rule and cover the same portion of the input string.

The modified algorithm works the following way:

1) Initialisation:
Create [S, Ø, S, 0, 0, 0, 0, Ø], set j := 0.

2) Modification of item-list I(j):
Repeat step 2.1 and 2.2 until no new items can be created.

2.1) Predictor: for all [A, y, Bz, i, j, U, V, g] and rules B -> x create
[B, Ø, x, j, j, U, U, Ø].

2.2) Completer: for all [B, x, Ø, i, j, U, V, g] and
[A, y, Bz, k, i, W, X, h] create
[A, yB, z, k, j, W + U - V, X, hg].

3) Hypo-Words: for all [A, x, ay, i, j, U, V, g] give a, U and j to the acoustic level, where a new entry in the 'active-word-list' is created. If a is the next symbol of more than one item, take the minimal accumulative score U. U is the initial score to which the local distances between the reference pattern for word a and the input symbols are added.

4) Modification of the active-word-list:
Set j:= j+1. Carry out the comparison between the reference patterns of the words in the active-word-list and the j-th input symbol. Apply a dynamic programming method for nonlinear time-alignment, which computes

for each word the minimal cumulative score. If the end of the reference pattern for a word a is reached, which was hypothesized from item-list k and has Score W (difference between the initial and accumulated score of a), do step 5.

5) Scanner: for all [A, x, ay, i, k, U, V, g] create
[A, xa, y, i, j, U + W, V, ga].

If j = n, i.e. the end of the input is reached, look for the item [S, y, Ø, 0, n, U, 0, g] with minimal U and give out g. If j < n, then if list j is empty go to step 4, else go to step 2.

For the space and time complexity the same considerations are valid as in the original version of the algorithm. The length of the i-th item list is proportional to i, which restricts the space complexity for the grammar level to n^2, if n is the length of the input string.

The scanner executes at most $|T|*i$ for the i-th item list, if each word $a \in T$ is hypothesized at each position of the input string and no length restrictions for the reference patterns are given. The number of predictor operations for each item list is proportional to the list length. The completer has to do i^2 operations for the i-th list, since in the worst case it has to process for each item I in list i all items of the list k, to which I points back. Therefore the number of operations for processing the whole sentence has a cubic dependence on the number of input symbols.

The pruning of unlikely hypotheses was not explicitly mentioned in the formal description of the algorithm. It is easily implemented by first determining the best score after the processing of all words in the active-word-list for one input symbol. Then the sum of this best score and a certain value gives a threshold for pruning. All words that have a higher score than the threshold are removed from the list. In the same way no item is put into an item list that has an accumulated score higher than the threshold.

3. EXPERIMENTAL RESULTS

Recognition tests were performed on continuously spoken commands for a text editor. The context-free grammar consists of 84 rules. The vocabulary comprises 84 words. An acoustic preprocessor converted the input speech signal into a sequence of phonemes, which were the input to the recognition module. Since the phoneme recognition rate was rather high, word recognition errors occured only in 6 of 80 sentences.

In these experiments a drastic reduction of the number of operations was achieved by pruning. Instead of a cubic a linear dependence on the number of input symbols was observed. Tab. 1 reflects the influence of the beam search strategy on the number of operations.

Table 1:

Computational steps of scanner, completer, and predictor operations for a full search and beam search.

Length of input	No. of operations full search	beam search
10	21599	208
15	76248	374
25	327004	1389
59	2500894	3676

4. CONCLUSIONS

An algorithm based on Earley's method was developed that allows the use of a general context-free grammar for guiding the search for the best matching sequence of words for a spoken sentence. It preserves the cubic dependence of the number of operations on the number of symbols in the input string. Since for spoken sentences this number is much higher than for written sentences, a reduction of the number of operations has to be achieved. Therefore a scoring method is used that allows direct comparison of different hypotheses and thus is appropriate for a beam search strategy. In recognition experiments based on phoneme strings, on the average a linear dependence of the number of operations on the number of input symbols was achieved.

ACKNOWLEDGMENT

The work described was carried out in a joint Siemens-Philips-IPO (Eindhoven) project ('SPICOS') and sponsored by the German Federal Ministery for Research and Technology (BMFT) under grant No. 413-5839-ITM 8401. Only the author is responsible for the contents of this publication.

The author would like to thank Dominique Snyers of Philips Research Laboratories Brussels for supplying her with the data base and grammar rules for the text-editor task.

REFERENCES

/Ear 70/ : J. Earley, 'An Efficient Context-Free Parsing Algorithm', Comm. of the ACM, Vol. 13, No. 2, Feb. 1970, pp. 94-102.

/Fu 82/ : K. S. Fu, 'Syntactic Pattern Recognition and Applications', Prentice-Hall, Englewood Cliffs, 1982.

/Gra 76/ : S. L. Graham, M. A. Harrison, W. L. Ruzzo: 'On-Line Context-Free Language Recognition in less than Cubic Time', Proc. of the 8. Annual ACM Symposium on Theory of Computing, 1976.

/Lyo 74/ : G. Lyon, 'Syntax-Directed Least-Error Analysis for Context-Free Languages: A Practical Approach', Comm. of the ACM, Vol. 17, No. 1, Jan. 1974, pp. 3-14.

/Nak 87/ : S. Nakagawa, 'Spoken Sentence Recognition by Time-Synchronous Parsing Algorithm of Context-Free Grammar', Proc. of the Int. Conf. on Acoustics, Speech, and Signal Processing, Dallas, TX, April 1987, pp. 20.9.1-4.

/Ney 82/ : H. Ney, 'Dynamic Programming as a Technique for Pattern Recognition', Proc. 6th Int. Conf. on Pattern Recognition, Muenchen, S. 1119 - 1125, 1982.

/Ney 87/ : H. Ney, 'Dynamic Programming Speech Recognition using a Context-Free Grammar', Proc. of the Int. Conf. on Acoustics, Speech, and Signal Processing, Dallas, TX, 1987, pp. 3.2.1-4.

EXPECTATION-BASED SPEECH RECOGNITION

J. Mudler and E. Paulus
Institut für Nachrichtentechnik, TU Braunschweig
Schleinitzstr. 23, D-3300 Braunschweig
F.R. Germany

Keywords: continous speech recognition / knowledge-based system / optimal search / categorial search trees / S^*-algorithm

Abstract: Expectation-based speech recognition is a knowledge-based approach to recognize continously spoken German speech. The knowledge base mainly consists of a large comprehensive lexicon providing various informations about each word of the registered vocabulary. During the recognition process numerous weighted hypotheses are generated that enter into competition with each other. To succeed in recognition the task is to keep the number of alternative hypotheses low by making good choices among all alternatives. The S^*-algorithm performs an optimal search strategy regarding phrase hypotheses and using the information given by categorial search trees.

1. INTRODUCTION

Expectation-based speech recognition (ESR) has been developped at our institute* as a knowledge-based approach for the automatic recognition of continously spoken German speech /MUD 84, MUD 87/. The basic concept had been presented in /MUD 83/. Starting from the acoustic speech signal, the recognition process should correctly identify the spoken utterance in terms of a sequence of words. Like the HEARSAY-system /ERM 80/, the ESR-system works on several interpretation levels interacting bottom-up as well as top-down, but its architecture is not modularized according to all the interpretion levels and the respective knowledge sources. Instead, above word level all knowledge sources are almost completely integrated into a single large comprehensive lexicon with entries for each word of the registered vocabulary (see fig. 1). A significant feature is the classification of the words into fundamental grammatical categories as there are nouns, adjectives, pronouns, prepositions etc. Grammatical and syntactical knowledge was derived from the German grammar and semantic knowledge is based on a special semantic marker description that also incorporates knowledge from the discourse domain of the spoken utterances.

In the ESR-system expectation based analysis is preceded by signal analysis and the generation of weighted word hypotheses (see fig. 1). Signal analysis has been based upon a well-known demisyllable approach /RUS 84/. The generated set of weighted word hypotheses can be regarded as a word lattice

* This work was supported by the Deutsche Forschungsgemeinschaft (DFG)

NATO ASI Series, Vol. F46
Recent Advances in Speech Understanding
and Dialog Systems
Edited by H. Niemann et al.

on a syllable grid. Virtually each word of the admitted vocabulary may start at any syllable boundary, however, for feasibility reasons at each syllable boundary only a restricted number of words are hypothesized indeed. Assuming the boundaries of the utterance to be known, and the utterance to consist of exactly one sentence, expectation-based analysis should yield that path through the word lattice that represents the best possible sentence hypothesis with respect to the actually given speech signal. The hypothesized sentence has to be correct with respect to all knowledge sources considered within the lexicon.

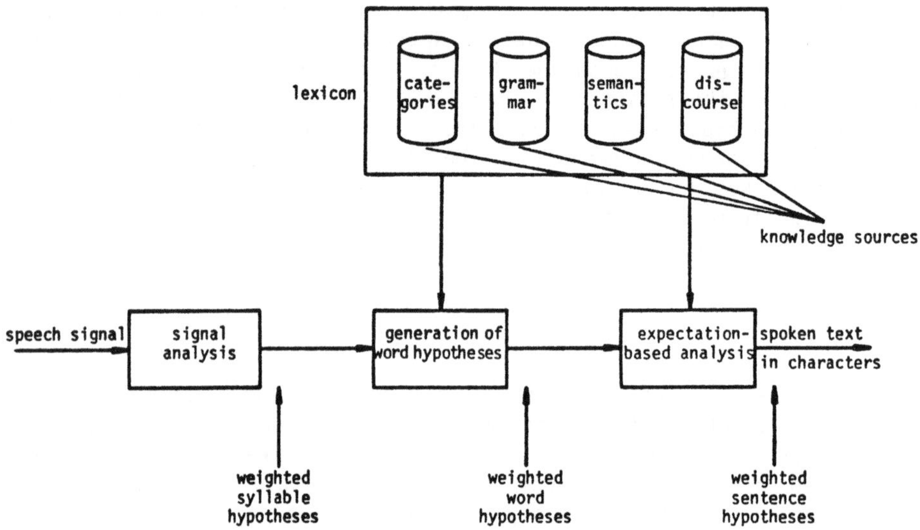

Figure 1: ESR-system architecture

2. RECOGNITION PROCESS

Expectation-based analysis is a search procedure operating in a "best-first manner" rather than from left to right. The procedure alternates between the generation and verification of hypotheses. Phrase hypotheses concerning e.g. noun phrases or prepositional phrases can be generated using reliable word hypotheses of any category as nuclei. Sentence hypotheses are assembled from phrase hypotheses according to structural descriptions of sentences placed at verb entries in the lexicon. At the generation of sentence hypotheses verb hypotheses resp. predicate hypotheses serve as nuclei. The hypotheses that are generated represent structures with slots for words or phrases, and verification of a hypothesis means that these slots can be filled with word hypotheses or with phrase hypotheses that have been already verified and that agree with the conditions associated with the slots. The weight of a verified hypothesis is computed by averaging the weights of the nucleus and of the hypotheses that are filling the slots.

At the start of the procedure the best word hypothesis within the word lattice is taken as a nucleus. For the nucleus under consideration a number of competing hypotheses is generated. Generation of hypotheses is governed mainly by the syntactical word category and a corresponding categorial search tree (see also section 3). Fig. 2 shows such a tree which applies if the category of the nucleus is "PRONOUN". The nodes of the tree represent slots for words of a certain category. Each path from the root to a leaf (labelled E) represents a correct sequence of word categories within a complete phrase hypothesis. The labels V and N indicate whether the next node extends the sequence to the left (V) or to the right (N). If the nucleus is a verb or a predicate, a number of competing phrase hypotheses is generated directly from respective entries within the lexicon.

In order to fit into a certain slot, a hypothesis must conform to specific syntactical and semantic constraints that are associated with the slot. For each slot of a generated hypothesis such constraints are compiled from lexicon entries and/or from information provided by a categorial search tree. Also, the constraints can depend upon features resulting from other slots that already have been filled. In order to test whether a hypothesis meets the actual contraints, its features must be tested. The features of a word hypothesis are provided by the lexicon. The features of a verified phrase or sentence hypothesis are resulting from the features of the nucleus and of the hypotheses filling its slots.

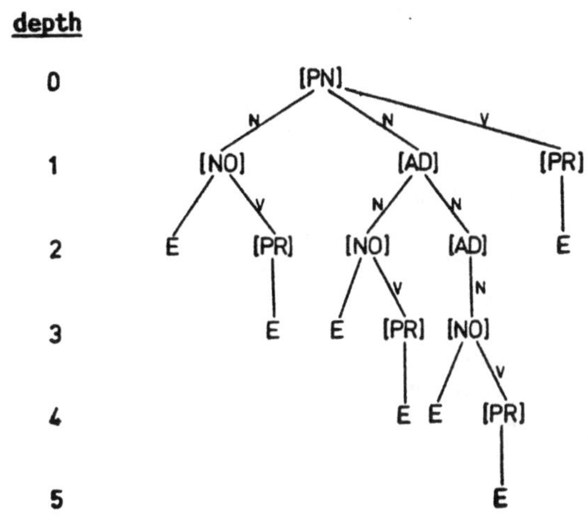

Figure 2: Categorial search tree for pronouns (PN)

Verification continues as long as existing slots can be filled. Then, generation of slots or hypotheses is resumed in a "best-first manner" either by further expanding a categorial search tree (see sect. 3.) or by selecting a new nucleus, which is found in the first position of a list of word hypotheses with increasing weights. Initially this WORDLIST contains all the word hypotheses that appear in the word lattice. For feasibility reasons the initial WORDLIST may be pruned in such a way that only word hypotheses with a weight lower than a certain value P are considered. Whenever a word hypothesis is selected as a nucleus it is discarded from WORDLIST.

3. S*-ALGORITHM

Although a large number of competing hypotheses may be generated, the procedure does not perform a complete search. One of the means for keeping the number of hypotheses within reasonable limits is the use of categorial search trees which provide a basis for utilizing the well-known A^*-algorithm, in order to persue only really promising phrase hypotheses. A suitably modified version of the A^*-algorithm is used which has been called S^*-algorithm /MUD 87/. This algorithm expands the categorial search tree that is indicated by the category of the nucleus and is used to determine the X best phrase hypotheses together with their weights, where X is a prespecified number. The algorithm maintains two lists, A-LIST and B-LIST, for generated and verified slots respectively. Operation is controlled by a function f^* as given below.

1. Put nucleus W on A-LIST. Calculate $f^*(W)$.
2. If A-LIST is empty and no goal has been reached so far, no solution exists. Otherwise no further solution exists.
3. Select from A-LIST that element i where f^* is minimum. If several elements qualify choose a goal element, otherwise choose the first.
4. Put element i on B-LIST and remove it from A-LIST.
5. Verify element i. If no verification is possible, remove element i from B-LIST. Go to 2.
6. If element i is a goal, a solution has been found. If it is the first solution, it is the optimal solution. Exit if parameter X is reached, otherwise go to 2.
7. If element i is not a goal, expand element i: Generate all possible successors N_i regarding the heuristic information given by the actual search tree. For each successor N_i, calculate $f^*(N_i)$. Put each successor N_i on A-LIST. Go to 2.

The function f^* is composed of two components. The first component g^* calculates the costs from the start node to a node n within the tree, and the second component h^* estimates the costs from the node n to a goal node, where a phrase hypothesis is completed. f^* is defined in such a way that the more promising a node is, the smaller is the value of f^*. f^* depends on the method of weighting hypotheses, and is defined in the ESR-system as follows:

$$f^*(n) = h^*(g^*(n)) \text{ with}$$

$$g^*(n) = \begin{cases} g^*(n-1) & \text{if goal node} \\ g^*(n-1)\,\dfrac{t}{t+1} + \dfrac{k(n)}{t+1} & \text{else} \end{cases}$$

$$h^*(g^*(n)) = \begin{cases} g^*(n) & \text{if goal node} \\ g^*(n)\,\dfrac{t+1}{t+2} + \dfrac{k_{min}}{t+2} & \text{else} \end{cases}$$

where k(n) is the weight of the actual word hypothesis (node n), $g^*(n-1)$ indicates the costs g^* of the predecessor node n-1 (predecessor of start node: $g^*(n-1)=0$), t is the depth of the search tree and k_{min} is the minimal weight of a word hypothesis.

According to the requirements of the A^*-algorithm, function f^* satisfies the admissibility condition as well as the consistency assumption.

4. EXPERIMENTAL RESULTS AND CONCLUSION

The ESR-system has been tested with a vocabulary of about 250 words (word forms) and a test set of 53 spoken utterances (sentences). About 200 word hypotheses for each spoken utterance were generated when a threshold for the word weights of 20 was given. The generation of phrase and sentence hypotheses were performed as two separate consecutive processes, in order to test the efficiency of the S^*-algorithm: First, the generation of phrase hypotheses was performed using the S^*-algorithm, and then the complete set of sentence hypotheses was determined. During the experiments the number of desired phrase hypotheses X and the pruning value P were varied. The experimental results are summarized in table 1.

		X					
		∞	5	3	2	1	
	∞	100	67,9	54,1	43,2	27,8	hypotheses[1)]
		96,4	92,9	88,6	75,7	36,2	recognition[2)]
P	12	45,9	23,4	16,7	----	----	hypotheses
		93,8	90,9	85,0	----	----	recognition
	10	30,7	14,5	10,1	----	----	hypotheses
		93,1	89,5	83,5	----	----	recognition

1) number of hypotheses in % compared to complete generation (X=∞, P=∞)
2) recognition rate on sentence level in %

Table 1: Experimental results using the S^*-algorithm

If all possible hypotheses are considered, the best possible recognition rate of 96,4% is archieved. Pruning of the WORDLIST, and also restricting the number of phrase hypotheses per nucleus to some value X, yields a significant reduction of the total number of hypotheses, however at the cost of a certain decrease of the recognition rate. Pruning of the WORDLIST regarding only hypotheses with a weight up to 10 reduces the number of hypotheses to about one third of the original number. Roughly, with X=5 the number of hypotheses can be halved. For the combination P=10, X=5 the number of hypotheses is reduced by a factor of 7, and the recognition rate decreases to 89,5%. This may be interpreted as substantial reduction of computational efforts at only a moderate loss in recognition performance. Current investigations shall reveal whether performance can be improved by incorporating prosodic analysis in order to assist the generation of phrase hypotheses.

REFERENCES

/ERM 80/ ERMAN, L.D., LESSER, V.R.: The HEARSAY-II Speech Understanding System: A Tutorial. In: Lea, W.A. (ed.): Trends in Speech Recognition, Prentice-Hall, Englewood Cliffs, 1980

/MUD 83/ MUDLER, J.: A System For Improving The Recognition Of Fluently Spoken German Speech. Proc. IJCAI-83, pp. 633-635

/MUD 84/ MUDLER, J., PAULUS, E.: Entwicklung und Erprobung der erwartungsorientierten Analyse für die automatische Spracherkennung. Sprache und Datenverarbeitung, 8. Jahrgang, 1984, Heft 1/2, S. 64-71.

/MUD 87/ MUDLER, J.: Erwartungsorientierte Spracherkennung. Dissertation, Technische Universität Braunschweig, 1987

/RUS 84/ RUSKE, G.: Halbsilben als Verarbeitungseinheiten bei der automatischen Spracherkennung. Sprache und Datenverarbeitung, 8. Jahrgang, 1984, Heft 1/2, S. 5-16

Merging Acoustics and Linguistics in Speech-Understanding

Gerh.Th.Niedermair
ZT ZTI INF 322
Siemens AG

Abstract:
The paper concentrates on the discussion of the interaction between acoustic and linguistic analysis. Recent approaches have either tried to master the number of acoustic hypotheses by applying successively syntactic and semantic restrictions on them. Other approaches have tried to have the acoustic recognition fully guided by these restrictions. The problems of both will be discussed. The paper will sketch a proposal for a closely linked , controlled interaction between linguistic prediction, acoustic recognition and linguistic verification in speech-understanding.

0. *Outset*

When processing spoken language, research has always been conscious of the fact that the recognition of words depends to a certain extent on what a listener expects; this refers to restrictions that are peculiar to the grammar he uses , second to what "makes sense " to him/her in a given situation, usually referred to as semantic restricions of the domain; and third by restrictions of what has been already said in a situation, known as pragmatics. Research in the latter field is only in the beginning (cf. Brietzmann/Ehrlich, 86).However, in speech-understanding systems the modelling of the mutual influence of these sources of restrictions has run into difficulties. Blackboard-architectures model the general aspect of this, but have so far failed to model the particular way of mutual influence. (cf. B.Hayes-Roth, 83).
In the following the focus will be on the central point of a close interaction between acoustic and linguistic analysis and not on system architectures as a whole, since they may look different depending on wether we have to deal with a dialogue-, QA-, or task oriented system.

1. *Bottom-up Flow*

1.1. *Syntax Oriented Analysis*

In a number of systems like Hearsay II, Spicos I, or EVAR a bottom -up acoustic analysis is followed by a syntactic analysis. The result of the first step is usually an undesireably large number of word-hypotheses scattered over the input. Prediction, if it plays a role at all, is used to select faster the proper hypotheses from the word lattice but not to guide acoustic recognition. For Spicos I , as for others, this number of hypotheses is 10 - 100 times the number of words in the spoken sentence, if the analysis is to guarantee that no more than 10 - 20 % of actually spoken words are missing entirely. What the system as a whole accomplishes is usually a bad compromise between what the syntactic analysis is still able to process, (not to forget that itself adds to the number of hypothesised structures [1]), and on the other hand how often one tolerates an interrupt of analysis because of missing words.

----

1) In Spicos I on average between 200 and 700 nominal constituents were produced out of the word-hypotheses. (cf. Dreckschmidt, 1987)

NATO ASI Series, Vol. F46
Recent Advances in Speech Understanding
and Dialog Systems
Edited by H. Niemann et al.

1.2. *Frame Oriented Analysis*

In frame oriented approaches, as developed at CMU (cf. Hayes, 86), the above mentioned difficulty of missing words is adressed by trying to fish for words in the hypotheses -lattice that are supposed to be central to the meaning of the sentence. These are to fill certain slots in case frames. Not all of the spoken words are necessary to completely fill a case frame. The hope is to be able to keep down the overall number of word hypotheses, that have to be considered and are needed to make up a sentence, because one can do without 'minor' words. However the consequence of such an approach is that:
- important syntactic restrictions are not taken into full account and therefore are not used for restricting possible word combinations. If frames are not used to supplement syntactic constraints by semantic restrictions, language analysis deteriorates to filling in sentence- or dialogue concepts by keywords.
- for each hypothesised keyword a frame has to be instantiated. When searching the whole sentence this leads to quite a number of partly instantiated frames. Apart from the considerable volume of datastructures the question of priority between fully or partly instantiated frames still remains a problem.
- since frame analysis is mainly oriented towards the main verb of a sentence, it is hard to see how, in a time-synchronous analysis from 'left to right' it could cope with domains that use other constructs than imperatives with verb initial position.

2. *Top-down Oriented Flow*

The need to restrict the search space for acoustic analysis by syntactic and semantic restrictions led to a number of techniques . Given a certain point of time in the signal analysis they produce a number of possible word successors within the given domain of application.

Semantic grammars have been used to accomplish this in a rather straight forward way. Since they are in fact only a very economic compression of sentence patterns, valid in the area of application, they implicitely contain syntactic regularities, but to the outside they only represent the result of these regularities as a condensed set of possible word-sequences. (cf. G.Thurmair 87, p.70). This set has to be rewritten for every new application.

Language-models, usually represented as finite state networks, are statistically constructed from a large number of examples in the application domain (cf. F.Jelinek , 82), or intellectually set up by a syntactic surface description based on a semanitically oriented model of the domain . They have been sucessfully implemented for top-down guided acoustic analysis. It was possible in SPICOS I to restrict the search space for acoustic analysis in such a way that an error-rate of about only 20% at the sentence level could be achieved. (cf. D.Mergel, 87). However, for the modelling of regularities the same is true here as above. Above that, when modelling sentence sequences, which depend on each other, as it is the case in dialogues, these models are facing serious difficulties.

Strictly top down oriented analysis in general has the disadvantage that :
- It always must project the acoustic signal on to the hypothesis that comes from the top model. This precludes the possibility of analysing previously unknown input (for instance with database updates). All utterable cases have explicitely to be foreseen. This seems to be a very contra-intuitive model of understanding.
- Linguistic analysis is only seen as a means to come to a yes/no decision wether a word is a possible successor or not, but not as itself a motor or supplier of heuristic clues for the ongoing analysis.
- It neglects the facts that with growing syntactic coverage and potentially richer domain the number of predicted items at a given place grows (potentially the complete lexicon). With it grows the cost to produce them . At the same time the

profit for the acoustic analysis decreases, since the hypotheses to be taken into account as possible successors of a given state are to many.

The above mentioned models in particular suffer from some disadvantages, namely that they:
- disregard the fact, that natural language is not finite state (cf. G.Thurmair, 87)
- have the tendency to get oversized, if they take into account all syntactic and semantic restrictions and do not artificially recombine nodes to shrink the complexity .
-make no distinction between syntactic and semantic restrictions , and therefore do not account for their respective regularities.

Before one considers an integration of
topdown linguistic hypotheses + acoustic verifikation on one hand and
bottom-up acoustic recognition + linguistic verification on the other
one has to be aware of some current boundary conditions.

3. *Current Boundary Conditions*

When thinking of future solution for a appearantly necessary interaction between acoustic and linguistic analysis that is not just serial one has to consider the following points:
A) - The blackboard-model forwards the idea of comprising different processes for a problem solution. Yet the model itself deliberately provides no constraints as to the interaction of the components. So far all implementations of a blackboard-model for speech understanding have run into control problems and ended up with a serial implementation of the processes involved. Besides that, the scheduling problem gets treated as an entirely separate problem, independent of the problem at hand (cf. Briscoe / Boguraev, 84).
B) - Given the current state of the art, the acoustic analysis has to search a large number of hypotheses in parallel in order to come to reasonable results. This requires rather intensive interaction with the linguistic components. Because of efficiency this interaction has to be kept to the possible minimum.
C) - a depth oriented search guided by linguistic plausibility and acoustic weight could only be sucessfull if from the linguistic point of view there is strong evidence that one hypotheses overrules the other. There will be very few places where this is possibly the case . Being guided by acoustic evidence only one may often run along the wrong track because the weights of the hypotheses in question are equally good.
Depth-oriented heuristic search needs the following conditions to be fullfilled:
- very strong linguistically motivated heuristics
- a high rate of certainty in acoustic recognition , which needs only a few items to compare in order to arrive at a reliable probability-score or
- a function that well estimates the cost of the paths not taken into account. This again presupposes the existence of all hypothesis over the whole input, which is not the case if linguistic analysis works time-synchronously from left to right .
- a measure to classify an acoustic signal as being below the level of recognition (here it seems rather impossible to distinguish between a bad match or just noisy data)

4. *Communication of Components*

In the light of the above mentioned points I will suggest an analysis procedure where the involved processes in turn make use of each others result and such proceed from left to right through the input signal. The arrangement, neither purely bottom up nor top down involves three major processes (figure 1):

Linguistic Prediction, which, based on a given path, computes restrictions on following words or wordchains. It should draw on syntactic as well as semantic restrictions. It may also produce probability scores that add up in some way or other to the acoustic score and help deciding which paths are most promising.
Acoustic Analysis, based on prediction (which may in certain cases be the full lexicon), produces word- or wordchain candidates with probability scores for a given path.
Linguistic Verification tries to verify the candidates according to full grammatical and semantic restriction and builds up a syntactic representation.

(fig. 1)

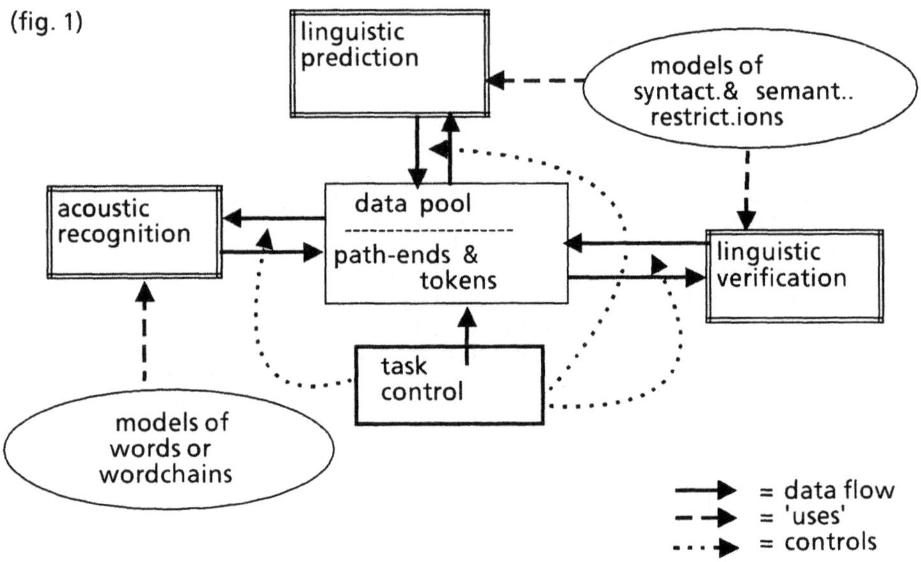

4.1 Linguistic Prediction

The linguistic prediction can either work on networks which are precompiled from a syntactic and semantic rule description of the domain in question (to what extent this will be feasible remains open), or could dynamically produce its hypotheses out of these descriptions. Predictions may overgeneralize, e.g. if they are only deduced from ensuing syntactic categoeries, as stated in the phrase structure part of the rule which is just being applied for a particular phrase. In either case two important factors need to be observed:
a) The communication with the other modules should be kept to a minimum (see 3. B)) This makes it desireable to precompile syntactically and semantically fairly stable sub-structures, that contain only local dependencies (e.g. dates). As subnetworks these should be available to the acoustic analysis just as wordmodels are. For dynamic prediction this would mean that the grammar treats those parts, for which subnetworks were precompiled, as terminal elements.

b) Prediction should be able to decide when it is too costly or of too little effect to produce the hypotheses in question (e.g. in case of undetermined places in the syntax). As a consequence, prediction must be allowed to overgeneralize. Apart from that, dynamically inferring complete information from syntactic and semantic description at every place is not in sight, nor (as a consequence) is full precompilation of a full fledged syntactic grammar, which is not written in a context free way.

4.2. *Acoustic Analysis*

Acoustic analysis takes these predictions to limit the number of possible continuations for a given path. If there is no restriction from prediction, it is up to the acoustic analysis to decide on acoustic data only, which hypotheses it wants to bring up as possible candidates. From the point of interaction the acoustic analysis works on word-models or other closed models of locally bounded structures (subnetworks). It delivers however many top candidates that belong to a certain path. Which paths are followed is due to the requirements of acoustic search (see above 3. C)). Due to overgeneralization in prediction, the candidates may contain some, that do not fit into the tight syntactic and semantic context of the path they were given for.

4.3 *Linguistic Verification*

Linguistic verification therefore takes these candidates and eliminates those who are no valid continuations of the path in question. This has of course to be the same path that they were predicted for (since acoustic analysis also has to take into acount the left context for interword assimilation.) . The verification should in one step make use of all syntactic and semantic restrictions, that it can get hold of . (cf G.Thurmair , 87).
There is no point in continuing syntactically correct structures if they are, up to this point, not within the semantic constraints of the domain. This makes it necessary to strongly couple syntactic and semantic analysis, yet maintaining a clear cut seperation between the two in terms of representing their own constraints. (This in turn complicates of course the process of dynamic prediction) . Spicos II will aim at clear solutions for this problem.
Linguistic verification is also in a position to apply linguistically motivated heuristics, such as plausibility measures for given structures. (e.g. near the end of a sentence a structure that has already gathered all obligatory arguments is more likely to 'win' than one with a number of free adverbs). These may come to bear when it is decided that only plausible structures are passed on for further prediction. Who passes on and who decides?

4.4. *Task Control*

The task controller has to watch over incoming and outgoing data from each of the processes. The data in essence consist of identifications of paths, which must be known by all processes, together with identifiers for verified or predicted items. The controller passes them on to the process whose turn it is next. Depending on the requirements of the processes involved, (they may well vary with different acoustic analysis procedures) it administrates the data and regulates their proper selection for passing them on.

Gaining greater transparency of the exchanged data and their flow allows to:

1. Explicitely model the successive invocation of the processes involved

2. Adapt the flow of information to the requirements of the processes, when experimenting with different approaches.

3. Model the invocation of processes and the data they are supplied with such that they are based on certain conditions, which may be
- local (e.g. the above mentioned linguistic plausibility before passing on verified results) or
- global, such as current system resources like memory space and computing time, or overall phenomena, like too many hypotheses under consideration;
just like humans do when they say : "eh ? "

References:

Brietzmann, A.: Semantische und pragmatische Analyse im Erlanger Spracherkennungsprojekt. Arbeitsberichte des Instituts f. Mathem. Maschinen und Datenverarbeitung. Bd.17, Nr.5 , 1984

Brietzmann, A., Ehrlich, U.,:The Role of Semantic Processing in an Automatic Speech Understanding System. Proceed. of the COLING Conf. 1986

Briscoe, E., Boguraev, B.,: Control Structures and Theories of Interaction in Speech Understanding Systems. Proceed. of the COLING Conf. 1984

Dreckschmidt,G.: The Linguistic Component in the Speech Understanding System SPICOS. in: Tillmann,H., Willée,G., ed.: Analyse und Synthese gesprochener Sprache, Hildesheim 1987

Erman, L., Hayes-Roth, F., Lesser, V., Reddy, R.: The Hearsay II Speech Understanding System . in: Computing Surveys, vol. 12, 1980

Hayes, Ph., Hauptmann, A., Carbonell, J., Tomita, M.: Parsing Spoken Language: A Semantic Case Frame Approach. Proceed. of the COLING Conf. 1986

Hayes-Roth, B.: The Blackboard Architecture: A General Framework for Problem Solving. Stanford University Report, May 1983

Jelinek, F.: Self Organised Continuous Speech Recognition. in: Haton, J-P.,ed.: Automatic Speech Analysis and Recognition. 1982

Mergel, D., Paesseler, A.: Construction of Language Models for Spoken Database Queries. to appear at ICASP 87

Thurmair, G.: Linguistische Analyse im Projekt SPICOS. in: Kleinheubacher Berichte 29, 1986

Thurmair, G.: Der Einsatz semantischer Verfahren in sprachverstehenden Systemen. in: Tillmann,H., Willée,G., ed.: Analyse und Synthese gesprochener Sprache, Hildesheim 1987

USING SEMANTIC AND PRAGMATIC KNOWLEDGE FOR THE INTERPRETATION OF SYNTACTIC CONSTITUENTS

Ute Ehrlich, Heinrich Niemann
Lehrstuhl für Informatik 5 (Mustererkennung)
Universität Erlangen-Nürnberg
Martensstr. 3, 8520 Erlangen, F. R. Germany

Abstract: In the speech understanding and dialogue system EVAR /NIEMANN 85/ linguistic knowledge is used for the interpretation of the meaning of a sentence and finding the user's intention for uttering it /BRIETZMANN 86/. Another very important point especially for the semantic and pragmatic knowledge is using it as early as possible for filtering hypotheses produced during the different steps of analysis, i.e. for example word recognition and syntactic anlaysis. This can be done also for hypotheses about single syntactic constituents like nominal or prepositional phrases. In this paper it is shown how special semantic features in our system are used for compatibility checks within the words of a syntactic constituent. On the other hand complex constituents built up of several simple syntactic constituents are sought (like "the train | to Hamburg"). For all so found "semantic" constituent hypotheses the possible referential objects are determined using information about the dialogue context, or if no referent can be found, they are rejected.

1. Introduction

The task of the semantic analysis in the speech understanding and dialogue system EVAR /NIEMANN 85/ is not only the semantic interpretation of structures like single syntactic constituents or whole sentences. Other tasks are the discovery of semantic inconsistencies between words building such a structure, the combination of some (semantically consistent) units which do not cover the whole range of the speech signal to bigger units and finding and interpreting an underlying structure of these units. In the following it is assumed that the syntactic analysis produces only hypotheses about simple constituents which themselves do not contain other constituents. Hypotheses about sentences covering the whole range of the speech signal are not used. Since the word recognition module does not find all actually spoken words, it is impossible to find the spoken sentence by parsing methods without allowing gaps. On the other hand the number of hypotheses found if gaps would be allowed would become too high to manage. But it even does not seem to be necessary to recognize all words. For example in the utterance "I want to go *to*

NATO ASI Series, Vol. F46
Recent Advances in Speech Understanding and Dialog Systems
Edited by H. Niemann et al.

Hamburg tomorrow." the really important words to understand the sentence in the situation of an information dialogue about intercity trains are "tomorrow to Hamburg". For these reasons the finding of longer word chains is left to the semantic module which can integrate semantic (and also pragmatic) knowledge in the search algorithm. In this paper the main point of interest is the semantic and pragmatic analysis of constituent hypotheses produced by the syntax module. Further steps of the semantic analysis are described in /EHRLICH 87/.

In our approach the semantic analysis of whole sentences is based on the caseframe theory (see for example /TESNIERE 66/) and the deep case theory (based on /FILLMORE 68/). These caseframes are modelled in a semantic network (strongly influenced by the formalism of *Structured Inheritance Networks,* see /BRACHMAN 78/). This approach gives us also the possibility to start the analysis with the actants of a verb, not only with the head verb of the sentence itself (which is important if this verb was not detected or was not articulated in the case of an ellipsis). The casesframe approach is also used in /HAYES 86/, but there it is integrated into a parsing strategy which covers also the syntactic analysis. Also /NIEDERMAIR 86/ uses caseframes (implemented as a chart parser) after the parsing of syntactic constituents. This mehtod has the disadvantage that the analysis is strongly left-to-right so that incomplete utterances cannot be handled (as they can in /HAYES 86/ and /EHRLICH 87/).

2. Filtering of Constituents

2.1 Semantic Consistency

For the represention of the meaning of a word semantic classes like 'LOCation' ('Hamburg') or 'TRAnsport' ('train') are used. These classes are ordered hierarchically, for example the class 'THIng' comprises also the class 'TRAnsport', i.e. the word 'train' can represent also the class 'THIng'. For some words (prepositions, adjectives) there exist selectional restrictions for the possible combinations with other words, especially nouns. For example the word 'fast' in the meaning of 'a fast train' requires a noun which describes an object with the property that it can be moved or can move itself. So the noun phrase 'the fast tree' has to be rejected as semantically inconsistent. The selectional restrictions between the words of a syntactic constituent are checked by bit operations. Therefore the semantic classes of a word and all their generalizations are coded in a bitvector. Each bit of this vector represents one semantic class. The selectional restrictions are represented by a bitvector that encodes only the classes themselves without their generalizations so that the checking of the restrictions is done by the operation 'logical and' which can be executed very fast.

2.2 The Semantic Features TYPE and REFERENCE

In addition to these semantic classes words also can have other semantic features. One of them is the feature REFERENCE which indicates whether a constituent refers to an object in the real world that is known a priori in the situational context (REFERENCE: deictic), for example "I" or "here", or if the object has been mentioned before during the dialogue (REFERENCE: anaphoric), for example "he" or "it". Another feature is the TYPE which can have values like 'possessive' (for example "my") or 'definite' (for example "this"). Not all the values of these two features can be combined. If contradictions occur, the constituents are rejected. Fig. 1 shows some examples of constituents where a feature of one word of the constituent is not compatible with the same or another feature of another word within the constituent, for example the article "one" with "TYPE indefinite" cannot be used together with the adjective "next" with "superlative" form like in (*) "one next train".

REFERENCE	TYPE	EXAMPLE
	question, indefinite	*"which a child?"*
	possessive, indefinite	*"a my car"*
	demonstrative, indefinite	*"this a man"*
anaphoric	**indefinite**	*"several all"*
anaphoric	**question**	*"which he?"*
deictic	**question**	*"how today?"*
	indefinite +ordinal	*"all first trains"*
	indefinite +superlative	*"one next train"*

Fig. 1: Contradiction of Semantic Features (part)

2.3 Constituents without Articles

Singular constituents without an article or a numeral are only accepted if they describe limited sets or unique things. This can be checked using the syntactic class (proper nouns can always be used without an article) or the semantic classes (for example words with the class 'COnTinous' - e.g. substances like 'water' - or with the class 'ACting_ Person' - e.g. describing the profession, the function or the nationality of a person - in German need not be combined with an article).

3. Finding Complex Constituents

Constituents that can be accepted as parts of a sentence dependent on the head verb can also be combined of several single constituents. In the following three different possibilities for the combination of constituents are presented.

3.1 Genitive Constructions

Dependent on nearly each noun there can be a genitive constituent describing a possessive relation (like "Peter's car") or the part of a whole (like "the room of the house"). These relations can be realized by a post positive genitive noun phrase, for example "der Speisewagen *des IC's 502*" (the dining car of the intercity train number 502) or a post positive prepositional phrase with the preposition "von" for example "der Hut *von diesem Mann*" (the hat of this man). The realization by the -s genitive before the head noun phrase for example "(mit) *Peters* Auto" (with Peter's car) is neglected because it cannot be found by chaining simple syntactic constituents ("with ... car" - "Peter's"). Another possibility, a possessive pronoun, for example, "*mein* Auto (my car), is already found during syntactic analysis. Therefore there is no need to consider it for finding complex constituents.

3.2 Denominal Actants

Nouns and adjectives can open slots to be filled with special constituents as do verbs. This is called the "valency" of a word. For the realization of the single slots (called actants) morpho-syntactic and semantic restrictions (see for example /TESNIERE 66/) can be given.

In principle it is tried to find for each constituent all possible actants before the constituent (with regard to the speech signal) if its head is an adjective respcetively after it if its head is a noun. These complex constituents then can be dependent on the head verb of the sentence like the simple constituents can. At the time all actants of nouns (for example "the train | to Hamburg") and of predicative adjectives (like "This ticket costs *more than the other.*") are analyzed. Actants of attributive adjectives ("die 2 Meilen lange Straße" - the 3 miles long road) and multilevel dependencies between constituents ("the waggon ← of the train ← to Hamburg", where a← b means "b is dependent on a") are not considered, although the analyzation would not require any difficulty (it would be only new data for just implemented algorithms). But such constructions seem to be too unnatural for spoken communication, as at least our own sample survey shows.

3.3 Temporal Constituents

For the application "information about intercity trains" the recognition and interpretation of temporal constituents are very important. Temporal constituents can be chained together. This chaining results in new temporal constituents which have to be interpreted as a whole (for example "on Friday | morning | at nine o' clock"). The combination of the single constituents is strictly limited by morpho-syntactic, semantic and pragmatic rules. The analysis is implemented as an ATN parser (see Fig. 2).

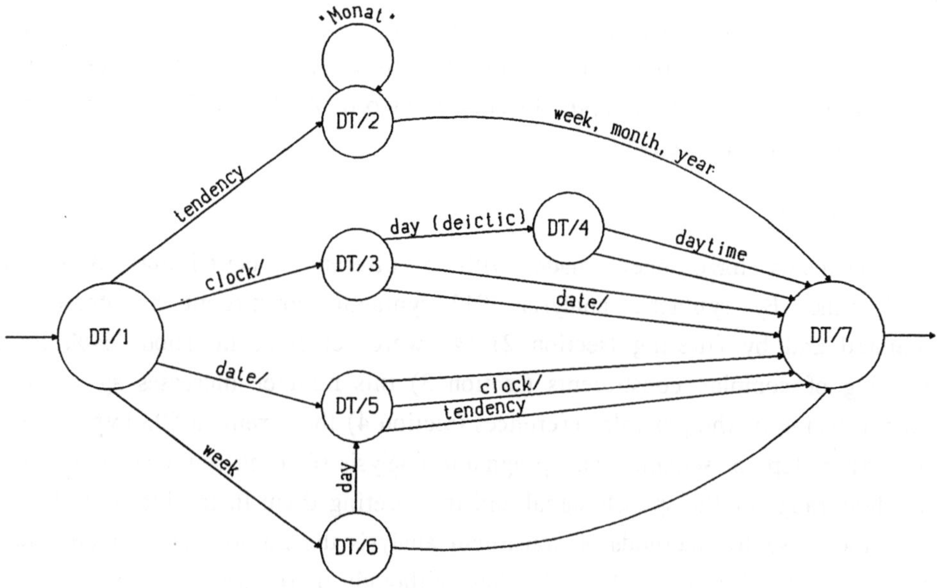

Example:
DT/1 - at nine o' clock - DT/3 - tomorrow - DT/4 - morning - DT/7

Fig. 2: Determination of Time

4. Resolving of Anaphoric References

During a dialogue it is possible and often used to refer back to a just mentioned entity by uttering anaphoric pronouns (like "it") or descriptive noun phrases (like "the - just mentioned - train"). In our system this is used for filtering the constituent hypotheses once more. At the time all possible referents for pronouns, adverbs (like "then") and definite noun phrases are resolved including the reference to a member of a just mentioned set. The information for this process is generated by a dialogue memory module. All hypotheses that are neither known in the dialogue situation (like proper names) nor have at least one possible referent are rejected as not interpretable.

Example:

U1: Ich möchte morgen früh nach *Hamburg* fahren. (I want to go to Hamburg tomorrow morning.)

S1: Sie können den *Intercity* um 8.30 h nehmen. Der kostet aber *Zuschlag*.
(You can take the intercity train at 8.30. But you have to buy an additional ticket.)

U2: Was kostet der? (What does it cost?)

U2': Hat *der Zug* auch einen Speisewagen? (Does the train have a dining waggon?)

In this example the possible referents of the pronoun "der" (U2) are the "Intercity" (S1) or the "Zuschlag" (S1). The decision between these alternatives is made for every possible context during the further steps of analysis. Also the definite noun phrase "der Zug" (U2') would be accepted because the word "Zug" describes a generalization of the referent of "Intercity".

5. Experiments

Experiments have been made with 5 utterances containing 13 syntactic constituents. By syntactic analysis 1012 syntactic constituent hypotheses were generated and by filtering (section 2) 645 were rejected, i.e about 64% By the analyzing of complex constituents (section 3) this number increases again to 557. After resolving of the possible references (section 4) there remain 503 hypotheses for the further steps of semantic and pragmatic analysis (finding sentences which cover the whole range of the speech signal and interpreting them in the intercity domain). So by the presented methods of consituent analysis the number of syntactic correct constituents can be reduced to the half although there are added new complex constituent hypotheses combined of several single syntactic constituents.

REFERENCES

/BRIETZMANN 86/ A. Brietzmann, U. Ehrlich: The Role of Semantic Processing in an Automatic Speech Understanding System. In: Proceedings of the 11th International Conference on Computational Linguistics, Bonn, F.R. Germany, p.596-598.

/EHRLICH 87/ U. Ehrlich: Multilevel Semantic Analysis in an Automatic Speech Understanding System. In: Proceedings of the 3rd Conference of the European Chapter of the ACL, to appear.

/FILLMORE 68/ C.F. Fillmore: The Case for Case. In: E. Bach, R.T. Harms (eds.). Universals in Linguistic Theory. Holt, Rinehart & Winston, New York, p. 1-88.

/HAYES 86/ P.J. Hayes, A.G. Hauptmann, J.G. Carbonell, M. Tomita: Parsing Spoken Language: a Semantic Caseframe Approach. In: Proceedings of the 11th International Conference on Computational Linguistics, Bonn, F.R. Germany, p.587-592.

/NIEDERMAIR 86/ G.T. Niedermair: Divided and Valency-oriented Parsing in Speech Understanding. In: Proceedings of the 11th International Conference on Computational Linguistics, Bonn, F.R. Germany, p.593-595.

/NIEMANN 85/ H. Niemann, A. Brietzmann, R. Mühlfeld, P. Regel, E.G. Schukat: The Speech Understanding and Dialog System EVAR. In: New Systems and Architectures for Automatic Speech Recognition and Synthesis, R.de Mori & C.Y. Suen (eds). NATO ASI Series F16, Berlin, p. 271-302.

/TESNIERE 66/ L. Tesniere: Elements de syntaxe structurale. 2nd edition. Klincksieck, Paris.

This work was carried out in cooperation with Siemens AG, München

TASK-ORIENTED DIALOGUE PROCESSING IN HUMAN-COMPUTER VOICE COMMUNICATION

N. Carbonell and J.M. Pierrel
CRIN / INRIA-Lorraine
B.P. 239 - 54506 Vandoeuvre cedex, France

Abstract : For three years we have been developing a voice dialogue system capable of continuous speech recognition, natural language understanding, task-oriented dialogue managing. First, the architecture of the system is surveyed. Then, the dialogue component is described. Finally, a dialogue execution trace produced by a prototype implementation is discussed by way of illustration.

We are developing a knowledge-based system capable of understanding oral task-oriented dialogues in a multi-speaker environment. This system should be able to process pseudo-natural sublanguages, that is subsets from natural language with few syntactic restrictions and large vocabularies (several thousand words).

Information Centers provide a wide range of potential applications for the general public. In order to test and validate design choices, we are implementing an automatic Administrative Information center.

We will first survey the overall architecture of the system, which is fully described in /CAR 86b/. Then we shall focus on the dialogue component.

1. INTRODUCTION : THE SYSTEM FUNCTIONALITIES AND ARCHITECTURE

Knowledge has been split up into several separate bases, in order to achieve :

- **flexibility** : the knowledge sources relating to a specific application (namely the lexicon and the application universe) can be defined as parameters to the system.

- **modularity** : our system is made up of five autonomous processors, each of them accessing only one of the knowledge sources involved in the understanding of continuous speech, thus preventing knowledge access conflicts between processors and making incremental development possible. These processors are described on Figure 1 together with the flow of information between them ; their functionalities, which are summarized here are detailed in /CAR 86b/ :

. APHON (acoustic-phonetic) :
segmentation of the signal and phonetic labeling (cf. /CAR 86a/).

. PROSO (prosodic) :
detection of prosodic markers indicating word or syntagm boundaries and statement type (assertion, question, contestation).

. SYN-SEM (syntactic-semantic) :
elaboration of semantic representations from the word lattice corresponding to a statement ; procedural node networks are used to perform local/global syntactic analysis ; semantic representations are generated by a case grammar.

NATO ASI Series, Vol. F46
Recent Advances in Speech Understanding and Dialog Systems
Edited by H. Niemann et al.

. DIAL (dialogue) :
for each interaction with the user :
. interpretation of the semantic structures generated by SYN-SEM, using the dialogue history, current goal, active script(s) and pragmatic knowledge ;
. generation of an appropriate reply to the user.

The recognition and understanding of a statement from the user may proceed from left to right or from anchor points outwards, depending on the reliability of available acoustic data. At any stage, the system may choose between bottom-up and top-down approaches, according to the nature of currently available data.

2. THE DIALOGUE COMPONENT (DIAL)

Figure 2 shows the structure of the dialogue component, with an emphasis on the different types of knowledge and dynamic information used by each subcomponent.

2.1. Knowledge sources used by DIAL and their representation

a. the application universe

It is represented by a set C of concepts.

ex : isa (identity_card, identification_document), isa* (identity_card, document).

b. Interpretation rules

These production rules help the interpreter to transform a case structure generated by SYN-SEM into a scored formula.

A scored formula is a pair (f,s) where f is a typed formula on C and s a global plausibility score that takes into account word recognition scores : typed formulas are represented here using functional denotation.

ex : . obtain (speaker, identity_card) is an elementary typed formula of type "obtain", whereas obtain (passport, fiscal stamp) is invalid, passport being inanimate ;
. and (nationality (speaker, not (France)), minor (speaker)) is a typed formula as well as apply (speaker, or (city_hall, police station)).

Questions are formulas containing one occurence of the concept "?" at least.

ex : . cost (fiscal stamp (identity_card), ?) corresponds to an open question ;
. ? minor (speaker) is a possible yes-no question from the system.

Thanks to interpretation rules, semantic representations of statements are contextually interpreted in relation to the dialogue history ; in particular, references and ellipses are solved.

ex : given the following dialogue extract :
system : Are you of age ?
speaker : yes.

and the interpretation rule :

if type (preceding_reply) = yes-no_question and type (current_reply) = agreement
then validation (preceding_reply_formula)

the interpreter replaces "yes" by the elementary formula major (speaker).

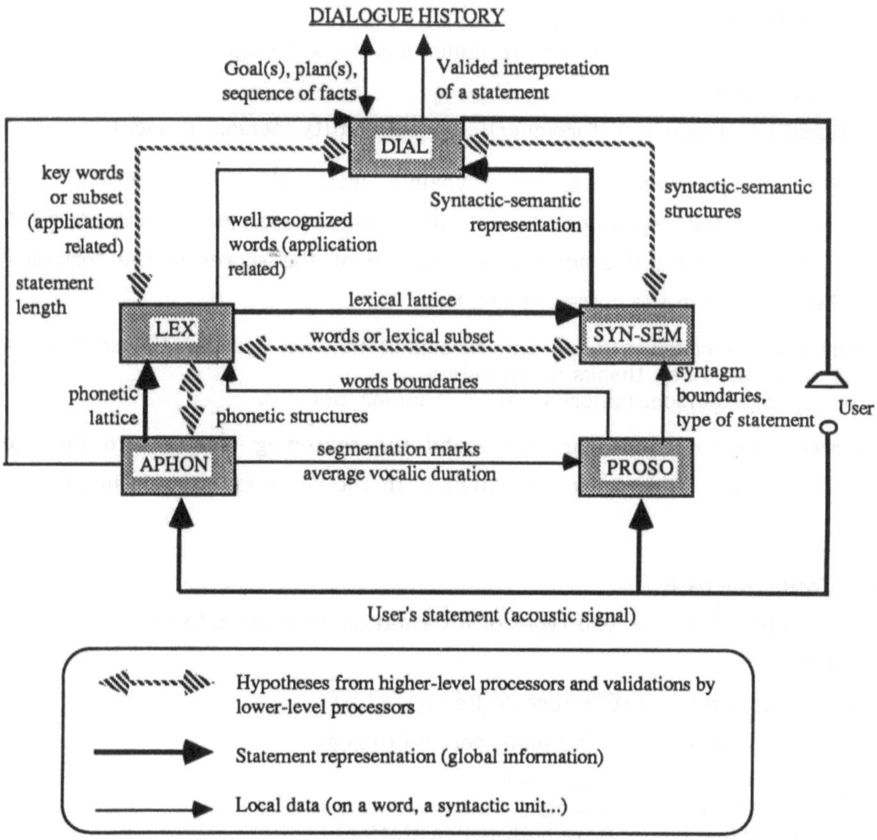

Figure 1 : General architecture of the dialogue system.

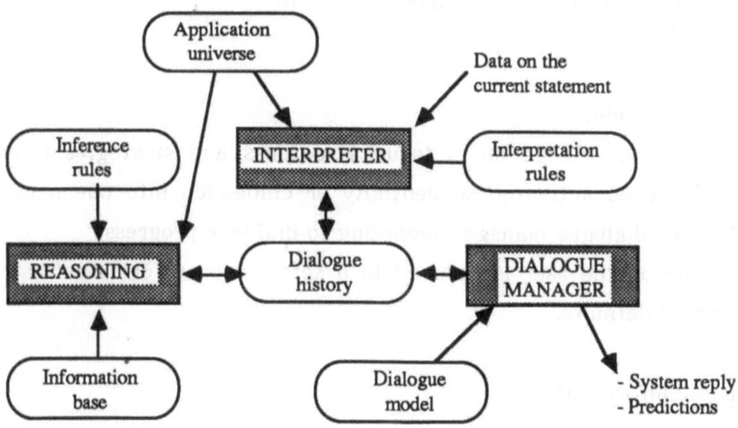

Figure 2 : Structure of the Dialogue component.

c. inference rules

f_1 ---> f_2, where f_1 and f_2 are formulas and "--->" designates logical implication, is an inference rule.

ex : nationality (person, not (foreigner)) ---> nationality (person, France).

Thanks to inference rules, new dynamic information is elaborated from an interpretation of the user's current statement and the dialogue history. Any inferred formula gets a score ; this score is a function of the scores in the formulas that match the premices in the corresponding rule.

ex : from (age (speaker, 20), s), the reasoning module deduces the scored formula (major (speaker), s), thanks to the rule :
greater (age (person, majority_age) ---> major (person).

Inferred scored formulas are stored by the reasoning module into the dialogue history if and only if they are consistent with the formulas already in this working memory.

d. the information base

This data base contains two types of information relating to the task :

- formulas :

ex : telephone_number (Préfecture_de_Région, 87...)

- conditional expressions (on formulas) related to goals :

```
goal obtain (person, identity_card)
  if nationality (person, France)
  then (apply (person, or (city_hall, police_station)
       bring ( person, and (fiscal_stamp,
                 or family_record_book, identification_sheet)))
       if minor (person)
       then accompany (person, parent (person))
       endif
endif.
```

e. the dialogue model

At present, knowledge on dialogue structures and strategies is represented by plans that may be activated sequentially or embedded into one another. Plans are selected by the dialogue manager according to dialogue progress.

Knowledge on the user is reduced to a set of scored formulas that the reasoning module uses as defaults.

2.2. Dynamic information

It consists of :

- scored syntactic-semantic representations of the current statement from the user ; they constitute DIAL inputs.

- scored formulas elaborated by the interpreter from syntactic-semantic representations of the user's current statement ; together with the dialogue history, they are used by the reasoning module as a fact base.

- the dialogue history : this working memory stores four types of information :

. scored formulas representing the contents of the user's statements (up to the current one), as well as information inferred from them ;
. formulas corresponding to the former replies from the system ;
. successive active goals in the form of scored formulas deduced by the reasoning module from interpretations of specific requests from the user ;
. successively activated plans up to the current one.

- the system reply to the user, which constitutes one of the output of DIAL and is elaborated by the dialogue manager.
If the user's statement concerns communication management (such as : "could you repeat, please ?"), no reasoning is performed.
If it is related to the task, it is processed by the reasoning module which, in the case of a question, has to access the information base and to copy out retrieved information into the dialogue history, besides validated interpretations and inferred formulas. Then, the dialogue manager selects the content of the system reply among the various formulas in the dialogue history, according to current goal, plan and dialogue strategy. At present, the linguistic generation module being not yet implemented, the system replies are given in the form of formulas.

- DIAL other outputs are predictions on the form of the next statement from the user ; they are elaborated by the dialogue manager from the system reply and the dialogue model. These predictions are sent to the understanding and recognition components in the system, making top-down analysis possible (cf. /CAR 86b/.

3. CONCLUSION

As a summary and an illustration of DIAL description, a dialogue execution trace produced by the present incomplete prototype implementation is given and commented in appendix. For the moment, semantic representations of statements from the user are entered interactively ; scoring has not been yet integrated into the system.

/CAR 86a/ N. Carbonell, J.P. Damestoy, D. Fohr, J.P. Haton, F. Lonchamp : APHODEX, design and implementation of an acoustic-phonetic decoding expert system. Proceedings of IEEE-ICASSP, Tokyo, Japan, 1986.

/CAR 86b/ N. Carbonell, J.M. Pierrel : Architecture and knowledge sources in a human computer oral dialogue system. Proceedings of NATO Workshop : structure of multimodal dialogues including voice. Corsica, France, 1986.

APPENDIX

Target dialogue	**Comments on the trace of the system inputs, outputs and reasoning**
S : Hello! Administrative Information Center speaking.	<-- greeting_statement
U : Hello! To whom can I apply for an identity card ?	--> goal (speaker, obtain (speaker, identity_card))[1] apply (speaker, current_goal, ?) *. selection of structure st matching goal in IB and replacement of person by speaker in st.* *. selection (in st) of formula matching speaker's question, using default = nationality (speaker, France)*
S : To the police station or the city hall	<-- or (city_hall, police_station)
U : What are the formalities ?	--> formality (current_goal, ?) *. selection (in st) of the whole conditional structure c* *. test of conditiion : minor (speaker) in c* *. result of test being undefined (no value in dialogue history, no default), dialogue strategy = ask for undefined value*
S : Are you under-age ?	<-- ? minor (speaker)
U : No, no.	--> not minor (speaker) *. not minor(speaker) is added to the dialogue history* *. selection (in c) of formulas verifying not minor(speaker) and not already communicated to the user.*
S : You have to produce your family record book or an identification sheet and bring a fiscal stamp.	<-- bring (speaker, and (fiscal_stamp, or (family_record_book, identifying_sheet)))
U : How much does a fiscal stamp cost ?	--> cost (fiscal_stamp (identity_card), ?) *. selection in IB of the requested price*
S : 115 F.	<-- cost (fiscal_stamp (identity_card), 115)
U: Thank you	--> satisfaction_of_the_user *. suppression of the current goal (since no new request)* *. request for a new goal (since no active goal)*
S : Do you want anything else ?	--> goal (speaker, ?)
U : No. Thank you. Goodbye.	<-- goal (speaker,$\wedge$) and farewell_statement [2]
S : Goodbye.	--> farewell_statement

1. cf the example page 3.
2. $\wedge$ designate the empty formula.

N.B. Characters typed on the keyboard or displayed on the screen are in bold type whereas comments are in italics.

EXPERIMENTATION IN THE SPECIFICATION OF AN ORAL DIALOGUE

M. GUYOMARD - J. SIROUX
CNET LAA/TSS/RCP
BP 40 22301 LANNION FRANCE

KEYWORDS.

Oral dialogue/ experimentation/ cooperation/ pragmatics/ speech recognition/ corpus/ dialogue strategy

ABSTRACT.

With the aim of achieving a system for oral interrogation of a telephone information type application, we have carried out experimental work* on dialogue between subjects and a simulated machine. This work was carried out in two phases in order to yield a definition of the dialogue making it possible to undertake its implementation. In the first phase we used both a highly constrained dialogue and an unrestricted dialogue. The second phase was based on the conclusions drawn from the previous dialogues and on a strategy for cooperation. In this paper we describe and analyse both phases. Particular attention is paid to the dialogue strategy (cooperation, phatic management).

0. INTRODUCTION.

Research in areas such as speech signal analysis, acoustics, phonetics and syntax have enabled different laboratories to develop prototype speech recognition and understanding systems applied to data base inquiries (BIERMANN,85), (NIEMANN,86), (SIROUX,85), (PECKHAM,86). These first systems lead to an awareness of the handicap that constitute the quasi-non-existence of theoretical foundations (dialogue models) vis-a-vis the development of man-machine oral dialogue systems.

So, in order to design a new realistic oral system, we decided to carry out an experimentation on oral dialogue. More precisely, we have attempted, through our experimental work, to: (1) check that the constraints arising through the limitations imposed by the use of automatic speech recognition (ASR) don't constitute an insurmountable obstacle to the system's viability; (2) make a list of the constraints that were overlooked initially and originating from the subjects' linguistic and strategic behaviour, whilst trying to make a distinction between those which can't be got round and those which can be overcome by supplying a few simple instruction to the user; (3) specify the future system, taking account of the above points, so as to produce: the ASR system's vocabulary, the syn-

---

* This work was carried out in the framework of the ESPRIT P1015 "Palabre" project, partially financed by the EEC.

NATO ASI Series, Vol. F46
Recent Advances in Speech Understanding and Dialog Systems
Edited by H. Niemann et al.

tactic constructions and the description of the oral dialogue that the system will be able to manage.

1. METHODOLOGY USED IN EXPERIMENTAL WORK.

Because the application (Yellow Pages verbal information service) doesn't exist, we assemble our own experimental dialogue system. In order to avoid imposing a priori constraints that it would be impossible to adhere to, we decided to conduct the work in two phases, the findings from the first being used as a basis for implementing the second. The first phase was itself divided into two parts covering the spectrum of the possible types of dialogue: firstly, a highly-directed dialogue, secondly, a completely unrestricted dialogue; this being done in order to find the constraints that won't be respected by the majority of users and the dialogue functions that are used spontaneously by the typical user. A judicious compromise can then lead to an acceptable dialogue both from the user's point of view as well as from the point of view of the state of the art in ASR and dialogue management.

Equipment setup: it was designed to give the subject the impression he was conversing with a machine. To achieve this, the announcer's voice was deformed as the result of passing through two vocoders. Additionally, in order to approach speech recognition conditions, the announcer's listening signal was deteriorated by insertion of a noise generator.

The application and the documentation: the subject is able to obtain information (name, address, telephone number, locality) about traders by supplying a certain amount of data (parameters). We restricted ourselves to 24 headings having a bearing on the transport and vehicles field and, from a geographical aspect, to ten localities around the town of Lannion.

The subjects: they were selected from voluntary, paid students. In all, 30 subjects were chosen, 15 for each phase.

The scenarios: the subject was put (artificially) in the position of someone requiring the name and other details of a trader, starting out from one of 41 possible scenarios.

2. THE EXPERIMENTAL WORK.

2.1 First phase of experimental work.

The directed dialogue protocol: the directed dialogue was formalized by a finite state automaton. In principle, the dialogue was fairly similar to that described by Van Katwijk et al. (VAN KATWIJK,79). It can be characterized by four points:

- The "system" only accepts strict responses on the part of the subject.
- For its part, the "system" responds strictly to the request formulated by the subject.
- Certain short utterances by the "system" are followed by a short pause, giving the subject the possibility of intervening (implicit utterance).
- A few simple commands ("repeat", "end", "more details") allowed the subject to partially control running of the dialogue.

The unrestricted dialogue protocol: the instructions are less clear-cut here: the announcer should rather follow the line of the dialogue whilst remaining cooperative.

Directed dialogues - Analysis and results:

- The directed dialogue as designed isn't viable for an occasional user: as an example, strict answers to yes/no questions from the announcer were not obtained.
- In line with Van Katwijk, we consider it indispensable to take account of indirect responses by the user.
- For phase 2 it is desirable to integrate the deviations which are frequently observed (spelling, user's dialogue control).

Unrestricted dialogues - Analysis and results:

- The majority of utterances made by subjects were marred by hesitations, false starts, re-starts and self-corrections. These phenomena are currently the object of study with a view to particular modelling.
- The size of vocabulary gathered is reasonable (353 terms).
- The "system's" behaviour must imperatively be made more cooperative. In the management of the succession of utterances, it is indispensable to provide instants for possible intervention by the user and to handle non-interventions in a satisfactory manner.
- The structure of the dialogues is sufficiently regular for modelling to be undertaken.

2.2 The second phase of the experimental work.

Protocol of the second phase: the emphasis was put on specifying the dialogue aimed at. Rather than going for an exhaustive approach, we shall limit our description to the pragmatic aspect of the dialogue and to phatic management.

Cooperation: the cooperative principles applied in this phase of the work arise from Kaplan's work (KAPLAN,82) and are discussed in more detail in (GUYOMARD,86). They are founded on the following pragmatic rule: when a wh-question would yield a strict answer that is empty, then it is preferable: to refute the false presuppositions that the question contains and then, to try and re-start the dialogue by proposing the answer to a weakened (less strict) question arising out of the initial question. This general framework finds its application both in the request negotiation phase as well as during answer negotiation.

Follow-on dialogues: these are dialogues that follow at the user's initiative through the utterance of a new request. During a session, the influence of a dialogue can become felt after it is completed. It is necessary to take account of this if the dialogue is to remain natural. We have formalized this influence of the context by drawing up rules, one example of which is: "If the new request uses a parameter that is in the field of the corrective or suggestive answer of previous requests (all other parameters being otherwise equal), the cooperative answer process is inhibited for this new request".

Implicit utterances: we have maintained the principle of implicit utterances and systematized their use.

Phatic management: we adopted for the following strategy: a poor understanding of the system produces an en-bloc request for repetition ("Pardon?"). The system accepts and interprets requests for premature termination, requests to spell out and requests for partial repetition. Like Waterworth (WATERWORTH,86), we have based the confirmation-correction process on a set of rules:

- particularly informative items are repeated by the "system".
- the tone employed for repetition by the "system" is either confirmative or interrogative depending on the degree of confidence attached to the information by the "system". In the first case (confirmative), a response by the user isn't obligatory whilst in the second case a response is expected.
- a user utterance carrying more than one informative item inhibits the confirmation-correction process (opposite to Waterworth's choice).

Instructions given to participants: the instructions proposed to the subject required him to produce simple and short phrases. In each session, the first intervention was constructed mentally before being given orally to the assistant.

Phase 2 - Analysis and results: the 15 subjects chosen enabled 70 conversations to be acquired. The general impression obtained from phase 2 is that the options chosen for the specification are the right ones: the dialogue structure envisaged wasn't found to be faulty, the rules for cooperation as drawn up played their role, the principle of optional interventions is an important factor for naturalness and for making things go more easily.

Analysis of the initial request showed that the subjects had observed the rules for conciseness. New requests (i.e. requests that lead into a follow-on dialogue) were clarified and classified into three categories : slidings (modification to the preceding request), mutations (usage of a heading not raised in the preceding dialogue) and reproductions (form of repetition of the preceding request).

The vocabulary used by subjects during this phase comprised 324 terms. "Erratic" phenomena (failure to end words, hesitations, etc.) in spontaneous oral output were also numerous here.

3. CONCLUSION.

The findings that result from our experimental work are various, mixed with hope and with fears. The influence it will bring to bear on our work on man-machine dialogue design are numerous and far-reaching.

The work carried out made it possible to experiment on and validate a cooperation mechanism and a dialogue structure which, as the evidence shows, can be generalised to a wide class of applications using finalised dialogues. The structure of the dialogue had been formalised by a dialogue grammar (PALABRE,87). The underlying semantics includes the notions of cooperation and phatic management described in this paper.

Let us also recall our concern about the realism of an application within the occasional user context. Two more difficulties increase our cause for concern: firstly, there is the problem of hesitation confirming that it is impossible to escape this, and secondly there is the problem of prediction. ASR researchers founded their hope on the predictive capacity of dialogues to avoid problems of combinational explosion with which they are confronted. However, the predictive power of a dialogue is an inverse function of the degree of freedom envisaged for the user in the dialogue's definition.

Finally, this experimental work brings the existence of expertise related to the dialogue to light, independent of the linguistic "expertise" and expertise related to the application. It possesses its own rules and ends, among which the following can be mentioned: its faculty for structuring a conversation, its user-friendliness objectives and its capacity for facilitating the task of automatic speech recognition, by reducing the number of user utterances and their length without harming the dialogue's quality.

Acknowledgements

We wish to thank Miss J. Damay and Messrs. J. Bluteau, A. Cozannet, E. Dalila, and R. Descout for their collaboration in this work.

REFERENCES

(BIERMANN,85) A.W. BIERMANN, R.D. RODMAN, D.C. RUBIN. Natural Language with Discrete Speech as a Mode of Human-to-Machine Communication. CACM June 1985, Vol 28, No 6, 628-636.

(GUYOMARD,86) M. GUYOMARD, J. SIROUX. Suggestive and Corrective Answers: a Single Mechanism. Structure of Multimodal Dialogues Including Voice. NATO Workshop, Sept 1-5 1986, Vénaco France.

(KAPLAN,82) S.J. KAPLAN. Cooperative Responses from a Portable Natural Language Query System. Artificial Intelligence 19 (1982), 165-187.

(NIEMANN,86) H. NIEMANN, A. BRIETZMANN, U. EHRLICH, G. SAGERER. Representation of a Continuous Speech Understanding and Dialogue System in a Homogeneous Semantic Net Architecture. ICASSP 86, Tokyo, 1581-1584.

(PALABRE,87) ESPRIT Project P 1015, Palabre. Deliverable WP 4.3.

(PECKHAM,86) J. PECKHAM. VODIS a Voice Operated Data Base Inquiry System. Speech Technology, Sept-Oct 1986, 56-61.

(SIROUX,85) J. SIROUX, D. GILLET. A System for Man-Machine Communication Using Speech. Speech Communication. Vol 4 No 4, 1985, 289-315.

(VAN KATWIJK,79) A.F.V. VAN KATWIJK, F.L. VAN NES, H.C. BUNT, H.F. MULLER, F.F LEOPOLD. Naive Subjects interacting with a Conversing Information System. IPO Annual Progress Report 14, 1979, 105-112.

(WATERWORTH,86) J. WATERWORTH. Interactive Strategies for Conversational Computer Systems. Structure of Multimodal Dialogues Including Voice. NATO Workshop, Sept 1-5 1986, Vénaco France.

List of Participants

NATO Advanced Study Institute
Recent Advances in Speech Understanding and Dialog Systems
Bad Windsheim, F.R. Germany, July 5 - July 18, 1987
Director: Prof. Dr. H. Niemann

Al-Dakkak, O., Institut de la Communication Parlée, I.C.P. - Unité Associée au CNRS, INPG-ENSERG 46 Av. Felix Viallet, 38100 Grenoble, France

Van Alphen, P., Institute of Phonetic Sciences, University of Amsterdam, Herengracht 338, 1016 CG Amsterdam, Holland

Atalay, A., TUBITAK-TETM, Ataturk Bulvari 221, Kavaklidere Ankara, Turkey

Beck, P., Daimler Benz AG, Abt. E6W, Mercedesstr., Postfach 303, 7000 Stuttgart, F.R. Germany

Bunt, H., Prof. Dr., Tilburg University, Postbus 90153, Tilburg, Netherlands 500

Cardin, R., McGill University, School of Computer Science, 805 Sherbrooke Street West, Montreal Quebec H3A 2K6, Canada

Carbonell, N., CRIN INRIA, BP 239, 54506 Vandoeuvre-les-Nancy Cedex, France

Casacuberta, F., Universidad Politécnica de Valencia, Camino de Vera, 46071 Valencia, Spain

Chollet , G., Ph.D., ENST-Dept. SIG, CNRS-UA 820, 46 Rue Barrault, 75634 Paris Cedex 13, France

Colla, A.M., Elettronica San Giorgio - ELSAG S.p.A, Via Puccini 2, 16154 Genova, Italy

Cooke, M.P., Department of Computer Science, University of Sheffield, Sheffield S10 2TN, Great Britain

Cozannet, M.A., CNET Lannion, Route de Tregastel - BP 40, 22301 Lannion Cedex, France

Derouault, A., IBM France Scientific Center, 36 avenue Raymond Poincaré, 75116 Paris, France

Dundar, E., Dept. of Computer Eng., Middle East Technical University, Inonu Bulvari, Ankara, Turkey

Eck, R., Fraunhofer Institut für Informations- und Datenverarbeitung, Sebastian-Kneipp-Str. 12-14, 7500 Karlsruhe 1, F.R. Germany

Euler, S., Institut für Angewandte Physik, Universität Frankfurt, Robert-Mayer-Str. 2-4, 6000 Frankfurt, F.R. Germany

Galiano, I., Universidad Politécnica de Valencia, Camino de Vera, 46071 Valencia, Spain

Gooding, F.G., Dr., Department of Linguistics, University College of North Wales, Bangor Gwynedd LL57 2UWL, Great Britain

Green, P.D., Dr., Department of Computer Science, University of Sheffield, Sheffield S10 2TN, Great Britain

Hackbart, H., Dr., SEL Forschungszentrum, Abt. ZT/FZS C3, Lorenzstrasse 10, 7000 Stuttgart 40, F.R. Germany

Haton, J.P., Prof. Dr., INRIA/CRIN, BP 239, 54506 Vandoeuvre les Nancy, France

Hoege, H., Dr., Siemens AG, ZT ZTI INF 11, Otto-Hahn-Ring 6, 8000 Muenchen 83, F.R. Germany

Hoeppner, W., Prof. Dr., EWH Rheinland Pfalz in Koblenz; Universität Hamburg, Fachbereich Informatik, Jungiusstrasse 6, 2000 Hamburg 36, F.R. Germany

Laface, P., Prof. Dr., Dip. Automatica e Informatica, Politecnico di Torino, C. Cuca Degli Abruzzi 24, 10129 Torino, Italy

Lang, M., Dr.rer.nat, Siemens AG, ZT ZTI INF1, Otto-Hahn Ring 6, 8000 Muenchen 83, F.R. Germany

Laprie, I., CRIN, BP 239, 54506 Vandoeuvre les Nancy, France

Lee, K.F., Computer Science Department, Carnegie Mellon University, Pittsburgh, PA 15213, USA

Lleida Solano, E., E.T.S.E. Telecomunicacio, Universidad Politécnica de Catalunya, Jorge Girona Salgado s/n, 08034 Barcelona, Spain

Martens, J.P., Dr., Electronics Laboratory, University of Gent, Sint-Pietersnieuwstraat 41, 9000 Gent, Belgium

Massia, G., Ing. C. Olivetti & C., S.p.A., D.O.R. Laboratory, Corso Svizzera 185, 10149 Torino, Italy

Merlo, E., School of Computer Science, McGill University, Burnside Hall, 805 Sherbrooke St. W., Montreal Quebec H3A 2K6, Canada

De Mori, R., Prof. Dr., School of Computer Science, McGill University, 805 Sherbrooke Street West, Montreal Quebec H3A 2K6, Canada

Mudler, J., Dr.-Ing., Institut für Nachrichtentechnik, Universität Braunschweig, Schleinitzstraße 23, 3300 Braunschweig, F.R. Germany

Ney, H., Dr., Philips Forschungslabor Hamburg, Vogt-Koelln-Straße 30, 2000 Hamburg 54, F.R. Germany

Niedermair, G., Siemens AG, Otto-Hahn-Ring 6, 8000 München 83, F.R. Germany

Niemann, H., Prof. Dr.-Ing., Lehrstuhl für Informatik 5 (Mustererkennung), Universität Erlangen-Nürnberg, Martensstraße 3, 8520 Erlangen, F.R. Germany

Paeseler, A., Philips Forschungslabor Hamburg, Vogt-Koelln-Straße 30, 2000 Hamburg 54, F.R. Germany

Palakal, M., Dr., IUPUI, Dept. of Computer Science, 1201 East 38th Street, P.O. Box 647, Indianapolis, Indiana 46223, USA

Pieraccini, R., Dr., CSELT, Via G. Reiss Romoli 274, 10148 Torino, Italy

Prieto, N., Universidad Politécnica de Valencia, Camino de Vera, 46071 Valencia, Spain

Rabiner, L.R., Dr., Head Speech Research Department, AT&T Bell Laboratories, 600 Mountain Avenue, Murray Hill, New Jersey 07974, USA

Ragazzini, S., Fondazione Ugo Bordoni, Via Baldassarre Castiglione 59, 00142 Roma, Italy

Reetz, H., Max-Planck-Institut für Psycholinguistik, Wundtlaan 1, 6525 XD Nijmegen, Netherland

Reininger, H., Institut für Angewandte Physik, Universität Frankfurt, Robert-Mayer-Str. 2-4, 6000 Frankfurt, F.R. Germany

Rolling, L., Abteilungsleiter GD XIII/B/3, Commission of European Communities, Bat. J.Monnet - Plateau du Kirchberg, L-2920 Luxembourg

Rubio-Ayuso, A., Departamento de Electrónica y Sistemas Informticos, Universidad de Granada, 18071 Granada, Spain

Sagerer, G., Dr.-Ing., Lehrstuhl für Informatik 5 (Mustererkennung), Universität Erlangen-Nürnberg, Martensstraße 3, 8520 Erlangen, F.R. Germany

Sanchis, E., Universidad Politécnica de Valencia, Camino de Vera, 46071 Valencia, Spain

Scheffers, M., Institut für Phonetik, Universität Kiel, Olshausenstr. 40-60, 2300 Kiel 1, F.R. Germany

Schukat-Talamazzini, E.G., Dr.-Ing., Lehrstuhl für Informatik 5 (Mustererkennung), Universität Erlangen-Nürnberg, Martensstraße 3, 8520 Erlangen, F.R. Germany

Schwartz, R.M., Senior Scientist, Speech Signal Processing Department, BBN Laboratories, 10 Moulton Street, Cambridge, MA 02238, USA

Sendlmeier, W., Max-Planck-Institut für Psycholinguistik, Wundtlaan 1, 6525 XD Nijmegen, The Netherlands

Soudoplatoff, S., Compagnie IBM France, Scientific Center, 36 avenue Raymond Poincaré, 75116 Paris, France

Taral, S., TUBITAK-TETM, Ataturk Bulvari 221, Kavaklidere Ankara, Turkey

Thurmair, G., Dr., Siemens AG, Bereich Datentechnik D AP 323, Postfach 830951, 8000 München 83, F.R. Germany

Vaissière, J., Dr., CNET Lannion - Division TSS/RCP, Route de Tregastel, 22301 Lannion, France

Varga, A., Royal Signals and Radar Establishment, St. Andrews Road, Malvern, Worcestershire WR14 3PS, Great Britain

Vidal, E., Universidad Politécnica de Valencia, Camino de Vera, 46071 Valencia, Spain

Wolf, D., Prof. Dr., Institut für Angewandte Physik, Universität Frankfurt, Robert-Mayer-Str. 2-4, 6000 Frankfurt, F.R. Germany

Yarman-Vural, F., Prof. Dr., Vaniköy Cad. 59 Cengelköy, Istanbul, Turkey, (presently at Drexel University, Philadelphia, USA)

Zanellato, G., Département d'Electricité, Faculté Polytechnique de Mons, Rue de Houdain 9, 7000 Mons, Belgium

Author Index

Subject Index

NATO ASI Series F

Vol. 1: Issues in Acoustic Signal – Image Processing and Recognition. Edited by C. H. Chen. VIII, 333 pages. 1983.

Vol. 2: Image Sequence Processing and Dynamic Scene Analysis. Edited by T. S. Huang. IX, 749 pages. 1983.

Vol. 3: Electronic Systems Effectiveness and Life Cycle Costing. Edited by J. K. Skwirzynski. XVII, 732 pages. 1983.

Vol. 4: Pictorial Data Analysis. Edited by R. M. Haralick. VIII, 468 pages. 1983.

Vol. 5: International Calibration Study of Traffic Conflict Techniques. Edited by E. Asmussen. VII, 229 pages. 1984.

Vol. 6: Information Technology and the Computer Network. Edited by K. G. Beauchamp. VIII, 271 pages. 1984.

Vol. 7: High-Speed Computation. Edited by J. S. Kowalik. IX, 441 pages. 1984.

Vol. 8: Program Transformation and Programming Environments. Report on an Workshop directed by F. L. Bauer and H. Remus. Edited by P. Pepper. XIV, 378 pages. 1984.

Vol. 9: Computer Aided Analysis and Optimization of Mechanical System Dynamics. Edited by E. J. Haug. XXII, 700 pages. 1984.

Vol. 10: Simulation and Model-Based Methodologies: An Integrative View. Edited by T. I. Ören, B. P. Zeigler, M. S. Elzas. XIII, 651 pages. 1984.

Vol. 11: Robotics and Artificial Intelligence. Edited by M. Brady, L. A. Gerhardt, H. F. Davidson. XVII, 693 pages. 1984.

Vol. 12: Combinatorial Algorithms on Words. Edited by A. Apostolico, Z. Galil. VIII, 361 pages. 1985.

Vol. 13: Logics and Models of Concurrent Systems. Edited by K. R. Apt. VIII, 498 pages. 1985.

Vol. 14: Control Flow and Data Flow: Concepts of Distributed Programming. Edited by M. Broy. VIII, 525 pages. 1985.

Vol. 15: Computational Mathematical Programming. Edited by K. Schittkowski. VIII, 451 pages. 1985.

Vol. 16: New Systems and Architectures for Automatic Speech Recognition and Synthesis. Edited by R. De Mori, C.Y. Suen. XIII, 630 pages. 1985.

Vol. 17: Fundamental Algorithms for Computer Graphics. Edited by R.A. Earnshaw. XVI, 1042 pages. 1985.

Vol. 18: Computer Architectures for Spatially Distributed Data. Edited by H. Freeman and G.G. Pieroni. VIII, 391 pages. 1985.

Vol. 19: Pictorial Information Systems in Medicine. Edited by K. H. Höhne. XII, 525 pages. 1986.

Vol. 20: Disordered Systems and Biological Organization. Edited by E. Bienenstock, F. Fogelman Soulié, G. Weisbuch. XXI, 405 pages.1986.

Vol. 21: Intelligent Decision Support in Process Environments. Edited by E. Hollnagel, G. Mancini, D.D. Woods. XV, 524 pages. 1986.

Vol. 22: Software System Design Methods. The Challenge of Advanced Computing Technology. Edited by J.K. Skwirzynski. XIII, 747 pages. 1986.

NATO ASI Series F

Vol. 23: Designing Computer-Based Learning Materials. Edited by H. Weinstock and A. Bork. IX, 285 pages. 1986.

Vol. 24: Database Machines. Modern Trends and Applications. Edited by A.K. Sood and A.H. Qureshi. VIII, 570 pages. 1986.

Vol. 25: Pyramidal Systems for Computer Vision. Edited by V. Cantoni and S. Levialdi. VIII, 392 pages. 1986.

Vol. 26: Modelling and Analysis in Arms Control. Edited by R. Avenhaus, R.K. Huber and J.D. Kettelle. VIII, 488 pages. 1986.

Vol. 27: Computer Aided Optimal Design: Structural and Mechanical Systems. Edited by C.A. Mota Soares. XIII, 1029 pages. 1987.

Vol. 28: Distributed Operating Systems. Theory und Practice. Edited by Y. Paker, J.-P. Banatre and M. Bozyiğit. X, 379 pages. 1987.

Vol. 29: Languages for Sensor-Based Control in Robotics. Edited by U. Rembold and K. Hörmann. IX, 625 pages. 1987.

Vol. 30: Pattern Recognition Theory and Applications. Edited by P.A. Devijver and J. Kittler. XI, 543 pages. 1987.

Vol. 31: Decision Support Systems: Theory and Application. Edited by C.W. Holsapple and A.B. Whinston. X, 500 pages. 1987.

Vol. 32: Information Systems: Failure Analysis. Edited by J.A. Wise and A. Debons. XV, 338 pages. 1987.

Vol. 33: Machine Intelligence and Knowledge Engineering for Robotic Applications. Edited by A.K.C. Wong and A. Pugh. XIV, 486 pages. 1987.

Vol. 34: Modelling, Robustness and Sensitivity Reduction in Control Systems. Edited by R.F. Curtain. IX, 492 pages. 1987.

Vol. 35: Expert Judgment and Expert Systems. Edited by J.L. Mumpower, L.D. Phillips, O. Renn and V.R.R. Uppuluri. VIII, 361 pages. 1987.

Vol. 36: Logic of Programming and Calculi of Discrete Design. Edited by M. Broy. VII, 415 pages. 1987.

Vol. 37: Dynamics of Infinite Dimensional Systems. Edited by S.-N. Chow and J.K. Hale. IX, 514 pages. 1987.

Vol. 38: Flow Control of Congested Networks. Edited by A.R. Odoni, L. Bianco and G. Szegö. XII, 355 pages. 1987.

Vol. 39: Mathematics and Computer Science in Medical Imaging. Edited by M.A. Viergever and A. Todd-Pokropek. VIII, 546 pages. 1988.

Vol. 40: Theoretical Foundations of Computer Graphics and CAD. Edited by R.A. Earnshaw. XX, 1246 pages. 1988.

Vol. 41: Neural Computers. Edited by R. Eckmiller and Ch. v. d. Malsburg. XIII, 566 pages. 1988.

Vol. 42: Real-Time Object Measurement and Classification. Edited by A.K. Jain. VIII, 407 pages 1988.

NATO ASI Series F

Vol. 43: Sensors and Sensory Systems for Advanced Robots. Edited by P. Dario. XI, 597 pages. 1988.

Vol. 44: Signal Processing and Pattern Recognition in Nondestructive Evaluation of Materials. Edited by C.H. Chen. VIII, 344 pages. 1988.

Vol. 45: Syntactic and Structural Pattern Recognition. Edited by G. Ferraté, T. Pavlidis, A. Sanfeliu, H. Bunke. XVI, 467 pages. 1988.

Vol. 46: Recent Advances in Speech Understanding and Dialog Systems. Edited by H. Niemann, M. Lang, G. Sagerer. X, 521 pages. 1988.

ProductSafety@springernature.com
Springer Nature Customer Service Center
Europaplatz 3, 69115 Heidelberg, Germany

FSC
www.fsc.org
MIX
Papier aus verantwortungsvollen Quellen
Paper from responsible sources
FSC® C105338

If you have any concerns about our products,
you can contact us on
ProductSafety@springernature.com

In case Publisher is established outside the EU,
the EU authorized representative is:
Springer Nature Customer Service Center GmbH
Europaplatz 3, 69115 Heidelberg, Germany

Printed by Libri Plureos GmbH
in Hamburg, Germany